Financial Forecasting
Volume II

The International Library of Critical Writings in Financial Economics

Series Editor: Richard Roll

Allstate Professor of Economics
The Anderson School at UCLA, USA

This major series presents by field outstanding selections of the most important articles across the entire spectrum of financial economics – one of the fastest growing areas in business schools and economics departments. Each collection has been prepared by a leading specialist who has written an authoritative introduction to the literature.

For a list of all Edward Elgar published titles visit our site on the World Wide Web at www.e-elgar.com

Financial Forecasting Volume II

Interest Rates, Exchange Rates and Volatility

Edited by

Roy Batchelor

HSBC Professor of Banking and Finance
Cass Business School, City of London, UK

and

Pami Dua

Professor of Economics
Delhi School of Economics, India

THE INTERNATIONAL LIBRARY OF CRITICAL WRITINGS IN FINANCIAL ECONOMICS

An Elgar Reference Collection
Cheltenham, UK • Northampton, MA, USA

Published by
Edward Elgar Publishing Limited
Glensanda House
Montpellier Parade
Cheltenham
Glos GL50 1UA
UK

Edward Elgar Publishing, Inc.
136 West Street
Suite 202
Northampton
Massachusetts 01060
USA

A catalogue record for this book is available from the British Library

Library of Congress Cataloguing in Publication Data
Financial forecasting / edited by Roy Batchelor and Pami Dua.
        p. cm. — (The international library of critical writings in financial economics ; 13)
    Includes bibliographical references and index.
    Contents: v. 1. Stock market forecasting — v. 2. Interest rates, exchange rates, and volatility.
    1. Business enterprises—Finance. 2. Business forecasting. I. Batchelor, R. A. II. Dua, Pami. III. Series.

    HG4026.F495 2003
    332'.01'12—dc21

                                                                                    2003054172

ISBN   1 84064 034 0 (2 volume set)

Printed and bound in Great Britain by MPG Books Ltd, Bodmin, Cornwall

Contents

Acknowledgements   ix

An introduction by the editors to both volumes appears in Volume I

PART I   FORECASTING INTEREST RATES

1. R.A. Kolb and H.O. Stekler (1996), 'How Well Do Analysts Forecast Interest Rates?', *Journal of Forecasting*, **15** (5), 385–94   3
2. Gordon Leitch and J. Ernest Tanner (1991), 'Economic Forecast Evaluation: Profits versus the Conventional Error Measures', *American Economic Review*, **81** (3), June, 580–90   13
3. Tae H. Park and Lorne N. Switzer (1997), 'Forecasting Interest Rates and Yield Spreads: The Informational Content of Implied Futures Yields and Best-fitting Forward Rate Models', *Journal of Forecasting*, **16** (4), 209–24   24
4. John T. Barkoulas and Christopher F. Baum (1997), 'Fractional Differencing Modeling and Forecasting of Eurocurrency Deposit Rates', *Journal of Financial Research*, **XX** (3), Fall, 355–72   40
5. Jun Woo Kim, H. Roland Weistroffer and Richard T. Redmond (1993), 'Expert Systems for Bond Rating: A Comparative Analysis of Statistical, Rule-based and Neural Network Systems', *Expert Systems*, **10** (3), August, 167–72   58

PART II   FORECASTING EXCHANGE RATES

6. Richard A. Meese and Kenneth Rogoff (1983), 'Empirical Exchange Rate Models of the Seventies: Do They Fit Out of Sample?', *Journal of International Economics*, **14**, 3–24   67
7. Don Alexander and Lee R. Thomas, III (1987), 'Monetary/Asset Models of Exchange Rate Determination: How Well Have They Performed in the 1980's?', *International Journal of Forecasting*, **3** (1), 53–63   89
8. Ronald MacDonald and Ian W. Marsh (1994), 'Combining Exchange Rate Forecasts: What is the Optimal Consensus Measure?', *Journal of Forecasting*, **13** (3), 313–32   100

A   Statistical Models

9. Nicholas Sarantis and Chris Stewart (1995), 'Structural, VAR and BVAR Models of Exchange Rate Determination: A Comparison of Their Forecasting Performance', *Journal of Forecasting*, **14** (3), 201–15   123

10. Francis X. Diebold and James A. Nason (1990), 'Nonparametric Exchange Rate Prediction?', *Journal of International Economics*, **28**, 315–32   138

11. Chung-Ming Kuan and Tung Liu (1994), 'Forecasting Exchange Rates Using Feedforward and Recurrent Neural Networks', *Journal of Applied Econometrics*, **10**, 347–64   156

12. Christian C.P. Wolff (1987), 'Time-Varying Parameters and the Out-of-Sample Forecasting Performance of Structural Exchange Rate Models', *Journal of Business and Economic Statistics*, **5** (1), January, 87–97   174

13. Andrew Berg and Catherine Pattillo (1999), 'Are Currency Crises Predictable? A Test', *IMF Staff Papers*, **46** (2), June, 107–38   185

B   Technical Analysis

14. Christopher J. Neely (1997), 'Technical Analysis in the Foreign Exchange Market: A Layman's Guide', *Federal Reserve Bank of St. Louis Review*, **79** (5), September/October, 23–38   219

15. Richard J. Sweeney (1986), 'Beating the Foreign Exchange Market', *Journal of Finance*, **XLI** (1), March, 163–82   235

16. Richard M. Levich and Lee R. Thomas, III (1993), 'The Significance of Technical Trading-Rule Profits in the Foreign Exchange Market: A Bootstrap Approach', *Journal of International Money and Finance*, **12** (5), October, 451–74   255

17. Carol Osler (2000), 'Support for Resistance: Technical Analysis and Intraday Exchange Rates', *Federal Reserve Bank of New York Economic Policy Review*, **6** (2), July, 53–68   279

PART III   FORECASTING RISK

18. Elroy Dimson and Paul Marsh (1990), 'Volatility Forecasting Without Data-Snooping', *Journal of Banking and Finance*, **14**, 399–421   297

19. Timothy J. Brailsford and Robert W. Faff (1996), 'An Evaluation of Volatility Forecasting Techniques', *Journal of Banking and Finance*, **20**, 419–38   320

20. Robert F. Engle, Che-Hsiung (Ted) Hong, Alex Kane and Jaesun Noh (1993), 'Arbitrage Valuation of Variance Forecasts with Simulated Options', *Advances in Futures and Options Research*, **6**, 393–415   340

A   Statistical Models

21. Adrian R. Pagan and G. William Schwert (1990), 'Alternative Models for Conditional Stock Volatility', *Journal of Econometrics*, **45**, 267–90   365

22. Stephen J. Taylor (1987), 'Forecasting the Volatility of Currency Exchange Rates', *International Journal of Forecasting*, **3** (1), 159–70   389
23. Jon Danielsson and Casper G. de Vries (2000), 'Value-at-Risk and Extreme Returns', *Annales d'Economie et de Statistique*, **60**, 239–70   401
24. Robert F. Engle and Jeffrey R. Russell (1997), 'Forecasting the Frequency of Changes in Quoted Foreign Exchange Prices with the Autoregressive Conditional Duration Model', *Journal of Empirical Finance*, **4** (2–3), June, 187–212   433

B   Options-implied Volatility
25. Christopher G. Lamoureux and William D. Lastrapes (1993), 'Forecasting Stock-Return Variance: Toward an Understanding of Stochastic Implied Volatilities', *Review of Financial Studies*, **6** (2), 293–326   461
26. Linda Canina and Stephen Figlewski (1993), 'The Informational Content of Implied Volatility', *Review of Financial Studies*, **6** (3), 659–81   495
27. Xinzhong Xu and Stephen J. Taylor (1995), 'Conditional Volatility and the Informational Efficiency of the PHLX Currency Options Market', *Journal of Banking and Finance*, **19**, 803–21   518

Name Index   537

Acknowledgements

The editors and publishers wish to thank the authors and the following publishers who have kindly given permission for the use of copyright material.

American Economic Review for article: Gordon Leitch and J. Ernest Tanner (1991), 'Economic Forecast Evaluation: Profits versus the Conventional Error Measures', *American Economic Review*, **81** (3), June, 580–90.

American Statistical Association for article: Christian C.P. Wolff (1987), 'Time-Varying Parameters and the Out-of-Sample Forecasting Performance of Structural Exchange Rate Models', *Journal of Business and Economic Statistics*, **5** (1), January, 87–97.

Annales d'Economie et de Statistique for article: Jon Danielsson and Casper G. de Vries (2000), 'Value-at-Risk and Extreme Returns', *Annales d'Economie et de Statistique*, **60**, 239–70.

Blackwell Publishing Ltd for articles: Richard J. Sweeney (1986), 'Beating the Foreign Exchange Market', *Journal of Finance*, **XLI** (1), March, 163–82; Jun Woo Kim, H. Roland Weistroffer and Richard T. Redmond (1993), 'Expert Systems for Bond Rating: A Comparative Analysis of Statistical, Rule-based and Neural Network Systems', *Expert Systems*, **10** (3), August, 167–72; John T. Barkoulas and Christopher F. Baum (1997), 'Fractional Differencing Modeling and Forecasting of Eurocurrency Deposit Rates', *Journal of Financial Research*, **XX** (3), Fall, 355–72.

Elsevier Science for articles: Richard A. Meese and Kenneth Rogoff (1983), 'Empirical Exchange Rate Models of the Seventies: Do They Fit Out of Sample?', *Journal of International Economics*, **14**, 3–24; Don Alexander and Lee R. Thomas, III (1987), 'Monetary/Asset Models of Exchange Rate Determination: How Well Have They Performed in the 1980's?', *International Journal of Forecasting*, **3** (1), 53–63; Stephen J. Taylor (1987), 'Forecasting the Volatility of Currency Exchange Rates', *International Journal of Forecasting*, **3** (1), 159–70; Adrian R. Pagan and G. William Schwert (1990), 'Alternative Models for Conditional Stock Volatility', *Journal of Econometrics*, **45**, 267–90; Francis X. Diebold and James A. Nason (1990), 'Nonparametric Exchange Rate Prediction?', *Journal of International Economics*, **28**, 315–32; Elroy Dimson and Paul Marsh (1990), 'Volatility Forecasting Without Data-Snooping', *Journal of Banking and Finance*, **14**, 399–421; Richard M. Levich and Lee R. Thomas, III (1993), 'The Significance of Technical Trading-Rule Profits in the Foreign Exchange Market: A Bootstrap Approach', *Journal of International Money and Finance*, **12** (5), October, 451–74; Xinzhong Xu and Stephen J. Taylor (1995), 'Conditional Volatility and the Informational Efficiency of the PHLX Currency Options Market', *Journal of Banking and Finance*, **19**, 803–21; Timothy J. Brailsford and Robert W. Faff (1996), 'An Evaluation of Volatility Forecasting Techniques', *Journal of Banking and Finance*, **20**, 419–38; Robert F. Engle and Jeffrey R.

Russell (1997), 'Forecasting the Frequency of Changes in Quoted Foreign Exchange Prices with the Autoregressive Conditional Duration Model', *Journal of Empirical Finance*, **4** (2–3), June, 187–212.

Robert F. Engle for article: Robert F. Engle, Che-Hsiung (Ted) Hong, Alex Kane and Jaesun Noh (1993), 'Arbitrage Valuation of Variance Forecasts with Simulated Options', *Advances in Futures and Options Research*, **6**, 393–415.

Federal Reserve Bank of New York for article: Carol Osler (2000), 'Support for Resistance: Technical Analysis and Intraday Exchange Rates', *Federal Reserve Bank of New York Economic Policy Review*, **6** (2), July, 53–68.

Federal Reserve Bank of St. Louis for article: Christopher J. Neely (1997), 'Technical Analysis in the Foreign Exchange Market: A Layman's Guide', *Federal Reserve Bank of St. Louis Review*, **79** (5), September/October, 23–38.

International Monetary Fund for article: Andrew Berg and Catherine Pattillo (1999), 'Are Currency Crises Predictable? A Test', *IMF Staff Papers*, **46** (2), June, 107–38.

Oxford University Press for articles: Christopher G. Lamoureux and William D. Lastrapes (1993), 'Forecasting Stock-Return Variance: Toward an Understanding of Stochastic Implied Volatilities', *Review of Financial Studies*, **6** (2), 293–326; Linda Canina and Stephen Figlewski (1993), 'The Informational Content of Implied Volatility', *Review of Financial Studies*, **6** (3), 659–81.

John Wiley & Sons Limited for articles: Ronald MacDonald and Ian W. Marsh (1994), 'Combining Exchange Rate Forecasts: What is the Optimal Consensus Measure?', *Journal of Forecasting*, **13** (3), 313–32; Chung-Ming Kuan and Tung Liu (1994), 'Forecasting Exchange Rates Using Feedforward and Recurrent Neural Networks', *Journal of Applied Econometrics*, **10**, 347–64; Nicholas Sarantis and Chris Stewart (1995), 'Structural, VAR and BVAR Models of Exchange Rate Determination: A Comparison of Their Forecasting Performance', *Journal of Forecasting*, **14** (3), 201–15; R.A. Kolb and H.O. Stekler (1996), 'How Well Do Analysts Forecast Interest Rates?', *Journal of Forecasting*, **15** (5), 385–94; Tae H. Park and Lorne N. Switzer (1997), 'Forecasting Interest Rates and Yield Spreads: The Informational Content of Implied Futures Yields and Best-fitting Forward Rate Models', *Journal of Forecasting*, **16** (4), 209–24.

Every effort has been made to trace all the copyright holders but if any have been inadvertently overlooked the publishers will be pleased to make the necessary arrangement at the first opportunity.

In addition the publishers wish to thank the Marshall Library of Economics, Cambridge University, the Library of the University of Warwick and the Library of Indiana University at Bloomington, USA for their assistance in obtaining these articles.

Part I
Forecasting Interest Rates

[1]

Journal of Forecasting, Vol. 15, 385–394 (1996)

How Well Do Analysts Forecast Interest Rates?

R. A. KOLB
US Military Academy, West Point, USA

H. O. STEKLER
George Washington University, USA

ABSTRACT

This paper examines interest rate forecasts made for the period 1982–90 and examines three issues: (1) Is there a general agreement among analysts about the level of interest rates six months in the future? (2) Are all the forecasters equally good? (3) Are the forecasts valuable to prospective users? We use distributions of the cross-sections of forecasts, Friedman's statistic for analysis of variance by rank, and tests of independence between forecasts and outcomes to examine these questions. We conclude that there usually was a consensus among analysts, that there was no significant difference in the ability to forecast short-term rates but there was a difference with respect to the long-term predictions, and that these forecasts were not significantly better than random walk forecasts.

KEY WORDS   Interest rate forecasts; forecast evaluation; consensus forecast;

INTRODUCTION

Since many financial institutions hire experts to make interest rate forecasts, it is of interest to evaluate the forecasts of these financial analysts, because little is known about their individual abilities to predict interest rates. The evaluation of the Goldsmith–Nagan (now known as the *Bond and Market Letter*) surveys by Dua (1988), Friedman (1979), Hafer and Hein (1989), and Prell (1973) focus exclusively on the mean of the forecasts of the survey participants. Another study (Belongia, 1987) examined a different set of forecasts, those published in *The Wall Street Journal*, but also considered only the mean forecasts.

In this paper, we analyse *individual analysts'* ability to forecast interest rates by examining the forecasts of prominent individuals whose predictions have been published in *The Wall Street Journal*. We do not focus on the mean forecast of the group, as Belongia did, but rather examine the entire distribution of the predictions issued at a particular time and then consider the complete records of individual analysts.

We will ask three basic questions. First, at any instant of time is there a consensus or general agreement among the analysts included in the survey about the level of interest rates that will be observed six months in the future? Second, are all the analysts equally good or are some better (worse)? Finally, are the forecasts valuable to the prospective user? The next section will

CCC 0277–6693/96/050385–10
© 1996 by John Wiley & Sons, Ltd.

Received March 1995
Accepted April 1996

386   *Journal of Forecasting*   *Vol. 15, Iss. No. 5*

describe the methodologies of this analysis. This is followed by a description of the data, our results, and our conclusions.

METHODOLOGIES

Is there a consensus forecast?

At a given point in time, a number of financial analysts predict the levels of interest rates which will prevail at some other point in the future. It has been customary to classify the median of a set of such predictions as the consensus forecast, even though few studies have examined such distributions of predictions to determine whether the median could actually be considered a 'consensus'.[1] Our methodology for determining whether, at any instant of time, there is a consensus among the financial analysts is identical to that used by Schnader and Stekler (1991) in examining the distributions of macroeconomic predictions.

In order to develop a statistical procedure for determining whether a consensus exists, it is necessary to describe the distribution of the forecasts. If the distribution were bimodal, there are at least two distinct collective opinions, and it is not reasonable to say that a consensus, standard, or representative forecast exists. Unimodality is a necessary but not sufficient condition. The distribution of forecasts should be symmetric and relatively peaked when there is a consensus. A set of cross-sectional forecasts which is normally distributed would yield a consensus, for the normal distribution has the three above-mentioned characteristics.

If the distribution of forecasts is not normal, it might be more skewed, more peaked or flatter. If a distribution is symmetrical but more peaked, it is leptokurtic, and most of the forecasts are even more tightly clustered around the mean than they are when the distribution is normal. Thus, if normality implies a consensus, when the forecasts are even closer together, there is also a consensus. In both the skewed and the symmetrical platykurtic cases we assume that there is no consensus, for the platykurtic distribution is characterized by a flatter top and more abrupt tails than the normal. If the distribution of forecasts is unimodal but skewed, there is no consensus, for the longer tail of the distribution indicates that there is a significant minority opinion. This statistical procedure thus involves a test for normality. This is followed by tests for skewness and kurtosis if the original distribution is non-normal.

Are all the forecasters equally good?

The test for determining whether all financial analysts were equally good in forecasting interest rates is again based on evaluations of macroeconomic predictions (Stekler, 1987; Batchelor, 1990; Kolb and Stekler, 1990; Batchelor and Dua, 1990). The Friedman (1937, 1940) statistic for analysis of variance by ranks has been used to compare the accuracy of individuals' predictions and test the hypothesis that all forecasters are equal. The use of this statistic requires that the population of forecasters remain constant over the entire period. Since we do not have such a balanced design, we use the Skillings and Mack (1981) extension of the Friedman statistic to the case of 'unbalanced' designs in our analysis. (See the Appendix for a description of that statistic.)

Are some analysts superior forecasters?

We will evaluate the performance of individual analysts to determine whether a particular individual did better than the average. When all individuals in each time period are ranked by the

---

[1] If there is no consensus, any evaluation which examines only the median would not provide insights about the 'representative' forecaster but would only yield information about how well the middle forecaster did. With a consensus, looking at the median does provide information about the 'representative' forecaster.

size of their absolute errors, the number of times that a particular analyst was in the top half of the distribution is determined. Then the binomial distribution is used to calculate the probability that this number could have occurred by chance on the assumption that there was a 0.50-0.50 likelihood of being either above or below the average. Similarly, the binomial distribution with a 0.25 probability is used to test whether an individual was superior in the sense of having a larger than expected number of occurrences in the top quartile and a smaller than expected frequency in the bottom quartile.

Are the forecasts useful?

Merton (1981) was the first to derive the conditions required for forecasts to have value to a user. His analysis involved market timing financial predictions and used statistical tests based on the hypergeometric distribution. Schnader and Stekler (1990) and Stekler (1994) modified this procedure to determine whether some macroeconomic forecasts could have been useful to their users. The modified procedure, based on contingency tables, will be applied to these interest rate forecasts. These tests compare only the *direction of change* of the predicted and actual movements of interest rates. The magnitude of the errors made in forecasting these variables is not considered, partially because of the importance of predicting the direction of change (see Pfeifer, 1985).[2]

Schnader and Stekler (1990) and Stekler (1994) used 2×2 contingency tables to determine whether the predicted changes were independent of the observed changes. Either Fisher's Exact Test, or for large samples, a χ^2 statistic may be used to test the hypothesis that the forecasts are independent of the observed events. If this hypothesis is rejected, then the forecasts can be said to have value.[3]

Both the forecasts and actual events are placed in one of two categories: $\Delta i > 0$, or $\Delta i \leq 0$. If a small change in one direction is predicted and if a small change in another direction occurred, this arbitrary division might provide misleading results. We therefore also constructed a 3×3 contingency table where a predicted or actual change of 25 basis points was considered small. Now there were three classifications: $\Delta i > 0.25$, $\Delta i < -0.25$, and $-0.25 \leq \Delta i \leq 0.25$.

THE DATA

Since January 1982, *The Wall Street Journal* has published the interest rate forecasts obtained of prominent financial analysts. These surveys appear semi-annually (early in January and July) and present estimates of the levels of two interest rates which are expected to prevail 6 months in the future.[4] These interest rates are the 90-day T-bill rate and the yield on 30-year government bonds. Consequently, we are able to examine forecasts of both short- and long-term interest rates.

Between January 1982 and January 1990 there were 17 surveys, with the number of responses per survey varying from 12 in the earliest to 40 in the latest. There were 64 individuals who

---

[2] It would also be possible to calculate the profits or losses that would be generated on the basis of investment strategies derived from these forecasts. (For a study that used this type of methodology in evaluating forecasts, see Leitch and Tanner, 1991.)

[3] Schnader and Stekler (1990) provided another interpretation of this test. They argued that testing whether the forecasts have value is the same as determining whether (in the sense of predicting the direction of change) the forecasts differed significantly from the results obtained from a naive model.)

[4] We do not test for the serial independence of the forecasts because the forecasts are for six-month lead times and the surveys are conducted at six-month intervals. Moreover, we do not utilize any methods where overlapping periods would pose a problem.

Table I. Number of consensus and non-consensus forecasts

	Consensus			
	Normal	Non-normal non-skewed leptokurtic	Non-consensus	Indeterminate
Short-term (T-bill)	13	1	2	1
Long-term (30-Year Treasury)	13	0	4	0

made predictions for these surveys, with 40 participating in 5 or more and 20 responding in 10 or more. In examining the individual forecasting records, we shall only consider those analysts who have provided at least five predictions.

RESULTS: CONSENSUS FORECASTS

Most of the predictions of short-term rates are consensus forecasts. Table I shows that normality could not be rejected at the 5% level of significance in 13 of 17 cases.[5] Of the other four surveys, two were skewed, thus yielding clear evidence of non-consensus. One of the remaining cases was leptokurtic, thus falling into the consensus group while the other was indeterminate. Thus 14 of 17 surveys yielded results that we would classify as consensus forecasts, one was indeterminate, while the remaining two were non-consensus. The predictions of long-term rates showed similar results. At the 5% level of significance, normality could not be rejected in 13 of 17 cases (Table I). However, all four of those surveys showed a skewed distribution of the forecasts.

Thus we may conclude that in most instances, there was a consensus or general agreement among the analysts participating in each of the surveys. This finding thus permits us to use the median forecasts as 'representative' of the particular cross-section.

RESULTS: ARE ALL FORECASTERS EQUAL?

The Skillings–Mack procedure was used to test whether all the forecasters were, on average, equal or whether some were superior. The procedure was applied to the rankings of all 40 forecasters who made at least five predictions. The results obtained from the short- and long-term predictions differ.

We cannot reject the hypothesis that all forecasters are equal, on average, in predicting the 90-day T-bill rate. The test T-statistic (equation (A6) of the Appendix) was 38.03, which can be compared with the χ^2 distribution with 39 degrees of freedom. The probability of obtaining such a value is 0.51. Thus we have not found any significant differences in the forecasters' abilities to predict short-term interest rates six months in advance. (However, this result does not indicate whether the individuals were all good or all equally bad.)

On the other hand, when the same procedure was applied to the forecasts of the 30-year Treasury rate, we obtained entirely different results. The value of the T-statistic was 55.12, which when compared to the χ^2 with 39 degrees of freedom was significant at the 0.05 level.

---

[5] In one additional case, normality was rejected at the 10% but not at the 5% level. That particular case did not exhibit skewness or kurtosis.

Thus, we can conclude that there were significant differences among the forecasters in their ability to predict the yield on 30-year Treasury bonds.[6]

RESULTS: ARE SOME ANALYSTS SUPERIOR?

Even if it is impossible to reject the hypothesis that all forecasters are about average, it is still possible that a small number of individuals are superior. To examine this question, we ranked the forecasters by size of absolute error and determined the number of times that any individual was in the top quartile of all the surveys in which the person participated, The probability that this number of appearances in the top quartile could have occurred by chance was calculated.

Table II presents the list of individuals who had the largest percentage of appearance in the top quartile of the surveys in which they participated.[7] The results show that the five forecasters who were best in forecasting the short-term interest rate were in the top quartile from 38% to 50% of the surveys in which they participated. The other analysts had lower success ratios. The hypothesis that these results could be attributed to chance (based on a 25% probability of being in the top quartile) could not be rejected for any analyst at the 10% or lower level of significance.[8] Even at higher levels of significance there are few individuals who could be judged superior.

Table II. Percentage of times that individuals appeared in top quartile of distributions in which they participated

Name	No. of surveys	No. of times in top quartile	%	Prob. due to chance
		Short-term forecasts		
Kahan	6	3	50	0.17
Nathan	6	3	50	0.17
Reynolds	7	3	43	0.24
Kellner	15	6	40	0.15
Schott	16	6	38	0.19
		Long-term forecasts		
Leisenring	5	5	100	0.001
Straszheim	7	4	57	0.07
Harris	7	4	57	0.07
Levy	9	5	56	0.05
Wyss	12	6	50	0.05
Hyman	13	6	46	0.08

[6] It has been suggested that the differing results for the short- and long-term rates may be due to separate phenomena. First, short-term rates may not move as much as long-term rates over a six-month horizon. Second, many more factors must be taken into account in predicting the long-term rates. Consequently, analysts may have different abilities to process information.

[7] These percentages are based on *all* the forecasters who participated in a given survey, but only those individuals who made at least five predictions are included in these tabulations.

[8] The exact probabilities, $P(X > x)$, presented in the last column of Table II were calculated from the binomial distribution $(0.25, N)$, where X is the number of observations in the top quartile out of the N surveys in which the individual participated.

390   *Journal of Forecasting*   *Vol. 15, Iss. No. 5*

The analysts with the best success ratios in forecasting the long-term rates are presented in the bottom panel of Table II. There are six individuals whose success ratios range from 46% to 100%. For each individual it is possible to reject at the 10% level the hypothesis that the observations could have occurred by chance and thus conclude that some forecasters are above average.

To be superior, an analyst should also have a smaller than expected number of observations in the lower quartile or at least not have a larger than expected number in that quartile. Of the six individuals appearing in the bottom panel of Table II, the 'best', in having fewer observations in the lower quartile than expected, were Wyss with only 1 out of 12 (8.3%) and Leisenberg with 0 out of 5 (0%). However, these were only equivalent to chance significance levels of 0.16 and 0.24, respectively. Moreover, one of the six, Hyman, had a significantly larger number of outcomes in the lowest quartile (6 of 13) than could be attributed to chance, equivalent to a 0.08 significance level. On the basis of this evidence, we can conclude that there are very few analysts who could be identified as being consistently superior.[9]

ARE THE FORECASTS VALUABLE?

Our criterion for determining whether the forecasts were useful was shown to depend on the relationship between the *direction of change* of the predicted and actual movements of interest rates. Table III presents the 2×2 table showing the association between the direction of change of the median forecast of each survey and the actual change that was observed six months later. The median forecast was used because our analysis indicated that a consensus existed in a

Table III. Association between the direction of predicted change of the *median* forecast and the actual change (short- and long-term forecasts), January 1982 to January 1990

Short-term forecasts

	Actual change	
Predicted change	≤ 0	> 0
≤ 0	3	6
> 0	5	3

Fisher Exact Test, $P = 0.956$.

Long-term forecasts

	Actual change	
Predicted change	≤ 0	> 0
≤ 0	4	6
> 0	4	3

Fisher Exact Test, $P = 0.883$

---

[9] There were, however, a number of forecasters whom we shall not identify, who were in the bottom quartile an inordinate number of times, e.g. A: 8 of 12, $p = 0.001$; B: 7 of 12, $p = 0.01$; C: 4 of 6, $p = 0.04$; etc.

majority of the surveys. Accordingly, a central moment is a representative forecast, and the median has generally been used as the 'consensus' forecast. The forecasts would be valuable if the hypothesis that the predicted changes were independent of the actual movements could be rejected.

Of the 17 median forecasts of the T-bill rate 6 months in the future, only six predicted the direction of change correctly. Intuitively, one could surmise that these forecasts were not useful. This is confirmed by Fisher's Exact Test, which indicates that the probability of obtaining such a result when there is independence is 0.956. Consequently, the hypothesis of independence could not be rejected.

To test that these findings did not result from analysts predicting a small change in one direction while a small change in the other occurred, we added, as previously noted, another classification: small change. The results using this new classification are presented in Table IIIA. There are only four observations along the diagonal, and we again do not reject the hypothesis of independence, for χ^2 is only 2.43. The results (Tables III and IIIA) also indicate that the independence hypothesis could not be rejected for the median forecasts of the interest rate on the 30-year Treasury bond. We therefore conclude that these median forecasts are not valuable for predicting interest rate changes.

Individual analysts' forecasts

Even though we concluded that the median forecasts were not valuable and were not clearly superior to no-change, random walk forecasts, we must also determine whether the same results apply to the predictions of individual analysts. Table IV presents the distribution of the values of the Fisher Exact statistic for all forecasters who participated in at least five surveys.

For the short-term forecasts it was not possible to reject the independence hypothesis for any of the analysts at a probability of 0.10 or lower. The probabilities for only two individuals were

Table IIIA. Association between the direction of predicted change of the *Median* forecast and the actual change, adjusted for small changes (short- and long-term forecasts), January 1982 to January 1990

	Short-term forecasts		
		Actual change	
Predicted change	< -0.25	$[-0.25, 0.25]$	> 0.25
< -0.25	1	2	2
$[-0.25, 0.25]$	2	3	3
> 0.25	2	2	0

$\chi^2 = 2.429$, with 4 d.f., $p = 0.658$

	Long-term forecasts		
		Actual change	
Predicted change	< -0.25	$[-0.25, 0.25]$	> 0.25
< -0.25	1	1	6
$[-0.25, 0.25]$	3	2	1
> 0.25	2	1	0

$\chi^2 = 7.497$, with 4 d.f., $p = 0.112$

392   *Journal of Forecasting*   *Vol. 15, Iss. No. 5*

in the range of 0.11 to 0.20. Consequently, we can conclude that there were few (if any) analysts whose predictions were useful to users in the sense of being significantly superior to the naive model. The results for the individual analysts' forecasts of the long-term rate are similar.[10]

CONCLUSIONS

This paper has examined the interest rate forecasts of a substantial number of noted financial analysts. These forecasts were contained in surveys published by *The Wall Street Journal*. We concluded that, in most surveys, there was a consensus among these analysts as to the direction of movement of both short- and long-term interest rates. We also showed that there was no significant difference in the ability of these financial analysts to predict short-term rates but that there was a difference when it came to forecasting the 30-year Treasury yields 6 months in the future.

The fact that the analysts agreed with each other need not be viewed positively, for neither the median not the individual analysts predictions were considered valuable. Given our interpretation, we can conclude that these predictions are not significantly superior to naive no-change random walk type of forecasts.

APPENDIX

Assume that each of n forecasters predicts a specific interest rate for several (at least five) of m periods. For each period, t, the errors of each forecaster are ranked according to their accuracy. The most accurate prediction receives a rank value of 1; the least accurate receives a rank equal to the number of individuals participating in that period, k_t. Ties are accommodated by averaging over the two or more ranks. Formally, R_{it} denotes the rank assigned to the tth prediction of forecaster i. When a forecaster does not participate during a time period, the corresponding R_{it} is given a value equal to the average rank for that time period; i.e.

$$R_{it} = (k_t + 1)/2 \tag{A1}$$

The usual Friedman statistic procedure sums the ranks for each forecaster and compares this to an expected sum. Using the Skillings–Mack procedure, we provide the following formula for a weighted adjusted sum for each forecaster:

$$A_i = \sum_{t=1}^{m} [12/(k_t + 1)^{1/2} [R_{it} - (k_t + 1)/2] \qquad i = 1, 2, \ldots, n \tag{A2}$$

This sum is a weighted measure of how good each forecaster performs relative to the other forecasters. The weights compensate for the different number of forecasters for each time period.

In order to calculate an inferential statistic, the covariance matrix, Σ, of the random vector $A' = (A_1, A_2, \ldots, A_n)$ is calculated under the null hypothesis that there is no difference in forecast

---

[10] Although participating in only five surveys, Leisenring correctly predicted the two positive and three negative changes in long-term interest rates that actually occurred.

R. A. Kolb and H. O. Stekler   *How Well Do Analysts Forecast Interest Rates ?*   393

errors. Following Skillings and Mack, this matrix $\Sigma \equiv (\sigma_{ik})$ can be formed by defining m_{ik} to be the number of years containing forecasts from both forecaster i and forecaster j. Then

$$\sigma_{ik} = -m_{ik} \qquad 1 \leq i \neq k \leq n$$

and   (A3)

$$\sigma_{ii} = \sum_{\substack{k=1 \\ k \neq 1}}^{n} m_{ik} = -\sum_{\substack{k=1 \\ k \neq 1}}^{n} \sigma_{ik} \qquad i = 1, 2, \ldots, n$$

As Skillings and Mack suggest, Σ is easy to construct since the off-diagonal elements are equal to $-m_{ik}$ and the diagonal elements are negative the sum of the off-diagonal elements in that row (or column).

The test statistic is then

$$T = A' \Sigma^- A \tag{A4}$$

where Σ^- is any generalized inverse of Σ. In our application (unless, pathologically, two forecasters provide equal forecasts over all time periods), the rank of Σ is $n - 1$, so that a generalized inverse can be formed as

$$\begin{pmatrix} \overset{-1}{\underset{11}{\Sigma}} & 0 \\ 0 & 0 \end{pmatrix}$$

where Σ_{11} is a $n - 1$ by $n - 1$ submatrix of Σ formed by deleting the last row and column of Σ. With this generalized inverse,

$$T = A'_* = (A_1, A_2, \ldots, A_{n-1}). \tag{A6}$$

where $A^* = (A_1, A_2, \ldots, A_{n-1})$.

Skillings and Mack show that this statistic has an asymptotic chi-squared distribution with $n - 1$ degrees of freedom. For our procedure a rejection of the null hypothesis would indicate that the forecasters were not equal; or rather that some were better while others were worse.

AUTHORS' NOTE

The opinions expressed in this paper are those of the authors and are not the views of the US Department of Defense.

REFERENCES

Batchelor, R. A., 'All forecasters are equal', *Journal of Business and Economic Statistics*, **8** (1990), 143–4.
Batchelor, R. A. and Dua, P., 'Forecaster ideology, forecasting technique, and the accuracy of economic forecasts', *International Journal of Forecasting*, **6** (1990), 3–10.
Belongia, M. T., 'Predicting interest rates: a comparison of professional and market based forecasts', Federal Reserve Bank of St Louis, *Review*, **69** (1987), 9–15.
Dua, P., 'Multiperiod forecasts of interest rates', *Journal of Business and Economic Statistics*, **6** (1988), 381–4.
Friedman, B. M., 'Interest rate expectations versus forward rates: evidence from an expectations survey', *Journal of Finance*, **34** (1979), 965–73.

Friedman, M., 'The use of ranks to avoid the assumptions of normality implicit in the analysis of variance', *Journal of the American Statistical Association*, **32** (1937), 675–701.

Friedman, M., 'A comparison of alternative tests of significance for the problem of *M* rankings', *Annals of Mathematical Statistics*, **11** (1940), 86–92.

Hafer, R. W. and Hein, S. E., 'Comparing futures and survey forecasts of near-term Treasury bill rates', Federal Reserve Bank of St Louis, *Review*, **71** (1989), 33–42.

Kolb, R. A. and Stekler, H. O., 'The lead and accuracy of macroeconomic forecasts', *Journal of Macroeconomics*, **12** (1990), 111–23.

Leitch, G. and Tanner, J. E., 'Economic forecast evaluation: profits versus the conventional error measures', *American Economic Review*, **81** (1991), 580–90.

Merton, R. C., 'On market timing and investment performance 1: An equilibrium theory of value for market forecasts', *Journal of Business*, **54** (1981), 363–406.

Pfeifer, P. E., 'Market timing and risk reductions', *Journal of Financial and Quantitative Analysis*, (1983), 451–9.

Prell, M. J., 'How well do the experts forecast interest rates?', Federal Reserve Bank of Kansas City, *Monthly Review*, September–October (1973), 3–13.

Schnader, M. H. and Stekler, H. O., 'Evaluating predictions of change', *Journal of Business*, **63** (1990) 99–107.

Schnader, M. H. and Stekler, H. O., 'Do consensus forecasts exist?', *International Journal of Forecasting*, **7** (1991), 165–70.

Skillings, J. H. and Mack, G. A., 'On the use of a Friedman-type statistic in balanced and unbalanced block designs', *Technometrics*, **23** (1981), 171–7.

Stekler, H. O., 'Who forecasts better?', *Journal of Business and Economic Statistics*, **5** (1987), 155–8.

Stekler, H. O., 'Are economic forecasts valuable?', *Journal of Forecasting*, **13** (1994), 495–505.

Authors' biographies:
R. A. Kolb is Professor of Mathematics at the US Military Academy. He is particularly interested in the application of statistical techniques to forecasting and has written a number of papers on this subject.
H. O. Stekler was a visiting professor at George Washington University when this paper was written. He has interests in all aspects of forecasting with an emphasis on forecast evaluations.

Authors' addresses:
R. A. Kolb, Department of Mathematics, US Military Academy, West Point, NY 10996-1786, USA.
H. O. Stekler, Department of Economics, George Washington University, Washington, DC 20052, USA.

[2]

Economic Forecast Evaluation:
Profits Versus The Conventional Error Measures

By GORDON LEITCH AND J. ERNEST TANNER*

Economists are often puzzled as to why profit-maximizing firms buy professional forecasts when statistics such as the root-mean-squared error or the mean absolute error often indicate that a naive model will forecast about as well. This paper argues that the reason is that these traditional summary statistics may not be closely related to a forecast's profits. Using profit measures, we find only very weak relationships between such summary error statistics and forecast value. If these results are robust, then least-squares regression analysis may not be appropriate for many studies of economic behavior. (JEL C52, C10)

Economists are often puzzled as to why seemingly profit-maximizing firms buy economic forecasts. Summary statistics such as the average absolute error (AAE), the root-mean-squared error (RMSE), and the Theil "U" statistic (which is free from the dimension problems of the other two) rarely reveal major differences between professional forecasting services and a simple naive approach of no change in the variable being forecast.[1] Yet, millions of dollars are spent annually both producing and purchasing these apparently worthless forecasts.

In this paper, we argue that the conventional criteria used in these evaluations may

well be inappropriate. In empirical tests of interest rate forecasts for the 1980's, we find that the conventional criteria, based upon some measure of the size of the forecast error, have no systematic relationship to profits. Perhaps because of some embarrassing forecasts and generally poor performance on the basis of conventional criteria, few forecasters are willing to allow extensive evaluations of their historical forecasts of interest rates.[2] However, we did have access to the entire record of one professional service and have used it as a basis for comparison. Moreover, with interest rate forecasts, a profit measure can easily be calculated, thereby permitting tests of the relationship between profits and the conventional measures of forecast-error magnitudes. It is naturally better to examine profits directly than to examine a proxy that is at

*Graduate student and Professor, respectively, Department of Economics, Tulane University, New Orleans, LA 70118. We are grateful to Vittorio Bonomo for many insightful discussions in evaluating economic forecasts. In addition, Ron Batchelder, John Boschen, Tom Mayer, Michael Parkin, Ed Tower, Terry Wilford, Jeff Zabel and three anonymous referees offered many helpful comments on earlier drafts. However, they are not responsible for any of the paper's shortcomings.

[1]Among those who accept the null hypothesis of no value added by most sophisticated forecasts over simple ARIMA-type models are Charles R. Nelson (1972), J. P. Cooper and Nelson (1975), G. V. L. Narashimhan (1975), J. R. Schmidt (1979), A. C. Petto (1981), and David Ahlers and Josef Lakonishok (1983). However, some evaluators do find that the larger models do supply valuable information not contained in the simple forecasts. See, for example, the evidence contained in Carl F. Christ (1975), Stephen K. McNees (1975, 1979), Roger Craine and Arthur M. Havenner (1988), and E. Philip Howrey et al. (1974).

[2]The semiannual *Wall Street Journal* survey occasionally makes mention of these problems. For example, in the July 1987 survey, it was noted that the strong economy produced sharply higher bond yields during early 1987, and many forecasts "proved widely inaccurate during the first half." A possible consequence of this was that one forecaster bowed out after predicting "anemic economic growth ... as well as a sharp decline in bond yields (July 6, 1987, p. 2) The *Blue Chip Economic Indicators* service has experienced similar difficulties as many of their interest rate forecasters do not permit identification, while all of their GNP forecasters are explicitly identified next to their forecasts.

best indirectly related to profits. Economists generally assume that firms use forecasts because they add to profits. Thus, a more appropriate test of forecast accuracy is profitability, and not the size of the forecast error or its squared value.

The paper proceeds as follows. Section I reviews the commonly used criteria to evaluate forecasts, while Section II describes a number of ways to calculate profit measures of an interest rate forecast. In Section III, we describe the interest rate forecasting approaches used in our evaluations, including the professional service and the more naive approaches. In Sections IV and V, we evaluate the forecasts in terms of the alternative profitability measures described in Section II and in terms of the conventional error-measures criteria widely used in the literature. In Section VI, we summarize the paper and offer some tentative conclusions.

I. Widely Used Forecast-Evaluation Criteria

Economic forecasts are typically evaluated by comparing the errors obtained when measuring the forecast values against the actual outcomes. The three commonly used statistics evaluating forecasts in this manner are the average absolute error (AAE), the root-mean-squared error (RMSE), and the Theil "U" coefficient.

The more familiar AAE and RMSE criteria can be misleading in certain cases. For example, a forecaster using the unit of measurement of thousands of dollars will have different error values than another forecaster using millions of dollars. Theil's U statistic is free of these problems. It can be viewed as the RMSE of a forecast divided by the RMSE of a naive forecast of no change:

$$(1) \quad U = \sqrt{\frac{\sum_{t=1}^{N} (\Delta F_{t+j} - \Delta A_{t+j})^2}{\sum_{t=1}^{N} (\Delta A_{t+j})^2}}$$

where F_{t+j} is the forecast value j periods ahead, A_{t+j} is the actual realized value of a variable, N is the number of forecasts, $\Delta F_{t+j} = F_{t+j} - A_t$, and $\Delta A_{t+j} = A_{t+j} - A_t$. $U = 0.0$ when the prediction is perfect, $U = 1.0$ when the RMSE of the predicted change equals the accuracy of the baseline forecast of no change, and statistics greater than 1.0 indicate that the forecasts have higher RMSE's than the no-change forecast. Because of the appeal of least squares based on a quadratic loss function, in which larger errors receive proportionately more weight, the RMSE and the Theil U coefficient have been the most popular criteria in the literature.[3] Other criteria have been proposed, but cataloging them would be a distraction.

II. Profit Measures of Using an Interest Rate Forecast

While there are many ways to calculate profits for an interest rate forecast, most alternatives cannot be studied, because the data are not available. For example, while the professional service's forecasts that we studied were issued monthly for 14 interest rates covering each of the succeeding 12 months,[4] few of these interest rates are represented by a corresponding forward rate and a futures contract. An exception, the three-month Treasury bill rate, has received the most attention in the literature. Since there is a liquid futures market for this security, we analyzed only this rate in our

---

[3] We know of one prominent forecaster who purposely was pessimistically biased in his forecasts. Because he believed that the profit-maximizing firms wanted to protect themselves from the "worst-case scenario," his forecasts were purposely biased. Clearly, since he believed that his clients' loss functions were not symmetrical, the conventional criteria would not be appropriate for judging the accuracy of his forecasts. The implications of this forecaster's beliefs have much more significance, for if he is correct, then least-squares regression analysis may not be appropriate for many empirical studies of economic behavior.

[4] The monthly forecasts on 14 interest rates for the period 1–12 months ahead are done by the Commonwealth Research Group and released through the *Money Rate Report* on the final trading day of each month. We should note that one of the authors is a cofounder of this firm and retains a financial interest in it.

tests. Moreover, this is one of the interest rates for which we had access to a monthly survey of money managers, economists, corporate treasurers, and other forecasters up to a year ahead of each of the futures contract months (March, June, September, and December).

Even narrowing the available data set to this extent leaves many measures of profit available. Are profits calculated from the cash market, the futures market, or the forward market? What is the size of the position assumed, and does it change depending upon the forecast? What are the transaction costs including brokers' fees and bid–ask spread?

To simplify matters, but to preserve the maximum level of realism corresponding to that for a user of interest rate forecasts, we did our profit calculations in the futures market for Treasury bills. We assume that the size of the position is always one unit;[5] all transactions were executed at the closing price at the end of the month,[6] when the

---

[5] Vittorio Bonomo (1989) finds that professional commodity-market traders do not vary the size of their bet, but amateurs, who end up as losers, do vary the size of their positions. He argues that if the odds are in one's favor, a series of constant-sized bets virtually guarantees success, and the professionals profit by making a large number of bets so that the odds work for them. On the other hand, traders who lose their money tend to assume different-sized bets over time. This result is obvious if one thinks of "doubling up" when the odds get high. In this case, unless the forecast is certain, such a strategy eventually always would result in losing money. For counterexamples to Bonomo's assertions, see Richard A. Epstein (1977 Ch. 3). In the context of a log utility function, a strategy of proportional betting, in which the size of the bet is proportional to expected profits, could dominate the constant-bet strategy we use. Such a strategy may make profits more highly correlated with the RMSE criterion.

[6] For most traders, placing a buy or sell "on-close" order would not have any appreciable effect on price. Given our assumption of one contract, it is very unlikely that our profit calculations would be materially affected by the effect such an order would have on this relatively fluid market. In fact, our broker at Shearson says there is a 99-percent probability of a fill at this price as several thousand contracts were traded on a typical day during the sample period used. Thus, the assumption that fills are done at closing prices gives the most accurate *ex post* prices available.

professional service's forecasts became available; and the positions were always evaluated at one-month intervals. New positions, based upon the updated forecasts, were assumed to have been taken at the closing price of each month.

For trading in Treasury-bill futures, round-trip broker's fees would range from about $8.50 each for large traders to about $85.00 for full-service retail brokers. The initial margin requirement for trading the $1 million Treasury-bill contract is set by the broker and usually ranges between $2,000 and $2,500, but falls to $1,500 at most brokers for maintenance purposes. To deal in such a contract, the usual procedure is to deposit with the broker between $10,000 and $20,000 in a money-market fund earning a competitive short-term interest rate. As one trades, funds are removed from and deposited to the trading account as needed. Thus, for most practical purposes, the $2,000–$2,500 margin earns no interest while the rest of the funds earn a competitive rate of return. If the market moves unfavorably, funds are transferred from the money-market fund to the trading account in order to meet the maintenance margin. However, should the market move in a favorable direction, excess funds will be pulled from the trading account and placed in the money-market fund earning additional interest. No interest will be earned on the maintenance margin required to hold the position in a "speculation" account. However, the same is not true for hedgers who have lower margin requirements.

In short, if a nonhedger uses a discount broker and the market fluctuates randomly, then round-trip costs amount to about $40 per month ($25 broker's fees and $15 lost interest on $2,000) to speculate on the price change of a single $1 million Treasury-bill futures contract. In our tests, and in actual practice, the transactions costs would be less, because we assumed new trades only when the new forecast calls for one to reverse positions or to roll over from an expiring contract.

In this environment, there are still many ways to use an interest rate forecast. Our approach for the first profit calculation (profit-rule A) was straightforward: if interest rates are forecast to rise, go "short" or sell a futures contract; conversely, if rates are forecast to fall, go "long" or buy a futures contract. This approach implicitly assumes that the market does not expect interest rates to change. On a $1 million three-month Treasury bill, each basis-point change in the interest rate changes the gross return by $25 ($1 million × 0.01 percent × 0.25 years). Thus, for each basis-point change in interest rates on the futures contract, the price of the contract changes by $25. Gross returns, before costs, are calculated directly using $25 per basis-point change and the position taken. A $15 opportunity cost on the margin funds per month and $25 per round-trip trade were then subtracted to obtain trading profits.

Our second profit calculation (profit-rule B) is similar but takes the futures-market forecast explicitly into account. This profit calculation assumes that, if interest rates are forecast to be above the rate implied by the futures market, one will short the contract; and conversely, if rates are expected to be below the rate implied by the futures contract, one will go long the contract. After this position is taken, profits are calculated in the same manner as above.

Our third profit calculation (profit-rule C) assumes a position only if interest rates are expected to change. If the forecast is for no change in rates (saying one doesn't know what to do), then the action is not to take a position. Otherwise, positions are assumed as in the second profit calculation above by comparing the forecast with the market's forecast.

Our fourth profit calculation (profit-rule D) assumes a position only if the forecast change in interest rates is opposite in sign to that of the market's forecast change. In other words, we take a long position in the futures contract only if we forecast rates to fall while the futures market is forecasting a rise, and conversely. At other times, no position is taken.

Because the professional interest-rate-forecasting service offers a prediction of the three-month Treasury bill rate for each of the next 12 months, we could theoretically estimate profits for each of the 12 forecast horizons. However, because we wanted to use the Treasury-bill forward market as an alternative forecasting system, we used only the forecasts up to nine months ahead. This is because the longest-maturing cash Treasury bill is only for one year. As a result, the longest readily estimated forward rate for three-month Treasury bills is nine months.

In predicting ahead nine months for the forecasts, we matched the forecast month with the nearest contract that would not expire before the end of the month (e.g., the December, January, and February forecasts were matched with the March futures contract; the March, April and May forecasts were matched with the June contract). Depending upon the current month, this means that the nearest three or the nearest four contracts are traded.

III. Forecasting Systems

For the tests made in this paper, we employed seven different forecasting systems. The first forecasting system was based upon the professional service whose forecasts were published in the *Money Rate Report*. Although the complete set of forecasts started in 1980, we only used the period beginning with their year-end 1981 forecast. At that point, the service began consistently including executive survey forecasts for interest rates. The survey, usually done during the last 10 days of the month, provides a "consensus" forecast for the three-month Treasury-bill rate for each month of the futures contracts up to a year ahead and fits well with our tests. Upon introducing the survey, the service indicated that the survey respondents included "[c]orporate financial officers, banking executives, and operating heads of firms ... [because] many analysts feel that market derived forecasts do not fully nor accurately represent informed opinion as to the future course of interest rates ..." (*Money Rate Report*, January 1981, p. 1). Because the survey results for the three-month Treasury bill rate were available monthly only since year-end 1981, we use the sample period from January 1982 through December 1987 for our tests.

The other forecasting systems are more conventional. An ARIMA model was estimated initially over the seven-year period beginning in January 1975 and ending in December 1981. The structure of the one-month change in three-month Treasury-bill interest rate appeared to be of the form AR(2). The fitted initial equation was estimated to be

$$(2) \quad r_t = 0.337 + 1.220 \, 3\text{MoTBill}_{t-1}$$
$$\qquad\qquad (1.00) \quad (10.16)$$

$$\qquad - 0.255 \, 3\text{MoTBill}_{t-2}$$
$$\qquad\quad (2.06)$$

($R^2 = 0.886$). For the purposes of the tests in this paper, we used a rolling regression with a fixed beginning point but ending with the month in which the above forecasts were made. Thus, aside from the general structure, only information available in the marketplace at the time the positions were assumed to have been taken was used in our *ex post* ARIMA forecasts. The final one-month-ahead ARIMA-forecast equation, estimated from January 1975 until December 1987 and looking very similar to the initial equation, was

$$(3) \quad r_t = 0.387 + 1.133 \, 3\text{MoTBill}_{t-1}$$
$$\qquad\qquad (1.91) \quad (14.25)$$

$$\qquad - 0.181 \, 3\text{MoTBill}_{t-2}$$
$$\qquad\quad (2.27)$$

($R^2 = 0.918$). This methodology was followed for the other forecast horizons using the ARIMA technique.

For the forward rate, we used the end-of-month Treasury-bill yield curve, as reported in the *Wall Street Journal*. The implicit rate up to nine months ahead for the three-month Treasury-bill rate was estimated from the Treasury-bill yield curve's bid price using the appropriate maturity dates up to one year ahead.

The futures rate forecasts were derived from the historical prices of the four nearest Treasury-bill future contracts. For forecasts nearer than the nearest contract, we interpolated between the current spot rate and the rate implied by the nearest contract.

For forecast dates between contract dates, we interpolated between the implied forecasts of the adjoining contract dates.

The other two forecasting systems are the naivest of models. The "naive no-change" technique forecasts that all future rates will equal the current spot rate. The "constant rate of growth" technique forecasts that the change in interest rates over the next *x* months is compounded from the most recent one-month change. Thus, rising interest rates are expected to continue to rise, while falling rates are expected to continue to fall.

IV. A First Look at the Data for Economic Forecasts: Profits and Other Criteria

In most evaluations of economic forecasts, profits are totally ignored. In Table 1, we present summary figures on the six-year average for the nine forecast horizons using the six forecasting techniques. The profitability of the forecast appears to bear little relationship to the conventional size-of-error criteria.

For the purpose of the table, we assumed that any forecast for interest rates to rise was associated with selling the appropriate futures contract and any forecast for interest rates to fall involved buying the contract. The no-change forecast involved sitting on the sidelines. Thus, the naive no-change forecast produces no profits or losses. As described in Section II, profits were calculated using the four nearby contracts corresponding to interest rate forecasts up to nine months ahead. We will show later that the lack of a clear relationship between profits and the conventional criteria is not due to the way we calculated profits, as all profit-calculation methods produced similar results. First, we need to explain what we did more fully.

The column labeled "average directional accuracy" shows the percentage of interest rate changes in the futures market that were accurately forecast by each technique over the one-month observation interval until the new forecasts were available. The results are not surprising because the forecasts are predicting revisions in what is essentially the market's full-information forecast. If the

TABLE 1—PROFITS AND OTHER FORECAST-EVALUATION CRITERIA, JANUARY 1982–DECEMBER 1987

Forecasting technique	Six-year average annual profits	Average directional accuracy (percentage)	Average absolute error (percentage)	Average root-mean-squared error (percentage)	Average Theil U statistic
Professional service	$1,643	49.3	0.781	0.932	1.93
ARIMA	− $928	47.9	0.739	0.902	1.82
Forward rate	− $3,050	43.7	0.656	0.848	1.62
Naive no-change	$0	37.9	0.410	0.530	1.00
Constant rate of growth	− $674	46.6	2.013	2.514	4.72
Survey forecast	− $3,262	43.8	0.811	1.081	2.06

Profit Rule

Buy a $1 million Treasury-bill futures contract if interest rates are forecast to fall, and sell a contract if rates are expected to rise. Profits are calculated based on a $25-per-basis-point change in the futures contract over a one-month period, until a new forecast is made at the close of each month.

Note: Although the level of profits, directional accuracy, and size of forecast error are different depending on the profit rule, the general pattern is very similar across trading rules, and in no case does there seem to be a strong and theoretically correct relation between profits and the error criteria. Thus, for brevity, we summarize the data using profit-rule A, as it seems to be the most straightforward.

interest-rate market is efficient, which most studies find it to be, then predicting changes in interest rates by any system should be equivalent to flipping a coin. The possible exception is the naive no-change forecast, which predicts that the futures market rate will move toward the spot rate. The fact that it appears to forecast the wrong direction almost two-thirds of the time suggests that the spot rate probably moves to the futures market, rather than conversely, but that is not the subject of this paper.[7]

The "average absolute error" column is the average difference between the forecast value as made at the end of the previous month and the futures-market value at the end of the current month for the forecast month in question. Note that, instead of the actual realized interest rate, we have used only the next month's new futures-market forecasts for the realization in this table. However, the results are not affected by doing the calculations this way, as the cash markets give essentially identical results. The root-mean-squared error and the Theil U statistics are calculated from the same

month-end data of the futures market and forecasts.

The data presented in this table are consistent with previous research. The only reference to a profit criterion that we find in the literature suggests that profits do not appear to be related to lowest root-mean-squared error. In Stephen Figlewski and Thomas Urich (1983), profits of a Treasury-bill forecast, when corrected for bias, are directly related to the size of the forecast error; but when they are not corrected for bias, profits and error measures are inversely related. However, the authors do not draw attention to this aspect of their research. Similarly, Scott Hein and Raymond Spudeck (1988) find no relation between cost and the conventional error criteria; but since they are concerned with using forecasts to minimize interest borrowing costs, they ignore the implications for forecast evaluation.

The columns on the size of the forecast error are also consistent with previous research; that is, in general, the smaller the forecast error, the better the Theil statistic. Moreover, as in the findings of James Pesando (1978), the naive forecast of no change has the smallest error, followed by predictions based on the forward rate and the ARIMA model. The worst forecasts, ranked from worst to best in terms of error magnitudes, are the constant-interest-rate-change forecasts followed by the survey forecasts, and then the professional-service forecasts.

---

[7] Michael T. Belongia (1987) found similar results for the cash market in Treasury bills. Using the results of the professional forecasters surveyed semiannually by the *Wall Street Journal*, he found they had an accuracy rate of 42 percent in predicting the direction of change over a six-month horizon. The comparable rate for the futures market was 55 percent.

TABLE 2—CORRELATIONS BETWEEN PROFITS AND THE VARIOUS FORECAST
CRITERIA FOR TREASURY-BILL FUTURES MARKET TRADING AVERAGED
OVER FORECAST HORIZONS OF 1–9 MONTHS

Profit rule	DA		AAE		RMSE		Theil U	
	r	t	r	t	r	t	r	t
A	+0.428	2.76	−0.077	0.45	−0.094	0.55	−0.156	0.92
B	+0.842	9.11	+0.185	1.10	+0.210	1.25	−0.230	1.38
C	+0.598	4.35	+0.226	1.35	+0.253	1.52	−0.148	0.87
D	+0.578	4.13	+0.326	2.01	+0.322	1.99	+0.009	0.05

Profit Rules

A: forecast rates to rise, short the futures contract; forecast rates to fall, buy the futures contract

B: forecast rates to be above implied forecast of futures, go short; forecast rates to be below implied forecast of futures, go long.

C: same as B, except no position if forecast is for no change in rates

D: take position only if forecast change has opposite directional sign to market forecast.

Notes: DA = directional accuracy of forecast; AAE = average absolute error of forecast; RMSE = root-mean-squared error of forecast; Theil U = Theil's forecast-evaluation statistic; r = simple correlation coefficient; and t = absolute value of the t statistic on the slope coefficient. For all analyses, $N = 36$ (forecasts for all nine forecast horizons were grouped together in each year, yielding six years of data on six forecasting systems, or 36 observations per profit rule).

Based upon the usual error-magnitude criteria, the results of this table confirm the major conclusions of the literature that firms appear to waste money on economic forecasts.

However, if profits were the criterion for whether or not to purchase forecasts, then the conclusion might be different. In the case summarized in Table 1, the only profitable system finished fourth out of six, based on the conventional criteria. There is nothing in these "error" criteria that would have caused firms to choose this profitable forecasting technique over the others. Yet, since the profitable forecasts were available only at a price while the others were essentially free, the market test did indicate that this forecast service's clients were probably not using the economists' criteria of lowest mean absolute error to evaluate the forecasts.

V. Statistical Relationships Between Profits and Error Measures

Although these results, which were based on six-year averages for one relatively arbitrary use of interest rate forecasts, are interesting and informative, are they statistically significant, and do they hold up for other plausible ways of using interest rate forecasts? To answer these questions, we calculated correlations between the various criteria and profits as measured by each of the profit rules discussed in Section II.

In Table 2, we present the results of averaging each forecast system over all nine forecast horizons for each year. Thus, the data are based on 36 observations: six forecasting systems for six years. In Table 3, we present the results for each of the nine forecast horizons. Since the data are still averaged over each year, we have 324 observations, corresponding to the six forecast systems and nine forecast horizons over six years.

As Table 2 shows, regardless of the profit rule followed, there is little systematic relationship between profits and the conventional measures of forecast quality. The only conventional measure of forecast quality that is related to profits is "directional accuracy" (DA), and it is infrequently used.[8]

----

[8]To the best of our knowledge, only James Cicarelli (1982) and E. Philip Howrey et al. (1974) use direc-

TABLE 3—CORRELATIONS BETWEEN PROFITS AND VARIOUS FORECAST CRITERIA
FOR TREASURY-BILL FUTURES-MARKET TRADING AVERAGED OVER EACH
YEAR BUT WITH EACH OF THE NINE FORECAST HORIZONS
TREATED SEPARATELY

Profit rule	DA		AAE		RMSE		Theil U	
	r	t	r	t	r	t	r	t
A	+0.441	8.81	−0.095	1.72	−0.101	1.82	−0.144	2.60
B	+0.819	25.66	+0.074	1.34	+0.096	1.72	−0.202	3.70
C	+0.619	14.14	+0.100	1.80	+0.123	2.23	−0.148	2.69
D	+0.572	12.51	+0.212	3.90	+0.216	3.97	−0.038	0.68

Profit Rules

A: forecast rates to rise, short the futures contract; forecast rates to fall, buy the futures contract.
B: forecast rates to be above implied forecast of futures, go short; forecast rates to be below implied forecast of futures, go long.
C: same as B, except no position if forecast is for no change in rates.
D: take position only if forecast change has opposite directional sign to market forecast.

Notes: DA = directional accuracy of forecast; AAE = average absolute error of forecast; RMSE = root-mean-squared error of forecast; Theil U = Theil's forecast-evaluation statistic; r = simple correlation coefficient; and t = absolute value of the t statistic on the slope coefficient. For all analyses, $N = 324$ (six forecasting systems, nine horizons, and six years of data).

The standard criteria show no consistent relationship with profits. Indeed, the average-absolute-error and root-mean-squared-error criteria have perverse signs (better forecasts should have lower average errors and higher profits, and thus, the simple correlations should be negative) in three-quarters of the cases. While the Theil statistic has the correct sign in three cases out of four, it is never statistically significant at conventional levels of significance.

Increasing the data set to 324 observations by treating each forecast horizon separately, but still averaging the data over the year, produces similar results (Table 3). However, the sizes of the error criteria are now occasionally significantly related to profits. However, of the six statistically significant correlations, three have incorrect signs. Nevertheless, directional accuracy re-mains highly significant as a proxy for forecast profits.

In Table 4, we present the correlations and related absolute t values between the conventional criteria using profit rule B. For brevity, the other profit rules have been omitted, but the results are very similar. As we would expect based upon the earlier tables, directional accuracy and the error-measure criteria are only weakly related. However, the various error-measure criteria are all closely related, confirming the usual result that the accuracy of the forecast is not likely to be dependent upon which error criterion is used. Unfortunately, none of the error criteria is reliably related to the profitability of the forecast.[9]

tional accuracy in evaluating forecasts. While Cicarelli was proposing the criterion, rather than extensively evaluating forecasts, Howrey et al. were using it to bolster the record of the Wharton forecasts over the 1969–1970 recession.

[9] Because many previous studies used professional forecasts in comparisons with the ARIMA-type forecast, we have followed their example. However, in the present case, it is conceivable that our results depend upon some fortunate outliers of the particular professional forecasting service we used. To test this conjecture, we redid the tests excluding the forecasts of the professional service. In this reduced sample, all the correlation coefficients and all the t values were extremely close to those reported in Tables 2, 3, and 4.

TABLE 4—CORRELATIONS AMONG VARIOUS FORECAST CRITERIA

N	Statistic	Correlation					
		DA–AAE	DA–RMSE	DA–Theil U	AAE–RMSE	AAE–Theil U	RMSE–Theil U
36	r	+0.061	+0.077	−0.129	+0.997	+0.675	+0.657
	t	0.36	0.45	0.76	71.83	5.33	5.08
324	r	+0.012	+0.024	−0.104	+0.996	+0.744	+0.726
	t	0.22	0.42	1.88	202.7	19.96	18.92

Notes: DA = directional accuracy of forecast; AAE = average absolute error of forecast; RMSE = root-mean-squared error of forecast; Theil U = Theil's forecast-evaluation statistic; r = simple correlation coefficient; and t = absolute value of the t statistic on the slope coefficient.

Since the forecasts we have used pertain to the cash market, conclusions based on the futures market about the reliability of conventional forecast-evaluation criteria may be flawed, because the two markets do not track exactly. As a consequence, we redid the tests using the cash market. In doing so, we were forced to make some very severe and unrealistic assumptions. First was the obvious problem that any three-month Treasury bill automatically turns into a two-month Treasury bill over the one-month observation interval. To overcome this problem, we assumed a perpetual three-month Treasury bill. With this theoretical construct, profits were calculated by multiplying $25 by the change in the three-month bill rate. Second, opportunity and trading costs in the cash market can differ widely, depending upon the characteristics of the trader, such as the bid–ask spread or the "cost of carry." To avoid these problems, we assumed trading costs identical to those applicable to futures trading with all transactions being made at the "bid" price.

While these assumptions are limiting, they do allow an operational method with which to calculate profits in the cash market, and the results are essentially identical to those derived from using the futures market. Profits and the directional accuracy of the forecast systems are highly correlated with a high degree of statistical significance. However, the relationships between profits (or directional change) and the conventional size-of-forecast-error criteria appear to be

very poorly related. In just over half the experiments tried, the relationships between profits and the root-mean-squared error have the anticipated correct negative sign; but individually, the level of significance is higher for the theoretically incorrect positive signs than for the correct negative signs. Like the futures-market evaluations, only the Theil U statistics generally have the theoretically appropriate signed relationship to profits, but often the level of significance is less than satisfactory as a reliable forecast-evaluation criterion.

VI. A Tentative Conclusion

Forecast evaluations made on the basis of conventional error-magnitude criteria often find little justification for profit-maximizing firms to allocate resources to professional forecasters, as naive models often predict as well. Unfortunately, the size of the conventional forecast-error criteria frequently has unpredictable relationships to the forecasts' profitability, rendering these criteria unreliable indicators of profits. Indeed, in evaluating the quality of interest rate forecasts, where forecast profits are readily calculated, we find no systematic relationship between the widely used *ex post* error criteria and *ex post* profits. The only substitute criterion for profits found in the literature that appears to be closely related is directional accuracy. The relationship between directional accuracy and profits appears to be almost as close as the relationships of the various error criteria are to each other. However, because the root-mean-squared error, the average absolute error, and the Theil U statistic appear to be tenuously linked to profits and directional accuracy, it is not surprising that profit-maximizing firms buy forecasts in spite of their seemingly large forecast errors.

The results of this paper suggest that, if profits are not observable, directional accuracy of the forecasts might be used as the evaluation criterion. All the conventional forecast-error-magnitude criteria are only marginally related to profitability, while directional accuracy consistently demonstrates a high degree of statistical association.

A more disturbing implication of our findings is that conventional least squares may not be the appropriate estimation technique for economic behavior. If profits are not related to the size of the error, then it may be that our empirical estimates of economic relationships should not be based upon a squared error loss function.

REFERENCES

Ahlers, David and Lakonishok, Josef, "A Study of Economists' Consensus Forecasts," *Management Science*, October 1983, *29*, 1113–25.

Belongia, Michael T., "Predicting Interest Rates: A Comparison of Professional and Market-Based Forecasts," *Review* (Federal Reserve Bank of St. Louis), March 1987, *69*, 9–15.

Bonomo, Vittorio, "The Behavior of Commodity Traders: Winners and Losers," mimeo, Virginia Polytechnic Institute and State University, September 1989.

Christ, Carl F., "Judging the Performance of Econometric Models of the U.S. Economy," *International Economic Review*, February 1975, *16*, 54–74.

Cicarelli, James, "A New Method of Evaluating The Accuracy of Economic Forecasts," *Journal of Macroeconomics*, Fall 1982, *4*, 469–75.

Cooper, J. Phillip and Nelson, Charles R., "The *Ex Ante* Prediction Performance of the St. Louis and FRB-MIT-PENN Econo-

metric Models and Some Results on Composite Predictors," *Journal of Money Credit and Banking*, February 1975, *7*, 1–32.

Craine, Roger and Havenner, Arthur M., "Forecast Comparisons of Four Models of U.S. Interest Rates," *Journal of Forecasting*, January-March 1988, *7*, 21–9.

Epstein, Richard A., *The Theory of Gambling and Statistical Logic*, New York: Academic Press, 1977.

Figlewski, Stephen and Urich, Thomas, "Optimal Aggregation of Money Supply Forecasts: Accuracy, Profitability, and Market Efficiency," *Journal of Finance*, June 1983, *38*, 695–710.

Hein, Scott E. and Spudeck, Raymond E., "Forecasting the Daily Federal Funds Rate," *International Journal of Forecasting*, 1988, *4* (4), 581–91.

Howrey, E. Philip, Klein, Lawrence R. and McCarthy, Michael D., "Notes on Testing the Predictive Performance of Econometric Models," *International Economic Review*, June 1974, *15*, 366–83.

McNees, Stephen K., "An Evaluation of Economic Forecasts," *New England Economic Review* (Federal Reserve Bank of Boston), November/December 1975, 3–39.

_____, "The Forecasting Record for the 1970's," *New England Economic Review* (Federal Reserve Bank of Boston), September/October 1979, 33–53.

Narashimhan, G. V. L., "A Comparison of Predictive Performance of Alternative Forecasting Techniques: Time Series versus Econometric Models," *Proceedings of the American Statistical Association, Business and Economic Statistics Section*, August 1975, 459–64.

Nelson, Charles R., "The Prediction Performance of the FRB-MIT-PENN Model of the U.S. Economy," *American Economic Review*, December 1972, *62*, 902–17.

Pesando, James A., "On the Efficiency of the Bond Market: Some Canadian Evidence," *Journal of Political Economy*, December 1978, *86*, 1057–76.

Petto, A. C., "Comparing the Relative Accuracy of Seasonal Sales Forecasting Models—A Case Study of an Urban Hotel," unpublished paper presented at the First International Symposium on Forecasting, Quebec, Canada, May 27–29, 1981.

Schmidt, J. R., "Forecasting State Retail Sales: Econometric Versus Time Series Models," *Annals of Regional Science,*

November 1979, *13*, 91–101.

Blue Chip Economic Indicators, Washington, DC: Capitol Publications, various issues.

Money Rate Report, New Orleans: Commonwealth Research Group, various issues.

Wall Street Journal, 6 July 1987, p. 2.

[3]

Journal of Forecasting, Vol. 16, 209–224 (1997)

Forecasting Interest Rates and Yield Spreads: The Informational Content of Implied Futures Yields and Best-fitting Forward Rate Models

TAE H. PARK[1] AND LORNE N. SWITZER[2*]

[1] *Fuji Capital Markets Co., USA*
[2] *Concordia University, Canada*

ABSTRACT

Forecasts of interest rates for different maturities are essential for forecasts of asset prices. The growth of derivatives markets coupled with the development of complex theories of the term structure of interest rates have provided forecasters with a rich array of variables for predicting interest rates and yield spreads. This paper extends previous work on forecasting future interest rates and yield spreads using market data for T-bills, T-Notes, and Treasury Bond spot and futures contracts. The information conveyed in technical models that use market data is also assessed, using a recent innovation in interest rate modelling, the maximum smoothness approach. Forecasts from this model are compared with predicted yields and yield spreads derived from futures prices as well as with those of the random walk model. The results show some evidence of market segment- ation, with more arbitrage evident for nearby maturities. Market partici- pants appear to show a greater degree of consensus on short-term interest rates than on longer-term interest rates. There is some indication that forecasts from the futures markets are marginally better than those provided by those of the maximum-smoothness approach, consistent with the informational advantages of futures markets. Finally, futures and maximum-smoothness market forecasts are shown to outperform those of the random walk model. © 1997 by John Wiley & Sons, Ltd.

J. forecast. **16**: 209–224, 1997

No. of Figures: 1. No. of Tables: 6. No. of References: 27.

KEY WORDS   forecasting interest rates and spreads; futures markets; maximum smoothness forward rates

Contract grant sponsor: SSHRC; Contract grant number: # 410-96-0748.

---

* Correspondence to: Lorne N. Switzer, Finance Department, Faculty of Commerce and Administration, Concordia University, 1455 De Maisonneuve Blvd W, Montreal, Quebec, Canada H3G 1M8. E-mail: switz@vax2.concordia.ca.

Received April 1996
Accepted January 1997

210   *Journal of Forecasting*   *Vol. 16, Iss. No. 4*

INTRODUCTION

Forecasts of interest rates for different maturities are essential for forecasts of asset prices. For example, the forecast value of any bond for time t can be derived as the forecasted value of a combination of zero-coupon (or pure discount) instruments with specific maturities as below (see e.g. Carleton and Cooper, 1976):

$$B_t = \sum_{j=1}^{T} \frac{CF_j}{(1 + RS_j)^j} \qquad (1)$$

where

B_t = the price of the bond at time t
CF_j = the cash flow from the bond at time j (coupon payment and/or principal payment)
RS_j = the discount rate for period j
T = the maturity of the bond.

The discount factor, RS_j, is the yield on a *zero-coupon or pure discount* instrument with maturity j. This yield is also called the *spot rate*. The *term structure of interest rates* depicts the historical relationship between spot rates and maturities and is illustrated in Figure 1 for the period 1988–94, for US government bonds. As can be seen, the term structure can take on a variety of shapes, from downward sloping (as in various periods in 1988) to humped (as in 1988–91) to upward sloping (as in various periods in 1992).

The growth of derivatives markets coupled with the development of complex theories of the term structure of interest rates have provided corporate treasurers, government policy makers,

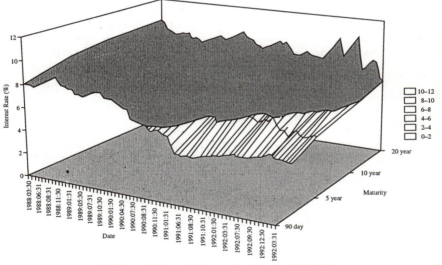

Figure 1. Term structure of spot rates, 1988–93

J. forecast. **16**: 209–224, 1997

homeowners, hedgers, and speculators with a rich array of variables for forecasting interest rates and yield spreads, defined as differences between spot rates for different maturities (see e.g. Cox, Ingersoll, and Ross, 1985; Hull and White, 1993). The unbiased expectations/fair game model of interest rate determination predicts that implied yields and yield spreads from market determined *futures* and *forward* prices should provide meaningful forecasts of spot yields and yield spreads in the future. Future prices are prices for bonds for future delivery that are set in organized market exchanges. In the unbiased expectations models, forward yields f_j are market expectations of future spot yields. For example, for a two-period discount bond, the forward rate f_1 is the market's forecast of the one period spot rate in the second period, and solves:

$$(1 + RS_2)^2 = (1 + RS_1)(1 + f_1) \tag{2}$$

From equation (2) a negatively sloped yield curve (as in 1988, when short spot rates were above long rates) would suggest that future spot rates should decline. Otherwise, arbitrageurs could make risk-free profits by borrowing the long bond (at a rate $(1 + RS_2)$) and investing in the one-period bonds.[1] The arbitraging activities of traders should also cause forward rates to closely cohere to those implied by the futures markets prices.

Forward rates and implied spot rates from futures prices for commodities have often been advocated for their price discovery functions (e.g. Grossman, 1986, 1989), and have been used by policy makers as direct forecasts in recent years.[2] The main advantage of such forecasts, of course, is that they are inexpensive. However, this should be weighed against their potential biases. French (1986, p. 29) notes that if the current spot rate equals the true expectation of the futures spot rate, the futures market cannot provide a better forecast than the random walk model. He demonstrates that futures prices cannot provide forecasts that are reliably better than the current spot prices unless the variation of the expected spot price change is a large fraction of the variation of the actual spot price change. Some work has been done indicating that futures contracts provide reasonably accurate forecasts for some commodities, such as animal products, but not others, such as wood products and metals (see Fama and French, 1987) and foreign exchange (e.g. Thomas, 1986). Kamara (1990) shows that for the period 1976–85, Treasury bill futures provide a more accurate forecast than simple forward rates for Treasury bills. Cole and Reichenstein (1994) provide evidence that, in recent years, Eurodollar futures rates serve as

---

[1] In general, in the case of discrete compounding, the T period spot rate is related to the current spot rate RS_1 and forward rates f_j as:

$$(1 + RS_T)^T = (1 + RS_1) * \prod_{i=1}^{T-1} (1 + f_i)$$

For the case of continuous compounding, with the current time set as $t = 0$, the spot rate is determined from: $P(t) = e^{-t \cdot RS(t)}$, where $P(t)$ is the price of a zero coupon bond maturing at $t \geqslant 0$; the instantaneous forward rate $f(t)$ is determined, using

$$B_t = -\exp\left(\int_0^t f(s)\, ds\right)$$

as: $f(t) = RS(t) + t * RS'(t)$.

[2] For example, in a recent news conference called to express the US administration's reaction to gas and oil market price increases, Laura D'Andrea Tyson, director of the White House's National Economic Council, stated: 'If you've been following gas, oil prices over the past few days, actually over the past ... week, there is already some sign that they are beginning to come down ... they've come down from about $24 a barrel to under $21 a barrel. All the *futures markets* suggest that the price of oil will be coming down later this year' (White House Economic News Conference, 2 May 1996).

rational expectations in the Muth (1961) sense since they reflect public information and are unbiased forecasts of later short-term interest rates. However, to date, no extensive work has been done to test the forecasting prowess of market implied *futures* yields and yield spreads for the term structure of interest rates for US government notes and bonds.

Fama (1984) demonstrates that over certain time periods, market-implied forward rates have reliable forecasting power for one-month spot rates up to one month in the future. Fama and Bliss (1987) extend this work and show that although forward rates do not forecast near-term interest rate changes well, they perform well for long-term horizon forecasts. Jorion and Mishkin (1991) also provide evidence that forward rates can serve as useful forecasts. Market-implied forward rates that are used in such studies can produce unacceptable yield patterns, however, such as forecasted spot rates that are unstable, and even negative, rendering them problematic in practical usage.

Some of these problems may be due to the simple fact that business conditions, fed policy, and government spending are important fundamental determinants of interest rates, and such factors must be taken into account directly.[3] However, forecasting fundamental business conditions and government policy responses is not straightforward. One could argue, on the other hand, that such fundamental factors are embedded in market (spot, futures and implied forward) prices. Grossman (1989) develops a rational expectations equilibrium model which shows that the spot price will not reveal all of the informed trader's information since there are many other factors ('noise') that determine the price along with the informed traders' information. Thus, futures prices should have incremental benefits to the information-revelation process.

An alternative approach to using implied forward prices is to introduce refined *technical* forecasts that are based on 'smoothed' forward prices. Best-fitting, maximum smoothness forward rates, introduced by Adams and Van Deventer (1994), represent a recent innovation in this direction. This approach is based on a common technique from numerical analysis used widely in engineering applications. However, the forecasting performance of this approach in comparison to the forecasts provided by market-implied futures yields and yield spreads for the term structure of interest rates remains an open question.

This paper attempts to fill this gap by examining the links between T-Bill, 5-Year T-Notes, 10-Year T-Notes, and T-bond futures yields, their smoothed forward rates, and actual spot market interest rates. Several models are subjected to a battery of tests for forecasting power. In particular, we examine the linkages between the futures yields and smoothed forward yields for possible causation. We also test whether or not the absolute difference between futures rates and implied forward rates decreases as the futures maturity date approaches, consistent with a greater degree of arbitrage for nearby maturities. In addition, we test whether the current forward and futures yields significantly predict actual future spot yields. Finally, we test whether the slope of the term structure implied by current forward and futures yields can predict future spot yield spreads. The results of this study show that actual spot rates as well as spot rate term premia that materialize in the future are significantly related to maximum smoothness forward rates, as well as rates implied from current futures prices. In addition, smoothed forwards and futures forecasts demonstrably outperform those of the random walk model.

The paper is organized into six sections. In the next section, we provide a description of the underlying data and the method of estimation of the forward and futures yields used in the

---

[3] We would like to thank the referee for pointing this out. The Cole and Reichenstein (1994) results support the contention that futures prices may indeed incorporate this type of information.

J. forecast. **16**: 209–224, 1997

analysis. In the second section we provide the results of the unit root and cointegration tests for the forward and futures yields as well as for the respective yield spreads. In the third section, causality tests between forward and futures yields as well as causality tests between the forward and futures yield spreads are shown. In the fourth section, we examine the nature of arbitrage between forward and futures markets. Specifically, we test whether the absolute differences between forward and futures yields and spreads tends to narrow, as the futures maturity approaches. In the fifth section, we examine the predictive power of the forward and futures yields and yield spreads. The final section provides a brief summary and conclusions.

A DESCRIPTION OF THE DATA

Our data consist of settlement prices for the Chicago Board and Trade (CBOT) Treasury bond, ten-year Treasury note, five-year Treasury note, and Chicago Mercantile Exchange (CME) T-bill futures contracts for the period from 1 June 1988 to 30 November 1993, a total of 1384 observations. As indicated above (and illustrated in Figure 1), this period spans a large variety of yield curve shapes. The time frame chosen also embraces both expansionary and contractionary business cycle conditions, and hence allows our models to capture the effects of cyclical trends in interest rates and term premia. The time period chosen also is free from price limit days for all the futures contracts examined, which are the most heavily traded bond futures contracts in the world.[4] All futures prices were obtained from Commodity Service Inc. The spot yields were determined using the common bootstrapping procedure for coupon and non-coupon bonds, as described, for example, in Fabozzi (1996, pp. 89–92).[5]

In implementing this procedure, all treasury note and bond prices for non-callable issues that traded on the market in the sample period were included, and were obtained from Bloomberg. The bond prices are at the closing of the spot market in New York. As Kamara (1990, p. 399) notes, since the closing spot rates are observed for up to an hour after the closing of the futures markets, this gives forward rates an advantage over the futures rates in examining informational effects and forecasting performance.[6] Over the sample period, new bonds are issued and older

---

[4] Price limits are exchange restrictions on the amount that contracts are permitted to change in price (up or down) each day. Such limits will, of course, prevent futures prices from incorporating market conditions fully. The CME abolished price limits on the T-bill futures contract in November 1985, before the start of our sample. Since 26 October 1986 price limits for the CBOT bond futures and the CBOT Ten Year futures contract have been set at 3 points ($3000 per contract). On 20 October 1987, during the stock market crash, the Bond Futures and Ten Year Note Futures Contracts experienced price limit days, as a consequence of the 'flight to quality' from the equities. However, these limits were lifted the next day. From that day (which predates our sample) until the end of our sample, neither the CBOT bond futures contract nor the CBOT Ten Year futures contract experienced limit days. The CBOT Five Year futures contract, whose introduction coincides with the start of the sample (June 1988) also has a 3-point price limit, which has yet to be reached.

[5] This procedure is implemented as follows. Using equation (1), if we know the cash flows of a bond maturing at $t = 1$ (coupon and/or principal) are CF_1 and CF_2, respectively, and we know the current spot rate at $t = 1$, RS_1 (from a zero-coupon or discount bond that is outstanding), given the 2-period bond price, B_2, we can solve for the two-period spot rate, RS_2 from:

$$B_1 = \frac{CF_1}{(1 + RS_1)} + \frac{CF_1}{(1 + RS_2)^2}$$

Once we have solved for RS_2, given the market price of a 3-period bond, we can solve for RS_3, and so forth.

[6] Hill, Schneeweis, and Yau (1990, p. 419) find that most informational effects for bond futures contracts are observed when both the cash or spot markets and futures markets are simultaneously open in the USA. Kamara (1990) finds that, notwithstanding the extra trading time of the spot market, futures rates for T-bills still provide superior forecasting

---

bonds mature, and hence the identity of the bonds changes each day. On average, there are 93 bonds used per day to calculate the spot rates. The current forward rate for period n-1 to period n is calculated from the current spot rate for a t_n period bond, $RS(t_n)$, and the current spot rate for a t_{n-1} period bond, $RS(t_{n-1})$, as

$$f(t_n) = RS(t_n) + t_n*\left(\frac{RS(t_n) - RS(t_{n-1})}{t_n - t_{n-1}}\right)$$

Futures yields, FY, are calculated from futures prices, P, for contracts with days to maturity DTM, according to the following formulae:

(a) *Treasury bill futures yields*:

$$FY = -4*\log\left[1 - (100 - P)*\left(\frac{DTM}{360}\right)\right] \tag{3}$$

(b) *Five-Year Treasury note futures yields*:

$$P = \sum_{t=1}^{10}\frac{4}{(1 + FY/2)^t} + \frac{104}{(1 + FY/2)^{10}} \tag{4}$$

(c) *Ten-Year Treasury note futures yields*:

$$P = \sum_{t=1}^{20}\frac{4}{(1 + FY/2)^t} + \frac{104}{(1 + FY/2)^{20}} \tag{5}$$

(d) *Treasury bond (20-year) futures yields*:

$$P = \sum_{t=1}^{40}\frac{4}{(1 + FY/2)^t} + \frac{104}{(1 + FY/2)^{40}} \tag{6}$$

---

performance relative to market-implied forwards. He does not look at T-Notes or T-Bonds or yield spreads or smoothed forward rates, however. The presumption of this paper, similar to Kamara (1990), is that informational effects are to be observed in the period known as the *trading time period*, which is when the principal markets for the securities are open. This, of course, ignores trading overseas and off-hours on the exchanges, which effectively permits trading for 23 hours per day around the world. Bond futures trade in London (LIFFE), Singapore (SIMEX), and Sydney (SFE), while spot contracts trade in Tokyo and London during the period that the US markets are closed. However, due to transactions costs and liquidity problems, such trading is limited (see e.g. Hill, Schneeweis and Yau, 1990). Night trading began on the CBOT on 30 April 1987. Off-hours trading has been facilitated further through the trading system known as GLOBEX, which is an international automated order-entry and matching system launched by Reuters in conjunction with the CBOT and the CME on 25 June 1992. GLOBEX trading has been very limited, representing less than 2% of the CME regular trading hour volume, since its inception. On 20 May 1994 the CBOT withdrew from the GLOBEX system, replacing it in October of that year with its Project A. Project A is a system designed for electronic trading off-hours for low-volume products. To date, the total of all Project A as well as off-exchange trading of CBOT bond and note futures contracts remains at below 1.5% of the total trading volume during regular trading hours. Commenting on the thin market for after-hour trading, CBOT Chairman Patrick Arbor stated: 'The appetite for 24 hour trading is not there yet'. See 'It's showdown time for GLOBEX', *New York Times*, 14 April 1994, D1.

J. forecast. **16**: 209–224, 1997

T. H. Park and L. N. Switzer   Forecasting Interest Rates and Yield Spreads   215

The fitted forward yields for time t, $f(t)$, are obtained, as in Adams and Van De Venter (1994) using the parameters a_j, b_j, and c_j provided from the fourth-order spline functions,[7] along with the k knot points:

$$f(t) = a_j + b_j * t + c_j * t^4 \tag{7}$$

for $t_{j-1} < t \leqslant t_j$, $j = 1, 2, \ldots, k + 1$ with the constraints:

$$c_{j+1} * t_j^4 + b_{j+1} * t_j + a_{j+1} = c_j * t_j^4 + b_j * t_j + a_j \tag{8}$$

for $j = 1, 2, \ldots k$

$$4 * c_{j+1} * t_j^3 + b_{j+1} = 4 c_j * t_j^3 + b_j * t \tag{9}$$

for $j = 1, 2, \ldots k$

$$-\log\left(\frac{B_j}{B_{j-1}}\right) = \frac{1}{5} * c_j * (t_j^5 - t_{j-1}^5) + \frac{1}{2} * b_j * (t_j^2 - t_{j-1}^2) + a_j * (t_j - t_{j-1}) \tag{10}$$

for $j = 1, 2, \ldots k$ and

$$c_{k+1} = 0 \tag{11}$$

The constraints in equation (8) ensure that the spline function (7) is continuous at the knot points, while equation (9) ensures that the slope of the spline function is continuous at the knot point. Constraints (10) and (11) are obtained from the definition of the forward curve, and the maximum smoothness constraint, respectively.

The method of estimation of the smoothed forward functions is restricted least squares. A key consideration in the estimation of spline functions as in this system is the choice of the number of knot points. Poor estimates may result from using too many or too few. Our strategy is to use the same ratio of knot points to data points as in Buse and Lim (1977). The empirical smoothed forward curves are thus obtained by setting $k = 4$, adding an error term to equation (7) and estimating the regression subject to the 13 constraints (8) to (11). In turn, the smoothed forward yield series that are fitted, based on the estimation, are adjusted to provide equivalent futures yields. We match the futures on an N-year Treasury that matures in n days with a forward rate for N years, n days in the future. The forward rate for N years, n days in the future that match the maturity of the futures contract that trades on the same calendar day, $f_{n,n+N}$ is calculated as:

$$f_{n,n+N} = \frac{\sum_{s=n}^{n+N} f(s)}{N} \tag{12}$$

TESTS FOR UNIT ROOTS AND COINTEGRATION FOR FORWARD AND FUTURES YIELDS AND YIELD SPREADS

As a first step to the analysis of market interrelationships, we tested each forward yield series, forward yield spread series, and futures yields series, as well as future yield spread series for

---

[7] The maximum smoothness properties of the fourth-order spline functions are shown in Adams and Van Deventer (1994).

© 1997 by John Wiley & Sons, Ltd.   J. forecast. 16: 209–224, 1997

Table I. Unit root tests for yield series

	Rates				Differences			
	DF	*DFT*	*PP*	*PPT*	*DF*	*DFT*	*PP*	*PPT*
90-day futures	−0.302	−2.840	−0.333	−2.876	−92.365	−92.264	−91.263	−91.241
90-day forward	−0.295	−2.832	−0.242	−2.527	−111.725	−111.586	−118.110	−118.068
5-year futures	−0.517	−2.574	−0.522	−2.782	−139.300	−139.117	−139.896	−139.803
5-year forward	−2.322	−6.203	−1.873	−5.546	−60.419	—	−67.786	—
10-year futures	−0.810	−2.759	−0.798	−2.763	−165.251	−163.024	−165.683	−165.529
10-year forward	−5.282	−8.780	−4.549	−8.198	—	—	—	—
20-year futures	−1.006	−2.643	−0.981	−2.622	−167.384	−0.981	−171.104	−170.939
20-year forward	−11.68	−12.39	−11.109	−11.953	—	—	—	—
95% critical value	−3.37	−3.80	−3.37	−3.80	−3.37	−3.80	−3.37	−3.80

Here and in Tables II and III, DF (PP) is the Dickey–Fuller (Phillips–Perron) *t*-statistic in an estimated model without a time trend. DFT and PPT are the corresponding *t*-statistics in estimated models with a time trend. Critical values can be found in Engle and Granger (1987) and Phillips and Ouliaris (1990). Differencing is not performed when unit roots are not detected.

Table II. Unit root tests for yield spread series

	Rates				Differences			
	DF	*DFT*	*PP*	*PPT*	*DF*	*DFT*	*PP*	*PPT*
5-yr–90-day fut.	−0.572	−1.993	−0.614	−2.044	−27.388	−28.334	−27.534	−28.204
5-yr–90-day fwd	−2.169	−3.790	−1.79	−3.152	−37.289	−37.297	−37.316	−37.337
10-yr–90-day fut.	−0.402	−2.121	−0.460	−2.174	−29.701	−30.086	−29.722	−29.967
10-yr–90-day fwd	−2.007	−3.848	−1.655	−3.233	−38.009	—	−38.028	−38.027
20-yr–90-day fut.	−0.454	−2.044	−0.516	−2.107	−31.722	−31.812	−31.715	−31.738
20-yr–90-day fwd	−3.359	−6.378	−2.637	−5.387	−38.406	—	−38.418	—
20-yr–5-yr fut.	−0.787	−2.809	−0.814	−2.853	−37.859	−37.975	−37.885	−38.031
20-yr–5-yr fwd	−8.247	−11.175	−7.436	−10.727	—	—	—	—
20-yr–10-yr fut.	−1.559	−2.890	−1.532	−2.868	−36.882	−35.975	−35.905	−35.973
20-yr–10-yr fwd	−9.778	−12.540	−8.762	−12.002	—	—	—	—
95% critical value	−3.37	−3.80	−3.37	−3.80	−3.37	−3.80	−3.37	−3.80

stationarity (the existence of unit roots). For non-stationary 'random walk' series, temporary shocks will have permanent effects. In addition, without due care, performing regressions with variables that behave individually as random walks in order to assess causality could lead to spurious results: classical significance tests will incorrectly identify relationships between the variables.

Table I shows the stationarity test results for the forward and futures yields using the classic Dickey–Fuller (1976) (DF) as well as Phillips and Perron (1988) (PP) tests for unit roots for models estimated with as well as without a time trend.[8] Table II shows the corresponding results for the yield spread series. If the DF and PP *t*-statistics are below the critical value, the null hypothesis of the presence of a unit root cannot be rejected.

From Tables I and II we note that unit roots prevail for all the futures and forward yields and yield spreads, with the exception of the implied 10-year forward rate, the implied 20-year forward

---

[8] For a description of these tests, see e.g. Maddala (1992).

T. H. Park and L. N. Switzer   *Forecasting Interest Rates and Yield Spreads*   217

Table III. Cointegration tests: estimation of equation (9)

Data series	DF	DFT	PP	PPT
90-day fut.–fwd	−7.427	−7.463	−6.946	−6.986
5-yr fut.–fwd	−12.648	−12.643	−12.446	−12.446
10-yr fut.–fwd	−11.864	−11.880	−11.658	−11.680
20-yr fut.–fwd	−13.007	−13.031	−12.681	−12.714
5-yr–90-day spread	−9.978	−9.999	−9.435	−9.460
10-yr–90-day spread	−10.432	−10.455	−9.987	−10.016
20-yr–90-day spread	−11.830	−11.826	−11.411	−11.412
20-yr–5-yr spread	−12.538	−12.534	−12.325	−12.326
20-yr–10-yr spread	−12.491	−12.641	−11.990	−12.174
95% critical value	−3.37	−3.80	−3.37	−3.80

rate, the 20-year–5-year implied forward yield spread, and the 20-year–10-year implied forward yield spread.[9] In all cases where unit roots are found, stationarity is achieved on taking first differences. These results imply that a standard regression to test for causation between most of the yields and yield spreads is misspecified. However, when non-stationary variables are cointegrated, a long-run equilibrium relationship exists between them that prevents them from moving far apart, and modified causality tests can be devised. Formally, if the two series FOR_t and FUT_t (in our case, these variables are forward and futures yields (or spreads)) show a long-run or equilibrium relationship, the error term e_t should be stationary:

$$FUT_t = \delta + \gamma * FOR_t + e_t \tag{13}$$

even when the two series FOR_t and FUT_t are non-stationary.[10]

Table III shows the cointegration tests for the futures yields and forwards yields, as well as corresponding yield spreads based on equation (13).

It is evident that all the futures yields and corresponding forward yields are found to be cointegrated (i.e. the 90-day forward–futures yields, the 5-year futures–forward yields, the 10-year futures–forward yields, and 20-year forward–futures yields exhibit significant co-integration). This implies that the forward and futures yields follow an equilibrium relationship that prevents them from drifting apart, suggesting the effectiveness of arbitrage of market participants in the futures and spot markets. The yield spreads (5-year over 90-day forward and futures, 10-year over 90-day forward and futures, 20-year over 90-day forward and futures, 20-year over 5-year forward and futures, and 20-year over 10-year forward and futures) are also found to be cointegrated, again suggesting strong arbitrage at all segments of the yield curve.

---

[9] This result is consistent with the pattern of mean reversion found by Park and Switzer (1996) for Note over Bond Spreads. Park and Switzer demonstrate, using simulated and out-of-sample spread data, that profitable trading strategies can be devised to exploit the apparent returns predictability in the data.
[10] It is generally true that any linear combination of two non-stationary time series is non-stationary.

CAUSALITY TESTS

The results on cointegration among the variables require that an error-correcting model (see e.g. Engle and Granger, 1987) be constructed when testing for causality for the variables. The error correction equations for Granger causality can be written as:

$$FOR_t = \alpha_0 + \sum_{i=1}^{m} \alpha_i {}^*FOR_{t-i} + \sum_{j=1}^{n} \beta_j FUT_{t-j} + \theta \hat{e}_{t-1} + v_t \tag{14}$$

$$FUT_t = \delta_0 + \sum_{k=1}^{p} \delta_k FOR_{t-k} + \sum_{l=1}^{q} \lambda_l FUT_{t-l} + \psi \hat{e}_{t-1} + w_t \tag{15}$$

where FOR_t and FUT_t are the forward yields (spreads) and futures yields (spreads) and $\hat{e}_{t-1}$ is the lagged value of the fitted error term in equation (13).

In each case, we have estimated optimal error-correcting models, with lags (m, n, p, and q) identified according to the Akaike and Schwartz Information Criteria (see e.g. Maddala, 1992, p. 540). The initial lag length tested was 24 trading days, which corresponds to approximately one calendar month. In markets that are as heavily traded as these, it is highly unlikely that autocorrelation patterns could persist for more than one month. We also used longer as well as shorter lag lengths. In all cases, whether looking at yield levels or spreads, we find that no more than two lags are necessary for characterizing the causality relationships. Thus, in the results reported here, m, n, p, and q are set to 2.

From equation (14), futures yields (spreads) will be found to lead or Granger-cause the forward yields (spreads) if $\beta_j = 0$. Similarly, from equation (15), forward yields (spreads) will lead or Granger-cause the futures yields if $\delta_k = 0$. The main results of the causality tests are shown in Table IV.

Based on the error-correction model estimates, it is apparent that there may be some information in futures markets yields that is not present in the spot (and forward) markets. In particular, for the 90-day T-bills, the futures yields lead (in the sense of Granger-cause) the forward yield. This result bolsters the view that futures traders appear to react faster to new information (see e.g. Schwert, 1990), suggesting that the futures market at this maturity has a higher percentage of informed traders relative to the spot market. Thus, for 90-day bills, the marginal trader in the spot market is more likely to be a less well-informed (e.g. noise) trader. This result is consistent with Kamara (1990). There is weaker evidence that the futures yields lead the forward yields at the 5-year maturity term. However, for all other maturities and for all yield spreads (5-year, 10-year and 20-year over 90-day; 20-year over 5-year; 20-year over 10-year) the forward and futures yields are co-determined, with no apparent lead–lag relationship. Hence, spread traders in the spot and distant maturity spot traders appear to not have any informational advantages over futures traders.

EVIDENCE ON ARBITRAGE BETWEEN FORWARD AND FUTURES YIELDS AND SPREADS

In this section we test whether the divergence between forward and futures yields and spreads tends to decline as the contract maturity approaches. Such a finding would be consistent with the

J. forecast. **16**: 209–224, 1997

Table IV. Error-correction Granger causality tests

$$FOR_t = \alpha_0 + \sum_{i=1}^{2} \alpha_i{}^* FOR_{t-i} + \sum_{j=1}^{2} \beta_j FUT_{t-j} + \theta \hat{e}_{t-1} + v_t$$

$$FUT_t = \delta_0 + \sum_{k=1}^{2} \delta_k FOR_{t-k} + \sum_{l=1}^{2} \lambda_l FUT_{t-l} + \psi \hat{e}_{t-1} + w_t$$

Direction of causation	F-statistics	
	$\beta_j = 0$	$\delta_k = 0$
90-day futures → 90-day forward	15.228[a]	—
90-day forward → 90-day futures	—	0.114
5-yr futures → 5-yr forward	2.149	—
5-yr forward → 5-yr futures	—	0.104
10-yr futures → 10-yr forward	0.005	—
10-yr forward → 10-yr futures	—	0.296
20-yr futures → 20-yr forward	0.006	—
20-yr forward → 20-yr futures	—	0.481
5-yr–90-day fut. spread → fwd spread	0.035	—
5-yr–90-day fwd spread → fut. spread	—	0.524
10-yr–90-day fut. spread → fwd spread	0.415	—
10-yr–90-day fwd spread → fut. spread	—	0.393
20-yr–90-day fut. spread → fwd spread	0.411	—
20-yr–90-day fwd spread → fut. spread	—	0.304
20-yr–5yr fut. spread → fwd spread	0.154	—
20-yr–5-yr fwd spread → fut. spread	—	0.551
10-yr–20-yr fut. spread → fwd spread	0.273	—
10-yr–20-yr fwd spread → fut. spread	—	1.435

[a] Significance at the 1% level. The null hypotheses of no causality are $\beta_{j=0}$ and $\delta_k = 0$ for equations (14) and (15) respectively. The test for causality is based on the computed F_1-statistic calculated by estimating equations (10) and (11) in restricted forms (with β_j and $\delta_k = 0$, giving $SSEr$) and unrestricted forms, (giving $SSEu$)

$$F_1 = \frac{(SSEr - SSEu)/m}{SSEu/(T - 2m - 1)}$$

which follows an F-distribution with m and T-$2m$-1 degrees of freedom.

hypothesis that traders have more consensus about nearby interest rates, which would tend to arbitrage away any systematic differences between futures and forward yields as well as futures and forward spreads for nearby maturity contracts.

To test this hypothesis, we perform the following regressions, for both forward and futures yields as well as for forward and futures spreads:

$$|FUT_t - FOR_t| = \lambda_0 + \lambda_1 DTM_t + e_t \tag{16}$$

where FUT_t and FOR_t are futures yields (spreads) and forward yields (spreads), respectively, DTM_t is the days to maturity of the futures contract, and e_t is the error term. These results, displayed in Table V, indicate that the absolute difference between futures and forward rates decreases as the futures maturity date approaches for the 90-day contracts alone. The absolute difference between future and forward spreads for the 5-year over 90-day and 10-year over 90-day contracts tends to decrease as the futures maturity date approaches. This suggests a greater degree

220   *Journal of Forecasting*   *Vol. 16, Iss. No. 4*

Table V. Absolute differences between futures and forward rates (spreads) as a function of futures contract maturity: least-squares estimates

$$|FUT_t - FOR_t| = \lambda_0 + \lambda_1 DTM_t + e_t$$

Differenced series	λ_0	λ_1	F
90-day futures–90-day forward	0.056 (4.247)[a]	0.003 (18.691)[a]	349.372[a]
5-yr futures–5-yr forward	0.236 (13.393)[a]	−0.0003 (1.367)	1.869
10-yr futures–10-yr forward	0.395 (16.111)[a]	−0.001 (3.477)[a]	12.029[a]
20-yr futures–20-yr forward	0.794 (12.903)[a]	−0.004 (4.034)[a]	16.275[a]
5-yr–90-day fut. spread–fwd spread	0.049 (10.915)[a]	0.0003 (5.420)[a]	29.374[a]
10-yr–90-day fut. spread–fwd spread	0.060 (13.254)[a]	0.0002 (3.066)[a]	9.399[a]
20-yr–90-day fut. spread–fwd spread	0.126 (11.433)[a]	−0.0001 (0.784)[a]	0.615
20-yr–5-yr fut. spread–fwd spread	0.139 (12.204)[a]	−0.0005 (2.866)[a]	8.213[a]
20-yr–10-yr fut. spread–fwd spread	0.068 (12.213)[a]	−0.0003 (3.935)[a]	15.482[a]

[a] Significant at the 5% level or better.
Absolute *t*-statistics in parentheses.

of arbitrage for nearby maturities, with traders having more consensus on short-term interest rates than on long-term ones. The results also suggest a larger degree of arbitrage at nearby maturities for spread traders across the short- and intermediate-term segments of the yield curve. The results for the other contracts and spread positions may be driven by the dynamics of a damped system, consistent with Samuelson's (1976) maturity hypothesis.[11]

FUTURES AND FORWARD YIELDS AND SPREADS AS PREDICTORS OF ACTUAL SPOT YIELDS AND SPOT TERM PREMIA

How well do the futures and forward yields predict the actual spot rates and term premia that prevail in the future? Are the futures or forward rate and forecasts better than the random walk forecasts, that project current values as the best predictors of the future? Given the reduction in uncertainty as contract maturity approaches, with the futures (and forwards) necessarily converging to the spot rates at maturity, we need to hold constant the period to maturity of the contract when determining forecasting performance. To assess the significance of futures and forward yields (and spreads) as predictors of the future spot rates (and spreads) in contrast to the spot rate (the random walk hypothesis) we perform the following least-squares regressions for each futures and forward yield as well as term spreads, for all of the 22 contracts that span our sample:

$$RS_T^i = \pi_0 + \pi_1 X_{t,T}^i + \pi_2 DTM_t^i + e_t^i \tag{17}$$

The dependent variable, RS_T^i, is the spot rate (or term spread) that prevails for contract i with a maturity at time T; $X_{t,T}^i$ is the futures or forward rate (or term spread) for contract i (that matures at time T) at time t, $DTM_{t,T}^i$ is the number of days to maturity for contract i as of day t, and $e_{t,T}^i$ is the random error term. The null hypothesis is that the forecasts provided by the futures and

---

[11] Samuelson (1976) demonstrates that for a damped system, the variability of nearby contracts can be greater than for more distant contracts.

J. forecast. **16**: 209–224, 1997

forward yields and yield spreads are unrelated to the spot rates and spreads that occur in the future. Forecasting power will be shown to the extent that the coefficient π_1 in equation (17) is found to be significantly different from 0. We also compare these forecasts to the simple random walk model given by:

$$RS_T^i = \gamma_0 + \gamma_1 RS_{t,T}^i + \gamma_2 DTM_t^i + e_t^i \tag{18}$$

where RS_T^i and DTM_t^i are defined as above, and $RS_{t,T}^i$ is the current spot rate (or spread) at time t for the bond (or spread position) underlying the delivery instrument of the futures contract that matures at time T.

Estimates of equation (17) given in Table VI show that holding constant the contract maturity, the futures yields today significantly forecast the 5-, 10-, and 20-year spot rates that actually prevail at contract maturity, but not the 90-day maturity contract. Only in the latter case is the estimated value of π_1 found not to be significantly different from zero. Similar predictive power is shown for corresponding 5-, 10-, and 20-year forward rates. Based on the estimated values of γ_1 and the goodness of fit of equation (18), it is evident that the random walk model is outperformed by the futures forecasts across all maturities and by the forward forecast for the 5-year forward forecasts. These results suggest that traders have greater uncertainty over short-term rates, reflected in less accurate forecasts. Our results also show that the forecast error of interest rates tends to decline as futures maturity approaches for the 5-, 10-, and 20-year contracts, suggesting better forecasting power from nearby futures contracts, as opposed to contracts of distant maturity. Such forecasting improvements are not shown, however, for the forecasts based on 10- and 20-year forward rates.

Table VI provides thus, two noteworthy results. First, when we hold constant the contract maturity, yield spreads based on the futures contracts as well as on the forward rates provide forecasting prowess: the futures market spreads prevailing in the market and forward rates (based on the maximum-smoothness model) are significantly related to actual spot spreads that materialize at contract maturity. This finding applies for all of the spread positions (for the 5-year over 90-day, 10-year over 90-day, 20-year over 90-day and 20-year over 5-year contracts), although it is less significant for the spread from the 20-year over 10-year forward rate forecasts. Finally, the random walk forecasts of spreads, where futures spreads are forecast to equal spot spreads that currently prevail, are outperformed in most instances by the futures- or forward-based forecasts except for spreads based on the 20-year bonds.

SUMMARY AND CONCLUSIONS

This paper provides new evidence on forecasting future interest rates and yields spreads using market data for T-bills, T-Notes, and Treasury Bond spot and futures contracts. The information contained in technical models is also assessed, using a recent innovation in interest rate modelling, the maximum-smoothness approach. Forecasts from this model are compared with implied yields and yield spreads derived from futures prices. Our results show the usefulness of forecasting market interest rates and the slope of the yield curve using data from futures markets, as well as from carefully modelled forward yield estimates.

There is some evidence of market segmentation, with more arbitrage apparently taking place for nearby maturities. Market participants appear to show a greater degree of consensus on short-term interest rates than on longer-term ones. There is an indication that forecasts from the

Table VI. (A) Least squares estimates of equation (17): the predictability of future spot yields and future spot term premia based on current futures and forward rates (spreads) and futures contract maturity; the dependent variable is the actual spot yield (or spot term premium) that will prevail at the maturity of the futures contract

$$RS_T^i = \pi_0 - \pi_1 X_{t,t}^i + \pi_2 DTM_t^i + e_t^i$$

RS_T^i is the spot rate (or term spread) that prevails for contract i with a maturity at time T, $X_{t,T}^i$ is the futures or forward rate (or term spread) for contract i (that matures at time T) at time t, $DTM_{t,T}^i$ is the number of days to maturity for contract i

Independent variable	π_0	π_1	π_2	F
90-day futures yield	8.015 (197.700)[a]	−0.002 (0.344)	−0.001 (2.726)[a]	3.780[a]
90-day forward yield	8.011 (201.205)[a]	−0.001 (0.196)	−0.001 (2.713)[a]	3.740[a]
5-yr futures yield	8.332 (109.027)[a]	0.058 (6.125)[a]	−0.001 (2.879)[a]	22.11[a]
5-yr forward yield	8.391 (123.048)[a]	0.050 (6.065)[a]	−0.001 (2.940)[a]	21.744[a]
10-yr futures yield	8.049 (74.928)[a]	0.140 (10.761)[a]	−0.001 (3.203)[a]	61.715[a]
10-yr forward yield	8.091 (73.119)[a]	0.131 (10.034)	−0.001 (2.646)[a]	54.117[a]
20-yr futures yield	7.985 (58.395)[a]	0.169 (10.481)[a]	−0.001 (2.971)[a]	58.330[a]
20-yr forward yield	8.955 (83.492)[a]	0.051 (4.154)[a]	−0.001 (2.580)[a]	11.809[a]
5-yr–90-day fut. spread	1.124 (1035.462)[a]	−0.021 (31.361)[a]	7×10^{-5} (0.906)	492.233[a]
5-yr–90-day fwd spread	1.124 (906.567)[a]	−0.021 (26.915)[a]	-7×10^{-5} (0.842)	362.637[a]
10-yr–90-day fut. spread	1.197 (1446.932)[a]	−0.032 (72.279)[a]	-8×10^{-5} (1.195)	2612.139[a]
10-yr–90-day fwd spread	1.189 (1445.551)[a]	−0.029 (70.436)[a]	-3×10^{-4} (5.347)[a]	2480.669[a]
20-yr–90-day fut. spread	1.208 (736.917)[a]	−0.023 (28.875)[a]	-4×10^{-5} (0.282)	416.958[a]
20-yr–90-day fwd spread	1.203 (828.475)[a]	−0.019 (30.439)[a]	-2×10^{-5} (1.400)	463.353[a]
20-yr–5-yr fut. spread	1.114 (223.487)[a]	−0.038 (9.039)[a]	-1×10^{-5} (0.796)	40.867[a]
20-yr–5-yr fwd spread	1.087 (511.062)[a]	−0.014 (8.858)[a]	-9×10^{-5} (0.631)	39.242[a]
20-yr–10-yr fut. spread	0.967 (84.264)[a]	0.054 (4.991)[a]	7×10^{-5} (0.608)	12.504[a]
20-yr–10-yr fwd spread	1.018 (314.622)[a]	0.005 (1.845)	3×10^{-5} (0.255)	1.753

(B) Least squares estimates of equation (18): the predictability of future spot yields and future spot term premia based on current spot rates (spreads) and futures contract maturity; the dependent variable is the actual spot yield (or spot term premium) that will prevail at the maturity of the futures contract

$$RS_T^i = \gamma_0 + \gamma_1 RS_{t,T}^i + \gamma_2 DTM_t^i + e_t^i$$

RS_T^i is the spot rate (or term spread) that prevails for contract i with a maturity at time T; $RS_{t,T}^i$ is the spot rate (or term spread) at time t for a bond underlying the deliverable instrument of futures contract i (that matures at time T), $DTM_{t,T}^i$ is the number of days to maturity for contract i

Independent variable	γ_0	γ_1	γ_2	F
90-day spot yield	8.022 (203.164)[a]	−0.022 (0.581)	−0.001 (2.714)[a]	3.890[a]
5-yr spot yield	8.410 (125.971)[a]	0.045 (5.907)[a]	−0.001 (2.778)[a]	20.751[a]
10-yr spot yield	8.083 (74.382)[a]	0.132 (10.308)[a]	−0.001 (2.524)[a]	56.911[a]
20-yr spot yield	8.945 (83.618)[a]	0.052 (4.258)[a]	−0.001 (2.527)[a]	12.500[a]
5-yr–90-day spot spread	1.122 (936.186)[a]	−0.019 (26.980)[a]	1×10^{-6} (0.114)[a]	346.206[a]
10-yr–90-day spot spread	1.186 (1486.733)[a]	−0.028 (64.471)[a]	2×10^{-5} (2.747)[a]	2413.186[a]
20-yr–90-day spot spread	1.201 (1850.186)[a]	−0.018 (30.365)[a]	-7×10^{-6} (0.471)	461.120[a]
20-yr–5-yr spot spread	1.086 (520.922)[a]	−0.014 (8.983)[a]	-7×10^{-6} (0.478)	40.366[a]
20-yr–10-yr spot spread	1.017 (323.992)[a]	0.006 (2.052)[a]	3×10^{-7} (0.251)	2.156[a]

[a] Significant at the 5% level or better.
Absolute t-statistics in parentheses.

J. forecast. **16**: 209–224, 1997

futures market are marginally better than those provided by the forward rates, consistent with the informational advantages of futures markets owing to lower transactions costs. Futures and forward market forecasts also tend to outperform those of the random walk model. However, there is only significant evidence that futures markets lead the forward rates for the shortest maturity instruments (90-day bills).

A consistent result from the cointegration tests is that a large degree of interdependence of the forward and futures rates is prevalent, suggesting that any tendency for these rates to drift apart will be only transient in nature. For the forecaster of future spot rates, this means that some reliability can be garnered from either well-fitted forward curves or from market futures data series. Of course, the usual caveat applies in time-series studies of this sort: that the results may be time-dependent. Since the sample examined incorporates periods of substantial variability in interest rates and in the slope of the yield curve, they may prove to be robust.

As a final note, the period coincides with the introduction of a new futures product, the CBOT Five-Year futures contract. We show that the forecasting performance of this new contract is similar to that of the other mature government bond and note futures contracts. The absence of a seasoning disparity is consistent with increased market efficiency through time.

ACKNOWLEDGEMENTS

We would like to thank Bob Shumway (the editor) and the anonymous referees for their helpful comments and suggestions. Financial support from the SSHRC (grant # 410-96-0748) to Switzer is gratefully acknowledged.

REFERENCES

Adams, K. J. and Van Deventer, D. R., 'Fitting yield curves and forward rate curves with maximum smoothness', *Journal of Fixed Income*, **4** (1994), 52–62.

Buse, A. and Lim, L., 'Cubic splines as a special case of restricted least squares', *Journal of the American Statistical Association*, **72** (1977), 64–8.

Carleton, W. T. and Cooper, I. A., 'Estimation and uses of the term structure of interest rates', *Journal of Finance*, **32** (1976), 1067–83.

Cole, C. S. and Reichenstein, W., 'Forecasting interest rates with Eurodollar futures rates', *Journal of Futures Markets*, **14** (1994), 37–50.

Cox, J. C., Ingersoll, J., Jr, and Ross, S. A., 'A theory of·the term structure of interest rates', *Econometrica*, **53** (1985), 385–407.

Dickey, D. A. and Fuller, W. A., 'Distribution of the estimators for autoregressive time series with a unit root', *Journal of the American Statistical Association*, **74** (1976), 427–31.

Engle, R. F. and Granger, C. W., 'Cointegration and error correction: representation, estimation, and testing', *Econometrica*, **55** (1987), 987–1007.

Fabozzi, F. J., *Bond Markets, Analysis, and Strategies*, 3rd edition, Upper Saddle River, NJ: Prentice Hall, 1996.

Fama, E. F., 'The information in the term structure', *Journal of Financial Economics*, **13** (1984), 509–28.

Fama, E. F. and Bliss, R. R., 'The information in long maturity forward rates', *American Economic Review*, **77** (1987), 680–92.

Fama, E. F. and French, K. R., 'Commodity futures prices: some evidence on forecast power, premiums, and the theory of storage', *Journal of Business*, **60** (1987), 55–74.

French, K. R., 'Detecting spot price forecasts in futures prices', *Journal of Business*, **59** (1986), s39–54.

Grossman, S. F., 'An analysis of the role of "insider trading" on futures markets', *Journal of Business*, **59** (1986), s129–46.

Grossman, S. F., *On the Informational Role of Prices*, Cambridge, MA: MIT Press, 1989.

Hill, J., Schneeweis, T., and Yau, J., 'International trading/non trading time effects on risk estimation in futures markets', *Journal of Futures Markets*, **10** (1990), 407–23.

Hull, J. and White, A., 'One factor interest rate models and the valuation of interest rate derivative securities', *Journal of Financial and Quantitative Analysis*, **28** (1993), 235–54.

Jorion, P. and Mishkin, F., 'A multicountry comparison of term-structure forecasts', *Journal of Financial Economics*, **29** (1991), 59–80.

Kamara, A., 'Forecasting accuracy and development of a financial market: the Treasury bill futures market', *Journal of Futures Markets*, **4** (1990), 397–405.

Maddala, G. S., *Introduction to Econometrics*, 2nd edition, Englewood Cliffs, NJ: Prentice Hall, 1992.

Muth, J. F., 'Rational expectations and the theory of price movements', *Econometrica*, **29** (1961), 315–35.

Park, T. H. and Switzer, L. N., 'Mean reversion of interest rate term premiums and profits from trading strategies with Treasury futures spreads', *Journal of Futures Markets*, **16** (1996), 331–52.

Phillips, P. C. B. and Ouliaris, S., 'Asymptotic properties of residual based tests for cointegration', *Econometrica*, **58** (1990), 165–94.

Phillips, P. C. B. and Perron, P., 'Testing for a unit root in time series regression', *Biometrika*, **75** (1988), 335–46.

Pindyk, R. S. and Rubinfeld, D. L., *Econometric Models and Econometric Forecasts*, 3rd edition, New York: McGraw-Hill, 1992.

Samuelson, P. A., 'Is the real-world price a tale told by the idiot of chance?' *Review of Economics and Statistics*, **58** (1976), 120–23.

Schwert, W., 'Stock volatility and the crash of 87', *Review of Financial Studies*, **3** (1990), 77–102.

Thomas, L. R., III, 'Random walk profits in currency futures trading', *Journal of Futures Markets*, **6** (1986), 109–26.

Authors' biographies:

Lorne N. Switzer is Professor of Finance and Director of the PhD and MSc in Administration Programs at Concordia University, Montreal, Canada. He obtained his PhD from the University of Pennsylvania in 1982. He has taught at the University of Saskatchewan, The University of Auckland (New Zealand), Tianjin University (People's Republic of China), The Hebrew University of Jerusalem, and Ben-Gurion University of the Negev (Israel). He has published several articles in the areas of futures markets, hedging, market efficiency, the economics of technological change, and real estate finance. He is on the Editorial Board of *European Financial Management* and is a technical consultant for the Caisse de Depot et Placement du Quebec and AMI Partners, Inc.

Tae H. Park is with the Risk Management Group, Fuji Capital Markets, New York, and is Associate Professor of Finance at Concordia University, Montreal, Canada. He obtained his PhD from the University of Michigan in 1990. His research interests include risk management, futures, options, and real estate finance.

Authors' addresses:

Lorne N. Switzer,
Finance Department, Concordia University, 1455 De Maisonneuve Blvd W, Montreal, Quebec, Canada H3G 1M8.

Tae H. Park,
Fuji Capital Markets Co., Two World Trade Center, 80th Floor, New York, NY 10048, USA.

The Journal of Financial Research • Vol. XX, No. 3 • Pages 355–372 • Fall 1997

FRACTIONAL DIFFERENCING MODELING AND FORECASTING OF EUROCURRENCY DEPOSIT RATES

John T. Barkoulas and Christopher F. Baum

Boston College

Abstract

Using the spectral regression method, we test for long-term stochastic memory in three- and six-month daily returns series of Eurocurrency deposits denominated in major currencies. Significant evidence of positive long-term dependence is found in several Eurocurrency returns series. Compared with benchmark linear models, the estimated fractional models result in dramatic out-of-sample forecasting improvements over longer horizons for the Eurocurrency deposits denominated in German marks, Swiss francs, and Japanese yen.

I. Introduction

Many economic and financial time series exhibit considerable persistence. Using standard unit-root tests of the $I(1)/I(0)$ variety, most of these series are best characterized as integrated processes of order one, denoted by $I(1)$. The assumption of an integer integration order is arbitrary, and relaxing it allows for a wider range of subtle mean-reverting dynamics to be captured. Allowing for the integration order of a series to take any value on the real line (fractional integration) leads to the development of long-memory models.

The long-memory, or long-term dependence, property describes the high-order correlation structure of a series. If a series exhibits long memory, persistent temporal dependence exists even between distant observations. Such series are characterized by distinct but nonperiodic cyclical patterns. The presence of long-memory dynamics gives nonlinear dependence in the first moment of the distribution and hence a potentially predictable component in the series dynamics. On the other hand, the short-memory, or short-term dependence, property describes the low-order correlation structure of a series. For short-memory series, observations separated by a long time span are nearly independent. Standard autoregressive moving average processes cannot exhibit long-term (low-frequency) dependence since they can only describe the short-run (high-frequency) behavior of a time series.

The presence of fractional structure in asset prices raises issues about theoretical and econometric modeling of asset prices, statistical testing of pricing models, and pricing efficiency and rationality. Applications of long-memory analysis include Greene and Fielitz (1977), Lo (1991), and Barkoulas and Baum (1996) for U.S. stock prices; Cheung (1993a) for spot exchange rates; and Fang, Lai, and Lai (1994) and Barkoulas, Labys, and Onochie (1997) for futures prices. The overall evidence suggests that stochastic long memory is absent in stock returns, but it may be a feature of some spot and futures foreign currency rates.

In the present study we extend the previous literature by investigating the presence of fractional dynamics in the returns series (yield changes) of three- and six-month Eurocurrency deposits denominated in eight major currencies: the U.S. dollar, Canadian dollar, German mark, British pound, French franc, Swiss franc, Italian lira, and Japanese yen. We emphasize the implications of long memory for predictability and market efficiency. According to the market efficiency hypothesis in its weak form, asset prices incorporate all relevant information, rendering asset returns unpredictable. The price of an asset determined in an efficient market should follow a martingale process in which each price change is unaffected by its predecessor and has no memory. If the Eurocurrency returns series exhibit long memory, they display significant autocorrelations between observations widely separated in time. Since the series realizations are not independent over time, past returns can help predict future returns, calling into question the validity of the efficient capital market hypothesis.

Using the spectral regression method of estimating the fractional integration parameter, evidence of long-memory dynamics is obtained in the Eurocurrency returns series for the Canadian dollar (three-month maturity only), German mark, Swiss franc, and Japanese yen. Except for the three-month Eurocanadian dollar returns series, long-memory forecasts are superior to linear predictors over longer forecasting horizons, thus establishing significant nonlinear mean predictability in these series.

II. Spectral Regression Method

The model of an autoregressive fractionally integrated moving average process of order (p,d,q), denoted by ARFIMA(p,d,q), with mean μ, may be written using operator notation as

$$\Phi(L)(1-L)^d(y_t - \mu) = \Theta(L)u_t, \qquad u_t \sim \text{i.i.d.}(0, \sigma_u^2) \tag{1}$$

where L is the backward-shift operator, $\Phi(L) = 1 - \phi_1 L - \ldots - \phi_p L^p$, $\Theta(L) = 1 + \vartheta_1 L + \ldots + \vartheta_q L^q$, and $(1-L)^d$ is the fractional differencing operator defined by

$$(1 - L)^d = \sum_{k=0}^{\infty} \frac{\Gamma(k-d)L^k}{\Gamma(-d)\Gamma(k+1)} \qquad (2)$$

where $\Gamma(\cdot)$ denotes the gamma, or generalized factorial, function. The parameter d is allowed to assume any real value. The arbitrary restriction of d to integer values gives rise to the standard autoregressive integrated moving average (ARIMA) model. The stochastic process y_t is both stationary and invertible if all roots of $\Phi(L)$ and $\Theta(L)$ lie outside the unit circle and $|d| < 0.5$. The process is nonstationary for $d \geq 0.5$, since it possesses infinite variance (see Granger and Joyeux (1980)). Assuming that $d \in (0,0.5)$ and $d \neq 0$, Hosking (1981) shows that the correlation function, $\rho(\cdot)$, of an ARFIMA process is proportional to k^{2d-1} as $k \to \infty$. Consequently, the autocorrelations of the ARFIMA process decay hyperbolically to zero as $k \to \infty$, which is contrary to the faster, geometric decay of a stationary ARMA process. For $d \in (0,0.5)$, $\sum_{j=-n}^{n} |\rho(j)|$ diverges as $n \to \infty$, and the ARFIMA process exhibits long memory, or long-range positive dependence. For $d \in (-0.5,0)$, the process exhibits intermediate memory (antipersistence), or long-range negative dependence. For $d = 0$, the process exhibits short memory, corresponding to stationary and invertible ARMA modeling. For $d \in [0.5,1)$, the process is mean reverting, even though it is not covariance stationary, since an innovation has no long-run effect on future values of the process.

Geweke and Porter-Hudak (1983) suggest a semiparametric procedure to obtain an estimate of the fractional differencing parameter d based on the slope of the spectral density function around the angular frequency $\xi = 0$. More specifically, let $I(\xi)$ be the periodogram of y at frequency ξ defined by

$$I(\xi) = \frac{1}{2\pi T} \left| \sum_{t=1}^{T} e^{it\xi}(y_t - \bar{y}) \right|^2. \qquad (3)$$

Then the spectral regression is defined by

$$\ln\{I(\xi_\lambda)\} = \beta_0 + \beta_1 \ln\left\{ 4 \sin^2\left(\frac{\xi_\lambda}{2}\right) \right\} + \eta_\lambda, \qquad \lambda = 1, \ldots, v \qquad (4)$$

where

$$\xi_\lambda = \frac{2\pi\lambda}{T} \quad (\lambda = 0, \ldots, T-1)$$

denotes the Fourier frequencies of the sample, T is the number of observations, and $v = g(T) \ll T$ is the number of Fourier frequencies included in the spectral regression.

Assuming that

$$\lim_{T \to \infty} g(T) = \infty, \quad \lim_{T \to \infty} \{g(T)/T\} = 0, \quad \text{and} \quad \lim_{T \to \infty} \ln(T)^2/g(T) = 0,$$

the negative of the ordinary least squares estimate of the slope coefficient in (4) provides an estimate of d. Geweke and Porter-Hudak (1983) prove consistency and asymptotic normality for $d < 0$, while Robinson (1990) proves consistency for $d \in (0,0.5)$. Hassler (1993) proves consistency and asymptotic normality for Gaussian ARMA innovations in (1). The spectral regression estimator is not $T^{1/2}$ consistent and will converge at a slower rate. The theoretical asymptotic variance of the spectral regression error term is known to be $\pi^2/6$.

To ensure that stationarity and invertibility conditions are met, we apply the spectral regression test to the returns series (yield changes) of the Eurocurrency deposit rates.

III. Data and Empirical Estimates

The data set consists of daily rates for Eurocurrency deposits denominated in U.S. dollars (US), Canadian dollars (CD), German marks (GM), British pounds (BP), French francs (FF), Swiss francs (SF), Italian lira (IL), and Japanese yen (JY) for three- and six-month maturities. These rates represent bid rates at the close of trading in the London market and are obtained from Data Resources Inc. The sample spans the period January 2, 1985, to February 8, 1994, for a total of 2,303 observations for the US, FF, and IL; 2,305 observations for the CD; 2,300 observations for the GM and JY; and 2,302 for the BP and SF. The last 347 observations of each series (roughly fifteen months) are reserved for out-of-sample forecasting while the remainder are used for in-sample estimation.

Table 1 presents the spectral regression estimates of the fractional differencing parameter d for the Eurocurrency deposit returns series. The number of low-frequency periodogram ordinates used in the spectral regression must be chosen carefully. Improper inclusion of medium- or high-frequency periodogram ordinates will bias the estimate of d; at the same time, a regression sample that is too small will increase the sampling variability of the estimates. To check the sensitivity of results to the choice of the sample size of the spectral regression, we report fractional differencing estimates for $v = T^{0.55}$, $T^{0.575}$, and $T^{0.60}$. The statistical significance of the d estimates is tested by performing two-sided ($d = 0$ versus $d \neq 0$) as well as one-sided ($d = 0$ versus $d > 0$) tests. The known

Fractional Differencing

TABLE 1. Estimates of the Fractional-Differencing Parameter d for the Eurocurrency Deposit Returns Series.

Series	$d(0.55)$	$d(0.575)$	$d(0.60)$
Three-month			
US dollar	0.092	0.106	0.037
	(1.137)	(1.333)‡	(0.526)
Canadian dollar	0.181	0.213	0.180
	(2.219)**‡‡	(2.679)***‡‡	(2.504)**‡‡‡
German mark	0.149	0.181	0.172
	(1.826)*‡‡	(2.262)**‡‡	(2.404)**‡‡‡
British pound	0.059	0.041	0.060
	(0.730)	(0.515)	(0.848)
French franc	−0.042	0.013	0.006
	(−0.516)	(0.171)	(0.093)
Swiss franc	0.215	0.210	0.152
	(2.635)***‡‡	(2.635)***‡‡	(2.114)**‡‡
Italian lira	0.054	0.064	0.069
	(0.669)	(0.805)	(0.962)
Japanese yen	0.244	0.250	0.190
	(2.996)***‡‡	(3.113)***‡‡	(2.645)***‡‡
Six-month			
US dollar	0.101	0.106	0.041
	(1.241)	(1.333)‡	(0.570)
Canadian dollar	0.086	0.108	0.053
	(1.059)	(1.358)	(0.739)
German mark	0.109	0.148	0.130
	(1.335)‡	(1.842)*‡‡	(1.821)*‡‡
British pound	0.028	0.025	0.031
	(0.344)	(0.325)	(0.435)
French franc	0.052	0.110	0.093
	(0.637)	(1.383)‡	(1.299)‡
Swiss franc	0.285	0.308	0.211
	(3.500)***‡‡	(3.862)***‡‡	(2.944)***‡‡
Italian lira	0.039	0.059	0.059
	(0.481)	(0.743)	(0.824)
Japanese yen	0.290	0.298	0.237
	(3.563)***‡‡	(3.707)***‡‡	(3.308)***‡‡

Notes: The sample corresponds to the in-sample number of observations (total number of observations minus 347, which are reserved for out-of-sample forecasting). $d(0.55)$, $d(0.575)$, and $d(0.60)$ give the d estimates corresponding to the spectral regressions of sample size $v = T^{0.55}$, $v = T^{0.575}$, and $v = T^{0.60}$. The t-statistics are given in parentheses and are constructed imposing the known theoretical error variance of $\pi^2/6$.

*Significant at the 10 percent level (two-tailed, $d = 0$ versus $d \neq 0$).
**Significant at the 5 percent level (two-tailed).
***Significant at the 1 percent level (two-tailed).
‡Significant at the 10 percent level (right-tailed, $d = 0$ versus $d > 0$).
‡‡Significant at the 5 percent level (right-tailed).
‡‡‡Significant at the 1 percent level (right-tailed).

theoretical variance of the regression error $\pi^2/6$ is imposed in the construction of the t-statistic for d.

As Table 1 indicates, robust evidence of fractional dynamics with long-memory features is obtained for the three- and six-month GM, SF, and JY returns series and the three-month CD returns series.[1] The fractional differencing parameters are similar in value across the two maturities considered for the GM, SF, and JY returns series. These series are not short-memory processes, which would exhibit a rapid exponential decay in their impulse response weights. However, they are clearly covariance stationary, as their d estimates lie below the stationarity boundary of 0.5. The presence of long memory is stronger, in terms of magnitude of the estimated fractional differencing parameters, for the SF and JY returns series, while it is milder for the GM and CD series. The implications of the long-memory evidence in these Eurocurrency returns series can be seen in both the time and frequency domains. In the time domain, long memory is indicated by the fact that the returns series eventually exhibit positive dependence between distant observations. A shock to the series persists for a long time even though it eventually dissipates. In the frequency domain, long memory is indicated by the fact that the spectral density becomes unbounded as the frequency approaches zero; the series has power at low frequencies.

The evidence of fractional structure in these returns series may not be robust to nonstationarities in the mean and short-term dependencies. Through extensive Monte Carlo simulations, Cheung (1993b) shows that the spectral regression test is robust to moderate ARMA components, ARCH effects, and shifts in the variance. However, possible biases of the spectral regression test against the no-long-memory null hypothesis may be caused by infrequent shifts in the mean of the process and large AR parameters (0.7 and higher), both of which bias the test toward detecting long memory. Agiakloglou, Newbold, and Wohar (1993) make a similar point. We now investigate the potential presence of these bias-inducing features in our sample series.

Graphs of the fractal Eurocurrency returns series do not indicate the data-generating process for the series in question underwent a shift in the mean.[2] Therefore, the evidence of long memory for these series should not be a spurious artifact of changes in the mean of the series. To examine the possibility of spurious inference in favor of long-term persistence due to strong short-term dependencies in the data, an autoregressive (AR) model is fit to each of the series

---

[1]We also applied the Phillips-Perron (PP) and Kwiatkowski, Phillips, Schmidt, and Shin (KPSS) unit-root tests to the returns series of Eurocurrency deposits. The combined use of these unit-root tests offers contradictory inference on the low-frequency behavior of several Eurocurrency returns series, which provides motivation for testing for fractional roots in the series. The long-memory evidence to follow reconciles the conflicting inferences derived from the PP and KPSS tests. To conserve space, these results are not reported here but are available upon request from the authors.

[2]These graphs are not presented here to conserve space, but they are available upon request from the authors.

in question according to the Schwarz information criterion. An AR(1) model is found to adequately describe dependence in the conditional mean of the three- and six-month GM, three-month SF, and three- and six-month JY returns series, while an AR(2) representation is chosen for the three-month CD and six-month SF returns series. All AR coefficient estimates are small in value, suggesting the absence of strong short-term dependencies.[3] Therefore, neither a shift in mean nor strong short-term dynamics appear to be responsible for finding long memory in the Eurocurrency returns series.

IV. A Forecasting Experiment

The discovery of fractional orders of integration suggests possibilities for constructing nonlinear econometric models for improved price forecasting, especially over longer forecasting horizons. An ARFIMA process incorporates this specific nonlinearity and represents a flexible and parsimonious way to model both the short- and long-term dynamical properties of the series. Granger and Joyeux (1980) discuss the forecasting potential of such nonlinear models, and Geweke and Porter-Hudak (1983) confirm this by showing that ARFIMA models provide more reliable out-of-sample forecasts than traditional procedures. The possibility of consistent speculative profits due to superior long-memory forecasts would cast serious doubt on the basic tenet of market efficiency, which states unpredictability of future returns. In this section we compare the out-of-sample forecasting performance of an ARFIMA model with that of benchmark linear models.

Given the spectral regression d estimates, we approximate the short-run series dynamics by fitting an AR model to the fractionally differenced series using Box-Jenkins methods. An AR representation of generally low order appears to be an adequate description of short-term dependence in the data. The AR orders are selected on the basis of statistical significance of the coefficient estimates and Q-statistics for serial dependence (the AR order chosen in each case is given in subsequent tables). A question arises as to the asymptotic properties of the AR parameter estimates in the second stage. Conditioning on the d estimate obtained in the first stage, Wright (1995) shows that the AR(p) fitted by the Yule-Walker procedure to the d-differenced series inherit the T^δ-consistency of the semiparametric estimate of d. We forecast the Eurocurrency deposit rates by casting the fitted fractional AR model in infinite autoregressive form, truncating the infinite autoregression at the beginning of the sample, and applying Wold's chain rule. Ray (1993) uses a similar procedure to forecast IBM product revenues.

---

[3] Full details of the AR representations of the fractionally integrated Eurocurrency deposit returns series are available upon request from the authors.

The long-memory forecasts are compared with those generated by two standard linear models: an AR model, described earlier, and a random walk with drift (RW) model. We reserve the last 347 observations from each series for forecasting. We analyze out-of-sample forecasting horizons of 1, 5, 10, 24, 48, 72, 96, 120, 144, 168, 192, 216, 240, 264, and 288 steps ahead, corresponding approximately to forecasting horizons of 1 day, 1 week, 2 weeks, and 1, 2, 3, 4, 5, 6, 7, 8, 9, 10, 11, and 12 months. These forecasts are truly ex-ante, or dynamic, since they are generated recursively conditioning only on information available at the time the forecast is made. Forecasting performance is judged by root mean squared error (RMSE) and mean absolute deviation (MAD) criteria.

Tables 2 through 8 report the out-of-sample forecasting performance of the competing modeling strategies for our fractal Eurocurrency returns series. Comparing the linear models first, the AR and RW forecasts are similar for all series across forecasting horizons. Table 2 reveals the long-memory forecasts for the three-month Eurocanadian dollar returns series to be inferior to linear forecasts across all forecasting horizons (with a few exceptions based on the MAD metric). The long-memory model may fail to improve upon its linear counterparts if the effect of long memory is considerably further into the future, and the adjustment to equilibrium takes considerable time to complete. Therefore, any improvement in forecasting accuracy over the benchmark models may only be apparent in the very long run.

A different picture is evident for the remaining fractal Eurocurrency returns series. As Tables 3 through 8 report, the long-memory forecasts for the GM, SF, and JY returns series significantly outperform the linear forecasts on the basis of both RMSE and MAD forecasting measures. The percentage reductions in the forecasting criteria attained by the long-memory models appear at very short horizons, they are dramatic, and they generally increase with the length of the forecasting horizon. The superior performance of the long-memory fits holds true across the various estimates of d for each returns series, suggesting robustness. It appears that the higher (lower) d estimates provide superior forecasting performance over longer (shorter) horizons.

To better reveal the relative forecasting performance of the alternative modeling strategies, Table 9 reports ratios of the forecasting criteria values (RMSE and MAD) attained by the long-memory model with the highest d estimate for each series to that obtained from the RW model. For the GM, SF, and JY series, the improvements in forecasting accuracy are sizable, while the long-memory forecasts of the Eurocanadian dollar returns series exhibit poor performance. The largest forecasting improvements occur for the SF and JY series with smaller, yet significant, improvements for the GM series.

The forecasting performance of the long-memory model for the GM, SF, and JY series is consistent with theory. As the effect of the short-memory (AR) parameters dominates over short horizons, the forecasting performance of the

TABLE 2. Out-of-sample Forecasting Performance of Alternative Modeling Strategies: Three-month Eurocanadian Dollar Rate.

Forecasting Model	k-Step-Ahead Horizon (Number of Point Forecasts)														
	1 (347)	5 (343)	10 (338)	24 (324)	48 (300)	72 (276)	96 (252)	120 (228)	144 (204)	168 (180)	192 (156)	216 (132)	240 (108)	264 (84)	288 (60)
Long memory															
d = 0.181. AR(6)	0.1939	0.3731	0.4995	0.6725	0.8967	1.1485	1.3511	1.5557	1.7288	1.9032	1.9885	2.1110	2.3994	2.8483	3.3485
	0.1184	0.2161	0.3066	0.4803	0.6882	0.8608	1.0067	1.1110	1.1883	1.3088	1.4638	1.6622	2.0837	2.5637	2.9942
d = 0.213. AR(6)	0.1940	0.3747	0.5055	0.6927	0.9216	1.1942	1.4131	1.6326	1.8166	2.0060	2.1031	2.2363	2.5307	3.0153	3.5864
	0.1185	0.2177	0.3098	0.4850	0.7041	0.8860	1.0419	1.1691	1.2446	1.3605	1.5130	1.7142	2.1422	2.6669	3.1703
AR(2)	0.1929	0.3648	0.4753	0.6117	0.5353	1.0171	1.1764	1.3453	1.5078	1.6587	1.7476	1.8680	2.1266	2.4250	2.6567
	0.1180	0.2108	0.3037	0.4808	0.6671	0.8064	0.8918	0.9989	1.1887	1.4044	1.5955	1.7616	2.0212	2.3054	2.4984
RW	0.1937	0.3637	0.4748	0.6160	0.8333	1.0145	1.1722	1.3392	1.4995	1.6487	1.7340	1.8524	2.1079	2.4065	2.6402
	0.1186	0.2110	0.3026	0.4801	0.6652	0.8042	0.8884	0.9909	1.1756	1.3889	1.5776	1.7413	2.0009	2.2857	2.4790

Notes: The test set consists of the last 347 observations for each series. The first entry of each cell is the root mean squared error (RMSE), while the second is the mean absolute deviation (MAD). AR(k) stands for an autoregressive model of order k. RW stands for random walk (with drift). The long-memory model consists of the fractional differencing parameter d and the order of the AR polynomial. The coefficient estimates and associated test statistics for the various AR models are available upon request. The RMSEs and MADs obtained from the long-memory models that are lower than those obtained from the RW model are underlined. The forecasting performance of the long-memory model corresponding to $d = 0.180$ is not reported since it is essentially identical to the one for $d = 0.181$.

TABLE 3. Out-of-sample Forecasting Performance of Alternative Modeling Strategies: Three-month Euromark Rate.

	k-Step-Ahead Horizon (Number of Point Forecasts)														
Forecasting Model	1 (347)	5 (343)	10 (338)	24 (324)	48 (300)	72 (276)	96 (252)	120 (228)	144 (204)	168 (180)	192 (156)	216 (132)	240 (108)	264 (84)	288 (60)
Long memory															
d = 0.149, AR(6)	0.0784	0.1659	0.2110	0.3305	0.4831	0.6360	0.8309	1.0574	1.3104	1.5316	1.7941	2.0119	2.2364	2.4591	2.6998
	0.0585	0.1262	0.1663	0.2657	0.4026	0.5626	0.7580	0.9895	1.2729	1.4713	1.7416	1.9858	2.2044	2.4149	2.6681
d = 0.181, AR(5)	0.0786	0.1664	0.2120	0.3304	0.4733	0.6084	0.7910	1.0046	1.2469	1.4624	1.7177	1.9246	2.1495	2.3696	2.6094
	0.0586	0.1263	0.1670	0.2665	0.3906	0.5298	0.7091	0.9263	1.2045	1.3946	1.6567	1.8900	2.1084	2.3130	2.5673
d = 0.172, AR(5)	0.0786	0.1660	0.2115	0.3299	0.4748	0.6140	0.7994	1.0159	1.2606	1.4770	1.7336	1.9427	2.1666	2.3867	2.6253
	0.0585	0.1262	0.1667	0.2659	0.3929	0.5366	0.7201	0.9408	1.2198	1.4115	1.6747	1.9108	2.1284	2.3340	2.5866
AR(1)	0.0781	0.1667	0.2195	0.3721	0.6120	0.8674	1.1336	1.4260	1.7284	1.9876	2.2885	2.5555	2.7886	3.0330	3.2888
	0.0584	0.1285	0.1717	0.2935	0.5488	0.8303	1.0966	1.3997	1.7106	1.9609	2.2689	2.5491	2.7778	3.0183	3.2804
RW	0.0778	0.1673	0.2194	0.3713	0.6105	0.8653	1.1307	1.4225	1.7244	1.9832	2.2836	2.5502	2.7830	3.0268	3.2835
	0.0583	0.1286	0.1719	0.2928	0.5470	0.8279	1.0935	1.3959	1.7065	1.9565	2.2637	2.5435	2.7720	3.0119	3.2749

Notes: The test set consists of the last 347 observations for each series. The first entry of each cell is the root mean squared error (RMSE), while the second is the mean absolute deviation (MAD). AR(k) stands for an autoregressive model of order k. RW stands for random walk (with drift). The long-memory model consists of the fractional differencing parameter d and the order of the AR polynomial. The coefficient estimates and associated test statistics for the various AR models are available upon request. The RMSEs and MADs obtained from the long-memory models that are lower than those obtained from the RW model are underlined.

TABLE 4. Out-of-sample Forecasting Performance of Alternative Modeling Strategies: Six-month Euromark Rate.

Forecasting Model	k-Step-Ahead Horizon (Number of Point Forecasts)														
	1 (347)	5 (343)	10 (338)	24 (324)	48 (300)	72 (276)	96 (252)	120 (228)	144 (204)	168 (180)	192 (156)	216 (132)	240 (108)	264 (84)	288 (60)
Long memory															
$d = 0.109$, AR(2)	0.0810	0.1582	0.2020	0.2966	0.4445	0.6086	0.7845	0.9899	1.2022	1.3968	1.6253	1.8441	2.0825	2.2994	2.5294
	0.0596	0.1226	0.1602	0.2387	0.3757	0.5502	0.7327	0.9464	1.1749	1.3554	1.5908	1.8208	2.0582	2.2699	2.5134
$d = 0.148$, AR(2)	0.0814	0.1600	0.2033	0.2942	0.4229	0.5593	0.7131	0.8995	1.0944	1.2764	1.4874	1.6866	1.9173	2.1237	2.3423
	0.0600	0.1240	0.1618	0.2397	0.3533	0.4919	0.6473	0.8402	1.0576	1.2195	1.4382	1.6522	1.8825	2.0804	2.3162
$d = 0.130$, AR(2)	0.0812	0.1591	0.2025	0.2947	0.4316	0.5807	0.7447	0.9400	1.1432	1.3310	1.5503	1.7588	1.9933	2.2047	2.4286
	0.0598	0.1233	0.1609	0.2388	0.3626	0.5179	0.6853	0.8882	1.1109	1.2819	1.5086	1.7302	1.9639	2.1685	2.4079
AR(1)	0.0806	0.1593	0.2136	0.3464	0.5850	0.8431	1.0944	1.3638	1.6327	1.8769	2.1613	2.4382	2.7071	2.9633	3.2349
	0.0590	0.1230	0.1665	0.2801	0.5293	0.8126	1.0712	1.3457	1.6211	1.8590	2.1482	2.4301	2.6973	2.9527	3.2305
RW	0.0815	0.1601	0.2137	0.3453	0.5827	0.8395	1.0896	1.3580	1.6261	1.8695	2.1526	2.4287	2.6966	2.9518	3.2235
	0.0592	0.1235	0.1670	0.2789	0.5270	0.8083	1.0659	1.3394	1.6140	1.8512	2.1391	2.4202	2.6867	2.9409	3.2188

Notes: The test set consists of the last 347 observations for each series. The first entry of each cell is the root mean squared error (RMSE), while the second is the mean absolute deviation (MAD). AR(k) stands for an autoregressive model of order k. RW stands for random walk (with drift). The long-memory model consists of the fractional differencing parameter d and the order of the AR polynomial. The coefficient estimates and associated test statistics for the various AR models are available upon request. The RMSEs and MADs obtained from the long-memory models that are lower than those obtained from the RW model are underlined.

TABLE 5. Out-of-sample Forecasting Performance of Alternative Modeling Strategies: Three-month Euroswiss Franc Rate.

Forecasting Model	k-Step-Ahead Horizon (Number of Point Forecasts)																	
	1 (347)	5 (343)	10 (338)	24 (324)	48 (300)	72 (276)	96 (252)	120 (228)	144 (204)	168 (180)	192 (156)	216 (132)	240 (108)	264 (84)	288 (60)
Long memory															
$d = 0.215$, AR(4)	0.1169	0.1781	0.2181	0.3195	0.3987	0.4436	0.4914	0.4876	0.5364	0.6280	0.6080	0.6567	0.7001	0.9051	1.1476
	0.0837	0.1292	0.1619	0.2492	0.3049	0.3138	0.3637	0.3469	0.4126	0.4702	0.4379	0.4741	0.5190	0.6892	0.9210
$d = 0.152$, AR(4)	0.1164	0.1747	0.2127	0.3081	0.3968	0.4685	0.5291	0.5549	0.6211	0.7135	0.7516	0.8345	0.9501	1.1778	1.4410
	0.0831	0.1263	0.1582	0.2402	0.3024	0.3403	0.3824	0.4104	0.4837	0.5469	0.5888	0.6751	0.8610	1.0653	1.3333
AR(1)	0.1156	0.1809	0.2222	0.3446	0.5395	0.7320	0.8911	1.0399	1.1981	1.3639	1.5476	1.7362	1.9685	2.2524	2.5640
	0.0815	0.1295	0.1680	0.2656	0.4375	0.6228	0.7908	0.9540	1.1224	1.2906	1.4879	1.6924	1.9508	2.2298	2.5452
RW	0.1142	0.1796	0.2213	0.3445	0.5405	0.7340	0.8938	1.0435	1.2027	1.3692	1.5538	1.7433	1.9766	2.2612	2.5734
	0.0800	0.1287	0.1674	0.2656	0.4388	0.6253	0.7943	0.9583	1.1276	1.2965	1.4947	1.7000	1.9592	2.2390	2.5550

Notes: The test set consists of the last 347 observations for each series. The first entry of each cell is the root mean squared error (RMSE), while the second is the mean absolute deviation (MAD). AR(k) stands for an autoregressive model of order k. RW stands for random walk (with drift). The long-memory model consists of the fractional differencing parameter d and the order of the AR polynomial. The coefficient estimates and associated test statistics for the various AR models are available upon request. The RMSEs and MADs obtained from the long-memory models that are lower than those obtained from the RW model are underlined. The forecasting performance of the long-memory model corresponding to $d = 0.210$ is not reported since it is essentially identical to the one for $d = 0.215$.

TABLE 6. Out-of-sample Forecasting Performance of Alternative Modeling Strategies: Six-month Euroswiss Franc Rate.

Forecasting Model	k-Step-Ahead Horizon (Number of Point Forecasts)														
	1 (347)	5 (343)	10 (338)	24 (324)	48 (300)	72 (276)	96 (252)	120 (228)	144 (204)	168 (180)	192 (156)	216 (132)	240 (108)	264 (84)	288 (60)
Long memory															
$d = 0.285$, AR(6)	0.1212	0.1777	0.2263	0.3170	0.3979	0.4740	0.5338	0.5398	0.5677	0.6374	0.5911	0.6308	0.6124	0.7706	0.9305
	0.0810	0.1316	0.1691	0.2477	0.3032	0.3406	0.4102	0.3889	0.4438	0.4950	0.4331	0.4903	0.4532	0.5935	0.7160
$d = 0.308$, AR(6)	0.1214	0.1789	0.2289	0.3239	0.4079	0.4844	0.5484	0.5604	0.6007	0.6842	0.6457	0.6882	0.6465	0.7860	0.9251
	0.0812	0.1323	0.1708	0.2518	0.3083	0.3509	0.4236	0.4043	0.4711	0.5374	0.4846	0.5449	0.4884	0.6173	0.7214
$d = 0.211$, AR(5)	0.1210	0.1765	0.2211	0.3028	0.3854	0.4734	0.5361	0.5457	0.5566	0.6050	0.5872	0.6550	0.7512	0.9613	1.1785
	0.0806	0.1306	0.1658	0.2394	0.2970	0.3351	0.4060	0.4088	0.4335	0.4505	0.4334	0.5072	0.5973	0.7969	1.0372
AR(2)	0.1203	0.1796	0.2290	0.3437	0.5552	0.7689	0.9434	1.0838	1.2058	1.3538	1.5381	1.7530	2.0228	2.3250	2.6317
	0.0789	0.1305	0.1715	0.2726	0.4663	0.6479	0.8234	0.9730	1.1217	1.2831	1.4785	1.7079	2.0041	2.3049	2.6213
RW	0.1241	0.1835	0.2327	0.3455	0.5570	0.7707	0.9461	1.0874	1.2101	1.3592	1.5439	1.7591	2.0299	2.3331	2.6419
	0.0799	0.1327	0.1730	0.2730	0.4673	0.6502	0.8263	0.9769	1.1264	1.2877	1.4835	1.7136	2.0108	2.3126	2.6309

Notes: The test set consists of the last 347 observations for each series. The first entry of each cell is the root mean squared error (RMSE), while the second is the mean absolute deviation (MAD). AR(k) stands for an autoregressive model of order k. RW stands for random walk (with drift). The long-memory model consists of the fractional differencing parameter d and the order of the AR polynomial. The coefficient estimates and associated test statistics for the various AR models are available upon request. The RMSEs and MADs obtained from the long-memory models that are lower than those obtained from the RW model are underlined.

TABLE 7. Out-of-sample Forecasting Performance of Alternative Modeling Strategies: Three-month Euroyen Rate.

Forecasting Model	k-Step-Ahead Horizon (Number of Point Forecasts)														
	1 (347)	5 (343)	10 (338)	24 (324)	48 (300)	72 (276)	96 (252)	120 (228)	144 (204)	168 (180)	192 (156)	216 (132)	240 (108)	264 (84)	288 (60)
Long memory d = 0.250, AR(5)	0.0484	0.0846	0.1161	0.1920	0.2675	0.3371	0.4096	0.4293	0.3682	0.3464	0.3663	0.3889	0.5098	0.5625	0.5102
	0.0345	0.0606	0.0856	0.1477	0.2156	0.2827	0.3313	0.3387	0.2807	0.2865	0.3101	0.3158	0.4387	0.5331	0.4890
d = 0.190, AR(4)	0.0483	0.0841	0.1149	0.1884	0.2639	0.3344	0.4060	0.4274	0.3776	0.3683	0.4000	0.4487	0.5730	0.6532	0.6248
	0.0343	0.0601	0.0840	0.1446	0.2111	0.2806	0.3323	0.3431	0.2873	0.2964	0.3332	0.3875	0.4983	0.6345	0.6112
AR(1)	0.0482	0.0844	0.1181	0.2022	0.3196	0.4361	0.5476	0.6177	0.6577	0.7293	0.8341	0.9758	1.1426	1.2814	1.3397
	0.0331	0.0576	0.0828	0.1479	0.2437	0.3634	0.4771	0.5539	0.6172	0.6956	0.8033	0.9579	1.1253	1.2768	1.3349
RW	0.0491	0.0847	0.1184	0.2023	0.3194	0.4358	0.5473	0.6175	0.6575	0.7289	0.8336	0.9752	1.1419	1.2808	1.3390
	0.0334	0.0578	0.0832	0.1481	0.2437	0.3632	0.4767	0.5536	0.6167	0.6951	0.8027	0.9572	1.1245	1.2761	1.3341

Notes: The test set consists of the last 347 observations for each series. The first entry of each cell is the root mean squared error (RMSE), while the second is the mean absolute deviation (MAD). AR(k) stands for an autoregressive model of order k. RW stands for random walk (with drift). The long-memory model consists of the fractional differencing parameter d and the order of the AR polynomial. The coefficient estimates and associated test statistics for the various AR models are available upon request. The RMSEs and MADs obtained from the long-memory models that are lower than those obtained from the RW model are underlined. The forecasting performance of the long-memory model corresponding to d = 0.244 is not reported since it is essentially identical to the one for d = 0.250.

TABLE 8. Out-of-sample Forecasting Performance of Alternative Modeling Strategies: Six-month Euroyen Rate.

Forecasting Model	k-Step-Ahead Horizon (Number of Point Forecasts)														
	1 (347)	5 (343)	10 (338)	24 (324)	48 (300)	72 (276)	96 (252)	120 (228)	144 (204)	168 (180)	192 (156)	216 (132)	240 (108)	264 (84)	288 (60)
Long memory d = 0.298, AR(6)	0.0458	0.0806	0.1129	0.1885	0.2725	0.3534	0.4447	0.4929	0.4805	0.4663	0.4105	0.3935	0.5175	0.5843	0.5375
	0.0325	0.0592	0.0836	0.1456	0.2259	0.2841	0.3585	0.3989	0.3693	0.3680	0.3416	0.3115	0.4209	0.5293	0.5154
d = 0.237, AR(4)	0.0455	0.0841	0.1149	0.1884	0.2639	0.3344	0.4060	0.4274	0.3776	0.3683	0.4000	0.4487	0.5730	0.6532	0.6248
	0.0323	0.0601	0.0840	0.1446	0.2111	0.2806	0.3323	0.3431	0.2873	0.2964	0.3332	0.3875	0.4983	0.6345	0.6112
AR(1)	0.0456	0.0808	0.1158	0.2024	0.3320	0.4583	0.5740	0.6518	0.7056	0.7755	0.8583	0.9830	1.1522	1.2996	1.3725
	0.0314	0.0579	0.0866	0.1631	0.2632	0.3829	0.4786	0.5492	0.6231	0.7132	0.8193	0.9582	1.1290	1.2898	1.3669
RW	0.0465	0.0809	0.1160	0.2020	0.3308	0.4563	0.5714	0.6486	0.7016	0.7706	0.8524	0.9762	1.1445	1.2912	1.3634
	0.0315	0.0583	0.0869	0.1627	0.2622	0.3810	0.4762	0.5455	0.6184	0.7078	0.8130	0.9512	1.1210	1.2812	1.3577

Notes: The test set consists of the last 347 observations for each series. The first entry of each cell is the root mean squared error (RMSE), while the second is the mean absolute deviation (MAD). AR(k) stands for an autoregressive model of order k. RW stands for random walk (with drift). The long-memory model consists of the fractional differencing parameter d and the order of the AR polynomial. The coefficient estimates and associated test statistics for the various AR models are available upon request. The RMSEs and MADs obtained from the long-memory models that are lower than those obtained from the RW model are underlined. The forecasting performance of the long-memory model corresponding to d = 0.290 is not reported since it is essentially identical to the one for d = 0.298.

TABLE 9. Relative Forecasting Performance of Long-Memory and Random Walk Models.

Forecasting Model	k-Step-Ahead Horizon														
	1	5	10	24	48	72	96	120	144	168	192	216	240	264	288
CD (3-month), d = 0.213	1.0015	1.0302	1.0647	1.1245	1.1060	1.1771	1.2055	1.2191	1.2115	1.2167	1.2129	1.2072	1.2008	1.2530	1.3584
	0.9992	1.0318	1.0238	1.0102	1.0585	1.1017	1.1728	1.1798	1.0587	0.9796	0.9591	0.9844	1.0706	1.1668	1.2789
GM (3-month), d = 0.181	1.0103	0.9946	0.9663	0.8898	0.7753	0.7031	0.6996	0.7062	0.7247	0.7374	0.7522	0.7547	0.7723	0.7829	0.7947
	1.0051	0.9821	0.9715	0.9102	0.7141	0.6399	0.6485	0.6636	0.7058	0.7128	0.7319	0.7431	0.8289	0.7680	0.7839
GM (6-month), d = 0.148	0.9988	0.9994	0.9513	0.8520	0.7258	0.6662	0.6545	0.6624	0.6730	0.6827	0.6910	0.6944	0.7110	0.7195	0.7266
	1.0135	1.0040	0.9689	0.8594	0.6704	0.6086	0.6073	0.6273	0.6553	0.6588	0.6723	0.6827	0.7007	0.7074	0.7196
SF (3-month), d = 0.215	1.0236	0.9916	0.9855	0.9274	0.7377	0.6044	0.5498	0.4673	0.4460	0.4587	0.3913	0.3767	0.3542	0.4003	0.4459
	1.0463	1.0039	0.9671	0.9383	0.6948	0.5018	0.4579	0.3620	0.3659	0.3627	0.2930	0.2789	0.2649	0.3080	0.3605
SF (6-month), d = 0.308	0.9782	0.9749	0.9837	0.9375	0.7323	0.6285	0.5120	0.5154	0.4964	0.5034	0.4182	0.3912	0.3185	0.3369	0.3502
	1.0163	0.9970	0.9873	0.9223	0.6597	0.5397	0.4247	0.4139	0.4182	0.4173	0.3267	0.3180	0.2429	0.2669	0.2742
JY (3-month), d = 0.250	0.9857	0.9988	0.9806	0.9491	0.8375	0.7735	0.7484	0.6952	0.5600	0.4752	0.4394	0.3988	0.4464	0.4392	0.3810
	1.0329	1.0484	1.0288	0.9973	0.8847	0.7784	0.6950	0.6118	0.4552	0.4122	0.3863	0.3299	0.3901	0.4178	0.3665
JY (6-month), d = 0.298	0.9849	0.9963	0.9733	0.9332	0.8238	0.7745	0.7783	0.7599	0.6849	0.6051	0.4816	0.4031	0.4522	0.4525	0.3942
	1.0317	1.0154	0.9620	0.8949	0.8616	0.7457	0.7528	0.7313	0.5972	0.5199	0.4202	0.3275	0.3755	0.4131	0.3796

Notes: The long-memory model for each series is the one corresponding to the highest d estimate. Similar results are obtained for the other long-memory models reported in previous tables. The first (second) entry in each cell is the ratio of the RMSE (MAD) value achieved by the long-memory model to that of the random walk (with drift) model.

long-memory and linear models is similar in the short run. In the long run, however, the dynamic effects of the short-memory parameters are dominated by the fractional differencing parameter d, which captures the long-term correlation structure of the series, thus resulting in superior long-memory forecasts. This evidence accentuates the usefulness of long-memory models as forecast-generating mechanisms for some Eurocurrency returns series, and it casts doubt on the hypothesis of the weak form of market efficiency for longer horizons. It also contrasts with the failure of ARFIMA models to improve on the RW model in out-of-sample forecasts of foreign exchange rates (Cheung (1993a)).

V. Conclusions

Using the spectral regression method, we find significant evidence of long-term stochastic memory in the returns series (yield changes) of three- and six-month Eurodeposits denominated in German marks, Swiss francs, and Japanese yen, as well as three-month Eurodeposits denominated in Canadian dollars. These series appear to be characterized by irregular cyclic fluctuations with long-term persistence. Except for the Canadian dollar returns series, the out-of-sample long-memory forecasts result in dramatic improvements in forecasting accuracy especially over longer horizons compared with benchmark linear forecasts. Price movements in these markets appear to be influenced not only by their recent history but also by realizations from the distant past. This is strong evidence against the martingale model, which states that, conditioning on historical returns, future returns are unpredictable.

We establish the practical usefulness of developing long-memory models for some Eurocurrency returns series. These results could be improved in future research via estimation of ARFIMA models based on maximum likelihood methods (e.g., Sowell (1992)). These procedures avoid the two-stage estimation process used in this paper by allowing for the simultaneous estimation of the long- and short-memory components of the series. Given the sample size of our series, however, implementing these procedures will be computationally burdensome, since closed-form solutions for these one-stage estimators do not exist. Additionally, in some cases, the maximum likelihood estimates of the fractional-differencing parameter appear to be sensitive to the parameterization of the high-frequency components of the series. Future research should investigate why certain Eurocurrency returns series exhibit long memory while others do not.

References

Agiakloglou, C., P. Newbold, and M. Wohar, 1993, Bias in an estimator of the fractional difference parameter, *Journal of Time Series Analysis* 14, 235–46.

Barkoulas, J. T. and C. F. Baum, 1996, Long term dependence in stock returns, *Economics Letters* 53, 253–59.

Barkoulas, J. T., W. C. Labys, and J. Onochie, 1997, Long memory in futures prices, *Financial Review*, Forthcoming.

Cheung, Y. W., 1993a, Long memory in foreign-exchange rates, *Journal of Business and Economic Statistics* 11, 93–101.

————, 1993b, Tests for fractional integration: A Monte Carlo investigation, *Journal of Time Series Analysis* 14, 331–45.

Fang, H., K. S. Lai, and M. Lai, 1994, Fractal structure in currency futures prices, *Journal of Futures Markets* 14, 169–81.

Geweke, J. and S. Porter-Hudak, 1983, The estimation and application of long memory time series models, *Journal of Time Series Analysis* 4, 221–38.

Granger, C. W. J. and R. Joyeux, 1980, An introduction to long-memory time series models and fractional differencing, *Journal of Time Series Analysis* 1, 15–39.

Greene, M. T. and B. D. Fielitz, 1977, Long-term dependence in common stock returns, *Journal of Financial Economics* 5, 339–49.

Hassler, U., 1993, Regression of spectral estimators with fractionally integrated time series, *Journal of Time Series Analysis* 14, 369–80.

Hosking, J. R. M., 1981, Fractional differencing, *Biometrika* 68, 165–76.

Lo, A. W., 1991, Long-term memory in stock market prices, *Econometrica* 59, 1279–1313.

Ray, B., 1993, Long range forecasting of IBM product revenues using a seasonal fractionally differenced ARMA model, *International Journal of Forecasting* 9, 255–69.

Robinson, P., 1990, Time series with strong dependence, *Advances in Econometrics*, 6th World Congress (Cambridge University Press, Cambridge).

Sowell, F., 1992, Maximum likelihood estimation of stationary univariate fractionally integrated time-series models, *Journal of Econometrics* 53, 165–88.

Wright, J. H., 1995, Stochastic orders of magnitude associated with two-stage estimators of fractional ARIMA systems, *Journal of Time Series Analysis* 16, 119–25.

[5]

Expert systems for bond rating: a comparative analysis of statistical, rule-based and neural network systems

Jun Woo Kim

Korea Telecommunication International (KTI), 676 Yeuksan Dong KangNam Ku, 135-080 Seoul, Korea

H. Roland Weistroffer and Richard T. Redmond

School of Business, Virginia Commonwealth University, Richmond, VA 23284–4000, USA

Abstract: *An important problem in financial investment is the classification of bonds based on the likelihood that the issuing company may default on the promised payments. Much effort has been invested into simulating the bond rating process using statistical tools. A weakness of these tools is the requirement of statistical assumptions which may not be appropriate for the bond rating problem. In this paper we present results of a study comparing an artificial neural network system, a rule-based expert system and statistical techniques applied to the bond rating problem. The bond rating process is simulated by using published financial data.*

1. Introduction

1.1. The bond rating problem

The default risk of a bond is the likelihood that the promised coupon and par value of a bond will not be paid. The commercial bond rating organizations such as Moody's and Standard & Poor's classify the bonds to represent the degree of default risk. These rating agencies conduct extensive committee analyses of the intrinsic characteristics of the issuing organizations. Investigations may be conducted in several areas, such as a business analysis, an analysis of accounting quality, a financial analysis and a legal analysis. The results are published in the form of ratings which provide information to the investors and the market in general. In the case of Standard & Poor's, the possible ratings are AAA, AA, A, BBB, BB, B, CCC, etc., where AAA is the best rating corresponding to the least risk of default.

The nature of the bond rating problem is similar to the general classification problem in that both deal with a set of input instances and output classes. Each instance is described by a suitable set of features and the classification process assigns each instance to one of the classes.

1.2. Classification tools

The various approaches to the classification problem can be grouped into two paradigms: statistical approaches based on statistical assumptions and mathematical processes, and human knowledge processing approaches which rely on artificial intelligence techniques. The latter can be further divided into *rule-based expert system* approaches and *artificial neural network* approaches. More details of these paradigms can be found elsewhere in the artificial intelligence literature, e.g. Lippmann (1987).

Even though the various classification methodologies are based on rather different paradigms, the algorithms based on these methodologies are all similar in that they all (1) require 'learning' from an already classified sample of input instances to obtain classification 'knowledge' and (2) then apply this knowledge on the input instances to be classified. The classification problem thus involves two important issues (see for example Fukunaga & Hayes (1989) and Kaplan & Urwitz (1979)): (1) feature extraction from the pool of data (i.e. selection of the important variables) and (2) selection of the tool (i.e. the specific classification methodology). The focus of this paper is on the second issue.

1.3. Previous studies

Previous bond rating research used almost exclusively statistical tools; published results utilizing artificial intelligence approaches are only recently becoming available (Dutta & Shekhar 1988; Kim 1992; Surkan & Singleton 1990). Kaplan & Urwitz (1979) and Ederington (1985) criticize the use of statistical tools as these require assumptions of parameter distributions and mathematical equation forms that are seldom satisfied by the bond rating applications.

The tools employed in previous studies are primarily linear regression analysis (Horrigan 1966; West 1970), logistic analysis (Ederington 1985; Kaplan & Urwitz 1979) and linear discriminant analysis (Belkaoui 1980; Pinches & Mingo 1973). Recent artificial intelligence approaches are reported by Dutta & Shekhar (1988) and by Surkan & Singleton (1990). In these studies the performance of the artificial neural network approach is compared with a simple regression approach and with discriminant analysis, respectively. Both studies conclude that the neural network approaches outperformed the statistical classification methods.

1.4. Purpose and overview of this paper

The purpose of this study is to help find a better approach to computer automated bond rating. As stated above, much effort has been expended in the past to simulate the bond rating process using statistical tools but not much has been published on alternate approaches, such as artificial neural networks. The statistical methods suffer from the requirements of statistical assumptions which are not normally satisfied by bond rating applications. Neural network and rule-based approaches may be better tools for these problems. In this paper we report on a comparative analysis of statistical, rule-based and neural network approaches for the bond rating problem, using published financial data.

The financial model used, the data samples used for the simulation and the implementation of the tools compared are presented in the following section under methodology. The results of the simulation are discussed in Section 3 and conclusions and future research are discussed in the final section.

2. Methodology

2.1. The model used

There are two major approaches that can be used in selecting the determinants of ratings (i.e. the independent variables): (1) use statistical techniques to identify those variables that have the highest correlation with the bond ratings and the least correlation with each other, and (2) choose the variables based on a bond rater's cognition. In this study we chose the latter approach because the derived model is independent of a particular data set and it does not favor any specific classification tool. As stated earlier in this paper, the focus of our study is on tool selection for a given model, not on feature extraction (i.e. determining the model).

Possible models of the second type, i.e. that are not derived statistically are: (1) use the ten financial factors employed in the rating guidelines of Standard & Poor's (Martin *et al.* 1984/85); (2) use accounting theory such as cash flow models (Gentry *et al.* 1988); and (3) use 'economic rationale' to link specific variables to the judgement of bond raters, as done by Belkaoui (1980).

For this study we chose the Belkaoui model because (1) it is a relatively recent model; (2) Belkaoui used discriminant

analysis in his study — the most common approach; (3) the reported performance was among the best; and (4) its variables are supported by finance theory. The model includes the following independent variables:

(1) total asset;
(2) total debt;
(3) long term debt or total invested capital;
(4) current asset or liability;
(5) (net income + interest) / interest;
(6) preferred dividend;
(7) stock price or common equity per share;
(8) subordination.

The dependent variable is the bond rating with a domain defined by the values 1 through 6, corresponding to Standard & Poor's ratings of AAA, AA, A, BBB, BB, and B. Lower ratings were not considered as such bonds would be of less interest to investors.

2.2. The data used

The training (learning) data samples and the test data samples were prepared from Standard & Poor's Compustat financial data tape. Data from companies with extreme high (5000 or more) financial ratios were discarded, as were data from companies with bond ratings below B.

The classification comparison in this study is performed on three data sets: (1) the training data itself; (2) separate classification test data collected from the same year as the training data; and (3) prediction test data collected from the subsequent year.

For the training data, 110 companies were randomly selected from the year 1988. Another 58 companies were randomly selected from the same year for the classification data. Finally, 60 companies were randomly selected from the year 1989 for the prediction data. The training data contained 10 AAA ratings and 20 of each of the other rating classes. The classification data contained eight AAA ratings and 10 of each of the other classes, and the prediction data contained 10 in each class (see Table 1).

Table 1:   *Sample sizes.*

	Training	Classification	Prediction
AAA	10	8	10
AA	20	10	10
A	20	10	10
BBB	20	10	10
BB	20	10	10
B	20	10	10
Total	110	58	60

2. 3. The classification tools used

Three analytical tool families are compared in this simulation study, with a total of five specific classification tools:

(1) regression analysis;
(2) discriminant analysis;
(3) ordinal logistic analysis;
(4) artificial neural network system (ANN);
(5) rule-based system.

For the three statistical tools, the SAS package was used. The package Neural Work Professional II Plus was used for ANN and the ID3 inductive learning algorithm was applied via the 1st Class expert system shell to implement the rule-based system. All computations were carried out on a 486-type microcomputer.

In applying the statistical tools, the following assumptions are made. For the regression analysis a normal distribution is assumed and for the logistic analysis a logistic distribution is assumed. For the discriminant analysis the assumption of multivariate normal distribution is made. Based on a test of homogeneity of the *within covariance matrices* (Kendall & Stuart 1961), which indicated significance at the 0.1 level, a quadratic discriminant function was used.

For the rule-based system, each instance in the training data was weighted at 0.5 under the assumption that all instances were equally important. In building the decision tree using the training data, each instance was sequentially applied.

The selected neural network model was a three-layered model, with seven nodes in the hidden layer (i.e. 8–7–6). The employed training method was the backpropagation learning rule and tanh was used as the threshold function.

A more detailed description of the implementation and training of the classification tools used in this research is given in Kim (1992).

3. Results

3. 1. Evaluation criteria

After completing the learning procedure using the training data, the other two test data samples were applied to measure the performance of the classification tools. The measures used in evaluating the tools are (1) the number of accurate classifications on the classification and prediction data samples, and (2) the number of classifications that differ by one rating class.

3. 2. Performance of the tools

Table 2, a–e, shows the performance results for the five classification tools on the classification data (same year as training data) and the prediction data (following year; in parentheses). *Number* is the number of input instances in that rating class (the sample size), and represents the desired outcome. *0-difference* indicates the number of input instances that were accurately classified into this rating class by the classification tool and *1-difference* shows the number of input instances that were classified one class away from the desired class.

Figure 1 summarizes the performance results for the classification data. The bar chart shows the total overall rating classes of both the accurate (0-difference) classifications and the 1-difference classifications, as percentages of the total sample sizes. Figure 2 shows the same for the prediction data.

Table 2: *Performance results on classification (prediction) data.*

Ratings	Number	0-difference	1-difference
AAA	8 (10)	1 (0)	2 (7)
AA	10 (10)	1 (4)	4 (4)
A	10 (10)	5 (6)	5 (3)
BBB	10 (10)	4 (7)	4 (3)
BB	10 (10)	5 (6)	5 (3)
B	10 (10)	5 (2)	2 (2)
Total	58 (60)	21 (25)	22 (22)
%	100	36.21 (41.67)	37.93 (36.17)

a: Regression Analysis

Ratings	Number	0-difference	1-difference
AAA	8 (10)	1 (1)	4 (7)
AA	10 (10)	4 (5)	5 (2)
A	10 (10)	4 (3)	5 (5)
BBB	10 (10)	1 (2)	7 (6)
BB	10 (10)	4 (2)	3 (4)
B	10 (10)	7 (3)	1 (6)
Total	58 (60)	21 (16)	25 (30)
%	100	36.20 (26.67)	22.73 (50.00)

b: Discriminant Analysis

Ratings	Number	0-difference	1-difference
AAA	8 (10)	6 (6)	0 (3)
AA	10 (10)	4 (6)	2 (2)
A	10 (10)	1 (3)	7 (7)
BBB	10 (10)	3 (4)	5 (5)
BB	10 (10)	3 (2)	7 (6)
B	10 (10)	8 (2)	1 (2)
Total	58 (60)	25 (23)	22 (25)
%	100	43.10 (33.33)	37.93 (41.67)

c: Logistic Analysis

Ratings	Number	0-difference	1-difference
AAA	8 (10)	5 (5)	2 (7)
AA	10 (10)	4 (3)	5 (4)
A	10 (10)	1 (3)	5 (3)
BBB	10 (10)	0 (0)	6 (3)
BB	10 (10)	2 (5)	3 (3)
B	10 (10)	6 (2)	2 (2)
Total	58 (60)	18 (18)	23 (28)
%	100	31.03 (30.00)	39.66 (46.67)

d: Rule Based (ID3)

Ratings	Number	0-difference	1-difference
AAA	8 (10)	4 (6)	2 (2)
AA	10 (10)	4 (6)	3 (3)
A	10 (10)	4 (4)	5 (5)
BBB	10 (10)	7 (8)	2 (1)
BB	10 (10)	4 (6)	4 (3)
B	10 (10)	9 (4)	1 (3)
Total	58 (60)	32 (34)	17 (17)
%	100	55.17 (56.17)	29.31 (28.33)

e: Artificial Neural Network

3.3. Comparative analysis

Table 2 and Figures 1 and 2 seems to indicate that the artificial neural network system outperforms the other classification tools overall. We use non-parametric statistics to compare the performance data from the neural network to the performance data from the other classifiers. Based on the null hypothesis that tool difference (e.g. regression versus ANN) is not related to the performance of the classifiers in terms of correct classifications, χ^2 statistics are calculated from 2×2 contingency tables, such as the one shown as Table 3. These χ^2 statistics, shown in Table 4, indicate that the null hypothesis cannot be accepted at the 0.1 significance level in most cases.

4. Conclusion

4.1. Discussion

In this paper we reported on a comparative study of statistical, rule-based and artificial neural network systems for computerized bond rating. The goal of the project was to help find a better tool than the conventional statistical approaches as a basis for bond rating expert systems. The series of experimentations and testings reported in this paper lead to the conclusion that the artificial neural network is a better tool than the statistical tools and the rule-based system for the bond classification problem.

A possible explanation for this conclusion may be that the statistical tools and the rule-based system require *a priori* assumptions of a certain type of distribution and functional form, but the bond rating data are typically noisy and incomplete and do not satisfy these assumptions. Artificial neural network systems do not assume specific distributions or functional forms.

4.2. Caveats

In generalizing from the results of this study, a number of limitations should be taken into consideration:

(1) Even though five tools were selected from three different kinds of tool families, the selected tools may not optimally represent the family from which they were selected.
(2) The training and classification data samples were randomly selected from Compustat 1988 year data. They

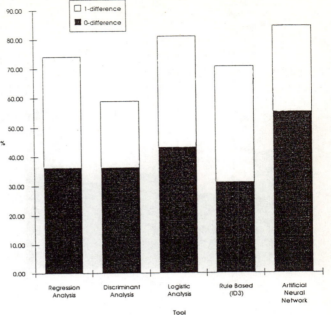

Figure 1: *Performance results on classification data.*

may have the weakness of small sample size and a lack of inter-year characteristics.

(3) Though the employed model was based on a recent and well-known bond rating study, there is no published research to prove that this model is the best of all proposed models, or that one model transcends method. It is possible that some tools perform better with some models than with others.

4.3. Future research

The results of this study show that neural network approaches for bond rating expert systems show great promise, and research into the application of this tool should continue. Further comparative studies, using different data sets and perhaps different implementations of statistical and rule-based tools (and possibly a different model) should be conducted, to confirm (or disprove) the results of this study. Optimal configuration of the neural network system should also be further investigated.

A further limitation of the current study is the assumption that the bond ratings provided by Standard & Poor's are in fact 'correct'. It is possible that in some cases where the expert systems classified bonds differently from the 'desired' rat-

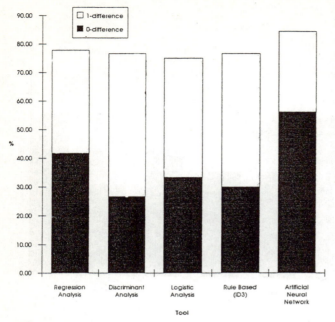

Figure 2:   *Performance results on prediction data.*

Table 3:   *2×2 contingency table on artificial neural network and regression analysis in 0-difference case.*

	Correct case	Not correct	Total
Regression	41.82	58.18	100
ANN	65.45	34.55	100
Total	107.27	92.73	200

Table 4: χ^2 *statistics from 2×2 contingency tables for artificial neural network and other tools in 0-difference case.*

	Regression Analysis	Discriminant Analysis	Logistic Analysis	Rule Based (ID3)
Classification	6.49953*	6.50688*	2.45163	10.9171*
Prediction	3.6467**	16.7379**	9.6461*	12.9176*

*   .05 significance
**   .10 significance

ings, the ratings provided by the expert systems are in fact the 'correct' ratings and the ratings provided by human experts are not. To evaluate the quality of the ratings provided by the expert system fully, the actual performance of the bonds should be analyzed. To the knowledge of the authors, no research of this kind has yet been published.

References

BELKAOUI, A. (1980) Industrial bond rating: A new look, *Financial Management*, Autumn.
DUTTA, S. and S. SHEKHAR (1988) Bond rating: A non conservative application of neural networks, in *Proceedings of the IEEE International Conference on Neural Networks, Vol. II.*
EDERINGTON, L. (1985) Classification models and bond ratings. *The Financial Review*, November, **20**.
FUKUNAGA, K. and R. HAYES (1989) Estimation of classifier performance. *IEEE Transactions on Pattern Analysis and Machine Intelligence*, **11**(10), 1087–1101.
GENTRY, J., P. NEWBOLD and D. WHITFORD (1988) Predicting industrial bond ratings with a probit model and funds flow components, *Financial Review*, **23**(3), 269–284.
HORRIGAN, J. (1966) The determination of long term credit sharing with financial ratios, *Journal of Accounting Research*, **4**, 44–62.
KAPLAN, R. and U. URWITZ (1979) Statistical model of bond ratings: A methodological inquiry, *Journal of Business*, April, 231–261.
KENDALL, M.G. and A. STUART (1961) *The Advanced Theory of Statistics*, Vol. 3, Chales, Griffin and Company Ltd, London.
KIM, J.W. (1992) A comparative analysis of rule based, neural network, and statistical classification systems for the bond rating problem. Unpublished dissertation, School of Business, Virginia Commonwealth University.
LIPPMANN, R. (1987) An introduction to computing with neural nets, *IEEE ASSP Magazine*, **16**, 4–22.
MARTIN, L., G. HERDERSON, L. PERRY and T. CRONAN (1984/85) Bond ratings: Predictions using rating agency criteria. Department of Finance Working Paper 1984/85–3, Arizona State University.
PINCHES, G. and K. MINGO (1973) A multivariate analysis of industrial bond ratings, *Journal of Finance*, **XXVIII**, 1–18.
SURKAN, A. and C. SINGLETON (1990) Neural network for bond rating improved by hidden layers, in *Proceedings of the IEEE International Conference on Neural Networks, Vol. II*, 157–168.
WEST, R. (1970) An alternative approach to predicting corporate bond ratings, *Journal of Accounting Research*, **7**, 118–127.

The authors

Jun Woo Kim

Jun Woo Kim is a senior researcher at Korea Telecommunication International (KTI) and an adjunct faculty member at Sogang University in Seoul, Korea. He received his PhD in Management Information Systems from Virginia Commonwealth University in Richmond, Virginia in 1992. His research interests focus on business applications of artificial intelligence technologies such as expert systems and neural network systems.

H. Roland Weistroffer

H. Roland Weistroffer is an Associate Professor of Information Systems at Virginia Commonwealth University. He holds a Doctor of Science degree from the Free University in Berlin, Germany, and a Master of Arts degree from Duke University in Durham, North Carolina. Prior to coming to VCU, he was a Chief Research Officer at the Council for Scientific and Industrial Research in Pretoria, South Africa. His primary research interests are in multiple criteria decision making, decision support systems and expert systems.

Richard T. Redmond

Richard T. Redmond is an Associate Professor of Information Systems at Virginia Commonwealth University. He received his Doctor of Business Administration from Kent State University and a Bachelor of Science in Business Administration from Shippensburg University. His research activities and publications include the areas of Image Data Base design, software engineering productivity metric, neural network applications and knowledge acquisition methods.

Part II
Forecasting Exchange Rates

[6]

Journal of International Economics 14 (1983) 3–24. North-Holland Publishing Company

EMPIRICAL EXCHANGE RATE MODELS OF THE SEVENTIES

Do they fit out of sample?

Richard A. MEESE*

University of California at Berkeley, Berkeley, CA 94720, USA

Kenneth ROGOFF

Board of Governors of the Federal Reserve System, Washington, DC 20551, USA

Received July 1981, revised version received April 1982

This study compares the out-of-sample forecasting accuracy of various structural and time series exchange rate models. We find that a random walk model performs as well as any estimated model at one to twelve month horizons for the dollar/pound, dollar/mark, dollar/yen and trade-weighted dollar exchange rates. The candidate structural models include the flexible-price (Frenkel–Bilson) and sticky-price (Dornbusch–Frankel) monetary models, and a sticky-price model which incorporates the current account (Hooper–Morton). The structural models perform poorly despite the fact that we base their forecasts on actual realized values of future explanatory variables.

1. Introduction

This study compares time series and structural models of exchange rates on the basis of their out-of-sample forecasting accuracy. We find that a random walk model would have predicted major-country exchange rates during the recent floating-rate period as well as any of our candidate models.[1] Significantly, the structural models fail to improve on the random walk model in spite of the fact that we base their forecasts on actual realized values of future explanatory variables.

*Both authors were at the Federal Reserve Board when this paper was written. This paper is a revised version of a paper presented at the International Monetary Fund and at the December 1981 Meetings of the Econometric Society. Robert Flood, Jeffrey Frankel, Robert Hodrick, Peter Hooper, and Julio Rotemberg gave us helpful comments on an earlier draft. We are indebted to Julie Withers and Catherine Crosby for research assistance. This paper represents the views of the authors and should not be interpreted as reflecting the views of the Board of Governors of the Federal Reserve System.

[1]Cornell (1977), Mussa (1979) and Frenkel (1981b) have noted that exchange rate changes are largely unpredictable. Mussa (p. 10) states that: 'The natural logarithm of the spot exchange rate follows approximately a random walk.' The present study systematically confirms this 'stylized fact'. Another point Mussa makes and the results of this study support, is that any serial correlation found in the exchange rates by in-sample tests is likely to be unstable over time.

4   *R.A. Meese and K. Rogoff, Exchange rate models of the seventies*

In our experiment, each competing model is used to generate forecasts at one to twelve month horizons for the dollar/pound, dollar/mark, dollar/yen and trade-weighted dollar exchange rates.[2,3] The parameters of each model are estimated on the basis of the most up-to-date information available at the time of a given forecast. This is accomplished by using rolling regressions to re-estimate the parameters of each model every forecast period.

As representative structural models we choose the flexible-price monetary (Frenkel–Bilson) model, the sticky-price monetary (Dornbusch–Frankel) model, and the Hooper–Morton model. The latter empirical model extends the Dornbusch–Frankel model to incorporate the effects of the current account. We estimate these models using ordinary least squares, generalized least squares, and Fair's (1970) instrumental variables technique. We also try specifications which incorporate lagged adjustment.

A variety of univariate time series techniques are applied to the data as well. None of these techniques, including estimation of a random walk with drift model, generally yields any forecasting improvement in root mean square error or mean absolute error over the random walk model. Nor does an unconstrained vector autoregression composed of the exchange rate and all the explanatory variables from the structural models.

The forward rate does not predict any better than the random walk model either. But the interpretation of its relative performance is somewhat tangential to the main issue here, which is: How well do existing empirical exchange rate models fit out-of-sample?

A description of the competing models and the techniques used to estimate them is presented in section 2 of the paper. Section 3 discusses our methodology for comparing models out of sample, and section 4 contains the main results. In section 5 we list some possible explanations of these results.

2. A description of the models

Here we discuss the specification and statistical estimation of the various competing models.

2.1. The structural models

From the 'asset' models that have come to dominate the recent literature on exchange rate determination we select three which, perhaps due to the relative tractability of their data requirements, have been subjected to

---

[2]Haache and Townend (1981), using different methods than ours, conclude that none of the structural models can explain the behavior of the effective pound sterling exchange rate over the seventies.

[3]The trade-weighted dollar is a weighted-average of U.S. dollar exchange rates with the Group of Ten Countries plus Switzerland; see the data appendix.

extensive (in-sample) empirical testing. These are the flexible-price monetary (Frenkel–Bilson) model, the sticky-price monetary (Dornbusch–Frankel) model, and the sticky-price asset (Hooper–Morton) model.[4] The quasi-reduced form specifications of all three models are subsumed in the general specification (1):

$$s = a_0 + a_1(m - \dot{m}) + a_2(y - \dot{y}) + a_3(r_s - \dot{r}_s)$$

$$+ a_4(\pi^e - \dot{\pi}^e) + a_5 \overline{TB} + a_6 \overline{\dot{TB}} + u, \tag{1}$$

where s is the logarithm of the dollar price of foreign currency, $m - \dot{m}$ the logarithm of the ratio of the U.S. money supply to the foreign money supply, $y - \dot{y}$ is the logarithm of the ratio of U.S. to foreign real income, $r_s - \dot{r}_s$ is the short-term interest rate differential and $\pi^e - \dot{\pi}^e$ is the expected long-run inflation differential.[5] TB and $\overline{TB}$ represent the cumulated U.S. and foreign trade balances, and u is a disturbance term. The disturbance term may be a serially correlated; we shall also consider allowing for lagged adjustment in eq. (1).

All of the models posit that, ceteris paribus, the exchange rate exhibits first-degree homogeneity in the relative money supplies, or $a_1 = 1$. The Frenkel–Bilson model, which assumes purchasing power parity, constraints $a_4 = a_5 = a_6 = 0$. The Dornbusch–Frankel model, which allows for slow domestic price adjustment and consequent deviations from purchasing power parity, sets $a_5 = a_6 = 0$. None of the coefficients in eq. (1) is constrained to be zero in the Hooper–Morton model. This model extends the Dornbusch–Frankel model to allow for changes in the long-run real exchange rate. These long-run real exchange rate changes are assumed to be correlated with unanticipated shocks to the trade balance.[6] Imposing the constraint that domestic and foreign variables (except for trade balances) enter eq. (1) in differential form implicitly assumes that the parameters of the domestic and

[4]See Bilson (1978, 1979), Frenkel (1976), Dornbusch (1976), Frankel (1979, 1981), and Hooper and Morton (1982). Our nomenclature, which identifies particular models with authors who contributed significantly to their development is a conventional one. But it is not comprehensive in that some of these authors have worked with more than one of the three models, and there are other researchers who have studied these models or closely-related ones.

[5]Proxies for the unobservable $\pi^e - \dot{\pi}^e$ are typically constructed from variables such as long-term interest rate differentials, the preceding twelve-month period CPI or WPI inflation rates, or with an inflation rate autoregression; see Frankel (1981) and Hooper and Morton (1982).

[6]Since current account data is available only on a quarterly basis, the monthly version of Hooper and Morton's empirical model uses the trade balance as a proxy. Cumulative deviations from trend balances (current accounts) enter Hooper and Morton's equation since they assume that deviations from trend balances are unanticipated. Frankel (1982b) employs a model with a very similar quasi-reduced form, in which the cumulated current accounts of both countries enter because of wealth terms in the money demand equations. Branson, Halttunen and Masson (1979) also include the cumulated current accounts in empirical exchange rate equations. Their justification derives from the joint assumptions of imperfect asset substitutability and differential asset preferences across countries.

foreign money demand and price adjustment equations are equal. While this parsimonious assumption is conventional in empirical applications, it is a potential source of misspecification; see Haynes and Stone (1981). As reported below, however, no gain in out-of-sample fit results from estimating separate coefficients for domestic and foreign money supplies and real incomes.

A conventional approach to comparing the models subsumed in eq. (1) involves estimating a model of the general form, and then testing the constraints implied by the competing models. When overall performance is measured by in-sample fit, regressions based on eq. (1) do reasonably well. [See, for example, Frankel (1979) or Hooper and Morton (1982).] One drawback to this approach is that it is difficult to deal with the statistical problems encountered in obtaining consistent estimates of the coefficients in eq. (1). Variables such as relative money supplies and relative incomes are typically treated as exogenous variables in the underlying theoretical models, but may be more realistically thought of as endogenous variables. Other variables, such as the short-term interest differential, are generally endogenous in these same theoretical models. Yet they are still treated as legitimate regressors in ordinary or generalized least squares regressions of eq. (1).

The possibility that the explanatory variables in eq. (1) are endogenous is supported by the vector autoregression results presented in Meese and Rogoff (1983), and by the block exogeneity specification tests presented in Glaessner (1982). Of course, endogeneity of the explanatory variables does not preclude consistent estimation of the structural parameters in eq. (1). If, for example, the error term follows an autoregressive process of known maximum order, then instrumental variables techniques such as Fair's (1970) method are available. Frankel (1979) takes this approach, assuming a first-order autoregressive process and treating long-term expected inflation differentials as endogenous; Frankel (1981) allows short-term interest rates to be endogenous as well. To also account for the possible endogeneity of the money supplies, he tries constraining the coefficient on relative money supplies to its theoretical value of one. Following Frankel, we estimate the models using ordinary least squares, generalized least squares (correcting for serial correlation),[7] and Fair's method. In the last case money supplies, short-term interest rates, and expected long-term inflation rates are treated as endogenous variables. Note that if one of the models summarized by eq. (1) is true, and if its structural and serial correlation parameters can be consistently estimated with instrumental variables techniques, then such techniques will outperform inconsistent techniques in large enough samples.

---

[7]Generalized least squares with a correction for a fifth-order autoregressive error term performs worse than GLS with a correction for a first-order autoregressive term (Cochrane–Orcutt). Cochrane–Orcutt also outperforms a stock-adjustment model.

However, generalized least squares parameter estimates did not yield inferior forecasts in our experiments.

While the forecasts generated in this study are based on models with freely-estimated coefficients, elsewhere [Meese and Rogoff (1983)] we try forecasting with the structural models using a grid of coefficient constraints drawn from the theoretical and empirical literature on money demand and purchasing power parity. Those results, which are discussed further below, do not lead to different conclusions than our experiments here with freely-estimated coefficients.

2.2. Univariate and multivariate time series models

Several univariate time series models involving a variety of prefiltering techniques and lag length selection criteria are employed in our experiments. All are estimated for the logarithm of the exchange rate.[8]

The prefiltering techniques involve differencing, deseasonalizing, and removing time trends. All six univariate time series techniques we consider are applied to both the actual and the prefiltered data. The first technique, the 'long AR', is an unconstrained autoregression (AR) where the longest lag considered (M) is a function of sample size (N), $M = N/\log N$. A deterministic rule like this has long been employed in spectral estimation [see Hannan (1970)] and has been applied to distributed lag models by Sims (1974b). If the true order of the autoregression is unknown but finite, this procedure is asymptotically inefficient relative to the Schwartz (1978) order selection criterion. We employ this procedure and the Akaike (1974) procedure in our study; the Schwartz criterion provides a consistent estimate of lag length, while the Akaike lag length criterion asymptotically produces minimum mean square prediction errors of the dependent variable. Our fourth procedure is like the long AR, except that in estimating the parameters more weight is given to recent observations. We arbitrarily choose to weight the observations by powers of 0.95. The fifth univariate technique involves direct application of the Wiener–Kolmogorov prediction formula in the frequency domain; see Sargent (1979).

A possible problem with all the techniques listed thus far is that they minimize criteria based on squared deviations. These type of criteria are inappropriate if, for example, exchange rates follow non-normal stable-Paretian distributions with infinite variance, as suggested by Westerfield (1977). Therefore, our final time series technique is based on minimizing absolute deviations. This 'MAD' estimator is more robust to fat-tailed distributions, and less sensitive to outlier observations.

---

[8]A Box–Cox transformation test indicates that the logarithmic transformation is slightly preferable to levels for all the exchange rates we consider. Theoretical reasons for preferring the logarithm of the exchange rate are given in section 3.

While the relative performance of the six univariate forecasting techniques is of interest in itself, we shall only report detailed results for the long AR model without trend, seasonal adjustment, or differencing. This model's performance characterizes those of the best univariate models; we will discuss the results of the other univariate models only to a lesser degree.

The random walk model, which uses the current spot rate as a predictor of all future spot rate is, of course, a univariate time series model. While the basic random walk model obviously requires no estimation, we also estimate a random walk model with drift parameter. The drift parameter is estimated as the mean monthly (logarithmic) exchange rate change.

An unconstrained vector autoregression (VAR), composed of the variables in eq. (1), serves as our representative multivariate time series model. A convenient normalization for estimation of the VAR is one in which the contemporaneous value of each variable is regressed against lagged values of itself and all the other variables, e.g. the exchange rate equation is

$$s_t = a_{i1}s_{t-1} + a_{i2}s_{t-2} + \cdots a_{in}s_{t-n} + B'_{i1}X_{t-1}$$

$$+ B'_{i2}X_{t-2} + \cdots B'_{in}X_{t-n} + u_{it}, \tag{2}$$

where X_{t-j} is a vector of the explanatory variables in eq. (1), lagged j periods. The error term u_{it} is serially uncorrelated, but may be contemporaneously correlated with the error terms in the other equations; thus the normalization used in (2) does not preclude contemporaneous interactions between variables. This normalization facilitates estimation since ordinary least squares equation by equation is an efficient strategy. The uniform lag length n across all (seven) equations is estimated using Parzen's (1975) lag length selection criterion.[9] To reduce the parameterization of the VAR, we also try constraining the domestic and foreign cumulated trade balances to enter in differenced form rather than separately. As is not unusual in a small sample, the more parsimoniously parameterized six-variable VAR yields better forecasts, so this is the model we report below. The VAR is important to include in our forecasting experiments since it does not restrict any variables to be exogenous a priori, and is therefore robust to some of the estimation problems that plague the structural models discussed in the previous section. We did not, however, experiment with algorithms designed to reduce the number of estimated coefficients in the profligately parameterized VAR; see Litterman (1979). Such algorithms can sometimes markedly reduce the mean square prediction errors produced by these models.

---

[9]Parzen's (1975) criterion asymptotically selects a lag order greater than or equal to the true order, assuming the true order is finite. The lag lengths chosen for the dollar/mark, dollar/pound, dollar/yen, and trade-weighted dollar VARs are 2, 2, 4, and 2.

2.3. Selecting the data

The data, which are described in an appendix, are chosen to conform to the theoretical assumptions underlying the specification of the structural models.

All of the raw data used in this study are seasonally unadjusted, which makes it possible to estimate seasonal and structural parameters on a consistent basis. The use of seasonally adjusted data is especially likely to distort structural parameter estimates when the variables are not all adjusted by the same method. [See Sims (1974a, 1974b) for a further discussion.] We experimented with two different seasonal adjustment procedures. One method uses seasonal dummy variables. The other is Sims' (1974a) method which explicitly allows the seasonal parameterization to expand with sample size. As the results of our experiment are robust to the choice between these two techniques, we only report the results for the more conventional dummy variables procedure. Another reason for using seasonally unadjusted data is to avoid the use of certain information not available at the time of a given forecast. Forecasts based on seasonally adjusted data, adjusted over the extended sample period or with a two-sided filter such as Census X-11, implicitly make use of information which would not have been available.

The dollar/mark, dollar/pound, and dollar/yen spot exchange rate data are monthly point-sample data. We use an average of daily rates for the trade-weighted dollar, partly because that data is more readily available and partly to be consistent with other work on the trade-weighted dollar. [See Hooper and Morton (1982).] For the purposes of this study, point sample data have a decided advantage over monthly average data. Suppose the exchange rate follows a random walk on a mid-day to mid-day basis. Then as Working (1960) observed, a series consisting of monthly averages of mid-day rates will exhibit positive serial correlation.

Bilateral forward rates of one, three, six, and twelve month maturities are drawn from the same day of the month as the spot rates; point-sample short-term and (where possible) long-term interest rate data also match the spot rate data. We use treasury bill rates and interbank rates for short-term interest rates. Using these interest rates makes sense when estimating models based on standard money demand specifications. However, Euromarket rates would be more likely to conform to another assumption underlying most of the structural models: perfect asset substitutibility. Some limited experimentation with Euromarket rates suggests that their use would have little effect on our results. As discussed below, the choice of monetary aggregates is potentially quite important. We try three different aggregates in our experiments: M1-B, M2, and the reserve-adjusted base. (Since the United Kingdom does not publish a series for M2, U.S. M3 and sterling M3 are employed in place of M2's for the dollar/pound rate experiments. Only M1-B type measures are used in the trade-weighted dollar experiments; we were unable to find or construct a reserve-adjusted base series for Japan.)

3. The methodology for comparing models out-of-sample

All the competing models are estimated over a monthly data series which starts in March 1973, the beginning of the floating rate period, and extends through June 1981. Each model is initially estimated for each exchange rate using data up through the first forecasting period, November 1976. Forecasts are generated at horizons of one, three, six, and twelve months; these forecast horizons correspond to the available forward rate data. Then the data for December 1976 are added to the sample, and the parameters of each model, including the seasonal adjustment parameters, are re-estimated using rolling regressions. New forecasts are generated at one, three, six, and twelve month horizons, etc.

The purpose of considering multiple forecast horizons in this type of experiment is to see whether the structural models do better than time series models in the long run, when adjustment due to lags and/or a serially correlated error term has taken place. Of course, when lags and serial correlation are fully incorporated into the structural models, a consistently-estimated true structural model will outpredict a time series model at *all* horizons in a large sample.

The choice of where to begin forecasting is predicted on our desire to have sufficient degrees of freedom available for initial parameter estimates of all the models, especially the profligately-parameterized vector autoregression. We also look at the subperiod beginning in November 1978, in part because that date marks a major change in U.S. intervention strategy, and in part to see whether the relative performances of the competing models are different over the recent subperiod than over the entire forecasting period. Finally, we try truncating the sample in November 1980 which, like November 1976, marks a U.S. presidential election.

The structural models require forecasts of their explanatory variables in order to generate forecasts of the exchange rate. To give these models the benefit of the doubt, we use actual realized values of their respective explanatory variables. This procedure directly addresses one possible defense of these models: structural exchange rate models have explanatory power, but predict badly because their explanatory variables are themselves difficult to predict.[10]

The methodology used here for comparing models out-of-sample is drawn from the macro literature; see, for example, Nelson (1972), Christ (1975),

---

[10]When the explanatory variables are endogenous they will in general be correlated with the error term in eq. (1). If available, information about this correlation could be used to construct better structural model forecasts.

Litterman (1979), or Fair (1979). Although out-of-sample comparisons have considerable intuitive appeal, formal tests of whether these differences are statistically significant generally require restrictive assumptions.[11] But this limitation of the experimental design does not turn out to be crucial for the interpretation of our major result. We shall postpone this discussion until the next section.

Out-of-sample accuracy is measured by three statistics: mean error (ME), mean absolute error (MAE) and root mean square error (RMSE). These are defined as follows:

$$\text{mean error} = \sum_{s=0}^{N_k-1} [F(t+s+k) - A(t+s+k)]/N_k, \tag{3a}$$

$$\text{mean absolute error} = \sum_{s=0}^{N_k-1} |F(t+s+k) - A(t+s+k)|/N_k, \tag{3b}$$

$$\text{root mean square error} = \left\{ \sum_{s=0}^{N_k-1} [F(t+s+k), - A(t+s+k)]^2/N_k \right\}^{1/2}, \tag{3c}$$

where $k = 1, 3, 6, 12$ denotes the forecast step, N_k the total number of forecasts in the projection period for which the actual value $A(t)$ is known, and $F(t)$ the forecast value. Forecasting begins in period t. Because we are looking at the logarithm of the exchange rate, these statistics are unit-free (they are approximately in percentage terms) and comparable across currencies. By comparing predictors on the basis of their ability to predict the logarithm of the exchange rate, we also avoid any problems arising from Jensen's inequality. Because of Jensen's inequality, the best predictor of the level of the dollar/mark rate might not be the best predictor of the mark/dollar rate.[12]

Root mean square error is our principal criterion for comparing forecasters. But because RMSE is an inappropriate criterion if, as mentioned

---

[11]Granger and Newbold (1977, p. 281) propose a formal test of two forecasting techniques; the test is applicable only when both forecast errors are independent and normally distributed with zero means and constant variances. Thus, the test can only be applied at forecast intervals greater than one month if overlapping multi-horizon forecasts are omitted.

[12]Siegel (1972) notes that because $1/x$ is a convex function of the random variable x, $E(1/x)$ is not in general equal to $1/E(x)$. McCulloch (1975) suggests that this problem is not important empirically, given the historical variance of the exchange rate. Both analyses are based on an erroneous Taylor expansion which yields $E(1/x) - 1/E(x) \approx \text{var}(x)/E(x).^3$ This approximation may be misleading because the Taylor expansion used to derive it is local, whereas the expectations integral is global. While the above approximation is precisely correct when x follows a lognormal distribution, it can be way off when the distribution of x is skewed. Consider the discrete probability density function: $P(x=1)=0.99$, $P(x=0.01)=0.01$. Then $E(1/x) - 1/E(x) = 1.99 - 1.01 = 0.98$. However, $\text{var}(x)/E(x)^3 \cong 0.01$. The order of magnitude of the Jensen's inequality term is more likely to be large in data sets where an outside chance of a major intervention is incorporated into expectations.

in subsection 2.2, exchange rates are governed by a non-normal stable Paretian process with infinite variance, it is important to include mean absolute error. MAE is also a useful criterion when the exchange rate distribution has fat tails, even if the variance is finite. The last criterion, mean error, provides another measure of robustness. By comparing MAE and ME we can ascertain whether a model systematically over- or underpredicts.

4. The results

Table 1 lists the root mean square error statistics at one and twelve month horizons over the full November 1976 through June 1981 forecasting period for exchange rate for representative versions of each model. The structural models in table 1 are estimated using Fair's method as described in subsection 1.1. The measure of money is M1-B and, in the two sticky-price models, the long-term interest differential serves as the proxy for the long-run expected inflation differential. In addition, table 1 gives RMSE for the spot rate, the forward rate, the vector autoregression, and a long univariate autoregression (with order a function of sample size).

Ignoring for the present the fact that the spot rate does no worse than the forward rate, the striking feature of table 1 is that none of the models achieves lower, much less significantly lower, RMSE than the random walk model at any horizon. Although RMSE at three month horizons are not listed in table 1, they give the same result.

The structural models in particular fail to improve on the random walk model in spite of the fact their forecasts are based on realized values of the explanatory variables. They predict much worse, especially at one month horizons, if serial correlation is not accounted for. We obtain very similar results to those presented in table 1 using Granger and Newbold's (1977) method of combining the forecasts of structural models (without serial correlation) and time series models.[13] Estimating the models in first difference form does not help, nor does using either a stock-adjustment formulation or generalized least squares with a correction for a fifth-order autoregressive process. Generalized least squares with a correction for first-order serial correlation (Cochrane–Orcutt) does frequently yield marginally better results than Fair's method. But this is not particularly encouraging

---

[13]Granger and Newbold's technique for optimally combining forecasts involves regressing the realized exchange rate against the forecasts of different models, with the weights constrained to sum to one, but not constrained to be positive. Even a bad predictor can sometimes be profitably combined with a good predictor; the forecasting gain depends on their covariation. An estimated combination of all seven forecasts never improves upon the random walk model alone, but estimated linear combinations of the different forecasts taken two at a time do sometimes outperform the random walk model. However, the same combination never works for more than one exchange rate. (These results are based on a November 1976–November 1980 forecasting period; linear combination forecasts were only generated at one month horizons.)

Table 1

Root mean square forecast errors.[a]

Exchange rate	Horizon	Random walk	Forward rate	Univariate autoregression	Vector autoregression	Frenkel-Bilson[b]	Dornbusch-Frankel[b]	Hooper-Morton[b]
$/mark	1 month	3.72	3.20	3.51	5.40	3.17	3.65	3.50
	6 months	8.71	9.03	12.40	11.83	9.64	12.03	9.95
	12 months	12.98	12.60	22.53	15.06	16.12	18.87	15.69
$/yen	1 month	3.68	3.72	4.46	7.76	4.11	4.40	4.20
	6 months	11.58	11.93	22.04	18.90	13.38	13.94	11.94
	12 months	18.31	18.95	52.18	22.98	18.55	20.41	19.20
$/pound	1 month	2.56	2.67	2.79	5.56	2.82	2.90	3.03
	6 months	6.45	7.23	7.27	12.97	8.90	8.88	9.08
	12 months	9.96	11.62	13.35	21.28	14.62	13.66	14.57
Trade-weighted dollar	1 month	1.99	N.A.	2.72	4.10	2.40	2.50	2.74
	6 months	6.09	N.A.	6.82	8.91	7.07	6.49	7.11
	12 months	8.65	14.24	11.14	10.96	11.40	9.80	10.35

[a]Approximately in percentage terms.
[b]The three structural models are estimated using Fair's instrumental variable technique to correct for first-order serial correlation.

since Cochrane–Orcutt estimates are less often of the theoretically correct sign. Constraining the coefficients to be of the correct sign does not, however, improve the structural model forecasts. Meese and Rogoff (1983) report extensive constrained-coefficient experiments in which the structural models still fail to beat the random walk model at horizons of one to twelve months; see section 5 below.

Allowing for separate coefficients on domestic and foreign real incomes and money supplies yields no gain in out-of-sample forecasting accuracy. Nor does including domestic and foreign price levels as additional explanatory variables. Replacing M1-B with either M2 or the reserve-adjusted base almost always yields worse results, and never an improvement on the random walk model. Replacing long-term interest rates by other inflationary expectations proxies, such as current period inflation differentials, a moving average of past inflation differentials, or future inflation differentials, yields comparable results in both constrained- and freely-estimated coefficient experiments. The past twelve-month-period inflation differential works somewhat better (over the present sample). With that proxy, at one month horizons for the dollar/mark rate the Dornbusch–Frankel and Hooper–Morton models predict better than the random walk model in RMSE by 0.02 and 0.05 percent, respectively. They do worse at longer forecast horizons, though. The Hooper–Morton model (with the past year inflation rate proxy) also exhibits marginal improvement over the random walk model for the dollar/yen rate at six months (but not at one month or twelve months), and for the trade-weighted dollar at six months. At twelve months, the Hooper–Morton model improves by a more substantial 2 percent over the random walk model for the trade-weighted dollar.

The failure of the univariate time series models to beat the random walk model is similarly quite robust. None of the various univariate techniques improve on the random walk model at any horizon for the dollar/mark rate. The random walk with drift model improves by about 0.5 percent at six and twelve month horizons for the dollar/pound rate, but is 0.1 percent worse at one month and does much worse at predicting the dollar/yen and trade-weighted dollar. Given that we use monthly average data for the trade-weighted dollar, one would expect that in a large enough sample, the estimated univariate models would predict it better than the random walk model, even if the latter model is true for point-sample data (see subsection 2.3). But here only the long AR model (detrended) ever predicts the trade-weighted dollar better; it is only 0.5 percent better at twelve months. Only the Schwarz criterion together with detrending yields an improvement over the random walk model for the dollar/yen rate. The improvement is 1.5 percent at six months and 4.8 percent at twelve months.

It is worth emphasizing that even though exchange rates probably do not follow a random walk exactly, an estimated univariate model may not forecast better due to sampling error. It is well known that imposing a coefficient restriction which is approximately correct tends to improve forecast accuracy. [See Sims (1980) or Litterman (1979) for further discussion.] This reason may similarly explain why the multivariate vector autoregression fails to outpredict the random walk model. It is thus possible that a non-structural method of reducing the number of estimated VAR parameters, such as the one Litterman (1979) proposes, would lead to an improvement on the random walk model.

At the risk of detracting from central issues such as how well existing empirical exchange rate models fit out-of-sample, we briefly turn to a comparison of spot and forward exchange rates. In table 1 the forward rate only improves on the random walk model in RMSE for the case of the dollar/mark rate at twelve month horizons. Given the joint assumptions of market efficiency and rational expectations, the relative performance of the forward rate may be interpreted as evidence on the existence of a risk premium.[14] For example, the forward rate could predict worse than the random walk model when there is a time-varying risk premium, even if the risk premium is zero on average.

The dominance of the random walk model over the other models in RMSE remains when forecasting begins in November 1978, or alternatively if it ends in November 1980. The mean absolute error statistics, which are generally 20–25 percent smaller than RMSE, are not listed here since they yield virtually the same rankings as RMSE. Even the univariate technique designed to minimize mean absolute deviations fails to improve on the random walk model in out-of-sample MAE.

The mean forecast errors of the various models are listed in table 2. These errors are generally much smaller than the corresponding mean absolute errors, indicating that the models do not systematically over- or underpredict. (The structural models do tend to go systematically offtrack if no serial correlation is allowed for.) Note that the random walk model is somewhat less dominant in ME than in RMSE and MAE in our experiments, particularly for the dollar/mark rate. Estimating the structural models in first difference form generally produces lower ME but higher RMSE than does estimating the models in levels with a correction for serial correlation.

The results presented above do not answer the question of whether the random walk is *significantly* better than the other models in root mean square error, our primary criterion. However, given our finding that the

---

[14]A number of recent authors, including Bilson (1981), Cumby and Obstfeld (1981), Geweke and Feige (1979), Hakkio (1981), Hansen and Hodrick (1980, 1983), Meese and Singleton (1980), and Tryon (1979), have found evidence of the divergence of forward rates from expected future spot rates over the recent floating-rate period. Bilson (1981), however, is the only author who uses an out-of-sample testing methodology. Although his model is not discussed, it too failed to outperform the random walk model at one month forecast horizons.

Table 2

Mean forecast errors[a]

Exchange rate	Model Horizon	Random walk	Forward rate	Univariate autoregression	Vector autoregression	Frenkel–Bilson[b]	Dornbusch–Frankel[b]	Hooper–Morton[b]
$/mark	1 month	0.04	0.35	0.26	-1.12	0.37	-0.17	0.07
	6 months	-0.92	1.31	1.99	-3.31	1.23	-0.59	-0.17
	12 months	-3.93	0.29	5.20	-5.22	0.55	-3.06	-1.52
$/yen	1 month	-0.46	-0.06	-0.15	-2.64	-1.36	-1.46	-0.18
	6 months	-3.32	-1.26	-3.17	-7.51	-8.00	-8.53	-1.81
	12 months	-6.48	-2.62	-8.91	-10.45	-14.05	-14.82	-2.38
$/pound	1 month	-0.31	-0.38	-0.12	-3.72	-0.48	-0.37	-0.52
	6 months	-3.09	-4.05	-1.32	-9.45	-5.55	-4.53	-5.30
	12 months	-7.75	-9.55	-4.17	-18.54	-13.21	-12.07	-11.69
Trade-weighted dollar	1 month	-0.03	N.A.	0.06	0.89	0.63	0.54	0.68
	6 months	0.77	N.A.	1.61	3.91	3.86	2.79	3.52
	12 months	3.18	7.66	6.44	7.11	7.69	5.30	5.78

[a]Approximately in percentage terms.
[b]The three structural models are estimated using Fair's instrumental variable technique to correct for first-order serial correlation.

random walk model almost invariably has the lowest root mean square error over all horizons and across all exchange rates, we *can* unambiguously assert that the other models do not perform significantly better than the random walk model. And while the random walk model may be as good a predictor as any of major-country exchange rates, it does not predict well. Even the RMSE in table 1 for the trade-weighted dollar — which as one might expect is more predictable than the bilateral rates — is 1.99 percent at one month and 8.65 percent at twelve months. The highest RMSE are for the dollar/yen rate: 3.70 percent at one month and 18.3 percent at twelve months.

One might hope to ultimately estimate a structural model which could perform substantially better than this, especially when forecasts are based on realized explanatory variable values. In the next section we address some possible explanations of our dissatisfying results. While the problem may lie in sampling error, it is also possible that these empirical models do not adequately capture expectations or other forces which influence exchange rates.

5. Possible reasons for the poor out-of-sample fit of the structural models

Since the structural model forecasts have been purged of explanatory variable uncertainty, their disappointing performance is most likely to be attributable to simultaneous equation bias, sampling error, stochastic movements in the true underlying parameters, or misspecification. Also, we make no attempt to account for possible non-linearities in the underlying models.

We have attempted to account for simultaneous equations bias by employing instrumental variables techniques, by estimating a vector autoregression, and by imposing theoretical coefficient constraints. The latter method is applied extensively in Meese and Rogoff (1983). There we develop and search a grid of coefficient constraints. The priors embodied in the grid are based on the fact that all the coefficients in the quasi-reduced form specification (1), except those on the cumulated trade balances, are functions of money demand parameters and the rate at which the real exchange rate returns to its long-run purchasing power parity level. [See Frankel (1979) or Hooper and Morton (1982).] Thus, we are able to base the coefficient on relative money supplies on the homogeneity postulate; the ranges for the income elasticity and interest rate semi-elasticity on the theoretical and empirical literature on money demand; and the range for the rate at which shocks to purchasing power parity are damped on empirical work on PPP.[15] Despite allowance for a serially correlated error term we find that no element of the grid yields a constrained-coefficient forecaster which improves on the

---

[15]The money demand and PPP literature is discussed and cited in Meese and Rogoff (1983).

random walk model for horizons under twelve months. While there is sometimes sporadic improvement at longer horizons, the overall results are similar to those presented here. (We examine longer forecasting periods in our other study, since the constrained coefficient models require estimation of only the intercept term.) These further results appear to demonstrate that simultaneous equations bias and/or sampling error cannot be regarded as the primary rationalization of the evidence presented here.

Another candidate explanation for the poor performance of the structural models is that their underlying parameters shifted over the course of the seventies due to the effects of the two oil shocks, changes in global trade patterns, or changes in policy regimes. But unless the structural model parameters themselves follow a random walk, it does not necessarily follow that parameter instability can explain why the random walk model outperforms the structural models. Nevertheless, it may be fruitful to account for parameter instability by utilizing a method such as Kalman filtering, which weights recent observations more heavily in forming parameter estimates; see Sargent (1979). We did employ one univariate technique along these lines, weighted least squares, but as we reported above this isolated effort failed. It should be noted that there is a sense in which parameter instability is equivalent to having omitted (perhaps binary) variables.

A useful approach to investigating the problem of omitted variables, or misspecification in general, is to examine the (not strictly independent) building blocks of the structural exchange rate models subsumed in eq. (1): uncovered interest parity,[16] the proxies for inflationary expectations, the goods market specifications, and the common money demand specification. Any or all of the above may be a source of misspecification; the discussion below is speculative.

Recent work on exchange rate risk premia has strongly challenged the assumption of uncovered interest parity. However, although the risk premia may be statistically significant, the evidence also suggests that the magnitudes are not large. (See the literature cited in footnote 14.) Therefore, it is not evident that deviations from uncovered interest parity can explain the poor forecasting performance of the structural models. [We note that empirical efforts to explain the risk premia in terms of portfolio-balance model variables have not been particularly successful; see, for example, Frankel (1982a).]

Measuring inflationary expectations presents many problems. The two sticky-price models, the Dornbusch–Frankel and Hooper–Morton models, are potentially quite sensitive to the proxy used for the long-run expected inflation differential. Proxies such as long-term interest rates and past inflation rates may be grossly inadequate. It is possible that the approach of

---

[16]Hooper and Morton allow for a risk premium as a function of central bank intervention in a more general version of their model.

estimating rational expectations versions of the models by imposing all the cross-equation restrictions, as in Driskell and Sheffrin (1981) or Glaessner (1982), will yield better expectations proxies. In that work, expectations of the exogenous forcing variables are formed using univariate or multivariate autoregressions. But it is not clear why autoregressions should necessarily yield good expectations proxies for the exogenous variables during a period when autoregressions yield poor proxies for the endogenous variables.

The goods market specifications of the models may also be suspect, though to differing degrees. There is little question that purchasing power parity did not hold in the short run during the seventies; see Isard (1977) or Frenkel (1981a). The Dornbusch–Frankel model assumes only long-run PPP; the evidence here is less clearcut [see Frenkel (1981b)]. The Hooper–Morton model attempts to empirically capture movements in the long-run real exchange rate, but it does not fit out-of-sample notably better than the other two models. Nevertheless, temporary or permanent movements in the PPP level of the exchange rate to real shocks may be a major cause of exchange rate volatility.

The final possible source of misspecification we shall discuss is the standard money demand function that underpins the models:

$$m - p = b_0 - b_1 r_s + b_2 y. \tag{4}$$

In (4), p is the logarithm of the price of the domestic good (using a different deflator for money balances would not alter the discussion below), and other variables are defined as in eq. (1). The breakdown of empirical money demand relationships is widespread, and the phenomenon is particularly acute for U.S. money demand equations; see Simpson and Porter (1980). In an attempt to control for unexplained shifts in velocity, we tried using eq. (4) and its foreign equivalent to substitute price levels for monetary variables in eq. (1). For the Frenkel–Bilson model the theoretical values of the coefficients in eq. (1) are the same as the corresponding coefficients in eq. (4), so price levels alone remain as regressors after the substitution. The transformed model is thus a purchasing power parity equation. In the two sticky-price models, the coefficient on short-term interest rates differs from the coefficient b_1 in (4). For those models, the coefficient on short-term interest rates in the quasi-reduced form exchange rate eq. (1) is the negative of the inverse of the goods market speed of adjustment parameter; see Frankel (1979). Therefore the price substitution only eliminates money supplies and real incomes in their quasi-reduced forms. In table 3 the models are estimated in the same fashion as in table 1, using Fair's method. The models still fail after the price levels substitution to improve on the random walk model in root mean square error. Implementing other estimation techniques and trying other expected inflation rate proxies yields qualitatively similar

20   *R.A. Meese and K. Rogoff, Exchange rate models of the seventies*

Table 3

Root mean square forecast errors with price levels substituted in for monetary variables.[a,b]

	Model:	Random walk	Modified Frenkel– Bilson (relative PPP)	Modified Dornbusch– Frankel	Modified Hooper– Morton
Exchange rate	Horizon				
	1 month	3.17	3.31	3.78	3.68
$/mark	6 months	8.71	9.78	11.28	10.51
	12 months	12.98	15.25	16.89	17.52
	1 month	3.70	3.70	4.42	4.18
$/yen	6 months	11.58	12.55	13.86	12.69
	12 months	18.31	21.80	20.55	20.65
	1 month	2.56	2.57	2.78	2.94
$/pound	6 months	6.45	7.83	8.64	8.92
	12 months	9.96	12.51	12.28	14.77
Trade-	1 month	1.99	2.18	2.29	2.48
weighted	6 months	6.09	6.63	6.33	6.80
dollar	12 months	8.65	10.48	9.52	9.45

[a]Approximately in percentage terms.
[b]The three structural models are estimated using Fair's instrumental variable technique to correct for first-order serial correlation.

results to those reported in section 3, where the models are estimated without the price level substitution.

As a final effort to investigate the money demand problem, we estimated the Dornbusch–Frankel model for the three cross-exchange rates, thereby abstracting from the particularly unstable demand for money in the U.S. The Dornbusch–Frankel model does not outperform the random walk model for the pound/yen or pound/mark rates, but does do 0.6 percent better at six months (12.0 vs. 12.6 percent for the random walk) and 3.4 percent better at twelve months (16.0 vs. 19.4 percent) for the yen/mark cross-rate. But even this improvement is not so great as to provide a basis for asserting that money demand instability or misspecification is the main problem with the models.

6. Conclusions

The random walk model performs no worse than estimated univariate time series models, an unconstrained vector autoregression, or our candidate structural models in forecasting three major bilateral rates (the dollar/mark, dollar/pound, and dollar/yen) and the trade-weighted dollar. The results of our paper contrast with those of previous studies based on in-sample fit. Thus, from a methodological standpoint, our paper supports the view that out-of-sample fit is an important criterion to consider when evaluating empirical exchange rate models.

The out-of-sample failure of the estimated univariate times series models and the vector autoregression suggests that major-country exchange rates are well-approximated by a random walk model (without drift). Of course, as long as the exchange rate does not exactly follow a random walk, we would expect one of the estimated time series models to prevail in a large enough sample.

Less certain is whether the failure of the stuctural models to outforecast the random walk model — even when uncertainty about the future values of the explanatory variables is removed — can similarly be attributed to sampling error. The constrained-coefficient experiments reported elsewhere in Meese and Rogoff (1983) suggest that neither sampling error nor simultaneous equations bias can fully explain the results presented here. We have listed other possible explanations without arriving at any definite conclusions. Structural instability due to the oil price shocks and changes in macroeconomic policy regimes, as well as the failure of the models to adequately incorporate other real disturbances, may be important. Misspecification of the money demand functions which underpin the structural models is another likely problem, although it is true that the structural models do not predict better when price levels are substituted in for monetary variables, or when M2 or the reserve-adjusted base are used in place of M1-B. Difficulties in modeling expectations of the explanatory variables are yet another obvious source of trouble. But determining the relative importance of the possible problems listed above, or any of the others listed in section 5, is at this point speculative.

Data appendix

The raw data consist entirely of seasonally unadjusted monthly observations over the period March 1973 to June 1981. In the bilateral data set for the United Kingdom, the spot and forward exchange rates, short-term interest rate, and long-term bond rate are all drawn from the same dates. Because daily long-term bond rate series are not readily available for Japan and Germany, only the exchange- and short-term interest rate dates correspond in those data sets. All other bilateral series as well as all of the series used in the trade-weighted data set are monthly data. All data are taken from publicly available sources. Data sources are listed below; a more detailed description of the data set can be found in Meese and Rogoff (1983).

United States data series
Long-term government bond yields, three-month Treasury bill rates, CPI,

industrial production, M1-B, M2 and the reserve-adjusted base: Federal Reserve Board data base.

Trade Balance: U.S. Department of Commerce, Highlights of U.S. Export and Import Trade.

Foreign data series for the bilateral data sets

Forward rates: Data Resources Inc. data base.

Spot rates: Federal Reserve Board data base.

Trade balances, monetary aggregates, and industrial productions: O.E.C.D. Main Economic Indicators.

Long-term bond yields and consumer prices: *Monthly Report of the Deutsche Bundesbank, Financial Times and Employment Gazette* (U.K.), *Economics Statistics Monthly* (Japan).

Interest rates (three-month): Frankfurter Allegemeine Zeitung (three-month German interbank rate), *Financial Times* (three-month British local authorities deposits), FRB data base ('Over two-month ends' bill discount rate, Tokyo stock exchange).

The trade-weighted data set

The weights utilized to determine the trade-weighted statistics are: German mark, 0.208; Japanese yen, 0.136; French franc, 0.131; United Kingdom pound, 0.119; Canadian dollar, 0.091; Italian lira, 0.090; Netherlands guilder, 0.083; Belgian franc, 0.064; Swedish Krona, 0.042; and Swiss franc, 0.036. These weights represent each country's share of the total trade (measured by the sum of imports plus exports) of all ten countries in the period 1972 through 1976. See Hooper and Morton (1978).

All the trade-weighted (foreign) data is drawn from O.E.C.D. Main Economics Indicators and the Federal Reserve data base.

References

Akaike, H., 1974, A new look at the statistical model identification, IEEE Transaction on Automatic Control AC-19, 716–723.

Amemiya, T., 1980, Selection of regressors, International Economic Review 21, 331–354.

Bilson, John F.O., 1978, Rational expectations and the exchange rate, in: J. Frenkel and H. Johnson, eds., The economics of exchange rates (Addison-Wesley Press, Reading).

Bilson, John F.O., 1979, The deutsche mark/dollar rate — A monetary analysis, in: Karl Brunner and Allan H. Meltzer, eds., Policies for employment, prices and exchange rates, Carnegie-Rochester Conference 11 (North-Holland Publishing Company, Amsterdam).

Bilson, John F.O., 1981, The 'speculative efficiency' hypothesis, Journal of Business 54, 435–451.

Branson, William H., Hannu Halttunen and Paul Masson, 1979, Exchange rates in the short run: Some further results, European Economic Review 12, 395–402.

Christ, Carl F., 1975, Judging the performance of econometric models of the U.S. economy, International Economic Review 16, 54–74.

Cornell, Bradford, 1977, Spot rates, forward rates and exchange market efficiency, Journal of Financial Economics 5, 55–65.

Cumby, Robert and Maurice Obstfeld, 1981, A note on exchange-rate expectations and nominal interest differentials, The Journal of Finance 36, 697–703.

Dornbusch, Rudiger, 1976, Expectations and exchange rate dynamics, Journal of Political Economy 84, 1161–1176.

Driskell, Robert A. and Steven M. Sheffrin, 1981, On the mark: Comment, American Economic Review 71, 1068–1074.

Fair, Ray C., 1970, The estimation of simultaneous equations models with lagged endogenous variables and first order serially correlated errors, Econometrica 38, 507–516.

Fair, Ray C., 1979, An analysis of the accuracy of four macroeconometric models, Journal of Political Economy 87, 701–718.

Frankel, Jeffrey A., 1979, On the mark: A theory of floating exchange rates based on real interest differentials, American Economic Review 69, 610–622.

Frankel, Jeffrey A., 1981, On the mark: Reply, American Economic Review 71, 1075–1082.

Frankel, Jeffrey A., 1982a, In search of the exchange rate risk premium: A six-currency test assuming mean variance optimization, University of California at Berkeley, mimeo.

Frankel, Jeffrey A., 1982b, The mystery of the multiplying marks: A modification of the monetary model, Review of Economics and Statistics 64, 515–519.

Frenkel, Jacob A., 1976, A monetary approach to the exchange rate: Doctrinal aspects and empirical evidence, Scandinavian Journal of Economics 78, 200–224.

Frenkel, Jacob A., 1981a, The collapse of purchasing power parities during the 1970's, European Economic Review 16, 145–165.

Frenkel, Jacob A., 1981b, Flexible exchange rates, prices, and the role of news: Lessons from the 1970's, Journal of Political Economy 89, 665–705.

Geweke, John and Edward Feige, 1979, Some joint tests of the efficiency of markets for forward foreign exchange, Review of Economics and Statistics 61, 334–341.

Glaessner, Thomas, 1982, Theoretical and empirical essays on spot and forward exchange rate determination, Ph.D. Dissertation, University of Virginia.

Granger, Clive and Paul Newbold, 1977, Forecasting economic time series (Academic Press, New York).

Hacche, Graham and John Townend, 1981, Exchange rates and monetary policy: Modeling sterling's effective exchange rate, 1972–1980, in: W. Eltis and P. Sinclair, eds., The money supply and the exchange rate (Oxford University Press, Oxford).

Hakkio, Craig S., 1981, Expectations and the forward exchange rate, International Economic Review 22, 663–678.

Hannan, E.J., 1970, Multiple time series (John Wiley & Sons, New York).

Hansen, Lars P. and Robert J. Hodrick, 1980, Forward exchange rates as optimal predictors of future spot rates: An econometric analysis, Journal of Political Economy 88, 829–853.

Hansen, Lars P. and Robert J. Hodrick, 1983, Risk averse speculation in forward exchange markets: An econometric analysis, forthcoming in: Jacob A. Frenkel, ed., Exchange rates and international macroeconomics (University of Chicago Press, Chicago).

Haynes, Stephen E. and Joe A. Stone, 1981, On the mark: Comment, American Economic Review 71, 1060–1067.

Hodrick, Robert J., 1979, On the monetary analysis of exchange rates: A comment, in: Kark Brunner and Allan H. Meltzer, eds., Policies for employment, prices, and exchange rates, Carnegie-Rochester Conference 11 (North-Holland, Amsterdam).

Hooper, Peter and John E. Morton, 1978, Summary measures of the dollar's foreign exchange value, Federal Reserve Bulletin 64, 783–789.

Hooper, Peter and John E. Morton, 1982, Fluctuations in the dollar: A model of nominal and real exchange rate determination, Journal of International Money and Finance 1, 39–56.

Isard, Peter, 1977, How far can we push the law of one price?, American Economic Review 67, 942–948.

Litterman, Robert B., 1979, Techniques of forecasting using vector autoregressions, Working paper no. 115, Federal Reserve Bank of Minneapolis.

Maddala, G.S., 1977, Econometrics (McGraw-Hill, New York).

McCulloch, J. Huston, 1975, Operational aspects of the Siegel paradox, Quarterly Journal of Economics 86, 303–309.

Meese, Richard A. and Kenneth J. Singleton, 1980, Rational expectations, risk premia, and the market for spot and forward exchange, International Finance Discussion Papers no. 165, Board of Governors of the Federal Reserve System.

Meese, Richard A. and Kenneth S. Rogoff, 1983, The out-of-sample failure of empirical exchange rate models: Sampling error or misspecification?, forthcoming in: Jacob A. Frenkel, ed., Exchange rates and international macroeconomics (University of Chicago Press, Chicago).

Mussa, Michael, 1979, Empirical regularities in the behavior of exchange rates and theories of the foreign exchange market, in: Karl Brunner and Allan H. Meltzer, eds., Policies for employment, prices and exchange rates, Carnegie-Rochester Conference 11 (North-Holland, Amsterdam).

Nelson, Charles, 1972, The prediction performance of the F.R.B.–M.I.T.–Penn. model of the U.S. economy, American Economic Review 62, 902–917.

Parzen, Emanuel, 1975, Multiple time series: Determining the order of approximating autoregressive schemes, Technical Report no. 23, State University of New York at Buffalo.

Sargent, Thomas J., 1979, Macroeconomic theory (Acadmic Press, New York).

Schwarz, Gideon, 1978, Estimating the dimension of a model, Annals of Statistics 6, 461–464.

Siegel, Jeremy J., 1972, Risk, interest rates, and the forward exchange, Quarterly Journal of Economics 86, 303–309.

Simpson, Thomas D. and Richard D. Porter, 1980, Some issues involving the definition and interpretation of the monetary aggregates, in: Controlling monetary aggregates, vol. III, Federal Reserve Bank of Boston conference series no. 23.

Sims, Christopher A., 1974a, Seasonality in regression, Journal of the American Statistical Association 69, 618–626.

Sims, Christopher A., 1974b, Distributed lags, in: Michael D. Intrilligator and David A. Kendrick, eds., Frontiers of quantitative economics (North-Holland, New York).

Sims Christopher A., 1980, Macroeconomics and reality, Econometrica 48, 1–48.

Tryon, Ralph, 1979, Testing for rational expectations in foreign exchange markets, International Finance Discussion Papers no. 139, Board of Governors of the Federal Reserve System.

Westerfield, Janice M., 1977, An examination of foreign exchange risk under fixed and floating rate regimes, Journal of International Economics 7, 181–200.

Working, Holbrook, 1960, Note on the correlation of first differences in a random chain, Econometrica 28, 916–918.

[7]

International Journal of Forecasting 3 (1987) 53–64
North-Holland

MONETARY/ASSET MODELS OF EXCHANGE RATE DETERMINATION
How Well Have They Performed in the 1980's?

Don ALEXANDER *

Citicorp Investment Bank, New York, NY 10043, USA

Lee R. THOMAS, III*

Goldman, Sachs & Co, New York, NY 10004, USA

Abstract: This study compares the performance of various structural exchange rate models based on the methodology developed by Meese and Rogoff (1983 a,b, 1985). The first part of the paper updates their study through 1985. The structural models examined include variations of the monetary/asset exchange rate model, and use realized values of future explanatory variables to produce their point forecasts. A second objective of the study is to evaluate the use of time-varying parameters estimated using a Kalman filter as a means of improving forecast performance.

Keywords: Exchange rates, Forecasting accuracy, Kalman filter, Random walk.

1. Introduction

Recent experience has supported those studies that earlier questioned the out-of-sample accuracy of time-series and structural models of exchange-rate determination. Moreover, the evidence is that professional currency forecasters' performance has been as disappointing as that of currency forecasting models (for example, see various Euromoney surveys). Among the most influential of the empirical studies of exchange rate forecasting models were those performed by Meese and Rogoff (1983a, 1983b, 1985) (M–R) who found that during the 1976–1984 period, no structural or time series technique could appreciably outperform the random-walk model at any forecasting horizon shorter than 12 months. Moreover, forecasts M–R constructed were based on the actual future values of the exogenous variables, and the models' coefficients were permitted to vary depending on the forecasting horizon adopted. Thus, two of the most serious difficulties in using structural models to produce forecasts were eliminated in the M–R examination of forecasting efficiency.

---

* The opinions expressed are those of the individuals and not necessarily those of Citibank and Goldman, Sachs respectively.

0169-2070/87/$3.50 © 1987, Elsevier Science Publishers B.V. (North-Holland)

These negative results raise several questions [1]. One of most obvious is whether the econometric models' poor exchange rate forecasting performances resulted from theoretical misspecification, or from inadequate estimation of the parameters of the candidate models. This question could obviously be most conclusively answered by finding econometric procedures that permit structural and/or time-series exchange rate models to forecast significantly better than does a random walk model.

M–R surmised that one likely explanation for their disappointing findings is structural instability. It is reasonable on theoretical grounds to surmise that the parameters of exchange rate models vary, rather than being fixed as conventional econometric practice assumes. Oil shocks, shifts in world patterns of trade, changes in monetary and other economic policies, and the Third-world debt crisis may all have changed the relationships among exchange rates and their explanatory variables during the last decade. Bilson (1978a), Frankel (1979) and Frenkel (1981) present evidence suggesting that the monetary model broke down, while Dornbusch (1980) and Frankel (1982, 1984) draw the same conclusion for the portfolio-balance approach. After empirically reviewing various monetary and asset approaches to exchange rate determination, Shafer and Loopesko (1983) conclude that no single model can adequately explain the dollar's fluctuations against other major currencies over the last decade. All of these results could be explained by changes in the nature of the process governing exchange rate evolution. The clear indication is to use estimation procedures that relax the assumption that the structures of exchange rate models are stable through time. This paper is primarily designed to evaluate the forecasting efficacy of standard exchange rate models estimated without imposing the usual assumption that their structural parameters are fixed.

2. Description of the data and econometric methodology

2.1. Data

The data set consists of seasonally-unadjusted monthly observations for the period January 1974 to October 1985, which yielded 142 observations per currency. Tests are performed on the dollar/pound, dollar/deutschemark and the dollar/yen exchange rates, and for each of these series the average of the London noon bid and offer rates was computed at the last business day of each month.

The money supply statistic used is M1 or its equivalent in Germany, Japan and the U.K.; M1-B was used for the U.S. when applicable. Short-term interest rates are three-month rates for either domestic interbank deposits or Government Treasury bills. Long-term interest rates represent yields on government bonds with a maturity of four years or longer. The industrial production index and trade balance for each country are based on OECD statistics.

The interested reader is referred to appendix A for a more complete description of the data.

---

[1] Also see Bilson (1978), Frankel (1979), Hansen and Hodrick (1983), Hodrick and Srivastava (1984), Meese (1986). Various explanations of the empirical failures of exchange rate models have been advanced. Melitz (1983) argues that in the attempt to simplify, the structural exchange models that have been estimated often diverge from those implied by a general theory of exchange rate determination. For example, he contends that properly-specified exchange rate equations may differ among currencies. Other often-cited sources of misspecification are unexplained shifts in money demand – which suggests that our exchange rate theory is inadequate because our understanding of monetary economics is inadequate, our difficulty in dealing with and measuring inflationary (and other) expectations, and the existence of speculative bubbles that are not accounted for in most exchange rate models. Finally the breakdown of uncovered interest rate parity documented by, among others, Cumby and Obstfeld (1984), suggest that there exists a time-varying risk premium embedded in forward exchange rates. This time-varying premium has yet to be fully integrated into exchange rate theories.

2.2. Structural models

The structural asset models used are identical to those previously considered by Meese and Rogoff (1983a, 1983b) and Shafer and Loopesko (1983). These are: the flexible price monetary model (Frenkel–Bilson), the sticky-price monetary model (Dornbusch–Frankel), and the sticky-price asset model (Hooper–Morton). By imposing the appropriate restrictions on the parameters, any of these models can be represented by the equation

$$S_t = b_0 + b_1(M - M*)_t + b_2(Y - Y*)_t + b_3(r_s - r_s*)_t$$

$$+ b_4(\Pi + \Pi*) + b_5(TB)_t + b_6(TB*)_t + u_t, \tag{1}$$

where S is the logarithm of the dollar price of the foreign currency, $M - M*$ is the logarithm of the ratio of the U.S. to foreign money supply, $Y - Y*$ is the logarithm of the ratio of the U.S. to foreign industrial production index, $r_s - r_2*$ and $\Pi - \Pi*$ respectively represent the ratio of short-term and long-term interest rate differentials between U.S. and the foreign country. The latter proxies for differences in inflationary expectations. TB and $TB*$ represent the cummulative U.S. and foreign trade balances and u is a disturbance term.

The Frenkel–Bilson (F–B), Dornbusch–Frankel (D–F) and Hooper–Morton (H–M) models can be distinguished by the restrictions they impose on the structural parameters b_2 through b_6. (All of the models predict $b_1 = 1$.) The F–B model is the most restrictive since it assumes purchasing-power parity; thus, it requires that $b_4 = b_5 = b_6 = 0$. In contrast, the D–F model assumes slow domestic price adjustment in the goods market relative to the rate of asset market adjustment, and permits short-term deviations from purchasing-power parity; it constrains $b_5 = b_6 = 0$. The Hooper–Morton (H–M) model is the most general specification. H–M relaxes the assumptions of the Dornbsch-Frankel model by permitting changes in the real exchange rate. These changes are assumed to be correlated with changes in the current account.

All variables in the structural models are subsequently treated as if they were strictly exogenous. In the case of some variables, such as the money supply or industrial output, this assumption appears heroic. However, relaxing this assumption has not beeen found to improve the forecasting performance of the models here or elsewhere.

2.3. Comparisons

The structural models were first estimated over the entire sample, from January, 1974 to October, 1985. The equations are then re-estimated over the January, 1974 to December, 1979 subperiod to ascertain if the parameters of models changed over the subsequently used hold out sample, from January, 1980 to October, 1985. Each model is evaluated on the basis of its standard error, t-statistics, coefficient of determination and root mean square error.

The second set of experiments involves assessing the out-of-sample performance of the F–B, D–F, and H–M models. Each out-of-sample forecast represents a point forecast at a time horizon of from 1 to 36 months. As in M–R, the actual values of the models' exogenous variables have been used to produce the predictions. As a result the forecasts reported below are better than those that available in practice.

Out-of-sample accuracy for each model is measured four ways: Mean Error (ME), Mean Absolute (MAE), Root Mean Square Error ($RMSE$) and Theil's U-Statistic.

2.4. Methodology

The problem of structural instability of the relationships among economic variables has been recognized in the empirical exchange rate literature, and also in more general contexts. There are many reasons that the OLS assumption of fixed parameters may fail. For example, model misspecification can lead to parameter drift; more substantively, economic theory indicates that changes in economic relationships are to be expected. Lucas' well-known argument for structural instability in the relationships among macroeconomic variables is even more telling when the dependent variables of interest are speculative prices.

In addition to these general reasons for macroeconomic relationships to be structurally unstable, there are particular reasons to expect an exchange rate model's parameters to change through time. For example, consider exchange market participants' response to an unexpected increase in the domestic money stock. Ordinarily, the domestic currency can be expected to depreciate. However, for the U.S. dollar exchange rates since 1979 the opposite relationship has been observed. [2] This is hardly mysterious: when the monetary authorities are believed to be targeting M1 closely, unexpected money growth produces expectations of Federal Reserve tightening; as a result, the dollar appreciates as a result of 'bad' money news. Thus, the relationship between money growth and exchange rate changes depends on the prevailing monetary regime, or, more rigorously, what exchange markets perceived the U.S. monetary authorities reaction functions to be. Clearly, the assumption that the parameters of dollar exchange rate equations are unchanging is unrealistic. In this example, we might even expect the partial derivative of dollar exchange rates with respect to U.S. money growth to change in the pre-and post-October, 1979 periods.

This section presents the empirical results of relaxing the standard OLS assumptions of fixed (unknown) parameters. The model is as follows.

The general form of the estimated equations is

$$S_t = X_t B_t + u_t, \tag{2}$$

where X_t and B_t are vectors containing the exogenous variables and coefficients from (1), and where the coefficient vector is assumed to evolve according to

$$B_t = B_{t-1} + v_t, \tag{3}$$

The v_t are identically, independently and normally distributed random variables. Each of the structural models was first estimated using OLS. The econometric procedure then utilized to update the forecasting equations, a Kalman filter, is equivalent to a rolling regression procedure.

Statistical results.   The first set of regressions constrains the estimated variance of v_t to be zero; that is, it uses standard OLS estimation techniques. The forecasting results achieved by the structural models are compared to those achieved by the following three naive models:

(i) The Random Walk model

$$S_t = S_{t-1} + u_t. \tag{4}$$

(ii) The AR(1) model

$$S_t - S_{t-1} = a + b(S_{t-1} - S_{t-2}) + u_t. \tag{5}$$

---

[2] See Cornell (1977).

Table 1
Out-of-sample forecasting results (Sterling: Root Mean Square Error).

Model	Horizon					
	1	3	6	12	24	36
(A) Fixed regression parameters						
AR(1)	3.4827	3.4113	3.3819	3.5001	3.2757	3.5832
AR(2)	3.4573	3.4127	3.3733	3.4893	3.2651	3.5785
F–B	17.4062	18.8163	20.2580	21.8358	27.2724	33.4578
D–F	18.1417	20.4307	23.5204	30.1603	43.6195	59.4408
H–M	15.7382	18.8305	23.0778	29.3095	42.5753	59.3158
(B) Time-varying regression parameters						
F–B	8.4624	12.3193	15.7220	16.2073	24.7687	37.7110
D–F	5.8398	8.9876	11.3500	15.8990	28.3816	45.6567
H–M	6.3458	9.7678	12.0778	18.1236	29.3839	46.4878

(iii) The AR(2) model

$$S_t - S_{t-1} = a + b(S_{t-1} - S_{t-2}) + c(S_{t-2} - S_{t-3}) + u_t. \tag{6}$$

These three naive models provide benchmarks against which the three structural models are compared.

The fixed coefficients forecasting OLS results for the pound sterling, deutschemark and Japanese yen are presented in tables 1–6, at horizons of 1, 3, 6, 12, 24, and 36 months. The out-of-sample estimates are based on data from January, 1980 through October, 1985.

OLS results. The regession results are broadly consistent with those reported for previous periods by M–R.

Table 2
Out-of-sample forecasting results (Sterling: Theil's *U*).

Model	Horizon					
	1	3	6	12	24	36
(A) Fixed regression parameters						
AR(1)	0.7274	0.7826	0.7152	0.6817	0.7325	0.7959
AR(2)	0.7221	0.7829	0.7134	0.6795	0.7301	0.7949
F–B	5.0072	2.8413	1.8682	1.3626	0.9949	0.8246
D–F	5.2182	3.0852	2.1691	1.8820	1.5912	1.4649
H–M	4.5273	2.8435	2.1283	1.8289	1.5531	1.4619
(B) Time-varying regression parameters						
F–B	2.4343	1.8603	1.4499	1.0133	0.9036	0.9294
D–F	1.6799	1.3572	1.0467	0.9921	1.0354	1.1253
H–M	1.8254	1.4750	1.1323	1.1309	1.0719	1.1457

Table 3
Out-of-sample forecasting results (Deutschemark: Root Mean Square Error).

Model	Horizon					
	1	3	6	12	24	36
(A) Fixed regression parameters						
AR(1)	3.9639	3.5323	3.2765	3.3362	3.1680	3.3399
AR(2)	3.9280	3.5547	3.2580	3.3187	3.1518	3.3286
F–B	11.0343	11.4256	11.2861	10.3192	12.2364	14.2083
D–F	11.5164	12.5019	13.3365	15.0987	19.8213	26.5419
H–M	10.7797	12.3145	13.6108	14.8464	23.0890	34.7397
(B) Time-varying regression parameters						
F–B	5.5226	10.6511	11.3832	8.7726	11.0992	13.6729
D–F	6.2865	8.4974	10.3340	10.7917	15.9157	20.5400
H–M	6.3157	9.3043	12.1430	10.4488	13.8436	25.1055

In general, the mean errors of the F–B model and of all the AR specifications are small relative to the mean absolute errors and root-mean-square errors. This indicates that these models are producing unbiased forecasts. In contrast, the D–F and H–M models appear to consistently under-forecast the pound and mark at all horizons, and to under-forecast the yen at six month and longer time horizons.

The Theil-U statistics are the primary indicators of forecasting efficacy subsequently examined. This statistic compares the *RMS* error of each model to that of eq. (4). (By definition, the Theil-U value for (4) equals 1.) A value of less than 1 indicates the model in question outperformed a random walk specification in out-of-sample forecasts. Since values less than 1 for Theil's U may not indicate that the structural models are performing impressively – it is easy to secure forecasts more accurate than those produced by (4) if, for example, the series is strongly trending – the values produced by these models should also be compared to those produced by eqs. (5)–(6).

Table 4
Out-of-sample forecasting results (Deutschemark: Theil's U).

Model	Horizon					
	1	3	6	12	24	36
(A) Fixed regression parameters						
AR(1)	0.6781	0.7032	0.6963	0.6461	0.6319	0.6794
AR(2)	0.6563	0.7077	0.6934	0.6472	0.6287	0.6771
F–B	2.8409	1.8149	1.2121	0.7645	0.5979	0.5108
D–F	2.9650	1.9858	1.4323	1.1186	0.9684	0.9542
H–M	2.7754	1.9561	1.4617	1.0999	1.1281	1.2489
(B) Time-varying regression parameters						
F–B	2.1942	1.6919	1.2225	0.6499	0.5423	0.4916
D–F	1.6185	1.3497	1.1098	0.7994	0.7776	0.7384
H–M	1.6260	1.4779	1.3041	0.7741	0.6764	0.9026

D. Alexander, L.R. Thomas, III / Monetary / asset models of exchange rate determination 59

Table 5
Out-of-sample forecasting results (Yen: Root Mean Square Error).

Model	Horizon					
	1	3	6	12	24	36
(A) Fixed regression parameters						
AR(1)	3.5556	3.4478	3.4062	3.4242	3.2421	2.7181
AR(2)	3.5777	3.4489	3.4036	3.4195	3.2360	2.7221
F–B	13.2317	14.2712	14.9675	15.5449	17.3370	17.4728
D–F	17.2936	18.5003	19.4774	21.6128	23.0306	25.9378
H–M	17.4484	19.0578	20.3063	22.8654	23.9643	26.3267
(B) Time-varying regression parameters						
F–B	7.6858	10.1820	12.1759	13.0010	16.3629	20.0366
D–F	10.8817	13.9676	15.3418	18.0680	20.4264	25.4791
H–M	12.8695	15.6434	17.8186	20.1055	22.6605	32.6267

Table 6
Out-of-sample forecasting results (Yen: Theil's U).

Model	Horizon					
	1	3	6	12	24	36
(A) Fixed regression parameters						
AR(1)	0.7348	0.7528	0.6959	0.7370	0.6369	0.6335
AR(2)	0.7394	0.7530	0.6954	0.7360	0.6357	0.6345
F–B	3.7729	2.4444	1.8501	1.6461	1.7758	1.8985
D–F	4.9311	3.1687	2.4076	2.2886	2.3589	2.8183
H–M	4.9752	3.2642	2.5101	2.4212	2.4546	2.8606
(B) Time-varying regression parameters						
F–B	2.1915	1.7440	1.5051	1.3767	1.6760	2.1771
D–F	3.1028	2.3924	1.8964	1.9132	2.0922	2.7685
H–M	3.6696	2.6794	2.2026	2.1290	2.3210	3.5451

The naive models' Theil's U statistics are uniformly close to 1 at short forecasting horizons. This indicates that all of the information contained in the historical series of exchange rates is reflected in the current exchange rate. This result, familiar from many asset market studies, is suggestive of exchange market efficiency [3].

At forecasting horizons of less than 1 year, the forecasting performance of the structural models are uniformly dismal. At the 1- and 3-month horizons, all three models' *RMS* errors are more than twice those of the random walk model(s). Neither was any structural model able to outperform a random walk for any currency at a 6-month forecasting horizon.

---

[3] Independence between the current and lagged values of the exchange rate is not itself a necessary or sufficient condition for market efficiency, but it is indicative.

At a one-year forecasting horizon the results are only slightly less clear. The random walk model outperformed the structural models for both the pound and yen. For the mark, only the flexible-price monetary model yielded an out-of-sample forecasting gain. The F–B model's reduction in forecast error variance for the mark – about 20% – is impressive.

The 2- and 3-year horizon results are more favorable for the structural models, but they must be interpreted with care. The out-of-sample period over which forecasts were constructed is only 70 months; thus, only 2 strictly independent forecast observations are available at the 24 month horizon, and only 1 is available at the 36 month horizon. Moreover, the structural models advantage from using the realizing values of the exogenous variables at these long forecasting horizons is probably substantial.

Bearing in mind these limitations, the F–B model appears to add forecasting power at longer horizons for two of the three currencies, the pound and the mark. The reduction in RMS errors are approximately 25% and 40% for these two currencies, respectively. The most likely explanation of this finding is that monetary surprises have been a significant determinent of U.S. dollar exchange rate changes during the 1980's. As a result, a prescient observer who correctly predicted the trajectory of U.S. money relative to foreign money growth could have used this information to produce exchange rate forecasts better than those represented by the spot rate.

The forecasting results for the time-varying parameter model are presented in tables 1–6. At forecasting horizons of less than 12 months, the forecasting performances of the structural models were all improved compared to the fixed coefficient, results, sometimes substantially. At longer horizons, the results were mixed, but generally the time-varying models produced lower Theil's U statistics. Overall, the results indicate that the assumption of fixed coefficients is inappropriate for these models. However, even after relaxing this assumption, the structural models generally under-performed the random walk model at forecasting horizons of 12 months or less. The only exception was in the case of the German mark, and then only at a 1 year horizon. In the case of the German mark, all three structural models outperformed both the random walk and the time-series models.

At longer horizons the time-varying model generally improved the quality of the forecasts. The F–B model was clearly the best performer at a 2- and 3-year horizon, registering the lowest Theil's U for both the pound and the mark. Once again these results suggest that previously unexpected growth in relative national money stocks has been a significant determinent of exchange rate fluctuations in the 1980's; there is little evidence in these experiments that unpredicability in long-term interest rates, and/or in trade balances, have been important. This assumes that we have correctly specified these variables in our exchange rate models. However, another possible explanation is that these variables are related to real exchange rates and are not accounted for in our models.

Overall the results suggest that the economic structure underlying dollar exchange rate equations is not stationary. But even after accounting for this factor by using a random coefficient regression model, the major findings reported by M–R stands: the three structural models examined here have been unable to consistantly outperform the random walk model at horizons of 12 months or less. At longer horizons, the simple (flexible price) monetary model was the best performer of a disappointing set of contending structural models.

3. Conclusions

Previous research has shown that structural exchange rate models are generally unable to outperform a random walk in out-of-sample experiments. Some doubt exists concerning whether this results from the theoretical inadequacies of exchange rate models or from problems in their econometric implementation. This study was designed to see if eliminating one dubious econometric assumption – fixed regression coefficients – would reverse the random walk model's dominance. The problem of structural instability has been cited by Meese and Rogoff as one likely explanation for their negative findings (1983 a, b, 1985).

Even using an estimation technique that assumes that regression coefficients describe random walks, the structural models still perform unimpressively out-of-sample. Their failure suggests that all historical information identified by these models as being potentially relevant – monetary growth rates, trade balances, national growth rates and interest rates – is already discounted in the existing structure of exchange rates. More strongly, even knowing the future trajectories for these variables would not have permitted improving on the current exchange rate as a predictor of the future exchange rates at forecasting horizons of less than 2 years during the early 1980's. Thus, it appears that our results suggest the problem in forecasting exchange rates may result from our inadequate understanding of exchange rate determination.

Appendix A

The data are all monthly observations that are not seasonally adjusted. Each data point represents a value taken at the end of each month or the last business day except where indicated for certain money supply figures. All data were taken from publicly available sources.

Forward rates. One, three six and twelve month.
Data source: Citibank database.
Series: One, three, six and twelve months forward rates are the mean rate between bit and offer rates expressed in U.S. dollars per local currency unit.
Description: Daily data based on a 10 : 00 A.M. opening New York market rates.

Spot exchange rates
Data source: Citibank database
Series: The mean rate between the bid and offer rate in U.S. dollars perlocal currency amount.
Description: Daily data based on London rate at noon.

Long term interest rates
U.S. Data source: International Financial Statistics
Series: U.S. government bonds
Description: Yields on government bonds with maturity of 5 years or more.

Japan Data source: Morgon Guaranty
Series: Long term bond rates for government bonds with a maturity of four years
Description: Yield on government bonds taken from the last business day of the month.

Germany Data source: Morgan Guaranty
Series: Long term bond rates for government bonds, maturity of greater than 5 years.
Description: Yield on government bonds taken on the last business day of the month.

United Kingdom
Data source: Morgan Guaranty
Series: Long term bond rates on gilts
Description: Yield on government bonds taken on the last business day of the month

Industrial production
Countries: U.S., U.K., Germany and Japan
Data source: OECD Main Ecnonomic Indicators
Series: Total Industrial Production
Description: Montly Index with 1980 = 100

Trade balance
Countries: U.S., U.K., Germany and Japan
Data source: OECD Main Economic Indicators
Series: Trade Balance (f.o.b.–c.i.f.) expressed in units of local currency

Money supply
Countries: U.S., U.K., Germany and Japan
Data source: OECD Main Economic Indicators
Series: M1 money supply or equivalent expressed in millions of local currency
Description: Monthly data taken from last weekly announcement of the month except in the U.K. where it is taken from the third Wednesday of the month.

Short term interest rates
U.S.
Data source: Citibank database
Series: Three month Treasury bill rates
Description: Monthly data taken from the last business day of the month

Germany
Data source: citibank database
Series: Three month domestic interbank deposit rate
Description: Monthly data taken from the last business day of the month

Japan
Data source: Citibank database
Series: Three month domestic interbank deposit rate
Description: Monthly data taken from the last business day of the month

United Kingdom
Data source: Citibank database
Series: Three month domestic interbank deposit rate
Description: Monthly data taken from the last business day of the month

References

Bilson, John, 1978a, A monetary approach to the exchange rate, some empirical evidence, IMF Staff Papers 25, 48–75.
Bilson, John, 1978b, Rational expectations and the exchange rate, in: J. Frenkel and H. Johnson, eds., The economics of exchange rates (Addison-Wesley, Reading, MA).
Bilson, John, 1979, The deutsche mark/dollar rate: A monetary analysis, in: Karl Brunner and Allan H. Meltzer, eds., Policies for employment, prices and exchange rates, Carnegie–Rochester Conference Series on Public Policy, Vol. 11 (North-Holland, Amsterdam).
Cornell, Bradford, 1977, Spot rates, forward rates and exchange market efficiency, Journal of Financial Economies, 5, 55–65.
Cumby, Robert and Maurice, Obstfeld, 1984. International interest rate and price level linkages under flexible exchange rates: A review of recent evidence, in: J.F.O. Bilson and R. Marston, eds., Exchange rate theory and practice. (NBER and University of Chicago Press, Chicago, IL).

Dornbusch, Rudiger, 1976, Expectations and exchange rate dynamics, Journal of Political Economy, 84, 1161–1176.

Dornbusch, Rudiger, 1980, Exchange rate economics: Where do we stand?, Brookings Papers on Economic Activity, no. 1, 145–185.

Frankel, Jeffrey, 1979, On the mark: A theory of floating exchange rates based on real interest differentials, American Economic Review 69, 610–622.

Frankel, Jeffrey, 1982, Monetary and portfolio-balance models of exchange rate determination, in: J. Bhandari, ed., Economic interdependence and flexible exchange rates (MIT Press, Cambridge, MA).

Frankel, Jeffrey, 1984, Testing of monetary and portfolio-balance models of exchange rate determination, in: J.F.O. Bilson and R.C. Marston, eds., Exchange rate theory and practice (NBER and University of Chicago, Chicago, IL).

Frenkel, Jacob A., 1976, A monetary approach to the exchange rate: Doctrinal aspects and empirical evidence, Scandinavian Journal of Economics 78, 200–224.

Frenkel, Jacob, A., 1981a, The collapse of purchasing power parities during the 1970's, European Economic Review 16 145–165.

Frenkel, Jacob A., 1981b, Flexible exchange rates, prices and the role of news: Lessons from the 1970's. Journal of Political Economy 89, 665–705.

Hansen, Lars P. and Robert J. Hodrick, 1980, Forward exchange rates as optimal predictors of future spot rates: An econometric analysis, Journal of Political Economy 88, 829–853.

Hansen, Lars P. and Robert J. Hodrick, 1983, Risk averse speculation in the forward foreign exchange market: An econometric analysis of linear models, in: J.A. Franekl, ed., Exchange rates and international macroeconomics (University of Chicago Press, Chicago, IL).

Hodrick, Robert, J. and Sanjay Srivastava, 1984, An investigation of risk and return in forward foreign exchange, Journal of International Money and Finance 3, 5–29.

Hooper, Peter and John E. Morton, 1982, Fluctuations in the dollar: A model of nominal and real exchange rate determination, Journal of International Money and Finance 1, 39–56.

Isard, Peter, 1983, An accounting framework and some issues for modeling how exchange rates respond to the news, in: J.A. Frenkel, ed., Exchange rates and international macroeconomics (University of Chicago Press, Chicago, IL).

Meese, Richard, 1986, Testing for bubbles in exchange markets: A case of sparkling rates? Journal of Political Economy 94, April, 345–374.

Meese, Richard and Ken Rogoff, 1983a, Empirical exchange rate models of the seventies: Do they fit out of sample?, Journal of International Economics, 14, 3–24.

Meese, Richard and Ken Rogoff, 1983b, The out-of-sample failure of empirical exchange rate models: Sampling error or misspecification?, in: J.A. Frenkel, ed., Exchange rates and international macroeconomics (University of Chicago Press, Chicago, IL).

Meese, Richard and Ken Rogoff, 1985, Was it real?: The exchange rate-interest differential relation, 1973–1984, International Finance Discussion Papers, Unpublished study (Federal Reserve Board of Governors, Washington, DC).

Melitz, Jacques, 1983, How much simplificiation is wise in modeling exchange rates?, in: Paul DeGrauwe and Theo Peters, eds., Exchange rates in multicountry econometric models (St. Martin's Press, New York)

Mussa, Michael, 1979, Empirical regularities in the behavior of exchange rates and theories of the foreign exchange market, in: Karl Brunner and Allan H. Meltzer, eds., Policies for employment, prices and exchange rates, Carnegie–Rochester Conference Series on Public Policy, Vol. 11 (North-Holland, Amsterdam).

Shafer, Jeffrey and Bonnie Loopesko, 1983, Floating exchange rates after ten years, Brookings Papers on Economic Activity, no. 1. 1–70.

Westerfield, Janice M., 1977, An examination of foreign exchange risk under fixed and floating rate regimes, Journal of International Economics 7, 181–200.

Williamson, John, 1983, The exchange rate system (Institute for International Economics, Washington, DC)

Biography: Don ALEXANDER is a Vice President at Citicorp Investment Bank in New York. He is involved in forecasting new developments in the foreign exchange and money markets. He is an associate editor of the International Journal of Forecasting.

Lee R. THOMAS III is a Vice President and the Director of Currency and Commodity Strategies at the J. Aron Division of Goldman, Sachs and Co. He has published in a number of economic and finance journals on monetary theory, portfolio theory, and the risk premium.

[8]

Journal of Forecasting, Vol. 13, 313–332 (1994)

Combining Exchange Rate Forecasts: What is the Optimal Consensus Measure?

RONALD MACDONALD and IAN W. MARSH
University of Strathclyde, U.K.

ABSTRACT

In this paper a high-quality disaggregate database is utilized to examine whether individual forecasters produce efficient exchange rate predictions and also if the properties of the forecasts change when they are combined. The paper links a number of themes in the exchange rate literature and examines various methods of forecast combination. It is demonstrated, *inter alia*, that some forecasters are better than others, but that most are not as good as a naive no-change prediction. Combining forecasts adds to the accuracy of the predictions, but the gains mainly reflect the removal of systematic and unstable bias.

KEY WORDS   Combining forecasts   Exchange rates   Information sets

Recently it has become popular to use survey-based measures of expectations to test a range of hypotheses about the behaviour of foreign exchange rates.[1] One particular advantage of such data is that, in principle, they enable a researcher to conduct tests of the efficiency of foreign exchange markets without imposing auxiliary assumptions about agents' risk preferences. However, the majority of research in this area uses some measure of the 'consensus' forecast, such as the mean or median. Often the use of such measures simply reflects the fact that the institution conducting the survey is unwilling to provide information on the individual responses. However, many interesting issues can only be addressed with the availability of the disaggregate data. For example, one common finding in the extant literature is that the consensus forecast measure is a biased predictor of the future exchange rate. But do all agents produce biased estimates or are some better than others? Also, is it possible to combine forecasts in such a way that an unbiased consensus forecast can be produced? These kinds of questions can only be addressed with a disaggregate survey database.

In this paper we use a novel database of disaggregate exchange rate forecasts, gathered from over 100 institutions in the leading financial centres of the world, to examine the issues referred to above. In particular, we examine whether individual forecasters produce expectations which are unbiased and orthogonal to a publicly available information set.[2] Although such tests are of interest in themselves, their presentation in this paper is more for motivational purposes;

---

[1] See, *inter alia*, Dominguez (1986), Frankel and Froot (1987, 1989), MacDonald (1990), and MacDonald and Torrance, (1988, 1990).

[2] This part of the paper may be viewed as an update of the estimates presented in MacDonald (1992).

CCC 0277–6693/94/030313–20
© 1994 by John Wiley & Sons, Ltd.

Received August 1992
Revised October 1993

our main objective is to examine whether such individual forecasts may be combined in ways which outperform other consensus measures. Our forecast combination strategy draws on a variety of techniques suggested by the optimal forecast combination literature.

The outline of the remainder of this paper is as follows. In the next section we present a brief survey of the literature on how best to combine forecasts and we relate this to the recent exchange rate modelling literature. The third section contains a description of the database used and also a discussion of the testing methodology employed. The issue of how well different forecast combinations perform is addressed in the fourth section. The paper closes with a summary and conclusions.

FORECAST COMBINATIONS AND EXCHANGE RATE FORECASTING

The optimal way of combining forecasts

Bates and Granger (1969) noted that the complexity of the economic system means that different forecasters will, in general, employ different information. While it would be best to combine this information and produce a forecast based upon this wider pool of knowledge, in practice only the forecasts themselves are available. Bates and Granger considered methods of using this one-step-removed data to provide better predictions. Earlier researchers had noted the strong performance of averages of forecasts, and Bates and Granger extended this idea by weighting the forecasts in various ways dependent on the quality of predictions in recent periods. The weights were restricted to sum to one, under the assumption that the forecasts were unbiased.

Newbold and Granger (1974) took up this theme empirically, and demonstrated that the in-sample performance of a weighted average forecast can indeed be superior to both individual forecasts and the simple average. In contrast, however, later studies found little advantage from sophisticated combination methods over simple averaging of forecasts.[3]

Granger and Ramanathan (1984) demonstrated how to analyse forecast combinations in a regression format.[4] Bates and Granger's earlier work, with presupposed unbiased forecasts, was seen to be equivalent to a linear regression of the actual variable on a set of forecasts with no constant and the constraint that coefficients sum to unity. However, this is an inefficient combination, because, as Granger and Ramanathan demonstrate, when forecast errors are stationary and the covariance matrix is constant optimal weights can be retrieved from an unrestricted regression with a constant included, even if forecasts are biased. By construction, this optimal combination will perform at least as well as the simple average within-sample. Empirical work has, however, cast doubt on the practical use of this method out-of-sample, when it cannot necessarily be assumed that the structure of forecast errors and the covariance matrix are invariant (see, for example, Figlewski and Urich, 1983; Winkler, 1984). The most often cited reasons for this breakdown are the actions of forecasters themselves. The performance of individual forecasters often determines their continued employment,[5] theoretical developments lead to major changes in the equations underlying the macroeconometric models of the economy,[6] and when a substantial amount of judgement is

---

[3] See, for example, Makridakis and Hibon (1979).

[4] This was not a totally innovative idea as it had been suggested as early as 1967 in the work of Crane and Crotty (1967), and revived by Reinmuth and Geurts (1979).

[5] Cyriax (1978) pointed out that over 70 organizations make macroeconomic forecasts in the UK alone, and while it needs few qualifications to provide such predictions, competition from the 'big' organizations whose forecasts are widely reported should force the correction of biases through time (see Webb, 1984).

[6] See, for example, Ball *et al.* (1979) for a history of the changes made to the London Business School model.

incorporated into a forecast there is no reason to suppose that optimal weights will remain constant through time. As a result, Clemen (1986) advocated the imposition of restrictions and used GNP forecasts to provide an example of how a regression with constrained coefficients can outperform an unrestricted 'optimal' forecast. Diebold and Pauly (1987) investigated the use of the most recent T^* observations in calculating optimal weights. They noted, however, that the choice of T^* is arbitrary and that the choice can have a large impact on the optimal weights.

Exchange rate forecasts

The problems of producing fundamentally determined exchange rate forecasts have been well documented since Meese and Rogoff (1983) compared the out-of-sample performance of several asset-based models of the exchange rate to a random walk for a range of currencies. The conclusion that emerged from their study was that none of the models could outperform the simple random walk over any forecast horizon considered, with the sole exception of one-month forecasts of the deutschmark. Furthermore, constrained combinations of all the forecasts (weights forced to sum to unity) failed to improve performance.[7] Meese and Rogoff (1984) produced forecasts from their models with coefficients constrained to values taken from the empirical literature on money demand functions which could outperform the no-change prediction, but only over horizons above one year. These results[8] may be interpreted as supporting the view that the exchange rate is an asset price determined in an efficient market. If this is the true representation of the way the foreign exchange market works, then trading on the basis of forecasts made by models or 'experts' cannot be profitable.

Evidence on this point is mixed. Boothe and Glassman (1987) found profitable trading rules based on a real interest differential model for the Canadian dollar and the deutschmark, though profits for the latter currency were highest from the random walk model. Boothe and Glassman noted, however, that the unexploited profit opportunities could be the result of risk bearing and did not necessarily indicate market failure. Bilson and Hsieh (1987) did account for risk and still found evidence of profitable speculation. However, their results were heavily influenced by a few highly profitable opportunities which could be associated with the 'peso' problem.[9] Guerard (1989) combined a time-series forecast, the forward rate and a forecast from a single US bank using a ridge regression technique but found the forward rate itself very hard to beat, indicating market efficiency.

Though the out-of-sample evidence may be unclear, the in-sample performance of most models is also unsatisfactory in terms of having wrongly signed coefficients, low R^2 values and insignificant magnitudes.[10] This has led some researchers to conclude that the operation of the foreign exchange market is influenced by technical analysts, or chartists, who base their predictions of currency movements on patterns in the history of exchange rate movements.

---

[7] Pairwise constrained combinations did beat a random walk over a one-month horizon, but never for more than one of the four exchange rates considered.

[8] Other researchers have managed to produce models capable of matching or beating a prediction of no change, but rarely for a wide range of currencies. Finn (1986) added partial adjustment dynamics to a flexible price model which subsequently performed as well as a random walk. Wolff (1987) repeated Meese and Rogoff's work using a Kalman filter which allowed coefficients to change with time. His results indicate an ability to predict the dollar/deutschmark rate, but a random walk model still outperformed the dollar–yen and dollar–sterling models at all forecast horizons. See MacDonald and Taylor (1992) for a more detailed discussion of the out-of-sample performance of economic models.

[9] That is, a small probability of an adverse event which did not occur within sample. In-sample occurrence of this event could then offset the profits made elsewhere. See Krasker (1980) for a more detailed discussion.

[10] See Dornbusch and Frankel (1987), MacDonald (1988), and MacDonald and Taylor (1992).

That these analysts play a role in the market is beyond doubt. Taylor and Allen (1992) found from survey results that over a short-term (intra-day to one week) forecasting horizon over 90% of chief foreign exchange dealers in London, the largest currency market in the world, use some type of chart analysis in formulating their expectations, and that over half of their respondents felt that these charts to be at least as important as fundamental determinants of the exchange rate. This is less surprising when one notes that Allen and Taylor (1990) found that some of the chart analysts could consistently outperform a random walk over a one-week and four-week forecast horizon. Theoretical models are now being devised which incorporate non-fundamentalist traders.[11]

Work carried out to date on the accuracy of exchange rate forecasts has used the forecasts of either econometric- or time-series-based models (economics-based), or technical analysts' predictions. Goodman (1979) used various measures of predictive power to evaluate the output of ten forecasting services; six used economics-based techniques and four used chartist-based methods. His broad conclusions were that the economics-oriented services did rather poorly and were not notably profitable, while the technical services did much better, producing high returns on speculated capital. Blake *et al.* (1986) investigated the performance of three British, economics-based forecasters and were able to reject the hypothesis of unbiasedness in both the individual forecast series and in an optimally combined series.

DISAGGREGATE INTERNATIONAL FORECASTS

To date, researchers have not systematically examined the performance of individuals who speculate in the foreign exchange market. We cannot, unfortunately, correct for this deficiency here, as market participants are, not surprisingly, reluctant to reveal their trading record.[12] What we can offer is an analysis of predictions made by traders and economists in banks, financial houses, and corporations from around the world, gathered by Consensus Economics of London. These predictions differ from the forecasts previously examined since our data consist of the survey respondents' subjective and potentially time-varying combinations of fundamentals-based forecasts, chartist predictions and other considerations.[13] Furthermore, most previous studies have concentrated on forecasters from one country, typically the United Kingdom or the U.S.A. A primary reason for combining forecasts is to capture a wider set of information. Focusing on a single country (or even worse, a single financial centre), where traders have largely common information sources, will limit potential gains.

Consensus Economics have surveyed leading financial institutions, forecasting units, and multinationals in the G7 countries on the first Monday of each month since October 1989, concerning their expectations of the dollar–sterling, mark–dollar, and yen–dollar spot exchange rates 3 and 12 months ahead. In this study we only use the 3-month forecasts for the period October 1989 to December 1991—a total of 27 overlapping observations. The number of forecasters surveyed differs from country to country; the response rate is not always perfect and varies across currencies. For this study we have only included those companies

---

[11] See Frankel and Froot (1986, 1990) for a model which helps to explain the behaviour of the US dollar in the mid-1980s, and Kirman (1991) for a model in which traders switch between chartist advice and fundamentalist predictions.
[12] Hartzmark (1991) analysed daily futures positions of large-volume traders in a variety of US exchanges using non-parametric techniques. He finds that returns to futures trading are randomly generated. However, he did not have any data on currency futures trades.
[13] In fact Goodman (1979) neglected to analyse the performance of 13 of his total sample of 23 forecasting agencies on the grounds that they combined both econometric and technical methods in making their predictions.

which responded to all surveys for a currency. We have also excluded specialist forecasting companies whose responses are likely to be model determined and not a mix of a variety of inputs. This has left us with 24 forecasters for the mark–dollar, 19 for the dollar–sterling, and 20 for the yen–dollar exchange rates. Thirteen of these are common to all three currencies. To preserve the anonymity of the survey respondents, we identify each by a country abbreviation and a number (thus F12 denotes company 12 for France).[14] Consensus, as their name suggests, also produce a variety of consensus forecasts. We follow their practice, but again only use our restricted data set, and produce mean forecasts from each country, a mean forecast for the entire sample, and the mean value from our core subset of thirteen forecasters.

In addition to the survey data, we collected data on spot exchange rates from the *Financial Times*. We took the closing spot rate (average of bid–ask spread) on the Monday the survey was made as the current spot rate, S_t. The corresponding 3-month forward rate was also collected. We also noted the spot rate which prevailed at the close of the day falling 3 calendar months from the survey date—the 'forecast day'. If this fell on a Saturday, the Friday rate was used, while if it fell on a Sunday we used the Monday rate. From this entire database we then calculated the actual and expected changes (in terms of our forecasts and the forward rate) for each currency.

Before turning to our forecast combinations, we first, as a preliminary exercise, test the individual forecasts for unbiasedness and error orthogonality. These tests were performed by running the following regressions:

$$\Delta S_{t+k} = \rho + \delta \, \Delta S_{t+k}^e + \varphi_{t+k} \tag{1}$$

$$S_{t+k}^e - S_{t+k} = \Phi_0 + \Phi_1 X_t + \zeta_{t+k} \tag{2}$$

where S denotes the (logarithm) of the spot exchange rate, superscript e denotes an expectation, Δ is the first difference operator, and X_t is the period-t information set available to agents at the time their k-period forecasts were formed. Unbiasedness in the forecasts implies that ρ should equal zero and δ should equal unity in equation (1), while error orthogonality implies that the Φ coefficients in equation (2) should jointly equal zero.[15] Since the forecast horizon of the forecasts is greater than the sampling frequency we have overlapping data, rendering estimated variance–covariance matrices inefficient. We therefore use Hansen's (1982) generalized method of moments (GMM), in its heteroscedasticity-consistent form, to correct the coefficient covariance matrix.[16]

The results of the OLS/GMM estimation of equations (1) and (2) are presented in Tables I and II. Unbiasedness is resoundingly rejected. Individual, country average, and sample average forecasts typically have point estimates of δ which are much closer to minus one than plus one. In only five of the 63 individual forecasts can we accept the hypothesis of no bias in the forecasts at the 5% level. The information set used in computing the orthogonality tests was the change in the spot exchange rate over the previous week. In the efficient markets sense this is a weak test, but still it appears that many of these forecasts do not fully incorporate such elementary information into their forecasts. More stringent tests, in terms of a wider

---

[14] The mnemonics are those attached to the entire database and so are not necessarily sequential. In future papers using the same database we plan to use the same identifying codes to facilitate comparison. C denotes Canada, F France, I Italy, J Japan, B Britain, U the USA and G Germany.

[15] Note that equation (1) is formulated in terms of rates of change rather than levels. This transformation is necessary as the stochastic process generating the spot exchange rate may be non-stationary, which would invalidate hypothesis testing in a levels equation. Further details can be found in Hodrick (1987, pp. 27–31).

[16] See MacDonald (1992) for details of the use of this correction.

information set, resulted in almost uniform rejection of error orthogonality. It is worth noting the difference between these results and those reported in MacDonald (1992). Although the general tenor of MacDonald's disaggregate results are similar to those noted here, he did report some results which indicated that German forecasters produced unbiased forecasts. We attribute the difference in the two sets of results to the different sample periods and the

Table I. Unbiasedness test of individual and average forecasts

	Deutschmark		Sterling		Yen	
	δ	T_2	δ	T_2	δ	T_2
C1	− 1.612	0.00	− 0.903	0.00	− 0.565	0.00
C5	− 0.063	0.00	− 0.084	0.00	− 0.802	0.00
F2	− 0.890	0.00				
F10	− 0.876	0.00	− 0.711	0.00	− 0.641	0.00
F12	− 0.318	0.00	− 0.706	0.00	0.196	0.15
I6	− 0.352	0.00			− 0.249	0.00
I10	− 0.094	0.00	− 0.752	0.00	− 0.625	0.00
J1					− 0.358	0.00
J3					− 0.697	0.00
J7					− 0.210	0.00
J14	− 0.025	0.00			− 0.302	0.00
J20	− 0.311	0.00	− 0.498	0.00	− 0.595	0.00
B16	− 0.403	0.00	− 0.183	0.00	− 0.747	0.00
B25			− 0.824	0.00		
B29	0.181	0.06	0.135	0.12		
B32			− 0.560	0.03		
B35	− 0.599	0.00	− 0.552	0.00	− 0.038	0.00
U1	− 0.773	0.01				
U5			− 0.211	0.00	− 0.206	0.01
U20	0.290	0.30				
U24	0.210	0.38				
G5	− 0.938	0.00	− 1.218	0.00	− 0.042	0.00
G8	− 0.573	0.00	− 0.523	0.00	− 0.533	0.00
G10	− 1.435	0.00			− 0.721	0.00
G12	− 0.312	0.00	− 0.127	0.00		
G13	− 0.623	0.00	− 0.678	0.00	− 0.281	0.00
G14	− 0.119	0.00	− 0.528	0.00	− 0.427	0.00
G15	− 0.268	0.00	− 0.145	0.00	− 0.376	0.00
G22	− 0.648	0.00	− 0.882	0.00		
G23	− 0.411	0.00				
Averages						
Canadian	− 0.887	0.00	− 0.818	0.00	− 0.787	0.00
French	− 1.150	0.00	− 1.015	0.00	− 0.600	0.00
Italian	− 0.341	0.00	− 0.752	0.00	− 0.430	0.00
Japanese	− 0.177	0.00	− 0.498	0.00	− 0.746	0.00
British	− 0.662	0.00	− 0.900	0.00	− 0.210	0.00
American	− 0.032	0.18	− 0.211	0.00	− 0.206	0.01
German	− 0.981	0.00	− 0.997	0.00	− 0.654	0.00
All	− 1.091	0.00	− 1.332	0.00	− 0.753	0.00
Forward	3.947	0.10	− 1.505	0.22	− 3.664	0.09

T_2 denotes the marginal significance of a chi-square test of $\rho = 0/\delta = 1$.

Ronald MacDonald and Ian W. Marsh   *Combining Exchange Rate Forecasts*   **319**

selection of different forecasters (because of the criterion required for combining forecasts).

Biased forecasts are, however, not necessarily bad forecasts and in order to evaluate the accuracy of our forecasters we have used two measures. First, the root mean squared error (RMSE) was calculated over the full sample period for each individual forecaster, each country consensus, the mean of the full sample, and for our core group of thirteen. We also computed

Table II. Orthogonality test of individual and average forecasts (information set X is change in spot rate over previous week)

	Deutschmark		Sterling		Yen	
	T_1	T_2	T_1	T_2	T_1	T_2
C1	0.007	0.019	0.035	0.044	0.002	0.005
C5	0.003	0.002	0.036	0.015	0.024	0.049
F2	0.001	0.001				
F10	0.019	0.045	0.056	0.050	0.057	0.163
F12	0.001	0.005	0.036	0.103	0.044	0.030
I6	0.001	0.003			0.035	0.093
I10	0.011	0.036	0.091	0.071	0.103	0.255
J1					0.098	0.214
J3					0.405	0.531
J7					0.086	0.051
J14	0.035	0.043			0.016	0.020
J20	0.004	0.013	0.065	0.159	0.054	0.031
B16	0.006	0.010	0.031	0.048	0.013	0.028
B25			0.011	0.025		
B29	0.000	0.000	0.008	0.016		
B32			0.260	0.227		
B35	0.001	0.003	0.023	0.054	0.000	0.000
US	0.043	0.072				
U5			0.126	0.197	0.037	0.110
U20	0.003	0.011				
U24	0.013	0.046				
G5	0.016	0.035	0.049	0.029	0.016	0.033
G8	0.003	0.003	0.025	0.009	0.017	0.049
G10	0.029	0.056			0.027	0.082
G12	0.092	0.238	0.676	0.304		
G13	0.000	0.001	0.009	0.027	0.001	0.001
G14	0.016	0.026	0.016	0.017	0.007	0.025
G15	0.000	0.000	0.000	0.000	0.014	0.037
G22	0.036	0.087	0.069	0.090		
G23	0.000	0.001				
Averages						
Canadian	0.005	0.007	0.033	0.027	0.007	0.025
French	0.002	0.004	0.039	0.072	0.029	0.059
Italian	0.002	0.009	0.091	0.071	0.060	0.170
Japanese	0.011	0.023	0.065	0.160	0.057	0.152
British	0.001	0.001	0.024	0.045	0.001	0.001
American	0.011	0.035	0.126	0.197	0.037	0.110
German	0.003	0.009	0.024	0.024	0.005	0.014
All	0.002	0.006	0.030	0.040	0.011	0.033
Forward	0.111	0.112	0.296	0.081	0.244	0.386

T_1 denotes the marginal significance of a chi-square test of $\Phi_1 = 0$, T_2 the marginal significance of a chi-square test of $\Phi_0 = 0/\Phi_1 = 0$.

320   *Journal of Forecasting*   *Vol. 13, Iss. No. 3*

the RMSEs using the forward and current spot rates as forecasts.[17,18] The distributions of these errors for each currency are presented graphically in Figures 1–3, and numerically in Table III. Only two individual forecasters managed to beat a forecast of 'no change', using this measure of accuracy.[19] These results are very supportive of the Meese and Rogoff (1983) findings, and indicate that the spot rate is efficient. The forward rate is always outperformed by the current rate, which, in turn, supports the findings of Goodhart *et al.* (1992), who conclude that the forward premium/discount contains no information about subsequent changes in the exchange rate. Note that (only) two forecasters manage to beat the forward rate and a random walk.

As a second measure, we calculated the profits accruing from speculation in the forward market. If the forecast was for a depreciation of the dollar in excess of that priced into the forward rate, a 3-month forward contract is deemed to have been sold, and vice versa. This is clearly only an approximate measure of trading profits as the possibility of an early closing of the contract (cutting of losses) is ignored, but it has the advantage of showing the importance of the qualitative predictions embedded in our forecasts.[20] That is, the accuracy of a forecast in terms of RMSE is possibly less important to a trader than correctly predicting

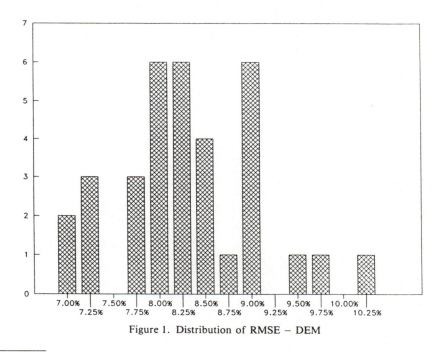

Figure 1. Distribution of RMSE – DEM

---

[17] The latter being the naive random walk forecast of no change.
[18] We initially transformed the data into logs which implies that the RMSE figures are approximately percentage measures.
[19] Unfortunately, these two forecasters, U20 and U24, only replied to the questionnaire regarding their forecasts of the deutschmark and so we cannot see whether they are equally good for the full range of currencies.
[20] An alternative measure would be the profits from a buy-and-hold strategy.

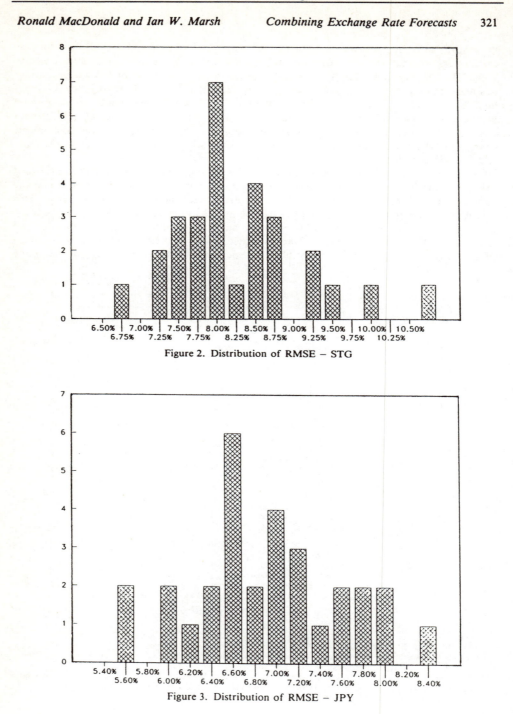

Figure 2. Distribution of RMSE – STG

Figure 3. Distribution of RMSE – JPY

Table III. Errors and profits from forward speculation (uncorrected)

	Deutschmark		Sterling		Japanese yen	
	RMSE	Profit/ (loss)	RMSE	Profit/ (loss)	RMSE	Profit/ (loss)
Individuals						
C1	8.09	(44.40)[a]	7.77	(16.59)	6.82	8.16
C5	7.96	(70.46)	7.59	(11.81)	6.67	(79.02)
F2	8.80	(130.00)				
F10	8.84	(121.68)	8.31	(70.39)	7.17	(46.04)
F12	8.18	19.40[a]	7.76	69.91	6.00	18.78
I6	8.19	(7.82)[a]			7.42	(14.63)
I10	7.70	(33.28)[a]	7.98	(54.99)	6.79	(42.48)
J1					7.53	(12.46)
J3					6.58	(60.32)
J7					6.58	44.66[a]
J14	8.87	(12.18)[a]			7.99	(68.60)
J20	8.18	26.98[a]	8.28	62.51	7.05	30.98[a]
B16	7.70	(2.24)[a]	7.48	135.77	6.42	26.06[a]
B25			8.13	(12.51)		
B29	7.53	(74.14)	7.07	54.97		
B32			7.80	(19.23)		
B35	8.18	(35.34)[a]	8.52	11.57	8.35	17.94
U1	7.87	(145.86)				
U5			7.31	(16.03)	5.89	(4.74)
U20	6.93[b]	31.40[a]				
U24	6.94[b]	35.90[a]				
G5	8.17	(32.24)[a]	8.33	(156.77)	6.38	(25.12)
G8	9.69	(186.28)	9.43	(156.65)	7.87	(125.72)
G10	8.80	(42.80)[a]			7.39	(86.06)
G12	8.34	(48.82)[a]	10.59	(15.83)		
G13	10.01	(79.28)	9.97	(73.89)	7.68	(24.36)
G14	8.36	22.60[a]	9.20	(136.29)	7.19	(38.16)
G15	9.38	(27.78)[a]	9.09	20.51	7.70	(45.90)
G22	8.94	(116.14)	8.73	(132.49)		
G23	8.55	(31.90)[a]				
Averages						
Canadian	7.88	(59.84)	7.54	(15.43)	6.54	2.04
French	8.28	(98.26)	7.77	(33.73)	6.23	35.56[a]
Italian	7.78	(14.40)[a]	7.98	(54.99)	6.96	(70.18)
Japanese	8.19	(12.08)[a]	8.28	62.51	6.52	(9.66)
British	7.78	(15.70)[a]	7.52	(5.31)	6.95	18.68
American	7.07	3.72[a]	7.31	(16.03)	5.89	(4.74)
German	8.49	(87.96)	8.67	(128.85)	6.94	(35.60)
All	7.94	(35.72)[a]	7.87	(43.35)	6.50	6.36
Random walk	7.03[a]	(56.38)	6.62[a]	142.03	5.46[a]	21.44
Forward	7.04		7.12		5.55	

In RMSE columns, [a] smaller value than forward rate, [b] smaller value than forward rate and random walk.
In Profit columns, [a] higher profit than random walk.

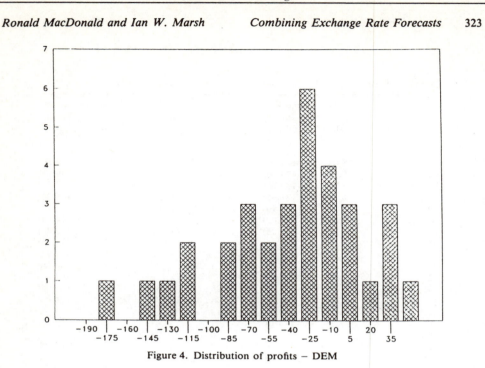

Figure 4. Distribution of profits – DEM

the direction of currency movements.[21] The results are given in Figures 4–6, and Table III. Comparison with the RMSE results is instructive. A random walk forecast no longer clearly dominates. Trading on the basis of a forecast of no change results in losses for the deutschmark, but is still the best strategy for the pound. It should also be noted that poor forecasts in terms of RMSE can be profitable. Forecaster B35, for example, has the highest RMSE for the yen and yet forward trading on the basis of his forecasts results in a profit. We leave for further research the question of whether these profits are a return for risk bearing, but we note that speculation based on individual forecasts resulted, on average, in losses, and that out of 63 forecast series only 17 forecasters (less than 27%) returned a profit. Of these 17, only eight outperformed their respective random walks.

If our forecasters are unable to clearly dominate a random walk forecast, can we detect any systematic difference between their performances? In analysing the performance of US forecasters, Stekler (1987) suggested the use of a non-parametric test which, when the analysis was corrected by Bachelor (1988), turned out to be Friedman's (1937) test for two-way analysis of variance by ranks. The procedure is as follows.

The absolute forecast errors are mapped into ranks for each forecast date. These ranks are then summed across time for each forecaster to produce a rank sum, r_i. Under the null hypothesis of no significant differences in rank, the expected value of r_i is $T(n + 1)/2$, where T is the number of observations and n the number of forecasters. Similarly, the sampling variance of an individual rank statistic is $n(n + 1)/12$ and so for T independent ranks is

---

[21] The authors are exploring the accuracy of forecast direction in current research.

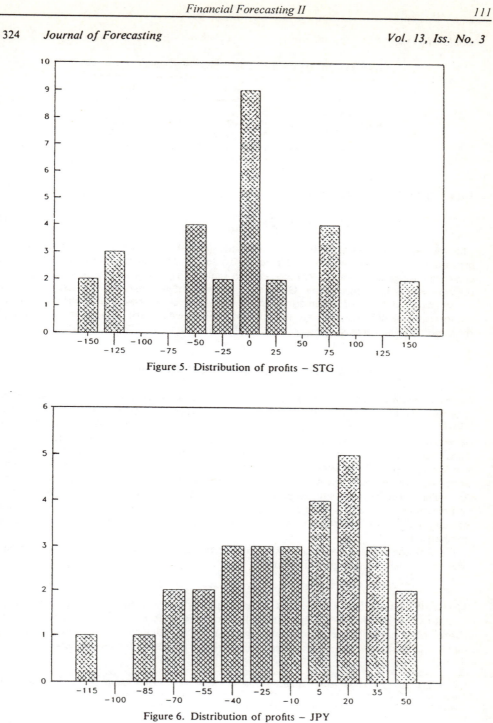

Figure 5. Distribution of profits – STG

Figure 6. Distribution of profits – JPY

Table IV. Friedman's test of independence of rank

	T	n	Φ	$\chi^2_{(n-1)}$	Marg. sig.
Deutschmark	27	24	41.43	35.2	0.011
Sterling	27	19	43.05	28.9	0.001
Yen	27	20	29.08	30.1	0.065
Pooled 13	81	13	39.23	21.0	0.000

$Tn(n + 1)/12$. The test statistic is:

$$\phi = \sum_{i=1}^{n} \frac{(r_i - T(n + 1)/2)^2}{Tn(n + 1)/12} \tag{3}$$

which under the null hypothesis of no systematic assignment of ranks will be asymptotically distributed as chi-square with $n - 1$ degrees of freedom.[22] The values of ϕ for each of the three currencies are given in Table IV, together with that for a pooling of the three currencies for the core group of 13 forecasters. Given the low power of non-parametric tests, these results are strongly indicative of systematic differences in forecasting power. Nevertheless, although the forecasts are different, they are still not very good. We now turn to the question of whether by combining the forecasts we can improve their accuracy.

THE PERFORMANCE OF FORECAST COMBINATIONS

We have demonstrated that individual forecasts are not very accurate, are biased, and do not take full account of available information. There are exceptions (most notably U20 and U24) and for some currencies even the least accurate are still profitable to follow. We have also demonstrated that the performance of our forecasters is not randomly generated. It would seem that at least some of our forecasts contain information. We have noted that ideally we would like to pool the information sets on which the forecasts are conditioned. As these data are clearly not available, the next best method is to combine the forecasts themselves. In order to evaluate these composite forecasts we must note that within-sample, unconstrained combinations of forecasts must match or outperform the components in terms of accuracy (though not necessarily profitability). The only true test of performance is an out-of-sample comparison.

We shall use the simple Granger–Ramanathan method to optimally combine the forecasts, whereby the following regression is run:

$$\Delta S_{t+k} = \alpha + \sum \beta_i \, \Delta S^c_{it+k}, \qquad i = 1, \ldots, n \tag{4}$$

That is, the actual change in the spot exchange rate is regressed on a constant and a set of n forecast changes. Due to the substantial location and scale biases[23] in the forecasts noted above, no constraints are imposed on equation (4). Running this regression to combine a number of forecasts will result in negative weights on some of the components. This is not

---

[22] Iman and Davenport (1980) suggest a small-sample version of the Friedman statistic which has an approximate F-distribution. Computing this alternative form had little effect on the marginal significance levels found.

[23] Alocation bias indicates a constant non-zero mean error ($\alpha \neq 0$), while a scale bias occurs when a forecaster systematically under- or over-predicts ($\beta \neq 1$).

necessarily a comment on the forecaster's ability but, rather, indicates the way the predictions should be combined given the correlations between forecasts. However, running equation (4) with just one forecast is equivalent to unbiasing the forecast. We do this for each of our individual forecasters and test the out-of-sample accuracy of these 'corrected' forecasts.

We have a total of 27 observations available, eight of which are saved for the out-of-sample tests. Our in-sample period, then, is October 1989 to April 1991, while our test period is May 1991 through December 1991. However, a researcher looking to combine forecasts in May 1991, the first of our test months, would only have outcome errors for the months up to February 1991.[24] This leaves just 17 in-sample observations in which to construct the weights. For each currency we have at least 19 forecasters—a severe shortage of degrees of freedom. We chose to split our forecasters into subgroups to overcome this problem. For example, for forecasts of the mark exchange rate we formed three groups consisting of nine German, eight other European and seven Other (Canadian, Japanese, and US) forecasters. Noting that we are seeking to pool information and that grouping homogeneous forecasters will not yield maximum benefits, we also combined the forecasts of our core group of 13 (which contains representatives from all seven countries) and the best five forecasters (in terms of in sample RMSE) for each currency. (Details of the groups are given in the Appendix.)

From equation (4) we retrieve the optimal weights attached to each forecast and use them to construct a set of out-of-sample 'optimal' forecasts. Three 'optimal' forecasts for each grouping of forecasters were constructed. In the first instance, the initial in-sample weights are taken as fixed throughout the out-of-sample period. We also compute weights which are updated as new information about the performance of our forecasters is received, using the full set of historical information. Finally, following Diebold and Pauly (1987), we update the weights using only the last T^* observations in an attempt to lessen the effect of any shifts in the structure of the forecast errors or covariance matrix. The size of our largest group constrains our choice of T^* and we use the most recent twelve observations. This, of course, precludes this type of weighting for G13.

The accuracy of these various combinations in terms of root mean squared errors and mean absolute errors (MAE) are detailed in Tables V to VII.[25] A few general results emerge. Exchange rates in our test period are more stable than in the rest of our sample period, since the random walk RMSEs are up to 2.1% lower than those computed over the full data period and shown in Table IV. Second, the Average forecast (an unweighed mean of all forecasts of each currency), while a worse predictor than the current spot or forward rate, is frequently as accurate as the 'optimal' combinations. The Average forecasts also perform better in the test period than in the full sample. Third, combining large numbers of forecasts tends to give poor results. For the G13 grouping the weights are unstable as correlations change, and the resultant errors are very large. This also holds true for the combined German forecasts of the pound and mark. Finally, updating weights as new information becomes available generally reduces errors whereas using only the most recent (twelve) observations in calculations appears to be detrimental. This last point, even more than the others, may be due to the small sample size available.

Turning to more specific results, no grouping is able to beat the RMSE and MAE scores of

---

[24] In fact, it is possible that January's forecast error is the latest available as the February forecast day may be later than the day on which the May predictions are made (see MacDonald, 1992, for more detail). We ignore this point as the overlap is only of the order of a couple of days.

[25] With a large enough sample we would have liked to calculate speculative profits from these combinations. This is something we hope to do as our data sample extends.

the random walk model for the deutschmark and pound sterling, no matter how the weights are chosen. Combinations of the Best 5 deutschmark forecasters come closest, and using full sample updating can marginally beat the RMSE of a random walk (but not the mean absolute error). Given that this grouping includes two individual forecasts which clearly outperform a no-change prediction over the full sample, U20 and U24, this is an indictment of the other three forecasts.[26,27] No combination comes close to challenging the pre-eminence of the random walk for sterling.

The yen tells a slightly different story. Both the groupings of the German and Best 5

Table V. Root mean squared and mean absolute errors no updating of weights

	Deutschmark		Sterling		Yen	
	RMSE	MAE	RMSE	MAE	RMSE	MAE
Random walk	5.90	4.63	4.52	3.43	3.45	3.03
Forward rate	6.55	5.25	5.41	4.21	3.76	3.38
Average[c]	7.20	5.82	5.92	4.95	4.99	4.26
G13	33.22	31.04	13.06	11.58	12.48	10.92
Best 5[c]	6.18[a]	5.49	8.40	7.28	2.12[b]	1.80[b]
German[c]	31.77	27.82	29.18	17.24	2.80[b]	2.52[b]
British			7.33	5.81		
Japanese					5.48	3.99
European	12.69	10.37				
Others[c]	6.23[a]	5.26	11.76	9.71	9.00	7.74

[a] Smaller value than forward rate.
[b] Smaller than forward rate and random walk.
[c] Note that the composition of these groups changes for different currencies. See Appendix for group compositions.

Table VI. Root mean squared and mean absolute errors updating of weights over full sample

	Deutschmark		Sterling		Yen	
	RMSE	MAE	RMSE	MAE	RMSE	MAE
Random walk	5.90	4.63	4.52	3.43	3.45	3.03
Forward rate	6.55	5.25	5.41	4.21	3.76	3.38
Average[c]	7.20	5.82	5.92	4.95	4.99	4.26
G13	22.64	18.92	10.80	8.95	10.52	7.60
Best 5[c]	5.84[b]	5.21[a]	6.80	5.04	2.36[b]	2.13[b]
German[c]	22.88	17.75	30.72	20.07	2.70[b]	2.21[b]
British			6.53	4.96		
Japanese					3.84	3.00[b]
European	13.07	9.65				
Others[c]	7.56	6.13	8.12	5.77	8.55	7.34

[a-c] As Table V.

---

[26] In fact, in the out-of-sample period, both of these forecasters are beaten by J14, which is also included in the Best 5.
[27] U20, U24, and J14 are also in the 'Other' group which explains the reasonably good performance of this combination.

Table VII. Root mean squared and mean absolute errors updating of weights using previous twelve observations

	Deutschmark		Sterling		Yen	
	RMSE	MAE	RMSE	MAE	RMSE	MAE
Random walk	5.90	4.63	4.52	3.43	3.45	3.03
Forward rate	6.55	5.25	5.41	4.21	3.76	3.38
Average[c]	7.20	5.82	5.92	4.95	4.99	4.26
G13	NA	NA	NA	NA	NA	NA
Best 5[c]	6.55	5.84	6.40	5.19	4.24	4.15
German[c]	33.95	23.88	32.00	17.62	5.97	4.67
British			8.64	6.37		
Japanese					4.86	3.50
European	26.52	21.32				
Others[c]	8.06	4.86[a]	15.48	13.37	9.81	7.30

[a,c] As Table V.

Table VIII. Out-of-sample errors ('corrected' individual forecasts)

	Deutschmark		Sterling		Japanese yen	
	RMSE	MAE	RMSE	MAE	RMSE	MAE
Random walk	5.90	4.63	4.52	3.43	3.45	3.03
Forward rate	6.55	5.25	5.41	4.21	3.76	3.38
C1	4.88[b]	4.01[b]	3.71[b]	3.23[b]	1.90[b]	1.25[b]
C5	4.62[b]	6.59	3.48[b]	4.02[a]	1.91[b]	1.45[b]
F2	4.67[b]	5.75				
F10	5.69[b]	5.75	3.89[b]	3.27[b]	1.60[b]	1.38[b]
F12	6.40[a]	7.85	4.29[b]	3.67[a]	3.74[a]	1.61[b]
I6	5.48[b]	6.75			1.86[b]	2.45[b]
I10	4.67[b]	5.14[a]	4.47[b]	2.97[b]	2.87[b]	1.58[b]
J1					2.70[b]	1.53[b]
J3					1.64[b]	1.34[b]
J7					2.91[b]	1.89[b]
J14	7.26	8.95			1.70[b]	2.78[b]
J20	5.66[b]	7.15	7.59	3.71[a]	3.93	1.89[b]
B16	4.71[b]	5.53	3.52[b]	3.52[a]	2.68[b]	1.87[b]
B25			3.83[b]	3.23[b]		
B29	4.61[b]	5.50	3.42[b]	3.67[a]		
B32			4.23[b]	3.36[b]		
B35	5.10[b]	5.06[a]	3.94[b]	3.32[b]	3.55[a]	2.30[b]
U1	5.72[b]	4.41[b]				
U5			3.76[b]	3.26[b]	2.79[b]	1.15[b]
U20	4.53[b]	5.04[a]				
U24	4.77[b]	4.53[b]				
G5	4.44[b]	4.64[a]	5.12[a]	3.76[a]	3.78	1.22[b]
G8	5.00[b]	7.21	6.39	3.53[a]	2.65[b]	1.90[b]
G10	4.55[b]	4.15[b]			2.41[b]	1.10[b]
G12	5.46[b]	6.28	14.96	6.43		
G13	8.73	8.04	8.73	3.58[a]	2.36[b]	2.66[b]
G14	4.61[b]	5.54	3.92[b]	3.71[a]	1.63[b]	1.56[b]
G15	5.00[b]	8.50	3.44[b]	3.90[a]	1.65[b]	1.83[b]
G22	6.67	6.60	7.27	3.88[a]		
G23	4.96[b]	6.15				

[a-c] As Table V.

forecasters convincingly outperform the current spot rate as a predictor of future rates when the full in-sample information is used to construct the weights. Interestingly, the Best 5 forecasters come from five different countries, and the only forecaster common to both groups, G5, does not have a dominant influence in either combination. It appears that combining information contained in some forecasts can lead to significant gains in forecast accuracy for the Japanese yen, though not for the two European currencies.

As we noted above, however, an unconstrained combination of forecasts also corrects for the bias in the forecasts. Have the gains in accuracy found from combining yen forecasts been because of information pooling or because we have removed bias? The errors of the corrected or unbiased individual forecasts are given in Table VIII. They indicate that by combining corrected forecasts we have actually lost accuracy. For all three currencies, merely correcting the in-sample bias of individual forecasters usually results in a better performance than the spot rate in an out-of-sample context.[28]

The fact that supposedly optimal combinations do so badly is due to changing correlations between forecasters. These changing correlations represent, we feel, the substantial amount of judgement that go into making these forecasts. For this reason, we do not feel that the good performance of our corrected individual forecasts is robust to extensions in the data sample. Furthermore, forecasters learn from, and work to correct, their mistakes, and the parameters used to unbias these forecasts will change.

SUMMARY AND CONCLUSIONS

In this paper we have used a high-quality disaggregate database to examine whether individual forecasters produce efficient forecasts and also whether the properties of the forecasts change when they are combined. In terms of the former testing strategy, we found that some are better than others, but that most are not as good as a naive no-change prediction. Further, available information is not efficiently incorporated into forecasts and this is interpreted as reflecting irrationality. In terms of the second part of our testing strategy, we found that pooling forecasters information sets by combining their forecasts possibly adds to the accuracy of the predictions, but the gains mainly reflect the removal of systematic bias. This bias does not appear to be stable over time, and this may explain the poor performance of combined forecasts. The fact that adjusted forecasts can be more accurate than the spot and forward rates as predictors indicates that there is information available to traders that is not incorporated into the market rates. However, with just two possible exceptions, the fact that individual forecasters are unable to beat these rates over an extended period implies that this information is widely scattered. Our non-parametric tests, which indicated differing abilities, could reflect one of two possibilities. There may just be some very bad forecasters which make the merely poor look good by comparison. On the other hand, scarce but unincorporated information may not be randomly scattered, but rather lies in the hands of a select few. We hope that this will show up as our data set extends over time.

---

[28] Holden and Peel (1989) address aspects of forecast bias and combination. They show that the unrestricted regression method of combination which we have used not only corrects for in-sample bias but also includes the unconditional mean of in-sample exchange rate changes as an additional forecast. They argue that including the mean of the dependent variable as an extra forecast may not be appropriate as it is typically a very poor predictor. In our situation, however, the mean change in exchange rates is very close to zero and so is in fact a good forecast.

APPENDIX: DETAILS OF GROUPINGS

All currencies
G13   C1 C5 F10 F12 I10 J20 B16 B35 G5 G8 G13 G14 G15

Deutschmark
Best 5   J14 U20 U24 G23 G5
German   G5 G8 G10 G12 G13 G14 G15 G22 G23
European   F2 F10 F12 I6 I10 B16 B29 B35
Other   C1 C5 J14 J20 U1 U20 U24

Sterling
Best 5   B29 U5 B25 B16 F12
German   G5 G8 G12 G13 G14 G15 G22
British   B16 B25 B29 B32 B35
Other   F10 F12 I10 J20 C1 C5 U5

Japanese yen
Best 5   U5 G5 J7 F12 I10
German   G5 G8 G10 G13 G14 G15
Japanese   J1 J3 J7 J14 J20
Other   C1 C5 F10 F12 I6 I10 B16 B35 U5

ACKNOWLEDGEMENTS

We are grateful to Michael Sykes of Consensus Economics for providing the survey data together with the Nuffield Foundation and ESRC (Grant No: R000232945) for financial support. We would also like to thank two anonymous referees for their helpful comments.

REFERENCES

Allen, H. L. and Taylor, M. P., 'Charts, noise and fundamentals in the foreign exchange market', *Economic Journal*, **100** (Supplement) (1990), 49–59.

Ball, R. J., Burns, T. and Warburton, P. S., 'The London Business School model of the UK economy: an exercise in international monetarism', in P. Ormerod (ed.), *Economic Modelling*, (London: Heinemann, 1979.

Batchelor, R. A., 'All forecasters are equal', *Journal of Business and Economic Statistics*, **8** (1988), 143–4.

Bates, J. M. and Granger, C. W. J., 'The combination of forecasts', *Operational Research Quarterly*, **20** (1969), 451–68.

Bilson, J. F. O. and Hsieh, D. A., 'The profitability of currency speculation', *International Journal of Forecasting*, 3 (1987), 115–130.

Blake, D., Beenstock, M. and Brasse V., 'The performance of UK exchange rate forecasters', *Economic Journal*, 96 (1986), 986–99.

Boothe, P. and Glassman, D., 'Comparing exchange rate forecasting models: accuracy versus profitability', *International Journal of Forecasting*, 3 (1987), 65–79.

Clemen, R. T., 'Linear constraints and the efficiency of combined forecasts', *Journal of Forecasting*, **5** (1986), 31–8.

Crane, D. B. and Crotty, J. R., 'A two-stage forecasting model: exponential smoothing and multiple regression', *Management Science*, 13 (1967), B501–7.

Cyriax, G. (ed.), *World Index of Economic Forecasts*, Farnborough: Gower Press, 1978.

Diebold, F. X. and Pauly, P., 'Structural change and the combination of forecasts', *Journal of Forecasting*, 6 (1987), 21–40.

Dominguez, K. N., 'Are foreign exchange forecasts rational? New evidence from survey data', *Economics Letters*, 21 (1986), 277–82.

Dornbusch, R. and Frankel, J., 'The flexible exchange rate system: experience and alternatives', in S. Borner (ed.), *International Trade and Finance in a Polycentric World*, London: Macmillan, 1987.

Figlewski, S. and Urich, T., 'Optimal aggregation of money supply forecasts: accuracy, profitability and market efficiency', *Journal of Finance*, 28 (1983), 695–710.

Finn, M. G., 'Forecasting the exchange rate: a monetary or random walk phenomenon?' *Journal of International Money and Finance*, 5 (1986), 181–93.

Frankel, J. and Froot, K., 'Understanding the dollar in the eighties: the expectations of chartists and fundamentalists', *Economic Record*, (1986), 24–38.

Frankel, J. and Froot, K., 'Using survey data to test standard propositions regarding exchange rate expectations', *American Economic Review*, 77 (1987), 133–53.

Frankel, J. and Froot, K., 'Interpreting tests of forward discount bias using survey data on exchange rate expectations', *Quarterly Journal of Economics*, 104 (1989), 139–61.

Frankel, J. and Froot, K., 'Chartists, fundamentalists, and the demand for dollars', in A. S. Courakis and M. P. Taylor (eds), *Private Behaviour and Government Policy in Interdependent Economies*, Oxford: Clarendon Press, 1990.

Friedman, M., 'The use of ranks to void the assumption of normality implicit in the analysis of variance', *Journal of the American Statistical Association*, 32 (1937), 675–701.

Goodhart, C. A. E., McMahon P. C. and Ngama, Y. L., 'Does the forward premium/discount help to predict the future change in the exchange rate?' *Scottish Journal of Political Economy*, 39 (1992), 129–40.

Goodman, S. H., 'Foreign exchange forecasting techniques: implications for business and policy', *Journal of Finance*, 34 (1979), 415–27.

Granger, C. W. J. and Ramanathan, R., 'Improved methods of forecasting', *Journal of Forecasting*, 3 (1984), 197–204.

Guerard, J. B., 'Composite model building for foreign exchange rates, *Journal of Forecasting*, 8 (1989), 315–29.

Hansen, L. P., 'Large sample properties of generalised method of moments estimators', *Econometrica*, 50, 1029–54.

Hartzmark, M. L., 'Luck versus forecast ability: determinants of trader performance in futures markets', *Journal of Business*, 64 (1991), 49–74.

Hodrick, R. J., *The Empirical Evidence on the Efficiency of Forward and Futures Foreign Exchange Markets*, Chur: Harwood, 1987.

Holden, K. and Peel, D. A., 'Unbiasedness, efficiency and the combination of economic forecasts', *Journal of Forecasting*, 8 (1989), 175–88.

Iman, R. L. and Davenport, J. M., 'Approximations of the critical region of the Friedman statistic', *Communications in Statistics*, A9 (1980), 571–95.

Kirman, A., 'Epidemics of opinion and speculative bubbles in financial markets', in M. P. Taylor (ed.), *Money and Financial Markets*, Cambridge, MA: Basil Blackwell, 1991.

Krasker, W. S., '"The peso problem" in testing the efficiency of forward exchange markets', *Journal of Monetary Economics*, 6 (1980), 269–76.

MacDonald, R., *Floating Exchange Rates: Theories and Evidence*, London: Unwin Hyman, 1988.

MacDonald, R., 'Are foreign exchange market forecasters "rational"? Some survey-based tests', *Manchester School of Economic and Social Studies*, 58 (1990), 229–41.

MacDonald, R., 'Exchange rate survey data: a disaggregated G—7 perspective', *Manchester School of Economic and Social Studies*, LX (Supplement) (1992), 47–62.

MacDonald, R. and Torrance, T. S., 'On risk, rationality and excessive speculation in the deutschmark–US dollar exchange market: some evidence using survey data', *Oxford Bulletin of Economics and Statistics*, 51 (1988), 107–23.

MacDonald, R. and Torrance, T. S., 'Expectations formation and risk in four foreign exchange markets', *Oxford Economic Papers*, 42 (1990), 544–61.

MacDonald, R. and Taylor, M. P., 'Exchange rate economics: a survey', *International Monetary Fund Staff Papers*, **39** (1992), 1–57.

Makridakis, S. and Hibon, M., 'Accuracy of forecasting: an empirical investigation', *Journal of the Royal Statistical Society. Series A*, **142** (1979), 97–145.

Meese, R. A. and Rogoff, K., 'Empirical exchange rate models of the seventies: do they fit out of sample?' *Journal of International Economics*, **14** (1983), 3–24.

Meese, R. A. and Rogoff, K., 'The out-of-sample failure of empirical exchange rate models: sampling error or misspecification?' in J. A. Frenkel (ed.), *Exchange Rates and International Macroeconomics*, Chicago, IL: University of Chicago Press, 1984.

Newbold, P. and Granger, C. W. J., 'Experience with forecasting univariate time series and the combination of forecasts', *Journal of the Royal Statistical Society, Series A*, **137** (1974), 131–49.

Reinmuth, J. E. and Guerts, M. D., 'A multideterministic approach to forecasting', in S. Makridakis and S. C. Wheelwright (eds), *Forecasting*, Vol. 12, TIMS Studies in the Management Sciences, New York, North-Holland, 1979.

Stekler, H. O., 'Who forecasts better?', *Journal of Business and Economic Statistics*, **5** (1987), 155–8.

Taylor, M. P. and Allen, H. L., 'The use of technical analysis in the foreign exchange market', *Journal of International Money and Finance*, **11** (1992), 304–14.

Webb, R. H., 'Inadequate tests of the rationality of forecasts', Paper presented at 1984 meetings of Western Economic Association, Las Vegas.

Winkler, R. L., 'Combining forecasts', in S. Makridakis *et al.* (eds), *The Forecasting Accuracy of Major Time Series Methods*, New York: Wiley, 1984.

Wolff, C. P., 'Forward foreign exchange rates, expected spot rates and premia: a signal-extraction approach', *Journal of Finance*, **42** (1987), 395–406.

Authors' biographies:
Ronald MacDonald is Professor of International Finance in the Department of Economics and the Centre for International Macroeconomic Modelling at the University of Strathclyde. He is the author of numerous books and journal articles on international economics.

Ian Marsh is a research assistant in the Economics Department at the University of Strathclyde. He is currently reading for his PhD on exchange rate forecasting and modelling.

Authors' address:
Ronald MacDonald and **Ian Marsh**, Department of Economics, University of Strathclyde, Curran Building, 100 Cathedral Street, Glasgow G4 0LN, Scotland.

A
Statistical Models

[9]

Journal of Forecasting, Vol. 14, 201–215 (1995)

Structural, VAR and BVAR Models of Exchange Rate Determination: A Comparison of Their Forecasting Performance

NICHOLAS SARANTIS AND CHRIS STEWART
Kingston University, UK

ABSTRACT

This paper compares the out-of-sample forecasting accuracy of a wide class of structural, BVAR and VAR models for major sterling exchange rates over different forecast horizons. As representative structural models we employ a portfolio balance model and a modified uncovered interest parity model, with the latter producing the more accurate forecasts. Proper attention to the long-run properties and the short-run dynamics of structural models can improve on the forecasting performance of the random walk model. The structural model shows substantial improvement in medium-term forecasting accuracy, whereas the BVAR model is the more accurate in the short term. BVAR and VAR models in levels strongly outpredict these models formulated in difference form at all forecast horizons.

KEY WORDS   exchange rate forecasting; structural models; vector autoregression; Bayesian vector autoregression

INTRODUCTION

This study compares the out-of-sample forecasting accuracy of a wide class of structural and time-series models of exchange rates over different forecast horizons. The existing literature on this subject has concentrated on US dollar bilateral exchange rates and focused mostly on the 1970s and early 1980s. In the present study, on the other hand, we examine the major bilateral exchange rates against the pound sterling (i.e. dollar/pound, D-mark/pound, yen/pound, and F-franc/pound) and cover the entire floating period up the end of the 1980s (i.e. 1973Q1–1990Q3).

The seminal work of Meese and Rogoff (1983a) revealed that the structural models failed to match the out-of-sample forecasting accuracy of the random walk model irrespective of the forecast horizon. Subsequent studies by Alexander and Thomas (1987), Wolf (1987), and Schinasi and Swamy (1989) have re-evaluated these models by adopting a methodology which allows for time-varying parameters, Meese and Rogoff (1983b) allowed for simultaneous equation bias, while Meese and Rose (1991) have assessed the importance of non-linearities in structural models using a variety of parametric and non-parametric techniques. Their findings were mixed, with Meese and Rogoff (1983b) and Alexander and Thomas (1987) confirming the original results by Meese and Rogoff (1987), Wolf (1987) showing that the *ex-post*

0277–6693/95/030201–15
© 1995 by John Wiley & Sons, Ltd

Received February 1994
Revised September 1994

202   *Journal of Forecasting*   *Vol. 14, Iss. No. 3*

predictions of the structural models are not uniformly dominated by the random walk, Schinasi and Swamy (1989) reporting that the structural models outperform the random walk model, and Meese and Rose (1991) concluding that accounting for non-linearities does not improve the ability of structural models to outpredict a random walk alternative. These studies have two important weaknesses. First, they only consider variants of the monetary approach to exchange rate determination.[1] They normally estimate three versions: the flexible price, sticky price, and sticky price with the current account monetary models. However, the literature on in-sample studies of exchange rate determination casts serious doubts on the monetary approach,[2] especially for the 1980s. Some of these authors themselves (e.g. Alexander and Thomas, 1987, p. 61) suggest that the structural models used may be inadequate. The second weakness concerns the dynamic specification of the structural models. Typically these models are estimated either in static form with or without first-order serial correlation or with a lagged dependent variable (e.g. Somanath, 1986; Schinasi and Swamy, 1989). This is a rather *ad hoc* and simplistic approach to a complex problem.

An important objective of this study is to address both these issues. Hence in addition to the monetary models we examine the portfolio balance model and a modified version of the uncovered interest parity hypothesis, both of which represent more recent theoretical developments. With regard to the specification of these models, we employ the cointegration-error correction methodology which allows us first, to investigate the existence of long-run equilibrium relationships consistent with alternative theoretical models, and second, to build the short-term dynamics by applying the error correction model and adopting the general to specific methodology.[3]

Another objective of the present study is to examine a wider class of time-series models. None of the previous studies has considered multivariate time-series models, except Meese and Rogoff (1983a), who applied a VAR (vector autoregressive) model. In this paper we examine both VAR and BVAR (Bayesian vector autoregressive) models composed of all the variables from the respective structural models.[4] An important issue that we wish to investigate is whether VAR and BVAR models should be estimated in level or difference form.

The paper is organised as follows. The next section describes the competing structural models and the methodology used in their estimation. The third and fourth sections present the VAR and BVAR models. The fifth section outlines our forecasting strategy for generating out-of-sample forecasts. In the sixth we compare the forecasting performance of the competing models. The final section draws the main conclusions.

STRUCTURAL MODELS

Our research plan was to investigate all major theories of exchange rate determination normally used in empirical studies: the flexible price monetary model, the sticky price monetary model, the Hooper–Morton model, the portfolio balance model, and the uncovered interest parity model. The first three models are different versions of the monetary approach, with the

---

[1] The one exception is the study by Meese and Rose (1991) which has also considered Hodrick's (1988) model.
[2] For an excellent survey of this literature, see MacDonald and Taylor (1992).
[3] The seminal papers on cointegration are those by Engle and Granger (1987) and Johansen (1988). An excellent analysis of the dynamic modelling methodology adopted in this paper can be found in Cuthbertson et al. (1992). A good analysis of the general to specific methodology can also be found in Pagan (1990).
[4] Notice that Diebold and Nason (1990) have investigated the forecasting performance of non-parametric autoregression exchange rate models, but they did not provide a comparison with predictions by structural models.

Hooper–Morton model (used by Meese and Rogoff, 1983; Alexander and Thomas, 1987; Schinasi and Swamy, 1989; and Meese and Rose, 1991) nesting the other two.

The exchange rate equations derived from the alternative theoretical models are essentially long-run equilibrium relationships. Therefore modelling should begin with an investigation of these equilibrium relationships. If we fail to uncover the existence of equilibrium relationships consistent with the respective theoretical models, the development of short-run structural equations based on such models will be inappropriate for forecasting exchange rates (see Baillie and Selover (1987)). Such an investigation can be carried out by applying the cointegration method (see Engle and Granger, 1987; Engle and Yoo, 1987; and Johansen, 1988).

The cointegration tests, together with a detailed analysis, for all the structural models mentioned above and all four sterling exchange rates over the period 1973Q1–1990Q3 are reported in Sarantis and Stewart (1993).[5] These tests rejected overwhelmingly the existence of a long-run equilibrium relationship consistent with the flexible price monetary model, or the sticky price monetary model, or the Hooper–Morton model. Our findings are similar to those reported by Baillie and Selover (1987) for five bilateral exchange rates against the US dollar. This dismal evidence seriously undermines the validity of monetary models used in exchange rate forecasting, and therefore the empirical results obtained by Meese and Rogoff (1983a,b) and others using monetary exchange rate models. The cointegration tests, on the other hand, uncovered long-run equilibrium relationships consistent with the portfolio balance model and a modified uncovered interest parity relationship with backward-looking expectations for three exchange rates: D-mark/pound, yen/pound, and F-franc/pound. Application of the Johansen (1988) maximum likelihood tests for cointegration confirmed the uniqueness of these cointegrating vectors.

Consequently, the structural models we have used in our forecasting study are as follows.

Modified uncovered interest parity (MUIP)

$$e_t = \alpha_0 - \alpha_1 (r^* - r)_t + \alpha_2 (\pi^* - \pi)_t + \alpha_3 (p^* - p)_t + \alpha_4 (CA/NY)_t - \alpha_5 (CA/NY)_t^* + u_t \qquad (1)$$

where e is the (natural) logarithm of the exchange rate, defined as the foreign currency price of domestic currency; r, π, p and (CA/NY) represent the logarithm of nominal short-term interest rate, expected price inflation rate, the logarithm of the price level, and the ratio of current account to nominal GDP for the domestic economy (i.e. UK), respectively; asterisks denote the corresponding foreign variables; u is the error term. The variables (CA/NY) and $(CA/NY)^*$ are proxies for the risk premium (see Fisher *et al.*, 1990, for a similar treatment).

Equation (1) is a modified version of the real UIP relationship (adjusted for risk) with backward-looking expectations, and is based on a similar model used by the Bank of England for modelling sterling's effective exchange rate. A detailed discussion and investigation of this model is given in Sarantis and Stewart (1993).

Portfolio balance (PB)

$$e_t = e[(p^* - p)_t, \ (vnso)_t, \ m_t^*, \ m_t, \ k_t^*, \ k_t, \ b_t^*, \ b_t, \ f_t^*, \ f_t] \qquad (2)$$
$$+ \qquad\qquad + \qquad\quad + \quad - \quad \pm \quad \pm \quad \pm \quad \pm \quad - \quad +$$

---

[5] Sarantis and Stewart (1993) provide a brief description of the main theoretical exchange rate models and a detailed econometric evaluation of these models using the cointegration-error correction methodology. Further evidence on variants of the monetary exchange rate model is also provided in Sarantis (1994).

where (*vnso*) is the value of North Sea oil; m, k, b and f are the nominal stocks (in natural logarithm) of UK money, equities, bonds, and foreign assets (held by the private sector), respectively; and asterisks denote the corresponding foreign variables.[6]

Equation (2) is derived from Sarantis (1987). That study developed a portfolio balance model which includes money, bonds, equity and foreign asset markets, as well as the influence of North Sea oil, and was applied to five sterling exchange rates with satisfactory results.

In applying the structural models (1) and (2) to each sterling exchange rate, we have made use of the two-stage modelling methodology proposed by Engle and Granger (1987). In the first stage we estimate the equilibrium or cointegrating equations (1) and (2) with the method of Ordinary Least Squares. The uniqueness of these cointegrating vectors is examined with the Johansen (1988) multivariate cointegration tests. These tests support the existence of unique long-run equilibrium relationships consistent with the respective structural models (see Sarantis and Stewart, 1993; and Sarantis, 1994). In the second stage we employ the error correction formulation to model the short-run dynamics of each sterling exchange rate, utilizing our prior estimates of the long-run parameters:

$$\Delta e_t = \beta_0 + \beta'_1 \Delta Y_{t-i} + \beta_2 \Delta e_{t-1-i} - \beta_3 RES_{t-1} + v_t \tag{3}$$

where Y is the vector of explanatory variables in the respective structural model: RES_{t-1} is the lagged residuals from the corresponding cointegrating relationship; and v is the error term. In specifying the dynamic model (3) we have used the general to specific methodology, starting with lags of up to four quarters and nested down to a parsimonious representation of data, so that the final regression model passes the various diagnostic tests of its error term, functional form and parameter stability. These econometric results are reported in Sarantis and Stewart (1993).

VECTOR AUTOREGRESSIVE (VAR) MODELS

In the VAR approach each variable is a linear function of lagged values of all variables in the system. Hence a VAR representation is given by

$$X_t = C + B(L)X_t + u_t \tag{4}$$

where X is an $(n \times 1)$ vector of all variables in the system, u is an $(n \times 1)$ vector of error terms, and $B(L)$ is an $(n \times n)$ polynomial matrix in the lag operator L.

Given that we are employing two structural models in our forecasting investigation, we have also estimated two VAR models; one includes the variables of the MUIP model, referred to as VAR1, and the other includes the variables of the portfolio balance model, referred to as VAR2. An important issue in VAR modelling is whether to transform the data to render all variables stationary or to conduct the analysis in levels. Pagan (1990) points out that 'the idea that $z_t(X_t)$ can be expressed as a VAR has its origin in the theory of stationary process' and hence suggests that 'the sensible response ... would be to focus upon growth rates rather than levels of variables'. On the other hand, Engle and Yoo (1987) argue that vector autoregressions estimated with cointegrated data will be misspecified if the data are differenced, and demonstrate that error correction and VAR in levels are competing specifications. To address the forecasting implications of this issue, we have used both level and stationary approaches. The VAR models in levels are denoted as LVAR1 and LVAR2 respectively, while VARs in difference (stationary) form are denoted by DVAR1 and DVAR2 respectively.

---

[6] Due to the unavailability of data on k^* and b^*, these variables were not included in the estimation of model (2).

Table I. LR tests for VAR lag lengths (levels)[a]

Model/lags	US dollar/ pound	D-mark/ pound	Yen/ pound	F-franc/ pound
LVAR1				
1→2	48.24 (51.0)	55.16 (51.0)	73.18 (51.0)	62.13 (51.0)
2→3	55.55 (51.0)	43.92 (51.0)	34.04 (51.0)	29.59 (51.0)
3→4	36.63 (51.0)	53.98 (51.0)	44.08 (51.0)	52.57 (51.0)
4→5	—	30.97 (51.0)	—	33.36 (51.0)
1→3	96.90 (92.8)	—	—	—
2→4	—	90.58 (92.8)	—	77.23 (92.8)
Chosen lag	$l = 3$	$l = 2$	$l = 2$	$l = 2$
LVAR2				
1→2	110.51 (66.3)	131.94 (83.7)	120.87 (83.7)	109.52 (83.7)
2→3	64.58 (66.3)	60.26 (83.7)	94.35 (83.7)	82.34 (83.7)
3→4	56.00 (66.3)	90.33 (83.7)	116.45 (83.7)	88.95 (83.7)
4→5	—	89.05 (83.7)	104.21 (83.7)	80.59 (83.7)
5→6	—	81.37 (83.7)	376.69 (83.7)	—
2→4	—	—	—	148.58 (155.4)
2→5	—	171.99 (225.3)	218.59 (225.3)	—
Chosen lag	$l = 2$	$l = 2$	$l = 2$	$l = 2$

[a] 5% critical values in parentheses.

Table II. LR tests for VAR lag lengths (differences)[a]

Model/lags	US dollar/ pound	D-mark/ pound	Yen/ pound	F-franc/ pound
DVAR1				
1→2	47.77 (51.0)	50.90 (51.0)	36.08 (51.0)	47.63 (51.0)
2→3	46.40 (51.0)	42.19 (51.0)	42.93 (51.0)	38.00 (51.0)
3→4	41.02 (51.0)	33.29 (51.0)	37.85 (51.0)	36.88 (51.0)
Chosen lag	$l = 1$	$l = 1$	$l = 1$	$l = 1$
DVAR2				
1→2	55.22 (66.3)	71.34 (83.7)	80.59 (83.7)	87.63 (83.7)
2→3	56.25 (66.3)	58.93 (83.7)	79.05 (83.7)	127.33 (83.7)
3→4	64.73 (66.3)	57.67 (83.7)	108.13 (83.7)	24.75 (83.7)
4→5	—	—	83.21 (83.7)	—
1→4	—	—	211.11 (225.3)	—
Chosen lag	$l = 1$	$l = 1$	$l = 1$	$l = 3$

[a] 5% critical values in parentheses.

206   *Journal of Forecasting*   *Vol. 14, Iss. No. 3*

To determine the optimal lag length of the VAR system we have employed the likelihood ratio test statistic, LR, suggested by Sims (1980).[7] The estimates of LRs for the two VAR models estimated in level and stationary form are shown in Tables I and II respectively. Given the number of observations, we have considered a maximum lag of four and then tested downwards to one lag. Where the test supports the four lag, we have estimated longer lag structures in order to confirm the significance of lag four. In cases where the LR statistics indicate two significant lags, we have tested one versus the other and the shorter lag is acceptable in all cases. The chosen lags for all exchange rates are indicated in the tables.

BAYESIAN VECTOR AUTOREGRESSIVE (BVAR) MODELS

To overcome the serious problem of over-parameterization associated with VAR models, Litterman (1986) and others have proposed the BVAR representation which provides a flexible method for incorporating prior information for all the coefficients.[8] Following Litterman (1986), we assume that each coefficient has an independent and normal distribution with zero mean, except for the coefficient on the first lag of the own variable which has a mean of unity.

The standard deviations of the prior distributions are given by

$$S(i, j, l) = \gamma f(i, j) g(l) s_j / s_i \qquad (5)$$

The function g describes the lag pattern and is assumed to be harmonic: $g(l) = l^{-d}$. The function f gives the tightness of the prior for variable j in equation i relative to the tightness on the own lags. This function is assumed to be symmetric and has the form, $f(i, j) = w$. The parameter γ is the overall tightness of the prior; it is the standard deviation of the prior on the first own lag in each equation.

The most important hyperparameters in the construction of BVAR models are w and γ. The parameter w measures the weight attached to the coefficients of other variables relative to that of the own lagged value. This parameter takes values between zero and one. When $w = 1$, all variables in each equation have equal weight when forecasting the own variable. As w approaches zero the model approaches a set of univariate autoregressions. In our experimentation we have considered three values for w: 0.3, 0.5, 0.8. For the parameter γ we have assumed a relatively 'loose' value of 0.2 and a 'tight' value of 0.1. This has given us six alternative specifications. Using lags up to the fourth order for all variables, each formulation was estimated both in levels and stationary form and used to produce out-of-sample forecasts.

We found that forecasting performance is sensitive to the choice of hyperparameters.[9] The

---

[7] If AR(m) is the unrestricted VAR and AR(l) the restricted one, where m and l are the respective lags, then the LR statistic for testing AR(l) against AR(m) is given by

$$LR = (T - c)(\ln|\Omega_l| - \ln|\Omega_m|)$$

where T is the number of observations, c is the correction factor which is equal to the number of regressors in each equation in AR(m), and Ω is the covariance matrix of residuals of AR(l) and AR(m) respectively. The statistic LR is asymptotically distributed as χ^2 with $k^2(m - l)$ degrees of freedom, where k is the number of regressions.

[8] As far as we are aware, this is the first application of BVAR models to exchange rates. It is worth noticing that Meese and Rogoff (1983a) suggest that application of this methodology may improve on the random walk model, but the authors do not pursue this investigation.

[9] Artis and Zhang (1990) have found a similar result in applications of the BVAR model to macroeconomic forecasting.

Table III. BVAR hyperparameters (levels)

Exchange rate	LBVAR1		LBVAR2	
	γ	w	γ	w
US dollar/pound	0.2	0.8	0.2	0.8
D-mark/pound	0.1	0.3	0.2	0.8
Yen/pound	0.2	0.3	0.2	0.8
F-franc/pound	0.2	0.8	0.2	0.5

Table IV. BVAR hyperparameters (differences)

Exchange rate	DBVAR1		DBVAR2	
	γ	w	γ	w
US dollar/pound	0.2	0.8	0.2	0.8
D-mark/pound	0.2	0.3	0.2	0.3
Yen/pound	0.1	0.8	0.1	0.3
F-franc/pound	0.2	0.3	0.2	0.3

combinations of values for w and γ producing the best forecast for each exchange rate are reported in Tables III (for BVARs in levels) and IV (BVARs in differences). A point worth making is that relatively 'loose' values for both γ and w produce better forecasts than 'tight' values for the overwhelming majority of models and exchange rates.

FORECASTING STRATEGY

Following Meese and Rogoff (1983a) and other researchers, we adopted the strategy of sequential estimation for generating out-of-sample forecasts for one to ten horizons. The parameters of the models are based on the most recent information available at the time the forecast is made. More precisely, the models were initially estimated using data from 1973Q2 (the beginning of the recent floating period) to 1986Q4. The choice as to where to begin forecasting was predicated on the desire to produce medium-term forecasts and have sufficient number of observations for each forecast step. This has enabled us to produce ten-steps-ahead (quarters) forecasts, which is normally the longest forecast horizon considered by professional forecasters in this area. Forecasts are then generated at horizons of one to ten quarters. Next, data for 1987Q1 are added to the sample and the parameters of each model are re-estimated. New forecasts are then generated for one- to ten-quarters-ahead. This process continues through to the last forecast period, 1990Q2.

The generation of forecasts with cointegration-error correction models requires the setting up of a simultaneous equation system to capture both the long-run equilibrium and short-run relationships. Hence the forecasting system for the MUIP (modified uncovered interest parity)

208   *Journal of Forecasting*   *Vol. 14, Iss. No. 3*

and PB (portfolio balance) structural models consists of the following equations:

$$\Delta e_t = \beta_0 + \boldsymbol{\beta'}_1 \Delta \mathbf{Y}_{t-1} + \beta_2 \Delta e_{t-1-i} - \beta_3 RES_{t-1} \tag{6a}$$

$$e_t = e_{t-1} + \Delta e_t \tag{6b}$$

$$RES_t = e_t - \boldsymbol{\alpha'} \mathbf{Y_t} \tag{6c}$$

Note that equation (6a) is the error-correction equation (identical to equation (3)), equation (6b) is used to obtain the predicted level (in logs) of the exchange rate, and equation (6c) is the cointegrating equation (i.e. equations (1) and (2) respectively) rearranged so that the residual term becomes the dependent variable.

It should be stressed that in the case of the structural models, both the cointegrating equation and the error correction models were re-estimated at each forecast point, as the data for the latest quarter were added to the sample. These parameter estimates (and the respective cointegrating residuals, RES) were used in the system (6a)–(6c) to generate one- to ten-quarters-ahead forecasts. These updated forecasts were stored in a separate file, which was subsequently used to construct the accuracy statistics described below. On the other hand, the updating of the VAR and BVAR models and forecasts was carried out with the Kalman filter which computes automatically all the accuracy statistics for different forecast steps.[10]

Following previous researchers in this area, we have used actual realised values of all explanatory variables in the prediction period to generate out-of-sample forecasts with the structural models. This problem does not arise in the case of VAR and BVAR models where all variables are endogenous.[11]

The accuracy of forecasts for each forecast horizon is measured by the root mean square error (RMSE) and the Theil U statistic, which are defined as follows:

$$\text{RMSE} = \left\{ \sum_{j=1}^{k} [A(t+j+k) - F(t+j+k)]^2 / N \right\}^{0.5} \tag{7}$$

$$U = \text{RMSE(model)} / \text{RMSE(random walk)} \tag{8}$$

where $k = 1, 2, \ldots 10$ denotes the forecast step; N is the total number of forecasts in the prediction period; $A(t)$ and $F(t)$ are actual and forecast values respectively.

The U statistic is the ratio of the RMSE for the estimated model to the RMSE of the simple random walk model which predicts that the forecast simply equals the most recent information. Hence if $U < 1$, the model performs better than the random walk model without drift; if $U > 1$, the random walk outperforms the model. The forecasted value used in the computation of the RMSE and U statistics is the level (in logarithm) of the exchange rate, so these statistics can be compared across the different models. In the case of the VAR and BVAR models formulated in stationary form, the generated forecasts were the changes in the log of the exchange rate. The latter were subsequently converted into forecasted levels using past levels and forecasted exchange rate changes.

---

[10] The estimation and simulation of the structural models were done on Microfit and PC-TSP, while the RMSE and U statistics for the forecasts produced by these models were computed on Quattro. The VAR and BVAR forecasts were produced on PC-RATS.
[11] The only exception is North Sea oil (*vnso*), which has been treated as an exogenous variable and, therefore, we have used its actual values during the prediction period.

EMPIRICAL RESULTS

The forecasting results for the competing models and each exchange rate over varied horizons are summarized in Table V–VII.[12] Also shown are RMSE and U averages for forecast steps one to four and one to ten. The most striking results from these tables concerns the relative forecasting performance of the two structural models. The modified UIP strongly outperforms the portfolio balance model for all exchange rates and forecast horizons. The average RMSE (over steps one to ten) for the MUIP is reduced by roughly 80% for the D-mark/pound, 84% for the F-franc/pound and by 31% for the yen/pound. Over the shorter horizon of one to four steps, the average RMSE for the MUIP is reduced by 72% for the D-mark/pound, 75% for the F-franc/pound and 28% for the yen/pound. This suggests that the gap between the two models becomes wider over longer forecasting horizons. We therefore choose the MUIP as our representative structural model.[13]. Similar evidence on the dominance of the MUIP model is also provided by the BVAR and VAR formulations of the variables included in the respective

Table V. Statistics on forecasting accuracy: deutschmark/pound

Forecast step Observations	One-step 15		Two-step 14		Three-step 13		Four-step 12		Five-step 11		Six-step 10	
	RMSE	U	RMSE	U	RMSE	U	RMSE	U	RMSE	U	RMSE	U
Modified UIP	0.027	0.900	0.045	0.939	0.056	0.900	0.063	0.847	0.065	0.776	0.066	0.736
Portfolio balance	0.076	2.511	0.139	2.924	0.201	3.209	0.263	3.551	0.325	3.871	0.362	4.056
LVAR1	0.037	1.223	0.065	1.364	0.087	1.392	0.108	1.458	0.128	1.521	0.144	1.611
LBVAR1	0.026	0.862	0.043	0.907	0.055	0.884	0.065	0.883	0.077	0.912	0.089	0.991
DVAR1	0.028	0.933	0.053	1.108	0.072	1.152	0.090	1.217	0.112	1.336	0.132	1.478
DBVAR1	0.031	1.032	0.055	1.163	0.074	1.183	0.087	1.180	0.108	1.283	0.128	1.427

Forecast step Observations	Seven-step 9		Eight-step 8		Nine-step 7		Ten-step 6		Average one to four		Average one to ten	
	RMSE	U	RMSE	U	RMSE	U	RMSE	U	RMSE	U	RMSE	U
Modified UIP	0.064	0.735	0.061	0.729	0.057	0.758	0.052	0.835	0.048	0.897	0.055	0.816
Portfolio balance	0.379	4.374	0.400	4.810	0.368	4.909	0.324	5.233	0.170	3.059	0.284	3.949
LVAR1	0.149	1.715	0.153	1.845	0.153	2.042	0.137	2.215	0.074	1.360	0.116	1.639
LBVAR1	0.094	1.083	0.098	1.175	0.099	1.325	0.088	1.419	0.047	0.884	0.073	1.044
DVAR1	0.146	1.680	0.158	1.902	0.171	2.281	0.175	2.824	0.061	1.103	0.114	1.591
DBVAR1	0.139	1.608	0.152	1.825	0.163	2.166	0.169	2.725	0.062	1.139	0.111	1.559

---

[12] Since we were unable to uncover any significant cointegrating vector, and consequently to develop a structural model, for the US dollar/pound rate, we decided to exclude this exchange rate from our forecasting comparison. Of course, one could still develop VAR and BVAR models for this exchange rate. This was done during our experimentation and the general finding was that the BVAR in levels tended to produce the most accurate forecasts.

[13] This evidence about the superiority of the modified UIP model over the portfolio balance model supports a similar result based on non-nested tests in Sarantis and Stewart (1993).

Table VI. Statistics on forecasting accuracy: yen/pound

Forecast step Observations	One-step 15		Two-step 14		Three-step 13		Four-step 12		Five-step 11		Six-step 10	
	RMSE	U	RMSE	U	RMSE	U	RMSE	U	RMSE	U	RMSE	U
Modified UIP	0.039	1.283	0.064	1.220	0.074	1.064	0.077	1.008	0.081	0.993	0.088	1.026
Portfolio balance	0.052	1.714	0.082	1.570	0.104	1.486	0.112	1.477	0.117	1.428	0.130	1.510
LVAR1	0.043	1.401	0.052	0.998	0.070	0.994	0.096	1.265	0.109	1.327	0.122	1.418
LBVAR1	0.025	0.802	0.043	0.823	0.060	0.853	0.074	0.970	0.085	1.037	0.100	1.166
DVAR1	0.034	1.110	0.062	1.187	0.090	1.286	0.106	1.392	0.120	1.469	0.127	1.474
DBVAR1	0.030	0.978	0.053	1.007	0.079	1.123	0.085	1.118	0.099	1.206	0.111	1.297

Forecast step Observations	Seven-step 9		Eight-step 8		Nine-step 7		Ten-step 6		Average one to four		Average one to ten	
	RMSE	U	RMSE	U	RMSE	U	RMSE	U	RMSE	U	RMSE	U
Modified UIP	0.094	1.087	0.100	1.173	0.103	1.266	0.101	1.272	0.063	1.144	0.082	1.139
Portfolio balance	0.141	1.620	0.147	1.723	0.151	1.843	0.150	1.887	0.088	1.562	0.119	1.626
LVAR1	0.130	1.496	0.133	1.558	0.139	1.697	0.135	1.695	0.065	1.165	0.103	1.385
LBVAR1	0.115	1.330	0.127	1.487	0.133	1.627	0.130	1.635	0.050	0.862	0.089	1.173
DVAR1	0.132	1.521	0.135	1.580	0.162	1.987	0.192	2.407	0.073	1.244	0.116	1.541
DBVAR1	0.122	1.403	0.144	1.696	0.177	2.170	0.193	2.429	0.062	1.057	0.109	1.443

structural models. Consequently, we do not report the forecasts produced by the BVAR and VAR formulations of the portfolio balance model (i.e. LVAR2, LBVAR2, DVAR2 and DBVAR2) in order to focus on the 'key contenders'.

Another issue of interest is whether the VAR and BVAR models should be estimated in level or difference (stationary) form. Looking at the VAR and BVAR formulations of the variables included in the MUIP model (VAR1 and BVAR1), the levels approach strongly outperforms the difference approach for all exchange rates and forecast horizons, except for the VAR model of the D-mark/pound rate over the short term horizon. It should be noted, however, that even these short-term VAR forecasts are considerably inferior to those produced by the BVAR model. The gap between the two modelling approaches is more striking in the case of the BVAR model. For steps one to ten, the average RMSE for the BVAR model in levels (LBVAR1) is reduced by 34% for the D-mark/pound, 18% for the yen/pound and by 25% for the F-franc/pound rate.[14]

Comparing the forecasting performance of the best structural, VAR and BVAR models, several observations are made. Looking at the forecasted levels of the D-mark/pound rate, the VAR model yields the largest RMSEs at all horizons, with its average value being 56% higher

---

[14] To our knowledge, the only study to have compared the out-of-sample forecasting performance of VAR models in level and difference form is that by Shoesmith (1992) for regional and state non-agricultural employment in the USA. The results of that study show that the stationary VAR produces more accurate forecasts than its level counterpart under different lag structures. We should note, however, that Shoesmith applied the VAR model to a non-integrated system, whereas our VAR and BVAR models are applied to cointegrated systems.

Table VII. Statistics on forecasting accuracy: french franc/pound

Forecast step Observations	One-step 15		Two-step 14		Three-step 13		Four-step 12		Five-step 11		Six-step 10	
	RMSE	U	RMSE	U	RMSE	U	RMSE	U	RMSE	U	RMSE	U
Modified UIP	0.026	0.877	0.043	0.873	0.051	0.765	0.053	0.647	0.051	0.540	0.047	0.465
Portfolio balance	0.096	3.215	0.152	3.080	0.200	2.980	0.268	3.251	0.341	3.614	0.399	3.912
LVAR1	0.034	1.143	0.047	0.944	0.052	0.767	0.055	0.666	0.061	0.650	0.066	0.650
LBVAR1	0.021	0.698	0.037	0.741	0.051	0.764	0.067	0.814	0.080	0.849	0.087	0.869
DVAR1	0.029	0.956	0.050	1.016	0.070	1.034	0.086	1.046	0.101	1.074	0.112	1.095
DBVAR1	0.028	0.948	0.049	0.991	0.069	1.023	0.086	1.037	0.102	1.082	0.116	1.140

Forecast step Observations	Seven-step 9		Eight-step 8		Nine-step 7		Ten-step 6		Average one to four		Average one to ten	
	RMSE	U	RMSE	U	RMSE	U	RMSE	U	RMSE	U	RMSE	U
Modified UIP	0.043	0.428	0.036	0.373	0.035	0.398	0.042	0.581	0.044	0.791	0.043	0.595
Portfolio balance	0.403	4.007	0.350	3.589	0.288	3.250	0.249	3.464	0.179	3.131	0.275	3.436
LVAR1	0.067	0.666	0.070	0.719	0.076	0.857	0.078	1.084	0.047	0.880	0.061	0.815
LBVAR1	0.089	0.886	0.085	0.874	0.083	0.937	0.079	1.101	0.044	0.754	0.068	0.853
DVAR1	0.111	1.109	0.107	1.100	0.099	1.116	0.086	1.195	0.059	1.013	0.085	1.074
DBVAR1	0.118	1.179	0.120	1.228	0.115	1.303	0.103	1.431	0.058	1.000	0.091	1.136

than that under the BVAR model. The BVAR model in levels produces the most accurate forecasts over steps one to three, while the structural MUIP model consistently outperforms the BVAR model for forecast steps one to ten. This is reflected in the average values of the RMSE. For steps one to four, the MUIP performs slightly worse than the BVAR, but for steps one to ten the MUIP improves on the BVAR by roughly 25%. A similar pattern is observed for the F-franc/pound rate. The BVAR model in levels is the most accurate over steps one and two, but the MUIP displays a considerable improvement over forecast steps three to ten, showing a reduction in the average RMSE (over steps one to ten) by 30% over the VAR and 37% over the BVAR model. In the case of the yen/pound rate, the BVAR model in levels is again producing the more accurate forecasts over steps one to four, whereas the structural MUIP model strongly outperforms all models over four to ten forecast steps. As a result of the widening gap over the longer horizons, the average RMSE (for steps one to ten) under the MUIP is reduced by 8% over the BVAR and 20% over the VAR. This contrasts with the short-term loss (over steps one to four) of 21% to the BVAR model. The VAR model is outperformed by the BVAR model at all forecast horizons, with its average RMSE value being 16% higher than that under the BVAR model for one to ten steps. The reported gains in medium-term forecasting accuracy under the structural model for all exchange rates, at the expense of loss of some short-term accuracy to the BVAR model, support *a priori* expectations about the relative performance of structural versus multivariate time-series models, and are also remarkably similar to the pattern obtained by Engle and Yoo (1987) through simulations.

A controversial issue in the literature is whether the random walk model yields more

212   **Journal of Forecasting**   *Vol. 14, Iss. No. 3*

accurate forecasts than the structural models.[15] The U statistics indicate that the best structural model (MUIP) outperforms consistently the random walk model at all forecast horizons in the cases of the D-mark/pound and F-franc/pound rates. On the other hand, the random walk model produces more accurate forecasts for the level of the yen/pound rate at all horizons. This finding is rather surprising, given the strong evidence of cointegration and error correction for the yen/pound rate reported in Sarantis and Stewart (1993). A potential explanation is the relative stability of the yen/pound exchange rate during the forecasting period 1987Q1–1990Q3; this rate exhibited a standard deviation of 0.055 and a coefficient of variation of 0.010, while the maximum and minimum values (in logs) were 5.599 and 5.412 respectively.

CONCLUSIONS

In this paper we have investigated the out-of-sample forecasting performance of a wide class of structural, BVAR and VAR models for bilateral sterling exchange rates. There are a number of empirical findings worth mentioning. The lack of statistical evidence in support of long-run relationships consistent with the various versions of monetary models used by previous researchers suggests that these structural models are inappropriate for exchange rate forecasting. Instead one should focus on the portfolio balance (PB) and a modified version of the uncovered interest parity (MUIP) as representative structural models. Our results show that the MUIP model produces more accurate forecasts than the portfolio balance model at all forecast horizons and all exchange rates. Proper attention to the long-run properties and the dynamics of structural models of exchange rate determination can improve on the forecasting performance of the random walk model. The best structural model strongly outperforms the random walk model at all forecast horizons for two out of three bilateral exchange rates (i.e. D-mark/pound, F-franc/pound). The only exception is the yen/pound rate which would have been predicted more accurately by the random walk model than by any structural model. These findings suggest that the dispute over structural versus random walk models is far from over and that the jury is still out. Any claim that exchange rates are not longer driven by fundamentals (Williamson, 1993) would seem to be premature, particularly for the European currencies.

The overall ranking of the models varies over different forecast horizons. The structural model shows substantial improvement in medium-term forecasting accuracy of exchange rate levels, whereas the BVAR model is more accurate in the short term (normally up to three or four quarters), though the average forecast errors for all steps (one to ten) are lower under the best structural model for all exchange rates. An implication of these results is that optimizing short- and long-term forecasting with cointegrated systems will often require separate efforts.

Our results show that the best VAR and BVAR models in levels improve considerably on the out-of-sample forecasting performance of these models formulated in difference form. This evidence provides support in favour of the levels approach in VAR and BVAR modelling. Worth mentioning is also the finding that the unrestricted VAR is generally outperformed by the restricted BVAR model.

---

[15] In contrasting our results with those of previous studies cited in the first section, we should bear in mind not only differences in the exchange rates and sample period covered but also in the frequency of data used. In the present study we have used quarterly data, while most previous researchers used monthly data.

APPENDIX: MEASUREMENT OF VARIABLES AND DATA SOURCES[16]

e (log) foreign currency/pound sterling spot exchange rate, average of daily telegraphic transfer rates in London—*Financial Statistics.*

m (log) UK money stock (M1) in pounds—data supplied by the Economics Division of the Bank of England.

m^* (log) foreign money stock (M1) in foreign currency (i.e. for the USA, West Germany, Japan and France)—*OECD Main Economic Indicators.*

r (log) UK interest rate on 3-month inter-bank loans, monthly averages—*Financial Statistics.*

r^* (log) foreign money market interest rate (Federal Funds interest rate for the USA), monthly averages—*OECD Main Economic Indicators* and *International Financial Statistics.*

π (log) UK long-term interest rate (yield of long-term government bonds), monthly averages—*OECD Main Economic Indicators.*

π^* (log) foreign long-term interest rate (USA: yield of government composite bonds > 10 years; Germany and Japan: yield of long-term government bonds; France: yield of long-term bonds guaranteed by government), monthly averages—*OECD Main Economic Indicators.*

p (log) UK producer price index—*OECD Main Economic Indicators.*

p^* (log) foreign producer price index (GDP implicit price deflator for France)—*OECD Main Economic Indicators.*

NY UK gross domestic product at current prices (in pounds)—*OECD Main Economic Indicators.*

NY^* foreign gross domestic product at current prices (in foreign currency)—*OECD Main Economic Indicators.*

CA UK current account balance in pounds—*OECD Main Economic Indicators.*

$(CA)^*$ foreign current account balance in foreign currency (data for Japan were in UK dollars and were converted in yen using the yen/dollar exchange rate)—*OECD Main Economic Indicators.*

f (log) foreign asset stock held by the UK private sector, F, computed as follows:

$$F_t = F_{t-1} + [CA_t - \Delta(RESERV)_t]$$

where $\Delta(RESERV)$ is the change in non-gold foreign reserves (these were in US dollars and were converted into pounds using the dollar/pound rate). The benchmark was 1971(1). For an explanation and use of this formula see Branson *et al.*, (1977) and Keating (1985). Data for RESERV were obtained from *International Financial Statistics.*

f^* (log) foreign asset stock held by the private sector of the foreign country, F^*, computed by the formula:

$$F^*_t = F^*_{t-1} + [CA^*_t - \Delta(RESERV)^*_t]$$

where the change in non-gold foreign reserves was converted from US dollars to that country's currency using the corresponding exchange rate between the US dollar and the country's domestic currency.

---

[16] Notice that all variables were tested for stochastic seasonality and that these seasonal roots (wherever found) were removed by applying appropriate filters. See Sarantis and Stewart (1993) for details about the measurement of variables.

214   *Journal of Forecasting*   *Vol. 14, Iss. No. 3*

k   (log) UK personal sector holdings of equity assets—data provided by the Centre of
        Economic Forecasting of the London Business School.
b   (log) UK personal sector holdings of public sector debt—data provided by the Centre
        for Economic Forecasting of the London Business School.
vnso   Value of North Sea oil production in pounds—data provided by the Centre for
        Economic Forecasting of the London Business School—expressed as a percentage of
        UK nominal GDP.

ACKNOWLEDGEMENTS

Financial support from the Kingston University Research Fund is gratefully acknowledged. We
thank an anonymous referee and the editor, Professor K. Holden, for their useful comments. As
usual, we are responsible for the organisation and contents of the paper.

REFERENCES

Alexander, D. and Thomas, L. R., 'Monetary/asset models of exchange rate determination: how well have
   they performed in the 1980's?' *International Journal of Forecasting*, **3** (1987), 53–64.
Artis, M. J. and Zhang, W., 'BVAR forecasts for the G-7', *International Journal of Forecasting*, **6**
   (1990), 349–62.
Baillie, R. T. and Selover, P. D., 'Cointegration and models of exchange rate determination', *International
   Journal of Forecasting*, **3** (1987), 43–51.
Branson, W. H., Haltunen, H. and Masson, P., 'Exchange rates in the short run: the dollar deutschmark
   rate', *European Economic Review*, **10** (1977), 303–24.
Cutherbertson, K., Hall, S. G. and Taylor, M. P., *Applied Econometric Techniques*, London: Harvester
   Wheatsheaf, 1992.
Diebold, F. X. and Nason, J. A., 'Nonparametric exchange rate prediction', *Journal of International
   Economics*, **28** (1990), 315–32.
Engle, R. F. and Granger, C. W. J., 'Co-integration and error correction: representation, estimation and
   testing', *Econometrica*, **55** (1987), 251–76.
Engle, R. F. and Yoo, B. S., 'Forecasting and testing in co-integrated systems', *Journal of Econometrics*,
   35 (1987), 143–59.
Fisher, P. G., Tunna, S. K., Turner, D. S., Wallis, K. F. and Whitley, J. D., 'Econometric evaluation of
   the exchange rate in models of the U.K. Economy', *Economic Journal*, **100** (1990), 1230–44.
Hodrick, R. J., 'Risk, uncertainty and exchange rates', *Jounral of Monetary Economics*, **23** (1988),
   433–59.
Johansen, S., 'Statistical analysis of cointegrated systems', *Journal of Economic Dynamics and Control*,
   12 (1988), 231–54.
Keating, G., *The Production and Use of Economic Forecasts*, London: Methuen, 1985.
Litterman, R. B., 'Forecasting with Bayesian vector autoregressions—five years of experience', *Journal
   of Business and Economic Statistics*, **4** (1986), 25–38.
MacDonald, R. and Taylor, M. P., 'Exchange rate economics: a survey', *IMF Staff Papers*, **39** (1992),
   1–57.
Meese, R. A. and Rogoff, K., 'Empirical exchange rate models for the seventies: do they fit out of
   sample?' *Journal of International Economics*, **14** (1983a), 3–24.
Meese, R. A. and Rogoff, K., 'The out-of-sample failure of empirical exchange rate models: sampling
   error or misspecification?', in Frankel, J. A. (ed.), *Exchange Rates and International Macroeconomics*,
   Chicago: University of Chicago Press, 1983b.
Meese, R. A. and Rose, A. K., 'An empirical assessment of non-linearities in models of exchange rate
   determination', *Review of Economic Studies*, **58** (1991), 603–19.
Pagan, A. R., 'Three econometric methodologies: a critical appraisal', in Granger, C. W. J. (ed.),
   Modelling Economic Series, Oxford: Clarendon Press, 1990.

Sarantis, N., 'A dynamic asset market model for the exchange rate of the pound sterling', *Weltwirtschaftliches Archiv*, (1987), 24–37.

Sarantis, N., 'The monetary exchange rate model in the long-run: an empirical investigation', *Weltwirtschaftlishes Archiv*, (1994), 698–711.

Sarantis, N. and Stewart, C., 'Monetary and asset market models for sterling exchange rates: a cointegration approach', *Economics Discussion Paper 93/1*, 1993, Kingston University (forthcoming in the *Journal of Economic Integration*, 1995).

Schinasi, G. J. and Swamy, P. A. V. B., 'The out-of-sample forecasting performance of exchange rate models when coefficients are allowed to change', *Journal of International Money and Finance*, **8** (1989), 373–90.

Shoesmith, G. L., 'Non-cointegration and causality: implications for VAR modelling', *International Journal of Forecasting*, **8** (1992), 187–99.

Sims, C., 'Macroeconomics and reality', *Econometrica*, **48** (1980), 1–48.

Somanath, V. S., 'Efficient exchange rate forecasts: lagged models better than the random walk', *Journal of International Money and Finance*, **5** (1986), 195–220.

Williamson, J., 'Exchange rate management', *Economic Journal*, **103** (1993), 188–97.

Wolf, C. C. P., 'Time-varying parameters and the out-of-sample forecasting performance of structural exchange rate models', *Journal of Business & Economics Statistics*, **5** (1987), 87–97.

Authors' biographies:

Nicholas Sarantis is Reader in Economics, and Course Director of the MSc in Business and Economic Forecasting, at the School of Economics, Kingston University. He has been a consultant on macroeconomic forecasting for Economic Models Ltd and DRI Europe Ltd. His research interests include macroeconomic modelling and forecasting, exchange rate modelling and forecasting, macroeconomics, international finance, and applied econometrics. He has published numerous articles in academic journals in the above areas.

Chris Stewart is part-time Lecturer and Research Assistant at the School of economics, Kingston University. He holds an MSc degree in economics from Birkbeck College. His research interests include time-series forecasting methods and applied econometrics. He has co-authored an article published in *Applied Economics*.

Authors' address:

Nicholas Sarantis and **Chris Stewart**, School of Economics, Kingston University, Penrhyn Road, Kingston-upon-Thames, Surrey KT1 2EE, UK.

[10]

Journal of International Economics 28 (1990) 315–332. North-Holland

NONPARAMETRIC EXCHANGE RATE PREDICTION?

Francis X. DIEBOLD*

University of Pennsylvania, Philadelphia, PA 19104-6297, USA

James A. NASON

University of British Columbia, Vancouver, British Columbia V6T 1W5, Canada

Received June 1989, revised version received August 1989

Conditional heteroskedasticity is frequently found in the prediction errors of linear exchange rate models. It is not clear whether such conditional heteroskedasticity is a characteristic of the true data-generating process, or whether it indicates misspecification associated with linear conditional-mean representations. We address this issue by estimating nonparametrically the conditional-mean functions of ten major nominal dollar spot rates, 1973–1987, which are used to produce in-sample and out-of-sample nonparametric forecasts. Our findings bode poorly for recent conjectures that exchange rates contain nonlinearities exploitable for enhanced point prediction.

1. Introduction

It is widely agreed that a variety of high-frequency asset returns are well described as linearly unpredictable, conditionally heteroskedastic, and unconditionally leptokurtic. Documentation of linear unpredictability may be traced at least to early work on efficient markets, such as Cootner (1964) and Fama (1965); similarly, leptokurtosis has been appreciated at least since Mandelbrot (1963). The early writers were also aware of the apparent occurrence of volatility clustering in asset returns, and the work of Engle (1982) provided a tool for its formal study. It is now agreed that many time series of asset returns, while approximately uncorrelated, are not temporally independent; dependence arises through persistence in the conditional variance and perhaps in other conditional moments.

*Diebold gratefully acknowledges financial support from the National Science Foundation and the University of Pennsylvania Research Foundation. An earlier version of this paper was presented at the 1988 North American Winter meetings of the Econometric Society, New York. We thank the participants there, as well as an anonymous referee, Buz Brock, Dee Dechert, Blake LeBaron, Andy Rose, and seminar participants at Boston College, Carnegie-Mellon, Wisconsin, Washington, LSU, and Stonybrook for useful comments. We especially thank William S. Cleveland, who generously provided his software, and Roberto Sella, who provided outstanding research assistance.

All of these results are manifest in exchange rates, which are the focus of the present study. The well-known work of Meese and Rogoff (1983a, b) provides graphic illustration of the failure of a variety of economic models to outperform a simple random walk in out-of-sample prediction.[1] Extensive reviews of linear unpredictability and leptokurtosis in exchange rates are contained in Westerfield (1977), Boothe and Glassman (1987), and Diebold and Nerlove (1989a). Conditional heteroskedasticity, in the form of ARCH and related effects, has also been repeatedly documented in exchange rates. Diebold (1988), for example, examines seven nominal dollar spot rates and finds little linear predictability but strong ARCH effects in all of them.

A number of explanations have been advanced for the leptokurtosis and volatility clustering, as well as reduction of excess kurtosis under temporal aggregation. The phenomena may be jointly explained, for example, by subordinating exchange rates to a process dictating information arrival. The seminal work of Clark (1973) shows that subordination to an i.i.d. information-arrival process produces leptokurtic returns. As mentioned by Diebold (1986) and formalized by Gallant, Hsieh and Tauchen (1988), Clark's analysis may be extended by allowing for persistence in the information-arrival process, which produces ARCH-like movements in higher-order conditional moments. Finally, Diebold (1988) uses central limit theorems for dependent observations to show that, under quite general conditions (not requiring, for example, existence of the fourth unconditional moment), the unconditionally fat-tailed behavior associated with stationary ARCH effects diminishes with temporal aggregation.

If the above characterization of exchange rate dynamics (linear conditional mean with nonlinearities working through the conditional variance) is correct, then the nonlinearities cannot be exploited to generate improved point predictions relative to linear models. It is not clear, however, that the ARCH effects are structural, i.e. that they are a characteristic of the true data-generating process (DGP). Instead, ARCH may indicate misspecification, serving as a proxy for neglected nonlinearities in the conditional mean.[2] A finding of significant conditional-mean nonlinearity would be important for both theoretical and empirical work: theoretically, a substantial challenge to our understanding of asset-price dynamics would be posed, and empirically, a source of improved point prediction relative to linear models would be provided.

Interestingly, recent empirical and theoretical results are consistent with

---

[1]Their candidate models include a flexible price monetary model, a sticky price monetary model, a sticky price monetary model with current account effects, six univariate time series models, a vector autoregressive model, and the forward rate.

[2]For an illustration of the difficulties involved in separating conditional-mean from conditional-variance dynamics, see Weiss (1986), who discusses ARCH and bilinearity.

the conjecture that nonlinearities may be present in asset-return conditional means. The empirical results may be categorized into two groups: (1) those using ideas from the theory of stochastic nonlinear time series, and (2) those using ideas from the theory of deterministic chaotic systems. In the nonlinear time series area, a number of studies, including Domowitz and Hakkio (1985), Hinich and Patterson (1985, 1987), Weiss (1986), Engle, Lillien and Robins (1987), Diebold and Pauly (1988), and others, appear to detect statistically significant nonlinearity in conditional means of various asset prices and other economic aggregates. Recent work on regime switching, including Flood and Garber (1983), Engel and Hamilton (1988), and Froot and Obstfeld (1989), is also squarely in the nonlinear tradition. Similar results have been obtained in the chaos literature, using tests based on estimated Lyaponov exponents and correlation dimensions, as developed in Brock, Dechert and Scheinkman (1987), inter alia. Scheinkman and LeBaron (1989), for example, find strong evidence of nonlinearity in common stock returns and suggest that it could be exploited for improved point prediction. Similarly, Gallant, Hsieh and Tauchen (1988) and Hsieh (1989) report evidence of residual nonlinearity in exchange rates, after controlling for conditional heteroskedasticity. These empirical results are provocative, because they challenge us to take seriously the possible existence of nonlinear conditional-mean dynamics in asset prices.

A number of recent theoretical developments are beginning, implicitly or explicitly, to address this challenge. Sims (1984), for example, shows that general-equilibrium asset-pricing models imply martingale asset-price behavior *only* at arbitrarily short horizons. Thus, economic theory cannot rule out the possibility of nonlinear dependence in conditional means (as well as in higher-order conditional moments) of asset returns. Moreover, substantial progress has been made in general equilibrium models with time-varying risk, such as Abel (1988), Hodrick (1987), Baldwin and Lyons (1988), and Nason (1988).

In summary, there appears to be strong evidence, consistent with rigorous economic theory, that important nonlinearities may be operative in exchange rate determination. Upon further consideration, however, it becomes clear that the literature is not in satisfactory condition, owing to a puzzle that immediately arises: Why is it that while statistically significant rejections of linearity in exchange rates routinely occur, no nonlinear model has been found that can significantly outperform even the simplest linear model in out-of-sample forecasting? Because a number of factors may be operative, a number of explanations may be offered. One, of course, is that the nonlinearities present may be in even-ordered conditional moments, and therefore are not useful for point prediction. Second, in-sample nonlinearities such as outliers and structural shifts may be present, and may cause various linearity tests to reject, while nevertheless being of no use for out-of-sample forecasting. Third, very slight conditional-mean nonlinearities might be truly present and be detectable with large datasets, while nevertheless yielding negligible ex ante forecast improvement.[3] Finally, even if conditional-mean nonlinearities are present and *are* important, the overwhelming variety of plausible candidate nonlinear models makes determination of a good approximation to the DGP a difficult task. The seemingly large variety of parametric nonlinear models that have received attention lately (e.g. bilinear, threshold, and exponential autoregressive) is in fact a very small subset of the class of plausible nonlinear DGPs.

In this paper we contribute to a resolution of this puzzling behavior of exchange rates by estimating conditional-mean functions nonparametrically. By so doing, we avoid the parametric model-selection problem; the class of potential models entertained is expanded greatly. In section 2 we discuss various aspects of nonparametric functional estimation, and the locally weighted regression procedure, which we use extensively, is highlighted. Section 3 contains empirical results; in particular, both in-sample LWR fits and out-of-sample LWR forecasts are compared to those arising from linear models. Section 4 concludes.

2. Nonparametric prediction

Nonparametric techniques may be used for estimation of a variety of densities and econometric functionals, including regression functions, first and higher-order derivatives of regression functions, conditional-variance functions, hazard and survival functions, etc.[4] We shall generally be concerned with nonparametric estimation of conditional expectation, or regression, functions,

$$E(y|x) = \int y f(y|x)\, dy = \int y[f(y,x)/f(x)]\, dy, \qquad (1)$$

which we use for nonparametric prediction.[5] This is achieved by (explicit or implicit) substitution of nonparametric estimates of the underlying joint and marginal densities into (1). In our dynamic models, the stochastic conditioning vector x is composed of lagged dependent variables:

$$x_t = \{y_{t-1}, \ldots, y_{t-p}\}. \qquad (2)$$

---

[3]In other words, *significance* of nonlinearity does not necessarily imply its *economic importance.*

[4]For surveys of various aspects of nonparametric and semiparametric estimation, see Ullah (1988) and Robinson (1988).

[5]Because the meaning is obvious from the context, we use lower-case letters for both random variables and their realizations, and we use f to denote all probability density functions.

We shall work with the very general nonlinear autoregressive structure:

$$y_t = g(y_{t-1}, \ldots, y_{t-p}) + \varepsilon_t,$$

(3)

$$\mathrm{E}(\varepsilon_t | y_{t-1}, \ldots, y_{t-p}) = 0,$$

$t = 1, \ldots, T$, so that (1) may be rewritten more specifically as:

$$\mathrm{E}(y_{t+1} | y_t, \ldots, y_{t-p+1}) = \int y_{t+1} f(y_{t+1} | y_t, \ldots, y_{t-p+1}) \, \mathrm{d}y_{t+1}$$

$$= \int y_{t+1} [f(y_{t+1}, y_t, \ldots, y_{t-p+1}) / f(y_t, \ldots, y_{t-p+1})] \, \mathrm{d}y_{t+1}.$$

(4)

The regression function estimates may be obtained by a variety of inter-related nonparametric methods, including kernel, series, and nearest-neighbor (NN) techniques, consistency results for which have been obtained in time series environments by Robinson (1983), Gallant and Nychka (1987), and Yakowitz (1987), respectively.

In this study we make use of a NN technique, known as locally-weighted regression (LWR). NN methods proceed by estimating $g(x)$, at an arbitrary point $x = x^*$ in p-dimensional Euclidean space, via a weight function:

$$\hat{g}(x^*) = \sum_{t=1}^{T} w_{k_T}(x_t) y_t,$$

(5)

where $w_{k_T}(x_t) = 1/k_T$ if x_t is one of the k_T nearest neighbors of x^*, and $w_{k_T}(x_t) = 0$ otherwise.[6] The LWR estimator, as proposed by Cleveland (1979) and refined by Cleveland and Devlin (1988) and Cleveland et al. (1988), is an important generalization of the NN estimator. Like a NN estimator, LWR fits the surface at a point x^* as a function of the y values corresponding to the k_T nearest neighbors of x^*. Unlike NN, however, LWR does not take $\hat{g}(x^*)$ as a simple average of those y values; rather, $\hat{g}(x^*)$ is the fitted value from a regression surface. This corresponds to a simple average only in the very unlikely case that the constant term is the sole regressor with explanatory power.

We now discuss the procedure in some detail. We compute the LWR estimate of the surface at a point $x^*, \hat{g}(x^*)$, as follows. Let ξ be a smoothing constant such that $0 < \xi \leq 1$, and let $k_T = \mathrm{int}(\xi \cdot T)$, where $\mathrm{int}(\cdot)$ rounds down to the nearest integer. Then rank the x_t's by Euclidean distance from x^*; call

---

[6]The subscript T of k_T serves as a reminder that the number of nearest neighbors used should depend on sample size, as discussed subsequently.

these $x_1^*, x_2^*, \ldots, x_T^*$. Thus, x_1^* is closest to x^*, x_2^* is second closest to x^*, and so on. Let $\lambda(a, b)$ measure Euclidean distance; then $\lambda(x^*, x_{k_T}^*)$ is the Euclidean distance from x^* to its k_Tth closest neighbor:

$$\lambda(x^*, x_{k_T}^*) = \left[\sum_{j=1}^{p} (x_{k_T j}^* - x_j^*)^2 \right]^{1/2}. \tag{6}$$

Form the neighborhood weight function:

$$v_t(x_t, x^*, x_{k_T}^*) = C[\lambda(x_t, x^*)/\lambda(x^*, x_{k_T}^*)], \tag{7}$$

where $C(\cdot)$ is the tricube function:

$$C(u) = \begin{cases} (1 - u^3)^3 & \text{for } u < 1, \\ 0 & \text{otherwise}. \end{cases} \tag{8}$$

The value of the regression surface at x^* is then computed as:

$$\hat{y}^* = \hat{g}(x^*) = x^{*\prime}\hat{\beta}, \tag{9}$$

where

$$\hat{\beta} = \operatorname{argmin} \left[\sum_{t=1}^{T} v_t(y_t - x_t'\beta)^2 \right]. \tag{10}$$

The LWR procedure, exactly as described above, is used in our subsequent empirical work. Obviously, it reflects a number of judgmental decisions, such as use of the Euclidean norm and tricube neighborhood weighting, as well as locally linear (as opposed to higher-order, such as quadratic) fitting. The Euclidean norm has obvious geometric appeal, as does the tricube weight function, which produces a smooth, gradual decline in weight with distance from x^*. Locally linear fitting is also highly reasonable (and computationally feasible) in the present context.[7]

Of greater interest is the choice of ξ, which determines the number of nearest neighbors used, and hence the degree of smoothing. Consistency of NN estimators (and hence LWR) requires that the number of nearest neighbors used go to infinity with sample size, but at a slower rate, i.e.

$$\lim_{T \to \infty} k_T = \infty, \qquad \lim_{T \to \infty} (k_T/T) = 0. \tag{11}$$

---

[7]See Cleveland, Devlin and Grosse (1988) for further discussion.

This implicitly creates a 'window' whose width becomes smaller as the sample size goes to infinity, but at a slower rate. In this way the shrinking window nevertheless contains progressively more neighbors, so that bias is reduced along with variance.

Similar issues arise in kernel and series estimation. In the kernel case, the window width corresponds to the bandwidth, which must shrink with sample size but at a slower rate. In the series case, the window width corresponds (inversely) to the number of included series terms; again, consistency requires that the truncation point increases with sample size, but at a slower rate. While the asymptotic mechanics of LWR estimators are similar to those of kernel and series estimators, it is interesting to note that their finite-sample properties are likely to be superior to those of kernel and series estimators. Series estimators produce global, as opposed to local, approximations, which is likely to make them inflexible in all but the largest samples. Kernel estimators do produce local approximations, but the approximation is locally *constant*, as opposed to locally *linear*, which may introduce substantial bias in finite samples.

It is interesting to note that the earlier-discussed LWR rule of $\xi \cdot T$ for selecting the number of nearest neighbors does not satisfy the second regularity condition for consistency. In any finite sample such as ours, however, this is of no consequence, since there exists a selection rule such as T^{α}, $\alpha < 1$, which *does* satisfy the regularity condition and results in the use of an identical number of nearest neighbors. For example, in a sample of size 800, the $\xi \cdot T$ rule with $\xi = 0.5$ selects approximately 400 nearest neighbors, as does the T^{α} rule with $\alpha = 0.9$.[8]

3. Empirical analysis

We study ten nominal New York interbank dollar spot rates, Wednesdays, 12.30 p.m., from the first week of 1973 (3 January) through the thirty-eighth week of 1987 (23 September). Sample size is therefore equal to 769. The rates are Canadian Dollar (CD), French Franc (FF), German Mark (DM), Italian Lira (LIR), Japanese Yen (YEN), Swiss Franc (SF), British Pound (BP), Belgian Franc (BF), Danish Kroner (DK) and Dutch Guilder (DG). All are measured in cents per unit of foreign currency and were obtained from the Federal Reserve Board database. Throughout, we use S_t as notation for a generic exchange rate at time t. Our interest centers on percent exchange rate changes, $\Delta \ln S_t$, on which we have 768 observations (second week of 1973 through thirty-eighth week of 1987); study of percent changes has the additional benefit of avoiding theoretical problems associated with estimation

---

[8] Moreover. in the empirical work that follows. we explore a wide range of ξ values.

322   F.X. Diebold and J.A. Nason, Nonparametric exchange rate prediction?

Table 1

In-sample analysis, $p = 1$.

ξ	CD	FF	DM	LIR	YEN	SF	BP	DG	DK	BF
0.10	2.7095	1.9321	2.1849	1.6824	1.7298	2.7994	1.9205	1.9462	3.3442	1.8685
	3.6230	0.9407	1.0192	0.8469	0.8512	1.1669	0.9329	0.9725	1.0139	0.9372
0.20	2.6906	1.9384	2.1857	1.6748	1.7310	2.7898	1.9200	1.9398	3.3383	1.8517
	3.6260	0.9328	1.0118	0.8411	0.8379	1.1713	0.9269	0.9680	1.0047	0.9343
0.30	2.6900	1.9379	2.1845	1.6731	1.7291	2.7886	1.9170	1.9332	3.3331	1.8481
	3.6379	0.9350	1.0133	0.8402	0.8326	1.1737	0.9242	0.9674	1.0065	0.9343
0.40	2.6923	1.9364	2.1787	1.6715	1.7311	2.7850	1.9143	1.9292	3.3292	1.8444
	3.6429	0.9375	1.0158	0.8390	0.8316	1.1719	0.9230	0.9684	1.0069	0.9355
0.50	2.6904	1.9336	2.1737	1.6712	1.7312	2.7778	1.9115	1.9221	3.3226	1.8361
	3.6418	0.9386	1.0179	0.8408	0.8328	1.1700	0.9237	0.9674	1.0062	0.9370
0.60	2.6848	1.9308	2.1674	1.6694	1.7288	2.7653	1.9074	1.9135	3.3156	1.8292
	3.6407	0.9398	1.0189	0.8429	0.8357	1.1683	0.9250	0.9665	1.0070	0.9399
0.70	2.6786	1.9262	2.1572	1.6653	1.7218	2.7477	1.8974	1.9026	3.3082	1.8225
	3.6419	0.9419	1.0193	0.8443	0.8385	1.1680	0.9256	0.9666	1.0077	0.9423
0.80	2.6728	1.9168	2.1445	1.6571	1.7034	2.7245	1.8841	1.8929	3.2983	1.8085
	3.6445	0.9437	1.0194	0.8468	0.8397	1.1684	0.9266	0.9680	1.0083	0.9444
0.90	2.6606	1.9055	2.1315	1.6501	1.6719	2.6974	1.8669	1.8755	3.2899	1.7937
	3.6409	0.9472	1.0206	0.8535	0.8388	1.1693	0.9274	0.9700	1.0087	0.9450
1.00	2.6645	1.9307	2.1488	1.6980	1.6663	2.6769	1.8717	1.8755	3.2905	1.8063
	3.6557	0.9714	1.0393	0.8833	0.8546	1.1838	0.9491	0.9902	1.0190	0.9629
2.00	2.6925	1.9421	2.1864	1.7189	1.6794	2.7086	1.8892	1.8890	3.2974	1.8200
	3.6712	0.9757	1.0489	0.8900	0.8575	1.1921	0.9556	0.9962	1.0218	0.9681
3.00	2.7089	1.9453	2.2029	1.7286	1.6858	2.7233	1.8975	1.8944	3.2998	1.8242
	3.6820	0.9769	1.0538	0.8935	0.8592	1.1956	0.9584	0.9983	1.0227	0.9697
10.00	2.7305	1.9486	2.2230	1.7409	1.6938	2.7410	1.9073	1.9003	3.3025	1.8286
	3.6964	0.9780	1.0599	0.8979	0.8612	1.1997	0.9616	1.0004	1.0238	0.9713
RW	2.9402	2.0736	2.3174	1.8046	1.9367	2.9265	1.9741	2.0519	3.4965	2.0176
	3.8568	1.0174	1.0879	0.9117	0.9153	1.2348	0.9819	1.0500	1.0903	1.0343

Notes: The first entry of each cell is MSPE, while the second is MAPE. MSPEs are $\times 10^4$, except for the CD, which is $\times 10^5$. MAPEs are $\times 10^2$, except for the CD, which is $\times 10^3$. Smallest MSPE and MAPE for each currency are underlined.

of nonstationary nonparametric regression functions, as well as numerical problems with highly collinear regressors.[9]

For each exchange rate we examine both in-sample 'fit' and out-of-sample predictive performance of the LWR nonparametric conditional-mean estimator. Observations 6 through 701 are used for in-sample analysis, while observations 702 through 768 are reserved for out-of-sample forecast comparison. Our out-of-sample forecasts are completely ex ante, using LWR estimates formed recursively in real time, using only information actually available.

The in-sample results for $p = 1$, 3 and 5 appear in tables 1, 2 and 3, respectively. We perform a sensitivity analysis with respect to ξ, exploring a

[9]Furthermore, as pointed out by Meese and Rogoff (1983a, b) the use of logs eliminates prediction problems arising from Jensen's inequality. For a discussion of issues related to unit roots, see Diebold and Nerlove (1989b).

Table 2

In-sample analysis, $p = 3$.

ξ	CD	FF	DM	LIR	YEN	SF	BP	DG	DK	BF
0.10	2.8388	1.9753	2.1892	1.6725	1.7711	2.8763	2.2728	1.9677	3.4300	1.8790
	3.7433	0.9338	0.9990	0.8450	0.8799	1.1642	0.9975	0.9613	1.0200	0.9377
0.20	2.7539	1.9291	2.0951	1.6455	1.7262	2.8388	2.1893	1.9236	3.3713	1.8240
	3.6637	0.9275	0.9886	0.8390	0.8604	1.1655	0.9848	0.9592	1.0102	0.9335
0.30	2.7174	1.9073	2.0613	1.6395	1.7149	2.7990	2.1431	1.8986	3.3451	1.8060
	3.6316	0.9236	0.9847	0.8362	0.8524	1.1634	0.9739	0.9561	1.0051	0.9336
0.40	2.6894	1.8854	2.0417	1.6343	1.7088	2.7652	2.1126	1.8804	3.3251	1.7948
	3.6160	0.9199	0.9824	0.8345	0.8489	1.1620	0.9669	0.9545	1.0016	0.9343
0.50	2.6629	1.8596	2.0153	1.6263	1.7019	2.7340	2.0797	1.8572	3.3043	1.7810
	3.6072	0.9153	0.9794	0.8329	0.8466	1.1601	0.9625	0.9516	0.9991	0.9338
0.60	2.6378	1.8286	1.9893	1.6151	1.6818	2.6952	2.0416	1.8330	3.2788	1.7617
	3.5998	0.9108	0.9771	0.8313	0.8419	1.1567	0.9583	0.9483	0.9966	0.9322
0.70	2.6114	1.7972	1.9670	1.6010	1.6501	2.6574	2.0036	1.8093	3.2548	1.7363
	3.5905	0.9063	0.9751	0.8306	0.8349	1.1529	0.9526	0.9452	0.9937	0.9278
0.80	2.5782	1.7589	1.9441	1.5896	1.6114	2.6249	1.9662	1.7734	3.2319	1.7008
	3.5769	0.9013	0.9728	0.8325	0.8264	1.1504	0.9482	0.9403	0.9911	0.9211
0.90	2.5341	1.7194	1.9256	1.5804	1.5760	2.5904	1.9316	1.7321	3.2097	1.6631
	3.5589	0.8980	0.9716	0.8361	0.8196	1.1493	0.9463	0.9351	0.9888	0.9139
1.00	2.5437	1.7022	1.9737	1.6117	1.5791	2.5764	1.9327	1.7146	3.1941	1.6392
	3.5812	0.9136	0.9966	0.8570	0.8271	1.1607	0.9644	0.9478	0.9947	0.9201
2.00	2.5961	1.7326	2.0139	1.6444	1.5987	2.6201	1.9753	1.7371	3.2131	1.6648
	3.6166	0.9242	1.0077	0.8682	0.8337	1.1728	0.9742	0.9569	1.0008	0.9291
3.00	2.6204	1.7422	2.0251	1.6582	1.6065	2.6391	1.9949	1.7454	3.2195	1.6733
	3.6336	0.9271	1.0108	0.8729	0.8363	1.1771	0.9785	0.9598	1.0027	0.9318
10.00	2.6502	1.7521	2.0367	1.6749	1.6155	2.6607	2.0174	1.7544	3.2264	1.6824
	3.6525	0.9299	1.0140	0.8785	0.8393	1.1818	0.9836	0.9626	1.0047	0.9346
RW	2.9402	2.0736	2.3174	1.8046	1.9367	2.9265	1.9741	2.0519	3.4965	2.0176
	3.8568	1.0174	1.0879	0.9117	0.9153	1.2348	0.9819	1.0500	1.0903	1.0343

Notes: The first entry of each cell is MSPE, while the second is MAPE. MSPEs are $\times 10^4$, except for the CD, which is $\times 10^5$. MAPEs are $\times 10^2$, except for the CD, which is $\times 10^3$. Smallest MSPE and MAPE for each currency are underlined.

wide range of values from 0.10 through 10.0.[10] In table 1 ($p = 1$) we find that mean squared prediction error (MSPE) is minimized for all currencies at either $\xi = 0.9$ or $\xi = 1.0$. The MSPE associated with the optimal ξ choice is always lower, often substantially so, than the random walk (RW) MSPE. Mean absolute prediction error (MAPE) is minimized for all currencies at generally smaller ξ values ranging from 0.1 to 0.6. Like MSPE, the MAPE associated with the optimal ξ choice is always smaller than the random walk MAPE.[11]

Similar results are obtained in table 2 ($p = 3$) and table 3 ($p = 5$):

[10]Note that $\xi = 1$ does not correspond to a linear autoregression, because the observations are still weighted. Rather, our algorithm is such that as ξ approaches infinity, the linear autoregression emerges. (In practice, $\xi = 10$ produces an approximately linear autoregression.)

[11]It is interesting to note that the MAPE-optimal ξ values are smaller than their MSPE-optimal counterparts, reflecting the willingness to accept higher variance in return for decreased bias under MAPE as opposed to MSPE loss.

Table 3

In-sample analysis, $p = 5$.

ξ	CD	FF	DM	LIR	YEN	SF	BP	DG	DK	BF
0.10	3.2387	2.1601	2.3172	1.7498	2.0348	3.1651	2.4893	2.1542	3.5454	2.1070
	3.9357	0.9764	1.0377	0.8762	0.9522	1.2282	1.0314	0.9913	1.0348	0.9927
0.20	3.0368	1.9977	2.1687	1.6525	1.8473	2.9726	2.3119	2.0008	3.4173	1.9375
	3.7960	0.9489	1.0187	0.8606	0.9011	1.1976	1.0053	0.9734	1.0188	0.9655
0.30	2.9215	1.9425	2.1218	1.6190	1.7864	2.8847	2.2363	1.9402	3.3744	1.8672
	3.7221	0.9359	1.0080	0.8487	0.8785	1.1859	0.9928	0.9651	1.0122	0.9530
0.40	2.8357	1.8983	2.0836	1.5856	1.7430	2.8227	2.1787	1.8947	3.3377	1.8166
	3.6693	0.9249	0.9995	0.8361	0.8634	1.1787	0.9808	0.9573	1.0074	0.9441
0.50	2.7724	1.8602	2.0433	1.5577	1.7010	2.7698	2.1174	1.8554	3.3026	1.7765
	3.6371	0.9175	0.9921	0.8254	0.8516	1.1723	0.9690	0.9517	1.0028	0.9365
0.60	2.7133	1.8194	2.0043	1.5409	1.6586	2.7157	2.0631	1.8183	3.2692	1.7388
	3.6116	0.9103	0.9848	0.8201	0.8399	1.1660	0.9606	0.9460	0.9968	0.9298
0.70	2.6589	1.7851	1.9668	<u>1.5337</u>	1.6153	2.6658	2.0208	1.7794	3.2408	1.7031
	3.5932	0.9047	0.9781	<u>0.8200</u>	0.8282	1.1583	0.9559	0.9400	0.9916	0.9222
0.80	2.6056	1.7479	1.9328	1.5372	1.5745	2.6223	1.9817	1.7409	3.2132	1.6715
	3.5766	0.8998	0.9726	0.8240	0.8175	1.1513	0.9522	0.9333	0.9864	0.9147
0.90	2.5511	1.7120	<u>1.9070</u>	1.5408	<u>1.5424</u>	2.5821	<u>1.9461</u>	1.7019	3.1853	1.6398
	<u>3.5617</u>	0.8969	<u>0.9701</u>	0.8287	<u>0.8102</u>	<u>1.1471</u>	<u>0.9482</u>	0.9275	0.9818	0.9085
1.00	<u>2.5333</u>	<u>1.7005</u>	1.9544	1.6059	1.5623	<u>2.5638</u>	1.9605	<u>1.6932</u>	<u>3.1805</u>	<u>1.6276</u>
	3.5891	0.9138	0.9899	0.8563	0.8236	1.1560	0.9614	0.9389	0.9888	0.9157
2.00	2.5874	1.7312	2.0027	1.6410	1.5854	2.6231	2.0085	1.7265	3.2074	1.6583
	3.6239	0.9428	1.0031	0.8682	0.8307	1.1713	0.9742	0.9523	0.9980	0.9268
3.00	2.6107	1.7420	2.0177	1.6548	1.5946	2.6457	2.0263	1.7388	3.2166	1.6688
	3.6384	0.9279	1.0077	0.8728	0.8336	1.1765	0.9792	0.9566	1.0010	0.9304
10.00	2.6390	1.7535	2.0339	1.6707	1.6054	2.6703	2.0464	1.7523	3.2263	1.6802
	3.6575	0.9310	1.0124	0.8782	0.8370	1.1822	0.9849	0.9612	1.0042	0.9342
RW	2.9402	2.0736	2.3174	1.8046	1.9367	2.9265	1.9741	2.0519	3.4965	2.0176
	3.8568	1.0174	1.0879	0.9117	0.9153	1.2348	0.9819	1.0500	1.0903	1.0343

Notes: The first entry of each cell is MSPE, while the second is MAPE. MSPEs are $\times 10^4$, except for the CD, which is $\times 10^5$. MAPEs are $\times 10^2$, except for the CD, which is $\times 10^3$. Smallest MSPE and MAPE for each currency are underlined.

nonparametric conditional-mean estimation leads to substantial reductions in loss, whether measured by MSPE or MAPE, relative to the random walk. Both MSPE- and MAPE-optimal ξ are almost always at 0.9 or 1.0. Finally, it is interesting to note the general tendency for both MSPE and MAPE to decrease and then level off as more lags are included. Although this need not happen (different nearest neighbors are used, in general, for different p), it is intuitively reasonable by analogy to the fact that inclusion of additional regressors in an OLS regression must lower (or, at worst, leave unchanged) the sum of squared residuals.

We now turn to the one-step-ahead out-of-sample analysis. Again, we estimate nonparametric autoregressions of order 1 through 5 using the LWR procedure, with values of the smoothing parameter ξ ranging from 0.1 through 10.0 for each p, corresponding to the use of roughly 70 nearest neighbors (with neighborhood weighting) through 'all' nearest neighbors

F.X. Diebold and J.A. Nason, Nonparametric exchange rate prediction?   325

Table 4

One-step-ahead out-of-sample forecast analysis, $p = 1$.

ξ	CD	FF	DM	LIR	YEN	SF	BP	DG	DK	BF
0.10	2.7119	2.0596	2.1725	2.1474	1.9619	3.0868	1.5960	2.2309	2.1069	2.4231
	3.8859	1.1435	1.1572	1.1895	1.0444	1.3759	1.0067	1.1638	1.1575	1.2047
0.20	2.5998	2.0606	2.2107	2.0917	1.9457	2.9372	1.5877	2.1936	2.1059	2.4041
	3.8181	1.1424	1.1656	1.1662	1.0365	1.3506	1.0005	1.1660	1.1635	1.2038
0.30	2.5515	2.0301	2.2238	2.0509	1.9351	2.8978	1.5960	2.1926	2.1209	2.3805
	3.7797	1.1348	1.1679	1.1546	1.0287	1.3420	1.0027	1.1660	1.1635	1.2038
0.40	2.5373	2.0097	2.2135	2.0317	1.9235	2.8984	1.6034	2.1740	2.1181	2.3543
	3.7603	1.1300	1.1680	1.1490	1.0252	1.3422	1.0070	1.1613	1.1657	1.1997
0.50	2.5322	1.9944	2.1985	2.0197	1.9104	2.9007	1.6074	2.1547	2.1163	2.3351
	3.7525	1.1276	1.1669	1.1460	1.0226	1.3439	1.0082	1.1577	1.1665	1.1951
0.60	2.5282	1.9795	2.1856	2.0080	1.9031	2.9092	1.6076	2.1467	2.1119	2.3193
	3.7518	1.1240	1.1650	1.1443	1.0204	1.3466	1.0079	1.1568	1.1655	1.1951
0.70	2.5269	1.9653	2.1711	1.9885	1.8989	2.9142	1.6078	2.1407	2.1091	2.3028
	3.7514	1.1211	1.1621	1.1423	1.0191	1.3488	1.0081	1.1566	1.1649	1.1930
0.80	2.5281	1.9473	2.1609	1.9646	1.8975	2.9069	1.6123	2.1343	2.1097	2.2789
	3.7471	1.1184	1.1603	1.1401	1.0204	1.3493	1.0090	1.1567	1.1661	1.1883
0.90	2.5392	1.9217	2.1466	1.9360	1.9070	2.8911	1.6155	2.1221	2.1097	2.2632
	3.7459	1.1147	1.1586	1.1367	1.0253	1.3497	1.0092	1.1565	1.1677	1.1867
1.00	2.5552	1.8533	2.0900	1.8717	1.9327	2.8195	1.5968	2.0785	2.0890	2.2167
	3.7549	1.1054	1.1621	1.1220	1.0369	1.3424	1.0006	1.1588	1.1683	1.1833
2.00	2.5458	1.8430	2.0725	1.8536	1.9271	2.7962	1.5933	2.0717	2.0809	2.2036
	3.7517	1.1030	1.1608	1.1147	1.0344	1.3385	0.9985	1.1588	1.1654	1.1798
3.00	2.5423	1.8430	2.0725	1.8536	1.9271	2.7962	1.5933	2.0717	2.0809	2.2036
	3.7501	1.1030	1.1608	1.1165	1.0352	1.3398	0.9852	1.1591	1.1661	1.1807
10.00	2.5387	1.8377	2.0557	1.8360	1.9228	2.7777	1.5888	2.0655	2.0756	2.1952
	3.7480	1.1014	1.1596	1.1126	1.0334	1.3371	0.9990	1.1584	1.1647	1.1788
RW	2.4368	1.7398	2.0431	1.7402	1.9433	2.7569	1.5483	1.9463	2.0183	2.0754
	3.6497	1.0703	1.1617	1.0847	1.0218	1.3407	0.9889	1.1514	1.1253	1.1506

Notes: The first entry of each cell is MSPE, while the second is MAPE. MSPEs are $\times 10^4$, except for the CD, which is $\times 10^5$. MAPEs are $\times 10^2$, except for the CD, which is $\times 10^3$. Smallest MSPE and MAPE for each currency are underlined.

(with no neighborhood weighting). For each ξ and each p, out-of-sample forecasts are computed by recursively estimating $E(\Delta \ln S_{702} | \Delta \ln S_{701}, \ldots, \Delta \ln S_{702-p})$, and then $E(\Delta \ln S_{703} | \Delta \ln S_{702}, \ldots, \Delta \ln S_{703-p})$ and so forth, in real time. This is continued until the sample is exhausted, resulting in a sequence of 67 ex ante one-step-ahead forecasts.

The one-step-ahead results for $p = 1$, 3 and 5 are contained in tables 4, 5 and 6, respectively. Here the random walk fares much better, indicating that the in-sample loss reduction may be the spurious result of overfitting. Out-of-sample loss reductions due to the use of LWR (with the best-performing ξ value) generally do not exist, and on the few occasions when they do, they are much smaller than those of the in-sample analysis. These qualitative conclusions hold regardless of the choice of p. In truly ex ante forecasting, in which even the ξ value must be chosen by the investigator (based upon a

326   *F.X. Diebold and J.A. Nason, Nonparametric exchange rate prediction?*

Table 5

One-step-ahead out-of-sample forecast analysis, $p = 3$.

ξ	CD	FF	DM	LIR	YEN	SF	BP	DG	DK	BF
0.10	2.3486	2.1847	2.4820	2.0735	1.9106	3.0651	1.4823	2.2189	2.2729	2.2872
	3.5420	1.1641	1.2178	1.1652	1.0188	1.3710	0.9738	1.1508	1.1977	1.1986
0.20	2.3839	2.0176	2.4108	2.0080	1.8601	2.9110	1.4627	2.1570	2.1936	2.2267
	3.5467	1.1115	1.2086	1.1425	0.9984	1.3622	0.9706	1.1520	1.1858	1.1878
0.30	2.4000	1.9693	2.3436	1.9825	1.8386	2.8567	1.4962	2.1485	2.1478	2.2334
	3.5747	1.0960	1.1970	1.1350	0.9902	1.3506	0.9805	1.1556	1.1747	1.1851
0.40	2.4280	1.9409	2.2890	1.9668	1.8367	2.8191	1.5299	2.1435	2.1217	2.2253
	3.6070	1.0890	1.1873	1.1350	0.9884	1.3405	0.9854	1.1577	1.1676	1.1797
0.50	2.4464	1.9132	2.2492	1.9505	1.8227	2.7993	1.5427	2.1328	2.1079	2.2232
	3.6291	1.0857	1.1799	1.1346	0.9872	1.3336	0.9847	1.1565	1.1650	1.1769
0.60	2.4609	1.8863	2.2137	1.9360	1.8073	2.7911	1.5533	2.1215	2.0945	2.2181
	3.6429	1.0842	1.1711	1.1331	0.9900	1.3298	0.9867	1.1521	1.1618	1.1748
0.70	2.4656	1.8607	2.1764	1.9210	1.8018	2.7815	1.5602	2.1015	2.0773	2.2055
	3.6381	1.0813	1.1656	1.1299	0.9951	1.3249	0.9880	1.1457	1.1592	1.1725
0.80	2.4581	1.8380	2.1403	1.9032	1.8042	2.7725	1.5714	2.0751	2.0605	2.1791
	3.6200	1.0788	1.1603	1.1250	1.0004	1.3220	0.9907	1.1419	1.1578	1.1674
0.90	2.4589	1.8211	2.1085	1.8804	1.8132	2.7666	1.5851	2.0473	2.0508	2.1495
	3.6152	1.0774	1.1554	1.1182	1.0043	1.3221	0.9983	1.1393	1.1574	1.1625
1.00	2.4971	1.7642	2.0120	1.8221	1.8503	2.7628	1.6047	1.9973	2.0209	2.0940
	3.6842	1.0746	1.1464	1.1071	1.0166	1.3343	1.0025	1.1414	1.1525	1.1595
2.00	2.5106	1.7638	1.9934	1.8121	1.8500	2.7547	1.6107	1.9940	2.0225	2.0977
	3.7047	1.0752	1.1438	1.1061	1.0153	1.3340	1.0009	1.1426	1.1510	1.1603
3.00	2.5167	1.7657	1.9884	1.8091	1.8493	2.7523	1.6125	1.9928	2.0231	2.0998
	3.7147	1.0756	1.1430	1.1063	1.0148	1.3336	1.0007	1.1425	1.1502	1.1605
10.00	2.5244	1.7685	1.9837	1.8063	1.8486	2.7505	1.6144	1.9918	2.0242	2.1026
	3.7270	1.0762	1.1423	1.1066	1.0141	1.3330	1.0007	1.1423	1.1493	1.1607
RW	2.4368	1.7398	2.0431	1.7402	1.9433	2.7569	1.5483	1.9463	2.0183	2.0754
	3.6497	1.0703	1.1617	1.0847	1.0218	1.3407	0.9889	1.1514	1.1253	1.1506

Notes: The first entry of each cell is MSPE, while the second is MAPE. MSPEs are $\times 10^4$, except for the CD, which is $\times 10^5$. MAPEs are $\times 10^2$, except for the CD, which is $\times 10^3$. Smallest MSPE and MAPE for each currency are underlined.

combination of prior information and previous sample information), the scope for improved prediction appears very limited.

The negative results uncovered thus far are for one-step-ahead conditional expectations; the possibility of nonlinear dependence at longer horizons remains. Such does not appear to be the case; the results for four-, eight- and twelve-step-ahead forecasts reported in an appendix (available from the authors on request) are qualitatively identical.

All of the results are summarized graphically in figs. 1 (MSPE) and 2 (MAPE). For each country, we display the in-sample loss, relative to that of the random walk, for nonparametric LWR forecasts based upon pth order models ($p = 1, 3, 5$). We also display the out-of-sample loss relative to the random walk for k-step ahead LWR forecasts ($k = 1, 4, 8, 12$) from pth order

Table 6

One-step-ahead out-of-sample forecast analysis, $p = 5$.

ξ	CD	FF	DM	LIR	YEN	SF	BP	DG	DK	BF
0.10	2.9123	2.5456	2.9236	2.6215	2.3325	3.3799	1.9555	2.4573	2.8317	2.6892
	4.1417	1.2889	1.3795	1.3076	1.1520	1.4933	1.0928	1.2349	1.3886	1.2547
0.20	2.6505	2.3117	2.6230	2.2931	2.0809	3.1792	1.8207	2.2870	2.5481	2.4742
	3.9257	1.2175	1.2974	1.2310	1.0697	1.4507	1.0469	1.1923	1.3113	1.2089
0.30	2.5028	2.1942	2.4743	2.1955	2.0016	3.0785	1.7494	2.2235	2.3913	2.3782
	3.8199	1.1829	1.2550	1.1972	1.0453	1.4162	1.0328	1.1720	1.2566	1.1892
0.40	2.4139	2.1025	2.3675	2.1214	1.9477	2.9925	1.6962	2.1836	2.2810	2.3299
	3.7456	1.1553	1.2190	1.1758	1.0285	1.3889	1.0209	1.1579	1.2200	1.1813
0.50	2.3949	2.0272	2.2714	2.0396	1.9088	2.9060	1.6593	2.1508	2.2026	2.2857
	3.7195	1.1310	1.1891	1.1497	1.0148	1.3605	1.0135	1.1422	1.1918	1.1716
0.60	2.4004	1.9606	2.11931	1.9760	1.8806	2.8413	1.6336	2.1036	2.1355	2.2363
	3.7092	1.1092	1.1688	1.1277	1.0048	1.3379	1.0106	1.1256	1.1670	1.1588
0.70	2.4216	1.9108	2.1267	1.9296	1.8656	2.7974	1.6164	2.0670	2.0902	2.1902
	3.6996	1.0930	1.1505	1.1150	1.0038	1.3218	1.0095	1.1124	1.1542	1.1461
0.80	2.4438	1.8816	2.0867	1.8902	1.8950	2.7652	1.6101	2.0403	2.0628	2.1536
	3.6950	1.0859	1.1404	1.1047	1.0048	1.3144	1.0079	1.1098	1.1465	1.1378
0.90	2.44609	1.8527	2.0615	1.8582	1.8530	2.7403	1.6154	2.0173	2.0542	2.1186
	3.6899	1.0826	1.1365	1.1000	1.0049	1.3161	1.0087	1.1163	1.1487	1.1351
1.00	2.4860	1.8015	2.0285	1.8303	1.8695	2.7587	1.6526	2.0041	2.0398	2.1037
	3.7133	1.0840	1.1498	1.1057	1.0172	1.3356	1.0082	1.1375	1.1534	1.1525
2.00	2.4636	1.7981	2.0087	1.8209	1.8860	2.7681	1.6526	2.0070	2.0363	2.1097
	3.7305	1.0846	1.1473	1.1067	1.0197	1.3394	1.0060	1.1434	1.1529	1.1575
3.00	2.4996	1.7987	2.0031	1.8182	1.8924	2.7705	1.6491	2.0070	2.0349	2.1119
	3.7407	1.0851	1.1465	1.1070	1.0199	1.3401	1.0052	1.1444	1.1523	1.1588
10.00	2.5083	1.8001	1.9980	1.8157	1.9000	2.7733	1.6443	2.0070	2.0334	2.1146
	3.7545	1.0855	1.1456	1.1074	1.0196	1.3410	1.0045	1.1453	1.1515	1.1602
RW	2.4368	1.7398	2.0431	1.7402	1.9433	2.7569	1.5483	1.9463	2.0183	2.0754
	3.6497	1.0703	1.1617	1.0847	1.0218	1.3407	0.9889	1.1514	1.1253	1.1506

Notes: The first entry of each cell is MSPE, while the second is MAPE. MSPEs are $\times 10^4$, except for the CD, which is $\times 10^5$. MAPEs are $\times 10^2$, except for the CD, which is $\times 10^3$. Smallest MSPE and MAPE for each currency are underlined.

models ($p = 1, 3, 5$). The MSPE and MAPE values, indicated with diamonds, correspond to use of the best ξ value.[12]

Clear and distinct patterns emerge. In-sample, MSPE and MAPE reductions in the neighborhood of 10–20 percent relative to the random walk are pervasive.[13] Out-of-sample, however, the nonparametric predictor fares much less well. Typically, the loss associated with the nonparametric predictor is

[12]To make matters concrete, consider the leftmost diamond of the Canada graph in fig. 1. It corresponds to in-sample analysis with $p = 1$, and its height of approximately -11 indicates that the nonparametric model fit by locally weighted regression has mean squared error approximately 11 percent smaller than that of the random walk. Now consider the first diamond to the right of the vertical dashed line. It corresponds to out-of-sample analysis with $k = p = 1$, and its height of approximately $+4$ indicates that the nonparametric model fit by locally weighted regression has mean squared error approximately 4 percent larger than that of the random walk.

[13]It is interesting to note that the marginal benefit of including more lags (i.e. increasing p) is diminishing.

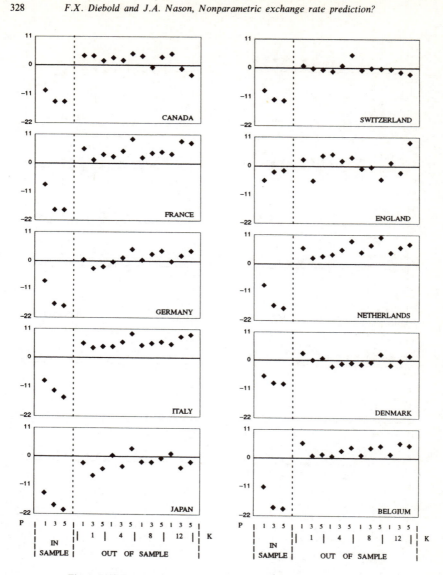

Fig. 1. MSPE comparisons: in-sample vs. out-of-sample performance.

F.X. Diebold and J.A. Nason, Nonparametric exchange rate prediction?   329

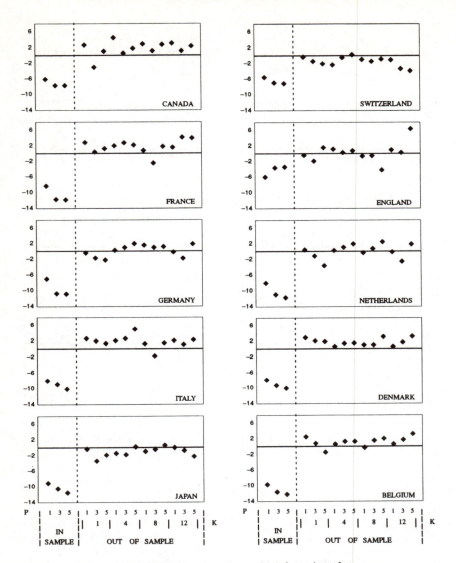

Fig. 2. MAPE comparisons: in-sample vs. out-of-sample performance.

larger than that of the random walk, regardless of the number of lags included (p) or the forecast horizon (k). When loss reduction does occur it is typically very small, and must be tempered by the fact that the loss reductions graphed correspond to the ex post optimal ξ values, which are not known in real time.

4. Summary and concluding remarks

Using a powerful nonparametric prediction technique, we are generally unable to improve upon a simple random walk in out-of-sample prediction of ten major dollar spot rates in the post-1973 float. Our exchange rate results therefore corroborate those of others using different techniques and different asset prices, such as Prescott and Stengos (1988), who find that kernel techniques deliver no improvement upon the random walk in the prediction of gold prices, and White (1988), who is unable to improve forecasts of IBM stock returns using a neural network. Taken together, these results constitute fairly strong evidence against the existence of asset price nonlinearities that are exploitable for improved point prediction.

Our reduced-form results carry important implications for structural models of exchange rate determination. In particular, it would appear unlikely that significant structural nonlinearities, whether of functional form or of regime-switching, have been operative in the post-1973 float. In complementary and independent work, Meese and Rose (1989) argue forcefully for this position.

The research could of course be extended in a number of directions. The analysis could be made completely ex ante by choosing ξ in real time by cross validation, and multivariate generalizations might be undertaken. Computational considerations render some of these extensions infeasible at the present time.

References

Abel, A.B., 1988, Stock prices under time varying dividend risk: An exact solution in an infinite horizon general equilibrium model, Journal of Monetary Economics 22, 375–393.

Baldwin, R. and R. Lyons, 1988, The mutual amplification effect of exchange rate volatility and unresponsive trade prices, NBER Working Paper no. 2677.

Boothe, P. and D. Glassman, 1987, The statistical distribution of exchange rates, Journal of International Economics 22, 297–319.

Brock, W.A., W.D. Dechert and J.A. Scheinkman, 1987, A test for independence based on the correlation dimension, SSRI Working Paper no. 8702 (Department of Economics, University of Wisconsin, Madison, WI).

Clark, P.K., 1973, A subordinated stochastic process model with finite variance for speculative prices, Econometrica 41, 135–155.

Cleveland, W.S., 1979, Robust locally weighted regression and smoothing scatterplots, Journal of the American Statistical Association 74, 829–836.

Cleveland, W.A. and S.J. Devlin, 1988, Locally weighted regression: An approach to regression analysis by local fitting, Journal of the American Statistical Association 83, 596–610.

Cleveland, W.S., S.J. Devlin and E. Grosse, 1988, Regression by local fitting: Methods, properties and computational algorithms, Journal of Econometrics 37, 87–114.

Cootner, P., ed., 1964, The random character of stock market prices (MIT Press, Cambridge, MA).

Diebold, F.X., 1986, Modeling persistence in conditional variances: A comment, Econometric Reviews 5, 51–56.

Diebold, F.X., 1988, Empirical modeling of exchange rate dynamics (Springer-Verlag, New York).

Diebold, F.X. and M. Nerlove, 1989a, The dynamics of exchange rate volatility: A multivariate latent-factor ARCH model, Journal of Applied Econometrics 4, 1–22.

Diebold, F.X. and M. Nerlove, 1989b, Unit roots in economic time series: A selective survey, in: T.B. Fomby and G.F. Rhodes, eds., Advances in econometrics: Co-integration, spurious regressions, and unit roots (JAI Press, Greenwich, CT) forthcoming.

Diebold, F.X. and P. Pauly, 1988, Endogenous risk in a rational-expectations portfolio-balance model of the deutschemark/dollar rate, European Economic Review 32, no. 1, 27–54.

Domowitz, I. and C.S. Hakkio, 1985, Conditional variance and the risk premium in the foreign exchange market, Journal of International Economics 19, 47–66.

Engel, C. and J.D. Hamilton, 1988, Long swings in exchange rates: Are they in the data and do markets know it?, Manuscript (Department of Economics, University of Virginia, VA).

Engle, R.F., 1982, Autoregressive conditional heteroskedasticity with estimates of the variance of U.K. inflation, Econometrica 50, 987–1008.

Engle, R.F., D.M. Lillien and R.P. Robbins, 1987, Estimating time-varying risk premia in the term structure: The ARCH-M model, Econometrica 55, 391–408.

Fama, E.F., 1965, The behavior of stock market prices, Journal of Business 38, 34–105.

Fama, E.F., 1976, Foundations of finance (Basic Books, New York).

Flood, R. and P. Garber, 1983, A model of stochastic process switching, Econometrica 51, 537–564.

Froot, F.A. and M. Obstfeld, 1989, Exchange rate dynamics under stochastic regime shifts: A unified approach, NBER Working Paper no. 2835.

Gallant, A.R. and D.W. Nychka, 1987, Semi-nonparametric maximum likelihood estimation, Econometrica 55, 363–390.

Gallant, A.R., D. Hsieh and G. Tauchen, 1988, On fitting a recalcitrant series: The pound/dollar exchange rate, 1974–1983, Manuscript (Graduate School of Business, University of Chicago, Chicago, IL).

Hinich, M. and D. Patterson, 1985, Evidence of nonlinearity in daily stock returns, Journal of Business and Economic Statistics 3, 69–77.

Hinich, M. and D. Patterson, 1987, Evidence of nonlinearity in the trade-by-trade stock market return generating process, Manuscript (Department of Government, University of Texas at Austin, TX).

Hodrick, R.J., 1987, Risk, uncertainty and exchange rates, NBER Working Paper no. 2429, forthcoming in Journal of Monetary Economics.

Hsieh, D.A., 1988, A nonlinear stochastic rational expectations model of exchange rates, Manuscript (Graduate School of Business, University of Chicago, Chicago, IL).

Hsieh, D.A., 1989, Testing for nonlinear dependence in foreign exchange rates: 1974–1983, Journal of Business 62, 339–368.

LeBaron, B., 1987, Nonlinear puzzles in stock returns, Manuscript (Department of Economics, University of Chicago, Chicago, IL).

Mandelbrot, B., 1963, The variation of certain speculative prices, Journal of Business 36, 394–419.

Meese, R.A. and K. Rogoff, 1983a, Empirical exchange rate models of the seventies: Do they fit out of sample?, Journal of International Economics 14, 3–24.

Meese, R.A. and K. Rogoff, 1983b, The out of sample failure of empirical exchange rate models: Sampling error or misspecification?, in: J. Frenkel, ed., Exchange rates and international economics (University of Chicago Press, Chicago, IL).

Meese, R.A. and A.K. Rose, 1989, An empirical assessment of nonlinearities in models of exchange rate determination, Manuscript (School of Business, University of California, Berkeley, CA).

Nason, J.M., 1988, The equity premium and time-varying risk behavior, Finance and Economics Discussion Series no. 8, Federal Reserve Board.

Prescott, D.M. and T. Stengos, 1988, Do asset markets overlook exploitable nonlinearities? The case of gold, Manuscript (Department of Economics, University of Guelph).

Priestley, M.B., 1980, State-dependent models: A general approach to nonlinear time series analysis, Journal of Time Series Analysis 1, 47–71.

Robinson, P.M., 1983, Nonparametric estimators for time series, Journal of Time Series Analysis 4, 185–207.

Robinson, P.M., 1988, Semiparametric econometrics: A survey, Journal of Applied Econometrics 3, 35–51.

Scheinkman, J.A. and B. LeBaron, 1989, Nonlinear dynamics and stock returns, Journal of Business 64, 311–338.

Sims, C.A., 1984, Martingale-like behavior of prices and interest rates, Discussion Paper no. 205 (Department of Economics, University of Minnesota, Minneapolis, MN).

Ullah, A., 1988, Nonparametric estimation of econometric functionals, Canadian Journal of Economics 21, 625–658.

Weiss, A.A., 1984, ARMA models with ARCH errors, Journal of Time Series Analysis 5, 129–143.

Weiss, A.A., 1986, ARCH and bilinear time series models: Comparison and combination, Journal of Business and Economic Statistics 4, 59–70.

Westerfield, J.M., 1977, An examination of foreign exchange risk under fixed and floating rate regimes, Journal of International Economics 7, 181–200.

White, H., 1988, Economic prediction using neural networks: The case of IBM daily stock returns, Working Paper no. 88-20 (Department of Economics, UCSD).

Yakowitz, S.J., 1987, Nearest neighbor methods for time series analysis, Journal of Time Series Analysis 8, 235–247.

[11]

JOURNAL OF APPLIED ECONOMETRICS, VOL. 10, 347–364 (1995)

FORECASTING EXCHANGE RATES USING FEEDFORWARD AND RECURRENT NEURAL NETWORKS

CHUNG-MING KUAN

Department of Economics, 21 Hsu-chow Road, National Taiwan University, Taipei 10020, Taiwan

AND

TUNG LIU

Department of Economics, Ball State University, Muncie, IN 47306, USA

SUMMARY

In this paper we investigate the out-of-sample forecasting ability of feedforward and recurrent neural networks based on empirical foreign exchange rate data. A two-step procedure is proposed to construct suitable networks, in which networks are selected based on the predictive stochastic complexity (PSC) criterion, and the selected networks are estimated using both recursive Newton algorithms and the method of nonlinear least squares. Our results show that PSC is a sensible criterion for selecting networks and for certain exchange rate series, some selected network models have significant market timing ability and/or significantly lower out-of-sample mean squared prediction error relative to the random walk model.

1. INTRODUCTION

Neural networks provide a general class of nonlinear models which has been successfully applied in many different fields. Numerous empirical and computational applications can be found in the *Proceedings* of the International Joint Conference on Neural Networks and Conference of Neural Information Processing Systems. In spite of its success in various fields, there are only a few applications of neural networks in economics. Neural networks are novel in econometric applications in the following two respects. First, the class of multilayer neural networks can well approximate a large class of functions (Hornik *et al.*, 1989; and Cybenko, 1989), whereas most of the commonly used nonlinear time-series models do not have this property. Second, as shown in Barron (1991), neural networks are more parsimonious models than linear subspace methods such as polynomial, spline, and trigonometric series expansions in approximating unknown functions. Thus, if the behaviour of economic variables exhibits nonlinearity, a suitably constructed neural network can serve as a useful tool to capture such regularity.

In this paper we investigate possible nonlinear patterns in foreign exchange data using *feedforward*, and *recurrent* networks. It has been widely accepted that foreign exchange rates are I(1) (integrated of order one) processes and that changes of exchange rates are uncorrelated over time. Hence, changes in exchange rates are not linearly predictable in general. For a comprehensive review of these issues, see Baillie and McMahon (1989). Since the empirical studies supporting these conclusions rely mainly on linear time series techniques, it is not unreasonable to conjecture that the linear unpredictability of exchange rates may be due to limitations of linear models. Hsieh (1989) finds that changes of exchange rates may be nonlinearly dependent, even though they are linearly uncorrelated. Some researchers also

CCC 0883–7252/95/040347–18
© 1995 by John Wiley & Sons, Ltd.

Received May 1992
Revised September 1994

provide evidence in favor of nonlinear forecasts (e.g. Taylor, 1980, 1982; Engel and Hamilton, 1990; Engel, 1991; Chinn, 1991). On the other hand, Diebold and Nason (1990) find that nonlinearities of exchange rates, if any, cannot be exploited to improve forecasting. Therefore, we treat neural networks as alternative nonlinear models and focus on whether neural networks can provide superior out-of-sample forecasts.

This paper has two objectives. First, we introduce different neural network modeling techniques and propose a two-step procedure to construct suitable neural networks. In the first step of the proposed procedure, we apply the recursive Newton algorithms of Kuan and White (1994a) and Kuan (1994) to estimate a family of networks and compute the so-called 'predictive stochastic complexity' (Rissanen, 1987), from which we can easily select suitable network structures. In the second step, statistically more efficient estimates for networks selected from the first step are obtained by the method of nonlinear least squares using recursive estimates as initial values. Our procedure differs from previous applications of feedforward networks in economics (e.g. White, 1988; Kuan and White, 1990) in that networks are selected objectively. Also, the application of recurrent networks is new in applied econometrics; hence its performance would also be of interest to researchers.

Second, we investigate the forecasting performance of networks selected from the proposed procedure. In particular, model performance is evaluated using various statistical tests, rather than crude comparison. Financial economists are usually interested in sign predictions (i.e. forecasts of the direction of future price changes) which yield important information for financial decisions such as market timing (see e.g. Levich, 1981; Merton, 1981). We apply the market timing test of Henriksson and Merton (1981) to justify whether the forecasts from network models are of economic value in practice; a nonparametric test for sign predictions proposed by Pesaran and Timmermann (1992) is also conducted. Other than sign predictions, we, as many other econometricians, are also interested in out-of-sample MSPE (mean squared prediction errors) performance. We use the Mizrach (1992) test to evaluate the MSPE performance of networks relative to the random walk model. Our results show that network models perform differently for different exchange rate series and that predictive stochastic complexity is a sensible criterion for selecting networks. For certain exchange rates, some network models perform reasonably well; for example, for the Japanese yen and British pound some selected networks have significant market timing ability and/or significantly lower out-of-sample MSPE relative to the random walk model in different testing periods; for the Canadian dollar and deutsche mark, however, selected networks exhibit only mediocre performance.

This paper proceeds as follows. We review feedforward and recurrent networks in Section 2. The network building procedure, including the estimation methods, complexity regularization criteria, and a two-step procedure, are described in Section 3. Empirical results are analysed in Section 4. Section 5 concludes the paper. Details of the recursive Newton algorithms are summarized in the Appendix.

2. FEEDFORWARD AND RECURRENT NETWORKS

In this section we briefly describe the functional forms of feedforward and recurrent networks and their properties; for more details see Kuan and White (1994a).

A neural network may be interpreted as a nonlinear regression function characterizing the relationship between the dependent variable (target) y and an n-vector of explanatory variables (inputs) x. Instead of postulating a specific nonlinear function, a neural network model is constructed by combining many 'basic' nonlinear functions via a multilayer structure. In a *feedforward* network, the explanatory variables first simultaneously activate q hidden units in an intermediate layer through some function Ψ, and the resulting hidden-unit activations h_i, $i = 1, \ldots, q$, then activate output units through some function Φ to produce the network output o (see Figure 1). Symbolically, we have

$$h_{i,t} = \Psi\left(\gamma_{i0} + \sum_{j=1}^{n} \gamma_{ij} x_{j,t}\right) \qquad i = 1, \ldots, q$$

$$o_t = \Phi\left(\beta_0 + \sum_{i=1}^{q} \beta_i h_{i,t}\right)$$

(1)

or more compactly,

$$o_t = \Phi\left(\beta_0 + \sum_{i=1}^{q} \beta_i \Psi\left(\gamma_{i0} + \sum_{j=1}^{n} \gamma_{ij} x_{j,t}\right)\right)$$

(2)

$$\equiv f_q(x_t, \theta)$$

where θ is the vector of parameters containing all β's and γ's, and the subscript q of f signifies the number of hidden units in the network.

This is a flexible nonlinear functional form in that the activation functions Ψ and Φ can be chosen quite arbitrarily, except that Ψ is usually required to be a bounded function. Hornik *et al.* (1989) and Cybenko (1989) show that the function f_q constructed in equation (2) can approximate a large class of functions arbitrarily well (in a suitable metric), provided that the number of hidden units, q, is sufficiently large. This property is analogous to that of nonparametric methods. As an example, consider the L_2 approximation property. Given the dependent variable y and some explanatory variables x, we are typically interested in the *unknown* conditional mean $M(x) = E(y \mid x)$. The L_2 approximation property asserts that if $M(x) \in L_2$, then for any $\varepsilon > 0$, there is a q such that

$$E \mid M(x) - f_q(x, \theta) \mid^2 < \varepsilon$$

(3)

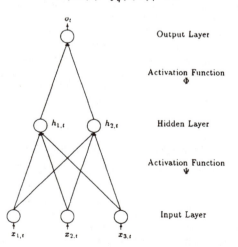

Figure 1. A simple feedforward network with one output unit, two hidden units, and three input units

Barron (1991) also shows that a feedforward network can achieve an approximation rate $O(1/q)$ by using a number of parameters $O(qn)$ that grows linearly in q, whereas traditional polynomial, spline, and trigonometric expansions require exponentially $O(q^n)$ terms to achieve the same approximation rate. Thus, neural networks are (asymptotically) relatively more parsimonious than these series expansions in approximating unknown functions. These two properties make feedforward networks an attractive econometric tool in (nonparametric) applications.

In a dynamic context, it is natural to include lagged dependent variables as explanatory variables in a feedforward network to capture dynamics. This approach suffers the drawback that the correct number of lags needed is typically unknown (this is analogous to the problem of determining the order of an autoregression). Hence. the lagged dependent variables in a network may not be enough to characterize the behaviour of y in some applications. To overcome this deficiency, various *recurrent* networks, i.e. networks with feedbacks, have been proposed. A recurrent network has a richer dynamic structure and is similar to a linear time-series model with moving average terms. In particular, we consider the following network due to Elman (1990) (see Figure 2):

$$h_{i,t} = \Psi\left(\gamma_{i0} + \sum_{j=1}^{n} \gamma_{ij} x_{j,t} + \sum_{l=1}^{q} \delta_{il} h_{l,t-1}\right)$$

$$\equiv \psi_i(x_t, h_{t-1}, \theta), \qquad i = 1, \ldots, q$$

$$o_t = \Phi\left(\beta_0 + \sum_{i=1}^{q} \beta_i \psi_i(x_t, h_{t-1}, \theta)\right)$$

$$\equiv \phi_q(x_t, h_{t-1}, \theta)$$

(4)

where θ denotes the vector of parameters containing all β's, γ's, and δ's, and the subscript q of ϕ again signifies the number of hidden units. Here, the hidden-unit activations h_i feed back

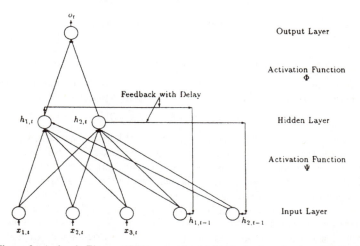

Figure 2. A simple Elman (1990) network with hidden-unit activations feedback

to the input layer with delay and serve to 'memorize' the past information (cf. equation (1)). From equation (4) we can write, by recursive substitution,

$$h_{i,t} = \psi_i(x_t, \psi(x_{t-1}, h_{t-2}, \dots, \theta), \theta) = \cdots = :r_i(x^t, \theta) \qquad i = 1, \dots, q \qquad (5)$$

where $x^t = (x_t, x_{t-1}, \dots, x_1)$, and ψ is vector-valued with ψ_i as its ith element. Hence, $h_{i,t}$ depends on x_t and its entire history. It follows that

$$o_t = \phi_q(x_t, h_{t-1}, \theta) =: g_q(x^t, \theta) \qquad (6)$$

is also a function of x_t and its history (cf. equation (2)). In view of equation (6), a recurrent network may capture more dynamic characteristics of y_t than does a feedforward network. In the L_2 context, a recurrent network may be interpreted as an approximation of $E(y_t | x^t)$. To ensure proper behaviour of the Elman (1990) network, Kuan and White (1994b) show that, aside from some regularity conditions on the data y and x and some smoothness conditions (such as continuous differentiability) on Φ and Ψ, the hidden unit activation function Ψ must also be a contraction mapping in h_{t-1}; otherwise, $h_{i,t}$ will approach its upper or lower bound very quickly when Ψ is a bounded function or will explode when Ψ is an unbounded function. Kuan *et al.* (1994) show that a sufficient condition assuring the contraction mapping property is $\delta_{il} < 4/q$, for all i, l.

3. BUILDING EMPIRICAL NETWORKS

In practice, there are basically two tasks in building neural networks: (i) unknown network parameters must be estimated, and (ii) a suitable network structure f_q or ϕ_q must be determined. We will discuss these two tasks in turn and propose a two-step procedure for constructing empirical neural networks.

3.1. Estimation methods

In view of equation (3), for a feedforward network f_q it is quite natural to estimate the parameters of interest θ_q^* which minimize mean squared approximation error, i.e.

$$\theta_q^* = \operatorname{argmin} E | E(y | x) - f_q(x, \theta) |^2$$

Observe that

$$E | y - f_q(x, \theta) |^2 = E | y - E(y | x) |^2 + E | E(y | x) - f_q(x, \theta) |^2 \qquad (7)$$

As $E(y | x)$ is the best L_2 predictor of y given x, the first term on the right-hand side of equation (7) cannot be minimized in L_2; hence θ_q^* is an MSE (mean squared error) minimizer:

$$\theta_q^* = \operatorname{argmin} E | y - f_q(x, \theta) |^2$$

where the function on the right-hand side is just the well-known least-squares criterion function. Practically, estimates of θ_q^* can be obtained using nonrecursive (off-line) or recursive (on-line) estimation methods. Econometricians are familiar with various nonrecursive, nonlinear least squares (NLS) optimization techniques. It is well known that NLS estimates are consistent for θ_q^* and asymptotically normally distributed under very general conditions. Recursive estimation methods include, e.g. the back-propagation (BP) algorithm of Rumelhart *et al* (1986) and the Newton algorithm of Kuan and White (1994a). Kuan and White (1994a) show that both the BP and Newton algorithms are root-t consistent for θ_q^* where t denotes the recursive step, but the Newton algorithm is statistically more efficient than the BP algorithm and is asymptotically equivalent to the NLS method. Although recursive estimates are not as efficient as NLS estimates in finite samples, they are useful when on-line information processing is important. Moreover, recursive methods can facilitate network selection, as discussed in the subsection below. White (1989) also suggests that one can perform recursive estimation up to certain time point and then apply a NLS technique to improve efficiency of estimates.

Similarly, the parameters of interest in a recurrent network ϕ_q are

$$\theta_q^* = \operatorname*{argmin}\ \lim_{t \to \infty} E\,|\,y_t - \phi_q(x_t, h_{t-1}, \theta)\,|^2$$

where limit is taken to accommodate the effects of network feedbacks h_{t-1} (Kuan and White, 1994b). The estimates of θ_q^* can also be obtained using nonrecursive or recursive methods. In view of equation (5) and (6), h_t and o_t depend on θ directly and also indirectly through the presence of lagged hidden-unit activations h_{t-1}. Thus, in calculating the derivatives of ϕ_q with respect to θ, parameter dependence of h_{t-1} must be taken into account to ensure proper search direction. Owing to this parameter-dependent structure and the constraints required for δ's (discussed in Section 2), NLS optimization techniques involving analytic derivatives are difficult to implement. Our experience shows that NLS estimation using numerical derivatives usually suffers the problem of a singular information matrix. Alternatively, one could use a recursive estimation method such as the 'recurrent Newton algorithm' of Kuan (1994), which is analogous to that of Kuan and White (1994a) for feedforward networks. This algorithm is also root-t consistent for θ_q^* (see e.g. Benveniste *et al.*, 1990). Kuan (1994) also shows that it is more efficient than the recurrent BP algorithm of Kuan *et al.* (1994). The recursive Newton algorithms for feedforward and recurrent networks used in our applications are described in the Appendix.

3.2. Complexity regularization criteria

The second task in practice is to determine a suitable network structure so that the unknown conditional mean function can be well approximated. As network functions Φ and Ψ can be chosen quite arbitrarily, this task amounts to determining network complexity, i.e. the number of explanatory variables and the number of hidden units. A very simple network may not be able to approximate the unknown conditional mean function well; an excessively complex network may over fit the data with little improvement in approximation accuracy. There is, however, no definite conclusion regarding how the complexity should be regularized. As neural network models are, by construction, some approximating functions, it is our opinion that the determination of network complexity is a model-selection problem. Thus, one possible criterion is the Schwarz (1978) Information Criterion (SIC). Note that selecting networks based on SIC is computationally demanding because NLS is required for estimating *every* possible network.

An alternative criterion to regularize network complexity is the 'Predictive Stochastic Complexity' (PSC) criterion due to Rissanen (1986a,b); see also Rissanen (1987). Given a function $m(x, \theta)$, where θ is a k-dimensional parameter vector, and a sample of T observations, PSC is computed as the average of squared, 'honest' prediction errors:

$$\frac{1}{T - k} \sum_{t = k + 1}^{T} (y_t - m(x_t, \hat{\theta}_t))^2 \tag{8}$$

where $\hat{\theta}_t$ is the predicted parameter obtained from the data up to time $t - 1$. The prediction error $y_t - m(x_t, \hat{\theta}_t)$ is 'honest' in the sense that no information at time t or beyond is used to calculate $\hat{\theta}_t$; in particular, the well-known recursive residual is a special case of honest prediction error. A model is selected if it has the smallest PSC within a class of models. If two models have the same PSC, the simpler one is selected. Clearly, the PSC criterion is based on *forward* validation, which is important in forecasting. Rissanen also shows that for encoding a sequence of numbers, the PSC criterion can determine the code with the shortest code length asymptotically. For a thorough discussion of the notion of stochastic complexity we refer to Rissanen (1989). Obviously, calculation of PSC is also computationally demanding if NLS is required to obtain θ_t for each t. Following the idea of Gerencsér and Rissanen (1992), we can compute θ_t using recursive estimation methods, which are more tractable computationally. Thus, recursive estimation methods are also useful for selecting appropriate network structures based on PSC.

3.3. Two-step procedure

In this paper we employ a two-step procedure to construct our empirical neural networks. We first choose the activation functions Ψ as the logistic function and Φ as the identity function in the networks equations (1) and (4). These choices are quite standard in the neural network literature. The dependent variables y are changes of log exchange rates, and for each exchange rate, networks explanatory variables x are own lagged dependent variables. The resulting networks are therefore nonlinear AR models. One could, of course, include other explanatory variables in networks to create nonlinear ARX models.

Specifically, our feedforward networks are of the form:

$$f_q(x_t, \theta) = \beta_0 + \sum_{i=1}^{q} \beta_i \left(\frac{1}{1 + \exp\left[-\left(\gamma_{i0} + \sum_{j=1}^{n} \gamma_{ij} y_{t-j} \right) \right]} \right)$$

and recurrent networks are:

$$\phi_q(x_t, \theta) = \beta_0 + \sum_{i=1}^{q} \beta_i \left(\frac{1}{1 + \exp\left[-\left(\gamma_{i0} + \sum_{j=1}^{n} \gamma_{ij} y_{t-j} + \sum_{l=1}^{g} \delta_{il} h_{l,t-1} \right) \right]} \right)$$

$$h_{i,t} = \frac{1}{1 + \exp\left[-\left(\gamma_{i0} + \sum_{j=1}^{n} \gamma_{ij} y_{t-j} + \sum_{l=1}^{g} \delta_{il} h_{l,t-1} \right) \right]}$$

The following two-step procedure is then used to determine the network structures and estimate their unknown parameters:

(1) Recursive estimation. A family of feedforward or recurrent networks with different n and q (the numbers of lagged dependent variables and hidden units) is estimated using the Newton algorithms (A1) or (A2) in the Appendix. For each network,
(a) Ten sets of initial parameters are generated randomly from $N(0,1)$, and the one that results in the lowest MSE is used as the initial values for recursive algorithms.
(b) We then let the Newton algorithms run through the data set once and compute the resulting PSC values.
Note that network structures are fixed during recursive estimation. After recursive estimation is complete, we select the three networks with the lowest PSC values and proceed to the second step.

(2) NLS estimation. The networks selected from the first step are estimated using a modification of the Levenberg–Marquardt algorithm (More, 1977). This algorithm is implemented using the FORTRAN subroutine LMDER in MINPACK distributed by Argonne National Laboratory.

(a) For each selected feedforward network, the final values of the Newton estimates from the first step are used as initial values for the NLS algorithm. The NLS estimates of β's and γ's are computed by minimizing

$$\frac{1}{T} \sum_{t=1}^{T} (y_t - f_q(x_t, \beta, \gamma))^2$$

(b) For each selected recurrent network, the NLS estimates of β's and γ's are computed by minimizing

$$\frac{1}{T} \sum_{t=1}^{T} (y_t - \phi_q(x_t, \bar{h}_{t-1}, \beta, \gamma, \delta))^2$$

where $\bar{h}_t = \psi(x_t, \bar{h}_{t-1}, \bar{\delta}, \bar{\gamma})$ is h_t evaluated at $\bar{\delta}$ and $\bar{\gamma}$, the final recursive estimates of δ and γ from the first step.

The first step in the proposed procedure implements a convenient network selection device based on recursive estimation results, in contrast with the White (1989) procedure. For feedforward networks, recursive estimation is needed to compute PSC, from which suitable networks can be selected; for recurrent networks, other than facilitating network selection, recursive estimation is crucial as NLS estimation is difficult to implement (Section 3.1). We use the Newton algorithms because they are statistically more efficient than the BP algorithm. We emphasize that for a feedforward network the first step is not needed when the desired network structure is known *a priori* or when other network-selection procedures are adopted. The second step in the proposed procedure performs NLS estimation to improve efficiency of parameter estimates. Note that for recurrent networks, fixing δ and h_{t-1} avoids troublesome constrained minimization. (Recall that δ's must be constrained suitably to ensure the desired contraction mapping property of h_t.) The resulting estimates are not full NLS estimates, and their convergence properties hold only conditional on $\bar{\delta}$ (see e.g., Kuan and Hornik, 1991).

4. EMPIRICAL RESULTS

In this paper five exchange rates against the US dollar, including the British pound (BP), the Canadian dollar (CD), the Deutsche mark (DM), the Japanese yen (JY), and the Swiss franc (SF), are investigated. The data are daily opening bid prices of the NY Foreign Exchange Market from 1 March 1980 to 28 January 1985, consisting of 1245 observations. All series except BP are US dollars per unit of foreign currency. This data set has also been used in Baillie and Bollerslev (1989). Let $S_{i,t}$ denote the ith exchange rate at time t, and $y_{i,t} = \log S_{i,t} - \log S_{i,t-1}$, $i = $ BP, CD, DM, JY, SF. By applying various unit-root tests, Baillie and Bollerslev (1989) find that $\log S_{i,t}$ are unit root processes without drift and that $y_{i,t}$ behave like a martingale difference sequence. We also estimated 36 ARMA models for $y_{i,t}$ from ARMA$(0,0)$ to ARMA$(5,5)$ and found that ARMA$(0,0)$ is the best model for all five series in terms of the SIC values. This is consistent with the results of Baillie and Bollerslev (1989). In what follows, we will abuse terminology and refer to ARMA$(0,0)$ as the random walk model.

Neural network models are constructed according to the two-step procedure described in

FORECASTING WITH NEURAL NETWORKS   355

Section 3. For each series, the network explanatory variables are lagged dependent variables; all variables are multiplied by 100 to reduce round-off errors. We have also constructed networks for each $y_{i,t}$ using lagged $y_{j,t}$, $j \ne i$, as additional explanatory variables, but the results are not particularly exciting. We therefore confine ourselves to networks of the present form which, as we have mentioned, are simply nonlinear AR models. In the first step, 30 feedforward and recurrent networks (with 1–6 lagged $y_{i,t}$ and 2–6 hidden units) are estimated using the recursive Newton algorithms, and the three networks with the best PSC values are selected.[1] In the second step, the selected networks are further 'smoothed' using the method of NLS. (We omit networks with one hidden unit because they are not practically interesting.) Ideally, we can construct a multiple-output network for all five series, analogous to a multivariate nonlinear regression model. A program implementing multiple-output networks is currently under development.

Table I. Out-of-sample RMSPE and sign predictions from selected networks: British pound

Net type	Test obs.	Selected network	Recursive result			NLS result			
			PSC	RMSPE	Sign	RMSPE	(Stat.)	Sign	(*p*-value)
FF	50	(1,2)	0·4355	0·5972[b]	64·0	0·6047[c]	(1·608)	62·0	(N/A)
		(1,4)	0·4358	0·6043[b]	72·0	0·6023[c]	(1·530)	58·0	(60·1)
		(2,2)	0·4365	0·6047[b]	72·0	0·6182	(0·905)	72·0	(N/A)
	100	(4,3)	0·4199	0·7718	59·0	0·7829[d]	(−1·699)	40·0	(97·8)
		(1,2)	0·4208	0·7437[b]	61·0	0·7405[b]	(1·970)	62·0	(11·2)
		(6,2)	0·4211	0·7508	62·0[c]	0·7475	(0·813)	61·0[b]	(1·2)
	150	(4,3)	0·4231	0·7174	56·6	0·7317[d]	(−1·866)	40·6	(99·0)
		(1,2)	0·4242	0·6971[b]	59·3	0·6942[a]	(2·536)	59·3	(15·7)
		(5,3)	0·4247	0·7022	62·0[b]	0·7090	(−0·075)	54·6	(50·5)
REC	50	(6,3)	0·4356	0·6104[c]	68·0	0·6405	(−0·701)	54·0	(97·1)
		(6,2)	0·4356	0·6065[b]	72·0	0·6173	(0·772)	50·0	(73·2)
		(1,3)	0·4357	0·6081[b]	72·0	0·6014[c]	(1·597)	74·0[c]	(6·4)
	100	(3,2)	0·4199	0·7683	58·0	0·7807	(−1·218)	54·0	(44·6)
		(1,2)	0·4210	0·7493[c]	61·0	0·7500[c]	(1·340)	61·0	(60·5)
		(2,3)	0·4212	0·7513	61·0	0·7560	(0·093)	52·0	(94·1)
	150	(3,2)	0·4237	0·7117	55·3	0·7213	(−0·937)	54·0	(41·0)
		(1,2)	0·4242	0·7016[b]	59·3	0·6953[a]	(2·328)	61·3[b]	(4·6)
		(6,2)	0·4248	0·7043	54·6	0·7270[d]	(−1·453)	54·0	(73·9)

Note: The selected networks are ordered from the best to the third best according to their PSC values. 'RMSPE' stands for the square root of out-of-sample MSPE; 'Sign' stands for the proportion of correct sign predictions in out-of-sample periods; 'Stat' is the Mizrach (1992) statistic; '*p*-value' is for the Henriksson and Merton (1981) test. If the forecasts are either all positive or all negative, the resulting *p*-value is listed as 'N/A'. Significance at 1%, 5%, and 10% is marked with superscripts a, b, and c, respectively; similarly, superscript d is used to indicate that a model is

---

[1] As we found in other simulations that huge prediction errors may occur in the very beginning of recursive estimation, we compute PSC according to equation (8) with k starting from $L + 65$, where L is the number of lagged dependent variables in the network, to get rid of beginning erratic prediction errors for all possible networks. This modification should not alter the asymptotic property of PSC.

C.-M. KUAN AND T. LIU

To evaluate the forecasting performance of different models of $y_{i,t}$, we reserve the last 50, 100, and 150 observations as out-of-sample testing periods and estimate models using 1194, 1144, and 1094 observations, respectively. These choices are arbitrary. The out-of-sample performances of network models are evaluated using two criteria: one based on sign predictions (i.e. forecasts of the direction of future price changes) and the other based on one-step-ahead MSPE. As sign predictions yield important information for financial decisions such as market timing, it is important to test whether they are of economic value in practice (see e.g., Levich, 1981; Merton, 1981; Henriksson and Merton, 1981). For this purpose, we apply the market timing test of Henriksson and Merton (1981), which is the uniformly most powerful test for market timing ability under their conditions. In this test, the number of correct forecasts has a hypergeometric distribution under the null of no market timing ability, and we use the IMSL subroutine HYPDF to compute the resulting p-values. We also apply a test proposed by Pesaran and Timmermann (1992) which is a Hausman-type of test designed to assess the performance of sign predictions. As the limiting distribution of this test is $N(0, 1)$, its one-sided critical values at 1%, 5%, and 10% levels are 2.33, 1.645, and 1.282, respectively. (We thank referees and the editor for these suggestions.) It is also typical in econometric applications to compare out-of-sample MSPE performance of a model relative to the random walk model. We therefore apply the MSPE-comparison test of Mizrach (1992) to evaluate statistical significance of network forecasts (cf. Diebold and Mariano, 1991). The limiting distribution of this test is also $N(0, 1)$; in our

Table II. Out-of-sample RMSPE and sign predictions from selected networks: Canadian dollars

Net type	Test obs.	Selected network	Recursive result			NLS result			
			PSC	RMSPE	Sign	RMSPE	(Stat.)	Sign	(p-value)
FF	50	(1,4)	0·6123	0·1372	54·0	0·1374	(0·361)	56·0	(N/A)
		(1,5)	0·6143	0·1374	54·0	0·1392	(−0·558)	56·0	(31·5)
		(1,3)	0·6165	0·1373	56·0	0·1373	(0·299)	54·0	(N/A)
	100	(1,4)	0·6212	0·1778	49·0	0·1770	(−0·293)	52·0	(71·0)
		(5,2)	0·6237	0·1817[d]	44·0	0·1875[d]	(−1·860)	52·0	(50·2)
		(2,2)	0·6244	0·1771	49·0	0·1756	(0·363)	53·0	(42·0)
	150	(1,4)	0·6214	0·2041	49·3	0·2038	(0·060)	52·0	(16·7)
		(2,2)	0·6242	0·2047	48·0	0·2036	(0·184)	50·0	(58·0)
		(1,2)	0·6242	0·2049	47·3	0·2040	(−0·050)	51·3	(34·5)
REC	50	(2,4)	0·6138	0·1367	56·0	0·1371	(0·500)	56·0	(N/A)
		(1,3)	0·6140	0·1365	56·0	0·1371	(0·602)	56·0	(N/A)
		(1,2)	0·6167	0·1372	56·0	0·1372	(0·711)	56·0	(N/A)
	100	(2,4)	0·6207	0·1762	52·0	0·1762	(0·218)	51·0	(63·7)
		(1,2)	0·6258	0·1761	52·0	0·1765	(0·095)	51·0	(84·6)
		(6,2)	0·6265	0·1770	49·0	0·1800	(−0·875)	50·0	(85·6)
	150	(1,4)	0·6227	0·2057[d]	48·6	0·2036	(0·223)	52·0	(16·7)
		(1,3)	0·6252	0·2042	50·0	0·2033	(0·429)	52·0	(23·6)
		(1,2)	0·6254	0·2039	50·0	0·2035	(0·347)	52·6	(14·2)

Note: PSC are the numbers in the table $\times 10^{-1}$.

computation, models with out-of-sample MSPE smaller than the random walk model have positive statistics. Out-of-sample forecasting results from recursive and NLS estimation are summarized in Tables I–V, where we use FF and REC to denote feedforward and recurrent networks and write a network with L lagged dependent variables and H hidden units as (L, H). We report only the Mizrach statistics and p-values for NLS results; complete tables including statistics and p-values for recursive results are available upon request. Note also that the Mizrach test is based on MSPE comparison, but our tables report the square root of MSPE (RMSPE).

We first observe that a wide variety of networks have been selected and that there is at least one common FF or REC network selected from three in-sample periods, except that for REC in BP and FF in JY the common networks are taken from the periods with 100 and 150 test observations. These common networks are:

BP: FF(1,2); REC(1,2).
CD: FF(1,4); REC(1,2).
DM: FF(2,2); REC(1,2).
JY: FF(6,2); REC(1,2).
SF: FF(2,2); REC(1,2) and REC(3,2).

Note that most of these common networks are not very complex; in particular, REC(1, 2) is the common recurrent network for all series. These results seem to suggest that there exists only mild nonlinearity in these series.

Table III. Out-of-sample RMSPE and sign predictions from selected networks: Deutsche marks

Net type	Test obs.	Selected network	Recursive result			NLS result			
			PSC	RMSPE	Sign	RMSPE	(Stat.)	Sign	(p-value)
FF	50	(2,2)	0·4990	0·4460[c]	62·0	0·4353	(0·973)	52·0	(72·0)
		(2,5)	0·5003	0·4431[b]	64·0	0·4407	(1·230)	64·0	(31·9)
		(5,2)	0·5006	0·4465[b]	60·0	0·4471	(0·943)	64·0	(27·4)
	100	(2,5)	0·4750	0·7726	61·0	0·8898	(−1·054)	58·0	(57·3)
		(2,2)	0·4766	0·7730	60·0	0·7785	(−0·024)	52·0	(57·9)
		(1,2)	0·4767	0·7875	59·0	0·7814	(−0·393)	53·0	(77·7)
	150	(2,2)	0·4819	0·7212	58·0	0·7307	(−0·464)	53·3	(62·5)
		(1,2)	0·4820	0·7322	56·6	0·7288	(−0·412)	52·6	(81·2)
		(5,2)	0·4827	0·7236	58·0	0·7303	(−0·385)	50·6	(33·0)
REC	50	(1,2)	0·4969	0·4479[c]	62·0	0·4488[c]	(1·569)	62·0	(N/A)
		(2,2)	0·4997	0·4455[b]	66·0	0·4481	(1·236)	50·0	(95·8)
		(1,3)	0·4999	0·4448[c]	66·0	0·4393[c]	(1·308)	60·0	(63·7)
	100	(1,2)	0·4734	0·7753	61·0	0·7780	(0·013)	57·0	(65·5)
		(3,2)	0·4755	0·7723	58·0	0·7731	(0·703)	59·0	(23·4)
		(2,3)	0·4769	0·7790	60·0	0·7682	(1·240)	59·0	(59·9)
	150	(1,2)	0·4787	0·7228	60·0	0·7214[c]	(1·504)	60·0	(N/A)
		(1,4)	0·4804	0·7249	60·0	0·7227	(0·322)	58·0	(44·0)
		(1,3)	0·4817	0·7215	59·3	0·7168	(0·874)	56·6	(41·9)

Table IV. Out-of-sample RMSPE and sign predictions from selected networks: Japanese yen

Net type	Test obs.	Selected network	Recursive result			NLS result			
			PSC	RMSPE	Sign	RMSPE	(Stat.)	Sign	(*p*-value)
FF	50	(1,6)	0·4489	0·3432[c]	64·0	0·3355[c]	(1·418)	60·0	(27·9)
		(2,6)	0·4538	0·3437[b]	64·0	0·3392	(0·895)	64·0[c]	(8·3)
		(5,2)	0·4608	0·3440[c]	56·0	0·3413	(0·629)	50·0	(61·3)
	100	(2,3)	0·4732	0·4149	50·0	0·4232	(−0·729)	49·0	(74·9)
		(6,2)	0·4742	0·4205	47·0	0·4335	(−1·062)	50·0	(50·3)
		(6,5)	0·4745	0·4242	52·0	0·4437[d]	(−1·348)	56·0	(16·5)
	150	(1,5)	0·4787	0·4788	58·0	0·4759	(1·059)	56·6	(11·8)
		(6,2)	0·4811	0·4793	52·6	0·4879	(−0·922)	54·0	(18·1)
		(6,3)	0·4811	0·4818	52·0	0·4866	(−0·671)	52·0	(45·2)
REC	50	(1,2)	0·4599	0·3417[c]	62·0	0·3441[b]	(1·983)	66·0[c]	(7·5)
		(1,3)	0·4609	0·3385[b]	66·0[c]	0·3426[c]	(1·633)	66·0[c]	(5·8)
		(5,4)	0·4614	0·3346[c]	64·0	0·3531	(−0·278)	60·0	(52·8)
	100	(1,3)	0·4645	0·4131[c]	61·0[a]	0·4140[b]	(1·687)	59·0[c]	(6·6)
		(1,2)	0·4705	0·4139[c]	60·0[b]	0·4142[c]	(1·547)	61·0[c]	(0·3)
		(6,3)	0·4713	0·4188	50·0	0·4243	(−1·041)	51·0	(50·6)
	150	(1,2)	0·4765	0·4785	57·3	0·4788	(0·435)	58·6[c]	(6·2)
		(6,3)	0·4772	0·4766	54·0	0·5021[d]	(−1·722)	50·6	(32·9)
		(6,2)	0·4773	0·4798	49·3	0·4916	(−1·240)	54·6	(33·0)

Our primary concern is whether selected network models have systematic, superior performance in out-of-sample testing periods. Some interesting NLS results are summarized below. Note that when models yield either all positive or all negative sign predictions, the Henriksson and Merton (1981) test cannot be computed, and their *p*-values are listed as 'N/A'.

(1) For the JY, Table IV shows that the common feedforward network does not perform well, and there is only one selected feedforward network has significant market timing ability. However, the common recurrent network, REC(1,2), has significant market timing ability in all three testing periods and has significant MSPE performance in the first two testing periods (with 50 and 100 observations). Note that REC(1,3), which is selected for the first two testing periods, is also significant in terms of both market timing ability and MSPE in these two periods.

(2) For the BP, it can be seen from Table I that the common feedforward network, FF(1, 2), does not have significant market timing ability, and that the common recurrent network, REC(1, 2), has significant market timing ability only in the last testing period. In terms of out-of-sample MSPE, FF(1, 2) and REC(1, 2) both perform significantly better than the random walk model in all periods (except that for the first testing period REC(1, 2) is not selected). Note that the market timing ability of FF(6, 2) is significant at the 5% level in the period with 100 observations, but it is not selected for other testing periods.

(3) For the SF, we find from Table V that common feedforward and recurrent networks do not have significant market timing ability. There is only one feedforward network, FF(3, 3),

Table V. Out-of-sample RMSPE and sign predictions from selected networks: Swiss franc

Net type	Test obs.	Selected network	Recursive result			NLS result			
			PSC	RMSPE	Sign	RMSPE	(Stat.)	Sign	(p-value)
FF	50	(3,3)	0·5745	0·4513[b]	60·0	0·4482[b]	(1·497)	66·0	(12·6)
		(2,5)	0·5752	0·4515[b]	66·0	0·4505[b]	(1·786)	62·0	(45·6)
		(2,2)	0·5757	0·4548[b]	62·0	0·4432[b]	(1·890)	66·0	(12·4)
	100	(3,3)	0·5718	0·6443	58·0	0·6471	(0·098)	59·0[c]	(10·0)
		(2,4)	0·5722	0·6498	55·0	0·6695	(−1·045)	53·0	(54·4)
		(2,2)	0·5732	0·6450	57·0	0·6469	(0·100)	54·0	(32·0)
	150	(2,5)	0·5782	0·6502	58·0	0·6683[d]	(−1·396)	56·6	(54·0)
		(2,2)	0·5795	0·6452	58·6	0·6490	(−0·092)	58·6	(21·4)
		(2,3)	0·5797	0·6428	57·3	0·6644[d]	(−1·330)	50·0	(57·3)
REC	50	(1,2)	0·5725	0·4513[b]	62·0	0·4552[b]	(2·227)	62·0	(N/A)
		(4,2)	0·5776	0·4565[b]	54·0	0·4494	(1·240)	62·0	(36·8)
		(3,2)	0·5791	0·4548[b]	62·0	0·4554[c]	(1·296)	64·0	(11·1)
	100	(1,2)	0·5698	0·6437	57·0	0·6437	(1·225)	57·0	(N/A)
		(3,2)	0·5723	0·6426	58·0	0·6461	(0·196)	48·0	(59·0)
		(4,2)	0·5743	0·6460	57·0	0·6472	(0·133)	55·0	(71·4)
	150	(1,2)	0·5796	0·6439	58·6	0·6501	(−0·367)	57·3	(42·4)
		(3,2)	0·5799	0·6453	56·6	0·6510	(−0·327)	55·3	(23·0)
		(1,3)	0·5817	0·6463	56·0	0·6610	(−0·941)	54·6	(71·3)

that has (marginally) significant market timing ability. In terms of MSPE, all three selected feedforward networks and two out of three selected recurrent networks are significant in the first testing period; they do not have similar performance in other testing periods, however.

(4) For the CD and DM, neither feedforward nor recurrent network has systematic good performance in all testing periods.

These results show that different network models perform differently in these series and that the PSC criterion is a quite sensible criterion to determine network structures. Although the CD and DM do not exhibit regularity that can be 'captured' by neural networks, we note that for the JY, the common recurrent networks perform well in terms of both market timing ability and MSPE, and that for the BP, the common feedforward and recurrent networks perform well in terms of MSPE. It is also interesting to note that for the BP and JY, most of networks with significant market timing ability also have significantly lower out-of-sample MSPE relative to the random walk model. This suggests that these two objectives need not be conflicting with each other. As our estimation methods are based on MSE minimization, which is not a loss function for sign predictions, it would be very interesting to construct estimation methods based on a suitable loss function and compare the resulting sign prediction results; this is beyond the scope of this paper, however.

We also observe from the tables that recursive results may be even better than the NLS results. In fact, for the BP, JY, and SF, recursive results that are significant usually agree with the NLS results. This indicates that the Newton algorithms for a sample of more than 1000 observations have quite satisfactory performance; some simulation results of the Newton algorithm can be found in Kuan (1994).

For the sake of comparison, we also evaluate out-of-sample performance of four commonly used ARMA models, including ARMA(1,0), (0,1), (1,1), and (2,2). The results are summarized in Table VI. Almost all ARMA models do not have significant market timing

Table VI. Out-of-sample RMSPE and sign predictions from ARMA models

Test obs.	ARMA model	BP RMSPE	BP Sign	CD RMSPE	CD Sign	DM RMSPE	DM Sign	JY RMSPE	JY Sign	SF RMSPE	SF Sign
	(0,0)	0·6232	48·2	0·1381	48·3	0·4581	46·5	0·3500	47·3	0·4644	46·8
	(1,0)	0·6239	60·0	0·1375^c	38·0	0·4580	46·0	0·3463	50·0	0·4651	52·0
50	(0,1)	0·6243	60·0	0·1374^c	46·0	0·4581	48·0	0·3467	50·0	0·4651	54·0
	(1,1)	0·6257	56·0	0·1373^c	46·0	0·4578	46·0	0·3461	52·0	0·4647	58·0^c
	(2,2)	0·6253	58·0	0·1377	44·0	0·4510	54·0	0·3467	50·0	0·4609	52·0
	(0,0)	0·7570	48·2	0·1766	48·1	0·7781	46·8	0·4171	47·1	0·6479	46·7
	(1,0)	0·7577	57·0^c	0·1773	39·0	0·7763	47·0	0·4133^c	55·0	0·6469	51·0
100	(0,1)	0·7578	59·0^c	0·1773	44·0	0·7765	48·0	0·4133^c	54·0	0·6470	51·0
	(1,1)	0·7580	56·0	0·1773	44·0	0·7764	47·0	0·4134^c	56·0	0·6468	54·0
	(2,2)	0·7625^d	48·0	0·1771	44·0	0·7747	55·0	0·4129^b	53·0	0·6473	53·0
	(0,0)	0·7082	48·4	0·2039	47·9	0·7262	47·0	0·4795	47·3	0·6481	47·1
	(1,0)	0·7087	54·0	0·2049^d	42·0	0·7248	49·3	0·4746^b	53·3	0·6484	47·3
150	(0,1)	0·7088	55·3	0·2049^d	45·3	0·7249	50·7	0·4746^b	52·7	0·6483	47·3
	(1,1)	0·7089	52·0	0·2049^d	45·3	0·7248	50·7	0·4748^b	55·3	0·6488	50·7
	(2,2)	0·7120^d	47·3	0·2049^d	44·0	0·7252	51·3	0·4744^b	54·0	0·6534	49·3

Note: For ARMA(0,0), 'Sign' is in-sample proportion of positive changes of log prices.

Table VII. The Pesaran and Timmermann (1992) test for sign predictions

Test obs.	Models for the BP FF(1,2)	REC(1,2)	ARMA(1,0)	ARMA(0,1)
50	62·0 (−1·95)	N/A	60·0 (−0·28)	60·0 (0·07)
100	62·0 (0·95)	61·0 (−1·10)	57·0 (0·73)	59·0 (1·36)^c
150	59·3 (0·79)	61·3 (1·48)^c	54·0 (0·37)	55·3 (0·89)

Test obs.	Models for the JY REC(1,2)	REC(1,3)	ARMA(1,0)	ARMA(1,1)
50	66·0 (1·94)^b	66·0 (2·21)^b	50·0 (0·30)	52·0 (0·60)
100	61·0 (2·99)^a	59·0 (1·81)^b	55·0 (1·08)	56·0 (1·27)
150	58·6 (1·81)^b	N/A	53·3 (0·97)	55·3 (1·45)^c

Note: The numbers in parentheses are the Pesaran and Timmermann (1992) statistic from NLS results. If a network was not selected for that testing period, it is listed as 'N/A'.

ability in these testing periods, except that ARMA$(1,0)$ and ARMA$(0,1)$ for the BP are significant in the period with 100 observations and ARMA$(1,1)$ for the SF is significant in the period with 50 observations. In terms of MSPE, all ARMA models for the JY have significant out-of-sample MSPE in testing periods with 100 and 150 observations, and three ARMA models for the CD have significant out-of-sample MSPE in the first testing period. Note that these significant ARMA models have almost identical MSPE.

We also apply the Pesaran and Timmermann (1992) test to evaluate sign predictions. To conserve space, we do not report all statistics here, but we summarize the results for some 'good' models discussed above in Table VII. For the BP, the test results for network models agree with those of the market timing test, but significance level is different. Note, however, that ARMA$(1,0)$ becomes insignificant in the second testing period under this test. For the JY, both REC$(1,2)$ and REC$(1,3)$ are still significant at the 5% level in all periods, whereas ARMA$(1,1)$ becomes significant at the 10% level in the last testing period. All the results we obtained suggest that REC$(1,2)$ and REC$(1,3)$ have systematic good performance for the JY series.

5. CONCLUSIONS

In this paper we propose a two-step procedure to estimate and select feedforward and recurrent networks and carefully evaluate the forecasting performance of selected networks in different out-of-sample periods. The forecasting results are mixed. We find networks with significant market timing ability (sign predictions) and/or significantly lower out-of-sample MSPE (relative to the random walk model) in only two out of the five series we evaluated. For other series, network models do not exhibit superior forecasting performance. Nevertheless, our results suggest that PSC is quite sensible in selecting networks and that the proposed two-step procedure may be used as a standard network construction procedure in other applications. Our results show that nonlinearity in exchange rates may be exploited to improve *both* point and sign forecasts, in contrast with the conclusion of Diebold and Nason (1990). Although some of the results reported here are quite encouraging, they provide only limited evidence supporting the usefulness of neural network models. We hope this paper will provoke more research in this direction in the future.

APPENDIX: RECURSIVE ESTIMATION METHODS—NEWTON ALGORITHMS

We describe recursive estimation methods for feedforward and recurrent networks. For feedforward networks we consider the following *stochastic Newton* algorithm:

$$\hat{\theta}_{t+1} = \hat{\theta}_t + \eta_t \hat{G}_t^{-1} \nabla f_q(x_t, \hat{\theta}_t)[y_t - f_q(x_t, \hat{\theta}_t)]$$
$$\hat{G}_{t+1} = \hat{G}_t + \eta_t [\nabla f_q(x_t, \hat{\theta}_t) \nabla f_q(x_t, \hat{\theta}_t)' - \hat{G}_t] \tag{A1}$$

where $\nabla f_q(x, \theta)$ is the (column) gradient vector of f_q with respect to θ, $\hat{G}_t$ is an estimated, approximate Newton direction matrix, and $\{\eta_t\}$ is a sequence of learning rates of order $1/t$. Here, $\nabla f_q(x, \theta)[y - f_q(x, \theta)]$ is the vector of the first-order derivatives of the squared-error loss: $[y - f_q(x, \theta)]^2$, and $\hat{G}_t$ is obtained by recursively updating the outer product of $\nabla f_q(x_t, \hat{\theta}_t)$. Thus, the algorithm (A1) performs a recursive Newton search in the parameter space. In practice, $\hat{\theta}_t$ is randomly initialized, and $\hat{G}_t$ is initialized using sI, where $s = 100/(\sum_t y_t^2/T)$ and I is the identity matrix. (The initial value for $\hat{G}_t$ is based on the suggestion of Ljung and Söderström (1983).) An algebraically equivalent form of (A1) which does not involve matrix inversion can be used to simplify computation; see Kuan and White (1994a) for more details.

We also note that if f is a linear function, the algorithm (A1) reduces to the well-known recursive least square algorithm.

A recurrent Newton algorithm analogous to (A1) is

$$
\begin{aligned}
\hat{e}_t &= y_t - \phi(x_t, \hat{h}_{t-1}, \hat{\theta}_t) \\
\nabla \hat{e}_t &= -\phi_\theta(x_t, \hat{h}_{t-1}, \hat{\theta}_t) - \hat{\Delta}_t \phi_h(x_t, \hat{h}_{t-1}, \hat{\theta}_t) \\
\hat{\theta}_{t+1} &= \hat{\theta}_t - \eta_t \hat{G}_t^{-1} \nabla \hat{e}_t \hat{e}_t \\
\hat{G}_{t+1} &= \hat{G}_t + \eta_t (\nabla \hat{e}_t \nabla \hat{e}_t' - \hat{G}_t)
\end{aligned}
\tag{A2}
$$

where ϕ_θ and ϕ_h are column vectors of the first-order derivatives of ϕ with respect to θ and h, respectively. Note that we have omitted the subscript q of ϕ for notational simplicity. In this algorithm, $\hat{\theta}_t$ and $\hat{G}_t$ are initialized as above, the ith $(i = 1, \ldots, q)$ hidden-unit activation is updated according to

$$
\hat{h}_{i,t} = \Psi\left(\hat{\gamma}_{i0,t} + \sum_{j=1}^{n} \hat{\gamma}_{ij,t} x_{j,t} + \sum_{l=1}^{q} \hat{\delta}_{il,t} \hat{h}_{l,t-1}\right) = \psi_i(x_t, \hat{h}_{t-1}, \hat{\theta}_t)
\tag{A3}
$$

with initial value $1/2$, and the jth $(j = 1, \ldots, q)$ column of $\hat{\Delta}_{t+1}$ is updated according to

$$
\hat{\Delta}_{j,t+1} = \psi_{j,\theta}(x_t, \hat{h}_{t-1}, \hat{\theta}_t) + \hat{\Delta}_t \psi_{j,h}(x_t, \hat{h}_{t-1}, \hat{\theta}_t)
\tag{A4}
$$

with initial values 0, where $\psi_{j,\theta}$ and $\psi_{j,h}$ are column vectors of the first-order derivatives of the jth hidden unit ψ_j with respect to θ and h, respectively. As Ψ is the logistic function in our application, it is bounded between 0 and 1. Setting the initial value of $h_{i,t}$ at $1/2$ is equivalent to assuming no knowledge of hidden units in the beginning. This algorithm is implemented with a truncation device to ensure $\hat{\delta}_{il} < 4/q$ for all i, l. More details of equation (A2) used in this study can be found in the Appendix of Kuan (1994).

Note that a recurrent network not depending on h_{t-1} is a feedforward network. In this case, the ϕ_h term is zero so that the updating equations of $\hat{\Delta}_t$ are not needed, and (A2) simply reduces to the standard Newton algorithm (A1).

ACKNOWLEDGEMENTS

We would like to thank Roger Koenker, Bill Maloney, Paul Newbold, four anonymous referees, and the editor for their invaluable suggestions and comments. We are most grateful to Richard Baillie for providing us with the data set and to Bruce Mizrach and Hal White for permitting us to access their programs. C.-M. Kuan also thanks the Research Board of the University of Illinois for research support. All remaining errors are ours. An early version of this paper (based on a different data set) was presented at the 1992 North American Winter Meeting of the Econometric Society in New Orleans, Louisiana.

REFERENCES

Baillie, R. T. and T. Bollerslev (1989), 'Common stochastic trends in a system of exchange rates', *Journal of Finance*, **44**, 167–181.
Baillie, R. T. and P. C. McMahon (1989), *The Foreign Exchange Market: Theory and Econometric Evidence*, Cambridge University Press, New York.
Barron, A. R. (1991), 'Universal approximation bounds for superpositions of a sigmoidal function', Technical Report No. 58, Department of Statistics, University of Illinois, Urbana-Champaign.

Benveniste, A., Métivier, M. and P. Priouret (1990), *Adaptive Algorithms and Stochastic Approximations*, Springer-Verlag, Berlin.

Chinn, M. D. (1991), 'Some linear and nonlinear thoughts on exchange rates', *Journal of International Money and Finance*, **10**, 214–230.

Cybenko, G. (1989), 'Approximations by superpositions of a sigmoidal function', *Mathematics of Control, Signals and Systems*, **2**, 303–314.

Diebold, F. X. and R. S. Mariano (1991), 'Comparing predictive accuracy I: An asymptotic test', Discussion Paper 52, Institute for Empirical Macroeconomics, Federal Reserve Bank of Minneapolis.

Diebold, F. X. and J. A. Nason (1990), 'Nonparametric exchange rate prediction?', *Journal of International Economics*, **28**, 315–332.

Elman, J. L. (1990), 'Finding structure in time', *Cognitive Science*, **14**, 179–211.

Engel, C. (1991), 'Can the Markov switching model forecast exchange rates?' Working Paper, University of Washington.

Engel, C. and J. Hamilton (1990), 'Long swings in the exchange rates: Are they in the data and do markets know it?' *American Economic Review*, **80**, 689–713.

Gerencsér, L. and J. Rissanen (1992), 'Asymptotics of predictive stochastic complexity', in D. Brillinger, P. Caines, J. Geweke, E. Parzen, M. Rosenblatt, and M. Taqqu (eds), *New Directions in Time Series Analysis*, Part 2, Springer-Verlag, New York.

Henriksson, R. D. and R. C. Merton (1981), 'On market timing and investment performance II: Statistical procedures for evaluating forecasting skills', *Journal of Business*, **54**, 513–533.

Hornik, K., Stinchcombe, M. and H. White (1989), 'Multi-layer feedforward networks are universal approximators', *Neural Networks*, **2**, 359–366.

Hsieh, D. A. (1989), 'Testing for nonlinear dependence in daily foreign exchange rates', *Journal of Business*, **62**, 329–368.

Kuan, C.-M. (1994), 'A recurrent Newton algorithm and its convergence property', *IEEE Transactions on Neural Networks*, forthcoming.

Kuan, C.-M. and K. Hornik (1991), 'Learning in a partially hard-wired recurrent network', *Neural Network World*, **1**, 39–45.

Kuan, C.-M., Hornik, K. and H. White (1994), 'A convergence result for learning in recurrent neural networks', *Neural Computation*, **6**, 620–640.

Kuan, C.-M. and H. White (1990), 'Predicting appliance ownership using logit, neural network, and regression tree models', BEBR Working Paper 90–1647, College of Commerce, University of Illinois, Urbana-Champaign.

Kuan, C.-M. and H. White (1994a), 'Artificial neural networks: An econometric perspective', *Econometric Reviews*, **13**, 1–91.

Kuan, C.-M. and H. White (1994b), 'Adaptive learning with nonlinear dynamics driven by dependent processes', *Econometrica*, forthcoming.

Levich, R. (1981), 'How to compare chance with forecasting expertise', *Euromoney*, August, 61–78.

Ljung, L. and T. Söderström (1983), *Theory and Practice of Recursive Identification*, MIT Press, Cambridge, MA.

Merton, R. C. (1981), 'On market timing and investment performance, I: An equilibrium theory of value for market forecasts', *Journal of Business*, **54**, 363–406.

Mizrach, B. (1992), 'Forecast comparison in L_2', Working paper, University of Pennsylvania.

More, J. (1977), 'The Levenberg–Marquardt algorithm, implementation and theory', in G. A. Watson (ed.), *Numerical Analysis*, Springer-Verlag, New York.

Pesaran, M. H. and A. Timmermann (1992), 'A simple nonparametric test of predictive performance', *Journal of Business and Economic Statistics*, **10**, 461–465.

Rissanen, J. (1986a), 'A predictive least-squares principle', *IMA Journal of Mathematical Control & Information*, **3**, 211–222.

Rissanen, J. (1986b), 'Stochastic complexity and modeling', *Annals of Statistics*, **14**, 1080–1100.

Rissanen, J. (1987), 'Stochastic complexity (with discussions)', *Journal of the Royal Statistical Society*, B, **49**, 223–239 and 252–265.

Rissanen, J. (1989), *Stochastic Complexity in Statistical Inquiry*, World Science Publishing Co., Singapore.

Rumelhart, D. E., Hinton, D. E. and R. J. Williams (1986), 'Learning internal representation by error propagation', in D. E. Rumelhart and J. L. McClelland (eds), *Parallel Distributed Processing: Exploration in the Microstructure of Cognition*, Vol. 1, 318–362, MIT Press, Cambridge, MA.

Schwarz, G. (1978), 'Estimating the dimension of a model', *Annals of Statistics*, **6**, 461–464.

Taylor, S. J. (1980), 'Conjectured models for trends in financial prices, tests and forecasts', *Journal of the Royal Statistical Society*, A, **143**, 338–362.

Taylor, S. J. (1982), 'Tests of the random walk hypothesis against a price trend hypothesis', *Journal of Financial and Quantitative Analysis*, **17**, 37–61.

White, H. (1988), 'Economic prediction using neural networks: The case of IBM Stock Prices', in *Proceedings of the IEEE Second International Conference on Neural Networks*, II, pp. 451–458, SOS Printing, San Diego.

White, H. (1989), 'Some asymptotic results for learning in single hidden-layer feedforward network models', *Journal of the American Statistical Association*, **84**, 1003–1013.

[12]

Journal of Business & Economic Statistics, January 1987, Vol. 5, No. 1

Time-Varying Parameters and the Out-of-Sample Forecasting Performance of Structural Exchange Rate Models

Christian C. P. Wolff

London Business School, Sussex Place, Regent's Park, London NW1 4SA, United Kingdom

Varying-parameter estimation techniques based on recursive application of the Kalman filter are used to improve the predictive performance of a class of monetary exchange rate models. I find that allowing estimated parameters to vary over time enhances the models' forecasting performance for the dollar–pound, dollar–mark, and dollar–yen exchange rates. Contrary to earlier results in the literature, ex-post forecasts for the dollar–mark rate compare favorably with those obtained from the naive random walk forecasting rule.

KEY WORDS: Exchange rate determination; Kalman filtering; Random walks; State–space models; Prediction; Forward exchange rates.

1. INTRODUCTION

This article deals with the out-of-sample forecasting performance of a class of empirical models of exchange rate determination. Although the literature has been flooded with in-sample studies of empirical exchange rate models since the breakdown of the Bretton Woods fixed-parity system in the early 1970s, systematic studies of the forecasting performance of structural or reduced-form models are relatively scarce.

Meese and Rogoff (1983a) studied the forecasting performance of several important monetary models. Although in-sample studies of these models usually show quite satisfactory fits, Meese and Rogoff's out-of-sample results were not very encouraging: the structural models failed to improve on the simple random walk forecasting rule, even though the models' forecasts were based on actual, realized values of future explanatory variables. A number of potential explanations for the unimpressive out-of-sample forecasting performance of the models have been offered in the literature (Isard 1983; Meese and Rogoff 1983a,b; Saidi 1983).

In this article I take up the possibility of parameter variation over time. The forecasting performance of a class of monetary exchange rate models is studied employing a methodology that allows for parameter variation. A number of different factors could lead to parameter instability. Some important ones are the following:

1. Instability in the conventional money demand functions that Meese and Rogoff (1983a) employed is an important potential explanation for the unimpressive out-of-sample forecasting performance of the structural

models. It should be noted that Meese and Rogoff performed joint tests of the out-of-sample validity of the exchange rate models *and* the money demand functions that they implicitly specified. It may well be that their rejections are, at least in part, due to inadequately specified money demand functions. In recent studies of the demand for money (Frankel 1982; Goldfeld 1976; Simpson and Porter 1980) instabilities in empirical money demand functions have been documented for the United States and for Germany. Money demand instabilities can be due to a number of factors, such as financial innovations (leading to improved money management techniques) and aggregation effects.

2. Another important potential source of parameter variation is the occurrence of changes in policy regimes (Lucas 1976).

3. Factors leading to changes in the long-run real exchange rate (such as changes in oil prices, global trade patterns, etc.) may lead to instability in the parameters of the class of structural exchange rate models that are studied in this article.

Following a suggestion by Meese and Rogoff (1983a), I will implement an empirical methodology based on recursive application of the Kalman filter in order to deal with parameter variation over time.

The presentation of the article is as follows: In Section 2 the basic structural models are described. As this is familiar ground, I will go through it as quickly as possible. Section 3 discusses the methodology that I employ, and in Section 4 the empirical results are presented for the basic models. As the basic models do not allow for changes in long-run real exchange rates, I augment these models in Section 5 with indicator variables for

88 Journal of Business & Economic Statistics, January 1987

equilibrium long-run real exchange rates. In Section 6 I compare the models' forecasting performance with the performance of an important benchmark, the forward exchange rate. Section 7 offers some concluding observations.

2. THE BASIC STRUCTURAL MODELS

The forecasting performance of two important structural (or quasi-reduced-form) models is studied in Section 4: the flexible-price monetary model (Bilson 1978, 1979; Frenkel 1976) and the sticky-price monetary model (Dornbusch 1976a; Frenkel 1979, 1981). Following Meese and Rogoff, I will refer to these as the Frenkel–Bilson and Dornbusch–Frankel models. For estimation purposes, the quasi-reduced-form equations of the Frenkel–Bilson and Dornbusch–Frankel models can be conveniently nested:

$$s = b_0 + b_1(m - m^*) + b_2(y - y^*)$$
$$+ b_3(i - i^*) + b_4(\pi - \pi^*) + u. \quad (1)$$

Here s is the natural logarithm of the spot exchange rate, defined as the price of a unit of foreign currency in terms of domestic currency; m and m^* are the logs of the domestic and foreign money supplies, respectively; y and y^* are the logs of domestic and foreign real income levels; i and i^* are the domestic and foreign nominal interest rates; and π and π^* are domestic and foreign long-run expected inflation rates. The b's in Equation (1) are parameters to be estimated, and u is a disturbance term. Unless I explicitly state otherwise, all variables are dated at time t. Both the Frenkel–Bilson and Dornbusch–Frankel models hypothesize that the exchange rate is homogeneous of degree 1 with respect to relative money supplies ($b_1 = 1$). The Frenkel–Bilson model, which assumes purchasing power parity (PPP), also posits the restrictions $b_2 < 0$, $b_3 > 0$, and $b_4 = 0$. The Dornbusch–Frankel model, which allows for short-run deviations from PPP due to prices that respond only gradually to excess demand, hypothesizes that $b_2 < 0$, $b_3 < 0$, and $b_4 > 0$.

The Frenkel–Bilson and Dornbusch–Frankel models represent an important class of empirically testable models of exchange rate determination. Extensive in-sample studies of the models' properties have appeared in the literature. These in-sample studies usually show quite satisfactory fits (see, e.g., Bilson 1978 and Frenkel 1979).

Predictive testing is an important aspect of econometric model building that is often neglected. In this article I focus on predictive testing in the context of varying-parameter versions of the monetary models. The empirical results of the article provide new evidence on the predictive performance of the models and indicate that a certain degree of parameter instability is present.

3. METHODOLOGY

3.1 The Statistical Model

To allow for parameter variation in Equation (1), assume that the natural logarithm of the spot exchange is generated by the following model [Eq. (2) is a representation of Eq. (1)]:

$$s(t) = x'(t) b(t) + u(t), \quad (2)$$
$$b(t + 1) = b(t) + v(t), \quad (3)$$

where $s(t)$ is the log of the spot exchange rate at time t, $x(t)$ is a $k \times 1$ vector of explanatory variables, $b(t)$ is a $k \times 1$ vector of time-varying coefficients, $u(t)$ is a scalar disturbance term, and $v(t)$ is a $k \times 1$ vector of disturbance terms. In addition, the following properties are assumed: (a) $Eu(t) = 0$, $\text{var}[u(t)] = R$ (R is a scalar); (b) $Ev(t) = 0$, $\text{var}[v(t)] = Q$ (Q is a $k \times k$ matrix); (c) $[u(t)]$ is an independent sequence; (d) $[v(t)]$ is an independent sequence; (e) $u(t)$ and $v(r)$ are independently distributed for all r, t; (f) the $x(t)$ are fixed, known regressors; and (g) $[u(t), v(t)]$ and $b(r)$ are independent for all $r \leq t$.

The system (2)–(3) is easily recognized as a state–space model, which can be recursively estimated by means of the Kalman filter (Kalman 1960) (see Sec. 3.2). Equation (2) is the observation equation, and (3) is the state transition equation. In Equation (3), it is assumed that the parameter vector $b(t)$ follows a multivariate random walk. Note that the elements of $b(t)$ are allowed to interact through the off-diagonal elements of the dispersion matrix Q. Clearly, many alternative stochastic processes could be imposed on the vector $b(t)$. My choice of the multivariate random walk is inspired by the empirical regularity that the natural logarithm of the spot exchange rate follows approximately a random walk (Mussa 1979).

It is interesting to derive the final time series process for the log of the spot exchange rate, $s(t)$, that is implied by Equations (2) and (3). If the elements of the vector of explanatory variables $x(t)$ are constant, nonstochastic numbers and the disturbance term $u(t)$ is identically equal to 0, then the implied times series process for $s(t)$ is exactly a random walk. If $x(t)$ is allowed to be stochastic, then a nonlinearity is introduced.

Throughout this article, I will use natural logarithms of exchange rates rather than their simple levels, as in Meese and Rogoff's (1983a,b) work. By comparing predictors on the basis of their ability to predict the logarithm of the spot exchange rate, I circumvent any problems arising from Jensen's inequality. Because of Jensen's inequality, the best predictor of the level of the spot exchange rate expressed as unit of currency i per unit of currency j may not be the best predictor of the level of the spot exchange rate expressed as units of currency j per unit of currency i. Because I consider logarithms of spot exchange rates, the summary statistics on the models' forecasting performance that I will present are unit-free (they are approximately in percentage terms) and comparable across currencies.

3.2 The Kalman Filter

Assume that the error terms $u(t)$ and $v(t)$ are normally distributed and that the vector $b(t)$ has a prior distribution that is normal with mean $b(0 \mid 0)$ and covariance matrix $\Sigma(0 \mid 0)$. At every time t, after the history of the process $S(t) = [s(t), s(t - 1), s(t - 2), \ldots, s(1)]$ has been observed, we want to revise the prior distribution of the unknown state vector $b(t)$. The Kalman filter algorithm allows us, given knowledge of R, Q, $b(0 \mid 0)$, and $\Sigma(0 \mid 0)$, to compute recursively the posterior mean and covariance matrix for each subsequent period. Note that I assume that the data do not go back in time forever but start at time $t = 1$.

Denote the conditional distribution of $b(t)$ given $S(t)$ by $p[b(t) \mid S(t)]$. Given my normality assumptions, $p[b(t) \mid S(t)]$ and $p[b(t + 1) \mid S(t + 1)]$ are also normal and completely characterized by their first two moments. If I denote the mean and covariance matrix of $p[b(t) \mid S(t)]$ by $b(t \mid t)$ and $\Sigma(t \mid t)$, respectively, and those of $p[b(t + 1) \mid S(t)]$ by $b(t + 1 \mid t)$ and $\Sigma(t + 1 \mid t)$, the Kalman filter recursions for $t = 0, 1, 2, \ldots$ are given by Equations (4)–(8) (see Abraham and Ledolter 1983; Anderson and Moore 1979):

$$b(t + 1 \mid t) = b(t \mid t), \tag{4}$$

$$\Sigma(t + 1 \mid t) = \Sigma(t \mid t) + Q, \tag{5}$$

$$b(t + 1 \mid t + 1) = b(t + 1 \mid t) + k(t + 1)[s(t + 1) \\ - x'(t + 1)b(t + 1 \mid t)], \tag{6}$$

$$\Sigma(t + 1 \mid t + 1) = \Sigma(t + 1 \mid t) \\ - k(t + 1)x'(t + 1)\Sigma(t + 1 \mid t), \tag{7}$$

where

$$k(t + 1) = [x'(t + 1)\Sigma(t + 1 \mid t)x(t + 1) + R]^{-1} \\ \times \Sigma(t + 1 \mid t)x(t + 1). \tag{8}$$

Without the normality assumptions, the preceding results hold for best linear unbiased predictions rather than for conditional expectations. The n-step-ahead forecast of $s(t + n)$, $s(t + n \mid t)$, is given by

$$s(t + n \mid t) = x'(t + n)b(t + n \mid t) \\ = x'(t + n)b(t \mid t). \tag{9}$$

The actual parameter estimates obtained can differ from their theoretical values for a number of reasons (see Wolff 1985). I will limit the discussion here to the problem of simultaneous equations bias. Application of the Kalman filter assumes that the explanatory variables are nonstochastic. In reality, however, I expect the explanatory variables to be stochastic and endogenous. Thus the parameter estimates are likely to be affected by simultaneous equations bias. This is unfortunate, but given the current state of knowledge it is not possible to deal with parameter variation and simultaneous equations considerations at the same time.

Given the presence of this problem, it is perhaps wise to consider my forecasting results as the outcome of an experiment with a flexible forecasting methodology rather than as a strict test of the models.

4. THE EMPIRICAL RESULTS

In this section the forecasting results of my varying-parameters model are presented. I study the same set of exchange rates as Meese and Rogoff (1983a): the U.S. dollar–German mark, U.S. dollar–Japanese yen, and U.S. dollar–British pound spot exchange rates. My monthly data set covers the period from March 1973, the beginning of the floating exchange rate period, through April 1984. The data are drawn from International Monetary Fund and Organization for Economic Cooperation and Development publications and are described in detail in the Appendix.

Following Meese and Rogoff (1983a,b) both structural models are first estimated for the period March 1973–June 1981. Initially, the models are estimated using data through the first forecasting period, November 1976, and forecasts are generated at horizons of 1, 3, 6, 12, and 24 months. Then December 1976 data are added to the sample, the parameters are updated, and new forecasts are generated. This recursive process continues until forecasts are generated using June 1981 data. Also following Meese and Rogoff, the forecasts of the structural models are based on actual, realized values of future explanatory variables (i.e., an ex-post forecasting experiment is performed).

Forecasting accuracy is measured by four summary statistics that are based on standard symmetric loss functions: the mean error (ME), the mean absolute error (MAE), the root mean squared error (RMSE), and the U statistic. The ME, MAE, and RMSE are defined as follows:

$$ME = \sum_{j=0}^{N-1} [A(t + j + k) - F(t + j + k)]/N,$$

$$MAE = \sum_{j=0}^{N-1} |A(t + j + k) - F(t + j + k)|/N,$$

$$RMSE = \left[\sum_{j=0}^{N-1} [A(t + j + k) \\ - F(t + j + k)]^2/N \right]^{.5},$$

where $k = 1, 3, 6, 12, 24$ denotes the forecast step; N denotes the total number of forecasts in the projection for which the actual value of the exchange rate, $A(t)$, is known; and $F(t)$ denotes the forecast value. Theil's

90   Journal of Business & Economic Statistics, January 1987

U statistic is the ratio of the RMSE to the RMSE of the naive random walk forecast. Because I am looking at the logarithm of the exchange rate, the ME, MAE, and RMSE are unit-free (they are approximately in percentage terms) and comparable across currencies.

The system (2)–(3) is estimated for both the Frenkel–Bilson and Dornbusch–Frankel models. No restrictions are imposed on the parameters, except that domestic and foreign variables enter (2) in differential form. Ideally, we would want to obtain fully efficient maximum likelihood estimates of R and Q along the lines of the procedures described in Harvey (1981). These estimates could then be used as inputs to the Kalman filter. In the case at hand, however, such an approach would be particularly unwieldy. For instance, estimating Q and R for the dynamic version of the Dornbusch–Frankel model that is proposed later in the article would introduce a nonlinear optimization problem involving 56 parameters. In a similar context, Garbade (1977) set all off-diagonal elements of Q equal to 0 in order to estimate only its diagonal elements. Although such a procedure, of course, dramatically reduces the number of parameters to be estimated, I choose not to follow this route because potentially important interactions between individual coefficients would be precluded arbitrarily. In the light of these considerations, I implement a procedure that can be viewed as a practical approximation to a full maximum likelihood setup. Before going into the details of my procedure, however, I will briefly discuss the "starting value" problem and ways of solving it.

Since I specified a nonstationary process (a vector random walk) for the parameter vector $b(t)$, starting values for the Kalman filter are not automatically available in the unconditional mean and covariance matrix of the parameter vector. Several methods of solving the starting value problem in this context are discussed in the literature. The filter can be initialized by using the first k observations to construct starting values, or a "diffuse prior" can be employed (see Harvey 1981). The latter involves setting $\Sigma(0 \mid 0) = \kappa I$, where κ is a large but finite scalar and I is the unit matrix. (Ansley and Kohn 1983 proposed more sophisticated ways to implement diffuse priors.) It is not clear which of the two methods is preferable. I have experimented with both initialization procedures, and the results were similar. Subsequently, I will report the results for starting values that are constructed from a set of initial observations.

The first step of my procedure consists of estimating Equation (1) for the period March 1973–March 1975 (25 observations) by ordinary least squares (OLS). The estimated parameter vector and its estimated covariance matrix were used as prior mean $b(0 \mid 0)$ and prior covariance matrix $\Sigma(0 \mid 0)$, respectively. The Kalman filter was then started for April 1975 and run for 20 periods before forecasts were generated. The squared standard error of estimate from the regression was used

as input for R. For the dispersion matrix Q, I consider a range of matrices that are proportional to the prior covariance matrix; that is, I specify $Q = \gamma \, \Sigma(0 \mid 0)$, where γ is a scalar. Values of .0 (which corresponds to no parameter variation), .01, .05, .10, and .25 are tried for γ.

Preliminary estimation of the state–space versions of the Frenkel–Bilson and Dornbusch–Frankel models indicates that residual first-order serial correlation is present in the error term $u(t)$. For the case of $\gamma = .0$, for instance, estimation of the Frenkel–Bilson (Dornbusch–Frankel) model results in Durbin–Watson statistics of .332 (.408) for the dollar–mark exchange rate, .304 (.257) for the dollar–yen rate, and .079 (.085) for the dollar–sterling rate. The usual approach in the literature to tackle this problem is to impose a first-order autoregressive error term on the model (see, e.g., Frankel 1979; Meese and Rogoff 1983a). Bearing in mind, however, the discussion by Hendry and Mizon (1978), who argued convincingly that this procedure may impose invalid restrictions on more general dynamic models with lagged variables, I do not arbitrarily impose a first-order autoregressive process on the error term $u(t)$. Instead I begin by considering a dynamic version of Equation (2):

$$s(t) = \alpha s(t - 1) + \beta' x(t) + \delta' x(t - 1) + \varepsilon(t),$$

$$(10)$$

where α is a scalar parameter, β and δ are vectors of parameters, and $\varepsilon(t)$ is a random error term with 0 mean and constant variance. Equation (10) will only reduce to the equivalent of (1) augmented with a first-order autoregressive process for the error term $u(t)$ if the restriction $\delta = -\alpha\beta$ is valid (see Hendry and Mizon 1978). If I define the vectors $z'(t) \equiv [s(t - 1), x'(t), x'(t - 1)]$ and $c' \equiv [\alpha, \beta', \delta']$ and if I again specify my multivariate random walk process for the parameters, I obtain the following two-equation model:

$$s(t) = z'(t) c(t) + \varepsilon(t), \qquad (11)$$

$$c(t + 1) = c(t) + \eta(t), \qquad (12)$$

where $\eta(t)$ is a vector of random disturbance terms with 0 mean and a constant dispersion matrix. If I assume that appropriately modified versions of previously mentioned assumptions (a)–(g) hold in the present context, Equations (11) and (12) are in state–space form, so the Kalman filter can again be used for recursive estimation and prediction. For forecasts at horizon n ($n > 1$), I employ the chain rule of forecasting to deal with the presence of the lagged exchange rate $s(t + n - 1)$ as an element of the vector of explanatory variables $z(t + n)$. The algorithm is started and predictions are generated as explained previously, the only difference being that one observation is lost for the estimation of the regression equation that I use to obtain a prior mean and covariance matrix for the state vector $c(t)$ (because of the dynamic specification of the model). Again, no restrictions are imposed on the parameters, except that domestic and foreign variables enter Equation (11) in differential form. Scaled-down versions of the prior covariance matrix of $c(t)$ are again used for the dispersion matrix that is associated with Equation (12), and the same values for the scalar γ are tried.

The model specification in Equations (11) and (12) solves the problem of residual first-order autocorrelation that was encountered previously. For the case of $\gamma = .0$, for instance, estimation of the dynamic version of the Frenkel–Bilson (Dornbusch–Frankel) model results in Durbin's (1970) h statistics of $-.061$ (.234) for the dollar–mark rate, 1.240 (1.202) for the dollar–yen rate, and .639 (.429) for the dollar–sterling rate. The values of these statistics are statistically insignificant at conventional levels. (I employ Durbin's h statistic in this context rather than the Durbin–Watson statistic because, in the presence of a lagged dependent variable, the latter is likely to have reduced power and is biased toward 2. See Durbin 1970.) The fitted models for the case of the dollar–mark exchange rate are presented in Table 1.

The model in Equations (11) and (12) combines a traditional dynamic model with lagged variables and a random-walk parameter model. It will be seen later that allowing for parameter variation leads to an improved forecasting performance relative to the traditional dynamic model without parameter variation. It is worthwhile to ask why this is the case or why I would expect this to be the case. In the introduction to this article several potential causes of parameter instability in the context of the monetary models were mentioned. I will consider each of the explanations in turn.

Table 1. *Estimated Dynamic Exchange Rate Equations for the Dollar–Mark Rate ($\gamma = .0$)*

	Frenkel–Bilson model	Dornbusch–Frankel model
Constant	$-.060$	$-.008$
	(.034)	(.045)
s_{-1}	.928	.875
	(.030)	(.043)
$(m - m^*)$	$-.009$	$-.006$
	(.100)	(.100)
$(m - m^*)_{-1}$	.196	.199
	(.100)	(.099)
$(y - y^*)$	.092	.082
	(.042)	(.042)
$(y - y^*)_{-1}$	$-.098$	$-.098$
	(.042)	(.042)
$(i - i^*)$	.004	.004
	(.002)	(.002)
$(i - i^*)_{-1}$	$-.001$	$-.001$
	(.002)	(.002)
$(\pi - \pi^*)$	—	$-.060$
		(.068)
$(\pi - \pi^*)_{-1}$	—	.021
		(.068)
R^2	.943	.944
SEE*	.032	.032
Durbin h	$-.061$	.234

NOTE: Standard errors are reported in parentheses.
* SEE = standard error of estimate.

In an influential paper, Lucas (1976) argued convincingly that changes in government economic policies will systematically alter the structure of econometric models in general. In this context varying-parameter models can play a useful role in tracking parameter changes over time and can help improve models' forecasting performance.

Here it is important to realize that formulations of the monetary models based on Equation (1) use the conventional Cagan (1956) functional form for the demand for money (see, e.g., Bilson 1978). If money demand functions of this type are not stable, as the evidence presented in the studies that were referenced in the introduction indicates, observed parameter variation for the monetary models may well be linked to money demand instabilities.

The Dornbusch–Frankel model does not allow for changes in long-run real exchange rates (or deviations from purchasing power parity) and the Frenkel–Bilson model does not allow for any changes in real rates. If real rates do change over time (as has clearly been the case in the period being studied) observed parameter variation for these models may also be due to these real rate movements.

I will now turn to the results of my forecasting experiments. As I move from $\gamma = .0$ to $\gamma = .01$, mean squared prediction errors fall uniformly (often substantially) for both structural models, for all three exchange rates, and for all prediction horizons. Allowing for parameter variation thus indeed enhances the models' forecasting performance. Increasing the value of γ beyond .01 affects the prediction results somewhat but does not lead to a systematic improvement or deterioration in the overall results. Summary statistics for $\gamma = .01$ are presented in Tables 2 and 3 (RMSE's and U statistics for $\gamma = .0$ are given for comparison).

It is interesting to look at the U statistics that are reported in Tables 2 and 3. U statistics are easily interpreted: If $U < 1$, the model performs better than the simple random walk forecast, and if $U > 1$, the random walk outperforms the model. The U statistics differ substantially across individual exchange rates. It is interesting and contrary to Meese and Rogoff's findings that both structural models for the dollar–mark exchange rate outperform the random walk model in a number of cases at horizons within 12 months (this result is obtained for all positive values of γ that we tried). The Dornbusch–Frankel model even outperforms the random walk forecasts at all horizons. It should be stressed that this observation depends on our choice of the value .01 for γ. This choice is essentially in-sample. As will be seen in what follows, however, the results for the dollar–mark rate are supported and even strengthened by the hold-out part of the sample (which was not consulted in choosing an appropriate value for γ).

The hold-out part of the sample consists of observations from July 1981 through April 1984 that have

92   Journal of Business & Economic Statistics, January 1987

Table 2. *Summary Statistics on the Forecasting Performance of the State–Space Version of the Frenkel–Bilson Model*

Horizon (months)	ME	MAE	RMSE	U statistic	N
			Dollar–Mark		
1	.44	2.62	3.65 (3.76)	1.00 (1.04)	55
3	1.48	4.83	5.73 (6.38)	.98 (1.09)	53
6	3.18	7.56	8.65 (10.13)	.97 (1.13)	50
12	7.12	11.60	12.82 (15.73)	.98 (1.20)	44
24	13.61	17.34	19.43 (23.76)	1.02 (1.25)	32
			Dollar–Yen		
1	.18	2.84	3.97 (4.00)	1.07 (1.08)	55
3	.76	6.45	7.87 (8.46)	1.15 (1.23)	53
6	2.54	12.38	15.41 (17.50)	1.34 (1.53)	50
12	5.08	22.51	26.40 (36.45)	1.43 (1.97)	44
24	.14	21.25	27.88 (84.81)	1.35 (4.67)	32
			Dollar–Pound		
1	.38	2.69	3.45 (3.68)	1.08 (1.15)	55
3	1.53	5.34	6.37 (7.35)	1.20 (1.38)	53
6	4.34	7.88	9.32 (11.77)	1.31 (1.65)	50
12	10.97	12.78	14.49 (19.84)	1.42 (1.94)	44
24	24.57	26.10	29.06 (36.53)	1.62 (2.03)	32

NOTE: Numbers in parentheses give the results for $\gamma = .0$ for comparison. Period—November 1976–June 1981 ($\gamma = .01$).

become available since Meese and Rogoff's (1983a) study. When the new data are combined with the original sample, 34 additional observations become available for the calculation of our summary statistics on the basis of the forecasting experiment that was described previously. The updated results corresponding to those in Tables 2 and 3 are presented in Tables 4 and 5.

Again the structural models are not consistently outperformed by random walks as earlier research suggests. For the dollar–mark exchange rate, both the Frenkel–Bilson and Dornbusch–Frankel models beat the random walk at all horizons. The opposite is true for the dollar–pound and dollar–yen exchange rates. The structural models' forecasts for the dollar–yen rate at longer horizons are very poor indeed compared with the results for the random walk. The mean errors are small in magnitude relative to the MAE's, indicating that the structural models did not systematically overpredict or underpredict over the course of the extended sample.

There are two ways of interpreting these results. On the one hand, the dollar–mark case may suggest that

Table 3. *Summary Statistics on the Forecasting Performance of the State–Space Version of the Dornbusch–Frankel Model*

Horizon (months)	ME	MAE	RMSE	U statistic	N
			Dollar–Mark		
1	.47	2.52	3.58 (3.66)	.99 (1.01)	55
3	1.56	4.53	5.46 (6.09)	.93 (1.04)	53
6	3.35	7.17	8.13 (9.60)	.91 (1.07)	50
12	7.27	11.03	12.09 (14.80)	.92 (1.13)	44
24	13.96	16.76	18.72 (22.27)	.99 (1.17)	32
			Dollar–Yen		
1	.18	2.80	3.99 (4.02)	1.07 (1.08)	55
3	.69	6.38	7.79 (8.48)	1.13 (1.23)	53
6	2.32	12.24	15.04 (17.33)	1.31 (1.51)	50
12	4.52	21.37	25.11 (34.06)	1.36 (1.84)	44
24	.30	17.80	24.44 (66.01)	1.53 (3.63)	32
			Dollar–Pound		
1	.39	2.68	3.52 (3.57)	1.10 (1.12)	55
3	1.55	5.55	6.72 (7.03)	1.26 (1.32)	53
6	4.31	8.17	9.74 (11.03)	1.37 (1.55)	50
12	10.85	12.93	14.56 (18.86)	1.42 (1.85)	44
24	24.30	25.73	28.56 (34.66)	1.59 (1.93)	32

NOTE: Numbers in parentheses give the results for $\gamma = .0$ for comparison. Period—November 1976–June 1981 ($\gamma = .01$).

Table 4.   Summary Statistics on the Forecasting Performance of the State–Space Version of the Frenkel–Bilson Model

Horizon (months)	ME	MAE	RMSE	U statistic	N
			Dollar–Mark		
1	.30	2.42	3.30	.98	89
3	.92	4.40	5.26	.95	87
6	1.57	5.94	7.19	.89	84
12	2.70	8.42	10.47	.82	78
24	3.04	12.13	14.94	.72	66
36	.24	13.89	16.85	.63	54
			Dollar–Yen		
1	.30	2.78	3.87	1.05	89
3	.90	6.11	7.75	1.18	87
6	1.76	11.40	14.26	1.39	84
12	2.97	19.54	23.54	1.55	78
24	− .99	21.60	30.36	2.05	66
36	− 4.74	22.03	39.67	2.82	54
			Dollar–Pound		
1	.13	2.59	3.39	1.08	89
3	.41	5.28	6.39	1.17	87
6	.64	7.90	9.63	1.18	84
12	1.06	13.34	15.16	1.14	78
24	− .79	25.35	27.78	1.19	66
36	− 3.69	32.03	35.90	1.18	54

NOTE: Period—November 1976–April 1984 (γ = .01).

the class of structural models studied may be of more value than Meese and Rogoff's results indicate. On the other hand, the results may be interpreted as a confirmation of Meese and Rogoff's dim assessment of the models, since the overall performance of the structural models remains quite unimpressive (the average U statistic reported in Tables 4 and 5 is about 1.17) despite the fact that I employ an estimation technique that al-

lows for parameter variation over time. I tend to favor the latter interpretation.

I have studied the time series of coefficients that result from estimation of the structural models (with γ = .01). (Efficient coefficient estimates were obtained by applying the fixed interval smoothing algorithm, which is described in, e.g., Harvey 1981.) Although considerable parameter variation is observed, coefficients do

Table 5.   Summary Statistics on the Forecasting Performance of the State–Space Version of the Dornbusch–Frankel Model

Horizon (months)	ME	MAE	RMSE	U statistic	N
			Dollar–Mark		
1	.43	2.40	3.28	.97	89
3	1.31	4.29	5.16	.93	87
6	2.43	6.09	7.04	.87	84
12	4.44	8.28	9.94	.78	78
24	6.17	11.50	14.16	.68	66
36	2.43	11.55	15.17	.57	54
			Dollar–Yen		
1	.19	2.74	3.85	1.04	89
3	.55	5.82	7.48	1.14	87
6	1.09	10.64	13.45	1.31	84
12	1.90	17.28	21.33	1.41	78
24	− 1.31	15.83	22.68	1.53	66
36	− 2.54	16.26	25.07	1.78	54
			Dollar–Pound		
1	.16	2.57	3.46	1.11	89
3	.54	5.44	6.64	1.21	87
6	.82	8.05	9.78	1.20	84
12	1.10	13.33	15.22	1.14	78
24	− .73	24.99	27.40	1.18	66
36	− 3.92	31.65	35.63	1.18	54

NOTE.   Period—November 1976–April 1984 (γ = .01).

94   Journal of Business & Economic Statistics, January 1987

Table 6. *The Dispersion Matrix Q for the State–Space Version of the Dornbusch–Frankel Model in the Case of the Dollar–Mark Exchange Rate ($\gamma = .01$)*

.101 E-02									
.255 E-03	.296 E-03								
−.487 E-03	.538 E-04	.180 E-02							
−.584 E-03	−.256 E-04	−.101 E-02	.175 E-02						
.284 E-04	−.278 E-04	−.303 E-03	.222 E-03	.258 E-03					
.462 E-04	.135 E-04	.232 E-03	−.278 E-03	−.131 E-03	.280 E-03				
.328 E-05	−.892 E-06	.294 E-05	−.722 E-05	−.556 E-06	.521 E-06	.263 E-06			
.525 E-06	−.110 E-05	.344 E-05	−.410 E-05	.261 E-06	.516 E-07	.646 E-07	.247 E-06		
.556 E-04	.130 E-04	−.698 E-04	−.865 E-05	−.260 E-04	−.644 E-04	.858 E-08	−.618 E-06	.331 E-03	
−.166 E-03	−.254 E-04	.824 E-04	.107 E-03	.291 E-04	.539 E-04	−.240 E-05	−.149 E-05	−.302 E-03	.344 E-03

not exhibit definite trends or swings that allow us to link the observed variation conclusively to one or more of the potential sources of parameter variation discussed previously. The fact that it is difficult to "unscramble" and attribute observed parameter variation is likely to be the result of many different factors operating simultaneously to change parameter values over the course of the time interval studied. To illustrate the degree of parameter variation that is allowed for in the estimation procedure, the dispersion matrix Q for the state–space version of the Dornbusch–Frankel model in the case of the dollar–mark rate is presented in Table 6. Note that off-diagonal elements are sizable in a number of cases, allowing for considerable interaction between individual coefficients. This is also the case for the Q matrices that are employed for the other currencies and for the state–space versions of the Frenkel–Bilson model.

5. INCORPORATING RELATIVE-PRICE VARIABLES INTO THE STATE–SPACE MODELS

The exchange rate models whose forecasting performance was studied in Section 4 did not allow for changes in the (long-run) real exchange rate. In the Frenkel–Bilson model, PPP is assumed to hold continuously, and in the Dornbusch–Frankel model PPP holds in the long run. Given the pronounced movements in real exchange rates that we have observed in recent years, it is desirable to augment the structural models to allow for changes in the equilibrium real exchange rate.

Meese and Rogoff (1983a) took a step in this direction by studying the forecasting performance of the model developed by Hooper and Morton (1982). The Hooper–Morton model extends the Dornbusch–Frankel model by allowing unanticipated shocks to current accounts to affect the long-run real exchange rate. Because monthly current account data are not available, Meese and Rogoff used the trade balance as a proxy. Meese and Rogoff's forecasting results with the Hooper–Morton model are not encouraging: The Hooper–Morton model did not do better than the Frenkel–Bilson and Dornbusch–Frankel models.

In this section I use an indicator variable for the equilibrium real exchange rate that is based on Balassa's

(1964) analysis of relative prices in a world with internationally traded and nontraded goods. This approach was subsequently introduced into modern exchange rate models by Dornbusch (1976b) and empirically implemented (in-sample) by Clements and Frenkel (1980) in a study of the dollar–pound exchange rate in the 1920s. I assume the existence of two categories of goods, those that are internationally traded and those that are not. The general price level in a country is assumed to be a linear homogeneous Cobb–Douglas function of the prices of traded and nontraded goods. For the case of the Frenkel–Bilson model, I replace the assumption of continuous PPP in terms of general price levels by the assumption that PPP applies to internationally traded goods only, and for the case of the Dornbusch–Frankel model, I assume that long-run PPP applies to traded goods only. Under these assumptions, together with some auxiliary assumptions, the following exchange rate equation can be derived:

$$s = b_0 + b_1(m - m^*) + b_2(y - y^*) + b_3(i - i^*) + b_4(\pi - \pi^*) + b_5 q + u \quad (13)$$

with

$$q = \ln[(p_t/p_n)/(p_t^*/p_n^*)], \quad (14)$$

where p_t is the domestic price level of traded goods, p_n is the domestic price level of nontraded goods, and starred price variables refer to the foreign country. For the case of the Frenkel–Bilson model $b_4 = 0$, as before. The exact derivation of Equation (13) can be found in Clements and Frenkel (1980) and Wolff (1985).

To be able to use Equation (13) for forecasting purposes, I need empirical proxies for prices of traded and nontraded goods. I proxy traded and nontraded goods prices by wholesale price indexes (WPI's) and consumer price indexes (CPI's), respectively. WPI's generally pertain to baskets of goods that contain large shares of traded goods relative to baskets of consumer goods that contain large shares of nontraded consumer services. The CPI's and WPI's are drawn from the *International Financial Statistics* and are described in greater detail in the Appendix.

In this section I present the empirical results of forecasting experiments on the basis of state–space versions

Table 7. Summary Statistics on the Forecasting Performance of the State–Space Version of the Frenkel–Bilson Model Augmented With an Index Variable for the Equilibrium Real Exchange Rate

Horizon (months)	ME	MAE	RMSE	U statistic	N
Dollar–Mark					
1	.25	2.44	3.36	1.00	89
3	.76	4.64	5.52	.99	87
6	1.24	6.14	7.35	.91	84
12	2.03	8.84	10.62	.84	78
24	1.55	13.24	15.20	.73	66
36	− 1.03	14.41	17.12	.64	54
Dollar–Yen					
1	.12	2.86	3.91	1.06	89
3	.34	5.78	7.52	1.14	87
6	.39	11.18	13.78	1.34	84
12	− .24	17.82	21.23	1.40	78
24	− 7.37	18.84	26.48	1.78	66
36	− 12.54	25.32	32.77	2.33	54
Dollar–Pound					
1	.16	2.66	3.48	1.11	89
3	.61	5.47	6.63	1.21	87
6	1.18	8.31	10.09	1.24	84
12	2.13	13.48	15.53	1.16	78
24	.01	24.88	27.80	1.19	66
36	− 4.77	31.52	35.37	1.17	54

NOTE: Period—November 1976–April 1984 ($\gamma = .01$).

of Equation (13). I use the same procedure as in Section 4, that is, forecasts are generated using an appropriately modified version of the state–space model that is defined by Equations (11) and (12). In Tables 7 and 8 the results are presented for the Frenkel–Bilson and Dornbusch–Frankel models augmented with the indexes for equilibrium real exchange rates. As in Section 4, these results are generated for a value of γ (the parameter that sets the degree of coefficient variation) of .01.

It is interesting to compare Tables 7 and 8 with Tables 4 and 5, respectively. On average, the forecasting results for the models with the real exchange rate index do not differ very much from the results without the index for the cases of the dollar–mark and dollar–pound

Table 8. Summary Statistics on the Forecasting Performance of the State–Space Version of the Dornbusch–Frankel Model Augmented With an Index Variable for the Equilibrium Real Exchange Rate

Horizon (months)	ME	MAE	RMSE	U statistic	N
Dollar–Mark					
1	.29	2.45	3.35	.99	89
3	.92	4.49	5.40	.97	87
6	1.79	6.02	7.15	.88	84
12	3.54	8.35	9.92	.78	78
24	4.63	12.18	14.24	.69	66
36	1.58	12.25	15.27	.57	54
Dollar–Yen					
1	.01	2.76	.38	1.04	89
3	− .03	5.31	6.98	1.06	87
6	− .13	9.26	12.14	1.18	84
12	− .58	14.49	18.57	1.22	78
24	− 5.01	13.97	20.29	1.37	66
36	− 7.06	16.98	24.28	1.73	54
Dollar–Pound					
1	.18	2.60	3.54	1.13	89
3	.69	5.53	6.82	1.25	87
6	1.26	8.29	10.09	1.24	84
12	1.89	12.92	14.93	1.12	78
24	− .60	23.20	26.06	1.12	66
36	− 5.90	30.15	33.67	1.11	54

NOTE: Period—November 1976–April 1984 ($\gamma = .01$).

96   Journal of Business & Economic Statistics, January 1987

Table 9.   *Summary Statistics on the Forecasting Performance of the Three-Month Forward Exchange Rate as a Predictor of the Subsequently Observed Spot Rate*

Rate	ME	MAE	RMSE	U statistic	N
		Initial Sample: November 1976–June 1981			
$/DM	.80	4.63	5.98	1.02	53
$/¥	− .61	6.02	7.10	1.03	53
$/£	− 1.62	4.76	5.71	1.07	53
		Full Sample: November 1976–April 1984			
$/DM	1.41	4.62	5.76	1.04	87
$/¥	.29	5.61	6.88	1.05	87
$/£	.30	4.82	5.80	1.06	87

exchange rates. The index variable makes quite a difference, however, for the case of the dollar–yen exchange rate. The U statistics for the dollar–yen case that are reported in Tables 7 and 8 are on average about .13 lower than those reported in Tables 4 and 5.

The fact that including the index variable improves the models' forecasting performance for the dollar–yen rate but not for the other exchange rates is perhaps not surprising in light of the fact that Japan has concentrated much more than Germany or the United Kingdom on growth through productivity gains in the tradables sector. Even with the index, however, the state–space structural models for the dollar–yen rate fail to improve on the simple random walk forecasting rule.

6. COMPARISON WITH FORWARD EXCHANGE RATES

In Sections 4 and 5 I have emphasized comparison of the models' forecasts with predictions from the simple random walk forecasting rule. The forward exchange rate is another important benchmark that deserves consideration. In a world in which expectations are formed rationally and financial markets are efficient, in the sense of Fama (1970), I would, in the absence of (risk) premia in the pricing of forward foreign exchange, expect the forward rate to be an unbiased prediction of the future spot rate.

My data source for spot exchange rates (*International Financial Statistics*, published by the International Monetary Fund) also reports corresponding three-month forward premia, from which three-month forward exchange rates can be constructed. In this section I compare the structural models' performance in forecasting three-month-ahead spot exchange rates with the performance of the three-month forward rate. Summary statistics for the case of the three-month forward rate are given in Table 9.

From the U statistics in Table 9, it is seen that the random walk model outperforms the forward rate in terms of RMSE. This result has been noted by, among others, Meese and Rogoff (1983a). In order to assess the performance of the structural models relative to performance of the forward rate, the entries in Table 9 can be compared with their counterparts in Tables 2–

5 and 7–8 (for a three-month forecasting horizon). The structural models for the dollar–yen and dollar–pound rates are generally outperformed by the forward rate, both in terms of MAE and RMSE, even though the structural models' forecasts are based on realized values of explanatory variables. For the dollar–mark case, however, the structural models dominate, as was the case in previous sections when the structural models' forecasting performance was compared with the performance of the random walk forecasting rule. Thus, comparison of the structural models' predictive ability with our two different benchmarks, the random walk model and the forward rate, leads to similar results, at least for the three-month horizon that is considered in this section.

7. CONCLUSIONS

In this article the out-of-sample forecasting performance of an important class of structural exchange rate models was studied, employing a varying-parameters estimation methodology. The introduction of time-varying parameters enhances the forecasting performance of the structural models, indicating that the kind of instability I am after is present in the data. I also find, and this finding is at variance with the results of earlier research, that the ex-post predictions of the structural models are not uniformly dominated by the simple random walk forecasting rule. The performance relative to the random walk is different for different exchange rates.

With respect to monetary-type models of exchange rate determination, my findings indicate that on average they leave a lot to be desired as descriptors of the behavior of relative prices of the currencies of the major industrial countries during the recent floating exchange rate period. This is true whether or not parameter variation or Balassa-type changes in real exchange rates are allowed for.

ACKNOWLEDGMENTS

This article is drawn from Chapters II and IV of my doctoral dissertation at the University of Chicago (Wolff 1985). I am very grateful to the members of my dissertation committee—Michael Mussa (chairman), Joshua

Aizenman, Robert Aliber, Jacob Frenkel, David Hsieh, John Huizinga, and Arnold Zellner—and to seminar participants at the University of Chicago, the London Business School, and the European Institute of Business Administration (INSEAD) for many helpful comments. Many valuable suggestions from an anonymous referee and an associate editor of this journal are also gratefully acknowledged.

APPENDIX: DATA SOURCES

In this appendix, I describe the sources for the data that are used in this study.

Exchange Rates. Spot exchange rates are taken from *International Financial Statistics* (IFS) (line ae), published by the International Monetary Fund. Forward rates are constructed from forward premia that are reported in the 1985 Supplement on Exchange Rates, IFS.

Money Supplies. Seasonally unadjusted M1 figures are used for all countries. United States: *Main Economic Indicators* (MEI), published by the Organization for Economic Cooperation and Development; Germany, Japan, and United Kingdom: IFS (line 34).

Real Income Levels. For all countries, seasonally unadjusted figures for industrial production were taken from the MEI.

Interest Rates. United Kingdom and United States: treasury bill rates as reported in the MEI, Germany and Japan: call money rates, IFS (line 60b).

Price Levels and Inflation Rates. Consumer price indexes: IFS (line 64); wholesale price indexes: IFS (line 63); expected long-run inflation rates are proxied by CPI inflation rates over the preceding 12-month period.

[*Received November 1985. Revised June 1986.*]

REFERENCES

Abraham, B., and Ledolter, J. (1983), *Statistical Methods for Forecasting*, New York: John Wiley.
Anderson, B. D. O., and Moore, J. R. (1979), *Optimal Filtering*, Englewood Cliffs, NJ: Prentice-Hall.
Ansley, C. F., and Kohn, R. (1983), "State Space Models and Diffuse Initial Conditions, I: Filtering and Likelihood," Technical Report 13, University of Chicago, Statistics Research Center, Graduate School of Business.
Balassa, B. (1964), "The Purchasing Power Parity Doctrine: A Reappraisal," *Journal of Political Economy*, 72, 584–596.
Bilson, J. F. O. (1978), "The Monetary Approach to the Exchange Rate," *International Monetary Fund Staff Papers*, 25, 48–75.
—— (1979), "The Deutsche Mark/Dollar Rate: A Monetary Analysis," *Carnegie-Rochester Conference Series on Public Policy*, 11, 59–101.
Cagan, P. (1956), "The Monetary Dynamics of Hyperinflation," in *Studies in the Quantity Theory of Money*, ed. M. Friedman, Chicago: University of Chicago Press, pp. 25–117.
Clements, K. W., and Frenkel, J. A. (1980), "Exchange Rates, Money

and Relative Prices: The Dollar/Pound in the 1920's," *Journal of International Economics*, 10, 249–262.
Dornbusch, R. (1976a), "Expectations and Exchange Rate Dynamics," *Journal of Political Economy*, 84, 1161–1176.
—— (1976b), "The Theory of Flexible Exchange Rate Regimes and Macroeconomic Policy," in *The Economics of Exchange Rates*, eds. J. A. Frenkel and H. G. Johnson, Reading, MA: Addison-Wesley, pp. 27–46.
Durbin, J. (1970), "Testing for Serial Correlation in Least-Squares Regression When Some of the Regressors Are Lagged Dependent Variables," *Econometrica*, 38, 410–421.
Fama, E. F. (1970), "Efficient Capital Markets: A Review of Theory and Empirical Work," *Journal of Finance*, 25, 383–417.
Frankel, J. A. (1979), "On the Mark: A Theory of Floating Exchange Rates Based on Real Interest Differentials," *American Economic Review*, 69, 610–622.
—— (1981), "On the Mark: Reply," *American Economic Review*, 71, 1075–1082.
—— (1982), "The Mystery of the Multiplying Marks," *Review of Economics and Statistics*, 64, 515–519.
Frenkel, J. A. (1976), "A Monetary Approach to the Exchange Rate: Doctrinal Aspects and Empirical Evidence," *Scandinavian Journal of Economics*, 78, 200–224.
Garbade, K. (1977), "Two Methods for Examining the Stability of Regression Coefficients," *Journal of the American Statistical Association*, 72, 54–63.
Goldfeld, S. M. (1976), "The Case of the Missing Money," *Brookings Papers on Economic Activity*, 3, 577–638.
Harvey, A. C. (1981), *Time Series Models*, Deddington, U.K.: Philip Alan.
Hendry, D. F., and Mizon, G. E. (1978), "Serial Correlation as a Convenient Simplification, Not a Nuisance: A Comment on a Study of the Demand for Money by the Bank of England," *Economic Journal*, 88, 549–563.
Hooper, P., and Morton, J. (1982), "Fluctuations in the Dollar: A Model of Nominal and Real Exchange Rate Determination," *Journal of International Money and Finance*, 1, 39–56.
Isard, P. (1983), "What's Wrong with Empirical Exchange Rate Models: Some Critical Issues and New Directions," International Finance Discussion Papers, No. 226, Washington, DC: Federal Reserve Board.
Kalman, R. E. (1960), "A New Approach to Linear Filtering and Prediction Problems," *ASME Journal of Basic Engineering*, 82, 35–45.
Lucas, R. E., Jr. (1976), "Econometric Policy Evaluation: A Critique," *Carnegie-Rochester Conference Series on Public Policy*, 1, 19–46.
Meese, R. A., and Rogoff, K. (1983a), "Empirical Exchange Rate Models of the Seventies: Do They Fit Out of Sample?" *Journal of International Economics*, 14, 3–24.
—— (1983b), "The Out-of-Sample Failure of Exchange Rate Models: Sampling Error or Misspecification?" in *Exchange Rates and International Macroeconomics*, ed. J. A. Frenkel, Chicago: University of Chicago Press, pp. 67–105.
Mussa, M. (1979), "Empirical Regularities in the Behavior of Exchange Rates and Theories of the Foreign Exchange Market," *Carnegie-Rochester Conference Series on Public Policy*, 11, 9–58.
Saidi, N. (1983), "Comment," in *Exchange Rates and International Macroeconomics*, ed. J. A. Frenkel, Chicago: University of Chicago Press, pp. 105–109.
Simpson, T. D., and Porter, R. D. (1980), "Some Issues Involving the Definition and Interpretation of the Monetary Aggregates," *Federal Reserve Bank of Boston Conference Series*, 23, 161–234.
Wolff, C. C. P. (1985), "Exchange Rate Models, Parameter Variation and Innovations: A Study on the Forecasting Performance of Empirical Models of Exchange Rate Determination," unpublished Ph.D. dissertation, University of Chicago, Graduate School of Business.

[13]

IMF Staff Papers
Vol. 46, No. 2 (June 1999)
© 1999 International Monetary Fund

Are Currency Crises Predictable? A Test

ANDREW BERG and CATHERINE PATTILLO*

This paper evaluates three models for predicting currency crises that were proposed before 1997. The idea is to answer the question: if we had been using these models in late 1996, how well armed would we have been to predict the Asian crisis? The results are mixed. Two of the models fail to provide useful forecasts. One model provides forecasts that are somewhat informative though still not reliable. Plausible modifications to this model improve its performance, providing some hope that future models may do better. This exercise suggests, though, that while forecasting models may help indicate vulnerability to crisis, the predictive power of even the best of them may be limited. [JEL F31, F47]

In recent years, a number of researchers have claimed success in systematically predicting which countries are more likely to suffer currency crises. The Asian crisis has stimulated further work in this area, with several papers already claiming to be able to "predict" the incidence of this crisis using pre-crisis data.[1]

It may seem unlikely that it should be possible to systematically predict currency crises. It is reasonable to doubt that sharp and predictable movements in the exchange rate are consistent with the actions of forward-looking speculators. Early theoretical models of currency crises suggested, however, that crises may

---

*Andrew Berg and Catherine Pattillo are Economists in the Research Department. They would like to thank, without implication, Graciela Kaminsky, Andy Rose, and Aaron Tornell for help reproducing and interpreting their results, Brooks Dana Calvo, Maria Costa, Manzoor Gill, and Nada Mora for superb research assistance, and Eduardo Borensztein, Robert Flood, Steve Kamin, an anonymous referee, and many IMF colleagues for useful comments.

[1]IMF (1998), Kaminsky (1998a and 1998b), Radelet and Sachs (1998b), Corsetti, Pesenti, and Roubini (1998a), and Tornell (1998), among others.

Andrew Berg and Catherine Pattillo

be predictable even with fully rational speculators.[2] In "second-generation" models, a country may be in a situation in which an attack, while not inevitable, might succeed if it were to take place; the exact timing of crises would be essentially unpredictable. Even here, though, it may be possible to identify whether a country is in a zone of vulnerability—that is, whether fundamentals are sufficiently weak that a shift in expectations could cause a crisis. In this case, the relative vulnerability of different countries might predict the relative probabilities of crises in response to a shock such as a global downturn in confidence in emerging markets.[3]

It is one thing to say that currency crises may be predictable in general, however, and another that econometric models estimated using historical data on a panel or cross section of countries can foretell crises with any degree of accuracy. It is an open question whether crises are sufficiently similar across countries and over time to allow generalizations from past experience. For example, models estimated over countries without capital mobility may not work in a world of capital mobility.[4] Moreover, many factors that may indicate a higher probability of crisis, such as inadequate banking supervision or a vulnerable political situation, are not easily quantified.

The possible endogeneity of policy to the risk of crisis may also limit the predictability of crises. For example, authorities within a country, or their creditors, might react to signals so as to avoid crises.[5] Policymakers are often fighting the previous battle, so they are likely to respond to the most obvious indicators from a previous crisis. On the other hand, a focus by market participants on a particular variable could result in its precipitating a crisis where one might not otherwise have occurred.

The flurry of work between the 1994 and 1997 crises and the large number of crises observed in 1997 provides an excellent opportunity to test existing state-of-the-art "early warning systems" out of sample. The 1997 Asian crises that we look at here present special challenges, however, on two grounds. First, many analysts have argued that the causes of the Asian crises lie not in the traditional macroeconomic fundamentals but rather in structural and microeconomic problems such as weak banking supervision, poor corporate governance, and even corruption.[6] Data on these are hard to come by, and the emphasis on these issues is somewhat new, so the available empirical models focus rather on the typical macroeconomic variables. This bodes ill for the predictability of the Asian crises with these models. A contrasting line of thought, but also with pessimistic

---

[2]Krugman (1979). In this model, though, the exchange rate does not jump and indeed there are no capital gains or losses of any sort at the point of crisis, so the relevance to the type of crises most people have in mind may be limited.

[3]See Flood and Marion (1998) for a survey of this literature.

[4]Flood and Marion (1994) discuss and present some evidence on the predictability of currency crises in capital-controlled developing economies.

[5]Initially successful early warning systems might thus cease to work following publication. This is a version of the Lucas critique.

[6]Radelet and Sachs (1998a) emphasize the inability of fundamentals to explain the crises, while Corsetti, Pesenti, and Roubini (1998b and 1998c) focus more on the structural and microeconomic explanations. See Lane and others (1999) and Berg (1999) and references therein for overviews.

ARE CURRENCY CRISES PREDICTABLE?

implications for us, is that the Asian crises were largely "bank run" phenomena—panic attacks against otherwise viable exchange rate regimes. This distinguishes these crises from those emphasized in most of the empirical models, and suggests that, at best, only a few variables that measure exposure to panicky capital outflows would be helpful predictors of crisis.[7] When a crisis will strike would be difficult or impossible to foretell.

On the other hand, the 1994 Mexico crisis, which was the immediate inspiration for much of the recent work on crises, does not in many respects look that different from Thailand's. Sachs (1997) argues that Thailand's 1997 crisis "has the same hallmarks [as the 1994 crisis]: overvaluation of the real exchange rate, coupled with booming bank lending, heavily directed at real estate." In any case, each set of new crises always presents some new features, so the existence of some novelty in the Asian crises does not invalidate them as tests of the models we consider.

Ultimately, the question of whether crises are predictable can only be settled in practice. The recent work claiming success in predicting crises has focused almost exclusively on in-sample prediction—that is, on formulating and estimating a model using data on a set of crises, and then judging success by the plausibility of the estimated parameters and the size of the prediction errors for this set of crises.[8] The key test is not, however, the ability to fit a set of observations after the fact, but the prediction of future crises. Given the relatively small number of crises in the historical data, the danger is acute that specification searches through the large number of potential predictive variables may yield spurious success in "explaining" crises within the sample. The possibility that the determinants of crises may vary importantly through time also suggests the importance of testing the models out of sample.

This paper evaluates three different models proposed before 1997 for predicting currency crises. The idea is to try to answer the question: if we had been using these models in late 1996, how well armed would we have been to predict the Asian crisis? For each of the three models, we duplicate the original results as closely as possible. We then reestimate the models using data through 1996, as would have a researcher who at the end of 1996 aimed to predict crises the following year. We use two samples of countries: the same as the original paper, and another common sample for purposes of comparing the three methods. We then use the models to forecast events in 1997. We generate a ranking of countries according to predicted probability or severity of crisis in 1997 for each model, and then compare the predicted and actual rankings.

We chose the following three approaches based on their promise as early warning systems, their potential applicability to the 1997 crises, and their success within sample:

---

[7] None of the precrisis models used a measure of short-term external debt relative to reserves, a variable much emphasized by many advocates of the "bank run" interpretation of these crises, such as Radelet and Sachs (1998b).

[8] Exceptions are Tornell (1998), discussed below, and Kaminsky (1998a), which, while it presents out-of-sample estimates of the probability of currency crisis, does not provide tests of whether these forecasts are better than, for example, guesswork. In addition, Furman and Stiglitz (1998) carry out an exercise similar to ours. Their conclusions are largely consistent with our own, with some differences as noted below.

Andrew Berg and Catherine Pattillo

- Kaminsky, Lizondo, and Reinhart (1998) (hereafter KLR) monitor a large set of monthly indicators that signal a crisis whenever they cross a certain threshold. This approach has the potential attraction that it produces thresholds beyond which a crisis is more likely. This accords with the common practice of establishing certain warning zones, such as current account deficits beyond 5 percent of GDP or reserves less than three months of imports. The authors claim some success in developing a set of indicators that reliably predict the likelihood of crisis. Moreover, Kaminsky (1998a and 1998b) and Goldstein (1998) have asserted that this method can be applied successfully to the 1997 crises.
- Frankel and Rose (1996) (FR) develop a probit model of currency crashes in a large sample of developing countries. Their use of annual data permits them to look at variables, such as the composition of external debt, that are available only at that frequency.
- Sachs, Tornell, and Velasco (1996) (STV) restrict their attention to a cross section of countries in 1995, analyzing the incidence of the "tequila effect" following the Mexico crisis. They concentrate on a more structured hypothesis about the cause of this particular episode, emphasizing interactions among weak banking systems, overvalued real exchange rates, and low reserves. They claim to explain most of the cross-country pattern of currency crisis in emerging markets in 1994–95. Their approach has also been applied to analyzing the Asian crisis.[9]

I. Three Methods for Predicting Crises

Kaminsky, Lizondo, and Reinhart (1998) Signals Approach

The Model

For KLR, a currency crisis occurs when a weighted average of monthly percentage depreciations in the exchange rate and monthly percentage declines in reserves exceeds its mean by more than three standard deviations.[10] KLR propose the monitoring of several indicators that may tend to exhibit unusual behavior during a 24-month window prior to a crisis. They choose 15 candidate indicator variables based on theoretical priors and on the availability of monthly data.[11] An indicator issues a signal whenever it moves beyond a given threshold level.

---

[9]Tornell (1998), Radelet and Sachs (1998b), Corsetti, Pesenti, and Roubini (1998a), and IMF (1998) estimate variants of STV for 1997, all with some success.

[10]Weights are calculated so that the variance of the two components of the index are equal. See Berg and Pattillo (1998) as well as KLR for further details regarding the methodology.

[11]Indicators are (1) international reserves in U.S. dollars; (2) imports in U.S. dollars; (3) exports in U.S. dollars; (4) terms of trade; (5) deviations of the real exchange rate from a deterministic time trend (in percentage terms); (6) the differential between foreign and domestic real interest rates on deposits; (7) "excess" real M1 balances, where excess is defined as the residuals from a regression of real M1 balances on real GDP, inflation, and a deterministic time trend; (8) the money multiplier of M2; (9) the ratio of domestic credit to GDP; (10) the real interest rate on deposits; (11) the ratio of (nominal) lending to deposit rates; (12) the stock of commercial bank deposits; (13) the ratio of broad money to gross international reserves; (14) an index of output; and (15) an index of equity prices measured in U.S. dollars. The indicator is defined as the annual percentage change in the level of the variable (except for the deviation of the real exchange rate from trend, "excess" real M1 balances, and the three interest rate variables).

ARE CURRENCY CRISES PREDICTABLE?

We can consider the performance of each indicator in terms of the matrix at right. Cell A represents the number of months in which the indicator issued a good signal, B is the number of months in which the indicator issued a bad signal or "noise," C is the number of months in which the indicator failed to issue a signal that would have been a good signal, and D is the number of months in which the indicator did not issue a signal that would have been a bad sig-

	Crisis within 24 months	No crisis within 24 months
Signal was issued	A	B
No signal was issued	C	D

nal. For each indicator, KLR find the "optimal" threshold, defined as that threshold that minimizes the noise-to-signal ratio B/A.[12]

The thresholds are calculated in terms of the percentiles of each country's distribution for the variable in question. An optimal threshold for a given predictor, such as domestic credit growth, might be 80, for example, meaning that a signal is considered to be issued whenever domestic credit growth in a given country is in the highest 20 percent of observations for that country. The optimal threshold is constrained to be the same across countries. Thus, minimizing the noise-to-signal ratio for the sample of countries yields an optimal threshold percentile for each indicator that is the same for all countries. The corresponding country-specific threshold value of the underlying variable associated with that percentile will differ across countries, however.

The KLR approach is bivariate, in that each indicator is analyzed, and optimal thresholds calculated, separately. Kaminsky (1998a) calculates a single composite indicator of crisis as a weighted sum of the indicators, where each indicator is weighted by the inverse of its noise-to-signal ratio. She then calculates a probability of crisis for each value of the aggregate index by observing how often within the sample a given value of the aggregate index is followed by a crisis within 24 months.

Table 1 presents an analog of a regression output for the KLR model, as estimated in the in-sample period of 1970 to April 1995.[13] The first column shows the noise-to-signal ratio estimated for each indicator (defined as the number of bad signals as a share of possible bad signals (B/(B+D)) divided by the number of good signals as a share of possible good signals (A/(A+C)). Column 2 shows how much higher is the probability of a crisis within 24 months when the indicator emits a signal than when it does not (within sample). When the noise-to-signal ratio is less than 1, this number is positive, implying that crises are more likely when the indicator signals than when it does not. Indicators with noise-to-signal ratios equal to or above unity are not useful in anticipating crises.

---

[12]If the absence of a crisis within 24 months is considered the null hypothesis, then observations of type B are Type I errors, while observations of type C are Type II errors. The procedure can be thought of as minimizing the ratio of Type I errors, as a share of tranquil periods (B/(B+D)) to 1 – Type II errors as a share of crisis periods (A/(A+C)).

[13]The in-sample period for the KLR model stops in April 1995 because of the 24-month prediction window. A person implementing the KLR model in April 1997 (right before the Thai crisis) would estimate the thresholds based on the performance of predictive variables measured only through April 1995, since after that month it would be impossible to know (yet) whether a crisis was to occur within 24 months.

Andrew Berg and Catherine Pattillo

Table 1. Performance of Indicators—In-Sample

23-Country Sample, 1970–April 1995

Indicator	Noise/signal (adjusted)[a] (1)	P(crisis/signal) –P(crisis)[b] (2)	Number of crises with data (3)
Real exchange rate[c]	0.25	29	70
M2/reserves growth rate	0.39	17	68
Export growth rate	0.60	9	68
International reserves growth rate	0.44	15	68
Excess M1 balances[d]	0.60	9	67
Domestic credit/GDP growth rate	0.78	4	65
Real interest rate	0.76	4	38
M2 multiplier growth rate	1.14	–2	68
Import growth rate	1.16	–2	68
Industrial production growth rate	1.14	–2	54
Terms of trade growth rate	0.93	1	55
Lending rate/deposit rate	1.04	–1	29
Bank deposit growth rate	1.63	–6	68
Stock price index growth rate	1.59	–6	44
Real interest differential	1.34	–4	38
Current account/GDP	0.42	16	70
M2/reserves (level)	0.45	14	51

[a]Ratio of false signals (measured as a proportion of months in which false signals could have been issued [$B/(B+D)$]) to good signals (measured as a proportion of months in which good signals could have been issued [$A/(A+C)$]).

[b]P(crisis/signal) is the percentage of the signals issued by the indicator that were followed by at least one crisis within the subsequent 24 months ([$A/(A+C)$] in terms of the matrix in the text). P(crisis) is the unconditional probability of a crisis. $(A+C)/(A+B+C+D)$.

[c]Deviation from deterministic trend.

[d]Residual from regression of real M1 on real GDP, inflation. and a deterministic trend.

We find eight indicators to be informative: deviations of the real exchange rate from trend. the growth in M2 as a fraction of reserves, export growth. change in international reserves, "excess" M1 balances, growth in domestic credit as a share of GDP, the real interest rate, and the growth in the terms of trade.[14]

Predicting 1997

We have already calculated the optimal thresholds and resulting noise-to-signal ratios for the different indicators. To forecast for the post-April 1995 period, we

---

[14]These indicators are also all informative in the KLR analysis. These results are quite similar to those obtained by KLR with a different sample of countries and time period. though they found a further four indicators to be informative. See the Appendix for more detail, as well as a full analysis of in-sample performance.

ARE CURRENCY CRISES PREDICTABLE?

apply these thresholds to the values of the predictive variables after this date, determining whether they are issuing signals or not. The first column of Table 2 shows the performance of the Kaminsky (1998a) composite measures of the probability of crisis based on the weighted sum of indicators signaling.

A natural question is whether the estimated probability of crisis is above 50 percent prior to actual crises. The summary statistics rows show that only 4 percent of the time was the predicted probability of crisis above 50 percent in cases when there was a crisis within the next 24 months, during the period May 1995 to December 1997. If we are more interested in predicting crises than predicting tranquil periods and are not so worried about calling too many crises, we may want to consider an alarm to be issued when the estimated probability of crisis is above 25 percent. Table 2 shows that the estimated probabilities are above 25 percent in 25 percent of the precrisis observations. Sixty-three percent of alarms, however, are false at the 25 percent cutoff.

This is not very good performance: most crises are missed and most alarms are false. These forecasts are, nonetheless, better than random guesses, both economically and statistically. The actual out-of-sample frequency of crisis following an alarm (defined as an estimated probability above 25 percent) is 37 percent. The frequency of crisis following periods without such alarms is 24 percent. And a χ^2 test of the goodness of fit results rejects at the 5 percent level of significance the hypothesis that the number of successfully called crises is no higher than if the warnings were uninformative.[15]

So far we have examined the ability of the model to predict the approximate *timing* of crises for each country.[16] We can also evaluate the cross-sectional success of the models' predictions in identifying which countries are vulnerable in a period of global financial turmoil such as 1997. The question here is whether the models assign higher predicted probabilities of crisis to those countries that had the biggest crises. We can then evaluate forecast performance by comparing rankings of countries based on the predicted and actual crisis indices. As we will see, this also allows us to compare forecasts across models with different definitions of crisis. Table 3 shows countries' actual crisis index and predicted probability of crisis in 1997 for the various different forecasting methods.[17] The table also shows the Spearman correlation between the actual and predicted rankings and its associated *p*-value, as well as the R^2 from a bivariate regression of the actual rankings on the predictions.

The KLR-based forecasts are somewhat successful at ranking countries by severity of crisis. The forecasted probabilities are significantly correlated with the actual rankings of countries in 1997 by their crisis index. They explain 28 percent of the variance.

To get a richer sense of how useful this general approach would have been, we now examine more closely the predictions of the KLR-based model for four Asian

---

[15]This is true for both the 50 percent and the 25 percent cutoff.

[16]We say approximate because the model only attempts to place the crisis within a 24-month window.

[17]The predicted crisis probability is the average of the probabilities during January to December 1996, using the out-of-sample estimates. The actual crisis index used to rank the countries for 1997 is the maximum value of the monthly crisis index for each country during 1997.

113

Andrew Berg and Catherine Pattillo

Table 2. Goodness-of-Fit of KLR Model—Out of Sample

Cutoff of 50 Percent

Goodness-of-Fit Table[a]

	Original specification				Augmented with current account and M2/reserves		
	Actual					Actual	
Predicted	Tranquil	Crash	Total	Predicted	Tranquil	Crash	Total
Tranquil	337	117	454	Tranquil	338	122	460
Crash	1	5	6	Crash	0	0	0
Total	338	122	460	Total	338	122	460

Summary Statistics

	Original	Augmented
p-value for χ^2 test of independence	0.002	No crisis called
Percent of observations correctly called	74	73
Percent of crises correctly called[b]	4	0
Percent of tranquil periods correctly called[c]	100	100
False alarms as a percent of total alarms[d]	17	No crisis called
Probability of crisis given:		
an alarm[e]	83	No crisis called
no alarm[f]	26	27

Cutoff of 25 Percent

Goodness-of-Fit Table[a]

	Original specification				Augmented with current account and M2/reserves		
	Actual					Actual	
Predicted	Tranquil	Crash	Total	Predicted	Tranquil	Crash	Total
Tranquil	286	91	377	Tranquil	279	83	362
Crash	52	31	83	Crash	59	39	98
Total	338	122	460	Total	338	122	460

Summary Statistics

	Original	Augmented
p-value for χ^2 test of independence	0.014	0.001
Percent of observations correctly called	69	69
Percent of crises correctly called[b]	25	32
Percent of tranquil periods correctly called[c]	85	83
False alarms as a percent of total alarms[d]	63	60
Probability of crisis given:		
an alarm[e]	37	40
no alarm[f]	24	23

[a]Table shows number of observations.

[b]A precrisis period is correctly called when the estimated probability of crisis is above the cutoff probability and a crisis ensues within 24 months.

[c]A tranquil period is correctly called when the estimated probability of crisis is below the cutoff probability and no crisis ensues within 24 months.

[d]A false alarm is an observation with an estimated probability of crisis above the cutoff (an alarm) not followed by a crisis within 24 months.

[e]This is the number of precrisis periods correctly called as a share of total predicted precrisis periods.

[f]This is the number of periods where tranquility is predicted and a crisis actually ensues as a share of total predicted tranquil periods (observations for which the predicted probability of crisis is below the cutoff).

ARE CURRENCY CRISES PREDICTABLE?

Table 3. Correlation of Actual and Predicted Rankings Based on KLR, FR, and STV

	KLR			FR			STV		
	Actual 1997 crises index	Predicted probabilities of crisis in 1997 Noise-to-signal weighted sum of indicators[a]		Actual 1997 crisis index	Predicted probabilities of crisis in 1997[d]		Actual crisis index April–Dec. 1997	Predicted probabilities of crisis in 1997	
		Original[b]	Augmented[c]		Table 4 Model 1	Table 4 Model 2		Table 5 Model 3	Table 5 Model 4
Thailand	1	16	7	3	7	11	2	7	5
Korea	2	4	5				3	12	11
Indonesia	3	18	11	2			1	14	9
Malaysia	4	8	13				4	6	6
Zimbabwe	5	3	3				5	23	12
Taiwan Province of China	6	5	4			7	9	11	22
Colombia	7	9	12	8	8	6	8	18	4
Philippines	8	1	1	7	6	8	6	1	1
Brazil	9	2	2	10	3	5	14	4	2
Turkey	10	7	10	1	10	2	7	9	21
Venezuela	11	14	16	5	11	12	21	22	13
Pakistan	12	10	9	6		9	10	17	20
South Africa	13	6	8				12	15	16
Jordan	14	15	18				17	20	15
India	15	20	21	14	13		13	5	19
Sri Lanka	16	17	19	11	14	13	15	16	17
Chile	17	19	20	15	9	10	16	19	14
Bolivia	18	23	22	13	12		22	13	10
Argentina	19	12	17	16	5	3	23	2	7
Mexico	20	13	14	12	4		18	21	18
Peru	21	11	6	9	1	4	20	8	23
Uruguay	22	22	23	4	2	1	11	3	3
Israel	23	21	15				19	10	8
Correlation[e]		0.54	0.60		0.33	0.12		0.11	0.23
p-value		0.007	0.003		0.253	0.694		0.612	0.295
R²		0.28	0.36		0.11	0.02		0.01	0.05

[a]Based on average of weighted sample conditional probabilities during 1996, using out-of-sample estimates.
[b]Original KLR variables.
[c]Addition of current account and M2/reserves in levels to original variables.
[d]Average predicted probabilities for 1996, where model was estimated up to April 1995.
[e]Spearman Rank Correlation of the fitted values and the actual crisis index and its p-value. The R² is from a regression of fitted values on actual values.

Andrew Berg and Catherine Pattillo

crisis countries (where crisis is identified according to the KLR definition): Korea, Indonesia, Malaysia, and Thailand, and one Asian and three Latin American noncrisis countries: Philippines, Argentina, Brazil, and Mexico.[18] Figure 1 presents the KLR composite measure of estimated probability of crisis, with vertical lines at crisis dates.

The KLR probability forecasts do not paint a clear picture of substantial risks in crisis compared to noncrisis countries. Two (then) noncrisis countries, Brazil and the Philippines, consistently present risks of crisis above 30 percent during 1996. One crisis country, Korea, also presents risks above 30 percent, though only in the first half of the year, while Malaysia is generally above 20 percent. Estimated crisis risks remain below 17 percent in 1996 for the crisis and noncrisis countries Argentina, Mexico, Indonesia, and Thailand.

In sum, the KLR is a mixed success. The fitted probabilities from the weighted sum of indicators are statistically significant predictors of crisis probability in 1997. Still, the overall explanatory power is fairly low, as demonstrated by the low R^2 statistic in the regression of the actual on the predicted crisis rankings and the overall goodness of fit for the out-of-sample predictions.

Frankel and Rose (1996) Probit Model

The Model

FR estimate the probability of a currency crash using annual data for more than 100 developing countries from 1971–92, a much broader sample of countries than the other two papers. The use of annual data may restrict the applicability of the approach as an early warning system, but it permits the analysis of variables such as the composition of external debt for which higher frequency data are rarely available. FR test the hypothesis that certain characteristics of capital inflows are positively associated with the occurrence of currency crashes: low shares of FDI; low shares of concessional debt or debt from multilateral development banks; and high shares of public-sector, variable-rate, short-term, and commercial bank debt.[19]

---

[18]These countries are an interesting but nonrandom subsample. We use them only to illustrate the conclusions from the broader sample.

[19]The complete list of variables is as follows. Domestic macroeconomic variables: (1) the rate of growth of domestic credit, (2) the government budget as percent of GDP, (3) and the growth rate of real GNP. Measures of vulnerability to external shocks include: (1) the ratio of total debt to GNP, (2) the ratio of reserves to imports, (3) the current account as a percentage of GDP, and (4) the degree of overvaluation, defined as the deviation from the average bilateral real exchange over the period. Foreign variables are represented by (1) the percentage growth rate of real OECD output (in U.S. dollars at 1990 exchange rates and prices), and (2) a "foreign interest rate" constructed as the weighted average of short-term interest rates for the United States, Germany, Japan, France, the United Kingdom, and Switzerland, with weights proportional to the fractions of debt denominated in the relevant currencies. Characteristics of the composition of capital inflows are expressed as a percentage of the total stock of external debt and include (1) amount of debt lent by commercial banks, (2) amount that is concessional, (3) amount that is variable rate, (4) amount that is public sector, (5) amount that is short-term, (6) amount lent by multilateral development banks (includes the World Bank and regional development banks but not the International Monetary Fund), and (7) the flow of FDI as a percentage of the debt stock.

ARE CURRENCY CRISES PREDICTABLE?

Figure 1. KLR Crisis Probabilities for Selected Countries

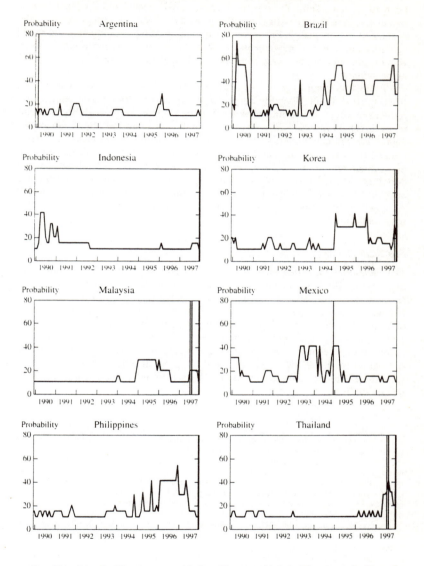

Note: The solid vertical lines represent crisis dates. The areas with dashed lines denote the 24 months prior to crises.

117

Andrew Berg and Catherine Pattillo

FR define a currency crash as a nominal exchange rate depreciation of at least 25 percent that also exceeds the previous year's change in the exchange rate by at least 10 percent. Thus, the type of currency crisis considered does not include speculative attacks successfully warded off by the authorities through reserve sales or interest rate increases. FR argue that it is more difficult to identify successful defenses, since reserve movements are noisy measures of exchange market intervention and interest rates were controlled for long periods in most of the countries in the sample.

Table 4 (column 1) presents the FR benchmark probit regression, estimated from 1970 through 1996 for purposes of forecasting 1997. The coefficients reflect the effect of one-unit changes in regressors on the probability of a currency crash (expressed in percentage points) evaluated at the mean of the data.[20] We can conclude that the probability of a crisis increases when foreign interest rates are high, domestic credit growth is high, the real exchange rate is overvalued relative to the average level for the country, the current account deficit and the fiscal surplus are large as a share of GDP, external concessional debt is small, and FDI is small relative to the total stock of external debt.[21] As noted in the Appendix, the in-sample goodness of fit of the FR model is reasonably high.

Predicting 1997

The FR model estimated through 1996 can easily generate out-of-sample predictions for 1997. We cannot directly analyze goodness of fit for this model, as there were no crisis countries in 1997 according to the FR definition.[22] Instead, we can compare the predicted probabilities of crisis and actual values of nominal exchange rate depreciation for 1997 for predictions based on model 1 of Table 4 (Table 3). Overall, the forecasts are not successful, with a correlation of 33 percent. The fraction of the variance of the rankings accounted for (measured by the R^2) is 11 percent, and the prediction is not significant.[23] In sum, the FR model fails to provide much useful guidance on crisis probabilities in 1997.

---

[20]Thus, an increase in the degree of exchange rate overvaluation by 1 percentage point would increase the estimated probability of crisis by 0.172 percentage points.

[21]This contrasts somewhat from the published FR results, particularly in the significance of the current account and the real exchange rate and the insignificance of reserves/imports. These changes result from several differences in specification. In addition to the inclusion of more recent years, the most important changes were that we exclude countries with a population below 1 million or annual per capita GDP below $1,000 and that we have fixed an error that resulted in a miscalculated real exchange rate measure. See the Appendix for details.

[22]This reflects the fact that the use of annual frequency does not work well here; because the devaluations happened toward the end of the year, none of the Asian countries are identified as crisis countries in 1997.

[23]This correlation is based on the 13 countries for which data are available that are part of the 23-country common sample. Based on the full sample where data are available (25 out of the 41 countries included in model 3A of Appendix Table A3), the forecasts are even less successful.

ARE CURRENCY CRISES PREDICTABLE?

Table 4. Frankel and Rose: Probit Estimates of Probability of a Currency Crash, 1970–96

	Model 1 FR specification		Model 2 Modified	
	dF/dx	$|z|^a$	dF/dx	$|z|^a$
Commercial bank share of total debt	0.022	0.1	0.121	1.0
Concessional share	−0.296	−2.3 **	−0.305	−3.3 ***
Variable rate share	0.020	0.1	−0.089	−0.6
Short-term share	0.106	0.6	0.161	1.1
FDI/debt	−0.795	−2.5 **	−0.576	−1.8 *
Public sector share	0.212	1.7 *	0.247	2.4 **
Multilateral share	0.021	0.1	0.045	0.4
Debt/GNP	−0.025	−0.5	0.021	0.6
Reserves/imports	−0.007	−1.3		
Reserves/M2			−0.206	−3.5 ***
Current account/GDP	−0.697	−2.4 **	−0.679	−2.8 ***
Overvaluation^b	0.172	2.9 ***	0.107	2.4 **
Government budget surplus/GDP	0.767	2.6 ***	0.595	2.6 **
Domestic credit growth	0.182	4.4 ***	0.119	3.1 ***
GDP growth rate	−0.058	−0.9	−0.017	−0.3
Foreign interest rate	1.007	2.0 **	0.909	2.3 **
Northern (OECD) growth	0.414	0.4	0.033	0.0
Open			−0.239	−4.1 ***
Sample size	464		448	
Pseudo R^2	0.20		0.32	

Goodness of Fit

	Model 1			Model 2 Actual		
	Tranquil	Crash	Total	Tranquil	Crash	Total
Cutoff probability of 50 percent^c						
Predicted tranquility	398	50	448	381	40	421
Predicted crash	6	10	16	7	20	27
Total	404	60	464	388	60	448
Cutoff probability of 25 percent^d						
Predicted tranquility	373	34	369	342	22	369
Predicted crash	31	26	57	41	38	79
Total	404	60	426	383	60	448

^{a}One, two, and three asterisks denote significance at the 10, 5, and 1 percent levels, respectively.
^{b}Defined as the deviation from the average real exchange rate over the period.
^{c}A crisis is correctly called when the estimated probability of crisis is above 50 percent if a crisis ensues within 24 months. A tranquil period is correctly called when the estimated probability of crisis is below 50 percent and there is no crisis within 24 months.
^{d}A crisis is correctly called when the estimated probability of crisis is above 25 percent if a crisis ensues within 24 months. A tranquil period is correctly called when the estimated probability of crisis is below 25 percent and there is no crisis within 24 months.

Andrew Berg and Catherine Pattillo

Sachs, Tornell, and Velasco (1996) Cross-Country Regressions

The Model

STV analyze the impact of Mexico's financial crisis of December 1994 on other emerging markets in 1995. They examine the determinants of the magnitude of the currency crisis in a cross section of 20 countries in 1995. This approach cannot hope to shed light on the timing of crises. Rather, it may answer the question of which countries are most likely to suffer serious attacks in the event of a change in the global environment. This approach is potentially attractive, even for our purposes, for a number of reasons. First, the timing may be much harder to predict than the incidence of a crisis across countries. Moreover, the determinants of crisis episodes may have varied importantly over time. STV can impose more economic structure on their analysis by focusing on a particular set of crises (those occurring at one time). STV argue that a key feature of the 1995 crises was that the attacks hit hard only at already vulnerable countries. In a rational panic, investors identify a country as being likely to suffer from a large devaluation in the face of an outflow, and validate their own concerns by fleeing the country. Thus, countries with overvalued exchange rates and weak banking systems were subject to more severe attacks, but only if they had low reserves relative to monetary liabilities (so that they could not easily accommodate the capital outflow) and weak fundamentals (so that fighting the attack with higher interest rates would be too costly).

The original STV model was not designed to predict future crises but rather to explain events in 1995. For our purposes, it is important for the crises that affected mostly Asian countries in 1997 to have been broadly similar to the 1995 crises. And in fact a number of researchers have argued since 1997 that the two sets of crises share many characteristics. Radelet and Sachs (1998a) argue that the 1997 and 1995 crises shared important characteristics, though their interpretation of post-Thailand Asian crises relies more heavily on contagion effects. The IMF (1998) argues that the STV results apply to the Asian crisis and constructs a composite indicator of crises on that basis. Radelet and Sachs (1998b), Tornell (1998), and Corsetti, Pesenti, and Roubini (1998a) also apply models in the STV spirit to both sets of crises.

Tequila Crisis Models

STV define a crisis index (*IND*) as the weighted sum of the percent decrease in reserves and the percent depreciation of the exchange rate, from November 1994 to April 1995. They argue that countries had more severe attacks when their banking systems were weak (proxied by a lending boom variable (*LB*) measuring growth in credit to the private sector from 1990 through 1994) and when the exchange rate was overvalued (measured as the degree of depreciation from 1986–89 to 1990–94 (*RER*)). Moreover, they find that these factors only matter for countries with low reserves (*DLR*), measured as having a reserves/M2 ratio in the lowest quartile, *and* "weak fundamentals" (*DWF*), which means having *RER* in the lowest three quartiles or *LB* in the highest three quartiles.

ARE CURRENCY CRISES PREDICTABLE?

Thus, they estimate across the *i* countries in their sample an equation of the form:

$$IND_i = \beta_1 + \beta_2 RER_i + \beta_3 LB_i + \beta_4 RER_i \cdot DLR_i + \beta_5 LB_i \cdot DLR_i +$$
$$\beta_6 RER_i \cdot DWF_i + \beta_7 LB_i \cdot DWF_i + \varepsilon_i.$$

Regression 1 of Table 5 reproduces the original STV benchmark regression, using their data.[24] The results emphasized by STV are, first, that the effect of *RER* is significantly negative for countries with low reserves and weak fundamentals (the sum of estimates of $\beta_2 + \beta_4 + \beta_6$ is negative), and the effect of *LB* is significantly positive for these same countries (the sum of estimates of $\beta_3 + \beta_5 + \beta_7$ is positive). They take the high R^2 of the regression (0.69) to indicate that the model explains the pattern of contagion well.

To apply this model to the 1997 crises, we run the model over the original STV sample (row 2 of Table 5) as well as the same sample of 23 countries to which we apply the KLR approach (row 3). The regression coefficients change substantially. The STV hypotheses now receive only mixed support. For example, when revised data are used (row 2), the effect of *RER* with low reserves and weak fundamentals ($\beta_2 + \beta_4 + \beta_6$) is now insignificantly different from zero, while the coefficient on *LB* with low reserves ($\beta_3 + \beta_5$) increases significantly.

The fragility of the STV results with respect to the data revisions that have taken place since their estimations and to the addition of three countries to the sample casts some doubt on the usefulness of this specification for the Asian crises. We nonetheless generate predictions for 1997 based on these estimates drawn from the Tequila crisis.

Predicting 1997

To implement the STV model for 1997, we mechanically update the STV variables and apply the coefficients from the STV regressions for the Tequila crisis to obtain predicted values for the 1997 crises. For the dependent variable that measures the severity of the crisis, we measure percent depreciation of the nominal exchange rate from April 1997 through December 1997. For the explanatory variables, we move all the definitions forward two years. We then calculate forecasts of devaluation using the coefficient estimates from the STV benchmark specification estimated for the Tequila crisis.

Column 7 of Table 3 shows the country rankings based on the actual value of the crisis index for 1997, defined, analogously to STV, as the change in the nominal exchange rate between April and December 1997. Column 8 presents country rankings based on applying the coefficients from the STV regression estimated over the 23-country sample to the updated *LB* and *RER* variables and associated dummy variables.

STV themselves try many variants of their benchmark regression, in their case to demonstrate robustness. For example, the STV definition in terms of the average level of the real exchange rate in the 1990 through 1994 period divided by the

---

[24]Regression 1 differs slightly from the published benchmark regression, as discussed in the Appendix.

Andrew Berg and Catherine Pattillo

Table 5. STV: 1994/95 Regressions

Results[a,b]

Regression Number	Regression	Number of Countries	R^2	$\bar{R}^2$	STV hypotheses: $\beta_2 = 0$	$\beta_2+\beta_4 = 0$	$\beta_2+\beta_4+\beta_6 < 0$	$\beta_3 = 0$	$\beta_2+\beta_3 = 0$	$\beta_2+\beta_3+\beta_7 > 0$
1	STV benchmark, rerun fixing Taiwan	20	0.69	0.55	**6.61** (2.311)	0.28 (0.539)	-2.16 (0.994)	**1.86** (0.810)	**-5.49** (2.648)	**3.88** (1.463)
2	STV with revised data	20	0.66	0.50	**6.46** (1.860)	-0.06 (0.228)	-1.59 (1.133)	**1.74** (0.654)	**-16.87** (7.292)	**3.75** (1.405)
3	23-country sample	23	0.44	0.22	**4.18** (1.811)	**-0.34** (0.205)	**-3.48** (1.615)	0.94 (0.617)	-8.11 (6.578)	1.89 (1.354)
4	Alternate RER definition (1) RER 1994/90	23	0.41	0.19	**-4.18** (2.329) (1.054)	0.78 (0.875) (1.216)	**-4.29** (1.784) (3.992)	**-0.42** (0.157) (0.724)	0.22 (0.771) (9.222)	2.15 (1.582) (0.731)

[a]Coefficients in bold are significant at the 5-percent level. Bolded coefficients are significantly inconsistent with the STV hypothesis. Figures in parentheses are standard errors.

[b]The βs are coefficients from the regression $IND = \beta_2 RER + \beta_3 LB + \beta_4 RER \cdot DLR + \beta_5 LB \cdot DLR + \beta_6 RER \cdot DWF + \beta_7 LB \cdot DWF$, where RER is the degree of real depreciation, LB is a measure of the lending boom, DLR is a dummy variable for countries with low reserves, and DWF is a dummy for countries with weak fundamentals (see text for explanations).

ARE CURRENCY CRISES PREDICTABLE?

average level during 1986 through 1989 clearly has an arbitrary element, and they also try other measures, such as the percent change in the real exchange rate from 1990 to 1994.

None of these forecasts performs well. The most successful specification, based on Table 5, regression 4, employs one of the alternative definitions of *RER*. Its forecast rankings of crisis severity are insignificant predictors of the actual rankings and explain only 5 percent of the variance of the actual country rankings.[25]

A recent paper (Tornell, 1998) may seem to contradict the results in this paper. Tornell estimates a model very similar to STV, stacking observations from the 1994/95 crisis and the 1997 crisis. He finds that his new model: (1) fits fairly well, with significant coefficients plausibly signed; (2) has coefficients that appear stable between the two sets of crises; and (3) when fitted with the 1994 observations only and forecasting for 1997, produces good predictions, much better than the STV forecasts examined here and comparable to the KLR-weighted sum of indicators-based probabilities.

Rather than providing a counterexample to the results presented here, this effort illustrates the importance of testing models out of the sample used to formulate them, as we do here. A variety of apparently small modifications characterizes the difference between the specification in STV and Tornell (1998), and yet these respecifications apparently make the difference between success and failure in predicting the incidence of the 1997 crises "out of sample."[26]

This suggests that specification uncertainty can be as important as parameter uncertainty across crisis episodes, at least for techniques such as STV that rely on a small number of observations and relatively complex models. Only the application of models to episodes that postdate the design of the model provides an appropriately tough test. Unfortunately for our purposes, the apparent need for a separate specification search for the new set of crises casts some doubt on the usefulness of this sort of approach for predicting future crises.

II. Do Additional Variables Help?

We have seen that even the most successful of the models under consideration (KLR) has fairly low explanatory power. None of these papers was meant to be the last word on forecasting, however, so it is reasonable to ask whether it would have been possible to do better with some relatively minor modifications. We have already corrected some errors in the previous versions, as would anyone

---

[25]In light of this predictive failure, we have also considered a much less ambitious test of the STV model, justified by the idea that we may reasonably expect some constancy of the general model of crisis episodes even if parameter constancy fails to hold. It turns out, however, that even when reestimated using 1996 and 1997 data to explain the 1997 results, the STV model applied to the 1997 crisis meets with little success. The results vary strongly depending on the exact specification, but the fit is always poor. Compared with its application to the 1994 crisis, the coefficients are economically and statistically different, and the explanatory power of the regressions is much lower. Naturally, the in-sample results for 1997 are superior to the out-of-sample predictions we have already analyzed. It is remarkable, though, that the STV regression reestimated with 1997 data performs somewhat worse than the KLR out-of-sample forecasts.

[26]Bussière and Mulder (1999) confirm this conclusion. They find that the Tornell (1998) model performs poorly at predicting 1998 crises.

Andrew Berg and Catherine Pattillo

implementing them in early 1997. We have also looked at robustness to alternate samples and, in the case of STV, to changes in the definition of some of the explanatory variables. Here, though, we go one step further and ask whether the addition of some plausible right-hand-side variables would have greatly improved the performance of the models. To some extent we are, then, deviating here from the approach of testing "pure" out-of-sample forecasts.

KLR omitted several variables that even prior to 1997 were clearly identified in the literature as important potential determinants of crisis, most notably the level of the ratio of M2 to reserves and the ratio of the current account to GDP. KLR used the rate of growth of M2/reserves, but most discussions of crisis vulnerability even then focused on the level of this variable. KLR did not use the current account. We find that in the KLR framework both the level of M2/reserves and the ratio of the current deficit to GDP are highly informative over the in-sample period, as Table 1 shows.[27] As shown in the second column of Table 2, the KLR model augmented with these two additional variables performs noticeably better out-of-sample than the original model. For example, 32 percent of the precrisis observations are called correctly at the 25 percent cut-off, compared with 25 in the original model. In the rank correlation test, the augmented model's predictions are more highly correlated with the actual ranking of crises, with a correlation coefficient of 0.60 compared with 0.54 for the original model (columns 2 and 3 of Table 3).

For the FR model, we also tried alternative explanatory variables, all estimated using data through 1996. We saw in the original FR specification that the ratio of reserves to imports does not seem to matter. Measuring reserves as a ratio to short-term external debt and to broad money (M2) have both been suggested as alternative ways of measuring the adequacy of reserves.[28] We find that both the ratio of reserves to short-term external debt and that of reserves to M2 are separately significant predictors of crisis. When all three reserve ratios are included, the ratio of reserves to M2 is significant at the 1 percent level, while the ratio of reserves to short-term external debt is significant at the 10 percent level. The ratio of reserves to imports is insignificant and wrongly signed. The degree of openness of the economy may indicate the flexibility of the adjustment mechanism in the country and hence the probability of crisis. We find that more open economies, as measured by the share of exports and imports in GDP, were significantly less likely to suffer a crisis.[29] Changes in the terms of trade had no apparent impact on the likelihood of crisis, while measuring the debt composition variables as a share of GDP rather than total debt also had no effect. Interacting short-term external debt with credit growth, in the spirit of STV, also did not help predict crises.

---

[27]The current account is measured as a moving average of the previous four quarters. We use our interpolated monthly GDP series to form the ratio of the current account to the moving average of GDP over the same period.

[28]See Calvo and Mendoza (1996) on Mexico for an emphasis on the ratio of M2 to reserves and Radelet and Sachs (1998a) on the Asian crises for a focus on short-term external debt/reserves. The inclusion of the ratio of reserves to short-term external debt is particularly in violation of the out-of-sample spirit of this paper, as most of the interest in this variable postdates the Asian crises.

[29]Milesi-Ferretti and Razin (1998) make this argument and include this variable in a similar regression with some success.

ARE CURRENCY CRISES PREDICTABLE?

As a result of this specification search, regression 2 of Table 4 includes the ratio of reserves to M2 and the degree of openness of the economy. These additions do not help performance in 1997, as shown in column 6 of Table 3, which shows that the correlation of predicted and actual rankings of crises in 1997 is still small and insignificantly different from zero.

We did not attempt to add variables to the STV model, partly because the small sample size renders the exercise particularly prone to data mining and also because STV themselves consider and reject the main alternative candidate explanatory variables. We noted above that we have investigated a variety of different specifications suggested by STV themselves, without success.

III. Is It Fair to Compare Such Different Models?

We have judged these models based on their forecasting performance. Only the KLR model was designed explicitly with this objective in mind, and so it is perhaps not surprising that it is the most successful. However, FR is also a panel-based approach, and it is a reasonable test of the model to ask how well it fits in more recent years. And the value of the STV model depends in part on its applicability to crises in general, not just to those over which it was estimated.[30]

We have analyzed and compared results from three models that differ in critical ways. Most fundamentally, they are models with different crisis definitions—that is, dependent variables—and different samples. Since each model is forecasting something different, the comparison of typical statistics such as the R^2 is not helpful. We have therefore relied on goodness of fit, where applicable, and more generally on the rank correlation of predicted probabilities and actual incidence of crisis in 1997 in assessing the models.[31]

It is nonetheless important to keep in mind that success has different meanings for each of the models. For STV, it would imply that the relative severity of crisis was predictable, given the time period during which attacks might be expected to occur. KLR (and even more so FR, because of the shorter forecast interval) attempt as well the more ambitious task of predicting the timing of crises. It is perhaps surprising that KLR achieves some success at both ranking (as measured by the correlations of predicted and actual for 1997) and timing, as measured by the goodness-of-fit statistics.

The three models embody different definitions of crisis. STV and KLR agree on looking at a crisis index that combines information on reserve losses and exchange rate depreciations, on the grounds that they are trying to measure pressure on the exchange regime, whether it results in a devaluation or not. FR measure only the exchange rate, though largely on the practical grounds that data on reserve changes are noisy. FR and KLR choose to look for discrete crises defined as extreme values of the underlying index. This approach may be justified on the

---

[30]Many have tried to apply the model to other crises, as mentioned in footnote 9.

[31]For the same reason, it is also not helpful to directly compare probabilities of crisis across models. Where the crisis events are more common, the unconditional probabilities, and hence the mean forecast probabilities in an unbiased model, are higher.

Andrew Berg and Catherine Pattillo

grounds that crises represent a structural break in the behavior of the exchange rate and reserves compared to other times; the models are attempting, then, to predict the breaks, not the behavior in between. STV do not predict crises as discrete events; rather, they try to predict the severity of crises as measured by the percent change in a crisis index over a particular period.

Different crisis definitions yield different results, and all operational definitions of crisis contain measurement error in that they only imperfectly capture whatever we have in mind by currency crises.[32] This may worsen the performance of the models, though it may mean that they "really" work better than reported, in that some of the false alarms or missed crises may have been due to measurement error of the dependent variable. We have not explored this issue here.

The models in their original forms were estimated over quite different samples: FR used the broadest possible sample of developing countries over 22 years; STV estimated over only a cross section of "emerging markets"—that is, countries in the IFC database—at a particular time characterized by contagion and crisis; and KLR included an eclectic mix of developing and developed countries, the latter in particular chosen partly because they had crises, over 25 years. We have to some extent tested whether these differences in sample were important, by reestimating the models over the original and over a common sample. We have found that the KLR results were fairly robust to this change, though we find fewer indicators to be informative. The FR specification changed in some important ways with the restriction of the sample.[33] The STV results turned out to be most fragile to changes in sample, both over the original time period and also with respect to future crisis episodes. It turns out, though, that this variation in performance of the STV and FR models across samples did not matter along one important dimension: in no case did the out-of-sample forecasts predict crises well.

The models forecast over different time horizons. FR and STV forecast roughly one year out, while KLR considers an alarm to be correct if a crisis happens any time within a 24-month window. This difference is not responsible for the superior performance of the KLR model, as it performs about as well when attempting to forecast crises 12 months ahead rather than 24.

Furman and Stiglitz (1998) apply the KLR methodology to predicting the Asian crisis and, while they do not systematically evaluate the results, conclude that it does not work well, noting some success but many false positives. They dismiss what success they do observe largely on the argument that the method of measuring predictive variables in terms of percentiles is biased in favor of predicting crises in countries that have previously had little volatility in predictive variables. For example, even relatively small real exchange rate appreciation results in a large percentile deviation in historically tranquil countries, such as the Asian crisis countries. We find this argument uncompelling. There are many reasons why measures that compare variables to their own history may pick up important trends efficiently.[34]

---

[32]See Milesi-Ferretti and Razin (1998) on sensitivity to alternative crisis definitions in the FR model.

[33]See the Appendix for details.

[34]A doctor may well ask whether a patient has lost weight, not how his weight compares to the standard charts, when looking for signs of sickness. (We thank Joseph Stiglitz for this analogy.)

ARE CURRENCY CRISES PREDICTABLE?

Ultimately, the question is empirical. In fact, the KLR model does not tend to systematically overpredict crises in-sample in relatively tranquil countries.

The models analyzed in this paper are, with the partial exception of STV,
reduced form and nonstructural. An alternative approach is to estimate a well-
defined structural model. Blanco and Garber (1986) estimate a model of currency
crisis probability for Mexico that achieves some success. The results of this sort
of model are hard to compare with those we consider here. First, their results are
essentially a special case, in that they fit a specific structural model. The first-
generation model they estimate, with excess domestic credit creation driving a
crisis, is more plausibly applied to the specific crises they consider (Mexico's in
the 1970s and 1980s) than in many other cases. Their estimation depends on
using the interest rate differential as a measure of expected devaluation. The
empirical relevance of this assumption is doubtful, despite its plausibility.[35]
Moreover, they estimate only one period ahead, a horizon that may be of limited
use for policymakers.[36]

IV. Conclusion

We have examined the extent to which models formulated and estimated prior to
1997 would have helped predict the 1997 currency crises. The exercise is thus "out
of sample" both in the sense that we estimate the models using data only through
1996 and, equally important, in that the models themselves were specified prior to
1997. The results of this unusually tough test are generally though not unambiguously negative. Two of the three models (STV and FR) provide forecasts that are
no better than guesswork. Ex ante plausible variations in sample and specification
did not change this result.

The KLR model, in contrast, achieved a measure of success. The probabilities
of crisis it generated during the period May 1995 to December 1996 were statistically significant predictors of actual crisis incidence over the subsequent 24
months. Moreover, its forecasted cross-country ranking of severity of crisis is a
significant predictor of the actual ranking. This success should not be exaggerated.
The model does not explain a large part of the actual variation in outcomes. When
this model issued an alarm during the May 1995 to December 1996 period, a crisis would actually have followed in 1997 37 percent of the time.[37] This compares
with a 27 percent unconditional probability of crisis in 1997. And the model
explains only 28 percent of the variation in actual crisis rankings.

We also tried adding various explanatory variables to the models. Plausible
modifications to the STV and FR models did not yield useful forecasts, even
some, such as the inclusion of short-term external debt, actually inspired by
events in 1997. The addition of two variables to the KLR model that were widely

---

[35]The interest differential did not signal an expected exchange rate change in advance of Mexico's
1994 crisis, as Werner (1996) discusses.

[36]Their estimated probabilities of crisis are generally somewhat lower than those of KLR largely
because they are trying to predict a much rarer event than KLR (a crisis next month, as opposed to a crisis sometime within the next 24 months).

[37]An alarm here is defined as a predicted probability above 25 percent.

Andrew Berg and Catherine Pattillo

considered good indicators prior to 1997—the level of the current account balance and M2/reserves—improves performance somewhat.

The answer to the question posed in the title of this paper is thus "yes, but not very well." The answer is "yes" since the KLR forecasts, and even more so the modified model, are clearly better than a naive benchmark of pure guesswork. We say "not very well" because even the KLR model issues more false alarms than accurate warnings, while it misses most crises.

We have judged the forecasts of these models against a naive alternative of pure guesswork, and the statistically significant results do not imply that the KLR model does better than the analysis of informed observers. Systematic comparisons against alternative benchmarks would be interesting. It is not easy to find more challenging comparators, however. First, ratings agencies such as Moody's did not warn markets against the East Asian crises of 1997.[38] Goldfajn and Valdés (1998) show that exchange rate expectations of currency traders do not help predict crises. And there is little evidence that interest differentials systematically predict crises.[39]

The out-of-sample comparison of different approaches provides some insight into important issues in the empirical modeling of currency crises. We have found that reestimating the panel-based KLR and FR models over different samples of countries and longer time periods has preserved most of the economically important results. The STV model has proved largely unstable. More recent efforts to apply STV-like models to the Asian crises have met with some success. While this may help explain the crisis, it seems that the approach of carefully fitting a small set of crises is not promising as a way to predict the next round. To put it another way, specification uncertainty appears to be as important as parameter uncertainty for STV-type approaches, which represent a more complex specification fitted to many fewer observations.

We have also shed some light on the styled facts about crises. All three approaches demonstrate that the probability of a currency crisis increases when domestic credit growth is high, the real exchange rate is overvalued relative to trend, and the ratio of M2 to reserves is high. Both FR and KLR also suggest that a large current account deficit is an important risk factor.[40] These conclusions imply that elements of both first- and second-generation models are relevant: M2/reserves would seem to play a more important role in second-generation models of crisis that emphasize multiple equilibria, while the other variables are more suggestive of traditional first-generation models.

Where do we go from here? In this paper we have seen that the addition of some plausible variables improves performance of the KLR model somewhat. In

---

[38]After years of stable or increasing ratings, the first downgrade in the Asian crisis countries was a negative outlook in Thailand in February 1997 (Moody's). The rest were not downgraded until mid- to late 1997. See Adams and others (1998).

[39]The nominal interest differential alone does not predict crises well in our sample of countries. In a bivariate probit regression (not shown), the nominal interest differential is statistically significant, but the goodness of fit is much worse than for the KLR model we have considered, and the out-of-sample forecasts are not helpful. The real interest differential does worse still.

[40]The real exchange rate and the current account are not significant in the original FR specification, as discussed in the Appendix.

ARE CURRENCY CRISES PREDICTABLE?

a related paper, we depart from the entire "indicators" methodology that looks for discrete thresholds and calculates signal-to-noise ratios.[41] Instead, we apply a probit regression technique to the same data and crisis definition as in KLR. In the process we test some of the basic assumptions of the KLR approach. Specifically, we embed the KLR approach in a multivariate probit framework in which the independent variable takes the value of one if there is a crisis in the subsequent 24 months and zero otherwise. These probit models provide generally better forecasts than the KLR models. In the process, we find also that the data do not generally support one of the basic ideas of the KLR indicator approach: that it is useful to interpret predictive variables in terms of discrete thresholds, the crossing of which is particularly significant for signaling a crisis.

A variety of specification issues appear worth exploring, particularly in the context of probit-based models estimated on panel data. We can be confident that future papers will predict past crises. This exercise suggests, though, that while crisis forecasting models may help indicate vulnerability, the predictive power of even the best of them may be limited.

APPENDIX

Issues in Reestimation and In-Sample Results

In the text we present the KLR, FR, and STV models estimated with a common sample, and analyze the success of the out-of-sample predictions for 1997. This appendix fills in some of the steps. First, we discuss issues involved in the reestimation of the models, including the effects of updating the estimation period, changing the sample, fixing any errors in the original estimates, and using more recently available and hence revised data. Second, we evaluate the in-sample performance of the models.

Kaminsky, Lizondo, and Reinhart (1998) Signals Approach

We first reproduce the KLR results using the same 20-country, 1970–95 sample they use.[42] Our results are broadly similar to those of KLR, though column 1 of Table A1 shows slightly weaker performance than reported by KLR for most of the indicators. Differences are starker for four indicators, for which KLR find a noise-to-signal ratio substantially below unity while we find a ratio above unity. Thus, although KLR find 12 informative indicators—that is, those with noise-to-signal ratios below unity—we find only 8 of these to be informative.[43]

Next, we modify the sample in two ways. First, we estimate only through April 1995. This reflects the information available to the analyst just before the Thai crisis of July 1997,

---

[41]See Berg and Pattillo (1998 and 1999).

[42]Argentina, Bolivia, Brazil, Chile, Colombia, Denmark, Finland, Indonesia, Israel, Malaysia, Mexico, Norway, Peru, the Philippines, Spain, Sweden, Thailand, Turkey, Uruguay, and Venezuela.

[43]There are a number of possible reasons for the differences in results. We have found that our implementation of the KLR definition of crisis results in a set of crisis dates that do not fully match the KLR crisis dates as reported in Kaminsky and Reinhart (1996). Specifically, we fail to match 14 out of 76 KLR crises. Some of this discrepancy may come from differences in the raw data. We have found that seemingly small differences due to revisions in International Financial Statistics (IFS) data can strongly influence the results, and furthermore they and we separately "cleaned" the data of errors.

Andrew Berg and Catherine Pattillo

Table A1. Performance of Indicators

Indicator	KLR Sample Rerun			Original KLR Estimates		
	Noise/signal (adjusted)[a] (1)	P(crisis/signal) −P(crisis)[b] (2)	Number of crises with data (3)	Noise/signal (adjusted)[a] (4)	P(crisis/signal) −P(crisis)[b] (5)	Number of crises with data (6)
Real exchange rate[c]	0.24	32	70	0.19	39	72
M2/reserves growth rate	0.46	16	69	0.48	17	70
Export growth rate	0.49	15	69	0.42	20	70
International reserves growth rate	0.53	13	69	0.55	16	72
Excess M1 balances[d]	0.69	7	68	0.52	15	66
Domestic credit/GDP growth rate	0.71	6	66	0.62	11	62
Real interest rate	0.74	5	42	0.77	6	44
M2 multiplier growth rate	0.80	4	69	0.61	11	70
Import growth rate	1.19	−3	69	1.16	−3	71
Industrial production growth rate	1.23	−3	58	0.52	16	57
Terms of trade growth rate	1.42	−5	63	0.77	6	58
Lending rate/deposit rate	1.44	−5	34	1.69	−9	33
Bank deposit growth rate	1.53	−6	69	1.20	−4	69
Stock price index growth rate	1.81	−9	47	0.47	18	53
Real interest differential	1.97	−9	42	0.77	6	44
Current account/GDP						
M2/reserves (level)						

[a]Ratio of false signals (measured as a proportion of months in which false signals could have been issued [B/(B+D)]) to good signals (measured as a proportion of months in which good signals could have been issued [A/(A+C)]).

[b]P(crisis/signal) is the percentage of the signals issued by the indicator that were followed by at least one crisis within the subsequent 24 months ([A/(A+C)] in terms of the matrix in the text). P(crisis) is the unconditional probability of a crisis, (A+C)/(A+B+C+D).

[c]Deviation from deterministic trend.

[d]Residual from regression of real M1 on real GDP, inflation, and a deterministic trend.

ARE CURRENCY CRISES PREDICTABLE?

since the evaluation of an observation requires knowing whether there will be a crisis within 24 months. Second, we change the sample of countries: we omit the five European countries from the sample and add other emerging market economies. This sample is more appropriate for our concern with crises in "emerging markets" and also serves as an informal test of robustness of the KLR approach.[44] Table 1 in the text shows that indicator performance over the larger sample is broadly similar to results using the KLR sample. The average noise-to-signal ratio falls a little for the informative indicators in the 23-country sample (as well as for the entire set of indicators).

So far we have looked at each indicator separately. Following Kaminsky (1998a), we next calculate the weighted-sum-based probabilities of crisis.[45] This produces a series of estimated probabilities of crisis for each country. These should be interpreted as the predicted probability of crisis within the next 24 months, based on the (weighted) number of indicators signaling in a given month.[46]

How good are these in-sample forecasts in predicting crises during January 1970 to April 1995? For zero/one dependent variables, it is natural to ask what fraction of the observations are correctly called. A cutoff level for the predicted probability of crisis is defined such that a crisis is predicted if the estimated probability is above this threshold. The resulting goodness-of-fit data are shown in the first two columns of Table A2 for two cutoffs: 50 percent and 25 percent.[47]

What can we conclude? The first column of Table A2 displays the goodness-of-fit measures for the KLR weighted-sum-based probabilities, using the original specification and our new sample. The model correctly calls most observations at the 50 percent cutoff, almost entirely through correct prediction of tranquil periods (i.e., those that are not followed by crises within 24 months). Almost all (91 percent) of the crisis months (i.e., observations followed by a crisis within 24 months) are missed. Even with so few crisis observations correctly called, 44 percent of alarms (i.e., observations where the predicted probability of crisis is above 50 percent) are false, in that no crisis in fact ensues within 24 months. Next, we add the two new variables, current account and M2/reserves in levels. As the second column of Table A2 shows, the addition of these variables only modestly improves the performance of the KLR-based probabilities. A χ^2 test rejects the null that the forecasts and actual outcomes are independent at the 1 percent level.

With a lower cutoff of 25 percent, 41 percent of crisis observations are correctly called by the original KLR model. The probability of a crisis within 24 months is now 37 percent if there is an alarm, much higher than the unconditional probability of crisis of 16 percent in this sample. Now, however, 63 percent of alarms are false. A χ^2 test also rejects the null that the forecasts and actual outcomes are independent at the 1 percent level here.

Our analysis of the in-sample success of the KLR-type models suggests that the approach can indeed be useful and the model does significantly better than guesses based on the unconditional probability of crisis. Nonetheless, most crises are still missed and most alarms are false.

---

[44]We add the following to the 15 KLR emerging market economies: India, Jordan, Korea, Pakistan, South Africa, Sri Lanka, Taiwan Province of China, and Zimbabwe.

[45]Two issues regarding the treatment of missing data in the KLR framework deserve mention. A key variable is c24, which is defined to equal one if there is a crisis in the next 24 months. This variable is defined as long as one observation is available (either a crisis or noncrisis month) in the relevant 24-month period. Secondly, the weighted sum of indicators signaling is calculated provided that data on at least one of the indicators is available. The weighted-sum-based probabilities are calculated using the same principle.

[46]Unlike Kaminsky (1998a), we use only the good indicators, that is, those with noise-to-signal ratio less than one.

[47]See Table 2 footnotes for precise definitions of "correctly called" and related terms.

Andrew Berg and Catherine Pattillo

Table A2. Goodness of Fit of KLR Model—In Sample

Cutoff of 50 Percent
Goodness-of-Fit Table[a]

| | Original Specification | | | | Augmented with Current Account and M2/reserves | | |
| | Actual | | | | Actual | | |
Predicted	Tranquil	Crash	Total	Predicted	Tranquil	Crash	Total
Tranquil	5,541	1,114	6,655	Tranquil	5,581	1,115	6,696
Crash	90	115	205	Crash	50	114	164
Total	5,631	1,229	6,860	Total	5,631	1,229	6,860

Summary Statistics

	Original	Augmented
Percent of observations correctly called	82	83
Percent of crises correctly called[b]	9	9
Percent of tranquil periods correctly called[c]	98	99
False alarms as a percent of total alarms[d]	44	30
Probability of crisis given:		
an alarm[e]	56	70
no alarm[f]	17	17

Cutoff of 25 Percent
Goodness-of-Fit Table[a]

| | Original Specification | | | | Augmented with Current Account and M2/reserves | | |
| | Actual | | | | Actual | | |
Predicted	Tranquil	Crash	Total	Predicted	Tranquil	Crash	Total
Tranquil	4,790	728	5,518	Tranquil	4,568	658	5,227
Crash	841	501	1,342	Crash	1,063	571	1,634
Total	5,631	1,229	6,860	Total	5,631	1,229	6,860

Summary Statistics

	Original	Augmented
Percent of observations correctly called	77	75
Percent of crises correctly called[b]	41	46
Percent of tranquil periods correctly called[c]	85	81
False alarms as a percent of total alarms[d]	63	65
Probability of crisis given:		
an alarm[e]	37	35
no alarm[f]	13	13

[a]Table shows number of observations.
[b]A precrisis period is correctly called when the estimated probability of crisis is above the cutoff probability and a crisis ensues within 24 months.
[c]A tranquil period is correctly called when the estimated probability of crisis is below the cutoff probability and no crisis ensues within 24 months.
[d]A false alarm is an observation with an estimated probability of crisis above the cutoff (an alarm) not followed by a crisis within 24 months.
[e]This is the number of precrisis periods correctly called as a share of total predicted precrisis periods.
[f]This is the number of periods where tranquility is predicted and a crisis actually ensues as a share of total predicted tranquil periods (observations for which the predicted probability of crisis is below the cutoff).

ARE CURRENCY CRISES PREDICTABLE?

Frankel and Rose (1996) Probit Model Using Multi-Country Sample

Table A3 (column 1) presents our reproduction of the FR benchmark probit regression, using the same sample of annual data for over 100 developing countries for 1970–92. FR conclude from this and a variety of similar regressions that the probability of a crisis increases when output growth is low, domestic credit growth is high, foreign interest rates are high, and FDI as a proportion of total debt is low. They also found support for the prediction that crashes tend to occur when reserves are low and the real exchange rate is overvalued.[48]

We made several revisions to the FR benchmark regression before updating it to 1996. As with the other papers, we used currently available, and hence revised, data from the same World Bank source as FR.[49] In addition, we corrected an error in the original FR calculation of the overvaluation variable.[50]

The net effect of all these changes is shown in the second regression of Table A3. Overall, the model performs somewhat better than the original FR regression. The corrected overvaluation variable now has a much stronger and more significant effect. Higher northern (OECD) growth now significantly decreases the risk of crisis, and the effect of foreign interest rates is smaller and insignificant.[51]

We now estimate the model through 1996 for purposes of generating predictions for 1997. As the third regression in Table A3 shows, the results are similar to the 1970 to 1992 regressions. A large share of debt which is concessional now reduces the risk of crisis.[52]

Next, we change the sample. The sample of countries used in the original FR regressions is substantially different from those in the KLR and STV regressions. In particular, a large number of least-developed countries (such as the countries of the Council for Mutual Economic Assistance) and small island economies (for example, São Tomé, Cape Verde, and Vanuatu) are included. Because of concerns that crises in these countries may have different determinants and to maximize comparability with the other papers, we have rerun the FR regression over a smaller sample of 41 countries made up of all developing countries with per capita incomes above $1,000 and population above 1 million for which there are data.[53]

---

[48]Although the authors highlight the importance of low reserves and overvaluation in their conclusion, their results show significant effects were not robust and were found in fewer than half of the specifications they tested. The result that faster domestic growth reduces the probability of crisis is also not robust, as illustrated by the benchmark regression itself.

[49]This changed not only some of the data but also the sample, because some of the data that had previously been available, largely from the early 1970s, are now considered to be of unacceptable quality, while other formerly unavailable observations now had data. The net effect is to increase the number of observations from 780 in FR to 881, though the overlap of common data points is only 729 observations.

[50]We also made two other technical modifications. First, we used percent changes instead of log differences in comparing the devaluations with the 25 percent crisis threshold. Second, we changed the implementation of the "windowing" procedure to more closely match the FR intent of ensuring that only the first of a sequence of crises was counted in the sample. See Milesi-Ferretti and Razin (1998), who recommended these two modifications.

[51]For the overvaluation variable itself, the correction is the source of the improvement. For the other variables, the changes in sample resulting from the data revision are more important than the data revisions themselves, the changes in the windowing procedure and definition of crisis, or the correction of the overvaluation variable in driving these changes in results.

[52]For purposes of predicting 1997 outcomes, we also estimate this regression with the government budget as a share of GDP excluded from this regression, because this variable is not available for 1996 as would be required for forecasting 1997. This omission makes little difference.

[53]Milesi-Ferretti and Razin (1998) raise these sample issues and extract this smaller sample, for which they get improved results compared with FR.

Andrew Berg and Catherine Pattillo

Table A3. Frankel and Rose: Probit Estimates of Probability of a Currency Crash

	Original 1970–92 Sample				1970–96 Sample	
	Model 1A FR benchmark		Model 2A revised		Model 3A FR benchmark	
	dF/dx	$|z|^a$	dF/dx	$|z|^a$	dF/dx	$|z|^a$
Commercial bank share of total debt	0.03	0.2	–0.07	–0.6	0.03	–0.3
Concessional share	–0.14	–2.1	–0.12	–1.6	–0.13	–1.9 *
Variable rate share	–0.03	0.2	0.20	1.5	0.13	1.1
Short-term share	0.23	2.0	0.28	2.3 **	0.27	2.2 **
FDI/debt	–0.31	–2.5	–0.53	–3.7 ***	–0.46	–3.3 ***
Public sector share	0.19	2.2	0.18	2.0 **	0.16	1.8 *
Multilateral share	–0.06	–0.8	0.08	1.0	0.06	0.8
Debt/GNP	–0.04	–1.7	–0.02	–1.5	–0.02	–1.4
Reserves/imports	–0.01	–3.4	–0.01	–3.3 ***	–0.01	–3.9 ***
Current account/GDP	0.02	0.2	–0.03	–0.3	–0.02	–0.2
Overvaluation[b]	0.08	2.5	0.15	4.0 **	0.12	3.3 ***
Government budget surplus/ GDP	0.16	1.1	0.10	0.7	0.11	0.8
Domestic credit growth	0.10	3.2	0.08	3.8 ***	0.08	3.7 ***
GDP growth rate	–0.16	–1.3	–0.07	–1.5	–0.08	–1.6
Foreign interest rate	0.80	2.6	0.48	1.4	0.33	1.0
Northern (OECD) growth	–0.85	–1.5	–1.17	–1.9 *	–1.52	–2.5 **
Sample size	780		881		940	
Pseudo R^2	0.17		0.17		0.15	

Goodness of Fit

	Model 1A			Model 2A			Model 3A		
	Tranquil	Crash	Total	Tranquil	Crash	Total	Tranquil	Crash	Total
Cutoff probability of 50 percent[c]									
Predicted tranquility	707	64	771	777	88	865	830	97	927
Predicted crash	4	5	9	7	9	16	5	8	13
Total	711	69	780	784	97	881	835	105	940
Cutoff probability of 25 percent[d]									
Predicted tranquility	678	52	730	743	62	805	792	72	864
Predicted crash	33	17	50	41	35	76	43	33	76
Total	711	69	780	784	97	881	835	105	940

[a]One, two, and three asterisks denote significance at the 10, 5, and 1 percent levels, respectively.
[b]Defined as the deviation from the average real exchange rate over the period.
[c]A crisis is correctly called when the estimated probability of crisis is above 50 percent if a crisis ensues within 24 months. A tranquil period is correctly called when the estimated probability of crisis is below 50 percent and there is no crisis within 24 months.
[d]A crisis is correctly called when the estimated probability of crisis is above 25 percent if a crisis ensues within 24 months. A tranquil period is correctly called when the estimated probability of crisis is below 25 percent and there is no crisis within 24 months.

ARE CURRENCY CRISES PREDICTABLE?

The results are broadly similar, as regression 1 of Table 4 shows. The most notable changes are that the ratio of reserves to imports is no longer significant whereas the current account and the fiscal balance now are.

The main text discusses our consideration of some alternative explanatory variables. Regression 2 of Table 4 includes the ratio to the reserves to M2 and the degree of openness of the economy, as a result of this specification search. This model suggests that the probability of a crash increases when concessional debt and FDI are small and public sector debt large as a share of total external debt, the ratio of reserves/M2 is low, the current account deficit is large, the real exchange rate is overvalued, domestic credit growth is high, foreign interest rates are high, and the country is not open to trade.

Model 3A of Table A3 is close to the original FR specification, with some corrections and minor revisions, while model 2 of Table 4 is our augmented specification using a more homogeneous sample. The diagnostic statistics show that, in-sample, these models rarely generate a predicted probability of crash above 50 percent. Model 3A correctly predicts only 8 out of the 105 crashes; model 2 (Table 4) does better, predicting one-third of the crashes in the sample. When an estimated probability of above 25 percent followed by a crash is considered success, the results look better. Model 2, for example, generates a probability above 25 percent before 63 percent of crises. About half of warnings defined this way (41 out of 79) were not followed by a crash.

The FR models thus show some promise for predicting crises based on this in-sample assessment. There is a fair amount of parameter stability across samples, and many sensible variables are significant predictors of crisis. The overall explanatory power is fairly low, though our modifications lead to some improvement here.

Sachs, Tornell, and Velasco (1996) Cross-Country Regressions

The text discussed reproduction of the original STV benchmark regression, using their data,[54] as well as results using revised data and estimating over the common 23-country sample (Table 5, regressions 1, 2, and 3, respectively). We also considered a revised specification based on a different definition of the real exchange rate (Table 5, regression 4).

Table A4 shows some further variants of the STV regressions for the 1994–95 sample. Regression 5 is another variant on the definition of the real exchange rate variable, measuring *RER* as the level of the real exchange rate in 1994 compared with its average over the 1986 to 1989 period. It is also quite similar to the benchmark specification in Table 5, regression 3.

The definitions of low reserves and weak fundamentals in terms of which quartile of the sample the country finds itself are somewhat arbitrary. For this reason, STV vary the definition of low reserves and weak fundamentals so that countries in different fractions of the sample qualify. For example, regression 6 of Table A4 reproduces the STV results for the

---

[54]Regression 1 differs slightly from the published STV benchmark, mainly because we have corrected an error in the calculation of *RER* for Taiwan Province of China, in STV. The resulting differences are statistically, numerically, and economically small. In addition, the data used both in the STV benchmark and regression 1 differ slightly from that described and published in STV. First, the data published in STV (but not that used in their regressions) contain several typographical errors, which we have corrected with the help of the authors. Second, here and in the STV regression the lending boom variable was calculated differently for Peru than for the other countries and as defined in the appendix of STV. Specifically, LB is defined as the growth from 1990 through 1994 in the ratio of domestic credit to the private sector to GDP. For Peru, however, the base year actually used is apparently 1991. This is presumably because the hyperinflation and stabilization of 1989/1990 led to a tiny base of credit/GDP and would have resulted in a large outlier for Peru if calculated as defined in STV. Third, the measure of reserves for South Africa apparently includes gold reserves, as is standard for that country but contrary to the description in the appendix of STV.

Andrew Berg and Catherine Pattillo

Table A4. STV: 1994/5 Regressions

Results[a, b]

Regression Number		Number of Countries	R^2	$\bar{R}^2$	STV hypotheses: $\beta_2 = 0$	$\beta_2+\beta_4 = 0$	$\beta_2+\beta_4+\beta_6 < 0$	$\beta_3 = 0$	$\beta_2+\beta_5 = 0$	$\beta_2+\beta_5+\beta_7 > 0$
With quartiles										
5	Alternate RER definition(2) RER 1994/average (1986–89)	23	0.43	0.21	2.22 (2.566)	**-0.30** (0.134)	**-2.69** (1.141)	0.46 (0.710)	-5.72 (5.779)	1.80 (1.351)
With halves										
6	STV benchmark from STV	20	0.68	0.54	-0.52 (1.545)	0.48	-6.58	0.26 (0.547)	-1.80	**3.32**
7	STV with revised data	20	0.66	0.50	-0.20 (0.952)	0.15 (0.881)	2.51 (4.657)	0.17 (0.399)	2.06 (3.832)	**4.94** (2.209)
8	23-country sample	23	0.64	0.51	-0.26 (1.054)	1.50 (1.216)	**-14.45** (3.992)	0.93 (0.724)	5.50 (9.222)	**1.93** (0.731)

[a] Coefficients in bold are significant at the 5-percent level. Bolded coefficients are significantly inconsistent with the STV hypothesis. Figures in parentheses are standard errors.

[b] The βs are coefficients from the regression $IND = \beta_2 RER + \beta_3 LB + \beta_4 RER \cdot DLR + \beta_5 LB \cdot DLR + \beta_6 RER \cdot DWF + \beta_7 LB \cdot DWF$, where RER is the degree of real depreciation, LB is a measure of the lending boom, DLR is a dummy variable for countries with low reserves, and DWF is a dummy for countries with weak fundamentals (see text for explanations).

ARE CURRENCY CRISES PREDICTABLE?

case where "low reserves" is defined as having a reserves/M2 ratio in the bottom *half* of the sample, while "weak fundamentals" is having low reserves or an exchange rate depreciation in the lower *half* of the sample. The main results continue to hold. Regressions 7 and 8 of Table A4 present the reestimation of regression 5 with revised data and correcting the Taiwan Province of China crisis variable. Unlike with the quartile regressions, this changes the results: most important, *RER* with low reserves and weak fundamentals ($\beta_2 + \beta_4 + \beta_6$) now has the wrong sign, though it is insignificant.[55]

A number of the STV results are not robust to the data revisions that have taken place since their estimations and to the addition of three countries to the sample. The fit of the models is generally poorer and the main hypotheses receive mixed support at best.

REFERENCES

Adams, Charles, Donald J. Mathieson, Garry Schinasi, and Bankim Chadha, 1998, *International Capital Markets* (Washington: International Monetary Fund, September).

Berg, Andrew, 1999, "The Asian Crisis: Causes, Responses, and Outcomes" (unpublished; Washington: International Monetary Fund).

―――― and Catherine Pattillo, 1999, "Predicting Currency Crises: The Indicators Approach and an Alternative," *Journal of International Money and Finance*, forthcoming.

――――, 1998, "Are Currency Crises Predictable?: A Test," IMF Working Paper 98/154 (Washington: International Monetary Fund).

Blanco, Herminio, and Peter M. Garber, 1986, "Recurrent Devaluation and Speculative Attacks on the Mexican Peso," *Journal of Political Economy*, Vol. 94 (February), pp. 148–66.

Bussière, Matthieu, and Christian Mulder, 1999, "External Vulnerability in Emerging Countries: The Trade-Off Between Fundamentals and Liquidity" (unpublished; Washington: International Monetary Fund)

Calvo, Guillermo A., and Enrique G. Mendoza, 1996, "Mexico's Balance-of-Payments Crisis: a Chronicle of a Death Foretold," *Journal of International Economics*, Vol. 41 (December), pp. 235–64.

Corsetti, Giancarlo, Paolo Pesenti, and Nouriel Roubini, 1998a, "Paper Tigers? A Model of the Asian Crisis," NBER Working Paper No. 6783 (Cambridge, Massachusetts: National Bureau of Economic Research).

――――, 1998b, "What Caused the Asian Currency and Financial Crisis? Part I: A Macroeconomic Overview," NBER Working Paper No. 6833 (Cambridge, Massachusetts: National Bureau of Economic Research).

――――, 1998c, "What Caused the Asian Currency and Financial Crisis?: Part II: The Policy Debate," NBER Working Paper No. 6834 (Cambridge, Massachusetts: National Bureau of Economic Research).

Flood, Robert, and Nancy Marion, 1998, "Perspectives on the Recent Currency Crisis Literature," NBER Working Paper No. 6380 (Cambridge, Massachusetts: National Bureau of Economic Research).

――――, 1994, "The Size and Timing of Devaluations in Capital-Controlled Developing Economies," NBER Working Paper No. 4957 (Cambridge, Massachusetts: National Bureau of Economic Research).

---

[55]In this case, part of the reason for the difference is that, even using the (typo-corrected) STV data, we were not able to reproduce regression 5.

Andrew Berg and Catherine Pattillo

Frankel, Jeffrey A., and Andrew K. Rose, 1996, "Currency Crashes in Emerging Markets: An Empirical Treatment," *Journal of International Economics*, Vol. 41 (November), pp. 351–66.

Furman, Jason, and Joseph Stiglitz, 1998, "Economic Crises: Evidence and Insights from East Asia," *Brookings Papers on Economic Activity: 1*, Brookings Institution, pp. 1–136.

Goldfajn, Ilan, and Rodrigo Valdés, 1997, "Are Currency Crises Predictable?" *European Economic Review*, Vol. 42 (May), pp. 873–85.

Goldstein, Morris, 1998, "Early Warning Indicators and the Asian Financial Crisis" (unpublished; Washington: Institute for International Economics).

International Monetary Fund, 1998, *World Economic Outlook* (Washington: International Monetary Fund, May).

Kaminsky, Graciela, 1998a, "Currency and Banking Crises: A Composite Leading Indicator," IMF Seminar Series No. 1998–6, February.

———, 1998b, "Financial Crises in Asia and Latin America: Then and Now," *American Economic Review, Papers and Proceedings*, Vol. 88 (May), pp. 44–48.

———, and Carmen M. Reinhart, 1996, "The Twin Crises: The Causes of Banking and Balance-of-Payments Problems," International Finance Discussion Paper No. 544 (Washington: Board of the Governors of the Federal Reserve System, March).

Kaminsky, Graciela, Saul Lizondo, and Carmen Reinhart, 1998, "Leading Indicators of Currency Crises," *Staff Papers*, International Monetary Fund, Vol. 45 (March), pp. 1–48.

Krugman, Paul, 1979, "A Model of Balance-of-Payments Crises," *Journal of Money, Credit and Banking*, Vol. 11 (August), pp. 311–25.

Lane, Timothy, and others, 1999, "IMF-Supported Programs in Indonesia, Korea and Thailand: A Preliminary Assessment," available via Internet: http://www.imf.org/external/pubs/ft/op/opasia/asia1.pdf (Washington: International Monetary Fund).

Milesi-Ferretti, Gian Maria, and Assaf Razin, 1998, "Current Account Reversals and Currency Crises: Empirical Regularities," IMF Working Paper 98/89 (Washington: International Monetary Fund).

Radelet, Steven, and Jeffrey Sachs, 1998a, "The Onset of the East Asian Financial Crisis," NBER Working Paper No. 6680 (Cambridge, Massachusetts: National Bureau of Economic Research).

———, 1998b, "The East-Asian Financial Crisis: Diagnosis, Remedies, Prospects," *Brookings Papers on Economic Activity: 1*, Brookings Institution, pp. 1–90.

Sachs, Jeffrey, Aaron Tornell, and Andrés Velasco, 1996, "Financial Crises in Emerging Markets: The Lessons from 1995," *Brookings Papers on Economic Activity: 1*, Brookings Institution, pp. 147–215.

Sachs, Jeffrey, 1997, "What Investors Should Learn from the Crisis That Has Forced Thailand to Seek an IMF Loan," *Financial Times* (London), July 30.

Tornell, Aaron, 1998, "Common Fundamentals in the Tequila and Asian Crises" (unpublished; Cambridge, Massachusetts: Harvard University).

Werner, Alejandro, 1996, "Mexico's Currency Risk Premia in 1992–94: A Closer Look at the Interest Rate Differentials," IMF Working Paper 96/41 (Washington: International Monetary Fund).

B
Technical Analysis

Christopher J. Neely is an economist at the Federal Reserve Bank of St. Louis. Kent A. Koch provided research assistance.

Technical Analysis in the Foreign Exchange Market: A Layman's Guide

Christopher J. Neely

Technical analysis suggests that a long-term rally frequently is interrupted by a short-lived decline. Such a dip, according to this view, reinforces the original uptrend. Should the dollar fall below 1.5750 marks, dealers said, technical signals would point to a correction that could pull the dollar back as far as 1.55 marks before it rebounded.

Gregory L. White
Wall Street Journal
November 12, 1992

Technical analysis, which dates back a century to the writings of *Wall Street Journal* editor Charles Dow, is the use of past price behavior to guide trading decisions in asset markets. For example, a trading rule might suggest buying a currency if its price has risen more than 1 percent from its value five days earlier. Such rules are widely used in stock, commodity, and (since the early 1970s) foreign exchange markets. More than 90 percent of surveyed foreign exchange dealers in London report using some form of technical analysis to inform their trading decisions (Taylor and Allen, 1992). In fact, at short horizons—less than a week—technical analysis predominates over fundamental analysis, the use of other economic variables like interest rates, and prices in influencing trading decisions.

Investors and economists are interested in technical analysis for different reasons.

Investors are concerned with "beating the market," earning the best return on their money. Economists study technical analysis in foreign exchange markets because its success casts doubt on the efficient markets hypothesis, which holds that publicly available information, like past prices, should not help traders earn unusually high returns. Instead, the success of technical analysis suggests that exchange rates are not always determined by economic fundamentals like prices and interest rates, but rather are driven away from their fundamental values for long periods by traders' irrational expectations of future exchange rate changes. These swings away from fundamental values may discourage international trade and investment by making the relative price of U.S. and foreign goods and investments very volatile. For example, when BMW decides where to build an automobile factory, it may choose poorly if fluctuating exchange rates make it difficult or impossible to predict costs of production in the United States relative to those in Germany.

Despite the widespread use of technical analysis in foreign exchange (and other) markets, economists have traditionally been very skeptical of its value. Technical analysis has been dismissed by some as astrology. In turn, technical traders have frequently misunderstood what economists have to say about asset price behavior. What can the two learn from each other? This article provides an accessible treatment of recent research on technical analysis in the foreign exchange market.

A PRIMER ON TECHNICAL ANALYSIS IN FOREIGN EXCHANGE MARKETS

Technical analysis is a short-horizon trading method; positions last a few hours or days. Technical traders will not hold

REVIEW
SEPTEMBER/OCTOBER 1997

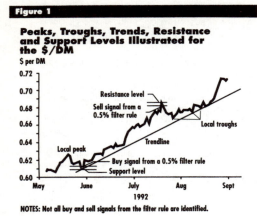

Figure 1

Peaks, Troughs, Trends, Resistance and Support Levels Illustrated for the $/DM

NOTES: Not all buy and sell signals from the filter rule are identified.

existence of trends: Trends in motion tend to remain in motion unless acted upon by another force. The third principle of technical analysis is that history repeats itself. Asset traders will tend to react the same way when confronted by the same conditions. Technical analysts do not claim their methods are magical; rather, they take advantage of market psychology.

Following from these principles, the methods of technical analysis attempt to identify trends and reversals of trends. These methods are explicitly extrapolative; that is, they infer future price changes from those of the recent past. Formal methods of detecting trends are necessary because prices move up and down around the primary (or longer-run) trend. An example of this movement is shown in Figure 1, where the dollar/deutsche mark ($/DM) exchange rate fluctuates around an apparent uptrend.[2]

To distinguish trends from shorter-run fluctuations, technicians employ two types of analysis: *charting* and *mechanical rules*. Charting, the older of the two methods, involves graphing the history of prices over some period—determined by the practitioner—to predict future patterns in the data from the existence of past patterns. Its advocates admit that this subjective system requires the analyst to use judgement and skill in finding and interpreting patterns. The second type of method, mechanical rules, imposes consistency and discipline on the technician by requiring him to use rules based on mathematical functions of present and past exchange rates.

Charting

To identify trends through the use of charts, practitioners must first find *peaks* and *troughs* in the price series. A peak is the highest value of the exchange rate within a specified period of time (a local maximum), while a trough is the lowest value the price has taken on within the same period (a local minimum). A series of peaks and troughs establishes downtrends and uptrends, respectively. For example, as

positions for months or years, waiting for exchange rates to return to where fundamentals are pushing them. In contrast, fundamental investors study the economic determinants of exchange rates as a basis for positions that typically last much longer, for months or years. Some traders, however, use technical analysis in conjunction with fundamental analysis, doubling their positions when technical and fundamental indicators agree on the direction of exchange rate movements.

Three principles guide the behavior of technical analysts.[1] The first is that market action (prices and transactions volume) "discounts" everything. In other words, all relevant information about an asset is incorporated into its price history, so there is no need to forecast the fundamental determinants of an asset's value. In fact, Murphy (1986) claims that asset price changes often precede observed changes in fundamentals. The second principle is that asset prices move in trends. Predictable trends are essential to the success of technical analysis because they enable traders to profit by buying (selling) assets when the price is rising (falling), or as technicians counsel, "the trend is your friend." Practitioners appeal to Newton's law of motion to explain the

[1] These principles and a much more comprehensive treatment of technical analysis are provided by Murphy (1986) and Pring (1991). Rosenberg and Shatz (1995) advocate the use of technical analysis with more economic explanation.

[2] Figure 1 shows only closing prices. In this, it differs from most charts employed by technical traders, which might show the opening, closing, and daily trading range.

Review

SEPTEMBER/OCTOBER 1997

shown in Figure 1, an analyst may establish an uptrend visually by connecting two local troughs in the data. A trendline is drawn below an apparent up trend or above an apparent downtrend. As more troughs touch the trendline without violating it, the technician may place more confidence in the validity of the trendline. The angle of the trendline indicates the speed of the trend, with steeper lines indicating faster appreciation (or depreciation) of the foreign currency.

After a trendline has been established, the technician trades with the trend, buying the foreign currency if an uptrend is signaled and selling the foreign currency if a downtrend seems likely. When a market participant buys a foreign currency in the hope that it will go up in price, that participant is said to be *long* in the currency. The opposite strategy, called *shorting* or *selling short*, enables the participant to make money if the foreign currency falls in price. A short seller borrows foreign currency today and sells it, hoping the price will fall so that it can be bought back more cheaply in the future.

Spotting the reversal of a trend is just as important as detecting trends. Peaks and troughs are important in identifying reversals too. Local peaks are called *resistance levels*, and local troughs are called *support levels* (see Figure 1). If the price fails to break a resistance level (a local peak) during an uptrend, that may be an early indication that the trend may soon reverse. If the exchange rate significantly penetrates the trendline, that is considered a more serious signal of a possible reversal.

Technicians identify several patterns that are said to foretell a shift from a trend in one direction to a trend in the opposite direction. An example of the best-known type of reversal formation, called "head and shoulders," is shown in Figure 2. The head and shoulders reversal following an uptrend is characterized by three local peaks with the middle peak being the largest of the three. The line between the troughs of the shoulders is known as the "neckline." When the exchange rate penetrates the neckline of a head and

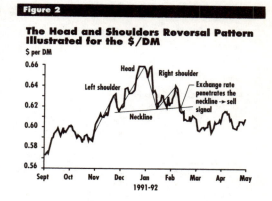

Figure 2

The Head and Shoulders Reversal Pattern Illustrated for the $/DM

$ per DM

shoulders, the technician confirms a reversal of the previous uptrend and begins to sell the foreign currency. There are several other similar reversal patterns, including the V (single peak), the double top (two similar peaks) and the triple top (three similar peaks). The reversal patterns of a downtrend are essentially the mirrors of the reversal patterns for the uptrend.

Mechanical Rules

Charting is very dependent on the interpretation of the technician who is drawing the charts and interpreting the patterns. Subjectivity can permit emotions like fear or greed to affect the trading strategy. The class of mechanical trading rules avoids this subjectivity and so is more consistent and disciplined, but, according to some technicians, it sacrifices some information that a skilled chartist might discern from the data. Mechanical trading rules are even more explicitly extrapolative than charting; they look for trends and follow those trends. A well-known type of mechanical trading rule is the "filter rule," or "trading range break" rule which counsels buying (selling) a currency when it rises (falls) x percent above (below) its previous local minimum (maximum). The size of the filter, x, which is

REVIEW
SEPTEMBER/OCTOBER 1997

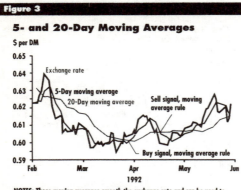

Figure 3

5- and 20-Day Moving Averages

$ per DM

NOTES: These moving averages smooth the exchange rate and can be used to generate buy and sell signals in the foreign exchange market.

Figure 4

The Oscillator Index

Normalized difference in moving averages

NOTES: The 5-day moving average minus the 20-day moving average can also be used to generate buy and sell signals.

exchange rate over a given number of previous trading days. The length of the moving average "window"—the number of days in the moving average—governs whether the moving average reflects long- or short-run trends.[3] Any moving average will be smoother than the original exchange-rate series, and long moving averages will be smoother than short moving averages. Figure 3 illustrates the behavior of a 5-day and a 20-day moving average of the exchange rate in relation to the exchange rate itself. A typical moving average trading rule prescribes a buy (sell) signal when a short moving average crosses a longer moving average from below (above)—that is, when the exchange rate is rising (falling) relatively fast. Of course, the lengths of the moving averages must be chosen by the technician. The length of the short moving average rule is sometimes chosen to equal one, the exchange rate itself.

A final type of mechanical trading rule is the class of "oscillators," which are said to be useful in *non-trending* markets, when the exchange rate is not trending up or down strongly. A simple type of oscillator index, an example of which is shown in Figure 4, is given by the difference between two moving averages: the 5-day moving average minus the 20-day moving average. Oscillator rules suggest buying (selling) the foreign currency when the oscillator index takes an extremely low (high) value. Note that the oscillator index, as a difference between moving averages, also generates buy/sell signals from a moving average rule when the index crosses zero. That is, when the short moving average becomes larger than the long moving average, the moving average rule will generate a buy signal. By definition, this will happen when the oscillator index goes from negative to positive. Therefore, an oscillator chart is also useful for generating moving average rule signals.

Other Kinds of Technical Analysis

Technical analysis is more complex and contains many more techniques than those described in this article. For

[3] For example, the five-day moving average of an exchange rate series is given by:

$$M(5)_t = \frac{1}{5} \sum_{i=0}^{4} S_{t-i}$$

where S_t denotes the closing price of the spot exchange rate at day t.

chosen by the technician from past experience, is generally between 0.5 percent and 3 percent. Figure 1 illustrates some of the buy and sell signals generated by a filter rule with filter size of 0.5 percent.

A second variety of mechanical trading rule is the "moving average" class. Like trendlines and filter rules, moving averages bypass the short-run zigs and zags of the exchange rate to permit the technician to examine trends in the series. A moving average is the average closing price of the

Review

SEPTEMBER/OCTOBER 1997

example, many technical analysts assign a special role to round numbers in support or resistance levels. When the exchange rate significantly crosses the level of 100 yen to the dollar, that is seen as an indication that further movement in the same direction is likely.[4] Other prominent types of technical analysis use exotic mathematical concepts such as Elliot wave theory and/or Fibonacci numbers.[5] Finally, traders sometimes use technical analysis of one market's price history to take positions in another market, a practice called inter-market technical analysis.

EFFICIENT MARKETS AND TECHNICAL ANALYSIS

Technical analysts believe that their methods will permit them to beat the market. Economists have traditionally been skeptical of the value of technical analysis, affirming the theory of efficient markets that holds that no strategy should allow investors and traders to make unusual returns except by taking excessive risk.[6]

Investing in the Foreign Exchange Market

To understand the efficient markets hypothesis in the context of foreign exchange trading, consider the options open to an American bank (or firm) that temporarily has excess funds to be invested overnight. The bank could lend that money in the overnight bank money market, known as the federal funds market. The simple net return on each dollar invested this way would be the overnight interest rate on dollar deposits. The bank has other investment options, though. It could instead convert its money to a foreign currency (e.g., the deutsche mark), lend its money in the overnight German money market (at the German interest rate) and then convert it back to dollars tomorrow. This return is the sum of the German overnight interest rate and the change in the value of the DM. Which investment should the bank choose? If the bank were not concerned about risk, it would choose

the investment with the higher expected return. While the U.S. and German interest rates are known, the bank must base its decision on its forecast of the rate of appreciation of the DM. If market participants expect the return to investing in the German money market to be higher than that of investing in the U.S. money market, they will all try to invest in the German market, and none will invest in the U.S. money market. Such a situation would tend to drive down the German return and raise the U.S. return until the two were equalized. The *excess return* on a German investment over an investment in the U.S. money market (R_t^{DM}), at date t, from the point of view of a U.S. investor is defined as

$$(1) \qquad R_t^{DM} \equiv i_t^{DM} + \Delta S_t - i_t^S,$$

where i_t^{DM} is the German overnight interest rate, ΔS_t is the percentage rate of appreciation of the DM against the dollar overnight, and i_t^S is the U.S. overnight interest rate.[7] If market participants cared only about the expected return on their investments, and if their expectations about the change in the exchange rate were not systematically wrong, the expected excess return on foreign exchange should equal zero, every day.

The assumption that market participants care only about the expected return is too strong, of course. Surely, participants also care about the *risk* of their investment.[8] Risk can come from either the risk of default on the loan or the risk of sharp changes in the exchange rate, or both. If investing in the German market is significantly riskier than investing in the U.S. market, investors must be compensated with a higher expected return in the German market, or they will not invest there. In that case, the expected excess return would be positive and equal to a risk premium. The expected risk-adjusted excess return would be equal to zero. That is,

$$(2) \qquad E[R_t^{DM}] - RP_t = 0,$$

where $E[*]$ is a function that takes the expected value of the term inside the

[4] "The 100 yen level for the dollar is still a very big psychological barrier and it will take a few tests before it breaks. But once you break 100 yen, it's not going to remain there for long. You'll probably see it trade between 102 and 106 for a while," said Jorge Rodriguez, director of North American Sales at Credit Suisse, as reported by Creswell (1995).

[5] Murphy (1986) discusses Elliot wave theory, Fibonacci numbers, and many other technical concepts.

[6] Samuelson (1965) did seminal theoretical work on the modern theory of efficient markets.

[7] The excess return may also be considered the return to someone borrowing in dollars and investing those dollars in German investments.

[8] Market participants may be concerned about the *liquidity* of their position as well as the expected return and risk. Liquidity is the ease with which assets can be converted into cash.

REVIEW
SEPTEMBER/OCTOBER 1997

brackets [*] and RP_t is the risk premium associated with the higher risk of lending in the German market.

Efficient Markets

The idea that the expected risk-adjusted excess return on foreign exchange is zero implies a sensible statement of the efficient markets hypothesis in the foreign exchange context: Exchange rates reflect information to the point where the potential excess returns do not exceed the transactions costs of acting (trading) on that information.[9] In other words, you can't profit in asset markets (like the foreign exchange market) by trading on publicly available information.

This description of the efficient markets hypothesis appears to be a restatement of the first principle of technical analysis: Market action (price and transactions volume) discounts all information about the asset's value. There is, however, a subtle but important distinction between the efficient markets hypothesis and technical analysis: The efficient markets hypothesis posits that the current exchange rate adjusts to all information to prevent traders from reaping excess returns, while technical analysis holds that current and past price movements contain just the information needed to allow profitable trading.

What does this version of the efficient markets hypothesis imply for technical analysis? Under the efficient markets hypothesis, only current interest rates and risk factors help predict exchange rate changes, so past exchange rates are of no help in forecasting excess foreign exchange returns—i.e., if the hypothesis holds, technical analysis will not work. Malkiel's summary of the attitude of many economists toward technical analysis in the stock market is based on similar reasoning:

> The past history of stock prices cannot be used to predict the future in any meaningful way. Technical strategies are usually amusing, often comforting, but of no real value. (Malkiel, 1990, p. 154.)

How do prices move in the hypothetical efficient market? In an efficient market, profit seekers trade in a way that causes prices to move instantly in response to new information, because any information that makes an asset appear likely to become more valuable in the future causes an immediate price rise today. If prices *do* move instantly in response to all new information, past information, like prices, does not help anyone make money. If there were a way to make money with little risk from past prices, speculators would employ it until they bid away the money to be made. For example, if the price of an asset rose 10 percent every Wednesday, speculators would buy strongly on Tuesday, driving prices past the point where anyone would think they could rise much further, and so a fall would be likely. This situation could not lead to a predictable pattern of rises on Tuesday, though, because speculators would buy on Monday. Any pattern in prices would be quickly bid away by market participants seeking profits. Indeed, there is considerable evidence that markets often *do* work this way. Moorthy (1995) finds that foreign exchange rates react very quickly and efficiently to news of changes in U.S. employment figures, for example.

Because the efficient markets hypothesis is frequently misinterpreted, it is important to clarify what the idea does *not* mean. It does not mean that asset prices are unrelated to economic fundamentals.[10] Asset prices may be based on fundamentals like the purchasing power of the U.S. dollar or German mark. Similarly, the hypothesis does not mean that an asset price fluctuates randomly around its intrinsic (fundamental) value. If this were the case, a trader could make money by buying the asset when the price was relatively low and selling it when it was relatively high. Rather, "efficient markets" means that at any point in time, asset prices represent the market's best guess, based on all currently available information, as to the fundamental value of the asset. Future price *changes*, adjusted for risk, will be close to unpredictable.

But if any pattern in prices is quickly bid away, how does one explain the

[9] There are a number of versions of the efficient markets hypothesis. This version is close to that put forward by Jensen (1978).

[10] For an example of an incorrect interpretation of the efficient markets hypothesis, see Murphy (1986, p. 20-21) who offers, "The theory is based on the *efficient markets hypothesis*, which holds that prices fluctuate randomly about their intrinsic value. . . . it's just unrealistic to believe that *all* price movement is random."

REVIEW
SEPTEMBER/OCTOBER 1997

apparent trends seen in charts of asset prices like those in Figure 1? Believers in efficient markets point out that completely random price changes—like those generated by flipping a coin—will produce price series that seem to have trends (Malkiel, 1990, or Paulos, 1995). Under efficient markets, however, traders cannot exploit those trends to make money, since the trends occur by chance and are as likely to reverse as to continue at any point. (For example, some families have—purely by chance—strings of either boys or girls, yet a family that already has four girls and is expecting a fifth child still has only a 50 percent chance of having another girl.)

EVALUATING TECHNICAL ANALYSIS

The efficient markets hypothesis requires that past prices cannot be used to predict exchange rate changes. If the hypothesis is true, technical analysis should not enable a trader to earn profits without accepting unusual risk. This section examines how two common types of trading rules are formulated and how the returns generated by these rules are measured. Problems inherent in testing the rules, measuring risk, and drawing conclusions about the degree of market efficiency are discussed.[11]

Finding a Trading Rule

A basic problem in evaluating technical trading strategies is that rules requiring judgement and skill are impossible to quantify and therefore unsuitable for testing. A fair test requires fixed, objective, commonly used trading rules to evaluate. An "objective" rule does not rely on individual skill or judgement to determine buy or sell decisions. The rule should be commonly used to reduce the problem of drawing false conclusions from "data mining"— a practice in which many different rules are tested until, purely by chance, some are found to be profitable on the data set. Negative test results are ignored, while positive results are

published and taken to indicate that trading rule strategies can yield profits. For example, there is a vast literature on pricing anomalies in the equity markets, summarized by Ball (1995) and Fortune (1991), but Roll (1994) has found that these aberrations are difficult to exploit in practice; he suggests that they may be partially the result of data mining.

Trading Rules

With these considerations, two kinds of trading rules have been commonly tested: *filter rules* and *moving average rules*. As a preceding section of this article explained, filter rules give a buy signal when the exchange rate rises x percent over the previous recent minimum. The analyst must make two choices to construct a filter rule: First, how much does the exchange rate have to rise, or what is the size of the filter? Second, how far back should the rule go in finding a recent minimum? The filter rules studied here will use filters from 0.5 percent to 3 percent and go back five business days to find the extrema.[12] A moving average rule gives a buy signal when a short moving average is greater than the long moving average; otherwise it gives a sell signal. This rule requires the researcher to choose the lengths of the moving averages. The moving average rules to be tested will use short moving averages of 1 day and 5 days and long moving averages of 10 days and 50 days. Both the filter rules and the moving average rules are extrapolative, in that they indicate that the trader should buy when the exchange rate has been rising and sell when it has been falling.

Profits

The trading rules switch between *long* and *short* positions in the foreign currency. Recall that a long position is a purchase of foreign currency—a bet that it will go up—while a short position is the reverse, selling borrowed foreign currency now in the hope that its value will fall. Denoting the percentage change in the exchange rate

[11] A number of previous studies have documented evidence of profitable technical trading rules in the foreign exchange market: Sweeney (1986); Levich and Thomas (1993); Neely, Weller, and Dittmar (1997).

[12] As with most aspects of technical analysis, the choice of filter size and window lengths has been determined by practitioners through a process of trial and error.

REVIEW

SEPTEMBER/OCTOBER 1997

Table 1

Technical Trading Rule Results for the $/DM
Moving Average Rule Results

Short MA	Long MA	Annual Return	Monthly Standard Deviation	Number of Trades	Sharpe Ratio	Estimated CAPM Beta	Standard Error of Est. Beta
1	10	6.016	2.979	928	0.583	−0.022	0.091
1	50	7.546	3.155	268	0.690	−0.135	0.085
5	10	6.718	3.064	576	0.633	−0.144	0.084
5	50	6.671	3.236	146	0.595	−0.134	0.080

Filter Rule Results

Filter	Annual Return	Monthly Standard Deviation	Number of Trades	Sharpe Ratio	Estimated CAPM Beta	Standard Error of Est. Beta
0.005	5.739	3.057	1070	0.542	−0.071	0.089
0.010	6.438	2.951	584	0.630	−0.092	0.093
0.015	3.323	3.255	382	0.295	−0.037	0.085
0.020	1.934	3.348	234	0.167	−0.128	0.087
0.025	0.839	3.236	142	0.075	−0.118	0.082
0.030	−1.541	3.578	92	−0.124	−0.086	0.077

NOTES: The first two columns of the top panel characterize the length of the short and long moving averages used in the moving-average trading rule. The third column is the annualized asset return to the rule, while the fourth column is the monthly standard deviation of the return. The fifth column is the number of trades over the 23-year sample. The sixth column is the Sharpe ratio, and the last two columns provide the CAPM beta with the S&P 500 and the standard error of that estimate. The lower panel has a similar structure, except that the first column characterizes the size of the filter used in the rule. All extrema for filter rules were measured over the previous five business days.

[13] The estimate of transactions costs used here is consistent with recent figures. Levich and Thomas (1993) consider a round-trip cost of 0.05 percent realistic, as do Osler and Chang (1995).

[14] The exchange rate data were obtained from DRI and were collected at 4:00 p.m. local time in London from Natwest Markets and S&P Comstock. Daily overnight interest rates are collected by BIS at 9:00 a.m. London time. Interest rates for Japan were unavailable before 3/1/82, so the interest rates before this date were set to 0 for the $/¥ case.

($ per unit of foreign currency) from date t to $t+1$ by ΔS_t, and the domestic (foreign) overnight interest rate by $i_t^\$$ (i_t^{DM}), then the overnight return from a long position is approximately given by Equation 1:

$$(1) \qquad R_t^{DM} \equiv i_t^{DM} + \Delta S_t - i_t^\$.$$

The return to a short position is the negative of the return to a long position. The return to a trading rule over a period of time is approximately the sum of daily returns, minus transactions costs for each trade. Transactions costs are set at 5 basis points (0.05 percent) for each *round trip* in the currency. A round trip is a move from a long position to a short position and back or vice-versa.[13]

Evidence from Ten Simple Technical Trading Rules

Six filter rules and four moving average rules were tested on data consisting of the

average of daily U.S. dollar bid and ask quotes for the DM, yen, pound sterling, and Swiss franc.[14] All exchange rate data begin on 3/1/74 and end on 4/10/97. These four series are called $/DM, $/¥, $/£, and $/SF. Because the results for the four exchange rates were similar, full results from only the $/DM will be reported in the tables.

Table 1 shows the annualized percentage return, monthly standard deviation (a measure of the volatility of returns), number of trades per year, and two measures of risk, the *Sharpe ratio* and the *CAPM beta*, for each of the 10 trading strategies for the $/DM. The Sharpe ratio and CAPM betas are discussed in some detail in the shaded insert. The mean annual return to the 10 rules was 4.4 percent, and 38 of the 40 trading rules were profitable (had positive excess return) over the whole sample. These results cast doubt on the efficient markets hypothesis, which holds that no trading strategy should be able to consistently earn positive excess

REVIEW
SEPTEMBER/OCTOBER 1997

returns. The number of trades over the 23-year sample varied substantially over the 10 rules, ranging from 4 trades per year to almost 50 trades per year. The moving average rules were somewhat more profitable than the filter rules.

There is little evidence that these excess returns are compensation for bearing excessive risk. The first measure of risk, the Sharpe ratio, is the mean annual return divided by the mean annual standard deviation. The moving average rules had higher Sharpe ratios (0.6 vs. 0.25) than the filter rules. Six of the 10 Sharpe ratios are better than the 0.3 obtained by a buy-and-hold strategy in the S&P 500 over approximately the same period. This result indicates that the average return to the rules is very good compared to the risk involved in following the rules.

The second measure of risk, the CAPM betas, reflects the correlation between the monthly trading rule returns and the monthly returns to a broad portfolio of risky assets (the S&P 500). Significantly positive betas indicate that the rule is bearing undiversifiable risk. These CAPM betas estimated from the 10 rules generally indicate negative correlation with the S&P 500 monthly returns. None of them is significantly positive, statistically or economically. In other words, there is no systematic risk in these rules that could explain the positive excess returns.

For Whom is Technical Trading Appropriate?

The discussion of risk and returns suggests that technical analysis may be very useful for banks and large financial firms that can borrow and lend freely at the overnight interbank interest rate and buy and sell in the wholesale market for foreign exchange, where transactions sizes are in the millions of dollars. Technical trading is much less useful for individuals, who would face much higher transactions costs and must consider the opportunity cost of the time necessary to become an expert on foreign exchange speculating and to keep

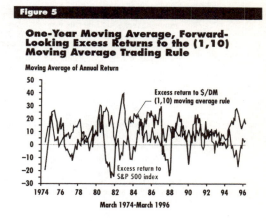

Figure 5

One-Year Moving Average, Forward-Looking Excess Returns to the (1,10) Moving Average Trading Rule

Moving Average of Annual Return

March 1974–March 1996

up with the market on a daily basis. How large would transactions costs have to be to eliminate the excess return to the technical rules? If we assume a 6 percent annual excess return to the rule and 230 trades (10 trades a year), round-trip transactions costs would have to be greater than 0.6 percent to produce zero excess returns.

In addition to higher transactions costs, individual investors following technical rules also must accept the risk that such a strategy entails. Figure 5 illustrates the risk by depicting, at monthly intervals, the one-year-ahead excess return from 1974 through 1996 for the (1,10) moving average rule on the $/DM and, for comparison, the total excess return on buying and holding the S&P 500 index, a popular measure of returns to a stock portfolio. The figure shows that the excess returns to both portfolios vary considerably at the annual horizon, often turning negative. While the technical trading rule excess return is less variable than the S&P excess return, it can still lead to significant losses for some subperiods. Two ways to measure losses over subperiods are the maximal single-period loss (maximum drawdown) and maximum loss in a calendar year. Over the period from March 1974 through March 1997, the maximum

REVIEW

SEPTEMBER/OCTOBER 1997

that an investor could have lost by using the moving average trading rule was −28.2 percent; this loss, which would have occurred between March 7, 1995, and August 2, 1995 (a period of 149 days), translates into an annual rate of −69.2 percent. In other words, an investor using this rule would have lost almost 30 percent of his capital over this five-month period. Similarly, the maximum loss for this technical trading rule in a complete calendar year was −9.8 percent in 1995, but −17.8 percent for the S&P 500 in 1981.[15]

Perhaps the biggest obstacle to exploiting technical rules is that while the returns to stocks depend ultimately on the profitability of the firms in which the stock is held, the *source* of returns to technical analysis is not well understood; therefore, the investor does not know if the returns will persist into the future or even if they continue to exist at the present. Indeed, Figure 5 shows that the post-1992 return to the (1,10) moving average rule for the $/DM has been negative.

Do These Results Measure the Degree of Market Efficiency?

There are a number of problems associated with inferring the degree of market efficiency from the apparent profitability of these trading rules. The first problem is the data. To test the profitability of a trading rule, the researcher needs actual prices and interest rates from a series of simultaneous market transactions. Unfortunately, simultaneous quotes for daily exchange rates and interest rates are not generally available for a long time span. For example, these exchange-rate data were collected late in the afternoon, while the interest rates were collected in the morning. Although most economists judge this problem to be very minor, some argue that the trading rule decisions could not have been executed at the exchange rates and interest rates used.

The second problem is that without a good model of how to price risk, positive excess returns resulting from the use of trading rules cannot be used to measure

the degree of inefficiency. Risk is notoriously difficult to measure. In fact, a major area of study for macro and financial economists for the last 10 years has been to explain why the return on stocks is so much higher than that on bonds, a phenomenon called the *equity premium puzzle*. Of course, at least part of the answer is that stocks are much riskier than bonds, but there is no generally accepted model of risk that will explain the *size* of the return difference.[16] Defenders of the efficient markets hypothesis maintain that the discovery of an apparently successful trading strategy may not indicate market inefficiency but, rather, that risk is not measured properly.

Another problem is that of "data mining": If enough rules are tested, some—purely by chance—will produce excess returns on the data. These rules may not have been obvious to traders at the beginning of the sample. In fact, the rules tested here are certainly subject to a data-mining bias, since many of them had been shown to be profitable on these exchange rates over at least some of the subsample. Closely related to the data-mining problem is the tendency to publish research that overturns the conventional wisdom on efficient markets, rather than research that shows technical analysis to be ineffective. One solution to the data-mining problem is suggested by Neely, Weller, and Dittmar (1997), who apply *genetic programming* techniques to the foreign-exchange market. Genetic programming is a method by which a computer searches through the space of possible technical trading rules to find a group of good rules (i.e., rules that generate positive excess return). These good rules are then tested on out-of-sample data to see if they continue to generate positive excess returns.

RETHINKING THE EFFICIENT MARKETS HYPOTHESIS

Early research in finance on the efficient markets hypothesis was very supportive; little evidence was found of profitable trading rules after transactions costs were accounted for (Fama, 1970).

[15] The returns for complete calendar years were available from 1975 through 1995.

[16] Kocherlakota (1996) and Siegel and Thaler (1997) discuss the equity premium puzzle extensively.

REVIEW
SEPTEMBER/OCTOBER 1997

The success of technical trading rules shown in the previous section is typical of a number of later studies showing that the simple efficient markets hypothesis fails in important ways to describe how the foreign exchange market actually functions. While these results did not surprise market practitioners, they have helped persuade economists to examine features of the market like sequential trading, asymmetric information, and the role of risk that might explain the profitability of technical analysis.

The Paradox of Efficient Markets

Grossman and Stiglitz (1980) identified a major theoretical problem with the hypothesis termed the *paradox of efficient markets*, which they developed in the context of equity markets. As applied to the foreign exchange market, the argument starts by noting that exchange rate returns are determined by fundamentals like national price levels, interest rates, and public debt levels, and that information about these variables is costly for traders to gather and analyze. The traders must be able to make some excess returns by trading on this analysis, or they will not do it. But if markets were perfectly efficient, the traders would not be able to make excess returns on any available information. Therefore, markets cannot be perfectly efficient in the sense of exchange rates' always being *exactly* where fundamentals suggest they should be. Of course, one resolution to this paradox is to recognize that market analysts can recover the costs of some fundamental research by profiting from having marginally better information than the rest of the market on where the exchange rate should be. In this case, the exchange rate remains close enough to its fundamental value to prevent less informed people from profiting from the difference. Partly for these reasons, Campbell, Lo, and MacKinlay (1997) suggest that the debate about perfect efficiency is pointless and that it is more sensible to evaluate the degree of inefficiency than to test for absolute efficiency.

Empirical Reasons to Suspect Failure of Efficient Markets

The miserable empirical performance of standard exchange rate models is another reason to suspect the failure of the efficient markets hypothesis. In an important paper, Meese and Rogoff (1983) persuasively showed that no existing exchange rate model could forecast exchange rate changes better than a "no-change" guess at forecast horizons of up to one year. This was true even when the exchange rate models were given true values of future fundamentals like output and money. Although Mark (1995) and others have demonstrated some forecasting ability for these models at forecasting horizons greater than three years, no one has been able to convincingly overturn the Meese and Rogoff (1983) result despite 14 years of research. The efficient markets hypothesis is frequently misinterpreted as implying that exchange rate changes should be unpredictable; that is, exchange rates should follow a *random walk*. This is incorrect. Equation 2 shows that interest rate differentials should have forecasting power for exchange rate changes, leaving *excess returns* unpredictable. There is, however, convincing evidence that interest rates are *not* good forecasters of exchange rate changes.[17] According to Frankel (1996), this failure of exchange rate forecasting leaves two possibilities:

- Fundamentals are not observed well enough to allow forecasting of exchange rates.

- Exchange rates are detached from fundamentals by (possibly irrational) swings in expectations about future values of the exchange rate. These fluctuations in exchange rates are known as *bubbles*.[18]

Which of these possibilities is more likely? One clue is given by the relationship between exchange rates and fundamentals when expectations about the value of the exchange rate are very stable, as they are under a *fixed exchange rate*

[17] Engel (1995) reviews the failure of this theory, called *uncovered interest parity.*

[18] Swings in expectations that are subsequently justified by changes in the exchange rate are known as *rational bubbles*. Swings that are not consistent with the future path of exchange rates are *irrational bubbles*.

REVIEW
SEPTEMBER/OCTOBER 1997

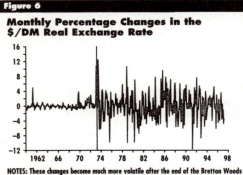

Figure 6

Monthly Percentage Changes in the $/DM Real Exchange Rate

NOTES: These changes become much more volatile after the end of the Bretton Woods system of fixed exchange rates in March 1973. The vertical line denotes this break date in the series. Data cover January 1960–February 1997.

regime. A fixed exchange rate regime is a situation in which a government is committed to maintaining the value of its currency by manipulating monetary policy and trading foreign exchange reserves. Fixed exchange rate regimes are contrasted to *floating* regimes, in which the government has no such obligation. For example, most countries in the European Union had a type of fixed exchange rate regime, known as a target zone, from 1979 through the early 1990s. Fixed exchange rates anchor investor sentiment about the future value of a currency because of the government's commitment to stabilize its value. If fundamentals, like goods prices, or expectations based on fundamentals, rather than irrationally changing expectations, drive the exchange rate, the relationship between fundamentals and exchange rates should be the same under a fixed exchange rate regime as it is under a floating regime. This is not the case. Countries that move from floating exchange rates to fixed exchange rates experience a dramatic change in the relationship between prices and exchange rates. Specifically, real exchange rates (exchange rates adjusted for inflation in both countries) are much more volatile under floating exchange rate regimes, where expectations are not tied down by promises of government intervention. Figure 6 illustrates a typical case:

When Germany and the United States ceased to fix their currencies in March 1973, the variability in the real $/DM exchange rate increased dramatically. This result suggests that, contrary to the efficient markets hypothesis, swings in investor expectations may detach exchange rates from fundamental values in the short run.

Why Do Bubbles Arise?

If traders might profit by anticipating swings in investor expectations, then the efficient markets hypothesis needs significant adjustment. The structure of the foreign exchange market has several features that might help drive these swings in expectations that produce bubbles. Most foreign exchange transactions are conducted by large commercial banks in financial centers like London, New York, Tokyo, and Singapore. These large banks "make a market" in a currency by offering to buy or sell large quantities (generally more than $1 million) of currencies for a specific price in another currency (e.g., the dollar) on request. The exchange rates at which they are willing to buy or sell dollars are known as the bid and ask prices, respectively. The market is highly competitive, and transactions occur 24 hours a day over the telephone and automated trading systems. The first feature of this market that might influence technical trading is that specific transactions quantities and prices are not public information; the market is *nontransparent*. But the bid and ask exchange rates are easy to track, as banks freely quote them to any participant. Second, the trades take place *sequentially*—i.e., there is time to learn from previous trades. Third, the participants in this market differ from one another in the information they have and their willingness to tolerate risk.[19] In other words, the participants are heterogeneous.

How might these features combine to produce bubbles? To the extent that some participants are better informed about certain fundamentals than other agents (for instance, they will know more about their own and their customers' demand for foreign exchange), the trading behavior of

[19] It has long been assumed that there is little or no private information in foreign exchange markets, but this view has been forcefully challenged with respect to intraday trading by Ito, Lyons, and Melvin (1997).

the informed participants will reveal some of their private information to the uninformed agents. For example, if the informed agents know of fundamental forces that are likely to make the exchange rate rise in the future, they are likely to buy the foreign currency and thereby bid up the publicly observed bid and ask prices. The uninformed agents might infer from the rise that the rate will continue to rise and, as a result, they might buy more foreign exchange, pushing the rate up themselves in a self-fulfilling prophecy.[20] This inference from past price behavior is extrapolative technical analysis: It assumes that the exchange rate will continue moving as it has in the recent past. The uninformed traders may continue to buy foreign exchange past the point where it is supported by fundamentals. Although this story is most plausible for very high-frequency (intraday) trading, it might also generate longer-term swings in the exchange rate.

There are other explanations for extrapolative trading that jettison the assumption of rational behavior in favor of the study of how people really make decisions. This field, called *behavioral finance*, has concentrated on examples of seeming irrationality in decision making. Two findings of this field are that (1) experimental participants seem unusually optimistic about their chances for success in games and (2) the behavior and opinions of members of a group tend to reinforce common ideas or beliefs.[21] For example, members of a jury may become more confident about their individual verdicts if the other members of the group agree.

Either explanation for extrapolative trading implies that bubbles may be produced by slow dissemination of private information into the market, coupled with extrapolative trading rules. There is some evidence to support this explanation. Eichenbaum and Evans (1995) found that foreign exchange markets reacted gradually to money supply shocks, over a period of many months, instead of instantly incorporating the new information. Surveys revealed that foreign exchange market participants' expectations are extrapolative at horizons up to six

months. That is, if the exchange rate has risen recently, market participants expect it to continue to rise in the near future (Frankel and Froot, 1987). Also, the success of extrapolative traders tends to feed on itself. Frankel and Froot (1990) argue that extrapolative traders' success during the early part of the large dollar appreciation of 1981-1985 convinced many other traders to follow extrapolative rules, driving the dollar up even further.

Central Bank Intervention

The other popular explanation for the apparent profitability of technical trading rules is that technical traders are able to profit consistently from central bank intervention. Some central banks frequently intervene (buy and sell currency) in the foreign exchange market to move the exchange rate to help influence other variables like employment or inflation.[22] Because these actions are designed to control macroeconomic variables rather than to make money, central banks may be willing to take a loss on their trading. Trading rule profits may represent a transfer from central banks to technical traders. Lebaron (1996) found that most trading rule profits were generated on the day before a U.S. intervention. Neely and Weller (1997) find that "intelligent" trading rules tend to trade against the Fed; that is, they tend to buy dollars when they find out the Fed is selling dollars. This tantalizing story does not fit all the facts, however. For example, Leahy (1995) finds that U.S. foreign exchange operations make positive profits, on average.[23] This finding is inconsistent with the idea that central banks are giving money away to technical traders.

Why Are the Profits Not Arbitraged Away?

Whether the trends or inefficiencies in exchange rates are created by swings in expectations or by central bank intervention, efficient market advocates would ask why any predictable returns in exchange rates

[20] Treynor and Ferguson (1985), Brown and Jennings (1989), Banerjee (1992), and Kirman (1993) construct models of behavior in which information is inferred from the actions of others. One easily understood example is the problem of consumers who must choose between two restaurants. One seemingly sensible strategy for choosing would be to go to the more crowded restaurant on the theory that it is likely to be crowded because it has better food. This phenomenon depends on *asymmetric information*.

[21] Shiller (1988) and Shleifer and Summers (1990) discuss behavioral finance in more detail. Ohanian (1996) considers the reasons for the collapse of bubbles.

[22] In the United States, the Federal Reserve and the U.S. Treasury generally collaborate on foreign exchange intervention decisions, and operations are conducted by the Federal Reserve Bank of New York on behalf of both.

[23] See Szakmary and Mathur (1996) for more on central bank intervention and trading rule profits.

REVIEW
SEPTEMBER/OCTOBER 1997

HOW TO MEASURE RISK?

The simplest widely used measure of risk is the *Sharpe ratio* or the ratio of the average annual excess return to a measure of excess return volatility called the standard deviation. Higher Sharpe ratios are desirable because they indicate either higher average excess returns or less volatility. A commonly used benchmark of a good Sharpe ratio is that of the S&P 500, which Osler and Chang (1995) estimated to be about 0.32 from March 1973 to March 1994.

A major drawback to Sharpe ratios is that they ignore an important idea in finance: An investment is risky only to the extent that its return is correlated with the return to a broad measure of the investments available. To see this, consider the risk associated with holding a portfolio of assets whose returns are each individually volatile but completely independent of each other. Each year, the assets in the portfolio that do unusually well will tend to offset those that do unusually poorly. The portfolio as a whole will be much less risky than any of the individual assets. The more assets in the portfolio, the less risky it will be. In fact, if enough of these independent assets are grouped together into a portfolio, the return on this portfolio becomes certain. This means that investors do not need to be compensated for holding risky assets that are not correlated with all the other assets they can buy (the market portfolio), because the risk of each uncorrelated asset can be reduced to zero if the portfolio contains a large enough variety of these assets. On the other hand, assets for which returns are positively correlated with those of the other assets on the market need a higher expected return to convince investors to hold them.

This idea motivates the second measure of riskiness, the *CAPM beta*: the coefficient from the linear regression of an asset's (or trading rule's) excess return on the excess return of a proxy for the market portfolio, the return to a broad equity index like the S&P 500. An estimated beta equal to zero means that the trading rule is bearing no systematic risk, while significantly positive betas indicate that a trading strategy is bearing some risk, and a beta equal to one means that the trading rule moves closely with the market, so that following it requires the investor to accept significant risk.

[24] Both Shleifer and Summers (1990) and Shleifer and Vishny (1997) discuss the importance of risk in speculating against bubbles.

should not be arbitraged away. One answer to this question is that speculators have short horizons and are deterred from speculating against the trends by the risk that such a strategy would incur. There are several reasons for this: First, traders typically operate on margin, borrowing some of the money with which they trade. With a limited line of credit, the borrowing costs would add up if traders were not able to turn a quick profit. Second, a trader's performance is typically evaluated on relatively short horizons (less than a year). Third, there may be institutional or legal restrictions that prevent some types of enterprises from taking on "excessive" exchange risk. And finally, traders do not

know the equilibrium value of the exchange rate with any certainty, so they cannot distinguish bubbles from movements in fundamentals. Investors who bet on long-run reversion to fundamental values in exchange rates may be wiped out by short-run deviations away from those values.[24]

Explaining the success of technical trading rules with bubbles begs one more question: Why do destabilizing extrapolative traders not lose their money? Friedman (1953) showed that destabilizing speculation is doomed to lose money and so drive the speculators out of the market. Friedman argued that speculation can only destabilize asset prices if the speculators consistently buy when the asset price is above its equilibrium value (driving the price up further) and sell when the asset price is below its equilibrium value; as the destabilizing speculators lose their money, he maintained, they will have less effect on the market. The corollary to this argument is that all successful speculation is stabilizing. Delong, Schleifer, Summers, and Waldman (1989) constructed a "noise trader" model that questioned this logic, however.[25] They showed that irrational ("noise") traders could create so much risk in asset markets that the returns to those assets would have to be unusually high for rational traders to trade in them at all. In other words, the irrational traders make unusually high returns (on average) by foolishly pursuing risky strategies. Some go out of business, but, on average, this group increases its market position.

CONCLUSION

Technical analysis is the most widely used trading strategy in the foreign exchange market. Traders stake large positions on their interpretations of patterns in the data. Economists have traditionally rejected the claims of technical analysts because of the appealing logic of the efficient markets hypothesis. More recently, however, the discovery of profitable technical trading rules and other evidence against efficient markets have led to a rethinking about the importance of institutional features that might justify extrapolative technical analysis such as private information, sequential trading, and central bank intervention, as well as the role of risk.

The weight of the evidence now suggests that excess returns have been available to technical foreign exchange traders over long periods. Risk is hard to define and measure, however, and this difficulty has obscured the degree of inefficiency in the foreign exchange market. There is no guarantee, of course, that technical rules will continue to generate excess returns in the future; the excess returns may be bid away by market participants. Indeed, this may already be occurring. Continued research on high-frequency

transactions data or experimental work on expectations formation may provide a better understanding of market behavior.

REFERENCES

Ball, Ray. "The Theory of Stock Market Efficiency: Accomplishments and Limitations," *Journal of Applied Corporate Finance* (Spring 1995), pp. 4-17.

Banerjee, Abhijit V. "A Simple Model of Herd Behavior," *Quarterly Journal of Economics* (August 1992), pp. 797-817.

Brown, David P., and Robert H. Jennings. "On Technical Analysis," *The Review of Financial Studies* (1989), pp. 527-51.

Campbell, John Y., Andrew W. Lo, and Archie Craig MacKinlay. *The Econometrics of Financial Markets*, Princeton University Press, 1997.

Creswell, Juli. "Currency Market Expects Rate Cut By Bank of Japan," *Wall Street Journal,* September 5, 1995, p. C16.

DeLong, J. Bradford, Andrei Shleifer, Lawrence H. Summers, and Robert J. Waldmann. "Noise Trader Risk in Financial Markets," *Journal of Political Economy* (August 1990), pp. 703-38.

Eichenbaum, Martin, and Charles L. Evans. "Some Empirical Evidence on the Effects of Shocks to Monetary Policy on Exchange Rates," *Quarterly Journal of Economics* (November 1995), pp. 975-1009.

Engel, Charles. "Why is the Forward Exchange Rate Forecast Biased? A Survey of Recent Evidence," Federal Reserve Bank of Kansas City Working Paper 95-06, September 1995.

Fama, Eugene F. "Efficient Capital Markets: A Review of Theory and Empirical Work," *Journal of Finance* (May 1970), pp. 383-417.

Fortune, Peter. "Stock Market Efficiency: An Autopsy?," *New England Economic Review,* Federal Reserve Bank of Boston (March/April 1991), pp. 18-40.

Frankel, Jeffrey. "How Well Do Foreign Exchange Markets Function: Might a Tobin Tax Help?," National Bureau of Economic Research Working Paper 5422, January 1996.

_____ and Kenneth A. Froot. "Using Survey Data to Test Standard Propositions Regarding Exchange Rate Expectations," *The American Economic Review* (March 1987), pp. 133-53.

_____ and _____. "Chartists, Fundamentalists and the Demand for Dollars," *Private Behavior and Government Policy in Interdependent Economies,* Anthony S. Courakis and Mark Taylor, eds., Clarendon Press, 1990.

Friedman, Milton. "The Case for Flexible Exchange Rates," *Essays in Positive Economics,* University of Chicago Press, 1953.

Grossman, Sanford J., and Joseph E. Stiglitz. "On the Impossibility of Informationally Efficient Markets," *The American Economic Review* (June 1980), pp. 393-408.

Ito, Takatoshi, Richard K. Lyons, and Michael T. Melvin. "Is There Private Information in the FX Market? The Tokyo Experiment," National Bureau of Economic Research Working Paper 5936, February 1997.

[25] Essentially the same argument is presented more simply in Shleifer and Summers (1990).

REVIEW

SEPTEMBER/OCTOBER 1997

Jensen, Michael C. "Some Anomalous Evidence Regarding Market Efficiency," *Journal of Financial Economics* (June/September 1978), pp. 95-101.

Kirman, Alan. "Ants, Rationality and Recruitment," *Quarterly Journal of Economics* (February 1993), pp. 137-56.

Kocherlakota, Narayana R. "The Equity Premium: It's Still a Puzzle," *Journal of Economic Literature* (March 1996), pp. 42-71.

Leahy, Michael P. "The profitability of US intervention in the foreign exchange markets," *Journal of International Money and Finance* (December 1995), pp. 823-44.

Lebaron, Blake. "Technical Trading Rule Profitability and Central Bank Intervention," National Bureau of Economic Research Working Paper 5505, March 1996.

Levich, Richard M., and Lee R. Thomas. "The Significance of Technical Trading-Rule Profits in the Foreign Exchange Market: A Bootstrap Approach," *Journal of International Money and Finance* (October 1993), pp. 451-74.

Malkiel, Burton G. *A Random Walk Down Wall Street*, Fifth Edition, W. W. Norton & Company, 1990.

Mark, Nelson C. "Exchange Rates and Fundamentals: Evidence on Long-Horizon Predictability," *The American Economic Review* (March 1995), pp. 201-18.

Meese, Richard A., and Kenneth Rogoff. "Empirical Exchange Rate Models of the Seventies: Do They Fit out of Sample?," *Journal of International Economics* (February 1983), pp. 3-24.

Moorthy, Vivek. "Efficiency Aspects of Exchange Rate Response to News: Evidence from U.S. Employment Data," *Journal of International Financial Markets, Institutions and Money* (1995), pp. 1-18.

Murphy, John J. *Technical Analysis of the Futures Markets*, New York Institute of Finance, Prentice-Hall, New York, 1986.

Neely, Chris, and Paul Weller. "Technical Analysis and Central Bank Intervention," Federal Reserve Bank of St. Louis Working Paper 97-002A, January 1997.

_____, _____, and Robert Dittmar. "Is Technical Analysis Profitable in the Foreign Exchange Market? A Genetic Programming Approach," Forthcoming in *Journal of Financial and Quantitative Analysis* (December 1997).

Ohanian, Lee E. "When the Bubble Bursts: Psychology or Fundamentals?," *Business Review*, Federal Reserve Bank of Philadelphia (January/February 1996), pp. 3-13.

Osler, Carol L., and P. H. Kevin Chang. "Head and Shoulders: Not Just a Flaky Pattern," Federal Reserve Bank of New York Staff Paper 4, August 1995.

Paulos, John Allen. *A Mathematician Reads the Newspaper*, Basic Books, 1995.

Pring, Martin J. *Technical Analysis Explained*, Third Edition, McGraw-Hill, 1991.

Roll, Richard. "What Every CFO Should Know About Scientific Progress in Financial Economics: What is Known, and What Remains to be Resolved," *Financial Management* (Summer 1994), pp. 69-75.

Rosenberg, Michael R., and Eric A. Shatz. *The Merrill Lynch Guide to Understanding and Using Technical Analysis*, Merrill Lynch and Co., Global Securities Research & Economics Group, 1995.

Samuelson, Paul A. "Proof that Properly Anticipated Prices Fluctuate Randomly," *Industrial Management Review* (1965), pp. 41-49.

Shiller, Robert J. "Fashions, Fads and Bubbles in Financial Markets," *Knights, Raiders and Targets: The Impact of the Hostile Takeover*, J. Coffee, S. Ackerman, and L. Lowenstein, eds., Oxford University Press, 1988. Reprinted in *Market Volatility*, by Robert J. Shiller, MIT Press, 1989.

Shleifer, Andrei, and Lawrence Summers. "The Noise Trader Approach to Finance," *Journal of Economic Perspectives* (Spring 1990), pp. 19-33.

_____ and Robert W. Vishny. "The Limits of Arbitrage," *Journal of Finance* (March 1997), pp. 35-55.

Siegel, Jeremy J., and Richard H. Thaler. "Anomalies: The Equity Premium Puzzle," *Journal of Economic Perspectives* (Winter 1997), pp. 191-200.

Sweeney, Richard J. "Beating the foreign exchange market," *Journal of Finance* (March 1986), pp. 163-82.

Szakmary, Andrew C., and Ike Mathur. "Central Bank Intervention and Trading Rule Profits in Foreign Exchange Markets," *Journal of International Money and Finance* (August 1997), pp. 513-35.

Taylor, Mark P., and Helen Allen. "The use of technical analysis in the foreign exchange market," *Journal of International Money and Finance* (June 1992), pp. 304-14.

Treynor, Jack L., and Robert Ferguson. "In Defense of Technical Analysis," *Journal of Finance* (July 1985), pp. 757-73.

[15]

THE JOURNAL OF FINANCE • VOL. XLI, NO. 1 • MARCH 1986

Beating the Foreign Exchange Market

RICHARD J. SWEENEY*

ABSTRACT

Filter rule profits found in foreign exchange markets in the early days of the current managed float persist in later periods, as shown by statistical tests developed and implemented here. The test is consistent with, but independent of, a wide variety of asset pricing models. The profits found cannot be explained by risk if risk premia are constant over time. Inclusion of the home-foreign interest rate differential in computing profits has little effect on the comparison of filter returns to those of buy-and-hold.

IN THE EARLY YEARS of the generalized managed floating that began in March 1973, filter rule profits in excess of buy-and-hold were found for many countries (Logue, Sweeney and Willett [18], Dooley and Shafer [6], Cornell and Dietrich [5]). It was unclear, however, whether such profits indicated inefficiencies. First, it was not clear that risk was adequately handled in such tests, and often risk was ignored. Second, there was no evidence such profits would be available postsample. And third, there was no statistical test of the significance of these profits.

This paper uses the logic of risk/return tradeoffs to analyze the role of risk in such tests and illustrates the logic in a discussion using the Sharpe-Lintner Capital Asset Pricing Model (CAPM), although a Breeden consumption-based CAPM, a Merton intertemporal CAPM, or an Arbitrage Pricing Model (APM) could easily be used. The paper develops a test of statistical significance appropriate to foreign exchange markets (Section I), analyzing the rate of return on foreign exchange speculation less the foreign-domestic interest rate differential. The test explicitly assumes that risk premia are constant over the sample. The excess rates of return observable in using filters in going from a risk-free dollar asset to a risk-free Deutsche Mark (DM) asset persist into the 1980's (Section II), and this is true even when taking account of transactions costs. It turns out that these results for the $/DM case do not depend very much on the interest-rate differential, but primarily on exchange rate behavior. This is useful to know because it is often quite difficult to find matching, interest-rate data of high quality. For a sample of nine other currencies, using only exchange rates, Section III shows that the excess returns made in the first 610 days of the float persist in the next 1,220 days, into the 1980's. (Dooley and Shafer [7] find similar persistence in experiments that do not use buy-and-hold and have no significance tests.)

When filter rule profits have been found in spot exchange markets, it has often been argued that the profits are due to risk. This paper uses the CAPM to analyze rates of return both to buy-and-hold and to filter strategies. It turns out that the

* Claremont McKenna College and Claremont Graduate School. Arthur D. Warga, Douglas Joines, and Thomas D. Willett offered helpful comments, and Ning-Ning Koo provided research assistance.

CAPM may be used to explain the return to both strategies, but not any excess filter returns; in fact, significant excess filter rule profits would be an indictment of the CAPM, since it does not predict such profits. Section IV illustrates how the CAPM has been misused to attempt to explain filter rules profits as due to risk. Section V offers some conclusions and possible reasons for existence of filter profits.

I. Filter Rule Profits in the Spot Exchange Market, Using Interest-Earning Assets[1]

This section develops a statistical test of filter rule rates of return in excess of buy-and-hold in the foreign exchange market; it then compares this test to the methodology used by Dooley and Shafer [7]. Section II applies the test to the dollar-DM case.

Consider a buy-and-hold strategy that puts funds in an overnight DM asset paying the (foreign) rate, r_f, which is riskless in terms of DMs. The daily return in terms of U.S. dollars is (approximately) the percentage appreciation of the DM (u) plus r_f, or is $u + r_f$ (ignoring the cross product, ur_f, and also transactions costs which are discussed in Sections II and III). The overnight riskless rate for, say, the U.S. is the (domestic) rate, r_d. Thus, the daily excess return to buy-and-hold over the U.S. risk-free rate is $u + r_f - r_d$. An alternative filter strategy earns the excess return $u + r_d - r_d$ for days "in" in the DM asset, and the excess return $r_d - r_d = 0$ for days "out" of the DM asset (and hence in the U.S. asset).

A. Risk, Buy-and-Hold Returns, and Filter Returns

This subsection develops expressions for average returns to the buy-and-hold and filter strategies and for an X statistic based upon these. All that is required is that the excess return to being "in" the DM be stationary. The development is made more intuitive, and is more connected with the literature, by being phrased in terms of an equilibrium asset pricing model. The development is consistent with a single-period Sharpe-Lintner CAPM with a beta on "the" market; with an intertemporal Merton [20] CAPM with betas on the market and every independent state variable; with a Breeden [4] CAPM with a single beta on an asset whose return is perfectly correlated with changes in aggregate consumption (or the portfolio with returns most highly correlated with changes in aggregate consumption); and with an APM with (potentially) multiple priced factors, none of which need be the market. In each case, the expected excess return to being "in" DMs when there is a risk-free rate is equal to betas times risk premia of underlying factors (refer to these products simply as risk premia for the investment). As long as the investment's risk premia are constant over time, the development below of the X statistic goes through for all of these models. While the development is stated in terms of a Sharpe-Lintner CAPM, any unfortunate overtones of phrasing the exposition in terms of a single-period model can be removed by viewing the model as a Breeden CAPM, with the return

---

[1] For a more detailed discussion of the following approach to filter rule tests, see Sweeney [23]. The development is related to Praetz [21]; see Sweeney [23] for a discussion of crucial differences.

Beating the Foreign Exchange Market 165

on an asset perfectly correlated with consumption changes substituted for the return on the market.

The CAPM can be used to give an explanation in terms of risk of the excess returns on either buy-and-hold or on days "in" the filter rule. As is well-known, international CAPMs often have no straightforward answer as to what "the" market index is or the appropriate risk-free rate, and both can depend on the country of residence of the investor considered.[2] Suppose the appropriate index, R_M, is known and for convenience suppose the risk-free rate applicable to the U.S. decision-maker is r_d. (The empirical work that follows does not assume knowledge of the "true" market.) Then, the CAPM implies

$$E(u) + r_f - r_d = b_f[E(R_M) - r_d] = g, \tag{1}$$

where $b_f = \mathrm{cov}(u, R_M)/\mathrm{var}(R_M)$ since r_f, r_d are given for any day. Call g the risk premium for this investment. g is explicitly assumed constant. The "market model" observational implementation of (1) is[3]

$$u + r_f - r_d = b_f(R_M - r_d) + e, \tag{2}$$

where by assumption $\mathrm{cov}(R_M, e) = 0$, $Ee = 0$, $\mathrm{cov}(e_t, e_{t+j}) = 0$ for $j \neq 0$.

Equation (1) implies that $E(u) + r_f - r_d \neq 0$ only in the case in which $b_f \neq 0$. This is the international CAPM result that expected appreciation (Eu) need not equal the interest rate differential $(r_d - r_f)$ if there is a risk premium. Equation (1) also implies that *if* both the expected premium on the market $(ER_M - r_d)$ and b_f are constant, then changes in expected appreciation must exactly equal changes in the interest rate differential. In this case, if $Eu \equiv \alpha$ and $r_d - r_f \equiv \alpha'$, then both α and α' may vary, but $\alpha - \alpha'$ must remain equal to the (possibly nonzero) constant g.

Equation (2) implies that systematic excess profits beyond the equilibrium excess returns in (1) can be obtained only by skill in forecasting R_M (market timing) or e (asset selection). Generally held views of market efficiency assume that neither can systematically be done.

Filter rule investigations in equity markets usually specify buy-and-hold as a standard of comparison (but see below for Dooley and Shafer's [7] methodology). The sample buy-and-hold arithmetic average excess rate of return,[4] over N periods, is

$$\bar{R}_{BH} = \frac{1}{N} \sum_{i=1}^{N} (u_i + r_{fi} - r_{di})$$

and hence $E\bar{R}_{BH} = g$ as long as b_f and $ER_M - r_d$ are constant. The sample mean

---

[2] See the discussion and references in Sharp [22].

[3] This assumes that the intercept $a = 0$ as the CAPM implies. Of course the estimate a is likely nonzero for any sample. The APM can be used to analyze cases where there are priced nonmarket factors, and hence a nonzero a in (2). Analysis based on the APM gives the same statistical test discussed later.

[4] These tests use the arithmetic rate of return rather than the geometric; the test is more easily developed and understood in the former case, but the latter is an obvious extension. Further, experiments suggest that the relative performance of a filter does not depend on which definition of the rate of return is used.

for a filter is[5]

$$\bar{R}_F = \frac{1}{N}\left\{ \sum_{i=1}^{N_{in}} (u_i + r_{fi} - r_{di}) + \sum_{j=1}^{N_{out}} (r_d - r_d) \right\},$$

where N_{in} is the number of days *"in"* the DM, and N_{out} the days *"out,"* with $N \equiv N_{in} + N_{out}$. Taking expectations, $E\bar{R}_F = \frac{1}{N} \sum^{N_{in}} g = (N_{in}/N)g = (1 - f)g$, where $f \equiv N_{out}/N$. Thus, the expected excess rate of return on the filter depends on beta and the ex ante market premium for days in, and is zero for days out (i.e., days in the domestic risk-free asset), with the overall excess rate of return a weighted average.[6]

B. Filter Returns in Excess of Buy-and-Hold

Instead of comparing the difference, $\bar{R}_f - \bar{R}_{BH}$, this paper uses the statistic

$$X = \bar{R}_F - \bar{R}_{BH} + f\bar{R}_{BH}, \tag{3}$$

for two reasons. First, comparing $\bar{R}_{BH}$ to $\bar{R}_F$ is biased in one direction or the other as long as $g \neq 0$. Second, suppose that $g = 0$, but for a given sample $\bar{R}_{BH} > 0$. Then, the investor would expect $\bar{R}_F > 0$, since this is an "up" market. But further, one would expect $\bar{R}_{BH} > \bar{R}_F$, since the filter is taking the investor out of an "up" market part of the time.

The adjustment factor, $f\bar{R}_{BH}$, in (3) ensures $EX = (1 - f)g - g + fg = 0$, since g is assumed constant (or risk premia are constant). Notice that (3) implies that X can be positive, and the filter thus beat the market even if $\bar{R}_F < \bar{R}_{BH}$. This is so because $\bar{R}_F$ includes some days when the filter is out of the market, bears no risk, and is thus paid a zero risk premium. For example, if the filter and buy-and-hold both return \$50, but the filter had $f = 0.5$ so the investor was out of DMs 50% of the time, then the investor bore risk only half as many days with the filter as with buy-and-hold, but made the same profit. Depending on g, the investor might well prefer the expectation of \$45 from the filter to \$50 from buy-and-hold.

Confidence bounds are needed to judge the significance of nonzero values of X. Assuming that $\alpha - \alpha'$ is constant, the variance of X is

$$\sigma_X^2 = (\sigma_u^2/N)f(1 - f), \qquad \text{so } \sigma_X = (\sigma_u/N^{1/2})[f(1 - f)]^{1/2},$$

where $\sigma_u^2 = E(u - \alpha)^2$ is assumed constant even though α may vary over time. The sampling distribution of X will be normal if σ_u exists. There is some evidence that u might be Paretian stable (Cornell and Dietrich [5]; Logue, Sweeney, and Willett [18]. If this is accepted, one may want to require higher than conventional levels of significance before rejecting the null $X = 0$.

---

[5] Alternatively, $\bar{R}_F$ could be averaged over N_{in} rather than N days, as for example in Fama and Blume [11]. Sweeney [23] shows that a test can be developed using this definition of $\bar{R}_F$, one with exactly the same properties as the one developed previously.

[6] If $\bar{R}_F$ is averaged over N_{in}, then $E\bar{R}_F = g$ (for $N_{in} > 0$) and hence $E\bar{R}_{BH} = E\bar{R}_F = g$. The prediction is equal returns to both strategies.

C. Comparison of Dooley and Shafer

An alternative approach is the zero-wealth pure-exchange-risk play used by Dooley and Shafer [7]. The two approaches are not as dissimilar as they might appear; they simply use different but related filter strategies. The present paper uses long positions while Dooley and Shafer use long *and* short positions. However, the test statistic used here is more robust than Dooley and Shafer's.

Suppose the investor has taken no position, and the DM rises enough to give a buy signal. In the strategy used here, the investors puts funds, say $1 million, in DM assets, earning a per day rate of return of $u + r_f$ and earning an excess rate of return of $u + r_f - r_d$ per day. The investor can either use his/her own money or borrow the funds (though the transactions costs are higher with borrowing). In the Dooley and Shafer strategy, the funds are borrowed and the net rate of return is $u + r_f - r_d$ per day. When the DM falls enough to give a sell signal, the strategy used here has the speculator sell his/her DM assets and buy dollar assets, giving an excess return of $r_d - r_d = 0$ (or simply close out the position if the funds were borrowed). Dooley and Shafer's strategy also has the speculator sell the DM assets but then borrow DMs at the rate, r_f, and invest in dollar assets at the rate, r_d. Thus, his net return is $r_d - r_f - u \equiv -(u + r_f - r_d)$. Thus, in both strategies, the speculator takes long positions in DM assets, but in the present paper holds dollar assets when not long in DMs, while in Dooley and Shafer's strategy she is short in DMs when not long. (The issue of whether the speculator uses his own funds or only borrows is irrelevant to the difference between the two strategies.)

In Dooley and Shafer's methodology, the daily rate of return on days "in" DM is $(u + r_f - r_d)$, and on days "out" of, or shorting, the DM is $-(u + r_f - r_d)$. Similar to Dooley and Shafer, form an average rate of return from the two positions as

$$Y = (1/N) \sum_{i=1}^{N_{in}} (u_i + r_{fi} - r_{di}) + (1/N) \sum_{j=1}^{N_{out}} - (u_j + r_{fj} - r_{dj}). \quad (4)$$

Then,

$$EY = (N_{in}/N)g - (N_{out}/N)g = (1 - f - f)g = (1 - 2f)g, \quad (5)$$

where $g = b_f[E(R_M) - r_d]$, as above, and

$$\sigma_Y^2 = (1/N)\sigma_u^2,$$

$$\sigma_Y = \sigma_u/N^{1/2}. \quad (6)$$

While Dooley and Shafer make explicit that they assume $E(u + r_f - r_d) = 0$, it is clear from (5) that their measure is biased if $E(u + r_f - r_d) \neq 0$. This, in turn, comes to the issue of the bias in the forward premium as a predictor of coming future spot rates. The evidence on this is mixed, but recent work provides some fairly strong evidence against the unbiasedness hypothesis (see Fama [10], Hodrick and Srivastava [16], and Sweeney [24]). The present test allows explicitly for $E(u + r_f - r_d) = g \neq 0$, though it assumes g is constant over time.

Similar to the development of the X statistic, Dooley and Shafer's statistic could be reformulated by subtracting an adjusted $\bar{R}_{BH}$ to give

$Y' = Y - (1 - 2f)\bar{R}_{BH}$, where

$$EY' = 0, \qquad \sigma^2_{Y'} = (\sigma^2_u/N)4f(1 - f), \qquad \sigma_{Y'} = (\sigma_u/N^{1/2})2[f(1 - f)]^{1/2}.$$

Thus, the present paper's comparison of filter returns to buy-and-hold is not only intuitively plausible, but also some comparison to (an adjusted) buy-and-hold is necessary to give an unbiased test statistic.[7]

The present test looks only at long positions unlike Dooley and Shafer who look at both long and short positions. Efficiency requires that neither strategy make systematic risk-adjusted profits. Fama and Blume [11] use a long-and-short strategy in examining U.S. equity markets. It is clear from their Table 3 (and pp. 236–40) that the shorting part of the strategy is generally unprofitable and indeed masks the evidence of profits (*before* commissions!) provided by the long part of the strategy. This suggested *not* running a long-and-short test in the foreign exchange markets. However, it is easy to show that[8] $Y' = 2X$ and $\sigma_{Y'} = 2\sigma_X$. Thus, if an appropriate measure of profits is used, the long and long-and-short strategies give identical t-statistics. The approach of Dooley and Shafer, appropriately modified, will give the same conclusions as this paper's.

II. Empirical Results for the X Test

The data used here were kindly provided by the Board of Governors of the Federal Reserve System. Daily data on the dollar-DM exchange rate, the overnight federal funds rate, and the one-day Frankfurt interbank loan rate were used; to avoid problems of political risk it might have been preferable to use Euro rates, but these were not readily available. The data were cleaned carefully and checked with other sources. After cleaning, there remained 1,289 trading days between 1975 and 1980 for which interest rate data were available.[9] The three series were not collected at exactly the same time as each other; further, some rates were averages across firms and may not be actual trading data. Nevertheless, the quality of the data seems adequate; in any case, it was not possible to obtain better data or indeed obtain data for comparable experiments for other countries. In particular, the intra-day variability of the interest rate differential seems small enough (on the basis of casual observation) that conclusions below would not be altered if simultaneously collected data on interest rates were used.

[7] Even if $EY = 0$, Y' is a better test statistic than Y in at least the following sense. Suppose the filter puts the speculator in DMs on the first day and keeps him or her there throughout ($f = 0$). Y' will, of course, say there are zero profits. Y will say there are profits equal to $\bar{R}_{BH}$; but we know this from $\bar{R}_F = \bar{R}_{BH}$ when $f = 0$. In such a case, Y will be significantly different from EY 5% of the time at the 95% confidence level. In other words, this would be a test of whether it was smart to pursue a buy-and-hold strategy for the DM this period, *not* a test of whether getting in and out of the DM produced profits beyond buy-and-hold.

[8] Under the null hypothesis, X has chances to be nonzero only on days "in," while Y' can also be nonzero on days "out" because of the shorting.

[9] Days with missing observations on any of the three variables were deleted from the sample. Since many of the missing observations were due to markets being closed, this amounts to a decision to run the filter only when all markets are open. The Board gathered these data at (approximately) noon from a number of firms and averaged the results. Further, these exchange rates were not collected at exactly the same time as the interest rates. All series are "indications" rather than necessarily actual trading data.

Table I shows that, for the dollar price of the DM, the mean percentage rate of change of the exchange rate on a daily basis is $[(Ex_t - Ex_{t-1})/Ex_{t-1}] \cdot 100 = 0.027$, while the mean interest rate differential on the basis of 262 business days per year is $(r_f - r_d)/262 = -0.0113$ (r_f and r_d are quoted at annual percentage rates). However, the variances are much more divergent, with that for the exchange rate 0.270, and the differential 0.0000875. In forming $(\Delta Ex/Ex) \cdot 100 + (r_f - r_d)/262$, the mean falls from that of $(\Delta Ex/Ex)/100$ to 0.016, while the variance rises marginally to 0.271. Table I shows that the autocorrelation function for $\Delta Ex/Ex$ is approximately white, save for spikes at lags 8 and 10; the Box-Pierce Q statistic (adjusted) is borderline significant. $r_f - r_d$ appears highly nonstationary. Nevertheless, the series for exchange rate changes adjusted for the interest rate differential is essentially that of $\Delta Ex/Ex$ adjusted for the mean of the differential.

The test developed above is, of course, independent of exactly how decisions are made to buy and sell assets. The actual filter rule used here is based on the long positions in Alexander [1] and Fama and Blume [11]. It says "buy when the dollar value of the DM rises $Y\%$ above its previous local low; sell when it falls $Z\%$ from its previous local high." Further, the Y and Z were set equal, and no attempts were made to find values that improved filter performance.

Table II shows results for seven different filters. The X statistics are reported as percent per day. Thus, the entry for the 0.5% rule shows profits of 0.016% per day or, on the basis of 250 trading days per year, profits of 4% per year (= 0.016% × 250). Table II shows that any filter but 10% beats buy-and-hold and that the X statistic is significant for filters of 0.5% and 1%. Note that the confidence bounds are contingent on the f for each particular rule.[10]

Similar to the results of Fama and Blume [11] on long positions, small filters seem to work best, but also have the largest number of transactions. However, unlike the Fama and Blume results, transaction costs do not seem to eliminate risk-adjusted excess filter returns. It is estimated (Sweeney and Lee [26]) that, in the foreign exchange-market, each round trip costs one-eighth of 1% of asset value on average for large, regular customers (separate bid/ask daily prices were not readily available).[11] Distributed over the 1,289 trading days of the sample,

---

[10] If $\alpha - \alpha'$ equals a constant, but α shifts over the sample, using the sample variance $(\Delta Ex/Ex) \cdot 100 + (r_f - r_d)/262$, as Table II does in the X test, gives a better estimate of σ_u^2 than does the sample variance of $(\Delta Ex/Ex) \cdot 100$. However, these two estimates of σ_u^2 are so close that the choice makes no practical difference.

[11] Frenkel and Levich [13, 14] use a method based on triangular arbitrage to estimate the cost of transactions in the market for foreign exchange. They emphasize that their "estimate should be interpreted to encompass the total cost associated with a transaction. Thus, it includes elements like brokerage fees, time cost, subscription costs, and all other components that compromise the cost of being informed" [14, p. 1212]. Using their method, McCormick [19] estimates spot market transactions costs for the period April–October 1976 to be 0.182 of 1% for the DM, based on triangular arbitrage from U.S. dollars to pounds sterling to DMs. However, the essence of McCormick's point is that the estimates require simultaneous quotes on the currencies involved in the triangular arbitrage, and this estimate for the DM has a difference of up to one hour. Using his estimates of transactions costs based on the Canadian dollar, transactions costs measured simultaneously are only 57% of those measured with a lag of up to one hour. Hence, the triangular arbitrage of the DM would imply transactions costs of 0.104 (= 0.57 × 0.182) of 1%, or about $\frac{1}{10}$ of 1%, less than the 0.125 or $\frac{1}{8}$ of 1% assumed in the text.

Financial Forecasting II

The Journal of Finance

Table I
Properties of Dollar-DM Exchange Rate, with and without Adjustment for Interest Rate Differentials

Panel A: Autocorrelation Function of $(\Delta Ex/Ex)\cdot 100$

Lag	1	2	3	4	5	6	7	8	9	10	11	12	Estimated Standard Error
Estimated Coefficient	0.02	0.00	0.02	-0.01	0.02	0.04	-0.01	0.08*	0.02	0.08*	-0.01	-0.02	0.03

Mean: 0.027   Variance: 0.270 $Q(12) = 22.8$

Panel B: Autocorrelation Function of $(r_f - r_d)/262$

Lag	1	2	3	4	5	6	7	8	9	10	11	12	Estimated Standard Error
Estimated Coefficient	0.95*	0.95*	0.90*	0.88*	0.87*	0.86*	0.85*	0.84*	0.82*	0.81*	0.80*	0.79*	0.03

Mean: -0.0113   Variance: 0.0000875 $Q(12) = 11,500$

Panel C: Autocorrelation Function of $\Delta(r_f - r_d)/262$

Lag	1	2	3	4	5	6	7	8	9	10	11	12	Estimated Standard Error
Estimated Coefficient	-0.30*	0.01	-0.08*	-0.05	-0.03	0.01	0.03	0.00	-0.02	0.03	-0.03	0.03	0.03

Mean: 0.45×10^{-5} Variance: 0.891×10^{-5} $Q(12) = 126$

Panel D: Autocorrelation Function of $(\Delta Ex/Ex)\cdot 100 + (r_f - r_d)/262$

Lag	1	2	3	4	5	6	7	8	9	10	11	12	Estimated Standard Error
Estimated Coefficient	0.02	0.00	0.02	-0.01	0.02	0.04	-0.01	0.08*	0.02	0.08*	-0.01	-0.02	0.03

Mean: 0.016   Variance: 0.271 $Q(12) = 23.4$

* Significant at the 95% confidence level.

Table II

Tests of Significance of Filter Rule Profits*

Filter (%)	$\bar{R}_F$	$\bar{R}_{BH}$	f	X	Transactions (Round Trips)	X (Net of Transaction)	$\bar{R}'_F$	$\bar{R}'_{BH}$	X'
0.5	0.024	0.0156	0.446	0.016** (0.002, 0.030)	94	0.0064	0.029	0.027	0.014** (0.000, 0.028)
1	0.028	0.0156	0.388	0.019** (0.005, 0.033)	42	0.0148**	0.034	0.027	0.017** (0.003, 0.031)
2	0.022	0.0156	0.422	0.013 (−0.001, 0.027)	18	0.0112	0.028	0.027	0.013 (−0.001, 0.027)
3	0.016	0.0156	0.423	0.007 (−0.007, 0.021)	13	0.0057	0.021	0.027	0.006 (−0.008, 0.020)
4	0.018	0.0156	0.250	0.007 (−0.006, 0.018)	8	0.0062	0.026	0.027	0.006 (−0.007, 0.018)
5	0.016	0.0156	0.265	0.005 (−0.008, 0.017)	6	0.0042	0.024	0.027	0.005 (−0.008, 0.017)
10	0.003	0.0156	0.396	−0.006 (−0.020, 0.008)	4	−0.0064	0.009	0.027	−0.007 (−0.021, 0.007)

* Bounds in parentheses ($n = 1,288$). $\text{Var}[(\Delta Ex/Ex)\cdot100] = 0.27041$; $\text{Var}[(\Delta Ex/Ex)\cdot100 + (r_I - r_d)/262] = 0.27063$; $\hat{\sigma}_X = \frac{1}{N}^{1/2}[f(1-f)(\text{Var}[(\Delta Ex/Ex)\cdot100 + (r_I - r_d)/262])]^{1/2}$, $\hat{\sigma}_{X'} = \frac{1}{N}^{1/2}[f(1-f)(\text{Var}[(\Delta Ex/Ex)\cdot100])]^{1/2}$.

** Significant at the 95% confidence level.

one round trip reduces $\bar{R}_F$ and hence X by $(\frac{1}{8})/1{,}289$ or by approximately 0.0001 on a daily basis. The column "X, Net of Transactions Costs" shows the adjusted Xs. All are smaller, of course, but all retain their previous signs. The 1% filter is still significant, and both the 1% and 2% filters look very good after transactions costs.

No explicit account is taken of the possible extra transactions costs of putting funds in interest-bearing assets. If all transactions are with a single bank, presumably the marginal cost of switching overnight interest-bearing assets among currencies is quite low and likely infra-marginal.

The period examined for the dollar-DM rate, adjusted for the interest rate differential, begins roughly around the end of the period for which Logue, Sweeney, and Willet [18], Dooley and Shafer [6] and Cornell and Dietrich [5] found excess filter rule profits. Hence, this test is evidence that profits persisted into the 1980's. Further, the present test takes account of risk as well as providing confidence bounds.

III. The Text When Interest-Rate Differentials Are Neglected

One problem with implementing the X test is that good data on the overnight differential, $r_d - r_f$, are hard to accumulate. Under certain circumstances, neglecting $r_d - r_f$ is low cost, e.g., if α' equals a constant. More generally, suppose that the average α' for days in ($\bar{\alpha}'_{in}$) equals the average for days out ($\bar{\alpha}'_{out}$), so $\bar{\alpha}' = \bar{\alpha}'_{in} = \bar{\alpha}'_{out}$. Then

$$X = (1/N) \sum^{N_{in}} (u - \alpha'_{in}) - [(1 - f)/N] \sum^N (u - \alpha)$$

$$= (1/N) \sum^{N_{in}} u - (N_{in}/N)\bar{\alpha}'_{in} - [(1 - f)/N] \sum^N u + (1 - f)\bar{\alpha}'$$

$$= (1/N) \sum^{N_{in}} u - [(1 - f)/N] \sum^N u. \tag{7}$$

In other words, when $\bar{\alpha}'_{in} \cong \bar{\alpha}'$, it is legitimate to simplify and instead of using X, use

$$X' = \bar{R}'_F - \bar{R}'_{BH} + f\bar{R}'_{BH}, \tag{8}$$

where $\bar{R}'_F = (1/N) \sum^{N_{in}} u_j$, $\bar{R}'_{BH} = (1/N) \sum^N u_j$, with $\bar{R}'_F$ the filter's sample return due solely to exchange rate appreciation and $\bar{R}'_{BH}$ the buy-and-hold return due to appreciation. Of course, when the dollar faces trend depreciation, $\bar{R}'_{BH} > \bar{R}_{BH}$ due to neglecting the fact than $r_f < r_d$. However, $\bar{R}'_F$ is similarly overstated, so on net X and X' are unaffected by omitting the differential as long as $\bar{\alpha}'_{in} \cong \bar{\alpha}'_{out}$.

As a practical matter, it should be true that $\bar{\alpha}'_{in} \cong \bar{\alpha}'_{out}$ whenever the out periods are scattered roughly evenly through the total, N. However, some insight into the difference in results due to neglecting the differential is available by considering the case of the \$/DM exchange rate, where results can be compared for both the X and the modified X' tests.

A. Empirical Results for the X' Test

Table II also shows the X' statistic for the same sample where X was calculated;[12] the X and X' are very close. The difference results from the fact

---

[12] X' has exactly the same days in and out as X. The difference is solely the exclusion in X' of the interest-rate differential in calculating all rates of return.

that the average interest rate differential for the sample is $\bar{\alpha}' = 0.0113$, while $\bar{\alpha}'_{in}$ is smaller for each rule and over the seven rules averages 0.0103; hence, on average $\bar{\alpha}' - \bar{\alpha}'_{in} = 0.0113 - 0.0103 = 0.001$. This implies $\bar{\alpha}'_{out} > \bar{\alpha}' > \bar{\alpha}'_{in}$. Inspection of (7) shows that $\bar{\alpha}'_{out} > \bar{\alpha}'_{in}$ makes the sample $X > X'$.

For the X' test, all filter rules save for 10% beat buy-and-hold, with both the 0.5 (borderline) and 1.0% rules beating buy-and-hold significantly, just as before.[13]

B. X' Test Results for 10 Countries

The results for the X and X' tests for the \$-DM exchange rate in Table II cannot, of course, prove that it is always safe to neglect interest-rate differentials. Nevertheless, since finding matching overnight interest rates is so difficult, the X' test is used here for 10 countries for 1,830 days of the floating rate period from April 1, 1973 into 1980. The period is broken into two parts, the first 610 days and the remaining 1,220 days.

Table III shows that for the first period, a substantial fraction of rules produced significant X' values. For example, the buy-and-sell filter of ½ of 1% for the Belgian franc gave an $X' = 0.035$ which is highly significant at the 95% confidence level; thus, the speculation earned an average 0.035% profits each day, or for a 250-day year, an annual rate of 8.75%. Of the 70 cases given by the seven rules and ten countries, 22 cases are significant.[14] A major question is whether knowledge of these results would have helped obtain profits after the first 610 trading days. Table IV shows that many rules gave significant X' values in the next 1,220 trading days; there are 21 significant cases of the 70 total.[15] In both Tables III and IV, adjustments for transactions costs affects results to about the same degree as in Table II.

Table V sheds light on how helpful the results in Table III are in exploiting the profit potential revealed in Table IV. First, eight rules significant in the first

---

[13] Use of X' in place of X will of course be misleading if $\bar{\alpha}'_{in} \neq \bar{\alpha}'_{out}$. For example, for a given value of X', inspection of (7) shows that if $\bar{\alpha}'_{in} < \bar{\alpha}'_{out}$, $X = X'$ and hence the filter rule's success is underestimated. However, this example may be misleading if α and α' tend to move in offsetting directions as theory suggests. Hence, when $\bar{\alpha}'_{in} > \bar{\alpha}'_{out}$, $\bar{\alpha}_{in}$ will tend to exceed $\bar{\alpha}_{out}$ and thus raise X'; in such cases, it is illegitimate to hold X' constant when conceptually increasing $\bar{\alpha}'_{in}$ relative to $\bar{\alpha}'_{out}$.

Using X requires, strictly speaking, stationarity of $u_t - \alpha'_t$, and using X' requires stationarity of u_t. If $\alpha' = $ constant, then $\bar{\alpha}'_{in} = \bar{\alpha}'_{out}$, and stationarity implies $\alpha_t - \alpha'_t = $ constant so $\alpha_t = $ constant, and it is economically and statistically legitimate to use X'.

Suppose X' is used when α_t varies over time but $\alpha - \alpha' = $ constant. Then X' may be either larger or smaller than the "true" X. This is ameliorated somewhat by the fact that the estimate $\hat{\sigma}_{X'}$ will tend to exceed the estimate $\hat{\sigma}_X$, because $\hat{\sigma}_u$ now includes not only the effect of random exchange rate changes but also the effect of the shifting mean α_t. Hence, any upward bias in X' is to some extent offset by an upward bias in $\hat{\sigma}_{X'}$.

[14] For any one country, the success of various filters will be correlated. Hence, the 70 cases are not independent, and no overall test can be done. Note that one of these cases, the Japanese yen for the 10% filter, produces significantly negative excess returns.

[15] The results for X' for the DM differ across Tables II and IV for two reasons. First, the beginning of the sample for Table II includes some of the (latter part of the) first 610 days. Second, Table II's sample does not include any days where the foreign exchange market was open but one of the money markets was closed (or interest rate data were unavailable.).

Again, the 10% filter produces significantly negative profits in one case, this time the Swedish krone.

Table III

Filter Rule Results: First 610 Observations*

	0.5%	1%	2%	3%	4%	5%	10%
Belgian franc	0.035**	0.029**	0.024	0.028**	0.026	0.033	0.007
	(2.80)	(2.32)	(1.92)	(2.24)	(1.93)	(2.64)	(0.74)
Canadian dollar	0.004	0.005	0.006**	0.004	0.003	0.002	0
	(1.60)	(1.67)	(2.40)	(1.60)	(1.50)	(1.00)	(0.00)
Deutsche mark	0.019	0.026	0.035**	0.018	0.043**	0.031**	−0.006
	(1.36)	(1.86)	(2.50)	(1.29)	(3.07)	(2.21)	(−0.46)
French franc	0.027**	0.034**	0.031**	0.027**	0.036**	0.041**	0.018
	(2.08)	(2.62)	(2.39)	(2.16)	(3.13)	(3.42)	(1.57)
Italian lira	0.028**	0.020**	0.016	0.016	0.008	−0.005	−0.005
	(3.11)	(2.86)	(1.88)	(1.88)	(1.07)	(−0.59)	(−0.63)
Japanese yen	0.005	0.007	0.017**	0.008	0	0.002	−0.015**
	(0.63)	(0.82)	(2.13)	(0.89)	(0.00)	(−0.24)	(−3.00)
Swiss franc	0.024	0.036**	0.023	0.030	0.027	0.026	0.013
	(1.50)	(2.25)	(1.48)	(1.88)	(1.69)	(1.63)	(0.93)
Swedish krone	0.013	0.030**	0.016	0.021	0.035**	0.025**	0.003
	(1.08)	(2.50)	(1.33)	(1.68)	(2.80)	(2.08)	(0.33)
Spanish peseta	−0.002	−0.007	0.002	0	−0.005	0	0
	(−0.36)	(−1.27)	(0.44)	(0.00)	(−1.11)	(0.00)	(0.00)
U.K. pound sterling	0.009	0.015	0.024**	0.017**	0.010	0.004	−0.006
	(1.13)	(1.89)	(3.00)	(2.27)	(1.25)	(0.50)	(−1.00)

* *t*-statistic in parentheses.
** Significant at the 95% confidence level.

Table IV
Filter Rule Results: Final 1,220 Observations*

	0.5%	1%	2%	3%	4%	5%	10%
Belgian franc	0.009	0.017**	0.010	0.006	-0.001	-0.001	-0.008
	(1.29)	(2.43)	(1.43)	(0.92)	(-0.17)	(-0.15)	(-1.60)
Canadian dollar	0.012**	0.012**	0.004	0	-0.003	0.004	0
	(3.43)	(3.43)	(1.14)	(0.00)	(-1.00)	(1.33)	(0.00)
Deutsche mark	0.008	0.014**	0.008	0	-0.001	-0.002	-0.007
	(1.14)	(2.00)	(1.14)	(0.00)	(-0.20)	(-0.44)	(-1.27)
French franc	0.013	0.014**	0.006	0.005	0.005	0.005	-0.016
	(1.86)	(2.15)	(0.86)	(0.77)	(0.77)	(-0.77)	(-1.52)
Italian lira	0.022**	0.015**	0	0.003	0.005	-0.004	0
	(3.14)	(2.14)	(0.00)	(0.43)	(0.77)	(-0.57)	(0.00)
Japanese yen	0.020**	0.027**	0.010	0.010	0.009	0.018**	0.022**
	(2.50)	(3.18)	(1.33)	(1.33)	(1.29)	(3.00)	(2.93)
Swiss franc	0.015	0.023**	0.012	0.019	0.015	-0.002	-0.002
	(1.50)	(2.42)	(1.20)	(1.90)	(1.43)	(-0.21)	(-0.20)
Swedish krone	0.009	0.015**	0.009	0.003	0.009	0.002	-0.014**
	(1.39)	(2.31)	(1.39)	(0.55)	(1.39)	(0.33)	(-2.33)
Spanish peseta (last 1,218 observations)	0.018	0.019**	0.023**	0.015	0.011	0.006	0.002
	(1.90)	(2.00)	(2.30)	(1.58)	(1.10)	(0.60)	(0.20)
U.K. pound sterling	0.019**	0.026**	0.015**	0.020**	0.018**	0.007	0.007
	(2.71)	(3.71)	(2.00)	(2.85)	(2.57)	(1.08)	(1.08)

* *t*-statistic in parentheses.
** Significant at the 95% confidence level.

Table V

Values of X': Final 1,220 Observations

Filter	Belgian Franc	Canadian Dollar	Deutsche Mark	French Franc	Italian Lira	Japanese Yen
0.5%	0.009*	0.012**	0.008	0.013*	0.022*,**	0.020**
1%	0.017*,**	0.012**	0.014**	0.014*,**	0.015*,**	0.027**
2%	0.010	0.004*	0.008*	0.006*	0.00	0.010*
3%	0.006*	0	0	0.005*	0.003	0.010
4%	−0.001	−0.003	−0.001*	0.005*	0.005	0.009
5%	0.001	0.004	−0.002*	−0.005*	−0.004	0.018**
10%	−0.008	0	0.007	−0.016	0	0.022**
Σ/7	0.005	0.004	0.005	0.003	0.006	0.017
Σ≠/N	0.008	0.004	0.002	0.006	0.019	0.010
Σ/3	0.011	0.007	0.002	0.005	0.010	0.016

Filter	Swiss Franc	Swedish Krone	Spanish Peseta	U.K. Pound Sterling
0.5%	0.015	0.009	0.018	0.019**
1%	0.023*,**	0.015*,**	0.019**	0.026**
2%	0.012	0.009	0.023**	0.015*,**
3%	0.019	0.003	0.015	0.020*,**
4%	0.015	0.009*	0.011	0.018**
5%	−0.002	0.002*	0.006	0.007
10%	−0.002	−0.014	0.002	0.007
Σ/7	0.011	0.005	0.013	0.016
Σ≠/N	0.023	0.009	0.000	0.018
Σ/3	0.017	0.009	0.019	0.020

* Rules that for this country generated *positive* values of X' significant at the 95% confidence level in the first 610 observations (22 did so).

** Rules that for this country generated *positive* values of X' significant at the 95% confidence level in the last 1,220 observations (20 did so).

period are also significant in the second. However, 15 rules were significant in the first period but not in the second, while there were 12 rules significant in the second period but not the first. Two further counts may be more revealing. The row "$\Sigma \neq/N$" shows the second period's average X' values for rules that were significant in the first period. In other words, suppose the first period's significant rules were used in the second period. For every country, $\Sigma \neq/N$ is positive. As a second experiment, for each country pick the three best rules in Table III, based on X' values, and use these in the second period. The resulting average X' values for the second period are shown in the row for $\Sigma/3$. For every country, $\Sigma/3$ is positive, and $\Sigma/3 > \Sigma/7$ for every country but Germany and Japan.

Finally, Table VI shows the average t-statistic across countries for each filter size. It is clear that smaller filters work somewhat better in the later than earlier period. If a finite variance exists for each exchange rate, the t-statistic for each is distributed $N(0, 1)$. Because the t-statistics should show no correlation across countries for the same filter,[16] the overall significance of the profits across countries from any filter can be tested by looking at the average t-statistic, $\bar{t}$, which is distributed $N(0, 1/N^{\frac{1}{2}})$ where N is the number of countries (10 in this case). The t-statistics for this test of $\bar{t}$ for each filter are in the third row of Table VI. For all filters of 4% or less, the profits are significant.

IV. Are Filter Rule Excess Profits Explicable by Risk?

A number of authors, e.g., Cornell and Dietrich [5], and Levich [17], have conjectured that existence of observed filter rule profits may be due to the risk involved in speculative efforts to exploit them (which would reduce them as a side effect). Indeed, this risk has sometimes been cast in the CAPM framework.

Cornell and Dietrich [5] estimated betas (b) for various currencies relative to the dollar in hopes of explaining their filter rule profits (Table VII). They argue that, in their tests, " . . . none of the rules led to annual profits of over 4% in the case of the British pound, Canadian dollar, or Japanese yen . . . For the German mark, Dutch guilder, and Swiss franc . . . the situation was quite different". This passage, however, fails to focus on the difference between the return to the filter rule versus buy-and-hold. The key issue is not how well the filter rule did, but how it did relative to buy-and-hold. Column (3) shows that, contrary to Cornell and Dietrich, filter rules did an impressive job for the mark and guilder *and also* the pound and yen vis-à-vis buy-and-hold, but *not* for the Swiss franc. Cornell and Dietrich go on to argue that "[o]ne explanation for the higher returns on the franc, mark and guilder positions is that the high returns are compensation for risk. The three currencies showing the highest rates of return also had the largest variance in daily rates of return . . . [M]odern finance theory indicates that only undiversified risk must be compensated for via higher expected rates of re-

---

[16] Movements in exchange rates are correlated, as are rates of return on equities in, say, the U.S. Nevertheless, excess rates of return on filter strategies should be virtually uncorrelated because the in-out positions are only randomly synchronized across currencies. For example, if the DM rises and the 1% filter has the investor "in," the yen may also rise but the speculator is equally likely to be "out" or "in" the yen: For details as applied to U.S. equities, see Sweeney [23].

Table VI

Average t-Statistics for X' for Various Filters

	0.5%	1%	2%	3%	4%	5%	10%
First 610 observations	1.49	1.75	1.95	1.59	1.53	1.27	0.15
Final 1,220 observations	2.09	2.58	1.28	1.03	0.87	0.42	−0.27
Final 1,220 observations; t-statistic multiplied by $\sqrt{10}$	6.60	8.15	4.05	3.26	2.75	1.33	−0.85

Table VII

Filter Rule Profits and Beta Risk

Currency	(1) Annual Rate of Return From Filter Rule, Net of Transactions Costs	(2) Annual Rate of Return from Buy-and-Hold	(3) = (1–2)	(4) $\hat{b}$	(5) $t(\hat{b})$
British pound	1.9	−6.4	8.3	0.03	0.85
Canadian dollar	1.4	−1.4	2.8	−0.003	0.22
Dutch guilder	13.0	4.8	8.2	0.12	2.18
German mark	15.7	4.3	11.4	0.11	1.85
Japanese yen	2.5	−4.6	7.1	0.08	1.71
Swiss franc	10.2	8.3	1.9	0.05	0.72

Source: Based on Tables 3 and 5, Cornell and Dietrich [5, pp. 116–17]. For (1), they report the *highest* rate. They do not compute (3).

turn . . . " They then provide the estimated betas and t-statistics in columns (4) and (5).

In conjunction with the risk premium on the market, $\hat{b}$ can be used to explain the buy-and-hold returns in (2). As a best guess, $\bar{R}_{BH}$ equals $\bar{r}_d + \hat{b}(\bar{R}_M - \bar{r}_d)$, where $\bar{R}_M$ is the sample return on the market and $\bar{r}_d$ the average risk-free rate. If $\bar{R}_F$ is measured over N_{in} rather than N (as in Section I), the best guess for $\bar{R}_F$ is also $\bar{r}_d + \hat{b}(\bar{R}_M - \bar{r}_d)$.[17,18] Thus, b can "explain" both columns (1) and (2) but cannot explain their difference, column (3). The issue is whether (3) is significantly different from zero, and judging this requires an explicit statistical test, such as Section I developed. The CAPM cannot "explain" (3), but worse, any significant values in (3) call for rejecting the CAPM since it predicts zero values in (3).

V. Conclusions

Major exchange markets showed grave signs of inefficiency over the first 1,830 days of the generalized managed floating that began in March 1973. This paper

---

[17] See footnote 6.

[18] As in footnote 3, this assumes the market model intercept is zero. Alternatively, one could use its estimate, $\hat{a}$, to form a best guess of R_{BH} as $\hat{a} + \hat{b} (\bar{R}_M - \bar{r}_d)$, and of R_F over N_{in} days as $\hat{a} + \hat{b} (\bar{R}_M - \bar{r}_d)$. This again, gives a best-guess difference of zero.

develops a test of the significance of filter rule profits that explicitly assumes constant risk/return trade-offs due to constant risk premia. While the test is discussed in terms of Sharpe-Lintner CAPM, it is fully consistent with Breeden or Merton CAPMs or with APMs. Excess filter rule returns over buy-and-hold are not explicable in terms of risk as modelled within CAPMs or APMs.

If one decides to judge filter rule profits on the basis of average daily rates of return versus buy-and-hold, it is theoretically more sound to use percentage exchange rate changes net of the interest rate differential, rather than just the percentage exchange rate changes themselves. However, there are instances when it does not matter which measure is used. In particular, if the interest differential is a constant, the two tests are identical. In the test performed on 1,289 daily observations of the dollar-DM exchange rate, net of the federal funds, and overnight Frankfurt interbank loan rate differential, both tests give virtually identical results, that the filter profits are often substantial and sometimes statistically significantly better than buy-and-hold's returns. While the differential is not constant, its day-to-day variability is orders of magnitude smaller than the percentage change in the exchange rate's and its average for "days in" versus "days out" is quite close. For practical purposes, then, the differential can be taken as constant and either test used. This seems likely to be the case in all of the major exchange markets under floating. This result is a great convenience, since it says filter tests need only look at exchange rates, and not also at the differentials which are more difficult to gather.

Some authors have argued that the filter profits found in exchange markets are explicable in light of the speculative risk involved in earning them and may perhaps not be excessive or indicative of inefficiency. Indeed, it is sometimes suggested that this issue should be looked at in terms of the CAPM. As shown previously, however, the CAPM explains returns to buy-and-hold, and to the filter, and implies that expected excess returns to the filter over buy-and-hold should equal zero. Thus, the significant returns previously found, rather than being explicable in terms of the CAPM, are evidence for rejecting the hypothesis that the CAPM describes exchange markets.

This evidence of excess speculative returns says nothing about why these returns exist. Two classes of explanations are of interest. One accepts the evidence of significant speculative profits and inefficiency, while the other class retains the efficient market hypothesis by explaining measured profits in terms of time-varying risk premia.

Discussions of exchange market behavior suggest three hypotheses to explain speculative profits and inefficiency. First, many policy discussions view exchange markets as subject to greater or lesser destabilizing speculation. Woo [28] has developed evidence of speculative "bubbles." He uses a rational expectations model where an explosive root governs exchange rate movements for a time. A difficulty with such a model is that knowledge of eventual shift to a stable path is inconsistent with the model's description of even temporary movement along an explosive path.

Second, the present generalized managed float has involved a great, although varying, amount of management. Ill-conceived government intervention can create profit opportunities such as those found above. There is substantial evidence suggesting at least some intervention to lean against the wind (Dornbusch [8], Genberg [15], Branson [3]). Some studies argue that central banks lose money on their intervention, and hence their actions are destabilizing (Taylor [27]). Whether this is so is a complicated and controversial issue, with definitive results not yet available (Federal Reserve Bulletin [12], Argy [2]). If appropriate data were made publicly available, the issue could be convincingly investigated along lines somewhat similar to those used previously. For example, suppose an exchange stabilization fund intervenes only with U.S. dollars. If one has daily figures on the fund's holdings of dollars and home currency, a statistic similar to the X statistic can be calculated and tested (Sweeney [25]). Significantly positive results would suggest the fund was stabilizing the exchange rate and reducing measured profits; further intervention might be beneficial. Significant negative results would suggest the fund contributed to the measured profits and that its intervention was counterproductive.

Third, the potential profits may be due to insufficient stabilizing speculation. Of course, in one sense this must be true, for with sufficient stabilizing speculative funds, even very great government intervention or private destabilizing speculation should leave no trace of profits in the data. However, some who hold this hypothesis point particularly to restrictions on the open positions that bank exchange traders can take. These restrictions are often imposed by the banks themselves, but many times with at least informal pressure by regulators. With access to daily data on banks' exchange positions, a test similar to that described for governments could be done (although this is more complicated with a portfolio of currencies). Significant positive results for such a test would suggest that increased activity by banks would reduce measured profits at the margin (while significant negative results would suggest that banks contribute to destabilizing the exchanges).

It is possible to reconcile this paper's results with generally held views of the efficient market hypothesis by asserting that risk premia vary over time, and hence expected returns both to the filter and to buy-and-hold also vary with time. In this view, the filter on average puts the investor "in" the foreign currency when the risk premia and hence the expected returns are larger than average. Positive X's are then a reflection of higher average risk borne, not true profits. This view can be tested if one is willing to specify a particular asset model and find estimates of premia. Fama [10], Hodrick and Srivasatava [16], and Sweeney [24] report evidence that risk premia in forward exchange rates vary over time; such premia are intimately related to the premia involved in spot market speculation.[19] Sweeney [22] reports preliminary results, using a single-period

---

[19] Assuming interest rate parity holds, as it does to a good approximation for *Euro* rates, speculative positions in the forward market are equivalent to borrowing and lending in the two currencies and taking a spot market position (if the transactions costs of borrowing and lending are neglected). The variable $u + r_f - r_d$, used in the text for spot market speculation, can be thought of as arising from borrowing dollars at r_d, converting them in the spot market to DMs, and investing the DMs at r_f. Thus, the risk premium in the forward speculation is in principle the same as that in $u + r_f - r_d$. However, the present paper analyzes overnight spot positions while Fama, Hodrick, and Srivastava and Sweeney look at thirty-day forward rates. Hence, the risk premia in these forward rates can only throw indirect light on the premia in overnight spot speculations.

Beating the Foreign Exchange Market 181

international CAPM, that do not very strongly support the view that variations in risk premia can be used to explain speculative profits in forward markets.

Many more tests of time-varying premia are possible and desirable, in the context of international CAPMs and other APMs. Since any test of efficiency is inevitably a test of a joint hypothesis (e.g., that an international CAPM holds), efficiency can always be preserved as an hypothesis in the face of negative evidence by abandoning other components of the joint hypothesis, as is well known. That is, one can stay a jump ahead of negative evidence, such as that presented here, by embodying efficiency in a joint hypothesis that has yet to be tested. From the practical point of view of evaluation of portfolio performance, one may be forced to proceed on the assumption of inefficiency. The portfolio manager may believe that the measured profits reported above may well be due to time-varying risk premia. But in the absence of measures of the extent to which this is true, a Bayesian manager is going to make some attempts to exploit these profits, i.e., act on the assumption of inefficiency. Indeed, in the absence of evidence that the profits are explicable by time-varying risk premia, the manager who forgoes these measured profits is going to have a hard sale justifying his or her behavior to those who put up the funds (see Dybvig and Ross' [9] example of market timing).

REFERENCES

1. S. S. Alexander. "Price Movements in Speculative Markets: Trends or Random Walks." *Industrial Management Review* V (Spring 1964), 25–46.
2. V. Argy. "Exchange-Rate Management and Practice." *Princeton Studies in International Finance* 50 (1982).
3. W. Branson. "A Model of Exchange Determination with Policy Reaction: Evidence from Monthly Data." National Bureau of Economic Research Working Paper No. 1135, June 1983.
4. D. T. Breeden. "An Intertemporal Asset Pricing Model with Stochastic Consumption and Investment Opportunities." *Journal of Financial Economics* 7 (September 1979), 265–96.
5. W. B. Cornell and J. K. Dietrich. "The Efficiency of the Market for Foreign Exchange Under Floating Exchange Rates." *Review of Economics and Statistics* LX (February 1978), 111–20.
6. M. Dooley and J. Shafer. "Analysis of Short-Run Exchange Rate Behavior, March 1973 to September 1975." International Finance Discussion Paper No. 76, Federal Reserve Board, 1976.
7. _____. "Analysis of Short-Run Exchange Rate Behavior: March 1973 to November 1981." In D. Bigman and T. Taya (eds.). *Exchange Rate and Trade Instability*. Cambridge, MA: Ballinger, 1983.
8. R. Dornbusch. "Exchange Rate Economics: Where Do We Stand?" *Brookings Papers on Economic Activity* No. 1, (1980), 143–206.
9. P. H. Dybvig and S. A. Ross. "Performance Measurement Using Differential Information and a Security Market Line." *Journal of Finance* 40 (June 1985), 383–400.
10. E. F. Fama. "Forward and Spot Exchange Rates." *Journal of Monetary Economics* 14 (December 1984), 319–38.
11. _____ and M. Blume. "Filter Rules and Stock-Market Trading." *Journal of Business* XXXIX (January 1966), 226–41.
12. Federal Reserve Bulletin. "Intervention in Foreign Exchange Markets: A Summary of Ten Staff Studies." November 1983, 830–36.
13. J. Frenkel and R. Levich. "Covered Interest Arbitrage: Unexploited Profits?" *Journal of Political Economy* 83, (April 1975), 325–38.
14. _____. "Transactions Costs and Interest Arbitrage: Tranquil versus Turbulent Periods." *Journal of Political Economy* 85 (December 1977), 1209–26.

15. H. Genberg. "Effects of Central Bank Intervention in the Foreign Exchange Market." *International Monetary Fund Staff Papers* 28 (September 1981), 451–76.

16. R. J. Hodrick and S. Srivastava. "The Covariation of Risk Premiums and Expected Future Spot Exchange Rates." *Journal of International Money and Finance*, forthcoming, 1986.

17. R. Levich. "Comment." In J. S. Dreyer, G. Haberler, and T. D. Willett (eds.). *The International Monetary System: A Time of Turbulence*. Washington, D.C.: American Enterprise Institute, 1982.

18. D. E. Logue, R. J. Sweeney, and T. D. Willett. "The Speculative Behavior of Foreign Exchange Rates During the Current Float." *Journal of Business Research* 6 (May 1978), 159–74.

19. F. McCormick. "Covered Interest Arbitrage: Unexploited Profits? Comment." *Journal of Political Economy* 87 (April 1979), 411–17.

20. R. C. Merton. "An Intertemporal Capital Asset Pricing Model." *Econometrica* 41 (September 1973), 867–87.

21. P. Praetz. "A General Test of a Filter Effect." *Journal of Financial and Quantitative Analysis* XIV (June 1979), 385–94.

22. P. Sharp. "Determinants of Forward Premia in Efficient Markets." In S. W. Arndt, R. J. Sweeney, and T. D. Willett (eds.). *Exchange Rates, Trade, and the U.S. Economy*. Cambridge, MA: Ballinger, 1985.

23. R. J. Sweeney. "Some New Filter Rule Tests: Methodology and Results." Claremont Working Paper, Claremont, CA, 1984.

24. ———. "Risk Premia in Forward Exchange Rates." Mimeo manuscript, Claremont, CA, 1985a.

25. ———. "A New Test of Portfolio Performance." Mimeo manuscript, Claremont, CA, 1985b.

26. ——— and E. J. Q. Lee. "Trading Strategies in Forward Exchange Markets." Mimeo manuscript, Claremont, CA, 1985.

27. D. Taylor. "Official Intervention in the Foreign Exchange Market or, Bet Against the Cental Bank." *Journal of Political Economy* 90 (April 1982), 356–68.

28. W. T. Woo. "Speculative Bubbles in the Foreign Exchange Markets." Brookings Discussion Paper in International Economics, Washington, D.C., 1984.

[16]

Journal of International Money and Finance (1993), **12**, 451–474

The significance of technical trading-rule profits in the foreign exchange market: a bootstrap approach

RICHARD M. LEVICH*

New York University, Stern School of Business, 44 West 4th Street, New York, NY 10012, USA and National Bureau of Economic Research

LEE R. THOMAS, III

Investcorp, Investcorp House, 65 Brook Street, London W1Y 1YE, UK

In this paper, we present new evidence on the profitability and statistical significance of technical trading rules in the foreign exchange market. We utilize a new data base, currency futures contracts for the period 1976–1990, and we implement a new testing procedure based on bootstrap methodology. Our results suggest that simple technical trading rules have very often led to profits that are highly unusual. Splitting the entire sample period into three 5-year periods reveals that on average the profitability of some trading rules declined in the latest period although profits remained positive (on average) and significant in many cases. (*JEL* F31, F47, G15).

Since the advent of floating exchange rates in the early 1970s, numerous empirical studies have investigated the time series behavior of exchange rates and the empirical distribution of exchange rates. A null hypothesis that features prominently in these studies is whether exchange rates can be characterized as serially independent drawings from a stationary distribution. Alongside these studies, tests of foreign exchange market efficiency have examined the profitability of various trading rules. A null hypothesis in these studies has been that mechanical rules for generating trading signals should not result in unusual (risk-adjusted) profits.

A variety of empirical studies (reviewed in Section I) support the notion that mechanical trading rules are often profitable when applied in the spot foreign exchange market. A drawback to these studies is that most do not measure the statistical significance of their results, while others measure

* We gratefully acknowledge Jo Jeffreys for diligent research assistance on this project. We also thank participants in seminars at the Second Summer Symposium of the European Science Foundation, University of Konstanz, and City University Business School who provided useful comments on earlier drafts. This paper is part of the research program in International Studies of the National Bureau of Economic Research. The opinions expressed in this paper are those of the authors and not those of any of the affiliated organizations.

0261–5606/93/05/0451–24 © 1993 Butterworth–Heinemann Ltd

statistical significance assuming that the volatility of exchange rates is constant. The latter assumption is questionable since recent evidence rejects the hypothesis that exchange rates can be described as random, independent drawings from a stationary distribution. Evidence is more consistent with the view that exchange rates are drawn from non-stationary distributions.

The purpose of this paper is to undertake new tests of the random behavior of exchange rates and the profitability of mechanical trading rules. Our tests do not rely on assumptions regarding the distribution of the process underlying exchange rate changes. Our approach involves the application of bootstrap methods—*i.e.* the generation of thousands of new series of pseudo exchange rates, each new series constructed from random reordering of the original series. We measure the profitability of the mechanical trading rules for each new series. The significance of the results from the original series can be assessed by comparison to the empirical distribution of results derived from the thousands of randomly generated series.

Overall, our empirical results suggest that mechanical trading rules have very often led to profits that are highly unusual relative to the profits earned by the same rules when applied to the randomly generated time series of exchange rates. Based on a sample of five currencies over the period January 1, 1976–December 31, 1990 and nine trading rules, we find that in 27 cases the original exchange rate series produced profits in the top 1 per cent of all times series, in 12 cases the original series produced profits in the top 5 per cent of all time series, and the remaining six cases produced profits that were positive but less significant. Splitting the entire 15-year sample period into three 5-year periods revealed that on average the profitability of mechanical trading rules has declined in the 1986–1990 period, although profits remained positive (on average) and significant in many cases.

The plan for the remainder of the paper is to review some of the earlier research on spot exchange rates and market efficiency in Section I. We present our own methodology and data sources in Section II. Our empirical results are presented in the following section. A summary and conclusions are in the final section.

I. Previous research

I.A. Efficient market theory

There are now a substantial number of empirical studies testing the efficiency of the foreign exchange market. Surveys of this literature have been prepared by Levich (1985, 1989) and Hodrick (1987). A critical point in the formulation of these studies is that all tests of market efficiency are tests of a joint hypothesis—first, the hypothesis that defines market equilibrium returns as some function of the available information set, and second, the hypothesis that market participants set actual prices or returns to conform to their expected values.

To be more specific, if we define $r_{j,t+1}$ as the actual one-period rate of return on asset j in the period ending at time $t + 1$, and $E(r_{j,t+1}|I_t)$ as the expected value of that return conditional on the information set available at time t, then the excess market return can be written as

$$\langle 1 \rangle \qquad Z_{j,t+1} = r_{j,t+1} - E(r_{j,t+1} | I_t).$$

The market is efficient if the expectational errors follow a fair game process such that $E(Z_{j,t+1} | I_t) = 0$ and $Z_{j,t}$ is uncorrelated with $Z_{j,t+k}$ for any value of k, In words, the market is efficient if, on average, expectational errors are zero, and these errors follow no pattern that might be exploited to produce profits.

In the case of speculative trading in spot or forward foreign exchange markets, risk is present but a risk premium may or may not be characteristic of equilibrium pricing and returns.[1] For example, in the monetary model of exchange rates, domestic and foreign currency bonds are assumed to be perfect substitutes once the interest differential between foreign and domestic assets offsets the foreign exchange rate change. In this case, there is no foreign exchange risk premium—any sustained speculative trading profits would be deemed unusual and a violation of market efficiency. However, in the portfolio balance model of exchange rates, domestic and foreign currency bonds are assumed to be imperfect substitutes, and in equilibrium investors require a risk premium (which could vary over time) in addition to the expected exchange rate change to compensate them for the uncertainty of exchange rate changes. In this case, some positive level of profits from trading rules would be consistent with an equilibrium. Since the equilibrium expected return in foreign exchange speculation could be zero or positive and time varying, it has been difficult to gauge what constitutes unusual or excessive profits as would be characteristic of an inefficient market.

The primary technique for testing spot market efficiency has been to compute the profitability of various mechanical trading strategies. One popular technique for generating buy and sell signals is the *filter rule*.[2] To illustrate the operation of a filter rule, assume that the speculator initially holds no currency positions, neither foreign nor domestic currency, neither long nor short. However, our speculator does have an initial stock of wealth that provides him with the necessary credit to trade foreign exchange contracts with a commercial bank, or the necessary collateral to trade foreign currency (FC) futures contracts on an exchange. An x per cent filter rule leads to the following strategy for speculating in the spot $/FC exchange market:

- Whenever FC rises by x per cent above its most recent trough (a buy signal), borrow $ and by converting the proceeds into FC at the spot exchange rate, take a long position in FC;
- Whenever FC falls x per cent below its most recent peak (a sell signal), sell any long FC position and take a short FC position by borrowing FC and converting the proceeds into $ at the spot exchange rate.

The flexibility to take both long FC positions (following buy signals) and short FC positions (following sell signals) is commonplace for currency traders and speculators in currency futures markets.[3] In addition, the strategy could be followed by American speculators whose wealth is denominated in dollars, as well as by foreign speculators with wealth denominated in FC. As we will show, the returns from the strategy would be added to the risk free rate of return on the speculator's initial wealth.

In the spot foreign exchange market, the return (R) from a *long* foreign currency (FC) position over the period $(t, t + 1)$ is measured by

$$\langle 2L \rangle \qquad R_{t,t+1} = \ln(S_{t+1}/S_t) - (i_\$ - i_{FC}),$$

where i_{FC} represents the interest earned on the long FC position, $i_\$$ is the interest expense of the short \$ position and S is the spot exchange rate in \$/FC.[4] By analogy, the return from a *short* foreign currency position over the period $(t, t + 1)$ is measured by

$$\langle 2S \rangle \qquad R_{t,t+1} = - \{\ln(S_{t+1}/S_t) - (i_\$ - i_{FC})\}.$$

The reader will recognize equations $\langle 2L \rangle$ and $\langle 2S \rangle$ as the uncovered interest parity condition, also known as the Fisher Open effect. Accordingly, under the joint null hypothesis of market efficiency and no foreign exchange risk premium, the expected return from following the trading strategy is zero.

Spot speculation of the sort described can be conducted using lines of credit or explicit margin secured by our speculator's initial wealth. With his wealth invested in Treasury Bills that earn interest for the speculator, it follows that the *entire* realized return from following a mechanical signal

$$\langle 3 \rangle \qquad R_{t,t+1} = d_t[\ln(S_{t+1}/S_t) - (i_\$ - i_{FC})],$$

where d_t is a dummy variable (defined $d_t = +1$ for long positions and $d_t = -1$ for short positions) should be interpreted as an unusual return—a risk premium, over and above the risk free rate of interest. However, under the joint null hypothesis of market efficiency and a time varying exchange risk premium (RP_t), expected returns from currency speculation will be positive. In this case, only the *excess* return

$$\langle 4 \rangle \qquad \pi_{t,t+1} = R_{t,t+1} - RP_t,$$

should conform to the conditions of a fair game if the market is efficient. The conundrum, then, in interpreting the empirical series of returns as in equation $\langle 3 \rangle$ is that occasional profits may be the result of chance, but sustained profits could either be indicative of market inefficiency or fair compensation for an exchange risk premium. The empirical support for a non-trivial exchange risk premium is mixed.[5] In practice, most empirical studies of spot market efficiency have not taken an exchange risk premium explicitly into account. One exception is Sweeney (1986) who measures the profitability of filter rules relative to a constant risk premium. In this paper we examine the effect of including a constant risk premium and find that there is no material effect on our results.

I.B. *Empirical evidence on exchange markets*

Studies by Dooley and Shafer (1976, 1983) report the filter rule trading profits for nine currencies using daily spot rates over the 1973–1981 period. Their calculations are adjusted to reflect the interest expense and interest income of long and short positions (as in equation $\langle 3 \rangle$) and transaction costs are incorporated by using bid and asked foreign exchange quotations. Their results indicate that small filters $(x = 1, 3$ or 5 per cent) would have been profitable for all currencies over the entire sample period. The authors also reported results for 10, 15, 20 and 25 per cent filters. These filters were profitable in more than one-half of the sub-periods but the results were more variable than for the smaller filters. However, even with the small filters there appears to be some element of riskiness in these trading rules since each filter would have generated losses in at least one currency during at least one sub-period. Even so, for three currencies (Yen, Guilder, and Pound sterling) every small filter was profitable in every sub-period. The authors did not report any measures of statistical or economic significance of these profits.

A study by Sweeney (1986) used a similar filter rule technique on daily exchange rates for ten currencies over the April 1973–December 1980 sample period and reached similar conclusions.[6] Filters of 0.5, 1, 2, 3, 4, 5, and 10 per cent led to trading profits in more than 80 per cent of the cases. The results for the smaller filters (0.5, 1, and 2 per cent) were again superior. Sweeney divided his sample into a 2.5-year estimation period followed by a 5-year post-sample period. Filter rules that were profitable in the first period tended to be profitable in the second. Under the assumption of constant exchange rate volatility, Sweeney calculated that in about one-third of the cases, the profits from filter trading were statistically significant. Again, the results were more pronounced for the smaller filters.

Schulmeister (1987, 1988) conducted an in-depth analysis of the $/DM rate over the April 1973–September 1986 period using several technical models in addition to the simple filter model.[7] In particular, Schulmeister tested a popular moving average rule that generates signals based on a cross-over between short-term and long-term moving average of past exchange rate. According to this rule, when the short-term moving average penetrates the long-term moving average from below (above) a buy (sell) signal is generated. Results for the 3 day–10 day, 5 day–10 day, and 4 day–16 day combinations are reported.

Schulmeister's results suggest that most of these technical models would have resulted in profitable trading strategies even after adjusting for interest expense and transaction costs. In particular, the moving average rules are profitable in each of the 10 sub-periods analyzed. Schulmeister suggests that the reason for his results is that exchange rate changes and speculative profits appear to be non-normally distributed. There are too many small exchange rate changes (relative to a normal distribution) but also too many large exchange rate swings (also relative to the normal). The implication from the latter is that once an exchange rate move has started, it is likely to proceed more or less uninterrupted, which allows market technicians time to identify a profitable investment opportunity.[8]

Two papers that analyze the statistical properties of exchanges rates are also worth noting. In an analysis of daily spot exchange rates over the period 1974–1983, Hsieh (1988) rejects the hypothesis that exchange rates are independently drawn from a fat-tailed distribution that remains fixed over time. While the usual tests do reveal the presence of serial correlation in exchange rates, Hsieh argues that this may be the result of heteroscedasticity. Once heteroscedasticity is removed from the data, very little serial correlation remains. Exchange rates appear more accurately characterized as drawings from distributions that vary over time with changing means and variances.[9]

Engel and Hamilton (1990) model the time-varying nature of exchange rate distributions as a Markov switching process between state 1 and state 2 where exchange rate movements are drawn from distributions

$$N(\mu_1, \sigma_1^2) \text{ in state 1, and}$$

$$N(\mu_2, \sigma_2^2) \text{ in state 2.}$$

Assume that these states evolve so that

$$\Pr(s_t = 1 | s_{t-1} = 1) = p_{11},$$

$$\Pr(s_t = 2 | s_{t-1} = 1) = 1 - p_{11},$$

$$\Pr(s_t = 1 | s_{t-1} = 2) = 1 - p_{22},$$

$$\Pr(s_t = 2 | s_{t-1} = 2) = p_{22}.$$

If p_{11} and p_{22} are high, and μ_1 and μ_2 have opposite signs, then there will be 'long swings' (*i.e.* uninterrupted trends) in exchange rates—the sort that might be susceptible to mechanical trading rules. Analyzing quarterly data for the period 1973:4–1988:1, Engel and Hamilton conclude that the long swings hypothesis (p_{11} and p_{22} high, and μ_1 and μ_2 with opposite signs) fits the data significantly better than a state independent model of a single distribution.

II. Data and methodology

A characteristic of exchange rates is that while it might be possible to model a series from one period as drawings from a fixed distribution, it is not possible to 'turn the clock back' and draw additional samples from the same time period. Instead, researchers typically 'turn the clock forward' and draw additional observations from an extended sample period. This technique may confound the analysis if the sampling distribution itself varies over time.

In classical statistics, statistical statements about population parameters are based only on the sample of data actually drawn in the context of an assumption about the distribution function that generated the sample. An alternative is the *bootstrap* approach, which assumes nothing about the distribution generating function.[10] The distribution generating function is determined empirically using numerical simulation. By drawing numerous random samples (with replacement) of size n from the original data itself, these new samples generate an empirical distribution. Probability statements regarding the original data (for example, the mean, standard deviation, or other moments) can now be made with reference to the empirical distribution.

In this paper, we have collected data on futures prices for five currencies (British pound (BP), Canadian dollar (CD), German mark (DM), Japanese yen (JY) and Swiss franc (SF)) for the period January 1, 1976 through December 31, 1990, or approximately 3800 daily observations. Our data source is I.P. Sharpe & Co., now a part of Reuters. Quotations are on closing settlement prices from the International Monetary Market of the Chicago Mercantile Exchange. A single time series is assembled by bringing together quotations on successive near-term contracts. For example, futures prices in January and February of 1976 reflect the March 1976 contract; futures prices in March, April and May of 1976 reflect the June 1976 contract; and so forth.[11] Since futures prices reflect the contemporaneous interest differential between the foreign currency and the US dollar, price trends and returns can be measured simply by

$$\langle 5 \rangle \qquad R_{t,t+1} = \ln(F_{t+1}/F_t)$$

where F_t is the currency futures price at time t.[12]

By the use of futures contracts, we eliminate the need for overnight interest rates on spot interbank deposits and we also obtain a reliable and consistent data set. However, each individual futures contract displays a deterministic decline in maturity from roughly 110 days to 20 days as we follow its price movements. Samuelson (1976) has proved that 'near futures contracts show more variability than (sufficiently far) distant ones', so there is some possibility that return variances may be rising as our contracts move toward maturity and then falling abruptly as we roll into the next futures contract. However, Samuelson (1976) also shows that for some stationary price generating processes, variance may rise over some intervals as time to maturity (T) rises, even though in the limit, variance of futures price changes is zero as $T \to \infty$. Thus, whether variance rises as our futures contracts move from $T = 110$ to 20 days to maturity remains an empirical question. As a practical matter, however, volatility in futures price changes, $\sigma^2(R_{t,t+1})$, will be heavily dominated by spot price changes (see Appendix). Our analysis of futures price changes reveals that there is no significant difference between volatility for 'far' maturities ($80 \leqslant T \leqslant 110$) and 'near' maturities ($20 \leqslant T \leqslant 50$).

In order to generate a vector of buy and sell trading signals, we utilize filter rules of size $x = 0.5$ per cent, 1 per cent, 2 per cent, 3 per cent, 4 per cent, and 5 per cent and three moving average cross-over rules: 1 day/5 day, 5 day/20 day, and 1 day/200 day. Each vector of signals is then applied to the original series of currency futures prices to measure the actual profitability of using these mechanical rules on the original sequence of price changes given in equation $\langle 5 \rangle$. The total return (TR) from following a trading strategy is measured by

$$\langle 6 \rangle \qquad TR_{1,N+1} = \sum_{t=1}^{N} R_{t,t+1} = \sum_{t=1}^{N} d_t \ln(F_{t+1}/F_t)$$

where $d_t = +1$ is a long FC position and $d_t = -1$ is a short FC position.[13] Under the hypothesis of no currency risk premium, TR should not be significantly different from zero.

If a risk premium is present, however, TR will overstate the true excess return from following the trading rule, especially if there is a prolonged trend in the currency over the sample period. To correct for this effect, we follow Sweeney (1986) and estimate the risk premium as a constant over the sample period and equal to the returns from a buy-and-hold strategy, or

$$\langle 7 \rangle \qquad RP_{1,N+1} = \sum_{t=1}^{N} \ln(F_{t+1}/F_t).$$

The benchmark for assessing unusual performance over a period is then the constant RP. Since our trading rules earn the RP over the fraction of days $(1 - f)$ long FC, and give up the RP over the fraction of days (f) short FC, the benchmark expected profit from the trading rule can be written as

$$\langle 8 \rangle \qquad R^* = (1 - f)RP - fRP.$$

If the fraction of days long FC is near 50 per cent or *RP* is small, *R** will approach zero. In our analysis, both conditions hold. Consequently the total return can be viewed again as an excess return.

As noted earlier, technical models employing filter rules and moving averages are popular models that have been analyzed in earlier studies. The filter sizes and moving average lengths are selected as they have been applied in earlier studies. Other filter sizes and moving average lengths along with other technical models could, of course, be analyzed. Data-mining exercises of this sort must be avoided. Rather than torture the data until a profitable rule materializes, we will report our empirical results for all of the popular models that we test.

We now describe our simulation technique. Each series of futures prices of length $N + 1$ corresponds to a series of log price changes of length N. These N observations could be arranged in $M = N!$ separate sequences, each sequence $(m = 1, \ldots, M)$ corresponding to a unique profit measure $(X[m, r])$ under trading rule r for $r = 1, \ldots, R$.[14] For each currency, we generate a new comparison series (a shuffled series), by making a random rearrangement of price changes in the original series. By operating on the sequence of price *changes*, the starting and ending price *levels* of the new series are constrained to be exactly as their values in the original data. And by randomly rearranging the original data, the new series is constrained to have identical distributional properties as the original series. However, the time series properties of the new data are made random. Our simulation, therefore, generates one of the many paths that the exchange rate might have followed from its level on the starting day of the sample until the ending day holding constant the original distribution of price changes.

This process of randomly shuffling the series of returns is repeated 10000 times for each currency, thereby generating 10000 i.i.d. drawings for all $m = 1, \ldots, M$ possible sequences. Each of the 10000 notional paths bears the same distributional properties as the original series, but the time series properties have been scrambled with each path, by construction, drawn independently of the other notional paths. Each technical rule (all filters and moving averages) is then applied to each of the 10000 random series and the profits, $X[m, r]$, are measured. This procedure generates an *empirical distribution* of profits. The profits of the original series can then be compared to the profits from the randomly generated, shuffled series. Under the null hypothesis, if there is no information in the original sequence of data, then the profits obtained from trading in the original series should not be significantly different from the profits available in the shuffled series. The null hypothesis that there is no information in the original time series of data is rejected at the α per cent level if the profits obtained in the original series are greater than the α per cent cutoff level of the empirical distribution.

III. Empirical results

In Table 1, we present descriptive statistics on the original time series of futures price returns. The mean daily return for all currencies is small and averages near zero. The largest (absolute) mean return was negative four basis points per day for the BP in the second sub-period, or roughly 10 per

TABLE 1. Sample statistics of daily returns: foreign exchange futures.

Currency and variable		Full sample	1976–80	1981–85	1986–90
DM	N	3786	1258	1264	1264
	Mu	0.000012	0.000073	−0.000338	0.000302
	Sigma	0.006740	0.005170	0.007579	0.007204
	T-value	0.11	0.50	−1.58	1.49
	Skewness	0.22	−0.09	0.52	−0.01
	s.e.	0.04	0.07	0.07	0.07
	Kurtosis	5.50	7.02	4.99	4.77
	s.e.	0.08	0.14	0.14	0.14
BP	N	3786	1258	1264	1264
	Mu	0.000077	0.000273	−0.000418	0.000377
	Sigma	0.007065	0.005626	0.008170	0.007137
	T-value	0.67	1.72	−1.82	1.88
	Skewness	0.82	−0.33	0.46	−0.20
	s.e.	0.04	0.07	0.07	0.07
	Kurtosis	6.22	7.19	6.08	4.89
	s.e.	0.08	0.14	0.14	0.14
CD	N	3785	1257	1264	1264
	Mu	0.000019	−0.000100	−0.000090	0.000246
	Sigma	0.002696	0.002512	0.002571	0.002968
	T-value	0.42	−1.40	−1.25	2.95
	Skewness	−0.21	−0.13	0.02	−0.47
	s.e.	0.04	0.07	0.07	0.07
	Kurtosis	7.33	4.33	6.66	9.07
	s.e.	0.08	0.14	0.14	0.14
JY	N	3533	1006	1263	1264
	Mu	0.000072	0.000230	−0.000190	0.000208
	Sigma	0.006964	0.007113	0.006532	0.007248
	T-value	0.61	1.02	−1.03	1.02
	Skewness	0.31	0.16	0.85	0.02
	s.e.	0.04	0.07	0.07	0.07
	Kurtosis	5.70	4.09	7.97	5.34
	s.e.	0.08	0.15	0.14	0.14
SF	N	3786	1258	1264	1264
	Mu	−0.000007	0.000045	−0.000345	0.000280
	Sigma	0.007856	0.006778	0.008517	0.008153
	T-value	−0.05	0.24	−1.44	1.22
	Skewness	0.16	−0.03	0.41	−0.01
	s.e.	0.04	0.07	0.07	0.07
	Kurtosis	4.86	5.48	4.80	4.28
	s.e.	0.08	0.14	0.14	0.14

Note: N = number of logarithmic returns; sample period for JY is 1977–1990.

TABLE 2. Autocorrelation functions of daily returns: foreign exchange.

	1	2	3	4	5	6	7	8	9	10	Sample Size
DM											
Full Sample	-0.0044	0.0270	0.0205	-0.0304	0.0113	0.0254	0.0039	0.0383[a]	0.0137	0.0028	3786
1976–1980	0.0478	0.0644[a]	-0.0375	-0.0420	0.0058	0.0434	0.0103	0.0511	0.0248	0.0658[a]	1258
1981–1985	-0.0266	0.0724[b]	0.0429	-0.0386	0.0029	0.0464	-0.0116	0.0430	0.0132	-0.0266	1264
1986–1990	-0.0107	-0.0430	0.0208	-0.0155	0.0153	-0.0138	0.0138	0.0170	0.0097	-0.0071	1264
BP											
Full Sample	0.0282	-0.0074	-0.0148	-0.0055	-0.0113	0.0183	-0.0027	0.0136	0.0288	-0.0180	3786
1976–1980	0.0292	-0.0176	-0.0143	-0.0212	-0.0227	0.0196	0.0157	0.0112	0.0544	0.0242	1258
1981–1985	0.0156	0.0351	-0.0016	-0.0222	-0.0418	0.0346	-0.0009	0.0160	0.0187	-0.0637[a]	1264
1986–1990	0.0368	-0.0628[b]	-0.0440	0.0238	0.0282	-0.0134	-0.0209	-0.0012	0.0266	0.0036	1264
CD											
Full Sample	0.0665[b]	-0.0310[a]	-0.0209	0.0196	0.0317[a]	0.0170	0.0183	0.0156	0.0149	-0.0215	3785
1976–1980	0.0449	-0.0176	0.0498	0.0237	0.0450	0.0099	0.0750[b]	0.0393	0.0194	0.0047	1257
1981–1985	0.1044[b]	-0.0296	-0.0656[a]	-0.0014	0.0447[a]	0.0551	0.0017	0.0454	0.0230	-0.0432	1264
1986–1990	0.0451	-0.0508	-0.0436	0.0245	0.0025	-0.0157	-0.0179	-0.0345	-0.0062	-0.0361	1264
JY											
Full Sample	0.0087	-0.0032	0.0324[a]	0.0078	0.0123	0.0215	-0.0044	0.0424[b]	0.0421[b]	0.0332[a]	3533
1976–1980	0.0184	-0.0401	0.0172	0.0072	0.0108	0.0137	-0.0210	0.0206	0.0839[b]	0.1083[b]	1006
1981–1985	-0.0207	0.0266	0.0485	0.0417	0.0108	0.0575[a]	-0.0051	0.0459	0.0419	-0.0382	1263
1986–1990	0.0230	-0.0019	0.0263	-0.0225	0.0166	-0.0025	0.0076	0.0550[a]	0.0113	0.0290	1264
SF											
Full Sample	0.0112	0.0234	0.0102	-0.0181	0.0033	0.0061	0.0025	0.0128	0.0225	0.0016	3786
1976–1980	0.0921[b]	0.0719[a]	-0.0018	-0.0055	-0.0113	0.0063	0.0188	-0.0060	0.0495	0.0516	1258
1981–1985	-0.0322	0.0620[a]	0.0127	-0.0273	0.0080	0.0272	-0.0115	0.0291	0.0120	-0.0310	1264
1986–1990	0.0007	-0.0518	0.0124	-0.0177	0.0037	-0.0206	0.0039	-0.0001	0.0155	-0.0050	1264

RICHARD M. LEVICH AND LEE R. THOMAS

461

	Original Autocorrelations				Heterosedasticity Consistent Autocorrelations			
	No. significant in 30 lags	Q(10)	Box–Pierce Q(20)	Q(30)	No. significant in 30 lags	Q(10)	Box–Pierce Q(20)	Q(30)
DM								
Full Sample	4	17.21	37.97	52.19	3	11.46	26.91	38.55
1976–1980	5	24.13	31.96	52.13	3	12.44	18.54	35.20
1981–1985	3	18.07	26.92	40.18	3	12.64	19.54	30.96
1986–1990	2	4.66	21.33	36.06	2	4.09	18.94	33.57
BP								
Full Sample	1	10.99	29.21	41.97	1	7.22	20.25	30.08
1976–1980	0	8.33	17.32	22.57	0	6.23	13.31	18.10
1981–1985	2	12.11	21.14	40.41	1	7.27	13.87	28.76
1986–1990	3	12.56	31.40	37.32	3	11.58	27.41	32.83
CD								
Full Sample	3	33.17	48.46	63.25	2	18.78	29.59	42.96
1976–1980	3	18.92	29.81	45.45	3	14.20	24.23	39.88
1981–1985	4	32.31	52.59	62.77	1	15.19	27.89	35.94
1986–1990	1	12.92	26.43	33.42	1	8.79	19.38	25.73
JY								
Full Sample	3	22.96	32.70	38.87	2	17.30	25.82	31.32
1976–1980	3	22.36	34.22	45.02	2	16.40	25.93	34.81
1981–1985	1	17.68	25.31	33.33	0	12.65	20.12	26.77
1986–1990	0	7.67	16.62	25.05	0	5.85	14.00	22.64
SF								
Full Sample	1	6.94	25.95	37.00	1	5.14	19.49	28.66
1976–1980	4	24.35	34.71	59.65	2	11.64	18.49	35.76
1981–1985	2	10.96	19.09	30.35	1	8.13	14.59	24.25
1986–1990	2	4.89	20.54	33.59	2	4.46	18.73	32.23

Notes: Q(10) $\sim X^2(10)$ with critical values 25.2, 20.5 and 18.3 at the 1%, 5% and 10% significance levels
Q(20) $\sim X^2(20)$ with critical values 40.0, 34.2 and 31.4 at the 1%, 5% and 10% significance levels
Q(30) $\sim X^2(30)$ with critical values 53.7, 47.0 and 43.8 at the 1%, 5% and 10% significance levels

[a]: significant at 5% level with standard error $= 1/\sqrt{N}$
[b] significant as above and with heteroscedasticity consistent standard error

cent per annum. The daily standard deviation in the full sample varies from 0.27 per cent for the CD to 0.79 per cent for the SF. For the CD and the JY, the standard deviation of returns is fairly constant across the three sub-periods. However, for the other three currencies, volatility rises sharply in the second sub-period.

Estimates of the skewness and kurtosis of daily returns are also reported in Table 1. In the full sample, four currencies display significant positive skewness while the CD reveals significant negative skewness. In the three sub-periods, however, there are many instances where skewness becomes insignificant, or as is the case for the BP, changes signs from negative to positive skewness and back to negative skewness—each one being significant. By comparison, positive kurtosis (measured against a value of 3.0 under the null hypothesis) is apparent for every currency during every sample period.

The autocorrelation of daily returns for lags 1–10 are reported in Table 2.[15] The estimates reveal a considerable amount of significant autocorrelation. For the DM, SF, and CD we find evidence of significant positive autocorrelation at lags 1 and/or 2. In more general tests for autocorrelation, we find significant Box–Pierce Q statistics for the DM and CD (over the full sample) and the JY and SF over the 1976–1980 sub-period.[16] No Q statistics are significant for the BP, or for any currency in the final 1986–1990 sub-period.

TABLE 3A. Profitability of filter rules, per cent per annum (sample period January 1976–December 1990)

Currency sample size	Filter size (percentage)						Average profit
	0.5	1.0	2.0	3.0	4.0	5.0	
DM ($N = 3786$)							
Actual profit	1.9	8.9	5.6	7.7	7.8	7.9	6.6
No. of trades	833	411	193	99	62	41	
Rank in 10000	7652	9998	9808	9975	9981	9991	
BP ($N = 3786$)							
Actual profit	10.0	6.6	6.2	7.8	6.7	4.9	7.0
No. of trades	793	432	192	108	69	53	
Rank in 10000	9994	9852	9850	9961	9907	9609	
CD ($N = 3785$)							
Actual profit	2.9	3.5	1.4	0.7	1.5	1.0	1.8
No. of trades	309	119	51	28	15	11	
Rank in 10000	9969	9989	9089	7845	9317	8672	
JY ($N = 3533$)							
Actual profit	6.7	7.8	8.0	7.3	10.2	8.5	8.1
No. of trades	777	412	170	98	60	44	
Rank in 10000	9883	9965	9973	9945	9997	9987	
SF ($N = 3786$)							
Actual profit	7.2	6.5	3.4	7.1	9.8	5.8	6.6
No. of trades	907	541	253	127	78	64	
Rank in 10000	9873	9808	9680	9872	9991	9702	

TABLE 3B. Profitability of moving average rules, per cent per annum (sample period, January 1976–December 1990).

Currency sample size	Moving average: short-term (days)/long-term (days)			Average profit
	1/5	5/20	1/200	
DM ($N = 3786$)				
Actual profit	5.6	11.1	7.6	8.1
No. of trades	950	212	79	
Rank in 10000	9786	10000	9990	
BP ($N = 3786$)				
Actual profit	8.1	8.8	9.4	8.8
No. of trades	935	192	42	
Rank in 10000	9975	9987	9993	
CD ($N = 3785$)				
Actual profit	3.1	2.6	2.1	2.6
No. of trades	957	190	91	
Rank in 10000	9977	9917	9804	
JY ($N = 3533$)				
Actual profit	7.8	10.5	8.7	9.0
No. of trades	866	190	87	
Rank in 10000	9957	10000	9994	
SF ($N = 3786$)				
Actual profit	7.5	4.4	8.7	6.9
No. of trades	975	213	71	
Rank in 10000	9912	9235	9987	

Sample autocorrelation may be spurious in the presence of heteroscedasticity.[17] Given the empirical evidence reviewed earlier on heteroscedasticity in currency movements, we follow the methodology of Hsieh (1988) and compute heteroscedasticity-consistent estimates of the standard error for each autocorrelation coefficient, $s(k) = \sqrt{(1/n)(1 + \gamma(x^2, k)/\sigma^4)}$, where n is the sample size, $\gamma(x^2, k)$ is the sample autocovariance of the squared data at lag k, and σ is the sample standard deviation of the original data. As expected, this adjustment reduces the number of significant autocorrelation coefficients (only those noted by the letter 'b' in Table 2). None of the adjusted Box–Pierce Q statistics are significant at the 5 per cent level.[18]

The profits associated with the generation of buy and sell signals using filter rules and moving average rules are reported in Tables 3A and 3B respectively. Over the entire 15-year sample period, every size filter results in positive profits for every currency. Average profit in the Canadian dollar across all filters is 1.8 per cent, substantially less than the average for other currencies where results range between 6.6 per cent and 8.1 per cent. The results are much the same for the moving average rules which led to average profits of 2.6 per cent for the CD, and between 6.9 per cent and 9.0 per cent for the other currencies.

As expected, small filters and trading rules based on short-term moving averages result in considerably more trading signals than larger filters and rules embodying long-term moving averages. The 0.5 per cent filter rule for the SF traded 907 times in 15 years, or about 60 trades per year; the 1/5 moving average rule for the SF produced 975 trades or 65 trades per year. We calculate that the likely cost of transacting in the currency futures market is about 2.5 basis points (0.025 per cent) per transaction for a large institution. A more conservative estimate would be roughly 4.0 basis points.[19] At 65 trades per year, a speculator would have his trading profits reduced by 1.62 per cent per year or 2.60 per cent per year if we take our more conservative measure. Transaction costs of this magnitude would nearly decimate the 3.1 per cent annual return for the 1/5 moving average rule in the Canadian dollar and take a considerable bite out of the other transaction generating rules. For the other trading rules we consider, the volume of trading is considerably smaller, and transaction costs do not significantly affect profits.

The rank of the filter rule profits for the actual series in comparison to the 10000 randomly generated series is also reported in Table 3A. The results are quite striking. In fifteen of the cases, the profits of the actual series rank in the top 1 per cent (9900 and above) of all the simulated series. In ten further cases, the rank is in the top 5 per cent (9500–9899). The remaining five cases rank lower, but in no case lower than the top 24 per cent of the

TABLE 4A. Statistics on the profitability of filter rules over 10000 simulated samples, 1976–1990 period, profits in per cent per annum.

| Currency | Filter size (percentage) | | | | | |
	0.5	1.0	2.0	3.0	4.0	5.0
DM						
Average profit	−0.008	−0.012	−0.022	−0.026	−0.034	−0.039
Median profit	−0.009	−0.015	−0.027	−0.021	−0.034	−0.038
Standard dev.	0.413	0.410	0.414	0.411	0.409	0.409
BP						
Average profit	0.003	−0.002	−0.011	−0.017	−0.012	−0.008
Median profit	−0.004	0.000	−0.012	−0.010	−0.013	−0.011
Standard dev.	0.433	0.435	0.431	0.436	0.430	0.425
CD						
Average profit	−0.005	−0.008	−0.010	−0.014	−0.021	−0.026
Median profit	−0.004	−0.010	−0.011	−0.016	−0.023	−0.026
Standard dev.	0.164	0.165	0.163	0.159	0.156	0.153
JY[a]						
Average profit	−0.014	−0.014	−0.011	−0.014	−0.011	−0.016
Median profit	−0.011	−0.009	−0.007	−0.013	−0.008	−0.017
Standard dev.	0.417	0.414	0.414	0.412	0.411	0.409
SF						
Average profit	0.000	−0.004	−0.019	−0.025	−0.032	−0.044
Median profit	−0.001	−0.013	−0.012	−0.028	−0.037	−0.047
Standard dev.	0.480	0.476	0.483	0.483	0.481	0.480

Note: [a] JY data is for 1977–1990 period.

TABLE 4B. Statistics on the profitability of moving average rules over 10 000 simulated samples, 1976–1990 period, profits in per cent per annum.

Currency	Moving average: short-term (days)/long-term (days)		
	1/5	5/20	1/200
DM			
Average profit	−0.005	−0.022	−0.064
Median profit	−0.005	−0.018	−0.062
Standard dev.	0.415	0.411	0.403
BP			
Average profit	−0.002	−0.016	−0.035
Median profit	−0.006	−0.016	−0.036
Standard dev.	0.435	0.434	0.416
CD			
Average profit	−0.004	−0.005	−0.020
Median profit	−0.006	−0.007	−0.019
Standard dev.	0.164	0.165	0.160
JY[a]			
Average profit	−0.009	−0.017	−0.043
Median profit	−0.008	−0.018	−0.045
Standard dev.	0.410	0.413	0.401
SF			
Average profit	0.000	−0.024	−0.074
Median profit	0.003	−0.021	−0.076
Standard dev.	0.478	0.482	0.468

Note: [a] JY data is for 1977–1990 period.

simulated series (rank 7600 and above). Thus in 25 of our 30 cases, we can reject the hypothesis that there is no information in the original series that can be exploited for profit by our filter rules.

The results are much the same for the moving average rules. We find twelve cases in which the profits of the actual series rank in the top 1 per cent of all of the simulated series and two additional cases that are significant at the 5 per cent level. The remaining case ranks lower, but still in the top 8 per cent of the simulated series (rank 9200 and above). Again, these results imply a strong rejection of the hypothesis that there is no information in the original series that can be exploited for profit by our moving average rules.

Summary statistics on profitability for the simulated series are shown in Table 4A for the filter rule trading strategies and in Table 4B for the moving average rules. In all cases, the average profit in the simulated series is very small and insignificantly different from zero. The average profit is positive for a sample of 10000 simulated series in only three cases. The other sample statistics for the simulated series suggest that average profits are normally distributed without skewness or kurtosis.

These results strongly suggest that the actual exchange rate series contained significant departures from serial independence that allowed technical trading rules to be profitable. If the actual series had been generated randomly, our simulations suggest that average profits would be close to zero. Gauged against these simulations, the actual path of exchange rates is seen to embody a significant degree of serial dependence.

To measure the stability of these results over time, we split the sample period into three, five-year sub-periods and repeated our analysis. We decided to split the sample in this arbitrary way rather than based on foreign currency strength and weakness, since the latter might exaggerate the profitability of trend-following rules. Our results for filter rules (in Table 5A) show that out of 90 cases (5 currencies × 6 filter rules × 3 periods) the application of filter rules to the original data resulted in profits in 78 cases and losses in the remaining 12 cases. Across all currencies, the average profitability of filter rules fell from 7.2 per cent in 1976–1980 to 6.6 per cent in 1981–1985, and fell again to 3.9 per cent in 1986–1990. Smaller filters appeared to be most

TABLE 5A. Profitability of filter rules, per cent per annum. Three sample sub-periods.

Currency	Filter size (percentage)						Average over all filters
	0.5	1.0	2.0	3.0	4.0	5.0	
DM							
1976–1980	5.2[c]	7.7[b]	4.9[c]	4.3[c]	4.8[c]	4.4[c]	5.2
1981–1985	6.1	18.1[a]	13.6[a]	12.2[b]	7.1	8.1[c]	10.9
1986–1990	−5.4	1.4	−2.5	5.9	9.8[b]	8.9[c]	3.0
BP							
1976–1980	8.1[b]	10.0[a]	7.3[b]	9.6[b]	10.8[a]	6.9[c]	8.8
1981–1985	13.1[b]	7.5	5.1	6.8[c]	5.6	5.7	7.3
1986–1990	9.1[c]	2.2	6.4	8.2[c]	1.7	1.3	4.8
CD							
1976–1980	3.7[b]	5.9[a]	0.2	−0.9	−1.8	−0.0	1.2
1981–1985	2.4	2.5[c]	3.2[b]	0.3	−0.3	−1.2	1.1
1986–1990	2.5	2.3	−0.1	1.6	5.4	5.3	2.8
JY							
1977–1980	7.4[c]	5.2	13.5[a]	14.2[a]	9.7[b]	8.2[c]	9.7
1981–1985	3.2	9.0[b]	4.4	2.0	10.2[b]	10.6[a]	.6.6
1986–1990	9.4[b]	8.6[b]	7.3[c]	6.4	9.8[b]	6.0	7.9
SF							
1976–1980	16.5[a]	11.1[a]	7.9[b]	13.6[a]	12.4[a]	5.0	11.1
1981–1985	6.0	12.3[b]	5.1	6.8	7.4	6.3	7.3
1986–1990	−0.7	−3.8	−1.6	−0.0	7.8[c]	4.0	0.9
All currencies							
1976–1980	8.2	8.0	6.8	8.2	7.2	4.9	7.2
1981–1985	6.2	9.9	6.3	5.6	6.0	5.9	6.6
1986–1990	3.0	2.1	1.9	4.4	6.9	5.1	3.9

Notes: [a] Significant at 1% level, rank >9900: 11 entries
          [b] Significant at 5% level, rank >9500: 18 entries
          [c] Significant at 10% level, rank >9000: 15 entries
   Not significant at 10% level, rank <9000: 46 entries
                                    90 entries total

profitable in the first two sub-periods, while in the final sub-period, the 3 per cent, 4 per cent and 5 per cent filters appeared to be more profitable on average. The recent decline in profitability is most apparent for the DM and SF, for which 0.5 per cent, 1 per cent and 2 per cent filters generally would have produced losses. Of the 90 cases in Table 5A, profits significant at the 10 per cent level or better were found in nearly half of the cases. However, the number of cases with significant profits declined from 24 to 12 to 8 across the three sub-periods.

A similar set of results for moving average rules during the three sub-periods is reported in Table 5B. All 45 cases (5 currencies × 3 rules × 3 periods) result in positive profits. On average, there is some deterioration over time in the profitability of these rules, but the overall decline is small. The most pronounced decline was for the 1 day/5 day rule in the third sub-period for

TABLE 5B. Profitability of moving average rules, per cent per annum. Three sample sub-periods.

Currency	Moving average: short-term (days)/long-term (days)			Average over all MA rules
	1/5	5/20	1/200	
DM				
1976–1980	6.1[b]	9.3[a]	5.2[b]	6.9
1981–1985	9.9[b]	11.4[b]	5.0	8.8
1986–1990	2.1	10.8[b]	5.5	6.1
BP				
1976–1980	6.8[c]	11.0[a]	4.6	7.5
1981–1985	9.8[c]	2.5	9.4[c]	7.2
1986–1990	8.8[c]	13.8[c]	8.7[c]	10.4
CD				
1976–1980	3.2[b]	5.1[a]	1.8	3.4
1981–1985	3.2[b]	1.4	0.4	1.7
1986–1990	2.6	1.5	5.4[c]	3.2
JY				
1977–1980	6.2	16.5[a]	12.6[a]	11.8
1981–1985	9.0[b]	6.7[c]	4.5	6.7
1986–1990	8.0[c]	9.9[b]	3.5	7.1
SF				
1976–1980	9.8[b]	1.7	6.2[c]	5.9
1981–1985	12.0[b]	5.8	6.2	8.0
1986–1990	0.9	6.1[c]	7.4	4.8
All currencies				
1976–1980	6.4	8.7	6.1	7.1
1981–1985	8.8	5.6	5.1	6.5
1986–1990	4.5	8.4	6.1	6.3

Notes: [a] Significant at 1% level, rank > 9900: 6 entries
    [b] Significant at 5% level, rank > 9500: 11 entries
    [c] Significant at 10% level, rank > 9000: 10 entries
    Not significant at 10% level, rank < 9000: 18 entries
    45 entries total

DM and SF. Despite this, more than half of the cases held significant profits at the 10 per cent level. And in the case of moving average rules, the number of cases with significant profits was fairly constant at 11, 8 and 8 across the three sub-periods.

These results for five-year sub-periods illustrate some of the risks that are entailed in technical trading, although it appears that some of these risks can be diversified by not operating in a single currency with a single technical rule.

The aforementioned results are unadjusted for a possible currency risk premium. Using equation $\langle 7 \rangle$ to estimate a constant risk premium for each currency over the 15-year period leads to the results in Table 6. The average per annum risk premium is negative for DM and SF and positive for the other three currencies. The estimated risk premia are small relative to the size of trading rule profits and none are significant.

In equation $\langle 8 \rangle$, we noted that the risk premium should be adjusted further for days long FC and days short FC. These calculations are reported in Table 7. In nearly all of the cases, the percentage of days long and short are in the 45–55 per cent range.[20] As a consequence, the expected return (R^*) from trading rules that permit both long and short positions is nearly zero. These results suggest that the adjustment needed for a constant risk premium would be small (a few basis points) and that our earlier results are unaffected by including a risk premium.

The methodology in Sweeney (1986) permits us to compute a significance level for excess returns (actual returns less the risk premium) under the assumption that both the risk premium and the standard deviation of returns are constant over the period. In Table 7, the t-values for excess returns are significant in 35 cases. It is interesting to note that the pattern and magnitude of t-values corresponds roughly to the pattern of significance values reported in Tables 3A and 3B using the bootstrap simulation approach.

IV. Summary and conclusions

The purpose of this paper was to update earlier evidence on the profitability of simple technical trading rules and to extend these results using a new

TABLE 6. Estimate of the currency risk premium, per cent per annum (sample period, January 1976–December 1990).

Currency	Risk premium	T-value
DM	− 0.32	− 0.11
BP	2.03	0.68
CD	0.49	0.49
JY	1.93	0.66
SF	− 0.17	− 0.17

Note: Risk premium estimated as the average return from a buy-and-hold strategy over the sample period. See equation $\langle 7 \rangle$ in text.

statistical test. Our results show that the profitability of simple technical models that was documented on data from the 1970s has continued on into the 1980s. Moreover, our statistical tests suggest that the profitability of these technical rules is highly significant in comparison to the empirical distribution of profits generated by thousands of bootstrap simulations.

The profitability of trend following rules strongly suggests some form of serial dependency in the data, but the nature of that dependency remains unclear.[21] Oddly, the BP series does not reveal any significant autocorrelation, yet the trading profits in the BP are consistently positive across all trading rules and sub-periods, broadly similar to the results for other currencies. Our technical rules for the DM, CD and SF are most profitable during sub-periods when there is no significant autocorrelation, rather than in other sub-periods when serial correlation is present. Only the JY has its most profitable sub-period when its autocorrelation is significant. Still the technical rules produced consistently positive and significant results for the JY in the 1986–1990 sub-period, when there is virtually no autocorrelation in daily returns. Thus the link between serial dependency in the data and the profitability of the technical rules is also an open question.

The persistence of trading profits over the 15-year sample period is itself a striking result. However, we also found evidence that these profits have declined somewhat over the most recent five-year sub-period. This decline was more pronounced for smaller filter rules (0.5 per cent, 1.0 per cent and 2.0 per cent), the returns from moving average rules being more consistent over time. A possible explanation for the persistence of trading profits is the presence of central bank intervention that tends to lean against the wind and retard exchange rate movements. The Federal Reserve Board has recently made available data on its historic daily intervention activity making possible a test of this hypothesis.[22] The profitability of trend following rules may instead be the result of excessive private speculation that causes prices to follow, at least temporarily, a speculative bubble path away from their fundamental equilibrium values. It is also, of course, possible that too little capital is committed to currency speculation making market prices slow to adjust to their equilibrium values. While commercial banks are exceedingly active in interbank market trading and intra-day positions may be large, far less capital is committed to overnight and longer-term currency positions.

The results presented here could be extended in several worthwhile directions. One would be to specify alternative models for generating exchange rates such as a univariate ARIMA time series model, a Markov switching model as discussed in Section I, or a GARCH model. Each specification could itself be taken as the null model, and we could then generate numerous simulated series using bootstrap techniques. Comparing the profitability of the original series with the empirical distribution of profits (and distributions of other sample statistics) would determine whether we can reject any null model.[23] While this technique could clarify which statistical model (or models) were consistent with the generation of currency prices, because these null models are not necessarily equilibrium economic models, they would not necessarily tell us whether the profits earned by technical trading rules were unusual in an economic, risk-adjusted sense.

TABLE 7. Excess returns from trading rules adjusting for a risk premium, days long, and days short.

Currency		Filter size						Moving average		
		0.5	1.0	2.0	3.0	4.0	5.0	1/5	5/20	1/200
DM	Total return	1.9	8.9	5.6	7.7	7.8	7.9	5.6	11.1	7.6
	Risk premium	−0.32	−0.32	−0.32	−0.32	−0.32	−0.32	−0.32	−0.32	−0.32
	Days long	1810	1747	1846	1881	2011	2093	1910	1893	1824
	% Days long	47.81%	46.14%	48.76%	49.68%	53.12%	55.28%	50.45%	50.00%	48.18%
	Days short	1975	2018	1914	1877	1596	1505	1857	1694	1943
	% Days short	52.17%	53.30%	50.55%	49.58%	42.16%	39.75%	49.05%	44.74%	51.32%
	R*	0.01	0.02	0.01	−0.00	−0.04	−0.05	−0.00	−0.02	0.01
	T-value	0.65	3.05	1.92	2.65	2.69	2.73	1.93	3.82	2.61
BP	Total return	10.0	6.6	6.2	7.8	6.7	4.9	8.1	8.8	9.4
	Risk premium	2.03	2.03	2.03	2.03	2.03	2.03	2.03	2.03	2.03
	Days long	2074	2048	2046	1888	1998	2057	1971	2063	1985
	% Days long	54.78%	54.09%	54.04%	49.87%	52.77%	54.33%	52.06%	54.49%	52.43%
	Days short	1711	1694	1696	1853	1741	1678	1796	1524	1774
	% Days short	45.19%	44.74%	44.80%	48.94%	45.99%	44.32%	47.44%	40.25%	46.86%
	R*	0.19	0.19	0.19	0.02	0.14	0.20	0.09	0.29	0.11
	T-value	3.28	2.15	2.01	2.61	2.20	1.57	2.68	2.85	3.11

RICHARD M. LEVICH AND LEE R. THOMAS 471

CD

Total return	2.9	3.5	1.4	0.7	1.5	1.0	3.1	2.6	2.1
Risk premium	0.49	0.49	0.49	0.49	0.49	0.49	0.49	0.49	0.49
Days long	2133	2209	2117	2352	2448	2279	2033	1861	1951
% Days long	56.35%	58.36%	55.93%	62.14%	64.68%	60.21%	53.71%	49.17%	51.55%
Days short	1645	1568	1646	1400	1271	1403	1730	1725	1820
% Days short	43.46%	41.43%	43.49%	36.99%	33.58%	37.07%	45.71%	45.57%	48.08%
R*	0.06	0.08	0.06	0.12	0.15	0.11	0.04	0.02	0.02
T-value	2.49	3.00	1.18	0.51	1.18	0.78	2.69	2.27	1.83

JY

Total return	6.7	7.8	8.0	7.3	10.2	8.5	7.8	10.5	8.7
Risk premium	1.93	1.93	1.93	1.93	1.93	1.93	1.93	1.93	1.93
Days long	1643	1598	1622	1758	1825	1905	1629	1690	1683
% Days long	46.50%	45.23%	45.91%	49.76%	51.66%	53.92%	46.11%	47.83%	47.64%
Days short	1880	1923	1886	1746	1678	1574	1884	1644	1837
% Days short	53.21%	54.43%	53.38%	49.42%	47.50%	44.55%	53.33%	46.53%	52.00%
R*	-0.13	-0.18	-0.14	0.01	0.08	0.18	-0.14	0.03	-0.08
T-value	2.34	2.73	2.79	2.49	3.46	2.84	2.71	3.58	3.00

SF

Total return	7.2	6.5	3.4	7.1	9.8	5.8	7.5	4.4	8.7
Risk premium	-0.17	-0.17	-0.17	-0.17	-0.17	-0.17	-0.17	-0.17	-0.17
Days long	1761	1789	1799	1564	1634	1660	1828	1660	1779
% Days long	46.51%	47.25%	47.52%	41.31%	43.16%	43.85%	48.28%	43.85%	46.99%
Days short	2024	1996	1959	2159	2066	2023	1938	1987	1994
% Days short	53.46%	52.72%	51.74%	57.03%	54.57%	53.43%	51.19%	52.48%	52.67%
R*	0.01	0.01	0.01	0.03	0.02	0.02	0.00	0.01	0.01
T-value	2.11	1.91	1.00	2.08	2.88	1.70	2.20	1.29	2.56

Note: R* is adjusted risk premium as in equation ⟨8⟩. T-value is for excess return measured by total return minus R*.

Appendix

Using the notation from the text, we can write the interest rate parity relation with continuous compounding as

$$\langle A1 \rangle \qquad F_t = S_t \exp(i_{S,t} - i_{FC,t}) = S_t \exp(D_t).$$

At time $(t-1)$, equation $\langle A1 \rangle$ can be re-written as

$$\langle A2 \rangle \qquad F_{t-1} = S_{t-1} \exp(D_{t-1}).$$

Dividing $\langle A1 \rangle$ by $\langle A2 \rangle$ and taking logarithms, we have

$$\langle A3 \rangle \qquad \ln(F_t/F_{t-1}) = \ln(S_t/S_{t-1}) + D_t - D_{t-1},$$

or

$$\langle A4 \rangle \qquad f_t = s_t + d_t,$$

where f_t is the price trend or the daily profit as defined in equation $\langle 5 \rangle$ in the text. The variance of f_t is

$$\langle A5 \rangle \qquad \sigma^2(f_t) = \sigma^2(s_t) + \sigma^2(d_t) + 2 \operatorname{Cov}(s_t, d_t).$$

As an empirical matter, it is well documented (see Levich, 1989) that the volatility of the interest differential, d_t, is far less than the volatility of the spot rate. Practically speaking, then, volatility in futures contracts will tend to be dominated by contemporaneous volatility in spot contracts rather than by changes in interest rates as the contract matures.

Notes

1. Asset models of exchange rates are discussed in Levich (1985) and Branson and Henderson (1985).
2. Filter rules were used by Alexander (1961) to test for trading profits in American equity markets. Follow up tests by Fama and Blume (1966) found that no profits were available after adjusting for transaction costs, dividends paid during short sales, and pricing discontinuities.
3. By comparison, portfolio managers may often face restrictions on their ability to execute short sales. For example, an American manager of a foreign currency bond fund might be allowed to hedge the currency risk in his foreign bonds, but not allowed to then short the currency. See Sweeney (1986) for an example of a currency filter rule with short sale restrictions.
4. For convenience, we follow the traditional practice in this field and measure the returns in logarithmic form. Returns could also be measured assuming simple interest, geometric compounding, or some other convention.
5. See Froot and Thaler (1990) for a discussion of the evidence on the foreign exchange risk premium.
6. Sweeney imposes a restriction on short FC positions. From an initial position in $, a buy signal triggers a move into FC while a sell signal results in a move back into $. Profits from this trading rule are evaluated *vis-à-vis* the benchmark of buying and holding the FC. The same methodology was used by Cornell and Dietrich (1978) in an analysis of five currencies over the March 1973–September 1975 period.
7. He also tested a momentum model, based on the rate of change in past exchange rate, and a combination model involving both moving average and momentum models.
8. A trend following rule in which the investor buys more as the currency goes up and sells more as the currency goes down is a dynamic call replicating strategy. As the strategy produces a synthetic currency call option, the profits from this strategy should be skewed. By comparison, the trading rules here entail a fixed position that is held until the next signal of opposite sign appears.
9. This result underlies the generalized autoregressive conditional heteroscedasticity (GARCH) model that includes the specification of a time-varying and serially correlated error term. An autoregressive integrated moving average (ARIMA) process is a more

restricted representation of a time series process with constant variance and time invariant parameters.

10. For more on the bootstrap method, see Efron (1979, 1982) and Hinkley (1988). For an application of bootstrap techniques to technical trading rules in the stock market, see Brock, Lakonishok and LeBaron (1991).

11. The June 1976 Japanese yen contract had extremely light trading volume and so there are no observations for yen during the months of March, April and May 1976. Data for the yen begin in June 1976 with prices for the September contract.

12. In this assumption, we rely on the interest rate parity relationship that is well established in the empirical literature. See Frenkel and Levich (1988).

13. In our calculations, d_t may also equal zero during the initial observations of a sample before a trend has developed.

14. In our case with N approximately 3800, M is, conservatively speaking, a huge number. With $N = 50$, for example, $M = 3.04 \times 10^{64}$.

15. Autocorrelations at lags 11–30 were computed but they are not reported here.

16. The Box–Pierce $Q(k)$ statistic tests the joint hypothesis that the first k autocorrelation coefficients are zero. We also computed Ljung–Box Q^* statistics which gave nearly identical results.

17. See Maddala (1988, pp. 218–219).

18. The adjusted Box–Pierce $Q(K)$ statistic reported in Table 2 is calculated as $\sum_{k=1}^{K} [\rho(k)/s(k)]^2$, which is asymptotically distributed as X^2 with K degrees of freedom.

19. We consider two elements in the cost of transacting: first, the bid/ask spread which we take as $0.0002 or $0.0001 per transaction, and second, the brokerage commission estimated at $11.00 per round-trip transaction. Since the sizes of currency futures contract are fixed and futures prices are variable, the percentage cost of transacting varies somewhat across currencies and over time. Our likely estimate reflects an average across these dimensions.

20. The Canadian dollar results for the 3.0%, 4.0% and 5.0% filters are an exception.

21. Bilson (1990) models the relationship between past and future exchange rate changes as a non-linear function of observable variables.

22. See Dominguez (1992) for a description of this data and a test of the impact of intervention on exchange rate volatility in the 1985–1991 period.

23. Brock, Lakonishok and LeBaron (1991) use technical models in concert with bootstrap simulation techniques to test the adequacy of alternative null models for the generation of stock market prices.

References

ALEXANDER, SYDNEY S., 'Price Movements in Speculative Markets: Trends or Random Walks,' *Industrial Management Review*, May 1961, **2**: 7–26.

BILSON, JOHN F.O., 'Technical Currency Trading,' in L. Thomas, ed, *The Currency Hedging Debate*, London: International Financing Review, 1990.

BLACK, FISCHER, 'Equilibrium Exchange Rate Hedging,' *Journal of Finance*, July 1990, **45**, 3: 899–907.

BRANSON, WILLIAM H. AND DALE HENDERSON, 'The Specification and Influence of Asset Markets,' in R. Jones and P. Kenen, eds, *Handbook of International Economics*, Amsterdam: North-Holland Publishing, 1985.

BROCK, WILLIAM, JOSEF LAKONISHOK AND BLAKE LEBARON, 'Simple Technical Rules and the Stochastic Properties of Stock Returns,' University of Wisconsin, Social Science Research Institute, Working Paper #9022, January 1991.

CORNELL, W. BRADFORD AND J. KIMBALL DIETRICH, 'The Efficiency of the Market for Foreign Exchange Under Floating Exchange Rates,' *Review of Economics and Statistics*, February 1978, **60**, 1: 111–120.

DOMINGUEZ, KATHRYN M., 'Does Central Bank Intervention Increase Exchange Rate Volatility?' working paper, Harvard University, April 1992.

DOOLEY, MICHAEL P. AND JEFFREY SHAFER, 'Analysis of Short-Run Exchange Rate Behavior: March 1973–September 1975,' International Finance Discussion Papers, No. 76. Washington, DC, Federal Reserve System, 1976.

DOOLEY, MICHAEL P. AND JEFFREY SHAFER, 'Analysis of Short-Run Exchange Rate Behavior: March 1973–November 1981,' in D. Bigman and T. Taya, eds, *Exchange Rate and Trade Instability*, Cambridge, Massachusetts: Ballinger Publishing, 1983.

EFRON, B., 'Bootstrap Methods: Another Look at the Jackknife,' *The Annals of Statistics*, 1979, **7**, 1: 1–26.

EFRON, B., *The Jackknife, the Bootstrap and Other Resampling Plans*, Philadelphia: Society for Industrial and Applied Mathematics, 1982.

ENGEL, CHARLES AND JAMES D. HAMILTON, 'Long Swings in the Dollar: Are They in the Data and Do Markets Know It?' *American Economic Review*, September 1990, **80**, 4: 689–713.

FAMA, EUGENE F. AND MARSHALL BLUME, 'Filter Rules and Stock Market Trading Profits,' *Journal of Business*, January 1966, **39**: 226–241.

FRENKEL, JACOB A. AND RICHARD M. LEVICH, 'Foreign Exchange Markets: Spot and Forward,' in *New Palgrave: A Dictionary of Economic Thought and Doctrine*, London: Macmillan, 1988.

FROOT, KENNETH A. AND RICHARD H. THALER, 'Anomalies: Foreign Exchange,' *Journal of Economic Perspectives*, Summer 1990, **4**, 3: 179–192.

HINKLEY, DAVID V., 'Bootstrap Methods,' *Journal of the Royal Statistical Society*, 1988, **50**, 3: 321–337.

HODRICK, ROBERT, *The Empirical Evidence of the Efficiency of Forward and Futures Foreign Exchange Markets*, Chur Switzerland: Harwood Academic Publishers, 1987.

HSIEH, DAVID A., 'The Statistical Properties of Daily Foreign Exchange Rates: 1974–1983,' *Journal of International Economics*, 1988, **24**: 129–145.

LEVICH, RICHARD M., 'Empirical Studies of Exchange Rates: Price Behavior, Rate Determination and Market Efficiency,' in R. Jones and P. Kenen, eds, *Handbook of International Economics*, Amsterdam: North-Holland Publishing, 1985.

LEVICH, RICHARD M., 'Is the Foreign Exchange Market Efficient?' *Oxford Review of Economic Policy*, Fall 1989, **5**, 3: 40–60.

MADDALA, G.S., *Introduction to Econometrics*, New York: Macmillan, 1988.

SAMUELSON, PAUL A., 'Is Real-World Price a Tale Told by the Idiot of Chance?' *Review of Economics and Statistics*, February 1976: 120–124.

SCHULMEISTER, STEPHAN, 'An Essay on Exchange Rate Dynamics,' unpublished working paper, Austrian Institute of Economic Research, 1987.

SCHULMEISTER, STEPHAN, 'Currency Speculation and Dollar Fluctuations,' *Quarterly Review*, Banca Nazionale del Lavoro, December 1988, **167**: 343–365.

SWEENEY, RICHARD, 'Beating the Foreign Exchange Market,' *Journal of Finance*, March 1986, **41**: 163–182.

Carol Osler

SUPPORT FOR RESISTANCE: TECHNICAL ANALYSIS AND INTRADAY EXCHANGE RATES

- Among the technical trading signals supplied to customers by foreign exchange trading firms are "support" and "resistance" levels. These levels indicate points at which an exchange rate trend is likely to be interrupted or reversed.

- A rigorous test of the levels specified by six trading firms during the 1996-98 period reveals that these signals were quite successful in predicting intraday trend interruptions.

- Although all six firms were able to identify turning points in exchange rate trends, some firms performed markedly better than others. As a group, the firms predicted turning points in the dollar-yen and dollar-pound exchange rates more accurately than turning points in the dollar-mark exchange rate.

- In addition, the predictive power of the support and resistance levels appeared to last at least five business days after they were first communicated to customers.

Early in the morning of each business day, the major foreign exchange trading firms send their customers lists of technical trading signals for that day. Timely technical signals are also supplied by major real-time information providers. These signals, which are based primarily on prior price and volume movements, are widely used by active foreign exchange market participants for speculation and for timing their nonspeculative currency transactions. In fact, 25 to 30 percent of foreign exchange traders base most of their trades on technical trading signals (Cheung and Chinn 1999; Cheung and Wong 1999). More broadly, technical analysis is used as either a primary or secondary source of trading information by more than 90 percent of foreign exchange market participants in London (Allen and Taylor 1992) and Hong Kong (Lui and Mole 1998).

The technical trading signals provided to customers vary over time and across technical analysts, but the vast majority of the daily technical reports include "support" and "resistance" levels. According to technical analysts, support and resistance levels are points at which an exchange rate trend is likely to stop and may be reversed. For example, a firm publishing a support level of $1.50/£ would claim that the dollar-pound exchange rate is likely to stop falling if it reaches $1.50/£. If the firm also provided another support level of $1.45/£, the firm would claim that if the exchange rate passes through $1.50/£, it is likely to stop falling at $1.45/£.

Carol Osler is a senior economist at the Federal Reserve Bank of New York.

The author thanks Franklin Allen, Alain Chaboud, and Charles Jordan for thoughtful comments, Gijoon Hong for excellent research assistance, and two anonymous referees. The views expressed are those of the author and do not necessarily reflect the position of the Federal Reserve Bank of New York or the Federal Reserve System.

Despite the almost universal use of support and resistance levels in short-term exchange rate forecasting, the ability of these trading signals to predict intraday trend interruptions has never been rigorously evaluated. This article undertakes such a test, using actual support and resistance levels published daily by six firms from January 1996 through March 1998. The firms include commercial banks, investment banks, and real-time information providers based in the United States and abroad. I examine the value of three currencies relative to the U.S. dollar: the German mark, the Japanese yen, and the British pound. Support and resistance levels for these exchange rates are tested against indicative exchange rate quotes sampled at one-minute intervals between 9 a.m. and 4 p.m. New York time.

These tests strongly support the claim that support and resistance levels help predict intraday trend interruptions for exchange rates. All six of the firms studied were able to identify

> *Despite the almost universal use of support and resistance levels in short-term exchange rate forecasting, the ability of these trading signals to predict intraday trend interruptions has never been rigorously evaluated.*

points where intraday trends were likely to end. However, some firms were better than others at identifying such points.

For most firms, the predictive power of support and resistance levels lasted at least five business days beyond the levels' publication date. Despite their overall success at identifying points of trend interruptions, none of the firms correctly assessed the relative likelihood of trend interruptions at the different levels. These results are consistent across firms and are sustained over a number of sensitivity analyses.

The statistical tests are based on the bootstrap technique (Efron 1979, 1982), a nonparametric method frequently used to evaluate technical trading strategies (Brock et al. 1992; Levich and Thomas 1993). To implement the tests, I compare the behavior of exchange rates upon reaching published support and resistance levels with the behavior upon reaching 10,000 sets of arbitrarily chosen support and resistance levels. If the outcome associated with the actual levels exceeds the average outcome for the arbitrary levels in a high proportion of months, I conclude that the published levels have significant predictive power.

To complement the analysis of these signals' predictive power, I also analyze the signals themselves. I show that support and resistance levels provided by individual firms tend to be fairly stable from day to day. Their range varies very little over time. Firms do not agree extensively with each other on the relevant signals.

The specific conclusion that exchange rates tend to stop trending at support and resistance levels has no precedent in the academic literature. The closest point of comparison is a study by Lo et al. (2000), which finds that the conditional distribution of financial prices is sensitive to the presence of a broad variety of technical trading signals, consistent with the results presented here.

The finding that support and resistance levels are able to predict trend interruptions is consistent with other studies of the usefulness of technical trading rules when applied to currencies. Filter rules were found to be profitable as early as 1984 (Dooley and Shafer 1984), less than a decade into the floating rate period, and this finding has been confirmed repeatedly (Sweeney 1986; Levich and Thomas 1993). Moving-average crossover rules have also been tested frequently on exchange rates, with similar results (Levich and Thomas 1993; Menkhoff and Schlumberger 1995). More recently, Chang and Osler (1998) find that a trading strategy based on the head-and-shoulders chart pattern is profitable for dollar exchange rates vis-à-vis the mark and the yen, although not for four other dollar exchange rates.

This study differs from those earlier studies in four notable ways. First, the technical trading signals used here are intended to anticipate trend reversals, rather than trend continuations. Second, this study uses a type of trading signal that is actively used by market participants. Third, it uses trading signals that were produced by market participants. Other academic studies of technical analysis have typically constructed technical trading signals of their own. Finally, this study uses data sampled at one-minute intervals throughout the New York trading day, while most earlier studies have used data sampled at daily or lower frequencies.

The two existing studies of support and resistance levels—Curcio et al. (1997) and Brock et al. (1992)—test the hypothesis that prices tend to move rapidly once the levels are breached. Curcio et al. find that the hypothesis is not true on average for currencies, but may hold true during periods of strong trending. Brock et al. find that the hypothesis is true for daily movements of the S&P 500 stock index, but the profits may not be sufficient to offset transaction costs. The hypothesis that prices will trend once a trading signal is breached is not unique to support and resistance levels and is not examined here.

TECHNICAL ANALYSIS

Technical analysts claim that they can predict financial price movements using an information set limited to a few variables, such as past prices. Many of the major technical indicators were described as early as 1930 by Shabacker, who based his conclusions on observations of U.S. stock prices. By now, technical indicators are widely used in major financial markets around the world, including foreign exchange and futures markets. There are two magazines devoted exclusively to the topic, each of which has more than 40,000 subscribers. To learn about technical analysis, one can consult myriad manuals, software, and on-line sources. Alternatively, one can take courses on technical analysis.

Casual observation and conversations with market participants indicate that support and resistance levels are the most widely used technical indicators in the foreign exchange market. This conclusion is also suggested by the fact that support and resistance levels are the only indicators provided by all six of the technical services covered in this research. In fact, some services provide no technical indicators at all other than support and resistance levels.

Support and Resistance Levels Defined

Before delving further into the analysis, it is important to explore the definition of support and resistance levels provided by technical analysts themselves. According to one major technical analysis manual, "support is a level or area on the chart under the market where buying interest is sufficiently strong to overcome selling pressure. As a result, a decline is halted and prices turn back again.... Resistance is the opposite of support" (Murphy 1986, p. 59).

A review of technical analysis manuals reveals that there is little disagreement among analysts on this definition (Arnold 1993; Edwards and Magee 1997; Hardy 1978; Kaufman 1978; Murphy 1986; Pring 1991; Sklarew 1980). For example, Pring states: "Support and resistance represent a concentration of demand and supply sufficient to halt a price move at least temporarily" (p. 199). Likewise, Arnold (1993) observes: "A support level is a price level at which sufficient demand exists to at least temporarily halt a downward movement in prices" (p. 67).[1]

To identify the support and resistance levels relevant for the coming day, practicing technical analysts consult a variety of information inputs. These include visual assessments of recent price performance, simple numerical rules based on recent

price performance, inference based on knowledge about order flow, and market psychology.

The simplest approach to visual assessment is to look at recent minima and maxima: "Usually, a support level is identified beforehand by a previous reaction low," and "a resistance level is identified by a previous peak" (Murphy 1986, p. 59). According to Pring (1991), one could also identify support and resistance levels by drawing a trendline,

> *To identify the support and resistance levels relevant for the coming day, practicing technical analysts consult a variety of information inputs.*

or "channel," in which recent peaks are connected by one line and recent troughs are connected by another: "A good trendline represents an important support and resistance zone" (p. 105).

One numerical rule used to infer support and resistance levels is the "50 percent rule," which asserts that a major market move will often be reversed by about 50 percent in the first major correction (Pring, p. 187). Fibonacci series, which are widely used, suggest that 38.2 percent and 61.8 percent retracements of recent rises or declines are common.

Market insiders sometimes identify support and resistance levels using private information or information circulated informally in the market about certain market participants. For example, if a technical analyst learned in conversation that Japanese exporters are selling at 100, he or she would report a resistance level at ¥100.00/$. Similarly, if a trader knew that his or her own firm had a large order at DM1.50/$, he or she might expect unusual price behavior at that point.

Simple market psychology is also used to help identify support and resistance levels. According to Murphy (1986): "Traders tend to think in terms of important round numbers . . . as price objectives and act accordingly. These round numbers, therefore, will often act as psychological support or resistance levels." As I will demonstrate later, published support and resistance levels are round numbers that end in 0 or 5 much more often than they would if they were chosen at random.

Some of the firms in the sample provided explanations for their chosen support and resistance levels. All of the approaches listed above are well represented among those explanations.

Properties of the Support and Resistance Database

The data examined here include support and resistance levels for the mark, yen, and pound in relation to the U.S. dollar, published daily by six firms from January 1996 through March 1998. Two of the firms did not report support and resistance levels for the pound. In total, there are approximately 23,700 support and resistance values (combined) for the mark, 22,800 for the yen, and 17,700 for the pound.

The six providers of technical analysis include commercial banks, investment banks, and news services. Some operate in the United States and others operate abroad. The commercial and investment banks provide the information free of charge to

> *The data examined here include support and resistance levels for the mark, yen, and pound in relation to the U.S. dollar, published daily by six firms from January 1996 through March 1998.*

their customers, hoping that customers will be encouraged to direct more business toward them. Some news services charge for the information. Since all the providers hope that the usefulness of their signals will generate additional business, they have every incentive to maximize accuracy. In the analysis that follows, the firms are assigned numbers to preserve anonymity.

TABLE 1
Average Total of Support and Resistance Levels per Reporting Day

Firm	Overall	German Mark	Japanese Yen	British Pound
1	10.0	10.0	10.0	10.0
2	6.0	6.0	6.0	6.0
3	17.8	18.1	18.0	17.5
4	9.0	9.2	8.8	—
5	4.2	4.8	3.8	4.0
6	2.5	2.7	2.3	—

Source: Author's calculations.

TABLE 2
Average Distance between Support and Resistance Levels

Firm	Overall	German Mark	Japanese Yen	British Pound
1	30	36	29	26
2	61	75	52	55
3	54	58	49	54
4	57	64	49	—
5	162	156	184	144
6	42	47	36	—

Source: Author's calculations.

Note: Distances are measured in points, or 0.0001 marks/dollar, 0.01 yen/dollar, and 0.0001 dollars/pound.

On any given day, technical indicators were likely to be received from about five of the six firms. Firms failed to report for reasons such as vacations, sickness, and equipment problems. For individual firms, the average number of support and resistance levels (combined) that were listed per reporting day per currency ranges from two to eighteen (Table 1).

The support and resistance levels were quite close together for some firms and quite far apart for others. As shown in Table 2, the average distance between levels varied from 30 to 162 points on average (where a point is the smallest unit used in quoting an exchange rate).

TABLE 3
Average Gap between Current Spot Rates and Outermost Support and Resistance Levels

Firm	German Mark	Japanese Yen	British Pound
1	3.45	2.56	2.38
2	3.71	2.38	2.63
3	8.32	6.73	7.15
4	5.52	3.79	—
5	4.96	5.13	4.52
6	1.24	0.74	—
Daily ranges			
Average	0.45	0.33	0.37
Maximum	3.23	3.88	3.28

Source: Author's calculations.

Note: Distances are measured in units of 100 points, or 0.01 marks/dollar, 1.0 yen/dollar, and 0.01 dollars/pound.

Firms also varied dramatically in the range over which they chose to present support and resistance levels applicable to a given day (Table 3). For Firm 6, the outermost support and resistance levels were typically only about 100 points away from current spot rates, while for Firm 3 the outermost support and resistance levels were typically more than 700 points away. The final two rows of the table show the average and maximum daily exchange rate moves away from their opening rates over the period. For all firms, the outermost support and resistance levels were substantially farther away from the opening rates than this average move. The correlation between daily exchange rate ranges and the gap between opening rates and outermost support and resistance levels was not statistically significant for any firm-currency pair.

Use of Round Numbers

More than 70 percent of the support and resistance levels in the sample end in 0, and a full 96 percent end in either 0 or 5 (Table 4). These proportions greatly exceed the proportions we would observe if levels were chosen randomly, which would be 10 or 20 percent, respectively. Levels ending in 00 or 50 were also disproportionately represented. This may be a manifestation of the psychological interpretation of support and resistance levels mentioned earlier. It is interesting to note that

Goodhart and Figliuoli (1991) observed that round numbers were also disproportionately represented in bid-ask spreads for major currencies.

Continuity

To analyze the extent to which support and resistance levels published by a given firm vary from day to day, I counted the number of support and resistance levels shared across days for a given firm, and compared it with the maximum number of levels that could have been shared. That maximum depends on the number of support and resistance levels provided on the two days: if the firm provided three support levels on the first day and four on the second day, the number of shared support levels, or matches, could not possibly exceed three. The maximum number also depends on the size of the exchange rate move from the first to the second day: if the exchange rate falls substantially between days one and two, then some of the support levels provided on day one might be irrelevant on day two. A shared level, or "match," was defined as a pair of support and resistance levels on contiguous days that differed by less than 5 points.

On average, about three-quarters of the still-applicable support and resistance levels from one day would be used again the next day (Table 5). This average masks a clear division of

TABLE 4
Support and Resistance Levels Ending in Round Numbers
Percent

	Support and Resistance Levels Ending in			
	00	00 or 50	0	0 or 5
Natural frequency	1.0	2.0	10.0	20.0
Firm 1	12.1	17.9	65.8	96.3
Firm 2	13.2	22.4	58.1	84.4
Firm 3	12.5	16.8	82.4	96.6
Firm 4	7.8	15.7	52.9	92.2
Firm 5	49.4	66.4	97.1	99.4
Firm 6	22.9	42.9	74.3	100.0
All firms	13.5	19.6	70.1	95.5

Source: Author's calculations.

TABLE 5
Continuity in Support and Resistance Levels

Firm	Overall	German Mark	Japanese Yen	British Pound
1	64.4	62.4	62.9	67.9
2	54.0	51.0	56.2	54.5
3	*91.4*	*89.8*	*91.7*	*92.6*
4	*81.9*	*81.2*	*82.7*	—
5	*80.8*	*77.5*	*85.0*	*81.3*
6	56.5	56.0	57.4	—
All firms	77.8	76.5	78.2	79.1

Source: Author's calculations.

Notes: The table shows the percentage of support and resistance levels shared across adjacent days. A pair of levels on adjacent days is defined as shared if the levels differ by at most 5 points. Numbers for firms showing particularly high continuity are italicized.

the firms into two groups. Firms 3, 4, and 5 showed the strongest continuity: more than three-quarters of their still-applicable support and resistance levels were used again the next day. For the remaining three firms, the corresponding proportions were lower, ranging from about one-half to two-thirds. These results do not change qualitatively if a match is defined as two levels within 2 points of each other.

Agreement across Firms

Firms do not agree extensively on the relevant support and resistance levels for a given day. To examine the extent of agreement across firms, I first counted the number of matches across each of the fifteen pairs of firms. For each day, the number of actual matches was then compared with the number of possible matches for that day. For a given day, the number of possible matches among support (resistance) levels was taken to be the minimum number of support (resistance) levels provided across the two firms.

On average, roughly 30 percent of all possible matches were realized as actual matches under the basic definition of a match (a maximum difference of 5 points), as shown in Table 6. Across firm pairs, the frequency of agreement varied from 13 to 38 percent (Table 7). Firm 5 stands out as the least likely to agree with its peers. Firms 1 and 2 stand out as agreeing particularly frequently with each other. Among the other firms, no strong patterns are distinguishable.

TABLE 6

Overall Agreement on Support and Resistance Levels across Firms

	Overall	German Mark	Japanese Yen	British Pound
Average possible matches per day	112.0	47.9	43.0	21.1
Average actual matches per day	33.5	14.3	12.3	6.9
Average actual matches per day as a percentage of possible matches	29.9	29.9	28.6	32.7

Source: Author's calculations.

Notes: The table shows the number of times all firms' support and resistance levels actually match as a percentage of the total number of possible matches. A match is defined as a pair of support and resistance levels that differ by at most 5 points.

TABLE 7

Pairwise Agreement across Firms on Support and Resistance Levels
All Currencies

Firm	Firm 2	3	4	5
1	*38*	33	27	17
2		35	31	13
3			32	25
4				23
5				

Source: Author's calculations.

Notes: The table shows the number of times a pair of firms' support and resistance levels actually match as a percentage of the number of possible matches. A match is defined as a pair of support and resistance levels that differ by at most 5 points. Numbers representing firm pairs for which agreement falls at or below 23 percent (mean overall agreement of 30 percent minus one standard deviation) are in bold. The italicized number represents firm pairs for which agreement falls at or above 37 percent (mean overall agreement of 30 percent plus one standard deviation).

If a match is defined as two levels within 2 points of each other, then roughly 18 percent of possible matches are actually realized. The same Firm 5 still stands out as the least likely to agree with its peers; the only strong agreement appears to be between Firms 3 and 6.[2]

EXCHANGE RATE DATA AND METHODOLOGY

This section presents the exchange rate data, some important definitions, and the statistical methodology used to test the ability of support and resistance levels to predict intraday trend interruptions.

Exchange Rate Data

The exchange rate data comprise indicative bid-ask rates posted on Reuters, captured at one-minute intervals from 9 a.m. to 4 p.m. New York time. The prices for a given minute were taken to be the last quote made prior to that minute.

The analysis in Goodhart, Ito, and Payne (1996) suggests that these indicative quotes are likely to correspond closely to actual transaction prices. The major divergences between quotes and actual prices seem most likely to occur at times of large, rapid price movements. During the sample period, these divergences often occurred at times of macroeconomic data announcements from the United States, which tended to happen at 8:30 a.m., before the exchange rate data used here begin. Recent research by Danielsson and Payne (1999) finds that quotes may differ from actual transaction prices in other, potentially important ways. This point is discussed in greater detail below.

The construction of the exchange rate data set was driven primarily by the need to capture as closely as possible the price sequence that would be observed by traders operating in the market. This explains why an interval of one minute was

> *The construction of the exchange rate data set was driven primarily by the need to capture as closely as possible the price sequence that would be observed by traders operating in the market.*

selected, rather than the more common interval of five minutes (for example, see Andersen and Bollerslev [1998]). It also explains why prices were not taken as an average of the immediately preceding and following quotes, another common technique in the literature (for example, see Andersen and Bollerslev [1998]): traders operating in real time could not know the immediately following quote.

The starting time for the data was chosen as 9 a.m. New York time for two reasons. First, by 9 a.m., the support and resistance levels in the data set have been transmitted to customers, including those from New York firms. Second, by 9 a.m., the reaction to macroeconomic data announcements from all the countries involved—including the United States, where, as noted, major announcements generally occurred at 8:30 a.m. New York time—would largely be over (see Andersen and Bollerslev [1998]).

The data end at 4 p.m. because very little trading takes place between then and the beginning of the next trading day in Asia. The 4 p.m. cutoff was also chosen because, in the underlying tick-by-tick exchange rate data set, quotes are not captured after 4 p.m. on Fridays.

Some Definitions

The exchange rate was defined as hitting a support (resistance) level if the bid (ask) price fell (rose) to within 0.01 percent of that level (see the chart for an illustration). Because the 0.01 percent figure is somewhat arbitrary, more than one definition was tried: the gap was also set at 0.00 percent and 0.02 percent in alternative tests. A trend interruption was defined as follows: once the exchange rate hit a support (resistance) level, the trend was interrupted if the bid (ask) price exceeded (fell short of) the support (resistance) level fifteen minutes later. Since the cutoff at fifteen minutes is also somewhat arbitrary, an alternative of thirty minutes was examined as well.

For brevity, a trend interruption will be referred to frequently as a "bounce," and the ratio of times the exchange rate bounces to the number of actual hits will be referred to as the "bounce frequency." In formal terms, the goal of the test described below is to ascertain statistically whether the bounce frequencies for the published support and resistance levels are high, as claimed by technical analysts.

Statistical Methodology

The statistical test evaluates whether or not published support and resistance levels are able to identify points of likely trend interruptions, as claimed by technical analysts. The central or "null" hypothesis is that the published levels have no special ability to identify such points. I begin with a summary of the methodology and then present details.

Hypothetical Exchange Rate Paths

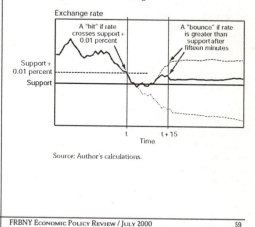

Source: Author's calculations.

Summary

The statistical methodology used to test this null hypothesis is a specific application of the bootstrap technique (Efron 1979, 1982). To apply this technique, I first calculate bounce frequencies for each firm for each month in the sample. I then build a statistical representation of what bounce frequencies for the published support and resistance levels would look like if the null hypothesis were true. In the present context, this representation is constructed by first creating 10,000 sets of artificial support and resistance levels for each day. For each of these artificial sets of support and resistance levels, I then calculate bounce frequencies for each month, using the criteria for hits and bounces listed above.

At this point, I have twenty-eight bounce frequencies for each firm, one for each month of the sample, and twenty-eight average bounce frequencies for the artificial support and resistance levels. In the final step of the test, I determine the number of months in which the bounce frequency for a given firm exceeds the average bounce frequency for artificial levels. If this number of months is quite high, I conclude that the published support and resistance levels have some ability to predict intraday trend interruptions. Additional details on this methodology are presented below.

Calculating Artificial Support and Resistance Levels

For each day, the artificial support and resistance levels are chosen at random from exchange rates within a certain range of the day's opening rate. The range for each month is based on the exchange rate's actual behavior, as follows: for a given month, I calculate the gap between the opening rate and intraday highs and lows for each day. The absolute value of the largest of these gaps is used as the range for calculating artificial support and resistance levels for that month.

For each day, twenty artificial support and twenty artificial resistance levels are calculated using the following algorithm:

$$R_{ti} = O_t + b_{ti} \, range \, .$$

$$S_{ti} = O_t - a_{ti} \, range \, .$$

Here, t represents time, $S_{ti}(R_{ti})$ is the ith artificial support (resistance) level, O_t is the day's opening rate, a_{ti} and b_{ti} are random numbers generated from a uniform distribution over $[0,1]$, and $range$ is the range for that month. These levels are then rounded off so that they have the same number of significant digits to the right of the decimal point as actual quoted exchange rates.[3]

The Statistical Test

The statistical test is based on comparing the bounce frequencies for the published support and resistance levels (B^P) with the average bounce frequencies for the artificial levels (B^A), month by month. To understand the test intuitively, suppose published support and resistance levels provide no more information than arbitrary levels. In this case, B^P should not consistently be higher or lower than B^A. However, if published support and resistance levels can predict points of likely trend interruptions, as claimed by technical analysts, then B^P should usually be higher than B^A.

This idea can be formalized into a rigorous statistical test. The comparison for each month can be viewed as a "Bernoulli trial," in which a random event occurs with a certain proba-

> *Consistent with the market's conventional wisdom, exchange rates bounced quite a bit more frequently after hitting published support and resistance levels than they would have by chance.*

bility. The random event here would be $B^P > B^A$. Under the null hypothesis that published levels have no special predictive power, the likelihood of that event is 50 percent. Over the entire twenty-eight-month sample, if it is true that published levels are not informative, the chance that $B^P > B^A$ for any given number of months will conform to the binomial distribution. This distribution is symmetrical around a single peak at fourteen months, where the probability is about 15 percent.

To understand how to use this distribution, suppose we find that $B^P > B^A$ in twenty of the twenty-eight months of the sample. We might naturally ask: Would it be unusual to get such an extreme outcome if the published levels are truly not informative? More concretely, what is the likelihood, if the published levels are not informative, of finding $B^P > B^A$ in twenty *or more* of the twenty-eight months of the sample? This likelihood is the area under the tail of the distribution to the right of the number 20. This is a very small number: in fact, it is 1.8 percent.

The likelihood of finding $B^P > B^A$ in twenty or more of the twenty-eight months, under the assumption that published levels are not informative, is called the "marginal significance level" associated with the number 20.[4] If the marginal significance level of some result is smaller than 5 percent, it is consistent with standard practice in the literature to conclude that the published numbers are better than arbitrary numbers at predicting trend interruptions. Such a result is said to be "statistically significant."

To summarize our example: it would be extremely unusual to find that $B^P > B^A$ in twenty or more of the twenty-eight months if the published support and resistance levels were truly not informative. In fact, we would realize such an outcome only 1.8 percent of the time. Since 1.8 percent falls below the common critical value of 5 percent, we would conclude that the predictive power of the published levels exceeds that of the arbitrary levels to a statistically significant degree.

Results

Consistent with the market's conventional wisdom, exchange rates bounced quite a bit more frequently after hitting published support and resistance levels than they would have by chance. Exchange rates bounced off arbitrary support and resistance levels 56.2 percent of the time on average.[5] By contrast, they bounced off the published levels 60.8 percent of the time on average (Table 8). Looking more closely, we find that in all sixteen firm-currency pairs, average bounce frequencies for published levels (across the entire sample period) exceeded average bounce frequencies for artificial levels.

The month-by-month breakdown shows that for most firm-currency pairs bounce frequencies for the published levels exceeded average bounce frequencies for artificial levels in twenty or more months. As noted above, these outcomes would be extremely unlikely if the support and resistance levels were truly not informative. More rigorously, the marginal significance levels indicate that the results are statistically significant at the 5 percent level for all but three firm-currency pairs.

The firms' ability to predict turning points in intraday trends seems to have been stronger for the yen and weaker for the mark and the pound. On average, bounce frequencies for published support and resistance levels exceeded those for arbitrary levels by 4.2 percentage points for the mark, 5.6 percentage points for the yen, and 4.0 percentage points for the pound. This relative ranking was maintained fairly consistently for individual firms.

Although all six firms seem to have the ability to predict exchange rate bounces, their performance varied considerably. The bounce frequencies of the best and worst firms differ by 4.0 percentage points on average. At one extreme, Firm 1's support and resistance levels for the yen had a bounce frequency 9.2 percentage points higher than that of the arbitrary levels.

Differences across firms are evaluated statistically in Table 9. Firm 1 is clearly the best overall: it had the highest bounce frequency for two of the three currencies and the second-highest bounce frequency for the third currency. Furthermore, the differences between Firm 1 and the other firms are statistically significant at the 5 percent level in seven of the thirteen possible firm-to-firm comparisons and are statistically significant at the 10 percent level in another comparison. Firm 5 did quite well for the mark, but did not do noticeably well for the other two currencies. No firm was consistently worst.

TABLE 8

Ability of Support and Resistance Levels to Predict Interruptions of Intraday Exchange Rate Trends

	Artificial Levels	Levels Published by Firm					
		1	2	3	4	5	6
		Bounce Frequency (Number of Hits)					
German mark	54.9	60.1	56.6	58.0	58.5	62.0	59.3
		(6,291)	(4,102)	(8,111)	(3,570)	(1,262)	(2,296)
Japanese yen	57.3	66.5	63.6	62.3	60.7	61.6	62.6
		(4,558)	(3,874)	(6,271)	(2,679)	(859)	(1,396)
British pound	56.3	63.0	58.8	59.6		60.0	
		(5,409)	(3,920)	(6,056)		(1,039)	
		Months $B^P > B^A$/Total Months (Marginal Significance)					
German mark		24/28	17/28	21/28	20/27	20/26	19/28
		(0.000)	(0.172)	(0.006)	(0.010)	(0.005)	(0.044)
Japanese yen		26/28	24/27	22/28	23/27	15/23	20/27
		(0.000)	(0.000)	(0.002)	(0.000)	(0.105)	(0.010)
British pound		27/28	19/28	24/28		16/26	
		(0.000)	(0.044)	(0.000)		(0.163)	

Source: Author's calculations.

Notes: The table compares the ability of published support and resistance levels to predict intraday trend interruptions with the distribution of predictive ability for 10,000 sets of arbitrary support and resistance levels. The measure of predictive ability is based on the "bounce frequency," or the number of times the exchange rate stopped trending after reaching support or resistance levels compared with the total number of times the rate actually reached such levels.

The table shows the bounce frequency for published and artificial support and resistance levels, the number of hits, the number of months in which the bounce frequency for published levels (B^P) exceeds the bounce frequency for artificial levels (B^A), and the marginal significance of this number of months under the null hypothesis that published support and resistance levels are not informative. "Total months" varies across firms and currencies because occasionally a firm contributed too few support and resistance levels to have any hits at all.

TABLE 9

Differences in Firms' Ability to Predict
Exchange Rate Bounces

Firm B	Firm A				
	1	2	3	4	5
German mark					
2	3.5**				
3	2.1**	-1.4			
4	1.5	-2.0	-0.6***		
5	-2.0**	-5.5**	-4.1***	-3.5	
6	0.8	-2.7	-1.3**	-0.7	2.8
Japanese yen					
2	2.8*				
3	4.1***	1.3			
4	5.7***	2.9	1.6		
5	4.9	2.0	0.7	-0.9	
6	3.8	1.0	-0.3	-1.9	-1.0
British pound					
2	4.2***				
3	3.5**	-0.8*			
5	3.1*	-1.2	-0.4		

Source: Author's calculations.

Notes: The table compares different firms' ability to predict intraday trend
interruptions in exchange rates. The measure of predictive ability is based
on the "bounce frequency," or the number of times the exchange rate
stopped trending after reaching support or resistance levels compared
with the total number of times the rate actually reached such levels. The
table presents the difference between bounce frequencies (measured as
Firm A minus Firm B).

* Statistically significant at the 10 percent level.
** Statistically significant at the 5 percent level.
*** Statistically significant at the 1 percent level.

Robustness

These results are robust to changes in the test methodology.[6]
They are not changed qualitatively if a hit is defined more
broadly or more narrowly (as described earlier) or if one looks
thirty minutes rather than fifteen minutes beyond a hit. The
results are also unchanged if one splits the sample into morning
and afternoon sessions (where the morning session is defined
to include positions entered before noon).

Interestingly, the results change somewhat if the sample is
split in half chronologically. During the first half of the sample
period, when volatility was fairly low by historical standards,
bounce frequencies were statistically significant for published
levels in all but one case. In the second half, when volatility
returned to more normal levels, firms' bounce frequencies still

exceeded those for the artificial levels, but the differences
were no longer statistically significant in half the cases.[7] This
outcome is consistent with the market's conventional wisdom
that rates tend to "range trade" in periods of low volatility, thus
making this type of trend reversal more common.

Quotes versus Transaction Prices

At this point, it is possible to discuss more fully the potential
implications of the differences noted by Danielsson and Payne
(1999) between exchange rate quotes and actual transaction
prices. The first important difference they note is that quotes
tend to be more volatile than actual transaction prices. This
should not be critical here, because these results concern the
direction of price changes, not their magnitude.

Second, Danielsson and Payne (1999) find that quotes tend
to be negatively autocorrelated while transaction prices are not.
In theory, this could affect the absolute frequency of bounces
presented in Table 8. Fortunately, the important qualitative

> *Could an analyst using support and
> resistance levels published today have any
> success predicting intraday trend reversals
> one week from today?
> The answer seems to be yes.*

conclusions of the paper are based on the *difference* between
bounce frequencies for published and simulated levels, rather
than the absolute size of those bounce frequencies. Furthermore, the negative autocorrelation in quote data may largely
have dissipated by the end of the fifteen-minute horizon of
interest. The reason is that if the exchange rate is required to
reach the actual level rather than some nearby level to achieve
a hit, bounce frequencies in the simulated support and
resistance levels fall slightly short of 50 percent. If negative
autocorrelation at the fifteen-minute horizon were an issue,
that proportion would presumably exceed 50 percent.

Duration of Predictive Power

Could an analyst using support and resistance levels published
today have any success predicting intraday trend reversals one
week from today? The answer seems to be yes. Five days after

TABLE 10

Ability of Support and Resistance Levels to Predict Interruptions of Intraday Exchange Rate Trends after Five Trading Days

	Artificial Levels	Levels Published by Firm					
		1	2	3	4	5	6
		Bounce Frequency (Number of Hits)					
German mark	53.8	58.0 (4,078)	59.0 (2,464)	57.5 (5,902)	56.9 (2,930)	58.3 (1,004)	55.5 (1,148)
Japanese yen	55.4	62.5 (3,531)	60.5 (2,112)	61.2 (4,392)	59.5 (2,373)	59.7 (703)	64.3 (635)
British pound	54.0	57.5 (3,661)	59.0 (2,400)	56.5 (4,641)		57.4 (622)	
		Months $B^P > B^A$/Total Months (Marginal Significance)					
German mark		22/27 (0.001)	22/27 (0.001)	21/27 (0.003)	16/26 (0.163)	16/23 (0.047)	16/25 (0.115)
Japanese yen		21/27 (0.003)	20/27 (0.010)	22/27 (0.001)	19/26 (0.014)	12/22 (0.416)	16/24 (0.076)
British pound		19/27 (0.026)	17/27 (0.124)	17/27 (0.124)		13/19 (0.084)	

Source: Author's calculations.

Notes: The table shows the results of using published support and resistance levels to predict intraday trend interruptions five business days after the levels' publication date. The measure of predictive ability is based on the "bounce frequency," or the number of times the exchange rate stopped trending after reaching support or resistance levels compared with the total number of times the rate actually reached such levels.

The table shows the bounce frequency for published and artificial support and resistance levels, the number of hits, the number of months in which the bounce frequency for published levels (B^P) exceeds the bounce frequency for artificial levels (B^A), and the marginal significance of this number of months under the null hypothesis that published support and resistance levels are not informative. "Total months" varies across firms and currencies because occasionally a firm contributed too few support and resistance levels to have any hits at all.

their publication, bounce frequencies for our six firms still exceeded those from arbitrary levels for all firms and currencies, and the differences were statistically significant in nine of the sixteen cases (Table 10). Not surprisingly, the published levels were not quite as useful at predicting intraday trend reversals five days after publication as they were on their actual publication day. On average, five days after publication, rates bounced at published levels 1.7 percentage points less frequently than they did on the actual publication day.[8]

The Power of Agreement

If many analysts agree that a particular level is likely to be important, does this imply that the level is more likely than others to be important? I addressed this question by comparing the predictive power of support and resistance levels provided by more than one firm ("agreed levels") on a given day with the predictive power of support and resistance levels provided by only one firm.

As shown in Table 11, the bounce frequencies associated with agreed levels are quite close to the bounce frequencies associated with levels provided by just one firm. Although the agreed levels tend to have higher bounce frequencies, the differences are generally not statistically significant. The one difference found to be statistically significant implies that agreed levels have *less* predictive power than other levels. Overall, these results suggest that, if agreed levels do provide additional predictive power, the benefit is too small to be of much practical importance.[9]

TABLE 11

Is There Power in Agreement?

	Narrow Agreement			Broad Agreement		
	German Mark	Japanese Yen	British Pound	German Mark	Japanese Yen	British Pound
Agreed levels	58.0	65.9	63.1	59.1	65.2	61.7
Other levels	59.0	63.7	60.6	58.6	63.5	60.3
Months agreed > other/total months	10/28	15/27	17/28	11/28	14/27	14/28
Marginal significance	0.96	0.35	0.17	0.91	0.50	0.57

Source: Author's calculations.

Notes: The table compares the predictive ability of support and resistance levels on which two or more firms agree ("agreed levels") with the predictive ability of support and resistance levels provided by only one firm. The measure of predictive ability is based on the "bounce frequency," or the number of times the exchange rate stopped trending after reaching support or resistance levels compared with the total number of times the rate actually reached such levels. If agreed levels were better able to predict intraday trend interruptions, the numbers would be positive and statistically significant. Two levels were in "narrow agreement" if they were within 2 points of each other; they were in "broad agreement" if they were within 5 points of each other.

Reliability of Estimated "Strengths"

Three of the firms regularly provided estimates of the "strength" of their published support and resistance levels. For example, levels could be categorized as having strength numbers "1," "2," or "3," with 3 being the strongest. The strength of a particular level can be interpreted as a crude measure of the likelihood that an exchange rate that arrives at the level will actually bounce off it.

Were the estimated strengths of support and resistance levels meaningful? To answer this question, I examined the relative frequency of bounces off support and resistance levels in three strength categories: (1) least strong, (2) somewhat strong, and (3) strongest. Unfortunately, in many months there were few observations in strength category 3, so the only reliable comparison was between categories 1 and 2.

Results for this comparison are shown in Table 12, where the reported differences would be positive and statistically significant if the strength categories were meaningful. In fact, the reported strength levels seem to have no consistent correspondence with the actual frequency with which exchange rates bounced off support and resistance levels. All but two of the differences are negative, and the three that are statistically significant are negative. In short, published estimates of the strength of the levels do not seem to be useful.

TABLE 12

The Meaning of Reported Strength Ratings

Comparison of Strengths 1 and 2	German Mark	Japanese Yen	British Pound
Firm 1	-2.3**	-4.1***	-6.5
	10/27	8/26	12/28
	(0.04)	(0.01)	(0.17)
Firm 2	-2.7**	-5.5	-3.9*
	10/27	10/25	10/26
	(0.04)	(0.11)	(0.08)
Firm 3	2.4	0.2	-0.1
	14/25	11/24	11/23
	(0.35)	(0.27)	(0.34)

Source: Author's calculations.

Notes: The table evaluates whether support and resistance levels considered somewhat strong by their publishers actually predict intraday trend interruptions better than those considered least strong. The measure of predictive ability is based on the "bounce frequency," or the number of times the exchange rate stopped trending after reaching support or resistance levels compared with the total number of times the rate actually reached such levels. Strength 1 corresponds to the support and resistance levels at which trend interruptions are least likely; strength 2 corresponds to support and resistance levels at which trend interruptions are more—but not most—likely.

For each firm listed on the left side of the table, the first row of numbers represents the difference between the predictive ability of support and resistance levels of the two different strengths. If the reported strength levels were reliable, then the numbers would be positive and significant. The first number in each second row represents the months in which the bounce frequency for strength 2 actually exceeded the bounce frequency for strength 1; the second number in each row (following the slash) represents the number of months in which the comparison was valid; the third row of numbers gives the marginal significance of the second row under the null hypothesis that there is no difference between the two sets of numbers.

* Statistically significant at the 10 percent level.
** Statistically significant at the 5 percent level.
*** Statistically significant at the 1 percent level.

CONCLUSION

This article has examined the predictive power of support and resistance levels for intraday exchange rates, using technical signals published by six active market participants from January 1996 through March 1998. The statistical tests, which use the bootstrap technique (Efron 1979, 1982), cover support and resistance levels for three currency pairs: dollar-mark, dollar-yen, and dollar-pound.

The results indicate that intraday exchange rate trends were interrupted at published support and resistance levels substantially more often than would have occurred had the levels been arbitrarily chosen. This finding is consistent across all three exchange rates and across all six firms studied. The predictive power of published support and resistance levels varies considerably across firms and across exchange rates. It lasts at least one week. The strength estimates published with the levels are not meaningful. These results are highly statistically significant and are robust to alternative parameterizations.

The predictive power of support and resistance levels has many possible sources, some of which are discussed in Osler (2000). Central bank intervention has been cited as a possible source of the predictive power of other technical trading strategies (Szakmary and Mathur 1997; LeBaron 1999). However, central bank intervention seems unlikely to be an important source of the predictive power of support and resistance levels since there was no reported intervention for the mark and the pound during the sample period. Other possible explanations include clustered order flow, which receives support in Osler (2000), and self-fulfilling prophecies.

The ability of support and resistance levels to predict trend reversals suggests that the intraday currency markets may not be fully efficient. To investigate this possibility, it would be natural to examine whether traders could profit from these predictable bounces on a fairly consistent basis. If it were indeed profitable to trade on these readily available technical signals, there would seem to be some incentive for rational traders to trade the profits away. This would be an appropriate subject for future research. It might also be appropriate to examine the claim of technical analysts that trends typically are sustained once support and resistance levels are "decisively" crossed.

ENDNOTES

1. Support and resistance levels are related to but not identical to trading ranges. A trading range has just one support level and one resistance level. The firms examined here usually provided multiple support levels and multiple resistance levels each day.

2. These results are available from the author upon request.

3. That is, all artificial support and resistance levels for the mark and the pound had the form x.xxxx00, while all artificial support and resistance levels for the yen had the form xxx.xx00000.

4. For some firms, there were few support and resistance levels in some months, and thus few hits and bounces. These months were excluded from the sample for those firms.

5. If intraday exchange rates followed a random walk, the tendency to bounce would, in the abstract, be about 50 percent. The tendency to bounce in the actual data exceeds this benchmark for two reasons. First, changes in the actual and the simulated data have a fairly strong negative first-order autocorrelation, as noted by Goodhart and Figliuoli (1991). Second, to "bounce," the exchange rate must first reach a level a little above (below) the actual support (resistance) level, and then remain above (below) the actual support (resistance) level for a certain interval. Thus, the exchange rate can continue trending slightly after officially hitting the level yet still be considered as having "bounced."

6. Results from these sensitivity tests are available from the author upon request.

7. The standard deviation of daily exchange rate changes rose by one-third on average between the first and second halves of the sample period. In the first half, these standard deviations were 0.199, 0.216, and 0.260 for the mark, yen, and pound, respectively. In the second half, the corresponding standard deviations were 0.252, 0.362, and 0.277 (all figures E+3).

8. The reader may also be interested to know whether the tendency of support and resistance levels to be selected as round numbers or as local highs/lows has any influence on the levels' predictive power. In Osler (2000), I examine whether round numbers or local minima/maxima (both of which are known to be sources of published support and resistance levels) have predictive power for exchange rate bounces. I find that they do, from which I conclude that at least some of the predictive power in the published levels comes from the firms' tendency to choose these types of numbers. I also show that the size of the typical move following a hit differs substantially between the published levels of some firms and the artificial levels. I conclude from this that round numbers and local minima/maxima do not incorporate as much information about intraday trend reversals as do some published support and resistance levels.

9. It would be desirable here to weight the advising firms by their order flow. However, order information is very closely guarded by the firms in question. Furthermore, some of the firms do not actually take orders.

REFERENCES

Allen, Helen, and Mark P. Taylor. 1992. "The Use of Technical Analysis in the Foreign Exchange Market." JOURNAL OF INTERNATIONAL MONEY AND FINANCE 11, no. 3 (June): 304-14.

Andersen, Torben, and Tim Bollerslev. 1998. "Deutsche Mark–Dollar Volatility: Intraday Activity Patterns, Macroeconomic Announcements, and Longer Run Dependencies." JOURNAL OF FINANCE 53 (February): 219-65.

Arnold, Curtis M. 1993. TIMING THE MARKET: HOW TO PROFIT IN BULL AND BEAR MARKETS WITH TECHNICAL ANALYSIS. Chicago: Probus Publishing Company.

Brock, W., et al. 1992. "Simple Technical Trading Rules and the Stochastic Properties of Stock Returns." JOURNAL OF FINANCE 48 (December): 1731-64.

Chang, P. H. Kevin, and C. L. Osler. 1998. "Methodical Madness: Technical Analysis and the Irrationality of Exchange Rate Forecasts." ECONOMIC JOURNAL 109, no. 458 (October): 636-61.

Cheung, Yin-Wong, and Menzie Chinn. 1999. "Traders, Market Microstructure, and Exchange Rate Dynamics." Unpublished paper, University of California at Santa Cruz, January.

Cheung, Yin-Wong, and Clement Yuk-Pang Wong. 1999. "Foreign Exchange Traders in Hong Kong, Tokyo, and Singapore: A Survey Study." ADVANCES IN PACIFIC BASIN FINANCIAL MARKETS 5: 111-34.

Curcio, Richard, et al. 1997. "Do Technical Trading Rules Generate Profits? Conclusions from the Intraday Foreign Exchange Market." Unpublished paper, London School of Economics.

Danielsson, Jón, and Richard Payne. 1999. "Real Trading Patterns and Prices in Spot Foreign Exchange Markets." Unpublished paper, London School of Economics, March.

Dooley, Michael P., and Jeffrey Shafer. 1984. "Analysis of Short-Run Exchange Rate Behavior: March 1973 to November 1981." In David Bigman and Teizo Taya, eds., FLOATING EXCHANGE RATES AND THE STATE OF WORLD TRADE AND PAYMENTS, 43-70. Cambridge, Mass.: Ballinger Publishing Company.

Edwards, Robert, and John Magee. 1997. TECHNICAL ANALYSIS OF STOCK TRENDS. 5th ed. Boston: John Magee.

Efron, B. 1979. "Bootstrap Methods: Another Look at the Jackknife." ANNALS OF STATISTICS 7: 1-26.

———. 1982. THE JACKKNIFE, THE BOOTSTRAP, AND OTHER RESAMPLING PLANS. Philadelphia: Society for Industrial and Applied Mathematics.

Goodhart, C., and L. Figliuoli. 1991. "Every Minute Counts in Financial Markets." JOURNAL OF INTERNATIONAL MONEY AND FINANCE 10, no. 1 (March): 23-52.

Goodhart, C., T. Ito, and R. Payne. 1996. "One Day in June 1993: A Study of the Working of the Reuters 2000-2 Electronic Foreign Exchange Trading System." In Jeffrey Frankel, Gianpaolo Galli, and Alberto Giovannini, eds., THE MICROSTRUCTURE OF FOREIGN EXCHANGE MARKETS, 107-79. National Bureau of Economic Research Conference Report Series. Chicago: University of Chicago Press.

Hardy, C. Colburn. 1978. THE INVESTOR'S GUIDE TO TECHNICAL ANALYSIS. New York: McGraw-Hill.

Kaufman, P. 1978. COMMODITY TRADING SYSTEMS AND METHODS. New York: Ronald Press.

LeBaron, Blake. 1999. "Technical Trading Rule Profitability of Foreign Exchange Intervention." JOURNAL OF INTERNATIONAL ECONOMICS 49 (October): 125-43.

Levich, R., and L. Thomas. 1993. "The Significance of Technical Trading Rule Profits in the Foreign Exchange Market: A Bootstrap Approach." JOURNAL OF INTERNATIONAL MONEY AND FINANCE 12 (October): 451-74.

Lo, Andrew W., et al. 2000. "Foundations of Technical Analysis: Computational Algorithms, Statistical Inference, and Empirical Implementation." NBER Working Paper no. 7613, March.

Lui, Yu-Hon, and David Mole. 1998. "The Use of Fundamental and Technical Analyses by Foreign Exchange Dealers: Hong Kong Evidence." JOURNAL OF INTERNATIONAL MONEY AND FINANCE 17, no. 3 (June): 535-45.

Menkhoff, Lukas, and Manfred Schlumberger. 1995. "Persistent Profitability of Technical Analysis on Foreign Exchange Markets?" Banca Nazionale del Lavoro QUARTERLY REVIEW 193 (June): 189-215.

References (Continued)

Murphy, John J. 1986. Technical Analysis of the Futures Market: A Comprehensive Guide to Trading Methods and Applications. New York: Prentice Hall.

Osler, C. L. 2000. "Are Currency Markets Efficient? Predictable Trend Reversals in Intraday Exchange Rates." Unpublished paper, Federal Reserve Bank of New York, February.

Pring, M. 1991. Technical Analysis Explained: The Successful Investor's Guide to Spotting Investment Trends and Turning Points. 3rd ed. New York: McGraw-Hill.

Shabacker, R. W. 1930. Stock Market Theory and Practice. New York: B. C. Forbes Publishing Company.

Sklarew, Arthur. 1980. Techniques of a Professional Commodity Chart Analyst. New York: Commodity Research Bureau.

Sweeney, R. J. 1986. "Beating the Foreign Exchange Market." Journal of Finance 41 (March): 163-82.

Szakmary, Andrew, and Ike Mathur. 1997. "Central Bank Intervention and Trading Rule Profits in Foreign Exchange Markets." Journal of International Money and Finance 16, no. 4 (August): 513-35.

The views expressed in this paper are those of the author and do not necessarily reflect the position of the Federal Reserve Bank of New York or the Federal Reserve System. The Federal Reserve Bank of New York provides no warranty, express or implied, as to the accuracy, timeliness, completeness, merchantability, or fitness for any particular purpose of any information contained in documents produced and provided by the Federal Reserve Bank of New York in any form or manner whatsoever.

Part III
Forecasting Risk

[18]

Journal of Banking and Finance 14 (1990) 399–421. North-Holland

VOLATILITY FORECASTING WITHOUT DATA-SNOOPING

Elroy DIMSON and Paul MARSH*

London Business School, London NW1 4SA, UK

Data-snooping arises when the properties of a data series influence the researcher's choice of model specification. When data has been snooped, tests undertaken using the same series are likely to be misleading. This study seeks to predict equity market volatility, using daily data on U.K. stock market returns over the period 1955–1989. We find that even apparently innocuous forms of data-snooping significantly enhance reported forecast quality, and that relatively sophisticated forecasting methods operated without data-snooping often perform worse than naive benchmarks. For predicting stock market volatility, we therefore recommend two alternative models, both of which are extremely simple.

1. Introduction

Data-snooping is a term used by Aldous (1989), Lo and MacKinlay (1990) and others to describe the bias which occurs when the properties of a data set influence the choice of estimator or test statistic. This leads to overstatement of the significance of estimated relationships. In turn, the out-of-sample performance of a fitted model is likely to be inferior to that which might be expected on the basis of classical test statistics.

The problem of data-snooping is endemic in Finance. A competent researcher will look at previous articles on the same subject, and will formulate models in the light of known attributes of the data set under investigation. This introduces pre-test biases such as those described by Leamer (1978). In the social sciences, where grounded empirical research is the norm, Merton (1987) has observed that, while the pervasiveness of data-snooping has been tacitly recognised, it is an issue which is often ignored.

Data-snooping is inevitable in many studies, and may therefore be differentiated from its more insidious manifestation, 'data-mining'. The latter refers to the selection of the model that provides the best fit between dependent and independent variables in a data set, followed by 'validation' of the estimated relationship using in-sample data. Despite early warnings of

*We wish to thank Mike Staunton for research assistance on an earlier version of this paper. Helpful comments on the latter were received from LBS colleagues and from participants at the 1988 European Finance Association Meetings (Istanbul) and LSE Capital Markets Workshop. The research was partially supported by the Securities and Investments Board.

the dangers of date-mining in Finance [e.g., Jensen and Bennington (1970)], this extreme form of data-snooping is relatively common. In many studies, the best fitting relationships are published, and reporting of other tested specifications is suppressed, while the quality of the final result is judged by test statistics (e.g., *t*-values or *R*-squareds) based on the sample data initially used to estimate the model.

Another common, but treacherous form of data-snooping is look-ahead bias. Banz and Breen (1986) pointed out that studies of accounting and financial data can reveal spurious 'anomalies' when the information source is retrospectively revised to provide 'updated' or 'corrected' data. They show that apparent relationships disappear when the dataset for each period is limited to only those figures which were available at the time. Similarly, Dimson and Marsh (1984) published a back-history for the FTSE 100 Share Index, based on index constituents that at each point in time had *previously* been amongst the largest 100 companies. They quote an alternative back-history computed by DataStream, based on 'looking ahead' to identify those stocks that were destined to be the actual constituents of the FTSE Index, which outperformed the Dimson–Marsh figures by an artefactual 4% per year. As Lo and MacKinlay (1990) indicate, tests of theoretically motivated models (for which empirical evidence is lacking) are likely to be biased least by data-snooping. Tests of data-driven models (for which a theoretical motivation is lacking) are most susceptible to data-snooping.

Levi (1988, p. 50) cautions that: 'Those who continue looking for patterns in returns for which they do not have a theory would do well to recall the fate of William Stanley Jevons. Mr. Jevons made a fundamental contribution to microeconomics via his use of marginal reasoning, but is better remembered for his attribution of cycles in the economy to sun spots. Jevons' explanation was basically empirically based, being supported only by reference to the effects of sun spots on weather and crop yields. The reduction in the importance of agriculture, and the lack of any solid foundations for his ideas, resulted in considerable discredit for Mr. Jevons'. With the extensive databases and computing power available to modern investigators, there is far greater scope for reading too much into regularities which are specific to the sample data which is under examination.

Any set of relationships which is presented as a model of financial asset price behaviour is, in a sense, a forecasting model. That is, the relationships are likely to be of interest insofar as they are considered to have out-of-sample validity. But explicit forecasting models are especially exposed to the risk of data-snooping. This is because such models are particularly likely to be empirically based. In this paper, we show how the predictive value of simple forecasting models can be misjudged, not as a result of inept or unscrupulous research techniques, but simply as a consequence of inadvertent snooping of the data.

Our investigation focuses on methods for forecasting equity market volatility. Recently, a number of newly developed techniques have received attention in this context [see, for example, Bollerslev (1986) and Engle and Bollerslev (1986)] but while these approaches provide interesting within-sample estimates, the evidence we present in this paper suggests that the more complex methodologies can actually perform the worst on out-of-sample data. Our focus, therefore, is on a number of simple conventional statistical forecasting procedures, which we use to generate a series of rolling forecasts.

These forecasts are not exposed to look-ahead bias, and are as free as possible from data-snooping. We measure the prediction error associated with each forecasting method; and we identify the incremental gain (in terms of reduced prediction errors) from selecting relatively sophisticated, in preference to relatively simplistic, variants of the same model.

We find evidence that commonplace forms of data-snooping can lead to substantial overestimation of the accuracy of a forecasting method. In particular, we note that:

(1) Even apparently innocuous data-snooping (for instance, ascertaining the long term mean of the series which is being predicted) significantly enhances reported forecast quality.

(2) Simple forecasting methods which incorporate data-snooping (i.e., selecting the parameters with the optimal in-sample performance) additionally enhance apparent forecast quality.

(3) But the same methods operated without data-snooping (by means of rolling forecasts with parameters updated each period) often perform *worse* than naive benchmarks.

At least in the context of this study, the best forecasting method, when the data are not snooped, turns out to be a simple one. For predicting stock market volatility, therefore, we recommend two alternative, but very straightforward formulae.

In the following section we review the motivation for, relevant literature on, and methods to be used, for forecasting stock market volatility. Section 3 describes our choice of data and methodology. Section 4 presents the evidence on the quality of alternative forecasting methods, both with and without the incorporation of data-snooping. In Section 5 we generalise our results by examining the impact of alternative criteria and forecasting horizons. Finally, in Section 6 we offer our conclusions, both in respect of preferred models for volatility forecasting and in relation to the impact of data-snooping.

2. Volatility forecasting

The volatility of the overall equity market is a crucial input to portfolio selection and to asset pricing models. Tactical investment decisions, and valuation of short-lived derivatives such as stock index options, frequently focus on short term predictions of volatility. If the time horizon for these forecasts is brief, alternative prediction rules can be tested out over a relatively short sample period. For example, if the forecast horizon is a week or so, then an acceptable test period might comprise 100 weeks, or only two years. If the time horizon for a longer term volatility forecast is a year, however, then a comparable number of independent test periods would run to no less than a century! The longer the horizon over which volatility is to be predicted, the longer the sample period required for empirical testing.

By contrast with tactical and short term decisions, strategic investment choices and valuation of long-lived assets require longer term predictions of volatility. In this study, we focus on such longer term predictions, and evaluate predictions by reference to realised levels of volatility. For this, we clearly require a long time-series of stock market volatilities, and this therefore rules out the use of implied standard deviations (ISDs) derived from stock index options through the use of option pricing models. This is because stock index option contracts are still relatively recent innovations. In the U.K., the FTSE 100 Share Index contract was, in fact, designed and introduced as late as 1984 [see Dimson and Marsh (1984b)]. Consequently, the availability of ISDs is limited to recent years. Researchers who require volatility data over a long interval therefore have little alternative but to utilise historical stock returns to generate the required series. For testing volatility forecasts over reasonably long prediction periods, the use of historical standard deviations (HSDs) is thus the norm.

The literature on the stochastic behaviour of market volatilities includes contributions by Rosenberg (1972), Officer (1973), Merton (1980), Poterba and Summers (1986), French et al. (1987), Schwert (1989) and Schwert and Seguin (1989) within the U.S. market; and Brealey et al. (1978) and Dickens (1987) within the U.K. market. There is clear evidence in these studies of stock market volatilities experiencing periodic shocks, with a subsequent return to more 'normal' levels of volatility. This pattern is witnessed also in studies of the time series properties of ISDs, including Black (1976), Beckers (1981), Franks and Schwartz (1990) and several of the authors mentioned above. The same pattern is revealed in research based on GARCH models [see Engle and Bollerslev (1986) and Bollerslev (1987)]. Summarizing, volatilities appear to wander over time. The question which concerns us is how best to forecast future volatilities?

In this study, we look at five volatility forecasting methods. These are the random walk model, the long-term mean, a moving average process, exponential smoothing and regression models. Our choice of these straightforward methods is driven by a desire to work, whenever possible, with a single parameter which can be estimated both with and without data-snooping. If the impact of data-snooping can be demonstrated in the context of simple, single-parameter forecasting techniques, the problem will be even more apparent when complex multivariate models are employed.

The forecasting parameter, labelled β in the paragraphs below, varies between zero (when forecasts give the greatest weight to the most recent evidence) and unity (when forecasts reflect observations which span as long an interval as possible). In our research, we examine the performance of forecasts based on all possible values for β which might conceivably have been selected ex ante; and we also identify the values for β which appear to have performed best if data-snooping is permitted. Later, we study the potential benefits from a program of continuously updating β to take advantage of the increasing volume of data available to an investigator who seeks to choose the best ex ante value for β. In the remainder of this section we explain the five forecasting methods which we investigate.

2.1. Random walk

If volatilities fluctuate randomly, then the optimal prediction is for there to be no change since the most recent observation. Our prediction is therefore

$$\hat{\sigma}_{t+1} = \sigma_t. \tag{1}$$

The random walk model for volatility provides us with a benchmark for judging the other forecasting methods outlined below.

2.2. Long-term mean

If the distribution of volatilities has a stationary mean, all variation in estimated volatilities will be attributable to measurement errors. In this case, our best estimate of each period's volatility will be the mean of the most recent and all previous observed volatilities, namely,

$$\hat{\sigma}_{t+1} = \bar{\sigma}_t = (\sigma_t + \sigma_{t-1} + \cdots + \sigma_1)/t. \tag{2}$$

The long-term mean is an additional standard of comparison for the other forecasting methods.

2.3. Moving average

The moving average involves forecasting volatilities as an unweighted average of previously observed volatilities. We assume there is some interval (in this study, five years) which contains the maximum number of periods, N, which would ever be incorporated into the moving average. If a proportion β

of these time periods are used in the forecast,[1] the moving average
prediction will be

$$\hat{\sigma}_{t+1}(\beta)=(\sigma_t+\sigma_{t-1}+\cdots+\sigma_{t-\beta N+1})/\beta N = \sum_{i=1}^{\beta N} \sigma_{t+1-i}/\beta N. \tag{3}$$

The parameter β is constrained to lie in the range $N^{-1} \leq \beta \leq 1$. When β is at
its minimum (i.e., close to zero), the prediction is that the following period's
volatility will equal the most recently observed volatility. This is the same
prediction as would be generated by the random walk model for volatility.
An a priori estimate for the value of β might lie somewhere in the middle of
the feasible range, at perhaps a value of $\beta=0.4$, i.e. a moving average based
on eight quarters' or two years' data.

2.4. Exponential smoothing

Exponential smoothing involves forecasting volatilities as a weighted
average of previously observed volatilities. The most recent observation
receives the largest weight $1-\beta$; while earlier observations are discounted
geometrically according to their age, with weights on observations from
$2, 3, 4, \ldots$ periods previously equal to $(1-\beta)\beta$, $(1-\beta)\beta^2$, etc. The quantity
$1-\beta$ is known as the exponential smoothing constant. To produce an
exponentially smoothed forecast, all that is required is to keep a record of
the latest period's prediction, $\hat{\sigma}_t$. At the end of each period, the forecast for
the following period is

$$\hat{\sigma}_{t+1}(\beta)=(1-\beta)\sigma_t+\beta\hat{\sigma}_t. \tag{4}$$

The parameter β is constrained to lie in the range $0 \leq \beta \leq 1$. When β is equal
to zero, the prediction is that the following period's volatility will be equal to
the most recently observed volatility. This is the same prediction as would be
generated by the random walk model for volatility. When β is small (say 0.2
to 0.5), the prediction gives major weight to the latest and other recent
periods. For large values of β (say 0.8 to 0.9), predictions are only slightly
influenced by the most recent period's volatility and largely reflect outcomes
over many previous time periods. As β approaches unity, the exponential
smoothing based forecast approaches the long-term mean. Brown (1962)
recommends that, in the absence of any other information, an a priori
estimate for the value of the smoothing constant would lie in the range of
0.05 to 0.30. Given that we would have known even in 1955 that stock
market volatility was subject to periodic shocks followed by a return to

---

[1]As we explain above, β can vary over time and should strictly be labelled β_t throughout the
remainder of this paper. For ease of exposition, however, we omit the time subscript, t, unless it
is required to avoid ambiguity.

normalcy, it would therefore be in the spirit of Brown's advice (op cit, pp. 106–122) to select as our naive prior a smoothing constant at the upper end of his range of prior values, of say 0.3, which corresponds to a parameter value of $\beta = 0.7$. Clearly, however, the most suitable value to use in relation to volatility forecasting remains an empirical question.

2.5. Regression model

Regression models also predict volatilities as a weighted average of previously observed volatilities. The weights are the estimated coefficients, $\gamma_0, \gamma_1, \gamma_2, \ldots$, in a regression of current on previously observed volatilities. A regression model would therefore predict a volatility for period $t+1$ of $\gamma_0 + \gamma_1 \sigma_t + \gamma_2 \sigma_{t-1} + \cdots$. In our empirical work, we examine the accuracy of multiple regression based forecasts such as this, as well as of a simple regression based model, with only a single lagged term (i.e., $\gamma_2 = \gamma_3 = \cdots = 0$). When a single lagged term is sufficient, the forecast is given by the simple regression model

$$\hat{\sigma}_{t+1}(\beta) = \gamma_0 + \gamma_1 \sigma_t = \beta \bar{\sigma}_t + (1-\beta)\sigma_t = \sigma_t + \beta(\bar{\sigma}_t - \sigma_t). \tag{5}$$

For expositional convenience, the parameter β is defined here to be equal to $1 - \gamma_1$; and hence, γ_1 is replaced by $1 - \beta$. If the forecasts are to be unbiased, then the expectation of both sides of this model must be $\bar{\sigma}_t$, the long term mean volatility; and hence, γ_0 is replaced by $\beta \bar{\sigma}_t$. Rearranging, the final equality above shows that the simple regression model implicitly predicts that each period's volatility will regress from its most recent level, σ_t, part way towards the long term average level, $\bar{\sigma}_t$. If $\bar{\sigma}_t$ is estimated from historical data, then the assumed long term mean will be that specified in eq. (2).

The parameter β specifies how fast volatilities regress towards the mean. As long as there is at least some regression towards the mean, β is constrained to lie in the range $0 \leq \beta \leq 1$. When β is zero, this model is predicting a random walk of volatility. When β is unity, the model is giving full weight to the assumed long term average $\bar{\sigma}_t$. In the absence of any data-snooping, one might choose an a priori estimate as lying midway between these two extremes, i.e., $\beta = 0.5$, though this is again a matter which requires empirical evidence.

3. Data and methodology

The value of the U.K. equity market is represented by the Financial Times–Actuaries (FTA) All Share Index. The FTA Index covers some 93% of the market capitalisation of the entire British equity market, and is available on a daily basis from the London Business School's financial database. Prior

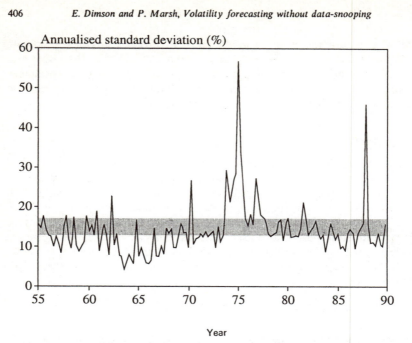

Fig. 1. Annualised standard deviations of the U.K. equity market, quarterly 1955–1989. [Note that on the assumption that true volatility is stationary and equal to 14%, the area shown shaded is the 95% confidence interval (see section 4).]

to the introduction of the FTA Index in 1962, the daily Financial Times Index is used instead.

Using the daily FTA returns, we estimate a series of non-overlapping volatilities for 140 successive calendar quarters, starting at the beginning of 1955 and ending at the close of 1989. Volatilities are expressed as annualised standard deviations of the daily returns within each quarter. Each quarterly volatility estimate is based on returns for approximately 63 trading days.

The time series plot in fig. 1 displays the quarterly volatilities we have computed. With a few exceptions, annualised standard deviations lie between 5 and 30%. The mean of all 140 volatilities is 14.0%; but the median is somewhat lower at 13.0%, reflecting the positive skewness of the distribution. The interquartile range runs from 10.0 to 15.5%.

The accuracy of each of the forecasting methods described above is gauged by generating, at the end of period t, a forecast, $\hat{\sigma}_{t+k}$, of volatility k periods hence. In most of the results reported in this paper, the period length is one quarter and k is set equal to a forecasting horizon of one period. For convenience, therefore, we present our methodology on the basis of judging the forecast error for one-period-ahead forecasts, $\hat{\sigma}_{t+1}$. The forecasts are made over the interval $t \in [1, T]$. They are evaluated using the mean squared error (MSE_i) for each forecasting method, i, by means of the following calculation:

$$MSE_i(\beta) = \sum_{t=1}^{T} [\hat{\sigma}_{t+1}(\beta) - \sigma_{t+1}]^2/T. \tag{6}$$

It will be recalled that the parameter β has a different meaning, but a similar interpretation, for each of the forecasting techniques (except the random walk and long term mean models, which have no such parameter). In each case, the value of β varies between (close to) zero and unity. The magnitude of β indicates how much weight is to be given to data prior to the current quarter. The time period covered in the MSE calculations initially runs from $t=1$ (the first quarter of 1955) to $t=T=140$ (the fourth quarter of 1989) inclusive.

The prediction errors, $MSE_i(\beta)$, for each forecast method are easier to interpret if we consider them in relation to a benchmark. The benchmark we adopt is the random walk model [eq. (1)]. We therefore judge the other methods by the relative mean squared error, defined as

$$RMSE_i(\beta) = MSE_i(\beta)/MSE_1. \tag{7}$$

The mean squared error for the first method, MSE_1, refers to the predictive accuracy of the random walk model. By definition, the latter therefore has an $RMSE$ value of one. In the following section, we report on the accuracy of the other approaches, for the full range of valid β values. Note that whatever value is selected here for β, this quantity is kept constant throughout the interval $t \in [1, T]$.

From the above, we are able to select the value for β which gives the lowest forecast error over the interval $t \in [1, T]$. This is the optimal ex post value, in the sense that an unvarying β of this value would have generated the lowest prediction errors over the entire sample period. Unfortunately, however, these optimal parameters (one for each forecasting method) are derived after snooping the data. It is important to know what the accuracy of the forecasting approaches would be on a true, ex ante basis.

We therefore calculate the optimal ex post value of β using data available over the variable length period $1, \ldots, t$, where t is set equal to the series of dates, $1, \ldots, T$, throughout the sample period. This gives rise to a sequence, for each forecast method, of β_t values covering the entire interval $t \in [1, T]$. Note that the β_t values vary over time;[2] but if used at (or after) period t, they

---

[2]The value of β_t is, however, constrained to remain at an 'initialisation value' for a number of periods, until sufficient observations accumulate for reliable estimates of β_t to be computed. The value is the a priori figure cited earlier in section 2.

involve no 'look-ahead' bias. They may therefore be used as a series of ex ante estimates of the optimal parameter value to be used for each forecasting method.

The remainder of our analysis focuses on forecasts produced with the help of this 'rolling update' technique for β_t. We provide a record of the variation over time of the β_t values. Finally, we compare forecasts generated using these ex ante 'optimal' parameters with forecasts generated by selecting an arbitrary, but non-time varying, value for β.

4. Empirical results

Fig. 1 displays a time plot of the quarterly volatilities we have computed, covering the period 1955 through 1989, and as already noted, the mean of all these observations is an annualised standard deviation of $\bar{\sigma} = 14.0\%$. Obviously, at least a part of the period-by-period variation in observed volatilities is a consequence of the limited amount of data used to compute each estimate (namely some 63 trading days per quarter). Conceivably, much of the variation in observed standard deviations is attributable to measurement error.

For normally distributed samples with a stationary variance, the observed variance follows the chi-square distribution. With a sample size of 63 returns, the 95% confidence interval for the variance therefore runs from a multiple of $62/\chi^2_{62,0.025}$ of the sample variance to a multiple of $62/\chi^2_{62,0.975}$, namely from 0.72 to 1.47. In terms of the observed standard deviation, $\bar{\sigma}$, this corresponds to lower and upper confidence limits of $0.85\bar{\sigma}$ and $1.21\bar{\sigma}$, respectively. Thus, the 95% confidence interval for the standard deviation runs from 11.9 to 16.9%.

If the changing levels of observed volatility were merely sampling fluctuations around a stationary mean, only 5% of all the observations would lie beyond the confidence limits marked on fig. 1. In fact, however, 53% of all the estimates fall outside these bounds. This evidence is consistent with the view that true volatilities vary over time, and are not drawn from a distribution whose mean remains constant.

Further clues regarding the non-stationarity of volatilities may be obtained by identifying times when volatility was below or above average. There were, in fact, prolonged periods when the measured volatility was below the 1955–1989 average, notably during the 1950s and 1960s. Likewise, there were periods when the measured volatility stayed above the 35-year average, in particular the mid-1970s.[3] Since these intervals of below or above average volatility appear to last for several years, there is scope for enhancing

---

[3] This evidence replicates a pattern which was previously identified in U.K. data covering a similar length sample period prior to 1955 [see Brealey et al. (1978)].

Table 1

Prediction error for all five forecasting methods, 1955–1989.[a]

Forecasting method	MSE	RMSE
1 Random walk	47.8	1.00
2 Long-term mean		
(a) Rolling ex ante	47.2	0.99
(b) Ex post	46.1	0.96
3 Moving average	39.7	0.83
4 Exponential smoothing	36.3	0.76
5 Regression model		
(a) One lag	35.4	0.74
(b) Two lags	34.2	0.72
(c) Three lags	34.1	0.71

[a]The table identifies the prediction error (*MSE* and *RMSE*) of each method for forecasting volatilities between 1955 and 1989. Note that forecasting rules 2(b) and 3–5 utilise parameter values estimated from data covering the same period as that used for computing the *MSE*.

volatility forecasts by using data which is relatively recent. On the other hand, since volatilities clearly tend to revert, at least after a while, to relatively normal levels, a pure random walk model will fail to capture this attribute of the market. One might expect both the random walk and long-term mean models to be dominated by the other three forecasting approaches.

4.1. Volatility forecasting with data-snooping

We judge the accuracy of each method by the size of its mean squared error (*MSE*), expressed relative to that of the random walk model (i.e., as a *RMSE*). Our conjecture certainly appears to be supported by the initial evidence, presented in table 1. The table shows that the *MSE* when each quarter's volatility is predicted to be the same as its predecessor (i.e., the random walk model) is approximately 48, corresponding to an average (non-squared) error in predicting annualised standard deviations of $\sqrt{48}$, or about 7%. The *MSE* of 48 may be expressed as a relative *MSE* of 1.00. By contrast, other forecasting methods appear superior (have a lower *RMSE*), especially in the case of the last three approaches in the table.

However, it has to be born in mind that the parameter β is required (in its various manifestations) by the moving average, exponential smoothing and simple regression model approaches (i.e., methods 3, 4, and 5(a), respectively). The appropriate value for β has been optimised for these three methods, using the data for 1955–1989. This falls short of 'best practice', though it is less subject to data-snooping biases than many attempts at stochastic modelling, since we have restricted the specification to one involving the use of only one parameter. If a full specification search were allowed, the reported in-sample MSEs would undoubtedly be lower. For example, when the regression model is estimated with more than one lagged term, the bottom two rows of table 1 show that we obtain an *MSE* which is appreciably smaller. The more complicated the forecasting equation and the more variables which are included, the lower the *MSE* is likely to be, as long as forecasting accuracy is judged over the sample period used to estimate the model.

This does not, of course, imply that these more sophisticated models will also perform better on an out-of-sample basis. Table 1 already provides one small clue to the likely biases from in-sample estimation of forecasting accuracy. When forecasts are based on the ex post long-term mean for the entire sample period, table 1 shows that the *RMSE* is 0.96. However, when forecasts are based on the rolling ex ante long-term mean, i.e., when there is no data-snooping, the *RMSE* rises to 0.99, or scarcely any lower than the random walk. Thus, even very modest forms of data-snooping, such as using knowledge of the long-term mean of the series being predicted, can help to enhance (overstate) forecasting ability.

To further quantify the biases from in-sample estimation of forecast accuracy, table 2 lists the *RMSE*s for a series of possible values for β for methods 3–5. The ex-post optimal *RMSE*s presented in table 1, are shown in boldface. Clearly, if the wrong parameter value were chosen in 1955 and were maintained throughout the sample period, the *RMSE* would be larger than that reported in table 1. In other words, only a clairvoyant could select the optimal value for β. Yet a clairvoyant would have no need for a forecasting model! In the absence of such perfect foresight, one clearly cannot expect to achieve the predictive accuracy implied by the in-sample test statistics.

Despite these reservations, the three forecasting methods analysed in table 2 are not without merit. There is a wide range of β values for which the *RMSE* is below 1.00, and a misjudgment about the appropriate magnitude of β need not necessarily have a hugh impact on predictive accuracy. We now seek to quantify the impact of the serious type of data-snooping which arises when in-sample testing is reported. We do this by examining the accuracy of forecasts which do not suffer from data-snooping biases.

4.2. Volatility forecasting without data-snooping

Data-snooping involves allowing detailed or fuzzy awareness of outcomes over the test period to influence estimation prior to the test period. The objection to the ex post optimal parameter values presented earlier to (1) is their use to judge predictive accuracy on an in-sample basis, and (2) the presentation of the resulting test statistics as being, in some sense, valid.

Table 2

Prediction error (*RMSE*) for three volatility forecasting methods, 1955–1989.[a]

Value of β	Moving average	Exponential smoothing	Regression model
Min[b]	1.00	1.00	1.00
0.10	0.86	0.93	0.91
0.15	0.84	0.90	0.88
0.20	0.84	0.88	0.84
0.25	**0.83**	0.85	0.82
0.30	0.84	0.83	0.80
0.35	0.85	0.81	0.78
0.40	0.85	0.80	0.77
0.45	0.86	0.79	0.76
0.50	0.87	0.78	**0.76**
0.55	0.88	0.77	0.76
0.60	0.88	0.76	0.76
0.65	0.90	**0.76**	0.78
0.70	0.91	0.76	0.79
0.75	0.92	0.77	0.81
0.80	0.94	0.78	0.84
0.85	0.94	0.80	0.87
0.90	0.95	0.84	0.90
0.95	0.94	0.90	0.94
1.00	0.94	0.99	0.99

[a]The table lists the prediction error (*RMSE*) for three volatility forecasting methods, identifying in boldface the smallest prediction error which could have been achieved over the period 1955–1989. The most accurate forecasts occur when: (1) moving averages are based on $\beta = 0.25$, i.e., using five of the 20 quarters of available data; (2) exponential smoothing is based on $\beta = 0.66$, i.e., using a 'smoothing constant' of 0.34; and (3) the regression model is based on $\beta = 0.52$, i.e., quarterly volatilities regress approximately halfway back to the mean.

[b]In the case of the moving average, the minimum value of β is $N^{-1} = 0.05$. For the other two methods, the minimum value of β is zero.

There is no such objection to the use of the estimated parameters for forecasting over a holdout period. It would indeed be interesting to know how well the ex post optimal forecasting procedure works during an interval *after* the estimation period.

Tables 3 and 4 provide valuable evidence on this question. In each period from 1956 onwards, all data from the beginning of the sample period (the first quarter of 1955) to date is used to estimate the optimal ex post value for β. This parameter estimate is recorded in table 3 for each for each year-end. It is interesting to note that the best-fitting values for β vary markedly over time. For the moving average, β varies between 0.10 and 0.95, implying the use of between 2 and 19 quarters' data to produce the optimal result. The β

Table 3

Optimal values for β_t at each year-end.[a]

Year end	Moving average	Exponential smoothing	Regression model
1955	0.20	0.70	0.50
1956	0.40	0.70	0.50
1957	0.15	0.54	0.67
1958	0.20	0.83	0.99
1959	0.60	0.78	0.90
1960	0.60	0.89	0.90
1961	0.60	0.95	1.00
1962	0.60	1.00	1.00
1963	0.20	0.93	0.91
1964	0.20	0.73	0.84
1965	0.50	0.79	0.82
1966	0.50	0.82	0.80
1967	0.50	0.82	0.80
1968	0.50	0.80	0.80
1969	0.50	0.79	0.79
1970	0.50	0.81	0.88
1971	0.50	0.82	0.87
1972	0.50	0.82	0.87
1973	0.50	0.82	0.91
1974	0.20	0.71	0.58
1975	0.25	0.64	0.43
1976	0.10	0.57	0.43
1977	0.10	0.61	0.43
1978	0.10	0.58	0.43
1979	0.10	0.59	0.43
1980	0.10	0.59	0.43
1981	0.10	0.59	0.43
1982	0.10	0.59	0.44
1983	0.10	0.59	0.43
1984	0.10	0.59	0.44
1985	0.10	0.59	0.43
1986	0.10	0.59	0.44
1987	0.15	0.60	0.43
1988	0.25	0.67	0.51
1989	0.25	0.66	0.52

[a]The table lists the values for β_t which generated the smallest prediction error ($RMSE$) from start-1955 to each specified year-end up to the end of the sample period. The 'initialisation values' of β_t were, however, constrained prior to end-1956 to have the following values: (1) moving average $\beta_t = \frac{1}{20}t$; (2) exponential smoothing $\beta_t = 0.70$; and (3) regression model $\beta_t = 0.50$.

Table 4

Prediction error (*RMSE*) for alternative β estimates, 1955–1989.[a]

Choice of parameter	Moving average β	RMSE	Exponential smoothing β	RMSE	Regression method β	RMSE
1 Ex post optimal	0.25	0.83	0.65	0.76	0.52	0.74
2 Time-varying ex ante	–[b]	0.80	–[b]	0.80	–[b]	0.81
3 A priori estimate	0.40	0.85	0.70	0.76	0.50	0.76
4 Alternative values:						
Lower decile	0.10	0.86	0.58	0.76	0.91	0.91
Lower quartile	0.10	0.86	0.59	0.76	0.87	0.88
Median	0.20	0.84	0.65	0.76	0.66	0.78
Upper quartile	0.50	0.87	0.74	0.77	0.44	0.76
Upper decile	0.60	0.88	0.77	0.77	0.43	0.76

[a]The table displays displays values for β and the associated prediction errors for: (1) the ex post optimal β identified in table 2; (2) the time-varying ex ante β_t values shown in table 3; (3) the a priori estimates of β recommended as 'initialisation values' in standard textbooks; and (4) alternative values, which are taken from the distribution of ex ante β_t, the year-end values of which are summarised in table 3.

[b]See table 3 for year-end values of β_t.

for exponential smoothing varies between 0.54 and 1.00, implying that, at one extreme, 46% weighting is given to the most recent observation, while at the other extreme, equal weights are given to all observations. Finally β for the regression model varies between 0.33 and unity, indicating wildly differing weights given to recent versus long-term volatility observations.

The β values in table 3 provide a sequence of 'up-to-date' estimates of the optimal ex post parameters for the forecasting models at the end of each calendar year. If quantity and recency of data are helpful, use of these continuously updated parameter values should provide useful forecasts. We therefore use these estimates as a set of time-varying ex ante β_t values for input into the forecasting process. Each β_t is calculated here using as much data as possible from periods prior to period t; and predictive accuracy is assessed by means of forecasting the out-of-sample volatility for period $t+1$. There is no danger of data-snooping.

For the two more sophisticated methods, exponential smoothing and regression, there is a marked decline in the *RMSE* when time-varying ex ante β_t are used in place of the ex post optimal β_t. The first two lines of table 4 show that for these two methods, the predictions based on the ex post optimal β, namely the volatility forecasts *with* data-snooping, achieve an *RMSE* of about 0.75, representing a 25% reduction in forecast error relative to our naive benchmark of 1.0. By contrast, the predictions based on the rolling update procedure for β_t, namely the volatility forecasts *without* data-snooping, achieve, an *RMSE* of around 0.80, offering only a 20%

reduction in forecast error relative to our benchmark. Quite clearly, with both exponential smoothing and regression, the results achieved with data snooping provide us with a misleading picture of the forecasting ability that would have been obtainable with truly ex ante predictions.

While, with exponential smoothing and regression, our rolling update procedure performs much less well than with ex post optimal estimates, it is surprising to observe in the third line of table 4 that the a priori estimates of β gives rise to considerably more accurate forecasts. These could, of course, simply represent a 'lucky' choice of parameter values, which are coincidentally close to the ex post optima for β. However, the final section of table 4 suggests that this result should not be summarily dismissed as simply 'luck'. This last section of the table shows, for each forecasting method, a range of β estimates which represent the 10th, 25th, 50th, 75th and 90th percentiles of the distribution of β_t (as specified in table 3 for the year-ends since 1955). For each β value, we record the *RMSE* associated with maintaining that level of β unchanged throughout the 1955–1989 period. In the vast majority of cases, the *RMSE* for both exponential smoothing and regression is lower than with the time-varying approach (second line of the table).

These results are so surprising, at least initially, that we feel it is worth restating them in different words:

> It is 1955. You have just had an accurate premonition of what the ex post optimal β values will be, quarter by quarter over the entire period until 1989 (though you unfortunately have had no other foresight). You are tempted to use these β values as an aid in forecasting. You would, in fact, have achieved roughly the same degree of forecasting ability with exponential smoothing and regression by selecting a naive prior and using that as your forecasting parameter, unchanged for the next 35 years! Furthermore, if you had selected almost any plausible prior value of β as your forecasting parameter and left if unchanged over the entire period, you would have achieved more accurate forecasts than if you had updated your parameters on a rolling basis, but without data-snooping.

Ironically, the only real exception to this rule occurs with the least sophisticated method of all, the moving average, which actually performs better on a time-varying ex ante basis. However, when β_t is left unchanged, this method is very clearly inferior to both exponential smoothing and regression, for virtually all choices of β – including, at one extreme, the naive prior, and at the other, the ex post optimal value.

We therefore endorse the 'Errata for the First Edition of *Long Range Forecasting*', in which Armstrong (1985) reports recent empirical evidence, based largely on non-financial databases, regarding the most effective forecasting techniques. He states that: 'In contrast to my original suggestions [...] adaptive parameters do not seem worthwhile for extrapolation, and exponential smoothing is more accurate than moving averages' (p. 450; also see pp. 494–495).

One further piece of evidence in favour of simplicity versus complexity is provided by table 5, which shows the results of using not only simple

Table 5

Prediction errors for regression analysis with additional lagged terms.[a]

Conditions	Statistic	Regression analysis with		
		One lag	Two lags	Three lags
Ex post optimal estimates	γ_0 (constant term)	7.2 (6.2)	5.8 (4.5)	5.4 (3.9)
	γ_1 (lag one coefficient)	0.48 (6.5)	0.39 (4.7)	0.38 (4.4)
	γ_2 (lag two coefficient)	n.a.	0.19 (2.2)	0.15 (1.7)
	γ_3 (lag three coefficient)	n.a.	n.a.	0.07 (0.8)
	R^2	0.23	0.25	0.25
	MSE	35.4	34.2	34.1
	RMSE	0.74	0.72	0.71
Time-varying ex ante measures	MSE	38.6	39.3	40.8
	RMSE	0.81	0.82	0.85

[a]The table displays the results from the regression, $\sigma_{t+1} = \gamma_0 + \gamma_1\sigma_t + \gamma_2\sigma_{t-1} + \gamma_3\sigma_{t-2} + \varepsilon_{t+1}$. The *t*-values for the regression coefficients are shown in parentheses. The top portion of the table shows the coefficients, R^2, *MSE* and *RMSE*, for the models which were ex post optimal over the sample period. The bottom panel shows how the *MSE* and *RMSE* change when the model is estimated with time-varying parameters on an ex ante basis.

regression, but also regression analysis with two or three lagged terms. The top panel of table 5 shows that using ex post optimal estimates for the regression coefficients, the *MSE* and *RMSE* improve steadily, the more complex the model used, and that with three lagged terms, the *RMSE* has fallen to 0.71. The bottom panel of table 5, however, shows that on a time-varying ex ante basis, the *simpler* the model, the better it performs. Adding additional lagged terms actually increases the *RMSE* from 0.81 to 0.82 with two lags, and to 0.85 with three.

We generalise these apparently counter-intuitive results in the following section. For the time being, we note that the evidence from this study strongly supports the 'keep it simple' approach to forecasting.

Finally, we conclude this section by indicating our preferred model for forecasting volatility. The essential attribute of an acceptable model has to be the capacity to represent the 'return to normalcy' behaviour of volatilities. Of our five approaches, only exponential smoothing and the regression model are likely candidates. As tables 3 and 4 show, the predictive accuracy of both methods is similar, not only if a priori parameters are used but also if plausible alternative parameters are substituted.

We therefore offer two formulae for volatility prediction: exponential smoothing [eq. (4)] with $\beta \approx \frac{2}{3}$ or the regression model [eq. (5)] with $\beta \approx \frac{1}{2}$. Our forecasting models are thus:

Volatility next quarter $= \frac{1}{3} \times$ Volatility this quarter $+ \frac{2}{3} \times$ Prediction for this quarter, (8)

Volatility next quarter $= \frac{1}{2} \times$ Volatility this quarter $+ \frac{1}{2} \times$ Long-term mean volatility. (9)

The first of these two formulae avoids the need for taking an explicit view on the average level of volatility which is likely over the long term. We therefore have a very marginal preference for eq. (8), the exponential smoothing formula, partly for reasons of practicality, but also because of its slightly superior performance on an ex ante basis and its robustness to prior values.

5. Discussion

In this section, we discuss two issues. First, we identify the impact on our results of focusing on squared prediction errors. What if we use some other criterion for judging forecasting accuracy? And second, we discuss the implications of our work for forecasting over an interval which differs from a quarter of a year. How should we predict volatilities when we have a semiannual or annual period, say, as our forecasting horizon?

5.1. Alternative criteria

From our approximate formulae [eqs. (8) and (9)] it is clear that each period's volatility comprises a medium-/long-term component, onto which is superimposed a short-term shock. Our models attempt to forecast not only shifts in the longer term element of volatility, but also the periodic shocks which are experienced. To some extent, we are seeking to predict the unpredictable. This gives rise to an apparently large forecasting error. In actual fact, since the *MSE* is dominated by the forecasting error in periods with the largest shocks, most periods have a predictive accuracy which is better than our *MSE* estimates suggest. In the case of the two best fitting ex post models [eqs. (4) and (5)] for example, no less than 86% of the forecasts with exponential smoothing, and 88% with the regression model, have a squared error which is below the *MSE* for these methods of 36 and 35, respectively.

A critical issue is thus the extent to which we value relative accuracy in predicting the extreme observations of volatility. This, in turn, must reflect the loss function associated with the magnitude of the errors in our forecasts. For many purposes, it is big jumps in volatility which are especially costly, and it may therefore be appropriate to seek to minimise the mean *squared* errors of our forecasts. For other purposes, it may be more appropriate to

Table 6

Relative prediction error over 1955–1989 using three criteria[a].

Forecasting method	RMSE	RMAE	RMAE$^{1.5}$
1 Random walk	1.00	1.00	1.00
2 Long-term mean	0.96	0.99	0.97
3 Moving average	0.83	0.97	0.90
4 Exponential smoothing	0.76	0.91	0.82
5 Regression model	0.74	0.86	0.78

[a]The table shows the relative prediction errors of each method based on the respective values for β which were ex post optimal over 1955–1989. The relative mean *squared* error (*RMSE*) is repeated from table 1; the other columns are the relative mean *absolute* error (*RMAE*), and a similar measure (*RMAE*$^{1.5}$) based on absolute forecasting errors raised to the power 1.5.

minimise the mean *absolute* error, or to minimise some other error function. In principle, this could significantly influence our choice of forecasting technique.

We therefore test the sensitivity of our rankings of forecasting methods $i = 1, \ldots, 5$ to the choice of error function. To do this, we estimate the mean absolute error (MAE_i) raised to the power k, for each of the volatility predictions. This is equal to

$$MAE_i^k(\beta) = \sum_{t=1}^{T} \text{Abs}[\hat{\sigma}_{t+1}(\beta) - \sigma_{t+1}]^k / T. \tag{10}$$

We then calculate, for each forecasting method i, the relative mean absolute error ($RMAE_i$) raised to the power of k. As previously [see eqs. (6) and (7) above], this is defined relative to the performance of the random walk model (forecasting method number 1):

$$RMAE_i^k(\beta) = MAE_i^k(\beta) / MAE_1^k. \tag{11}$$

Note that when $k = 2$, eq. (11) yields the *RMSE* [eq. (7)] reported previously. Note also that, for convenience of exposition, the power subscript k is omitted whenever it is superfluous, i.e., when $k = 1$.

Table 6 shows how the $RMAE_i^k$ for each forecasting technique varies with the choice of error criterion. The table repeats the relative mean squared error, *RMSE*, from table 1, and accompanies this with the relative mean absolute error (*RMAE*) and a similar measure (*RMAE*$^{1.5}$) based on giving an intermediate weight to forecasting errors (i.e., $k = 1.5$). Based on this ex post analysis of the time series, the ranking of prediction methods is invariant to the choice of loss functions considered in table 6. Naturally, however, the magnitude of the preferred value for β can change with the choice of criterion. Thus, for example, when $RMAE$ is the criterion, the ex post optimal β is 0.61 for exponential smoothing and 0.54 for the regression model.

As an alternative to focusing on the prediction errors when the ex post optimal β values are used, the table may be re-estimated on the basis of the a priori values proposed in section 2 for β. However, this does not alter the ranking of the forecasting methods when they are evaluated by means of eq. (11). We conclude that the choice of preferred prediction technique is insensitive to the error-minimisation criterion which has been selected.

5.2. Alternative forecasting horizons

Our study has focused on quarterly volatilities, balancing the need for a large number of volatility observations against the desire to have a relatively long interval length and a large number of observations comprising the estimate for the volatility in each time period. For some purposes, it may be helpful to make more distant volatility forecasts. An approximate method will involve taking our quarterly model, and making straightforward adjustments for successive quarters. For example, using the simplified version of the regression model [eq. (9)], the weighting given to the last quarter obviously declines from 1 (if one wishes to 'predict' the last quarter) to $\frac{1}{2}$ (for this quarter), then to $\frac{1}{4}$ (i.e., the square of $\frac{1}{2}$, for the next quarter), and so on. It may also be useful to convert figures from an interval of one quarter of a year to an alternative time horizon. Provided volatilities are computed from daily data (for which mean returns are very close to zero), the quarterly volatilities may be averaged to produce approximate semiannual figures, or estimates which correspond to alternative durations.

However, there is a complex relationship between the parameters for even the simplest models when the periodicity of the data is changed. We therefore conclude by presenting in table 7 the optimal, ex post parameters for our two favoured models over a variety of forecasting horizons. It can be seen that the value of β which best fits the entire sample varies, depending on the forecasting horizon. In the case of exponential smoothing, as the horizon is lengthened beyond one quarter, β appears to decline. This may be because increasing weight is given to the volatility observed in the most recent time interval, both because the longer time interval is more representative of long-term volatility and (perhaps more importantly) because it is estimated with greater precision from a larger number of daily returns. However, there does

Table 7

Optimal β parameter values for various forecasting horizons.[a]

Horizon	Exponential smoothing	Regression model
1 month	0.63	0.43
2 months	0.61	0.45
Quarter	0.66	0.52
4 months	0.65	0.53
5 months	0.56	0.48
Semiannual	0.59	0.52
7 months	0.60	0.56
8 months	0.64	0.61
9 months	0.58	0.54
10 months	0.61	0.61
11 months	0.40	0.49
Annual	0.49	0.53

[a]The table lists the ex post optimal parameter values over the period 1955–1989 for forecasts of volatility for the next 1,2,..., 12 months ahead.

not appear to be any similar tendency in the case of the regression model. Here, although the optimal values still vary depending on the differencing interval, β is always fairly close to $\frac{1}{2}$. This implies that our 'keep it simple' forecasting rule given by eq. (9) can be used *whatever* the differencing interval!

6. Conclusion

Data-snooping makes it dangerous to draw conclusions about the likely accuracy of a model from its performance over an estimation period. We have shown how, even for very simple forecasting models, there is substantial attenuation in their predictive accuracy once the latter is judged on an out-of-sample basis. We have also noted that more sophisticated models, incorporating a larger number of estimated parameters, can be even more likely to underperform during a holdout period. This might make it tempting to use ex post optimal parameter estimates to produce continuous updates of stock market volatility. Unfortunately, time-varying ex ante forecasting of this nature performs poorly. It appears to be better to select a sensible forecasting parameter on an a priori basis. This is likely to perform better than the time-varying alternative, except, perhaps, with extremely unsophisticated methods such as the moving average.

In this study, we find that two very simple models perform reasonably well as predictors of quarterly volatility. The exponential smoothing model involves giving a weight of one-third to observed volatility in the most recent time period, and two-thirds to the most recent prediction. The regression model involves giving equal weight to the most recent observation of volatility and to the long-term average volatility.

With the increasing interest in using complicated econometric techniques for volatility forecasting, our research strikes a warning bell. For those who are interested in forecasts with reasonable predictive accuracy, the best forecasting models may well be the simplest ones.

References

Aldous, D., 1989, Probability approximations via the Poisson clumping heuristic (Springer, New York).

Armstrong, J.S., 1985, Long range forecasting (Wiley, New York).

Banz, R.W. and W.J. Breen, 1986, Sample-dependent results using accounting and market data: Some evidence, Journal of Finance 41, 779–793.

Beckers, S., 1981, Standard deviations implied in option prices as predictors of future stock price variability, Journal of Banking and Finance 5, 363–381.

Black, F., 1976, Studies of stock price volatility changes, in: Proceedings of the 1976 meeting of the American Statistical Association, Business and Economics Section (American Statistical Association, Washington, DC) 177–181.

Bollerslev, T., 1986, Generalised autoregressive conditional heteroscedasticity, Journal of Econometrics 31, 307–327.

Brealey, R.A., J. Byrne and E. Dimson, 1978, The variability of market returns, The Investment Analyst 52, 19–23.

Brown, R.G., 1962, Smoothing, forecasting and prediction (Prentice-Hall, Englewood Cliffs, NJ).

Dickens, R., 1987, The ARCH model as applied to the study of international asset market volatility, Technical paper no. 13 (Bank of England, UK).

Dimson, E. and P.R. Marsh, 1984a, Hedging the market: The performance of the FTSE 100 Share Index, Journal of the Institute of Actuaries 111, 403–430.

Dimson, E. and P.R. Marsh, 1984b, Futures, options and the FTSE Index, The Investment Analyst 74, 14–26.

Engle, R.F. and T. Bollerslev, 1986, Modelling the persistence of conditional variance, Econometric Reviews 5, no. 1, 1–50.

Franks, J.R. and E. Schwartz, 1990, The stochastic behaviour of market variance implied in the price of index options, Working paper (Institute of Finance and Accounting, London Business School, UK).

French, K.R., G.W. Schwert and R.F. Stambaugh, 1987, Expected stock returns and volatility, Journal of Financial Economics 19, 3–29.

Jensen, M.C. and G.A. Bennington, 1970, Random walks and technical theories: Some additional evidence, Journal of Finance 25, 469–482.

Leamer, E., 1978, Specification searches (Wiley, New York).

Levi, M., 1988, Weekend effects in stock market returns: An overview, in: E. Dimson, ed., Stock market anomalies (Cambridge University Press, Cambridge) 43–51.

Lo, A.W. and A.C. MacKinlay, 1990, Date-snooping biases in tests of financial asset pricing models, MIT Sloan School working paper 3020-89-EFA, Feb.

Merton, R.C., 1987, On the current state of the stock market rationality hypothesis, in: R. Dornbusch, S. Fischer and J. Bossons, eds., Macroeconomics and finance: Essays in honor of Franco Modigliani (MIT Press, Cambridge, MA).

Merton, R.C., 1980, On estimating the expected return on the market: An exploratory investigation, Journal of Financial Economics 8, 323–361.

Officer, R., 1973, The variability of the market factor of the NYSE, Journal of Business 46, 434–453.

Poterba, J.M. and L.H. Summers, 1986, The persistence of volatility and stock market fluctuation, American Economic Review 76, 1142–1151.

Rosenberg, B., 1972, The behaviour of random variables with nonstationary variance and the distribution of security prices, Research Program in Finance working paper no. 11 (University of California, Berkeley).

Schwert, G.W., 1989, Why does stock market volatility change over time?, Journal of Finance 44, 1115–1153.

Schwert, G.W. and P.J. Seguin, Heteroskedasticity in stock returns, Working paper no. 2956 (National Bureau of Economic Research, Cambridge, MA).

[19]

ELSEVIER   Journal of Banking & Finance 20 (1996) 419–438

Journal of
BANKING &
FINANCE

An evaluation of volatility forecasting techniques

Timothy J. Brailsford [a,*], Robert W. Faff [b]

[a] *Department of Accounting and Finance, University of Melbourne, Parkville 3052, Australia*
[b] *Department of Accounting and Finance, Monash University, Clayton 3168, Australia*

Received 15 March 1992; accepted 15 January 1995

Abstract

The existing literature contains conflicting evidence regarding the relative quality of stock market volatility forecasts. Evidence can be found supporting the superiority of relatively complex models (including ARCH class models), while there is also evidence supporting the superiority of more simple alternatives. These inconsistencies are of particular concern because of the use of, and reliance on, volatility forecasts in key economic decision-making and analysis, and in asset/option pricing. This paper employs daily Australian data to examine this issue. The results suggest that the ARCH class of models and a simple regression model provide superior forecasts of volatility. However, the various model rankings are shown to be sensitive to the error statistic used to assess the accuracy of the forecasts. Nevertheless, a clear message is that volatility forecasting is a notoriously difficult task.

JEL classification: G12; G15

Keywords: Forecasting; Stock market volatility; ARCH models; Australia

1. Introduction

While traditional financial economics research has tended to focus upon the mean of stock market returns, in recent times the emphasis has shifted to focus

---

* Tel.: 61-3-9344-7662; fax: 61-3-9344-6681.

420   *T.J. Brailsford, R.W. Faff / Journal of Banking & Finance 20 (1996) 419–438*

upon the volatility of these returns. Moreover, the international stock market crash
of 1987 has increased the focus of regulators, practitioners and researchers upon
volatility. Large swings in price movements have apparently become more prevalent and some observers have blamed institutional changes for this apparent
increase in volatility. [1] These concerns have led researchers to examine the level
and stationarity of volatility over time. Specifically, research has been directed
toward examining the accuracy of volatility forecasts obtained from various
econometric models including the autoregressive conditional heteroscedasticity
(ARCH) family of models. [2]

Volatility forecasts have many practical applications such as use in the analysis
of market timing decisions, aid with portfolio selection and the provision of
estimates of variance for use in asset (and option) pricing models. Thus, it follows
that it is important to distinguish between various models in order to find the
model which provides the most accurate forecasts. This information is clearly of
particular value in economic decision-making. To this end, this study compares
various volatility forecasting models, including the ARCH class of models, in the
Australian stock market.

The investigation of conditional volatility of the US stock market has been
extensively undertaken. However, only recently have models of conditional
volatility been tested in other stock markets. Specifically, the application of these
models has been investigated by de Jong et al. (1992) (Holland), Tse (1991)
(Japan), Tse and Tung (1992) (Singapore), Poon and Taylor (1992) (United
Kingdom) and Brailsford and Faff (1993) and Kearns and Pagan (1993) (Australia).
The evidence in these non-US markets is limited and therefore examining the
Australian market, which has different institutional features, provides an important
opportunity to add to the accumulated evidence to date. [3]

Brailsford and Faff (1993) using the same Australian data as those employed in
the current paper, conducted an extensive model fitting exercise of stock market
volatility. On the basis of several model selection techniques, they initially found
in favour of the GARCH(3,1) model. However, the results from the asymmetry
based diagnostic tests of Engle and Ng (1993) showed that this model was unable
to adequately capture asymmetric responses in volatility to past innovations.
Consequently, Brailsford and Faff (1993) examined asymmetric volatility models
and found support for the Glosten, Jagannathan and Runkle (GJR; 1993) modified

---

[1] Program trading, the advent of trading strategies such as arbitrage trading, the introduction of
futures and options trading and the increased influence of institutional investors, have all been put
forward as possible causes. See Schwert (1990) for further discussion.

[2] See Bollerslev et al. (1992) for a comprehensive review of the theory and empirical evidence of
modelling ARCH in finance.

[3] Further support is provided by Ang (1991, pp. 201–203) who argues strongly in favour of
conducting financial research in Pacific Basin markets. Moreover, Bollerslev et al. (1992, p. 31) stress
the potential insights to be gained from examining volatility using international data.

T.J. Brailsford, R.W. Faff / Journal of Banking & Finance 20 (1996) 419–438   421

GARCH model. Specifically, they concluded that the GJR-GARCH(3,1) specification was the superior fitting model.

While such model fitting investigations provide useful insights into volatility, the models are usually selected on the basis of full sample information. For practical forecasting purposes, the predictive ability of these models needs to be examined out-of-sample. The few papers that have tested the forecasting ability of ARCH models out-of-sample have reached inconsistent conclusions. Akgiray (1989) found that a GARCH(1,1) specification exhibited superior forecasting ability of monthly US stock market volatility compared to more traditional models. However, Tse (1991) and Tse and Tung (1992) questioned the superiority of the GARCH model in the Japanese and Singaporean markets, respectively. These latter two studies found evidence strongly in favour of an exponentially weighted moving average (EWMA) model. Dimson and Marsh (1990) in an examination of the UK equity market, concluded that the simple models provide more accurate forecasts, and recommended the exponential smoothing and simple regression models. However, Dimson and Marsh did not subject ARCH models to examination. [4] Nevertheless, the conclusions of Dimson and Marsh have important implications for forecasts obtained from the relatively complex GARCH model: "With the increasing interest in using complicated econometric techniques for volatility forecasting, our research strikes a warning bell. For those who are interested in forecasts with reasonable predictive accuracy, the best forecasting models may well be the simplest ones" (Dimson and Marsh (1990, p. 420)).

Using daily Australian data, the aim of this paper is to examine the relative ability of various models to forecast monthly stock market volatility. The forecasting models which are employed range from naive models to the relatively complex ARCH class of models. The various model rankings are shown to be sensitive to the error statistic used to assess the accuracy of the forecasts. Notwithstanding this sensitivity, the results suggest superior forecasts of volatility are provided by the ARCH class of models and a simple regression model. Of further note is the poor performance of some other models which have previously been identified in the literature as good performers.

2. The Australian environment [5]

Brailsford and Faff (1993) identify several distinguishing features of the Australian stock market which are worthy of further discussion. Specifically, these

---

[4] Dimson and Marsh (1990) investigated five volatility forecasting models: (1) a random walk model, (2) a long-term mean, (3) a moving average model, (4) an exponential smoothing model and (5) regression models.

[5] This section extends a similar discussion in Brailsford and Faff (1993, pp. 111–112).

features relate to the size of the market; the relative dominance of the largest stocks; the significance of resource sector stocks; the dominance of institutional investors; the degree of regulation; and the observed empirical regularities.

The Australian stock market comprises 1030 stocks with a total capitalisation of around USD$135 billion (at December 1992). The Australian Stock Exchange represents a small market with a small number of listed companies, of small per unit economic size when compared to the USA. For example, at the end of 1992 the US market had in excess of 7,000 listed stocks with a total market capitalisation of USD$4,758 billion. [6] However, in the context of the Asia Pacific region within which the Australian market operates, with the exception of Japan it assumes a position of relative importance. For example, in comparison the Singapore stock market had 163 listed companies with a total capitalisation of USD$49 billion, in 1992. [7] An alternative measure of market size is the total value of stocks traded in any given year. In 1992, USD$2,679 billion, USD$46 billion and USD$14 billion worth of trading occurred in the US, Australian and Singapore markets, respectively. [8]

The second feature of the Australian market is the dominance of trading activity in a relatively small number of the largest corporations. For example, the largest stock in the Australian market is Broken Hill Proprietary Company Ltd which at any one time constitutes approximately 8 to 10 percent of total market capitalisation. Moreover, the largest 10 stocks represent some 40 percent of the market capitalisation and trading value. [9] In comparison, only 15 percent of the total market capitalisation in the US was concentrated in the ten largest stocks in 1992. [10] Furthermore, many of the smaller Australian companies are typified by prolonged periods of little or even no trading activity (see Hathaway (1986, p. 51)). This market characteristic suggests a need to recognise the potential effects of thin trading in any analysis of data.

The third feature of the Australian stock market is the substantial influence which resource based stocks have upon the market. Australia is a resource rich country and relies heavily upon its rural and mining sectors. Resource stocks comprise about one third of the total market capitalisation. The performance of these stocks is dependent on many highly variable factors including, for example, the variability of commodity prices, which tends to induce greater volatility in price changes compared to industrial companies. Indeed, Ball and Brown (1980) have shown that while Australian resource stocks earned approximately the same mean return as their industrial counterparts over the period 1958 to 1979, the standard deviation of resource sector stocks was almost double that of industrial

---

[6] Source: International Finance Corporation (1993).
[7] ibid.
[8] ibid.
[9] Source: Australian Stock Exchange, 1993.
[10] Source: International Finance Corporation (1993).

T.J. Brailsford, R.W. Faff / Journal of Banking & Finance 20 (1996) 419–438   423

sector stocks. A similar result holds in the later period. [11] To the extent that resource stocks experience more volatile price changes, the Australian market is potentially more volatile than it otherwise would be.

The fourth feature of the Australian stock market is the composition of the investment community in terms of the mix between personal and institutional investors. The Australian market is typified by a relatively low incidence of direct personal investment, particularly since the occurrence of the Crash of October 1987. For example, only 10 percent of adult Australians were direct share owners at December 1991. Furthermore, 94 percent of the top 330 companies have at least 50 percent of their stock held by no more than 20 investors. [12]

The fifth feature of the Australian stock market is the degree of regulation. During the 1980s the Australian economy operated under a regime of continuing financial market deregulation. For example, in late 1983 the Australian dollar was floated, while in late 1984 foreign banks were granted licences to operate in Australia. Notwithstanding the significant progress toward general financial market deregulation over the past decade, it is true that some specific regulatory restrictions are more prevalent in Australia than in the USA. For example, the ability of investors to short sell securities in Australia is far more restrictive than in the USA. Indeed short selling was outlawed in Australia over the period 1971 to 1986. Since 1986 only restrictive short selling opportunities have been available. This constraint on trading could suggest, all other things equal, that the volatility of stock returns may be higher in Australia. For example, there is empirical evidence that the standard deviation of the Australian market is 30 percent larger than the standard deviation of the US market, (see Jaffe and Westerfield (1985)).

Arguably, the Australian financial system represents one of the more deregulated markets of the developed countries in the Asia-Pacific region. This is particularly the case during the last decade or so for the reasons discussed in the preceding paragraph. In contrast, the governments of countries such as Japan and Singapore are well known for their stringent market controls.

The final distinguishing feature of the Australian stock market is several observed empirical regularities which differ from many other stock markets. For example, the Australian market does not only exhibit a strong January seasonal as in the USA, but exhibits January, July and August seasonals (see Brown et al. (1983)). Of greater relevance to the current study is the finding of a significantly negative average Tuesday return in the Australian market. A similar Tuesday effect has also been documented in Japan (Kato, 1990), in Singapore (Condoyanni et al., 1987) and some other South-East Asian markets (Wong et al., 1992). This

---

[11] Over the period 1980 to 1993, the resource sector earned an average monthly return of 0.62 percent with a standard deviation of 8.70 percent while the industrial sector earned 1.48 percent with a standard deviation of only 6.05 percent.

[12] Source: Australian Stock Exchange, 1991.

Tuesday effect is in contrast to the widely observed Monday effect in many other markets, including the USA. [13] Consequently, any analysis of Australian data using the daily measurement interval needs to consider the impact of such empirical regularities.

3. Data

In order to investigate aggregate stock market volatility, a market index is required. The index used in our study is the Statex-Actuaries Accumulation Index. This index comprises the 50 most actively traded companies listed on the Australian Stock Exchange. Further, the index is an accumulation index and therefore yields a measure of total return. Our sample consists of over 4900 observations encompassing the period from 1 January 1974 to 30 June 1993. [14]

A preliminary investigation of the data reveals that the series is skewed, leptokurtic and exhibits a high degree of autocorrelation in both levels and squares. Specifically, the skewness estimate is -4.81, [15] the excess kurtosis estimate is 139.54, the $Q(20)$ statistic is 336.50 and the $Q^2(20)$ statistic is 137.26. [16]

To ensure that the volatility models use only data contained in the current information set, the raw monthly volatility series (which is used in forecasting), is defined as the sum of squared daily returns, viz: [17]

$$\sigma_T^2 = \sum_{t=1}^{N_T} r_t^2 \tag{1}$$

where r_t is the daily rate of return and N_T is the number of trading days in month T.

---

[13] For example, see Jaffe and Westerfield (1985) and Jaffe et al. (1989).

[14] Further details on the data are provided in Brailsford and Faff (1993).

[15] When data from October 1987 crash are excluded the skewness estimate falls to 0.11.

[16] The $Q(20)$ and $Q^2(20)$ statistics are from the Box–Pierce–Ljung test for first to twentieth-order autocorrelation in the returns and squared returns, respectively. The test statistics are approximate chi-squares with 20 degrees of freedom.

[17] As the true underlying monthly volatility series is unobservable, the entire analysis was also conducted on other volatility series and very similar results were obtained. In particular, these alternative series were: (1) the daily returns were adjusted for the within-month mean return, and (2) a series based on the daily return data adjusted for the effect of non-synchronous trading through the addition of cross-product terms (see French et al. (1987, p. 5)). Furthermore, as partial autocorrelation estimates for the daily rate of return indicated significant autocorrelation, a moving average process (MA(1)) was used to take account of the autocorrelation which may be induced by non-synchronous trading in the daily return series. The empirical regularities of the day of the week and holiday effects were also accounted for in a return model by running an OLS regression of returns on independent dichotomous dummy variables for days of the week and before and after holidays.

T.J. Brailsford, R.W. Faff / Journal of Banking & Finance 20 (1996) 419–438 425

4. Volatility forecasting models

The focus of this paper is on the forecasting accuracy of monthly stock market volatility from various statistical models. The basic methodology involves the estimation of the various models' parameters using an initial set of data and the application of these parameters to later data, thus forming out-of-sample forecasts. Following Akgiray (1989), Dimson and Marsh (1990), [18] Tse (1991) and Tse and Tung (1992), several forecasting models of volatility are investigated. These are (1) a random walk model, (2) an historical mean model, (3) a moving average model, (4) an exponential smoothing model, (5) an exponentially weighted moving average model, (6) a simple regression model, (7) two standard GARCH models and (8) two Glosten–Jagannathan–Runkle (GJR) asymmetric GARCH models. [19]

For all forecasting approaches, the initial data used for the estimation of the models' parameters are drawn from the period 1974 to 1985 (months $T = 1, 2, ..., 144$). Thus, the first month for which out-of-sample forecasts are obtained is January 1986 ($T = 145$). As the sample period covers 234 months, out-of-sample forecasts are constructed for months 145 to 234. Note that this period includes 1987 which requires the models to predict volatility in a period when actual volatility was extremely high.

4.1. Random walk model

Under a random walk model, the best forecast of this month's volatility is last month's observed volatility.

$$\hat{\sigma}_T^2(\text{RW}) = \sigma_{T-1}^2 \quad T = 145, 146, ..., 234. \tag{2}$$

where σ_T^2 is the monthly volatility measure defined in expression (1).

4.2. Historical mean model

Under the assumption of a stationary mean, the best forecast of this month's volatility is a long-term average of past observed volatilities.

$$\hat{\sigma}_T^2(\text{LTM}) = \frac{1}{T-1} \sum_{j=1}^{T-1} \sigma_j^2 \quad T = 145, 146, ..., 234. \tag{3}$$

---

[18] Note that Dimson and Marsh (1990) examine models of standard deviation.

[19] An alternative approach would entail calculating implied standard deviations from option prices (see Day and Lewis (1992)). However, such an approach requires an active options market on the index which unfortunately, does not exist in Australia.

4.3. Moving average models

A moving average is often used by market analysts as a predictor of mean returns. Further, this technique is often used in traditional time-series analysis. Thus, a moving average model is employed. The choice of the moving average estimation period is arbitrary. In this paper, five (mid-term) and twelve years (long-term) are chosen as estimation periods to ensure consistency with the estimation period of later models which require large samples for estimation. The twelve-year moving average model can be expressed as:

$$\hat{\sigma}_T^2(\text{MA}) = \frac{1}{144} \sum_{j=1}^{144} \sigma_{T-j}^2 \quad T = 145, 146,..., 234. \tag{4}$$

A similar formulation is used for the five-year moving average model where the summation is conducted over 60 months.

4.4. Exponential smoothing model

Following Dimson and Marsh (1990), an exponential smoothing model is used to forecast volatility. In this model, the forecast of volatility is posited to be a function of the immediate past forecast and the immediate past observed volatility.

$$\hat{\sigma}_T^2(\text{ES}) = \phi\hat{\sigma}_{T-1}^2(\text{ES}) + (1 - \phi)\sigma_{T-1}^2 \quad T = 145, 146,..., 234. \tag{5}$$

The smoothing parameter (ϕ) is constrained to lie between zero and one. The optimal value of ϕ must be determined empirically. If ϕ is zero, then the exponential smoothing model collapses to the random walk model. As ϕ approaches unity, the major weight is given to the prior period forecast which itself is heavily influenced by its immediate past forecast and so on. When forecasting, the optimal value of ϕ is chosen by a search of values between zero and one using data from $T = 1, 2,..., 144$ and selecting the value of ϕ which corresponds to the minimum prediction error. [20] Three error metrics were used to assess the minimum prediction error, namely the root mean squared error, the mean absolute error and the mean absolute percentage error. Based on the similarity of selected values of ϕ generated by the three error metrics, the root mean squared error metric is employed for the selection of ϕ. The smoothing parameter selection procedure is performed annually, whereby the estimation period is updated, thus resulting in a rolling 12-year estimation window. [21]

---

[20] The initial exponential smoothing forecast is taken to be t estimated volatility over the first month of the estimation period.

[21] Dimson and Marsh (1990) in their study of UK stock market volatility found that the optimal value of ϕ was 0.76. In this study, the value of ϕ ranges between 0.51 and 0.98.

4.5. Exponentially weighted moving average model

Following the work of Tse (1991) and Tse and Tung (1992), an exponentially weighted moving average model (EWMA) is examined. This model is similar to the exponential smoothing model except that the past observed volatility in expression (5) is replaced by the five-year moving average forecast which can be formally expressed as: [22]

$$\hat{\sigma}_T^2(\text{EWMA}) = \psi \hat{\sigma}_{T-1}^2(\text{EWMA}) + (1 - \psi)\hat{\sigma}_T^2(\text{MA})$$

$$T = 145, 146,..., 234. \tag{6}$$

Again, the selection of the smoothing parameter (ψ) value is an empirical issue. The optimal value of ψ is chosen by a search of values between zero and one using pre-sample data and selecting the value of ψ which corresponds to the minimum prediction error. Similar to the exponential smoothing model, the selected values of ψ do not vary considerably across error metrics and therefore, the root mean squared error is employed. The parameter selection procedure is also updated annually, employing a rolling 12-year window. [23]

4.6. Simple regression model

This model employs an OLS regression of observed volatilities on immediate past observed volatility, and the resulting volatility forecasts are given by:

$$\hat{\sigma}_T^2(\text{SR}) = \hat{\gamma}_0 + \hat{\gamma}_1 \sigma_{T-1}^2 \quad T = 145, 146,..., 234. \tag{7}$$

The model parameters are initially estimated over the 12-year period (from 1974 to 1985). These parameter estimates are subsequently used to forecast the volatility of January 1986 ($T = 145$). Two approaches are then used to obtain the new parameter estimates. Under the first approach, the parameter estimation window is anchored at January 1974 ($T = 1$), while the end of the window is continually updated as the most recent month's data become available. The second approach uses a constant window length of 12 years. Under this latter approach, the window is rolled forward one month at a time as the more recent data become available resulting in a 12-year rolling estimation period. As the results from the two estimation procedures are very similar, only the results using the estimation period of a 12-year rolling window are reported.

---

[22] A twelve-year moving average forecast was also used in the EWMA model in expression (6). These results do not substantially differ from those of the EWMA model forecasts reported in the text.

[23] Tse (1991) found the optimal value of ψ to be 0.86 in his study on the Japanese market, while Tse and Tung (1992) do not report the optimal value of ψ in their study on the Singapore market. In this study, the value of ψ ranges between 0.0 (following October 1987) and 0.9.

4.7. Standard GARCH models

The GARCH model involves the joint estimation of a conditional mean and a conditional variance equation. As the GARCH(1,1) model has generally been found to be the most appropriate of the standard ARCH family of models for stock return data, [24] this model is employed, viz: [25]

$$r_t = \gamma + \epsilon_t \tag{8}$$

where $\epsilon_t \sim N(0, h_t)$ and

$$h_t = \omega + \beta_1 h_{t-1} + \alpha_1 \epsilon_{t-1}^2. \tag{9}$$

The conditional variance equation (expression (9)) models the time varying nature of the volatility of the errors derived from the conditional mean equation. [26] An initial test for ARCH errors using Engle's LM procedure (Engle, 1982) yields a test statistic significant at the 0.001 level.

Following Engle and Bollerslev (1986) a daily s-step ahead forecast can be formed based on the GARCH(1,1) model as follows:

$$\hat{h}_{t+s}(G) = \hat{\omega} \sum_{i=0}^{s-2} \left(\hat{\alpha}_1 + \hat{\beta}_1 \right)^i + \left(\hat{\alpha}_1 + \hat{\beta}_1 \right)^{s-1} \hat{h}_{t+1} \quad s = 1, 2, ..., N_T. \tag{10}$$

where $\hat{h}_{t+1}$ is the one-day ahead volatility forecast for the first day of each month generated by the empirical counterpart of expression (9).

Monthly volatility forecasts are then formed by aggregating the s-step ahead daily forecasts across trading days in each month as follows:

$$\hat{\sigma}_T^2(G) = \sum_{s=1}^{N_T} \hat{h}_{t+s}(G) \tag{11}$$

where a given month (T) has N_T daily observations.

The monthly GARCH(1,1) volatility forecasts therefore become: [27]

$$\hat{\sigma}_T^2(G) = \hat{\omega} \sum_{s=1}^{N_T} \sum_{i=0}^{s-2} \left(\hat{\alpha}_1 + \hat{\beta}_1 \right)^i + \sum_{s=1}^{N_T} \left(\hat{\alpha}_1 + \hat{\beta}_1 \right)^{s-1} \hat{h}_{t+1} \tag{12}$$

$$T = 145, 146, ..., 234.$$

---

[24] This conclusion is consistent with the majority of research in this area such as Akgiray (1989), Baillie and DeGennaro (1990), Lamoureux and Lastrapes (1990) and Schwert and Seguin (1990).

[25] The conditional mean specification was also used taking account of predictable influences which had been identified as the effects of non-synchronous trading, days of the week and holidays. These results do not substantially differ from those reported in the text.

[26] In this paper, all GARCH models are estimated using maximum likelihood techniques and the Berndt et al. (1974) algorithm employing numerical derivatives and the assumption of conditional normality.

[27] Alternatively, monthly returns could be used in the GARCH model to obtain one-step ahead forecasts of monthly volatility. However, there are no ARCH effects in the monthly return series (LM test is insignificant at the 0.001 level). Hence, such a procedure is not used in this paper.

Initially the GARCH model is estimated over the 12-year period from 1974 to 1985. The parameter estimates of ω, α_1 and β_1 are then used in (10) to obtain daily s-step ahead forecasts for each month. These volatility forecasts initially cover the trading days in January 1986 ($T = 145$) and their summation yields the monthly forecast for that month according to (11). The start and end dates of the parameter estimation period are then rolled forward one calendar month and the model parameters are re-estimated. These new estimates are used to forecast daily s-step ahead volatilities for each trading day over the next month (February 1986 or $T = 146$) and their summation yields that month's volatility forecast. This procedure is repeated, rolling forward the estimation window one calendar month at a time until the forecast for the final calendar month (June 1993 or $T = 234$) is obtained.

In a general investigation of fitting conditional volatility models in the Australian stock market. Brailsford and Faff (1993), using the same data as the current paper, considered higher order ARCH models, but concluded that the GARCH(1,1) specification was preferred. However, when higher order GARCH(p,q) models were examined, it was found that a GARCH(3,1) specification was preferred to the GARCH(1,1) counterpart. Hence, the forecasting ability of the GARCH(3,1) model is also examined here. The conditional variance equation becomes: [28]

$$h_t = \omega + \beta_1 h_{t-1} + \beta_2 h_{t-2} + \beta_3 h_{t-3} + \alpha_1 \epsilon_{t-1}^2. \tag{13}$$

A similar forecasting procedure to the GARCH(1,1) model is used to obtain daily volatility forecasts for the GARCH(3,1) model which are then summed over trading days in each month to obtain monthly volatility forecasts. Again, a rolling 12-year window is used as the estimation period commencing with the period 1974 to 1985, and forecasts are obtained for months $T = 145, 146,..., 234$.

4.8. GJR-GARCH models

The standard GARCH model is symmetric in its response to past innovations. However, there are theoretical arguments which suggest a differential response in conditional variance to past positive and negative innovations. The two main arguments are related to corporate leverage and information arrival. [29] Several alternative GARCH model specifications have been proposed in an attempt to capture the asymmetric nature of volatility responses. Engle and Ng (1993) in a test of volatility models on Japanese stock return data find strong support for the GJR-GARCH (Glosten et al., 1993) model which explicitly incorporates the

---

[28] The conditional mean equation of the GARCH(3,1) model remains the same as Eq. (8).

[29] Refer to Black (1976), Christie (1982) and Nelson (1991) for a discussion of the effects of corporate leverage on volatility, and Campbell and Hentschel (1992) for a discussion of the relationship between information arrival and volatility.

potential for asymmetry in the conditional variance equation. Similarly, Brailsford and Faff (1993) also find the GJR-GARCH models to be preferable to standard GARCH models using Australian stock return data.

Specifically, the GJR-GARCH model augments the conditional variance equation in the GARCH(p,q) model with a variable equal to the product of S_t^- and ϵ_{t-1}^2, where S_t^- is a dichotomous dummy variable that takes the value of unity if ϵ_{t-1} is negative and zero otherwise. In the case of the GJR-GARCH(1,1) version of the model, the conditional variance equation becomes: [30]

$$h_t = \omega + \beta_1 h_{t-1} + \alpha_1 \epsilon_{t-1}^2 + \gamma S_t^- \epsilon_{t-1}^2. \tag{14}$$

Brailsford and Faff (1993) also examined the fit of higher order GJR-GARCH(p,q) specifications. They found that the GJR-GARCH(3,1) model was preferred to all other models investigated. Hence, the forecasting ability of this model is also examined and the conditional variance equation becomes: [31]

$$h_t = \omega + \beta_1 h_{t-1} + \beta_2 h_{t-2} + \beta_3 h_{t-3} + \alpha_1 \epsilon_{t-1}^2 + \gamma S_t^- \epsilon_{t-1}^2 \tag{15}$$

A similar forecasting procedure to the standard GARCH models in Section 4.7 is used to obtain daily volatility forecasts for both GJR-GARCH specifications which are then summed over trading days in each month to obtain monthly volatility forecasts. Again, a rolling 12-year window is used as the estimation period commencing with the period 1974 to 1985, and forecasts are obtained for months $T = 145, 146,..., 234$.

5. Out-of-sample model forecast results

5.1. Definition of the forecast error statistics

Previous papers have used a variety of statistics to evaluate and compare forecast errors. [32] Consistent with this research, the 90 monthly forecast errors generated from each model in this study are compared by the mean error (ME), the mean absolute error (MAE), the root mean squared error (RMSE) and the mean absolute percentage error (MAPE) which are defined as follows:

$$\text{ME} = \frac{1}{90} \sum_{T=1}^{90} \left(\hat{\sigma}_T^2 - \sigma_T^2 \right) \tag{16}$$

$$\text{MAE} = \frac{1}{90} \sum_{T=1}^{90} |\hat{\sigma}_T^2 - \sigma_T^2| \tag{17}$$

---

[30] The conditional mean equation of the GJR-GARCH(1,1) model remains the same as Eq. (8).
[31] The conditional mean equation of the GJR-GARCH(3,1) model remains the same as Eq. (8).
[32] See Akgiray (1989), Dimson and Marsh (1990), Tse (1991) and Tse and Tung (1992).

Table 1
Error statistics from forecasting monthly volatility

	ME	MAE		RMSE		MAPE	
	Actual	Actual	Relative	Actual	Relative	Actual	Relative
Random walk	−0.00001	0.00427	0.951	0.01870	1.000	1.06022	0.449
Historical mean	−0.00102	0.00318	0.708	0.01441	0.771	1.39229	0.589
Moving average (5-year)	−0.00000	0.00405	0.902	0.01455	0.778	2.36392	1.000
Moving average (12-year)	−0.00101	0.00327	0.728	0.01446	0.773	1.47063	0.622
Exponential smoothing	0.00094	0.00449	1.000	0.01477	0.790	2.29353	0.970
EWMA	−0.00086	0.00361	0.804	0.01453	0.777	1.74513	0.738
Simple regression	−0.00107	0.00315	0.702	0.01441	0.771	1.37149	0.580
GARCH(1,1)	−0.00181	0.00324	0.722	0.01542	0.825	0.57398	0.243
GARCH(3,1)	−0.00082	0.00317	0.706	0.01537	0.822	0.86086	0.364
GJR-GARCH(1,1)	−0.00255	0.00292	0.650	0.01449	0.775	0.56895	0.241
GJR-GARCH(3,1)	−0.00108	0.00310	0.690	0.01527	0.817	0.76393	0.323

Calculated values are provided for four different error statistics across eleven models used to forecast monthly volatility. ME is a mean error statistic defined by expression (16); MAE is a mean absolute error statistic defined by expression (17); RMSE is a root mean squared error statistic defined by expression (18), and MAPE is a mean absolute percentage error statistic defined by expression (19). The error statistics are applied to forecasts obtained over the period January 1986 to June 1993. The relative error statistics are obtained by expressing the actual statistic as a ratio relative to the worst performing model for a given error measure.

$$\text{RMSE} = \sqrt{\frac{1}{90} \sum_{T=1}^{90} \left(\hat{\sigma}_T^2 - \sigma_T^2 \right)^2} \tag{18}$$

$$\text{MAPE} = \frac{1}{90} \sum_{T=1}^{90} |\left(\hat{\sigma}_T^2 - \sigma_T^2 \right)/\sigma_T^2|. \tag{19}$$

Dimson and Marsh (1990) further standardise each error statistic by the value of the error statistic obtained from the random walk forecast. The advantage of such a procedure is that the statistics can be more easily interpreted relative to a benchmark forecast. In this study, each error statistic is also expressed on a relative basis where the benchmark is the value of the statistic for the worst performing model.

5.2. Forecast results

Table 1 presents the actual and relative forecast error statistics for each model across the four error measures. An examination of Table 1 reveals that no single model is clearly superior. The ME does not allow for the offsetting effect of errors of different signs and as such, little credence should be placed upon it. However, the mean error can be used as a general guide as to the direction of over/under-prediction. All models are found to under-predict volatility, with the exception of the exponential smoothing model.

The MAE statistic indicates that the GJR-GARCH(1,1) model provides the most accurate forecasts. This forecast model is 35 percent more accurate than the benchmark model which, for this error statistic, is the exponential smoothing model. The GJR-GARCH(3,1) model ranks a close second. However, the MAE statistic does not allow for a clear distinction between the higher ranking models which is evidenced by the marginal (2.6 percent) difference in relative accuracy which separates the next five ranked models.

The RMSE statistic equally favours the historical mean and simple regression models which are 23 percent more accurate than the benchmark model which is the random walk model. The exponential smoothing model now ranks seventh. The GJR-GARCH(1,1) model now ranks fourth, but it is only slightly less accurate than the best model and is still 22.5 percent more accurate than the benchmark model. Furthermore, while the GJR-GARCH(3,1) model now ranks eighth, it too is not substantially worse than the best ranked model. Indeed, it is difficult to distinguish between the higher ranking models as evidenced by the top six ranking models which are separated by only 0.7 percent in forecasting accuracy.

The MAPE statistic gives a relative indication of overall forecasting performance. The GJR-GARCH(1,1) model has the best (actual) MAPE of 56.9 percent. The standard GARCH(1,1) model ranks second and is only marginally less accurate. Notably, the four GARCH models rank as the top four models. While the MAPE estimates for all four GARCH models may be considered as high in absolute terms, the corresponding estimates for the other models are all substantially higher. The worst performing model, as assessed by the MAPE statistic, is the moving average (5-year) model. The best GARCH class models are 76 percent more accurate than the benchmark model while the random walk model which is the next ranking non-GARCH model, is only 55 percent more accurate than the benchmark. Thus, the MAPE statistic clearly identifies the GARCH class models as superior.

In summary, the ranking of any one forecasting model varies depending upon the choice of error statistic. This sensitivity in rankings highlights the potential hazard of selecting the best model on the basis of an arbitrarily chosen error statistic. Notably, the RMSE statistic is equivalent to the primary error measure used by Dimson and Marsh (1990) to reach their conclusion that the simple regression model is superior. [33] Consistent with this finding, our results also indicate that the simple regression model is ranked (equal) first by the RMSE statistic. Furthermore, Dimson and Marsh find that the superiority of the simple

---

[33] Dimson and Marsh (1990) use the MSE (mean squared error) statistic.

T.J. Brailsford, R.W. Faff / Journal of Banking & Finance 20 (1996) 419–438   433

regression model is insensitive to the use of the MAE statistic which is again generally consistent with our MAE results. However, while Dimson and Marsh find an equivalent ranking across all models between their error statistics, our model rankings, while similar, are not entirely robust between the RMSE and MAE statistics. This inconsistency in rankings is exacerbated further when other error statistics, such as the MAPE statistic, are considered. For example, the random walk model ranks second last and last for the MAE and RMSE metrics respectively, yet ranks fifth (only behind the GARCH class models) for the MAPE metric. Hence, the results of Dimson and Marsh may not be robust to other error statistics, contrary to their claim (see Dimson and Marsh (1990, pp. 416–418)). Nevertheless, if the GARCH class model results are excluded from Table 1, the simple regression model ranks first for the MAE and RMSE metrics and second for the MAPE metric, generally consistent with the results of Dimson and Marsh (1990).

Also of note from Table 1 is the consistently poor performance of the EWMA model which ranks eighth, fifth and ninth out of the eleven models under the MAE, RMSE and MAPE statistics, respectively. This evidence is in direct conflict to the results of Tse (1991) and Tse and Tung (1992) which show the EWMA to be clearly superior under the same error metrics. [34] In conclusion, while it is difficult to claim superiority of any one model, the GJR-GARCH(1,1) model is our choice.

5.3. Asymmetric loss functions

The error statistics reported in Table 1 assume that the underlying loss function is symmetric. From a practical viewpoint, it is conceivable that many investors will not attribute equal importance to both over- and under-predictions of volatility of similar magnitude. For example, consider the positive relationship between the volatility of underlying stock prices and call option prices. An under-prediction of stock price volatility will lead to a downward biased estimate of the call option price. This under-estimate of the price is more likely to be of greater concern to a seller than a buyer. The reverse is true of over-predictions of stock price volatility. In the spirit of Pagan and Schwert (1990), [35] to account for the potential

---

[34] However, it should be noted that in highly regulated markets, such as Japan and Singapore, that the objectives of the regulators is often to dampen volatility. Hence, forecasting models which use a smoothing parameter may be expected to perform better in such markets than in less regulated markets. This may explain the inconsistency between our results and those of Tse (1991) and Tse and Tung (1992).

[35] The restrictions of the standard assumptions on loss functions has been recognised and relaxed in previous work, such as Pagan and Schwert (1990, p. 280) who employ a proportional loss function measure as opposed to a quadratic loss function.

asymmetry in the loss function, we construct an error statistic which penalises under-predictions more heavily and is called the mean mixed error (MME(U)): [36]

$$\text{MME}(U) = \frac{1}{90}\left[\sum_{T=1}^{O} |\hat{\sigma}_T^2 - \sigma_T^2| + \sum_{T=1}^{U} \sqrt{|\hat{\sigma}_T^2 - \sigma_T^2|}\right] \qquad (20)$$

where O is the number of over-predictions and U is the number of under-predictions.

Similarly, the above statistic can be redefined so to weight over-predictions more heavily and is constructed as follows:

$$\text{MME}(O) = \frac{1}{90}\left[\sum_{T=1}^{O} \sqrt{|\hat{\sigma}_T^2 - \sigma_T^2|} + \sum_{T=1}^{U} |\hat{\sigma}_T^2 - \sigma_T^2|\right]. \qquad (21)$$

A 'biased' forecast model can be viewed as one which systematically over- or under-predicts, whereas an 'unbiased' forecast model should, when not providing a perfect forecast, over-predict 50 percent of the time and under-predict 50 percent of the time. Table 2 presents the MME statistics and the number of times that the models over- and under-predict. From the number of over- and under-predictions reported in Table 2, only the random walk and the GJR-GARCH(3,1) models can be claimed to provide 'unbiased' forecasts. These models provide the only cases in which the null hypothesis of an equal number of over- and under-predictions can be accepted at standard significance levels. With the exception of the GJR-GARCH(1,1) model, the remaining models all systematically over-predict volatility. However, it is notable that systematic over-prediction of the other models is a result of decreasing average volatility in the out-of-sample test period compared to the estimation period. This feature arises because of the Crash of October 1987. [37] No doubt a different period could result in systematic under-prediction.

Recall that in Table 1, according to the ME statistic, with the exception of the exponential smoothing model, all models were found to under-predict volatility. This apparently contrasts with the results presented in Table 2 which indicate that all models except the random walk and GJR-GARCH(1,1) models over-predict volatility. The paradox is explained as the ME statistic takes into account the *magnitude* of forecasting errors, whereas Table 2 presents the *number* of over/under-predictions and ignores the magnitude of forecast errors. Hence, most of the models over-predict volatility more frequently but with relatively small

---

[36] As the absolute values of all forecast errors are less than unity, taking their square root will place a heavier weighting on the under-predictions. If the absolute value of all forecast errors were greater than unity, the MME(U) would need to square the errors in order to achieve the desired penalty.

[37] October 1987 is the 22nd month in the 90 month out-of-sample forecasting period. The surge in volatility over this month creates a dramatic increase in average volatility which subsequently declines from then on as volatility never reaches the same level again.

T.J. Brailsford, R.W. Faff / Journal of Banking & Finance 20 (1996) 419–438   435

Table 2
Mean mixed error statistics from forecasting monthly volatility and results of under- and over-prediction

	MME(U)		MME(O)		Under-predictions	Over-predictions	Binomial prob.
	Actual	Relative	Actual	Relative			
Random walk	0.02137	0.659	0.02284	0.516	45	45	0.458
Historical mean	0.01482	0.457	0.02944	0.665	23	67	0.000
Moving average (5-year)	0.01484	0.458	0.03965	0.895	21	69	0.000
Moving average (12-year)	0.01558	0.481	0.02979	0.673	24	66	0.000
Exponential smoothing	0.01281	0.395	0.04429	1.000	17	73	0.000
EWMA	0.01759	0.543	0.03241	0.732	26	64	0.000
Simple regression	0.01445	0.446	0.02773	0.626	24	66	0.000
GARCH(1,1)	0.01067	0.329	0.02847	0.643	27	63	0.000
GARCH(3,1)	0.01669	0.515	0.02202	0.497	34	56	0.007
GJR-GARCH(1,1)	0.03241	1.000	0.00654	0.148	76	14	0.000
GJR-GARCH(3,1)	0.01875	0.579	0.01922	0.434	39	51	0.085

Calculated values are provided for two different error statistics across eleven models used to forecast monthly volatility. MME(U) is a mean mixed error which penalises under-predictions more heavily and is defined by expression (20). MME(O) is a mean mixed error which penalises over-predictions more heavily and is defined by expression (21). These statistics are designed to capture potential asymmetry in the loss function. The error statistics are applied to forecasts obtained over the period January 1986 to June 1993. The number of under- and over-predictions are provided for each set of forecasts. The associated binomial probability is based on the test that the number of under-predictions and over-predictions are equal.

errors. In contrast, when the models under-predict volatility, they do so by a relatively large amount. Also note that in Table 1, the GJR-GARCH(1,1) model had the largest negative ME measure and it is the only model which under-predicts more frequently in Table 2. Conversely, the exponential smoothing model is the only model which had a positive ME measure in Table 1 and it has the highest frequency of over-predictions in Table 2.

The MME(U) statistics in Table 2 indicate superiority of the standard GARCH(1,1) model, while the GJR-GARCH(1,1) and random walk models provide the worst forecasts. This is not surprising as these models provide the greatest number of under-predictions which receive a heavier penalty than over-predictions in the computation of the MME(U) statistic. Also of note is the relatively good performance of models previously identified (in Table 1) as poor performers. For example, the exponential smoothing model was ranked last, seventh and tenth by the MAE, RMSE and MAPE statistics respectively, but is the second best forecasting model according to the MME(U) statistic.

The MME(O) statistic which penalises over-prediction errors more heavily, ranks the GJR-GARCH(1,1) model first while the exponential smoothing model is now ranked last. [38] This contrast in model rankings again illustrates that the forecasts are highly sensitive to the assessment criteria. Hence, caution should be exercised in the interpretation of the obtained rankings. Moreover, the choice of error measure should reflect an appropriate underlying loss function which in turn depends on the ultimate purpose of the forecasting procedure. For example, again using the call option context, a buyer of a call option being more concerned with over-predictions, would prefer the MME(O) statistic and hence would favour the GJR-GARCH model.

6. Summary

This paper has examined the ability of various models to forecast aggregate monthly stock market volatility in Australia. The models which were tested included a random walk model, an historical mean model, a moving average model, an exponential smoothing model, an exponentially weighted moving average (EWMA) model, a simple regression model, two standard GARCH models and two asymmetric GJR-GARCH models. Contrary to prior evidence, the results in this paper suggest that no single model is clearly superior. The rankings of the various model forecasts are sensitive to the choice of error statistic.

In addition to the traditional error measures, a mean mixed error statistic was constructed to allow for the asymmetry in the loss function of investors, and this measure also provided a conflict in model rankings. Given the conflicting nature of the results, we urge caution in the interpretation of various error measures and recommend that use be determined according to the purpose for which the forecasts are provided.

Nevertheless, consistent with the findings of Dimson and Marsh (1990), we find some support for a simple regression model. However, when ARCH class models are considered, they are found to be at least equal, if not superior to the simple regression model. In particular, the evidence favours the GJR-GARCH(1,1) specification.

Acknowledgements

We wish to thank Richard Baillie, Fischer Black, Tim Bollerslev, Jon Kendall, Keith McLaren, Alan Ramsay, anonymous referees of this journal, G.P. Szego (the

---

[38] Note that while the GJR-GARCH(1,1) and exponential smoothing models appear to almost reverse their extreme ranks, there is no consistent negative correlation in the comparative rankings of other models resulting from the MME(U) and MME(O) statistics. For example, the EWMA model ranks eighth and ninth under the respective MME(U) and MME(O) statistics.

editor), seminar participants at the Australian National University, Monash University, the Universities of Melbourne, New South Wales, Queensland, Southern Queensland and Tasmania, and participants at the Fourth Australasian Finance and Banking Conference (Sydney), the Third Asia Pacific Finance Conference (Singapore) and the 1993 Annual Conference of the Accounting Association of Australia and New Zealand (Darwin) for helpful comments on earlier versions of this paper. The first author gratefully acknowledges the financial assistance of a Coopers and Lybrand Travel Grant.

References

Akgiray, V., 1989, Conditional heteroscedasticity in time series of stock returns: Evidence and forecasts, Journal of Business 62, 55–80.

Ang, J.S., 1991, Agenda for research in pacific-basin finance, in: S.G. Rhee and R.P. Chang, eds., Pacific-Basin capital markets research, Volume II (Elsevier Science, North-Holland), 201–210.

Australian Stock Exchange, 1991, Australian share ownership.

Australian Stock Exchange, 1993, Fact book.

Baillie, R.T. and R.P. DeGennaro, 1990, Stock returns and volatility, Journal of Financial and Quantitative Analysis 25, 203–214.

Ball, R. and P. Brown, 1980, Risk and return from equity investments in the Australian mining industry: January 1958 to February 1979, Australian Journal of Management 5, 45–66.

Berndt, E.K., B.H. Hall, R.E. Hall and J.A. Hausman, 1974, Estimation and inference in nonlinear structural models, Annals of Economic and Social Measurement 4, 653–665.

Black, F., 1976, Studies of stock price volatility changes, American Statistical Association – 1976, Proceedings of the Business and Economic Section, Boston, 177–181.

Bollerslev, T., R.Y. Chou and K.F. Kroner, 1992, ARCH modelling in finance: A review of the theory and empirical evidence, Journal of Econometrics 52, 61–90.

Brailsford, T.J. and R.W. Faff, 1993, Modelling Australian stock market volatility, Australian Journal of Management 18, 109–132.

Brown, P., D. Keim, A. Kleidon and T. Marsh, 1983, Stock return seasonalities and the tax-loss selling hypothesis: Analysis of the arguments and Australian evidence, Journal of Financial Economics 12, 105–127.

Campbell, J.Y. and L. Hentschel, 1992, No news is good news: An asymmetric model of changing volatility in stock returns, Journal of Financial Economics 31, 281–318.

Christie, A.A., 1982, The stochastic behaviour of common stock variances: Value, leverage and interest rate effects, Journal of Financial Economics 10, 407–432.

Condoyanni, L., J. O'Hanlon and C.W.R. Ward, 1987, Day of the week effects on stock returns: International evidence, Journal of Business Finance and Accounting 14, 159–174.

Day, T.E. and C.M. Lewis, 1992, Stock market volatility and the information content of stock index options, Journal of Econometrics 52, 267–287.

de Jong, F., A. Kemna and T. Kloek, 1992, A contribution to event study methodology with an application to the Dutch stock market, Journal of Banking and Finance 16, 11–36.

Dimson, E. and P. Marsh, 1990, Volatility forecasting without data-snooping, Journal of Banking and Finance 14, 399–421.

Engle, R.F., 1982, Autoregressive conditional heteroskedasticity with estimates of the variance of United Kingdom inflation, Econometrica 50, 987–1007.

Engle, R.F. and T. Bollerslev, 1986, Modelling the persistence of conditional variances, Econometric Reviews 5, 1–50.

Engle, R.F. and Ng, V.K., 1993, Measuring and testing the impact of news on volatility, Journal of Finance 48, 1749–1778.

French, K.R., G.W. Schwert and R.F. Stambaugh, 1987, Expected stock returns and volatility, Journal of Financial Economics 19, 3–29.

Glosten, L.R., R. Jagannathan and D.E. Runkle, 1993, On the relation between the expected value and the volatility of the nominal excess return on stocks, Journal of Finance 48, 1779–1801.

Hathaway, N., 1986, The non-stationarity of share price volatility, Accounting and Finance 26, 35–54.

International Finance Corporation, 1993, Emerging stock markets factbook (IFC, Washington DC).

Jaffe, J. and R. Westerfield, 1985, The week-end effect in common stock returns: The international evidence, Journal of Finance 41, 433–454.

Jaffe, J., R. Westerfield and C. Ma, 1989, A twist on the Monday effect in stock prices: Evidence from the US and foreign stock markets, Journal of Banking and Finance 13, 641–650.

Kato, K., 1990, Weekly patterns in Japanese stock returns, Management Science 36, 1031–1043.

Kearns, P. and A.R. Pagan, 1993, Australian stock market volatility: 1875–1987, The Economic Record 69, 163–178.

Lamoureux, C.G. and W.D. Lastrapes, 1990, Persistence in variance, structural change, and the GARCH model, Journal of Business and Economic Statistics 8, 225–234.

Nelson, D.B., 1991, Conditional heteroscedasticity in asset returns: A new approach, Econometrica 59, 347–370.

Pagan, A.R. and G.W. Schwert, 1990, Alternative models for conditional stock volatility, Journal of Econometrics 45, 267–290.

Poon, S-H. and S.J. Taylor, 1992, Stock returns and volatility: An empirical study of the UK stock market, Journal of Banking and Finance 16, 37–59.

Schwert, G.W., 1990, Stock market volatility, Financial Analysts Journal 46, 23–34.

Schwert, G.W. and P.J. Seguin, 1990, Heteroskedasticity in stock returns, Journal of Finance 45, 1129–1155.

Tse, Y.K., 1991, Stock return volatility in the Tokyo stock exchange, Japan and the World Economy 3, 285–298.

Tse, Y.K. and S.H. Tung, 1992, Forecasting volatility in the Singapore stock market, Asia Pacific Journal of Management 9, 1–13.

Wong, K.A., T.K. Hui and C.Y. Chan, 1992, Day of the week effects: Evidence from developing stock markets, Applied Financial Economics 2, 49–56.

[20]
ARBITRAGE VALUATION OF VARIANCE FORECASTS WITH SIMULATED OPTIONS

Robert F. Engle,* Che-Hsiung (Ted) Hong,[†] Alex Kane,[‡] and Jaesun Noh*

I. INTRODUCTION

When probability distributions of asset rates of return are time varying, forecasts of portfolio variance will be desired by investors. Even those who pursue passive strategies would need periodic variance forecasts to calibrate efficient asset allocation (e.g., Bodie 1988). The criterion for choosing between any pair of competing algorithms to forecast the variance of an asset return would be the expected incremental profit of a switch from the lesser to the better one.

*Department of Economics, University of California, San Diego.
[†]Nomura Securities Inc , New York City.
[‡]Graduate School of International Relations and Pacific Studies, University of
  California, San Diego.

Advances in Futures and Options Research,
Volume 6, pages 393–415.
ISBN: 1-55938-492-1

394   ROBERT ENGLE, CHE-HSIUNG HONG, ALEX KANE, and JAESUN NOH

In this paper we propose a technique to assess incremental profits for a set of competing forecasts of the variance of a given portfolio. The proposed technique exploits the role of volatility in the pricing of contingent claims. It incorporates into the analysis considerations of hedge positions, which also depend on variance forecasts. We demonstrate the technique with the NYSE portfolio experience over the period of July 3, 1962, to December 29, 1989.

We estimate incremental profits of algorithms to forecast portfolio variance by setting up a hypothetical insurance market. Each forecasting algorithm is used exclusively by one hypothetical agent in an ex post forecasting exercise. The hypothetical agents prepare a forecast for every period of the exercise using past observations of the portfolio rates of return, and they set a price for one-period options on one dollar's worth of the target portfolio. In the beginning of each period, upon examination of the entire set of forecast-induced option prices, each agent buys any option believed to be underpriced. In the ex post part of the exercise, actual subsequent-portfolio returns are used to settle the agent accounts. The period profits and losses accumulate in the agent accounts over the entire exercise.

Profits and losses that accumulate over the exercise period represent the relative success of agents, and hence of the forecasting algorithms that they represent. In the present experiment, one-day options on \$1 shares of the NYSE are priced from the following specifications of the NYSE return process: (1) moving average of squared daily returns; (2) ordinary least squares: the variance rate is estimated from the standard error of an AR(1) on the daily rate; (3) ARMA(1,1) on squared errors; and (4) GARCH [autogregressive conditional heteroskedasticity] (1,1). Each of the four specifications is used by three algorithms that differ in the number of past observations in the rolling sample used to estimate the specification parameters. The three sample lengths are (1) 300 days, (2) 1,000 days, and (3) the entire available history, up to 5,000 observations.

The main objective of the work presented here is to introduce this preference-free approach to the economic evaluation of variance forecasts. We have no commitment to the algorithms that were chosen to compete, and we limit the investigation to options of short maturity to minimize the import of the adequacy of the Black–Scholes pricing model when the variance is stochastic. Aspects of the forecast horizon and option maturity are left to a subsequent investigation.

To preview the results in this experiment with the NYSE portfolio, the GARCH(1,1) specification is best. The worst performer of the specification set is ARMA(1,1). Because the economic performance of the various specifications in the experiment has been significantly different, inferences about the relationship between stock price and changes in volatility, as in Poterba and Summers (1986), should be reexamined. Evidence from the experiment also indicates that some restriction on the length of the rolling sample may lead to improved forecasts.

We allow agents to hedge their variance-forecast-driven transactions by taking positions in the NYSE stock. In a Black–Scholes framework these would be riskless portfolios. However, here they are not riskless. Evidence from the experiment suggests that imperfect hedge ratios due to variance-forecasting errors affect the risk reduction capacity in an economically significant way. The hedging activity itself helps to distinguish better forecasting algorithms.

Theoretical arguments in favor of the proposed forecasting valuation technique are presented in Section I. Section II develops the mechanics of the valuation method and describes the details of the experiment involving the forecasting of the variance of the NYSE portfolio. Discussion of the experiment results can be found in Section III. Summary and suggestions for future research conclude the paper.

II. THEORETICAL UNDERPINNINGS

In the genre of choosing of optimal forecasts, a comparison of return-variance forecasts is unique. The variance is unobservable and there is no natural metric for measuring the dollar value of forecast errors. But realized rates of return allow us to test the efficacy of variance-driven option prices, thus providing an appropriate loss function. The role of variance in no-arbitrage pricing of contingent claims suggests that the best forecast algorithm should be decided on performance in correctly pricing contingent claims on the asset in question.

This approach is different from testing the correlation between observed option-price implied volatility and some measure of subsequently realized variance. Instead we ask which forecast technique (which may include implied volatility from past option prices) would lead to better pricing of new options.

In efficient capital markets when the variance of the rate of return on a target asset is constant over time and where options on the asset are traded, an option price implies an estimate of the asset variance. Under such ideal circumstances, indeed by the definition of market efficiency, option prices would yield preferred estimates of asset variances. Schmalensee and Trippi (1978) and others have shown that call-option-implied variances yield better forecasts of standard deviation than do simple estimates of standard deviation from past returns.

When the variance is time varying, the hedge ratio that allows arbitrage pricing depends on the unknown variance. It may still be possible to compute the implied expected variance over the life of an efficiently priced option, if unexpected changes in variance over the life of the option are nonsystematic (see Wiggins 1987 and Hull and White 1987). Such circumstance is not guaranteed, particularly when the asset in question is a well-diversified portfolio.

Indeed, with time-varying variances, we cannot even take for granted that the market is efficient with respect to any variance forecast. Such determination can be reached only when no known variance-forecasting algorithm can be used to profit from trading in the asset and its derivatives. The technique proposed here can also be applied to the question of market efficiency with respect to specific variance forecasts.

As information asymmetry about asset variance develops, a natural strategy for an informed investor would be to set up a hedged position that includes the asset and options. This position cannot be made entirely risk free. However, a strategy that consistently employs superior variance forecasts may be expected to yield a superior risk-reward ratio.

We chose for our first experiment short-term variance forecasts utilized to price short-lived options. We realize that tests of longer-range forecasts, to be used for pricing longer-maturity options, may be of greater economic value. The experiment and analysis in this paper relates short (one day) variance forecasts to profit opportunities from pricing one-day options on the NYSE portfolio. The advantage of this framework is that the variance can be taken as constant over the day but allowed to vary from one day to the next.

Estimates of the relative profitability of alternative variance-forecast algorithms depend on which option-pricing formula is used. At the same time, the validity of the experiment does not depend on whether the user knows with certainty that the formula used is actually implicit in market prices; only that it is the one he or she would bet on if and when contingent claims had to be written on the asset. In this case we use the Black–Scholes formula since the horizon is so short. It is understood, however, that further experimentation will be required whenever a different option-pricing formula comes into favor.

Another issue of methodology is transitivity in the dominance relationship among variance forecasts. When the experiment is performed with more than two hypothetical agents, representing more than two competing forecast algorithms, the winner is not guaranteed to dominate every agent in a different grouping or in pair-wise competition. This issue has to be empirically addressed.

III.   APPLICATION OF THE VALUATION METHOD TO THE NYSE PORTFOLIO

It is best to describe the valuation methodology as it applies to a specific experiment. Here we apply it to the NYSE portfolio using daily returns from July 3, 1962, to December 29, 1989. We begin by describing the competing variance-forecast algorithms.

A.   The Set of Competing Variance Forecasts

We test four specifications for the return generating process of the NYSE portfolio, and three alternative lengths of rolling samples from past data to update estimates of the specification parameters. The four specifications are detailed below with the following notation: Z_t denotes the portfolio return; a subscript t dates observations and forecasts; a subscript n on a forecast, or parameter estimate, refers to the length of the rolling sample that is used every day to produce the variance forecast for the next day; finally σ^2 denotes a variance forecast.

1. *Moving Average Variance: The MA Model*

The forecast for the next-day variance, using the n most recent observations, is

$$\sigma^2_{n,t+1} = \frac{1}{n-1} \sum_{j=t-n+1}^{t} (Z_j - \bar{Z}_{n,t})^2 \tag{1}$$

where

$$\bar{Z}_{n,t} = \frac{1}{n} \sum_{j=t-n+1}^{t} Z_j. \tag{2}$$

2. *Ordinary Least Square: The OLS Model*

The rate of return is assumed to follow an AR(1),

$$Z_t = a_{n,t} + b_{n,t} Z_{t-1} + \varepsilon_t \tag{3}$$

and the forecast is

$$\sigma^2_{n,t+1} = \frac{1}{n-1} \sum_{j=t-n+1}^{t} \varepsilon_j^2. \tag{4}$$

3. *ARMA(1,1) in the squared residual: The ARMA Model*

As in the OLS model,

$$Z_t = a_{n,t} + b_{n,t} Z_{t-1} + \varepsilon_t \tag{5}$$

except that the squared residual follows:

$$\varepsilon_t^2 = w_{n,t} + v_{n,t} \varepsilon_{t-1}^2 + u_t - d_{n,t} u_{t-1}. \tag{6}$$

The inclusion of this process was motivated by the work of Poterba and Summers (1986), where the sample variance of the residual was assumed to follow an AR(1). This specification differs from the GARCH(1,1) only by the estimation method. In this case conventional unweighted Box Jenkins methods are used while the GARCH estimates recognize that the innovations are heteroskedastic. The variance forecast will be

398   ROBERT ENGLE, CHE-HSIUNG HONG, ALEX KANE, and JAESUN NOH

$$\sigma^2_{n,t+1} = w_{n,t} + v_{n,t}\varepsilon^2_t - d_{n,t}u_t. \tag{7}$$

4.   GARCH(1,1): The ARCH Model

The ARCH family of specifications was first proposed by Engle (1982). A sample of its increasing use for rates of return on capital assets can be found in Bollerslev, Chou, and Kroner (1990), Bollerslev, Engle, and Wooldridge (1988), Chou (1988), French, Schwert, and Stambough (1987), Hong (1987), and references cited there. As in the OLS model,

$$Z_t = a_{n,t} + b_{n,t} Z_{t-1} + \varepsilon_t \tag{8}$$

and the forecast will be

$$\sigma^2_{n,t+1} = w_{n,t} + v_{n,t}\varepsilon^2_t - d_{n,t}\sigma^2_{n,t}. \tag{9}$$

The parameters of Equations (8) and (9) are estimated by maximum likelihood, assuming ε_t to be conditionally normal. We note that Equations (7) and (9) provide identical forecast equations; they differ only in parameter estimation, where Equation (7) uses least squares whereas (9) is maximum likelihood, which optimally weights the observations.

We used three alternative sample lengths for n. In the first, we let n take the entire available set of past observations, but no fewer than 1,000. Thus, the forecasting experiment begins at June 23, 1966, for all three algorithms, leaving 5,913 test forecasts. The second and third alternatives assume that the parameters of the true specification change over time. Ideally, one would search for the best sample length. We chose, quite arbitrarily, 300 and 1,000, respectively, as short and intermediate alternatives to the long sample.

The four specifications and three sample lengths produce 12 competing daily forecasts. To these we added 3 more daily forecasts. The thirteenth is a simple average of all daily forecasts, and the fourteenth and fifteenth are the daily maximum and minimum forecasts.

A simple average of n equal-quality, conditionally independent forecasts will rapidly converge to a perfect forecast (see Kane and Marks 1987). Hence, failure of the average forecast indicates economically significant divergence in quality and mutual dependence of the 12 forecasts.

We added the maximum and the minimum of the daily forecasts to the set as a check for any forecast bias that affects profits significantly. If, for instance, a downward bias is indeed present and significant, then the maximum forecast will beat the minimum forecast and any of the individual forecasts that are more severely biased. If some forecasts are sufficiently upward biased, the minimum forecast will overcome the diversification effect of the average forecast and show a better cumulative profit. At the same time, both the minimum and maximum of the daily forecasts are expected to show greater profit volatility than the average forecast.

The two extreme forecasts will hereafter be referred to as MAXIMUM and MINIMUM, respectively.

B. Option-Pricing Formula and Hedge Ratio

The accuracy of the proposed valuation technique may be compromised if an inferior option-pricing formula is used in the experiment. We opted to use the Black–Scholes formula on the assumption that for maturities of one business day it will be sufficiently accurate.

Agents in the experiment trade one-day options on a $1 share of the NYSE portfolio. The exercise price of the options is taken to be $\exp(r_f)$, approximately $1 plus the risk-free rate. (Merton [1981] used this characterization and resultant option-pricing formula for his valuation of market timing ability.) The one-day excess rate of return (over the risk-free rate) on the NYSE portfolio is assumed to satisfy the required distributional assumptions. Under these conditions the Black–Scholes call (or put) option price reduces to

$$P_t = 2N(0.5\sigma_t) - 1, \tag{10}$$

where P_t is the call or put price, $N[\cdot]$ the cumulative normal density, and σ_t the standard deviation of the daily rate of return. For small σ_t the price is approximately linear in σ.

With this pricing formula, ignoring uncertainty about the variance, the hedge ratio for a riskless position involving the stock and call option (the number of shares per call), is given by $H_t = -N(0.5\sigma_t)$ (see Smith [1976, p. 21]).

C. Daily Round of Trade among Hypothetical Agents

Step 1: Agents set their call (= put) price. Every day of the exercise, each agent applies his or her designated algorithm to the sample of past observations (with the appropriate length) and computes a forecast for the variance of the NYSE index of the next day. From this forecast, using Equation (10), the agent determines his price for a one-day call/put on a $1 share of the NYSE portfolio.

The price of an option is increasing in the underlying asset variance. As a result, agents with low variance forecasts will believe that agents with high variance forecasts are overpricing call and put options, and vice versa.

Step 2: Agents execute trades. The following trades are executed each day.

1. Every agent buys one call and one put from every agent who offers them at a lower price. The transaction is executed at the average of the bid (seller's) and ask (buyer's) price. For every trade, the agent uses his own variance forecast to determine the appropriate hedge ratio. Each trade, call or put, is then separately hedged by each agent, taking the appropriate position in the stock of the NYSE index.

2. The trades in step 1 are repeated two more times with different transaction prices: instead of averaging the bid-ask spread, the first duplicate transactions are executed at the lower (seller's) price, and the second at the higher (buyer's) price.

Transacting at the lower price creates an asymmetry where upward-biased forecasts are preferred to downward-biased forecasts. The reverse is true when transactions are executed at the buyer's (higher) price. A separate account of these transactions serves two purposes. First, the difference in the relative profits of the duplicate transactions will help smoke out the algorithms that produce forecasts with a bias that is economically significant. Second, from these separate transactions we can compose a category that we call "trade at own price." Here, every agent transacts both buy and sell orders at his or her own price. This category is less sensitive to the price differentials between agents, and more sensitive to the rank order of forecasts, when compared with the average bid-ask price transactions. Each of these identical trades (at different prices) is also hedged (with the same ratio).

Step 3: Settle end-of-day accounts and accumulate profit/loss in individual agent accounts. At the end of each forecast day, the actual daily rate of return on the NYSE index is used to compute the profit/loss of each trade. For the purpose of future analysis, agent accounts are separated to subaccounts. There are 24 separate subaccounts in all, to distinguish the following 4 categories: (1) transaction price of the trade: bid, ask, average; (2) days of positive and negative return on the NYSE index; (3) unhedged and hedged trades; and (4) trades in puts and calls. Finally, each agent's subaccount is further partitioned by customer/competitor agent. This partition can be used to test any subgroup of competing forecasting agents.

For each agent, profits from all trades for the day are totaled in each subaccount. Because each pair of agents trades one straddle, absolute profits depend on the number of agents (algorithms) in the experiment. In computing agent profits we wish to eliminate the effect of the volume of transactions that is proportional to the number of participating agents. Hence, the total daily profit in each subaccount is averaged over the number of trades/competitors by dividing it by $k-1$, where k is the number of participating agents.

IV. A RELATIVE PROFITABILITY OF THE NYSE VARIANCE FORECASTS, 6/1966–12/1989

We report results of the experiment along the categories described in Section II.B, step 3, beginning with some forecast statistics and the rank order of profitability for the entire experiment.

A. Summary Statistics of the Variance Forecasts

Over the experiment period, June 23, 1966, to December 29, 1989, the annual excess return, compounded continuously, on the NYSE portfolio has been 4.18%, with a standard deviation of 14.08%. The ratio of daily standard deviation to average return was 20.11.

The annualized average daily forecasts of the standard deviation and the standard deviation of these forecasts, by algorithm, are presented in Table 1a. The first column shows that all algorithms' average forecasts of standard deviation were lower than the in-sample standard deviation of the NYSE return.

The second column of Table 1a shows that the variance of the forecasts was very different across specifications. For example, the standard deviation of forecasts from the OLS(5,000) is only 1.64%, indicating a smooth measure of variance, whereas that of the ARMA (300) is 8.65%, revealing a widely varying forecast.

The standard deviation of forecasts (and even the average) also varies quite significantly across sample lengths within each specification and is not always smallest for the longest sample length. Within the ARMA and ARCH specifications, the intermediate sample length (1,000) results in the least variable forecast.

The right-hand column in Table 1a displays the betas of the forecasts of standard deviation. They are estimated from regressions of the daily forecasts of standard deviation on the subsequent NYSE returns. The betas are practically zero, indicating that changes in the forecasts of standard deviation (not forecast errors) are nonsystematic.

As a proxy for the accuracy of the variance forecasts, a forecast error is often defined as the difference between the squared return and the variance forecast.

Table 1a.   Summary Statistics of the Annualized Percent
Daily Forecasts of Standard Deviation

Specification	Average	SD	Beta[a]
ARCH300	12.24	6.08	0.06
ARCH1,000	12.23	5.38	0.06
ARCH5,000	12.35	6.06	0.06
OLS300	12.88	4.19	0.05
OLS1,000	12.57	2.74	0.05
OLS5,000	11.11	1.64	0.04
ARM A300	9.24	8.65	0.04
ARMA1,000	10.14	7.35	0.04
ARMA5,000	10.38	8.51	0.05
MA300	13.18	4.48	0.05
MA1,000	12.91	2.72	0.05
MA5,000	11.44	1.67	0.04

Note: [a]The regression coefficient of the forecast of standard deviation on the subsequent
        excess return.

402   ROBERT ENGLE, CHE-HSIUNG HONG, ALEX KANE, and JAESUN NOH

Table 1b.   Summary Statistics of the Annualized Percent Daily Forecast Errors

Specification	June 23, 1966–Dec. 29, 1989			June 23, 1966–Sept. 29, 1987	
	MSE/AV[a]	SD/AV[b]	Beta[c]	SD/AV[b]	Beta[c]
ARCH300	0.0593	5.6076	−1.34	1.62	0.20
ARCH1,000	0.1009	5.3294	−1.27	1.61	0.21
ARCH5,000	0.0472	5.3277	−1.25	1.62	0.20
OLS300	0.0645	5.4067	−1.21	1.68	0.22
OLS1000	0.1671	5.4081	−1.20	1.72	0.23
OLS5,000	0.3664	5.3998	−1.19	1.71	0.23
ARMA300	0.1942	5.4150	−1.26	2.15	0.17
ARMA1,000	0.2081	5.3779	−1.24	1.94	0.18
ARMA5,000	0.0935	5.9161	−1.32	2.09	0.18
MA300	0.0251	5.4065	−1.21	1.68	0.21
MA1,000	0.1247	5.4084	−1.20	1.72	0.22
MA5,000	0.3283	5.3992	−1.19	1.71	0.23

Notes: [a]The ratio of squared realized return minus the variance forecast divided by the sample variance.
[b]Standard deviation of the daily forecast error divided by the sample standard deviation.
[c]The regression coefficient of the variance forecast error on subsequent excess return.

(With daily observations, taking the squared deviation from a daily mean would make no difference.)

The first column in Table 1b shows the mean forecast error of the variance as a percentage of the sample variance for the entire period. The second column of Table 1b measures the standard deviation of the variance "forecast error" divided by the

Table 1c.   Average Forecast-Driven Call (=Put) Prices and Average Profits from Long One Straddle[a]

Specification	Average Option Price[b]	Average Profit of Straddle	Standard Deviation of Profit
ARCH300	0.3089	0.0055	0.6075
ARCH1,000	0.3088	0.0057	0.5991
ARCH5,000	0.3116	0.0000	0.6027
OLS300	0.3248	−0.0265	0.6414
OLS1,000	0.3172	−0.0111	0.6448
OLS5,000	0.2802	0.0628	0.6365
ARMA300	0.2332	0.1569	0.6956
ARMA1,000	0.2560	0.1114	0.6606
ARMA5,000	0.2618	0.0996	0.6893
MA300	0.3325	−0.0417	0.6408
MA1,000	0.3256	−0.0280	0.6444
MA5,000	0.2886	0.0461	0.6363
MAXIMUM	0.4265	−0.2298	0.6468
MINIMUM	0.1572	0.3086	0.6399
AVERAGE	0.2958	0.0318	0.6065

Notes: [a]The underlying asset is $1 of the NYSE index, the exercise price is $e^{(1+r)}$, and the maturity is 1 day.
[b]Price is of cents per call and put.

average forecast. It shows that the forecast errors are quite large and, when normalized, are quite similar across algorithms.

The third column in Table 1b shows the beta for the forecast error. The magnitude of the negative betas suggests that large forecasting errors (as defined here) are more likely in down market, days when the NYSE return is negative, and result mainly from the crash of October 1987. Eliminating the week of the crash brings the betas down to practically zero.

The statistics in Tables 1a and 1b do not suggest a clear choice of specification. On the basis of mean square error, MA(300), ARCH(5,000), ARCH(300), and OLS(300) look best. But these are not best in terms of variance of forecast error.

Table 1c introduces the option valuations that we use to transform differences in variance forecasts to differences in pricing options on the NYSE index portfolio. First, the daily variance forecast of each algorithm is transformed to a one-day call price (which is equal to the one-day put price). The first column in Table 1c shows the average call price in cents per one-day call on a $1 share on the NYSE, with an exercise price of $1 plus the daily risk-free rate. Next we pretend that every day each forecaster buys one call and one put at his or her own price, based on his variance forecast. Holding this straddle, the end-of-day payoff to each forecaster is identical. Only the cost of the straddle differs. The day t profit to forecaster i equals

$$\pi_t = \max[\exp(r_t) - \exp(r_{ft}), \exp(r_{ft}) - \exp(r_t)] - 2P_{it},$$

where r_t is the daily NYSE return and P_{it} is the (ith forecast-driven) call price for day t because put and call prices are equal. This profit varies across forecasters as their forecasts differ.

Note that the objective here is to identify the best option-pricing forecast algorithm. Hence we are looking for the agent with the smallest cumulative profit from holding the straddle (pricing bias), and with the smallest variance of profit (squared pricing error).

The first column of Table 1c shows the average daily price in cents per day that agents assigned to a call (put) on a $1 share of the NYSE, with an exercise price of $1 plus the daily risk-free rate, over the entire forecast period. It is of an order of 0.30 cents as reflected by the average price of the AVERAGE forecast.

The second column in Table 1c shows the average daily profit from holding one straddle a day over the sample forecast period. The last column shows the standard deviation of the daily profit. The bottom panel in Table 1c introduces the additional forecasters, the MAXIMUM, MINIMUM, and AVERAGE forecasters.

The nonlinearity of the arbitrage-pricing loss function is reflected in that 4 of the 12 specification forecasters (as well as the MAXIMUM) show a negative profit, that is, an upward bias in pricing, while their average forecasts in Table 1a were smaller than the sample standard deviation. Using option prices in this way, too, does not indicate a winning forecast algorithm. ARCH(5,000) has an average profit of zero, that is, a zero pricing bias. Note from Table 1a that the average forecast of

404 ROBERT ENGLE, CHE-HSIUNG HONG, ALEX KANE, and JAESUN NOH

ARCH(5,000) is less than the in-sample standard deviation of the rate of return. Yet the standard deviation of profits of the ARCH(5,000) agent is not the lowest. It does appear, however, that the three ARCH forecasts are superior.

The AVERAGE forecast fails to dominate in either average profit or standard deviation, implying that the forecasts are significantly different in quality and not conditionally independent. MINIMUM has a better average profit than MAXIMUM as a result of a prevailing downward bias of the variance forecasts.

B. Rank Order by Overall Profit

The overall result of the experiment is given in Table 2a. It summarizes agent profits from all trades over the entire period, from trades at the average of the bid and ask prices.

Turning first to the question of whether the algorithms are of similar quality with independent pricing errors, we note from Table 2 that the AVERAGE forecast is inferior to ARCH(1,000), and only marginally superior to the two other ARCH specifications. This indicates that the 3 ARCH forecasts are distinctly better than the remainder of the 12. As for conditional independence of the forecasts, note that the standard deviation of the average daily profit of the AVERAGE forecast is by far the smallest. This indicates that the pricing errors of the competing agents offset one another for the most part, so that the average pricing error is small. For this to happen, the pricing errors of the agents must be quite independent.

Overall, the results indicate a potential for significant incremental profits from switching among variance-forecast algorithms in a competitive asset market. These

Table 2a. Annualized Daily Profits from All Trades[a]

Specification	Average	SD	Beta	Rank
ARCH300	8.76	2.80	−0.0183	4
ARCH1,000	10.38	2.22	0.0023	1
ARCH5,000	8.98	2.73	−0.0078	3
OLS300	3.29	2.34	0.0115	7
OLS1,000	0.74	2.85	0.0322	9
OLS.1,000	1.77	2.89	0.0087	8
ARMA300	−14.11	3.77	−0.0284	14
ARMA1,000	−3.70	2.13	−0.0205	11
ARMA5,000	−5.35	2.94	−0.0205	12
MA300	3.40	2.59	0.0101	5
MA1,000	−0.21	2.78	0.0286	10
MA5,000	3.31	2.40	0.0073	6
MAXIMUM	−9.12	4.51	−0.0242	13
MINIMUM	−17.36	4.51	0.0122	15
AVERAGE	9.14	1.19	−0.0001	2

Note: [a] The profits are in cents per competitor per straddle per year. Trades are at the average of the bid-ask spread.

Table 2b.   Annualized Daily Profits from All Trades[a]

Specification	June 23, 1966–Sept. 30, 1987 No. of obs. = 5,344			Oct. 1, 1987–Dec. 29, 1989 No. of obs. = 568		
	Profit	SD	Beta	Profit	SD	Beta
ARCH300	8.16	2.06	0.0173	14.37	6.41	−0.1467
ARCH1,000	9.52	2.11	0.0151	18.50	3.02	−0.0487
ARCH5,000	8.02	2.52	0.0109	18.05	4.18	−0.0778
OLS300	4.62	2.05	0.0028	−9.31	4.10	0.0379
OLS1,000	1.58	2.14	−0.0004	−7.13	6.40	0.1429
OLS5,000	1.44	2.46	−0.1513	4.88	5.47	0.0893
ARMA300	−15.29	3.42	−0.0096	−2.98	6.08	−0.0820
ARMA1,000	−3.71	2.59	−0.0041	−3.52	5.14	−0.0744
ARMA5,000	−7.40	2.82	−0.1908	13.99	3.71	−0.0188
MA300	4.24	2.39	0.0080	−4.53	3.97	0.0137
MA1,000	0.97	2.30	0.0062	−11.39	5.48	0.1043
MA5,000	3.10	2.10	−0.0100	5.34	4.28	0.0638
MAXIMUM	−6.90	3.96	0.0222	−30.10	7.88	−0.1793
MINIMUM	−16.19	3.99	−0.0275	−28.18	7.84	0.0161
AVERAGE	7.80	1.14	−0.0015	21.82	1.37	−0.0014

Notes: [a]Trades are at the average of bid-ask spread.

profits (which appear to be nonsystematic) are mostly driven by the variance of the variance forecasting errors, a property that is difficult to assess with standard statistics. (Admittedly this is a small, arbitrary set of specifications. See Pagan and Hong [1988], Pagan and Ullah [1988], and Pagan and Schwert [1989] for discussion of the quality of variance estimators.)

More specific indications of the quality of forecasts from Table 2a are as follows.

1. The ARMA specification appears as the experiment's worst performer. Poterba–Summers (1986) made a powerful argument that variance shocks should matter little to stock prices. Using an ARMA specification, they show that shocks to the variance of stocks do not persist and hence should have little effect on value. Our experiment suggests that in the context of asset prices vis-à-vis changes in variance, persistence needs to be examined with better forecast algorithms.

2. The results suggest that some restriction on the length of forecasting sample may be profitable. A straightforward application of the technique proposed here allows identification of a preferred sample length for the appropriate specification. The question of whether business cycles or shifts in monetary policies affect the parameters (particularly in terms of persistence) of various return process specifications can be addressed using the technique proposed here.

3. The dominance of the ARCH specification is quite striking. It justifies the new interest in testing asset pricing models with ARCH estimates in order to account for rational forecasts of market variance and asset covariances.

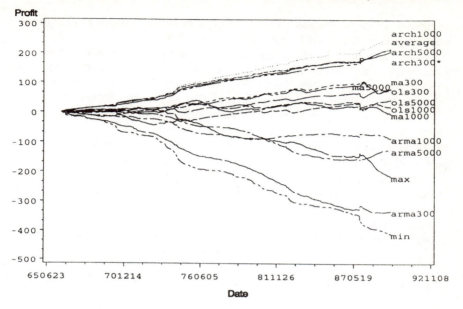

Figure 1.   Cumulative annualized profits from all trades,
June 23, 1966–December 29, 1989.

The significance of potential profits from better forecasting can be judged from the annualized average profit of the agents. From Table 1c, the average investment in one straddle (one call and one put on a $1 share of the NYSE) was in the order of 0.6 cents per day. Table 2a shows the annualized profit from an average daily trade from such average investment (actually less because the profit is stated per trade and agents could be taking offsetting positions). For the best three forecasters in Table 2a, the total annual profit (from 250 daily sessions per year) was in the order of 10 cents, with an annualized daily standard deviation of about 2 cents. Such large profits are obviously due in part to the even larger losses of the big losers. Still, bear in mind that none of the algorithms in the experiment has been condemned in the literature as inadequate, and empirical studies have made extensive use of these and similar ones. We shall show results from pairwise trades below. Figure 1 shows the time path of the cumulative profits for all forecasters. The graph shows that the profit behavior is quite consistent over time but that the crash of 1987 and its aftermath had a noticeable effect on profits.

Table 2b splits the forecasting period at October 1, 1987. The first set of columns presents profits from forecast-driven trades between June 23, 1966, and September 30, 1987. The results for this period are quite similar to the overall sample as reported in Table 2a. The second set of columns in Table 2b shows profits for the period from October 1, 1987, and December 29, 1989.

The results from the period that includes the crash are quite surprising. First, one would expect the shorter estimation-period forecast algorithms to do better in a period of changing volatility. But the 300-observation algorithms did much worse in this period, compared with the earlier period, in all four specifications.

The greater volatility of the period surrounding the crash would also lead one to expect that the MAXIMUM forecaster would improve its track record more than the MINIMUM forecaster. Rather, the reverse is true. The maximum is the worst performer over this period.

Another striking result is the large improvement in the profits of the AVERAGE forecaster. Forecasting errors across forecasters over the period surrounding the crash were more independent than usual.

While the ARMA forecasters had better results in the period surrounding the crash, particularly ARMA(5,000) with the longest estimation period, the ARCH forecasters garnered even more profits over this period than before.

C. Trade at Your Own Price and Ranking within Option Categories

Table 3 reports agent relative performance in a different way. It reports profit-ability in the four separate option-trade categories: sell/buy; call/put. The table reports profits from trades at their own prices: the sell transactions are executed at the low (seller's) price. The buy transactions are executed at the high (buyer's) price. Thus, each transaction between two agents is reported at a different price (with a different profit) in each trader's account.

If the net position of an agent were long one straddle (at own price) each day, then his or her average profit would be identical to that reported in Table 1c. The difference in profits as reported in Table 3 results from the frequency of long and short trades with the various agents. It is not affected by the difference in prices across agents, and hence profits cannot be driven by the magnitude of the forecast differences across agents. Rather, profits will be driven by the frequency and timing of above- and below-average forecasts. This measure of profitability is very sensitive to agent bias vis-à-vis other agents.

Average profits from all transactions at own price, as reported in Table 3, must be worse than those at average of bid-ask price in Table 2a. When transacting at own price, as compared with average of bid-ask prices, every transactor loses half the bid-ask spread.

Another reason why, at own prices, agents' profits are less than those reported in Table 1c is that now each agent gets to execute more net transactions on days when his or her forecast is more extreme relative to other agents. At own price, same-day transaction prices are the same for both buy and sell transactions. Hence, long positions exactly offset short ones. With an extreme forecast, the agent will be on the same side of most of all transactions. If more often than not, extreme

408   ROBERT ENGLE, CHE-HSIUNG HONG, ALEX KANE, and JAESUN NOH

Table 3.   Annualized Daily Profits from Trades at Own Prices[a]

Specification	Sell Call[b]	Sell Put[b]	Buy Call[c]	Buy Put[c]	Total	Rank
ARCH300	−3.31	0.26	2.94	−4.66	−2.38	3
ARCH1,000	−2.89	1.59	3.26	−3.20	−0.62	1
ARCH5,000	−3.70	0.77	1.74	−4.59	−2.88	4
OLS300	−4.72	−0.84	−2.44	−9.51	−8.76	6
OLS1,000	−7.26	−2.33	−3.30	−9.36	−11.12	9
OLS5,000	−11.37	−5.40	1.53	−3.38	−9.31	8
ARMA300	−30.06	−21.31	−6.40	−8.18	−32.98	14
ARMA1,000	−20.29	−12.25	−1.16	−4.02	−18.86	11
ARMA5,000	−21.60	−12.33	−3.81	−5.35	−21.55	12
MA300	−3.41	−0.72	−2.82	−10.91	−8.93	7
MA1,000	−6.54	−2.94	−4.09	−11.22	−12.39	10
MA5,000	−9.10	−4.37	2.14	−4.09	−7.71	5
MAXIMUM	0.00	0.00	−21.60	−31.81	−26.70	13
MINIMUM	−40.95	−30.73	0.00	0.00	−35.84	15
AVERAGE	−5.53	0.82	3.91	−0.74	−0.77	2

Notes: [a]Profits are in cents per competitor per straddle per year.
   [b]Trades are at the agent's (seller's) lower price.
   [c]Trades are at the agent's (buyer's) higher price.

forecasts are biased even for the better forecasters, then profits must be smaller in Table 3 than those in Table 1c.

The relative performance at own price, as reported in Table 3, is quite similar to profit from trading at bid-ask prices, as reported in Table 2a. Moving from average bid-ask to own price, we find a switch in ranks 3 and 4 of ARCH(5,000) and ARCH(300), as well as a switch among 5–7. This implies that the rank order of profitability is not mostly driven by the magnitude of the forecasting error of the big losers, but also by the number of positions on the correct side that agents take. Further evidence of that will be given in smaller groups and pairwise comparisons.

D.   Effect of Hedging Variance-drive Put and Call Option Trades

The overall portfolio positions of information traders will be affected by their variance forecasts in two ways: the desired (short vs. long) position, and the hedge ratio of the position. Agents with more accurate variance forecasts will also be able to hedge their positions more accurately. It is therefore interesting to see how the hedging activity affects the profitability of trading on variance forecasts.

Figure 2 conveys the order of magnitude of the risk reduction that hedging provides to a forecaster's position. It shows the kernel-density estimate of the daily profits from unhedged (the line marked 1) and hedged (the line marked 2) put positions for the ARCH(1,000) forecaster, the best performer. Figure 3 shows the kernel density for ARMA(300), the weakest forecaster.

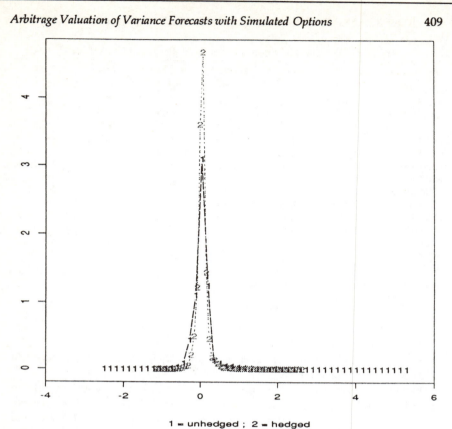

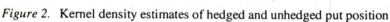

1 = unhedged ; 2 = hedged

Figure 2. Kernel density estimates of hedged and unhedged put position
of the daily Profits for the ARCH1000 forecaster.

Notes: The kernel density estimates are derived using the S-Plus program. The program uses the normal kernel and
a window width of 0.25.

In both cases the figure shows a significant reduction in risk: much shorter tails
and greater mass around the mean. The shift of the mass to the center of the
distribution is more pronounced for the hedged positions of the ARCH forecaster,
leading to an increase in the overall profits. The shift to the center of the
ARMA(300) forecaster is tilted to the left, and so, while reducing risk, hedging
further reduces profits. We see below that although hedging may reduce the average
profits of a successful forecaster, it will still improve the risk adjusted, that is, the
normalized profit.

Table 4a isolates the effect of the hedging activity for put and call trades. The
effect of hedging straddles is obviously negligible. In fact, for at-the-money
options, profits from hedged call trades are identical to profits from hedged put

410 ROBERT ENGLE, CHE-HSIUNG HONG, ALEX KANE, and JAESUN NOH

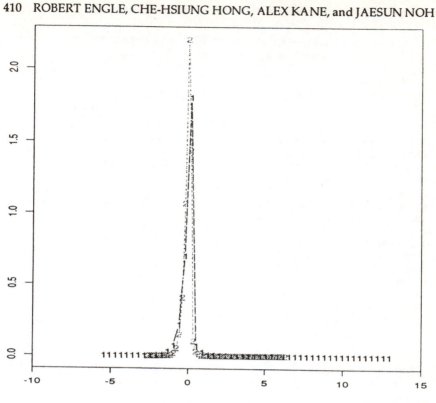

1 = unhedged ; 2 = hedged

Figure 3. Kernel density estimates of hedged and unhedged put position
of the daily profits for the ARMA300 forecaster.

Notes: The kernel density estimates are derived using the S-Plus program. The program uses the normal kernel and a window width of 0.25.

trades, and hence each is equal to the profit from straddles as reported in Table 2a. Table 4a shows the annualized average profit, its standard deviation, beta, and the normalized profit (profit divided by its standard deviation) for unhedged call and put positions. The last column shows the normalized profits for hedged positions resulting from the profit and its standard deviation as reported in Table 2a. The contribution of hedging forecaster positions in call or put options can be seen from the standard deviations, the betas, and the normalized profits. For all forecasters, for both puts and calls, the standard deviation is always lower for hedged trades (reported in Table 2a). The beta of the profits is smaller in absolute value. But the normalized profits are increased for significant positive-profit forecasters and decreased for the significant negative-profit forecasters.

Table 4a.   **Normalized Profits from Hedged and Unhedged Positions in Call and Put Options[a]**

	Unhedged Position								Hedged Position
	Call				Puts				
				Normalized				Normalized	Normalized Profits
Specification	Profit	SD	Beta	Profit	Profit	SD	Beta	Profit	Put or Call
ARCH300	10.79	4.14	0.0976	2.61	6.74	5.29	−0.1317	1.28	3.13
ARCH1,000	11.37	4.06	0.1018	2.80	9.40	3.93	−0.0957	2.39	4.68
ARCH5,000	9.92	4.88	0.1177	2.03	8.06	4.98	−0.1313	1.62	3.29
OLS300	4.89	4.09	0.0544	1.20	1.70	4.11	−0.0308	0.41	1.41
OLS1,000	1.31	4.26	−0.0315	0.31	0.18	5.31	0.0956	0.03	0.26
OLS5,000	1.24	5.03	−0.1792	0.25	2.29	5.15	0.1956	0.45	0.61
ARMA300	−17.59	6.43	−0.1310	−2.74	−10.62	6.76	0.0754	−1.57	−3.75
ARMA1,000	−6.29	5.02	−0.0678	−1.25	−1.11	5.22	0.0278	−0.21	−1.26
ARMA5,000	−9.21	5.37	−0.0909	−1.72	−1.49	5.01	0.0511	−0.30	−1.82
MA300	6.11	4.63	0.1472	1.32	0.71	4.57	−0.1259	0.16	1.31
MA1,000	1.56	4.53	0.0673	0.35	−1.97	5.05	−0.0098	−0.39	−0.08
MA5,000	4.06	4.20	−0.0716	0.97	2.57	4.35	0.0856	0.59	1.38
MAXIMUM	−3.99	7.71	0.4430	−0.52	−14.19	8.16	−0.4855	−1.74	−2.02
MINIMUM	−22.47	7.76	−0.4530	−2.90	−12.25	8.11	0.4756	−1.51	−3.85
AVERAGE	8.29	2.15	−0.0042	3.85	9.99	1.93	0.0042	5.18	7.68

Note: [a]Trades are at the average of bid-ask spread.

Table 4b summarizes the effect of hedging on the normalized forecasts of the best forecasters (the three ARCH specifications and the AVERAGE) and the weakest forecasters (the three ARMA specifications plus the MINIMUM and MAXIMUM forecasts). The last column in Table 4b shows the average hedged profit for these specifications, which was the basis for their selection.

Table 4b.   Normalized Profits with Hedged and Unhedged Positions for the Best and Worst Specification[a]

	Normalized Profits			Total Profits from Straddle
Specification	Hedged Call or Put	Unhedged Call	Put	(as in Table 2)
(Best)				
ARCH300	3.13	2.61	1.28	8.76
ARCH1,000	4.68	2.80	2.39	10.38
ARCH5,000	3.29	2.03	1.62	8.98
AVERAGE	7.68	3.85	5.18	9.14
(Worst)				
ARMA300	−3.75	−2.74	−1.57	−14.11
ARMA1,000	−1.26	−1.25	−0.21	−3.70
ARMA5,000	−1.82	−1.72	−0.30	−5.35
MAXIMUM	−2.02	−0.52	−1.74	−9.12
MINIMUM	−3.85	−2.90	−1.51	−17.36

Note: [a]Trades are at the average of bid-ask spread.

412   ROBERT ENGLE, CHE-HSIUNG HONG, ALEX KANE, and JAESUN NOH

The best forecasters (top panel of the table) always increase normalized profits by hedging their positions, whereas the weakest forecasters (bottom panel) always fare worse when hedging.

Note that the hedging activity, unlike trading in options, is not a zero sum game. An agent with a variance forecast that is too high will offer a high price for a put option. In addition, he will take a larger than called for long position in the stock. The entire portfolio will amount to a net long position in the stock that, if fairly priced, would have a positive expected rate of return.[1]

E.   Transitivity in the Relative Profitability of Forecasters

There is no reason to expect that the relative profit relation across forecasts is transitive. This issue is investigated in Table 5.

The first six columns of Table 5 show the ranking of agents within the forecasting groups as the least profitable are dropped out. The first column in Table 5 shows the ranks of all 15 forecasts. When the bottom three forecasts are dropped, there are some changes in the ranks. Along the way, dropping the 3 worst forecasters at a time, slight changes take place in the form of switches between forecasts that perform similarly. An expected change occurs in the rank of the AVERAGE, which deteriorates as the group becomes smaller and inferior forecasts are dropped.

Table 5.   Transitivity in Relative Profits across Forecasts and Pairwise Comparison of ARCH1,000 with the Competition

	Ranks in Groups by Size[a]						Annualized Profits of ARCH1,000 in Pairwise Trades with	
	15	12	9	6	3	2	Low Price[b]	High Price[c]
ARCH300	4	4	3	3	3		3.44	3.47
ARCH1,000	1	1	1	1	1	1	0.0	0.0
ARCH5,000	3	2	2	2	2	2	1.30	2.02
OLS300	7	6	6	6			5.65	9.68
OLS1,000	9	9	9				9.88	11.98
OLS5,000	8	8	8				11.35	4.22
ARMA300	14						28.83	9.93
ARMA1,000	11	11					20.90	7.69
ARMA5,000	12	12					22.31	10.58
MA300	5	5	5	5			4.83	10.76
MA1,000	10	10					8.94	13.16
MA5,000	6	7	7				10.03	4.98
MAXIMUM	13						−0.70	28.74
MINIMUM	15						38.40	0.52
AVERAGE	2	3	4	4			5.48	2.32

Notes: [a]Trades are at the average or bid-ask spread.
          [b]Trades are at the seller's price.
          [c]Trades are at the buyer's price.

The last two columns in Table 5 show how the best forecast in the tested group ARCH(1,000) fares in pairwise trades with all other forecasts, when traded at both the high and low price. These comparisons show that ARCH(1,000) is preferred to all other forecasts in the group. It is apparent that this forecast is downward biased, though. When trading at the low price ARCH(1,000) loses to MAXIMUM, which is always on the buy side. At the same time when trading at the high price, ARCH(1,000) still wins against MINIMUM, which is always on the sell side.

The magnitude of the gains of ARCH(1,000) against all other forecasts is striking. Even against the next best specification on a pairwise basis, ARCH(5,000), the gain at the average of bid-ask prices, would be 1.66 cents per year on an average investment of less than 0.6 cent.[2]

F. Sensitivity to Exercise Price

So far the exercise price was always set so that its present value equaled the current stock price. Tables 6a and 6b show that the foregoing results are not sensitive to the exercise price.

The shift in the exercise price was calibrated to induce a change in the option price by 25% on average. In Table 6a, the right- and left-hand columns use exercise prices that are shifted each day by four times the daily risk-free rate. The results are very similar. Table 6b uses exercise prices of 0.998, 1.0 and 1.002. Here, too, results do not show significant change.

Table 6a. Annualized Daily Profits from All Trades with Different Exercise Prices

	$K - e^{5r_f}$		$K - e^{r_f}$		$K - e^{-3r_f}$	
	Profit	Rank	Profit	Rank	Profit	Rank
ARCH300	8.64	4	8.76	4	8.17	4
ARCH1,000	10.12	1	10.38	1	9.94	1
ARCH5,000	8.77	3	8.98	3	8.70	3
OLS300	2.92	6	3.29	7	2.69	6
OLS1,000	0.34	9	0.74	9	0.27	9
OLS5,000	1.73	8	1.77	8	1.73	8
ARMA300	−14.56	14	−14.11	14	−10.48	13
ARMA1,000	−4.46	11	−3.70	11	−1.96	11
ARMA5,000	−5.91	12	−5.35	12	−3.58	12
MA300	2.86	7	3.40	5	2.44	7
MA1,000	−0.77	10	−0.21	10	−1.04	10
MA5,000	3.08	5	3.31	6	2.80	5
MAXIMUM	−10.07	13	−9.12	13	−10.80	14
MINIMUM	−17.31	15	−17.36	15	−12.38	15
AVERAGE	8.85	2	9.14	2	9.12	2

Table 6b. Annualized Daily Profits from All Trades with Different Exercise Prices

	K = 1.002		K = 1		K = 0.998	
	Profit	Rank	Profit	Rank	Profit	Rank
ARCH300	8.76	3	8.67	4	7.71	4
ARCH1,000	10.13	1	10.32	1	9.62	1
ARCH5,000	8.77	2	8.95	3	8.51	3
OLS300	2.81	5	3.22	7	1.89	6
OLS1,000	0.01	9	0.70	9	−0.57	10
OLS5,000	1.42	8	1.75	8	1.60	7
ARMA300	−14.19	14	−13.17	14	−7.36	13
ARMA1,000	−4.28	11	−3.22	11	−0.26	9
ARMA5,000	−6.15	12	−5.01	12	−1.77	11
MA300	2.65	7	3.28	5	1.01	8
MA1,000	−1.17	10	−0.29	10	−2.55	12
MA5,000	2.72	6	3.25	6	1.98	5
MAXIMUM	−10.53	13	−9.30	13	−13.54	15
MINIMUM	−16.73	15	−16.18	15	−7.62	14
AVERAGE	8.68	4	9.18	2	8.80	2

V. SUMMARY

The paper proposes a technique to compare variance-forecast algorithms using an economic value criterion. It takes advantage of the role of variance in pricing contingent claims. This is accomplished by setting up a hypothetical option market where each agent represents a competing variance-forecast algorithm.

The technique has been demonstrated with one-day options on the NYSE portfolio over the period 1966–1989. We show that the economic value to improved accuracy of variance forecasts, from switching across some widely used forecast algorithms, is large by any standard.

For the limited set of specifications tested here, it has been demonstrated that ARCH specifications appear the most suitable and that some restriction on the length of the rolling sample is preferred. We have shown that variance-forecast accuracy bears significant economic profits.

Examination of the relative forecast profits with the proposed technique reveals the economic significance of various statistical properties of the forecast errors. In particular, it appears that differences in the variance of the forecast errors may be generating most of the large economic losses from using inadequate variance forecasts.

In subsequent research we will apply this technique to longer-term options. There, the issue of the appropriate option-pricing formula will have to be reevaluated. Testing of the technique will include the introduction of new assets, such as currency and bond options.

ACKNOWLEDGMENT

We thank Robert L. McDonald for helpful discussions and suggestions, and participants in the UCSD conference on modeling the volatility in asset pricing for helpful comments.

NOTES

1.   The portfolio will still have a less than adequate risk premium, perhaps even a negative expected excess return, because of the overpricing of the put option.

2.   The profit at the average bid-ask price is not the simple average of the profits at high and low prices. Rather it is a weighted average with the number of sell/buy transactions as weights.

REFERENCES

Bodie, Zvi. "Inflation, Index-Linked Bonds and Asset Allocation." NBER Working Paper No. 2793, December 1988.

Bollerslev, Tim, Robert Engle, and Jeffrey Wooldridge. "A Capital Asset Pricing Model with Time Varying Covariances." *Journal of Political Economy* 96 (1988), pp. 116–131.

Bollerslev, Tim, Ray Chou, and Kenneth Kroner. "ARCH Modeling in Finance: A Selective Review of the Theory and Empirical Evidence." *Journal of Econometrics* 52 (1992), pp. 201–224.

Chou, Ray. "Volatility Persistence and Stock Valuation." *Journal of Applied Econometrics* 3 (1988), pp. 279–294.

Cox, John and Mark Rubinstein. *Option Markets.* Englewood Cliffs, NJ: Prentice Hall, 1985.

Engle, Robert. "Autoregressive Conditional Heteroskedasticity with Estimates of the Variance of U.K. Inflation." *Econometrica* 50 (1982), pp. 987–1008.

French, Kenneth, William Schwert, and Robert Stambaugh. "Expected Stock Returns and Volatility." *Journal of Financial Economics* 19, No. 1 (September 1987), pp. 3–29.

Hong, Ted. "The Integrated Generalized Conditional Heteroskedastic Model: The Process, Estimation and Monte Carlo Experiments." University of California, San Diego Discussion Paper No. 87–32, 1987.

Hull, John and Alan White. "The Pricing of Options on Assets with Stochastic Volatility." *Journal of Finance* 42(June 1987), pp. 281–300.

Kane, Alex and Stephen G. Marks. "The Rocking Horse Analyst." *Journal of Portfolio Management* 13, No. 3 (Spring 1987), pp. 32–37.

Merton, Robert. "On Market Timing and Investment Performance I: An Equilibrium Theory of Value for Market Forecasts." *Journal of Business* 54 (1981), pp. 302–406.

Pagan, Adrian and Y. Hong. "Non Parametric Estimation and the Risk Premium." University of Rochester, mimeo, 1988.

Pagan, Adrian and William Schwert. "Alternative Models for Conditional Stock Volatility." *Journal of Econometrics* 45 (1990), pp. 267–290.

Pagan, Adrian and Aman Ullah. "The Econometric Analysis of Models with Risk Items." *Journal of Applied Econometrics* 3 (1988) pp. 87–105.

Poterba, James and Lawrence Summers. "The Persistence of Volatility and Stock Market Fluctuations." *American Economic Review* 76 (1986), pp. 1124–1141.

Schmalensee, Richard and Robert Trippi. "Common Stock Volatility Implied by Option Premia." *Journal of Finance* 33, No. 1 (1978), pp. 129–147.

Smith, Clifford, "Option Pricing." *Journal of Financial Economics* 3 (1976), pp. 3–51.

Wiggins, James. "The Pricing of Options with Stochastic Volatility." *Journal of Financial Economics* 19 (1987), pp. 351–372.

A
Statistical Models

Journal of Econometrics 45 (1990) 267–290. North-Holland

ALTERNATIVE MODELS FOR CONDITIONAL
STOCK VOLATILITY*

Adrian R. PAGAN

University of Rochester, Rochester, NY 14627, USA
Australian National University

G. William SCHWERT

University of Rochester, Rochester, NY 14627, USA
National Bureau of Economic Research

This paper compares several statistical models for monthly stock return volatility. The focus is on U.S. data from 1834–1925 because the post-1926 data have been analyzed in more detail by others. Also, the Great Depression had levels of stock volatility that are inconsistent with stationary models for conditional heteroskedasticity. We show the importance of nonlinearities in stock return behavior that are not captured by conventional ARCH or GARCH models. We also show the nonstationarity of stock volatility.

1. Introduction

Over the last decade several models of conditional volatility in economic time series have been proposed. Basic to all these suggestions is the notion that volatility can be decomposed into predictable and unpredictable components, and interest has largely centered on the determinants of the predictable part. For financial series this concern with the predictable component of volatility is motivated by the fact that, in many models, the risk premium is a function of it.

By definition, the predictable component of volatility in a series is the conditional variance of that series, σ_t^2. The different ways of modeling σ_t^2 reflect different answers to two basic questions. First, how does σ_t^2 vary with information available at time t; that is, what is the nature of the conditioning set F_t? Second, what does the mapping between information and σ_t^2 look like? Of these two questions, the first has to be dispensed with summarily.

*We received useful comments from David Backus, John Campbell, Mahmoud El-Gamal, Robert Engle, James Hamilton, David Hendry, Andrew Lo, Robert Stambaugh, Richard Startz, the participants at the NBER Conference on New Empirical Methods in Finance, and from an anonymous referee. The National Science Foundation (Pagan, under grant SES-8719520) and the Bradley Policy Research Center at the University of Rochester (Schwert) provided support for this research.

Because of the large range of variables whose volatility has been measured, it is impossible to be precise about conditioning variables, other than to say that the history of the series being analyzed is the most popular choice. We also make that choice by focusing on univariate time series techniques. The debate over the mapping between σ_t^2 and conditioning variables can be more fruitfully analyzed out of the context of particular applications, and it is this question that we concentrate on in this paper.

Suppose we write the series y_t to be modeled as $y_t = x_t'\beta + u_t$, where x_t is a set of variables affecting the conditional mean of y_t, while u_t is an error term with zero mean and conditional variance $E(u_t^2|F_t) = \sigma_t^2$. Then Engle (1982) proposed that

$$\sigma_t^2 = \sigma^2 + \sum_{k=1}^{q} \alpha_k u_{t-k}^2,\tag{1}$$

the ARCH(q) model. Bollerslev (1986) generalized this to

$$\sigma_t^2 = \sigma^2 + \sum_{j=1}^{p} \beta_j \sigma_{t-j}^2 + \sum_{k=1}^{q} \alpha_k u_{t-k}^2,\tag{2}$$

the GARCH(p, q) model, and Engle and Bollerslev (1986) extended GARCH to the class of integrated GARCH (IGARCH) models that have the restriction $\sum\beta_j + \sum\alpha_k = 1$. As Bollerslev (1988) records, the class of GARCH models has been extensively applied with some success. Nevertheless, several authors have felt that these models are too restrictive, because of their imposition of a quadratic mapping between the history of u_t and σ_t^2. Nelson (1988) argued that stylized facts associated with Christie (1982) and Black (1976) imply that σ_t^2 be an asymmetric function of the past data, and he modified the conditional variance to

$$\ln \sigma_t^2 = \alpha_0 + \sum_{j=1}^{q} \beta_j \ln \sigma_{t-j}^2 + \sum_{k=1}^{p} \alpha_k \left[\theta \psi_{t-k} + \gamma \left(|\psi_{t-k}| - (2/\pi)^{1/2} \right) \right],$$

$$\tag{3}$$

where $\psi_t = u_t/\sigma_t$. By modeling the logarithm of the variance $\ln \sigma_t^2$, it is not necessary to restrict parameter values to avoid negative variances as in the ARCH and GARCH models. An obvious name for the model in (3) is the exponential GARCH (EGARCH) model. To identify the parameters, γ is set to 1.

Hamilton (1988, 1989) proposed a bivariate state model in which σ_t^2 was a linear function of the conditional probability that the economy was in a state

$S_t = 1$, rather than the alternative $S_t = 0$. Because the conditional probability is a nonlinear function of F_t, once again this represents a departure from the GARCH class of volatility measures. The exact mapping between σ_t^2 and F_t induced by his two-state approach depends on the data, and this raises the broader issue of whether one might allow the data to determine the unknown function. Pagan and Ullah (1988) argued that nonparametric estimation methods could be used for this purpose, and Pagan and Hong (1988) gave some examples of where there seemed to be gains in doing nonparametric estimation rather than following the parametric formulations such as GARCH. Very little of a comparative nature has emerged about these methods. For this reason it is of interest to apply each of the techniques mentioned above to the same data set, with the aim of investigating the different implications each might have for the predictability of volatility. The following section selects a series on monthly stock returns from 1834 to 1925 as the basis for such a comparison.

2. Estimation of stock return volatility

We concentrate on monthly stock returns from 1834–1925, previously analyzed by Schwert (1989b). He gives details on the construction of the data and places it in an historical context. In fact, the series extends through 1987 but, because French, Schwert, and Stambaugh (1987) and Nelson (1988) have previously worked with the data from 1926 onward, it is useful to concentrate on a sample that has not received much attention. Furthermore, many of the models and estimators we consider impose *covariance stationarity* on the data. There is strong evidence that the stock return series is not covariance stationary when the period of the Great Depression (1929–1939) is included.[1] If this is true, models such as Hamilton's can be immediately rejected as inappropriate. Moreover, the assumptions underlying nonparametric estimators would also be violated, and one could not justify their usage based on asymptotic theory. Some assessment of whether the data are covariance stationary is therefore mandatory.

2.1. Recursive variance plots

Because covariance stationarity implies that the unconditional variance of the data is a constant over time, a simple graphical view of the likelihood of such constancy is available from a plot of the *recursive* estimates of the variance of the series against time [see Mandelbrot (1963)]. If $\hat{u}_t$ is the difference between the stock return and an estimate of its conditional mean

---

[1]Schwert (1989a) stresses that stock volatility was unusually high during the Depression relative to the volatility of other important macroeconomic series.

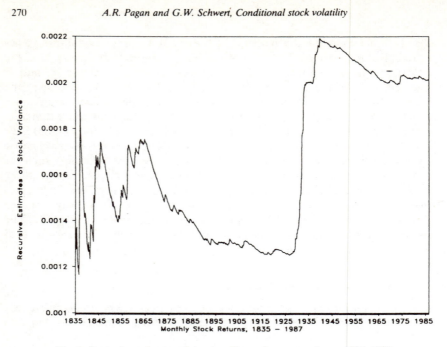

Fig. 1. Recursive estimates of the monthly stock return variance, 1835–1987.

described in section 2.2,

$$\hat{\mu}_2(t) = t^{-1} \sum_{k=1}^{t} \hat{u}_k^2 \qquad (4)$$

is the recursive estimate of the unconditional variance at time t. Fig. 1 displays the plot of this against t for 1835 to 1987. There are three distinct phases. In the first, ending around 1866, the unconditional variance estimate is quite erratic. After that, the estimate is very stable until it jumps to a much higher level around 1930. It is this latter jump that is the most striking feature of the data and it suggests that data before 1930 has a different variance from that after 1930. One might argue that the pre- and post-1866 data are also different, although the switch from the Macaulay (1938) to the Cowles (1939) data occurring near that time could explain part of the aberrant behavior.

We have done a variety of tests for whether the unconditional variance is constant over the 1834–1987 period, and they all reject at conventional levels. For the 1834–1925 period, however, most of these tests do not reject covariance stationarity at small significance levels. Hence, we use this sample period for the remainder of our analysis.

2.2. Modeling the conditional mean return

There is a long history of arguments in the analysis of stock returns that the mean return exhibits little predictability from the past. Qualifications to this conclusion are the existence of a possible moving average error term induced by nonsynchronous data and calendar effects. In the representation $y_t = x_t'\beta + u_t$, y_t being stock returns, x_t would be monthly dummies, and u_t would be an MA(1), $e_t + \theta e_{t-1}$. To account for these effects, we regressed out twelve monthly dummies to get $\hat{u}_t$, and then $\hat{u}_t$ was regressed against $\hat{u}_{t-1}, \ldots, \hat{u}_{t-12}$. Only lags 1, 2, 3 and 10 seemed to be significant. The point estimates for the first four lags are 0.27, -0.10, 0.07, -0.02. The alternating signs and size suggest that this is compatible with an MA(1) with parameter around 0.3. We decided to approximate this MA effect with an autoregression, so that $\hat{e}_t$ was computed as the residuals from the regression of $\hat{u}_t$ against $\hat{u}_{t-1}, \ldots, \hat{u}_{t-10}$. The $\hat{e}_t$ are then the raw data. Central to this procedure is the belief that there are no dependencies in the conditional mean other than linear ones. Nonparametric estimates of conditional mean functions reported later support this assumption.

The task is to model the conditional variance of the series $\hat{e}_t$. To do this, a set of conditioning variables F_t must be chosen and a decision made about how σ_t^2 relates to F_t. We decided to keep F_t as a function of the history of returns alone, and this meant that F_t could be constructed from either $\{\hat{u}_{t-j}\}$ or $\{\hat{e}_{t-j}\}$. If an infinite number of conditioning variables was possible there would be no difference between these, as they are just different linear combinations of y_{t-j}. Because we must restrict the lags to a finite set, differences can arise. We adopt $\{\hat{e}_{t-j}\}$ as the basis of the conditioning set, as this simplifies comparisons with GARCH models. Both $\{\hat{e}_{t-j}\}$ and $\{\hat{u}_{t-j}\}$ were always tried, however, and there were no important discrepancies in results. A finite number of lags was selected by considering the regression of $\hat{e}_t^2$ against $\hat{e}_{t-1}^2, \ldots, \hat{e}_{t-12}^2$. This regression yields the partial autocorrelation function of the $\hat{e}_t^2$. It is important to recognize that the error terms will be heteroskedastic and to adjust t-statistics with the method of White (1980). The difference in the ordinary and robust standard errors is dramatic, with t-statistics of the estimated coefficients of $\hat{e}_{t-1}^2$, $\hat{e}_{t-2}^2$, and $\hat{e}_{t-7}^2$ falling from (6.24, 4.63, and 3.15) to (2.16, 1.77, and 1.84), while that for $\hat{e}_{t-8}^2$ went from -1.45 to -2.03. The t-statistics for the remaining lags were small. Based on this evidence, we concluded that $F_t^4 = \{\hat{e}_{t-1}, \hat{e}_{t-2}, \hat{e}_{t-7}, \hat{e}_{t-8}\}$ should suffice as the broadest set of conditioning variables, but we also conducted experiments with $F_t^2 = \{\hat{e}_{t-1}, \hat{e}_{t-2}\}$ and $F_t^1 = \{\hat{e}_{t-1}\}$. To anticipate later developments, most of the information is in F_t^1, but the expansion to the larger set F_t^4 does improve the prediction of $\hat{e}_t^2$.

Having chosen F_t, it only remains to describe the set of methods employed to estimate σ_t^2. Because ten lags were used in constructing $\hat{u}_t$, and a further eight if F_t^4 was selected, the sample size was always July 1835 to December 1925, yielding 1086 observations. More observations were available when F_t^1 or F_t^2 are the conditioning sets, but working with a variable sample size makes it hard to compare the different results.

2.3. A two-step conditional variance estimator

Because $E(e_t^2|F_t) = \sigma_t^2$, a simple two-step estimator of σ_t^2 can be found as the predictions from the regression of $\hat{e}_t^2$ against $\{\hat{e}_{t-1}^2, \ldots, \hat{e}_{t-8}^2\}$ [see Davidian and Carroll (1987)]. The underlying model of volatility here is

$$\sigma_t^2 = \sigma^2 + \sum_{k=1}^{8} \alpha_k \hat{e}_{t-k}^2, \tag{5}$$

and all one does is replace σ_t^2 by $\hat{e}_t^2 + (\sigma_t^2 - e_t^2) + (e_t^2 - \hat{e}_t^2) = \hat{e}_t^2 + v_t$. It is easy to show that the term $(e_t^2 - \hat{e}_t^2)$ does not affect the limiting distribution of $\hat{\alpha}_{OLS}$, so v_t behaves like $(\sigma_t^2 - e_t^2)$, which is a martingale difference with respect to the sigma field generated by F_t. Ordinary least squares is therefore a consistent estimator, although not an efficient one. Efficiency could be improved by doing weighted least squares with $\hat{\sigma}_t^{-1}$ as weights, but the nonnormality of v_t also suggests that adaptive estimation of α might be preferable. The role of the two-step estimator is that of a benchmark, however, and the R^2 of 0.089 between $\hat{\sigma}_t^2$ and $\hat{e}_t^2$ sets a limit to which other models can be compared.

2.4. A GARCH model

The two-step estimator is effectively an eighth-order ARCH model and an obvious extension is to see if a GARCH specification would be superior. French, Schwert, and Stambaugh (1987) fitted a GARCH(1, 2) model to y_t over the period 1928–1984, although the second ARCH parameter α_2 was small. We estimated a GARCH(1, 2) model for $\hat{e}_t$ for 1835–1925. French, Schwert, and Stambaugh allowed for an MA(1), $u_t = e_t + \theta e_{t-1}$, and we did the same here, although since $\hat{e}_t$ has been purged of a tenth-order autoregression, the MA term was not significant. After estimation, the following model for σ_t^2 was found (t-values in parentheses):

$$\hat{\sigma}_t^2 = \underset{(3.65)}{0.000239} + \underset{(6.11)}{0.571} \, \hat{\sigma}_{t-1}^2 + \underset{(4.38)}{0.158} \, \hat{e}_{t-1}^2 + \underset{(1.35)}{0.064} \, \hat{e}_{t-2}^2. \tag{6}$$

A diagnostic test advocated by Pagan and Sabau (1987), involving the regression of $\hat{e}_t^2$ against unity and $\hat{\sigma}_t^2$, gave an estimated coefficient on $\hat{\sigma}_t^2$ of 0.827 in table 1, with a t-statistic of -0.60 for testing the null that the coefficient is unity [implied by the restriction $E(e_t^2|F_t) = \sigma_t^2$]. For this situation, however, where we are testing an ARCH rather than an ARCH-M model, results in Sabau (1988) show that the test is probably rather weak. A point to note is that the point estimates are compatible with the idea that σ_t^2 is generated by a GARCH rather than IGARCH process. The R^2 between $\hat{\sigma}_t^2$ and $\hat{e}_t^2$ is 0.067, which is less than the R^2 for the two-step method.[2]

2.5. An exponential GARCH model

The exponential GARCH(1,2) model allows lagged shocks to have an asymmetric effect on conditional volatility. In particular, the evidence in Black (1976), Christie (1982), French, Schwert, and Stambaugh (1987), Nelson (1988), and Schwert (1990) suggests that negative stock returns lead to larger stock volatility than equivalent positive returns. We estimate an EGARCH(1,2) model (t-values in parentheses):

$$\ln\hat{\sigma}_t^2 = \underset{(-3.90)}{-1.73} + \underset{(11.62)}{0.747} \ln\hat{\sigma}_{t-1}^2 + \underset{(5.21)}{0.262} Z_{t-1} + \underset{(2.06)}{0.124} Z_{t-2}, \quad (7)$$

where

$$Z_{t-k} = \left[\left(|\hat{\psi}_{t-k}| - (2/\pi)^{1/2} \right) - \underset{(-3.91)}{0.352} \hat{\psi}_{t-k} \right],$$

and $\hat{\psi}_t = \hat{e}_t/\hat{\sigma}_t$. The log-likelihood for this model is 2198.2 versus 2191.8 for the GARCH(1,2) model. Thus, the estimates of Nelson's EGARCH model confirm the previous evidence that conditional volatility increases more when return shocks are negative. The R^2 between $\hat{\sigma}_t^2$ and $\hat{e}_t^2$ is 0.118, which is a small improvement over the two-step method, but well above the GARCH(1,2) model.[3]

---

[2] French, Schwert, and Stambaugh (1987) also estimated a GARCH-in-mean model, where the conditional mean return was a linear function of either the standard deviation or variance. We estimated such models for the 1835–1925 data, and the R^2 statistics were 0.076 and 0.077. Thus, the GARCH-in-mean results are essentially equivalent to the GARCH results reported in the text.

[3] The log-likelihood is for the *returns* $\hat{e}_t$, while the R^2 pertain to the explanation of the *squared returns* $\hat{e}_t^2$. Hence, although the two measures point in the same direction, they are not comparable.

2.6. Hamilton's two-state switching-regime model

Hamilton (1989) proposes a switching-regime Markov model for GNP growth rates as a model for recessions and expansions. Briefly, consider a variable y_t that follows an AR(m) process,

$$y_t - \mu(S_t) = \phi_1[y_{t-1} - \mu(S_{t-1})] + \phi_2[y_{t-2} - \mu(S_{t-2})] + \cdots$$
$$+ \phi_m[y_{t-m} - \mu(S_{t-m})] + \sigma(S_t)v_t, \tag{8}$$

where v_t is n.i.d.$(0, 1)$. The mean, $\mu(S_t)$, and the residual standard deviation, $\sigma(S_t)$, are functions of the regime in period t. The regimes are assumed to follow a two-state first-order Markov process,

$$P(S_t = 1 | S_{t-1} = 1) = p,$$
$$P(S_t = 0 | S_{t-1} = 1) = 1 - p,$$
$$P(S_t = 1 | S_{t-1} = 0) = 1 - q, \tag{9}$$
$$P(S_t = 0 | S_{t-1} = 0) = q,$$

and the parameters of (8) are modeled as

$$\mu(S_t) = \alpha_0 + \alpha_1 S_t, \qquad \sigma(S_t) = \omega_0 + \omega_1 S_t. \tag{10}$$

Finally, the errors v_t are assumed to be independent of all S_{t-j}. Given this structure, it is straightforward to use numerical procedures to maximize the likelihood as a function of the parameters $\{\phi_1, \ldots, \phi_m, p, q, \alpha_0, \alpha_1, \omega_0, \omega_1\}$.[4] Besides point estimates and asymptotic standard errors, Hamilton's algorithm estimates the probability that the variable is in regime 1 conditional on data available at data t. The estimates of Hamilton's model from July 1835 through December 1925 are

$$\hat{e}_t - \hat{\mu}(S_t) = \underset{(1.09)}{0.035} [\hat{e}_{t-1} - \hat{\mu}(S_{t-1})] - \underset{(-0.24)}{0.007} [\hat{e}_{t-2} - \hat{\mu}(S_{t-2})]$$

$$- \underset{(-0.24)}{0.007} [\hat{e}_{t-3} - \hat{\mu}(S_{t-3})]$$

$$\underset{(-0.04)}{-0.001} [\hat{e}_{t-4} - \hat{\mu}(S_{t-4})] + \hat{\sigma}(S_t)v_t, \tag{11}$$

$$\hat{\mu}(S_t) = \underset{(0.58)}{0.0006} - \underset{(-0.68)}{0.0025} S_t, \qquad \hat{\sigma}(S_t) = \underset{(26.02)}{0.0246} + \underset{(8.84)}{0.0253} S_t,$$

[4] Hamilton (1988, 1989) provides additional information about the statistical model and the related estimation procedures. We are grateful to Jim Hamilton for providing the FORTRAN source code used to estimate these models.

with t-statistics in parentheses. The estimates of the Markov probabilities are $\hat{q} = 0.9619$ (with a standard error of 0.0125) and $\hat{p} = 0.9034$ (with a standard error of 0.0328). Thus, these estimates imply that the high variance regime is less likely than the low variance regime, although both regimes are likely to persist once they occur.[5] Schwert (1989b) shows how to compute the conditional variance from this model. Briefly, if the variable was in regime 1 at $t - 1$, the variance of the squared forecast error for period t is

$$E\{\sigma^2(S_t)|S_{t-1} = 1\} + \mathrm{var}\{\mu(S_t)|S_{t-1} = 1\}$$

$$= [E\{\sigma(S_t)|S_{t-1} = 1\}]^2 + \mathrm{var}\{\sigma(S_t)|S_{t-1} = 1\}$$

$$+ E\{[\mu(S_t) - E(\mu(S_t))]^2|S_{t-1} = 1\}$$

$$= [\omega_0 + \omega_1 p]^2 + \omega_1^2 p(1-p) + \alpha_1^2 p(1-p). \tag{12}$$

If the variable was in regime 0 at $t - 1$, the variance of the squared forecast error for period t is

$$E\{\sigma^2(S_t)|S_{t-1} = 0\} + \mathrm{var}\{\mu(S_t)|S_{t-1} = 0\}$$

$$= [E\{\sigma(S_t)|S_{t-1} = 0\}]^2 + \mathrm{var}\{\sigma(S_t)|S_{t-1} = 0\}$$

$$+ E\{[\mu(S_t) - E(\mu(S_t))]^2|S_{t-1} = 0\}$$

$$= [\omega_0 + \omega_1(1-q)]^2 + \omega_1^2 q(1-q) + \alpha_1^2 q(1-q). \tag{13}$$

Multiplying (12) and (13) by the estimates of the conditional probabilities of being in each regime given data through $t - 1$, $P(S_{t-1} = 1|\hat{e}_{t-1}, \ldots)$ and $P(S_{t-1} = 0|\hat{e}_{t-1}, \ldots)$ gives the estimate of the conditional variance of the forecast error at time t, $\hat{\sigma}_t^2$. The R^2 between $\hat{e}_t^2$ and $\hat{\sigma}_t^2$ is 0.057, which is the smallest among all the techniques we consider.

2.7. A nonparametric kernel estimator

Broadly there are two major philosophies in nonparametric estimation. The first is essentially a weighted average, that is

$$\hat{\sigma}_t^2 = \sum_{j=1}^{T} w_{jt} \hat{e}_j^2, \qquad \sum_{j=1}^{T} w_{jt} = 1, \tag{14}$$

[5]The expected durations of the regimes are $(1 - \hat{p})^{-1} = 10.4$ months and $(1 - \hat{q})^{-1} = 26.2$ months.

where T is the sample size. The weights w_{jt} are made to depend on F_j and F_t in such a way that, if F_j and F_t are 'far apart', w_{jt} is close to zero. What this does is make σ_t^2 equivalent to the sample variance of $\hat{e}_j$ using only those observations that are close to F_t. Since it is these observations that have variance σ_t^2, the method is analogous to the use of sample moments to estimate population moments. Many weighting schemes are possible. Letting z_t be the $r \times 1$ vector containing the elements in F_t, Nadaraya (1964) and Watson (1964) set

$$w_{jt} = K(z_t - z_j) \Big/ \sum_{k=1}^{T} K(z_k - z_t), \tag{15}$$

where the kernel $K(\cdot)$ has the properties that it is nonzero, integrates to unity, and is symmetric. The kernel used in this paper was the Gaussian one,

$$K(z_t - z_j) = (2\pi)^{-1/2}|H|^{-1/2}\exp\left[-\tfrac{1}{2}(z_t - z_j)'H(z_t - z_j)\right]. \tag{16}$$

$H = \operatorname{diag}(h_1 \ldots h_r)$ contains the bandwidths, that were set to $\hat{\sigma}_k T^{-1/(4+r)}$, where $\hat{\sigma}_k$ is the sample standard deviation of z_{kt}, $k = 1, \ldots, r$. Silverman (1986) shows that the minimum mean square error choice of the bandwidth is proportional to $\hat{\sigma}_k T^{-1/(4+r)}$. No experimentation with the kernel or bandwidth was done, and we did not look at other weighting schemes. Partly this was due to our preference for the Fourier nonparametric estimator described later. One important modification that was employed was to leave out the tth observation when computing $\hat{\sigma}_t^2$,

$$\hat{\sigma}_t^2 = \sum_{\substack{j=1 \\ j \neq t}}^{T} w_{jt}\hat{e}_t^2. \tag{17}$$

Generally, it is important to adopt the 'leave-one-out' estimator to avoid the situation where 'outliers' in the data force w_{tt} to be unity, while all other w_{jt} are close to zero. In these circumstances, $\hat{e}_t^2$ becomes the estimator of σ_t^2 if all observations are used. While there is a sense in which this is the best estimate of σ_t^2, it tends to overstate the predictability of volatility by making a perfect prediction at time t. Based on F_t^1 the R^2 between $\hat{e}_t^2$ and $\hat{\sigma}_t^2$ is 0.126 if $\{\hat{e}_{t-1}\}$ is the conditioning variable. There is a major improvement over the GARCH and Hamilton models, and it is somewhat larger than for the EGARCH model. The R^2 between $\hat{e}_t^2$ and $\hat{\sigma}_t^2$ is lower for F_t^2 and F_t^4. This difference occurs because some of the observations on $\hat{e}_t^2$ for which $\hat{\sigma}_t^2$ was not computed were very large.

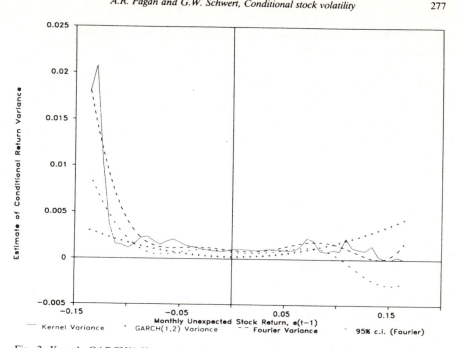

Fig. 2. Kernel, GARCH(1,2), and Fourier estimates of the monthly stock return variance conditional on the lagged unexpected stock return, e_{t-1}, 1834–1925 (with the lower 95 percent confidence interval for the Fourier estimate).

It is worth noting that the estimate of conditional variance in (17) is a function of all the data, not just observations before time t. This is no different, however, than estimating the regression parameters in (5) using all the data. In both cases, the predictions of the conditional variance $\hat{\sigma}_t^2$ are a function of all the data. In section 3 we will discuss the results of a post-sample prediction experiment where the forecast models are estimated using data from 1835–1899, then forecasts are made for 1900–1925. We also use the estimates from 1835–1925 to forecast for 1926–1937.

It is not easy to summarize the mapping between σ_t^2 and $\{\hat{e}_{t-j}\}$ when the conditioning set is F_t^4. Some insight is available by computing the variance of $\hat{e}_t$ when the conditioning set is F_t^1. Fig. 2 displays the mapping of $\hat{\sigma}_t^2$ into a grid of fifty values of $\hat{e}_{t-1}$, located within the range of $\hat{e}_{t-1}$ found in the sample. An outstanding characteristic of fig. 2 is the difference in implied volatility for negative and positive values of $\hat{e}_{t-1}$, a stylized fact alluded to in the introduction. Fig. 2 is also similar to the equivalent mapping found by Pagan and Hong (1988) in their analysis of monthly stock returns from 1953 to 1984. Also in fig. 2 is the σ_t^2 implied by the GARCH(1, 2) model if one just took the lead term in the distributed lag connecting $\hat{\sigma}_t^2$ and $\hat{e}_{t-j}^2$. Comparing the GARCH and kernel functions it is clear that the GARCH model is likely to exhibit different volatility patterns when $|\hat{e}_{t-1}|$ is large. For small values of $|\hat{e}_{t-1}|$, the two predictions should be close. Unfortunately, this fact makes it hard to discriminate between the two methods, because large values of $|\hat{e}_{t-1}|$ are only a small fraction of the sample.

In addition to the conditional variance, one could compute the mean of $\hat{e}_t$ conditional on $\hat{e}_{t-1}$ to see if there are nonlinearities present. Both the kernel and Fourier estimators discussed later were used to estimate the conditional mean. There was very little dependence of the mean on $\hat{e}_{t-1}$. Thus, for this series it seems that the linear model used to estimate conditional means is an adequate representation of the data. This outcome is to be contrasted with the situation for the conditional variance.

2.8. A nonparametric flexible Fourier form estimator

An alternative nonparametric scheme involves a global approximation using a series expansion, followed by an evaluation of σ_t^2 using F_t. Many series expansions exist in the numerical approximation literature and could be adopted here, but the one used most extensively in economics has been the Flexible Fourier Form (FFF) [Gallant (1981)], where σ_t^2 is represented as the sum of a low-order polynomial and trigonometric terms constructed from the elements of F_t, $z_{tj} = \hat{e}_{t-j}$. Applying this idea to our context gives a model for volatility of the form

$$\sigma_t^2 = \sigma^2 + \sum_{j=1}^{L} \left\{ \left(\alpha_j z_{tj} + \beta_j z_{tj}^2 \right) + \sum_{k=1}^{2} \left[\gamma_{jk} \cos(k z_{tj}) + \delta_{jk} \sin(k z_{tj}) \right] \right\},$$

$$(18)$$

where $L = 1$, 2, or 4 depending on whether F_t^1, F_t^2, or F_t^4 was used. In theory, the number of trigonometric terms must tend to infinity, but in terms of significance it did not seem worthwhile going above order two.

A disadvantage of the FFF is the possibility that estimates of σ_t^2 can be negative, and indeed this happens for a few points in the sample. It has the advantage, however, that when few observations are available in a region of the sample space, the FFF will interpolate the function from other data points, whereas the kernel estimate is only based on the few observations. One must be ambivalent about this property. On the one hand, since 'difficult' points are often concentrated around the origin in multivariate problems [e.g., the 'empty space' phenomenon discussed in Silverman (1986)], there is no 'extrapolation outside the sample', and the results should be reasonable. On the other hand, it is important to know that what we are seeing *is* just an interpolation. Joint viewing of output from both estimators is a prerequisite for an understanding of the behavior of nonparametric volatility measures.

Fig. 2 also shows the FFF estimates of $\hat{\sigma}_t^2$ as a function of $\hat{e}_{t-1}$ along with the lower part of the 95 percent confidence interval for the FFF estimates. The story of the mapping is much the same as for the kernel, except there is a larger estimate of volatility for large positive $\hat{e}_{t-1}$.[6] In this respect the FFF is closer to the GARCH estimate. Notice that across most of the range of $\hat{e}_{t-1}$, $\hat{\sigma}_t^2$ is constant, and it is only for large positive and negative values of $\hat{e}_{t-1}$ that any discrimination between the different ways of measuring σ_t^2 is possible. As there is only a small fraction of the sample featuring large $|\hat{e}_{t-1}|$, one must be sanguine about the possibility of differentiating between the techniques. Nevertheless, the F-statistic that the coefficients of the trigonometric terms in the FFF equal 0 is 6.47, compared with the 5% critical value of $F_{15,\infty} = 1.67$ (the actual degrees of freedom are 16 and 1061). Hence, the nonlinearities accounted for by the Fourier terms are important in explaining volatility. The R^2's between $\hat{e}_t^2$ and $\hat{\sigma}_t^2$ are 0.125 (F_t^1), 0.185 (F_t^2), and 0.205 (F_t^4). Because the EGARCH model has a conditioning set more like F_t^2 than F_t^1, it seems more appropriate to compare the fit of the different models with those R^2, and here the nonparametric estimator seems to represent a substantial improvement. Thus, it may be useful to consider extending the EGARCH model by the addition of Fourier terms in Z_{t-1} and Z_{t-2}.

2.9. Summary

Table 1 contains estimates of the regression

$$\hat{e}_t^2 = \alpha + \beta \hat{\sigma}_t^2 + v_t, \tag{19}$$

for 1835–1925, with heteroskedasticity-consistent standard errors in parentheses under the parameter estimates. If the forecasts are unbiased, $\alpha = 0$ and $\beta = 1$. For the two-step and the Fourier models, least squares estimation forces $\alpha = 0$ and $\beta = 1$. For the other methods, the estimates of α and β are within one standard error of their hypothesized values. The Box–Pierce (1970) statistics for twelve lags of the residual autocorrelations $Q(12)$, corrected for heteroskedasticity, are large for the Markov switching-regime model and the nonparametric kernel and Fourier (one lag) models, showing

---

[6]The close correspondence was another factor in deciding not to experiment with window width in kernel estimation.

Table 1

Comparison of within-sample predictive power for the conditional variance of stock returns, 1835–1925.[a]

$$\hat{e}_t^2 = \alpha + \beta \hat{\sigma}_t^2 + \upsilon_t$$

Model	α	β	R^2	$Q(12)$	R^2 for logs
1. Two-step	0.00000 (0.00036)	1.000 (0.3402)	0.089	0.69 (1.00)	0.022
2. GARCH(1,2)	0.00019 (0.00031)	0.8274 (0.2904)	0.067	17.3 (0.139)	0.033
3. EGARCH(1,2)	−0.00034 (0.00041)	1.318 (0.3911)	0.118	14.6 (0.265)	0.042
4. Markov switching-regime	−0.00009 (0.00021)	1.165 (0.2342)	0.057	23.3 (0.025)	0.034
5. Nonparametric kernel (1 lag)	0.00028 (0.00027)	0.7565 (0.2501)	0.126	29.2 (0.004)	0.012
6. Nonparametric Fourier (1 lag)	0.00000 (0.00033)	1.000 (0.3020)	0.125	29.0 (0.004)	0.015
7. Nonparametric Fourier (2 lags)	0.00000 (0.00018)	1.000 (0.1606)	0.185	13.2 (0.358)	0.028

[a]Standard errors using White's (1980) heteroskedasticity correction are in parentheses under the coefficient estimates. R^2 is the coefficient of determination. $Q(12)$ is the heteroskedasticity-corrected Box–Pierce (1970) statistic for twelve lags of the residual autocorrelations, with its p-value in parentheses below it. The corrected Box–Pierce statistic is calculated by comparing the sum of squared autocorrelation estimates, each divided by White's (1980) heteroskedasticity-consistent variance, and comparing this with a χ^2 distribution with twelve degrees of freedom. The R^2 for logs column shows the R^2 statistic from the regression of $\ln \hat{e}_t^2$ on $\ln \hat{\sigma}_t^2$.

serially correlated residuals υ_t. The serial correlation shows there is additional persistence in volatility that is not captured by these models.

As a check on the criterion function we use to compare alternative models, we also ran the regression

$$\ln \hat{e}_t^2 = \alpha + \beta \ln \hat{\sigma}_t^2 + \upsilon_t \tag{20}$$

to compare the R^2 statistics from these regressions.[7] These statistics, labeled 'R^2 for logs' in table 1, are motivated by the idea of a proportional loss function, rather than the quadratic loss function implicit in (19). Mistakes in predicting small variances are given more weight in (20) than in (19). All the R^2 statistics for logs are smaller than the R^2's for the raw data. The nonparametric estimates are affected the most, showing that their apparent

[7]We are grateful to the referee and to John Campbell for suggesting this analysis.

advantage in predicting $\hat{e}_t^2$ is for very large values, which is consistent with the plots in fig. 2.

3. Post-sample prediction

The previous comparisons involve within-sample estimates of R^2 between $\hat{e}_t^2$ and $\hat{\sigma}_t^2$. Since some of the methods use a large number of parameters to model the data, there is the possibility that 'over-fitting' can occur. One way to evaluate this question is to estimate the model parameters with a subset of data and create out-of sample forecasts for the remainder.

3.1. Predictions for 1900–1925

Table 2 contains estimates of (19) and (20) for 1900–1925, where the model parameters were estimated using data from 1835–1899. For the two-step, GARCH(1, 2), EGARCH(1, 2), Hamilton, and kernel forecasts, the estimates of α and β are within one standard error of the hypothesized values ($\alpha = 0$, $\beta = 1$). For the Fourier forecasts, however, the estimates of α are more than two standard errors above 0, and the estimates of β are more than two standard errors below 1. The two-step model has the highest R^2 of 0.110, while the GARCH, EGARCH, and Hamilton forecasts have R^2's of about 0.07. The nonparametric forecasts have R^2's below 0.035. The Box–Pierce (1970) statistics for twelve lags of the residual autocorrelations $Q(12)$, corrected for heteroskedasticity, are large for all the forecast models, showing serially correlated forecast errors.

One might be tempted to conclude that the nonparametric methods of modeling conditional volatility suffer from over-fitting, since the R^2 statistics are so low for the out-of-sample forecasts. To check this possibility, we also calculated the R^2 statistics for 1900–1925 using the fitted values from the models estimated over the entire 1835–1925 sample period. If over-fitting is a serious problem, these R^2 statistics should be much higher than the out-of-sample prediction R^2's. Since the in-sample R^2's are only slightly higher than their out-of-sample counterparts, however, and the differences are similar for all the models in table 2, it seems that over-fitting or parameter instability is not a serious problem. Rather, the nonparametric forecasting methods work poorly in this sample because there are few large returns in the 1900–1925 period. Fig. 2 shows that the kernel and Fourier models obtain explanatory power from a few extreme returns and, as will be shown in section 4, many of these occur in the earlier part of the sample. It is well-known that nonparametric estimators are inefficient compared with parametric estimators of a *correctly specified* model. For this part of the data, the predictions of all the models would be for small values of σ_t^2, since the minimum value of $\hat{e}_t$ was

Table 2

Comparison of out-of-sample predictive power for the conditional variance of stock returns, 1900–1925.[a]

$$\hat{e}_t^2 = \alpha + \beta \hat{\sigma}_t^2 + v_t$$

Model	α	β	R^2	$Q(12)$	In-sample R^2	R^2 for logs
1. Two-step	−0.00020 (0.00045)	1.112 (0.4329)	0.110	22.2 (0.035)	0.137	0.023
2. GARCH(1,2)	0.00018 (0.00035)	0.7752 (0.3427)	0.075	30.4 (0.002)	0.077	0.027
3. EGARCH(1,2)	0.00007 (0.00033)	0.8771 (0.3310)	0.074	30.2 (0.003)	0.077	0.033
4. Markov switching-regime	−0.00003 (0.00032)	1.042 (0.3555)	0.070	30.4 (0.002)	0.086	0.026
5. Nonparametric kernel (1 lag)	0.00027 (0.00059)	0.7720 (0.5626)	0.013	21.8 (0.040)	0.019	0.019
6. Nonparametric Fourier (1 lag)	0.00090 (0.00024)	0.1416 (0.1964)	0.002	23.5 (0.024)	0.009	0.012
7. Nonparametric Fourier (2 lags)	0.00051 (0.00021)	0.4978 (0.2129)	0.032	22.2 (0.036)	0.046	0.018

[a]Standard errors using White's (1980) heteroskedasticity correction are in parentheses under the coefficient estimates. R^2 is the coefficient of determination. $Q(12)$ is the heteroskedasticity-corrected Box–Pierce (1970) statistic for twelve lags of the residual autocorrelations, with its p-value in parentheses below it. The corrected Box–Pierce statistic is calculated by comparing the sum of squared autocorrelation estimates, each divided by White's (1980) heteroskedasticity-consistent variance, and comparing this with a χ^2 distribution with twelve degrees of freedom. The parameters for these models are estimated using data from July 1835 through December 1899, then forecasts of conditional variances $\hat{\sigma}_t^2$ are made for the January 1900 through December 1925 period. The in-sample R^2 statistic in the next-to-last column measures the relation between fitted values from the model estimated over the entire 1835–1925 period with $\hat{e}_t^2$ over the 1900–1925 subsample. The R^2 for logs column shows the R^2 statistic from the regression of ln $\hat{e}_t^2$ on ln $\hat{\sigma}_t^2$ for the forecasts from 1900–1925.

−0.09. As seen from the slope coefficients, the nonparametric estimates have more variable $\hat{\sigma}_t^2$ than necessary, a sign of an inefficient estimator.

The R^2 statistics for logs from (20) are again smaller than for the raw data. The ranking of alternative methods is similar, however. Nelson's EGARCH model has the highest R^2 for ln $\hat{e}_t^2$.

3.2. Predictions for 1926–1937

Table 3 contains estimates of (19) and (20) for 1926–1937, where the model parameters were estimated using data from 1835–1925. As mentioned earlier, the Great Depression from 1929–1939 was a period of unprecedented stock return volatility. The recursive variance estimates in fig. 1

Table 3

Comparison of out-of-sample predictive power for the conditional variance of stock returns, 1926–1937.[a]

$$\hat{e}_t^2 = \alpha + \beta \hat{\sigma}_t^2 + v_t$$

Model	α	β	R^2	$Q(12)$	R^2 for logs
1. Two-step	0.00373 (0.00170)	0.8146 (0.4409)	0.055	7.6 (0.813)	0.066
2. GARCH(1, 2)	0.00288 (0.00148)	0.9209 (0.3918)	0.078	8.4 (0.754)	0.091
3. EGARCH(1, 2)	0.00136 (0.00112)	1.895 (0.5478)	0.080	6.4 (0.893)	0.111
4. Markov switching-regime	−0.00406 (0.00184)	5.644 (1.490)	0.045	7.0 (0.861)	0.026
5. Nonparametric kernel (1 lag)	0.00670 (0.00160)	−0.0115 (0.2522)	0.000	24.0 (0.020)	0.025
6. Nonparametric Fourier (1 lag)	0.00631 (0.00120)	0.0074 (0.0077)	0.019	12.9 (0.374)	0.033
7. Nonparametric Fourier (2 lags)	0.00642 (0.00120)	0.0071 (0.0078)	0.016	15.8 (0.202)	0.047

[a]Standard errors using White's (1980) heteroskedasticity correction are in parentheses under the coefficient estimates. R^2 is the coefficient of determination. $Q(12)$ is the heteroskedasticity-corrected Box–Pierce (1970) statistic for twelve lags of the residual autocorrelations, with its p-value in parentheses below it. The corrected Box–Pierce statistic is calculated by comparing the sum of squared autocorrelation estimates, each divided by White's (1980) heteroskedasticity-consistent variance, and comparing this with a χ^2 distribution with twelve degrees of freedom. The R^2 for logs column shows the R^2 statistic from the regression of $\ln \hat{e}_t^2$ on $\ln \hat{\sigma}_t^2$.

strongly show that the unconditional variance is not constant between 1835–1925 and 1926–1937. Thus, we should expect that forecasting conditional variances in this sample period will be difficult. Nevertheless, the large changes in stock prices that occurred in this period provide an interesting out-of-sample experiment. If the 1900–1925 period was too quiet, the 1926–1937 period may be too volatile.

Indeed, the estimates (19) in table 3 show substantial bias in the forecasts. Most of the intercept estimates $\hat{\alpha}$ are more than two standard errors above 0, and the slope coefficient estimates $\hat{\beta}$ are more than two standard errors from 1. The two-step, GARCH(1, 2), and EGARCH(1, 2) models seem to work best, probably because they capture the persistence in volatility that was important in this period. Hamilton's model has an upper bound on the conditional variance that is too small, so the slope coefficient is over 5.5. While the Markov model correctly identifies periods of high variance, its estimate of volatility is too low. The nonparametric models also do poorly in this period. The large positive and negative monthly returns that occurred in the 1926–1937 period have no precedent in the 1835–1925 sample, so the kernel has no basis for making predictions of conditional variance. The Fourier model also does poorly because it has to extrapolate outside of the range of the data.[8]

The R^2 statistics from the log regressions (20) are generally larger for this sample period. The large values of $\hat{e}_t^2$ are difficult for all the models to predict. Nevertheless, the relative ranking of the methods is similar: the EGARCH model does best, followed by the other parametric models, and the nonparametric methods do worst in this out-of-sample prediction experiment.

4. Analysis of important episodes of stock volatility

Another way to contrast the behavior of the alternative variance estimators is to analyze their behavior during important subperiods in the sample. Fig. 2 shows that the main difference between the GARCH(1, 2) model and the kernel or Fourier estimator occurs for large negative returns. These data also explain the difference between Nelson's EGARCH model and the GARCH model. Thus, it is worthwhile to plot some of the variance estimates around major drops in stock prices from 1835–1925. Schwert (1989b) notes that many of the stock market 'crashes' during the 19th century occurred at about the same time as banking panics. Therefore, we will use the dates of the bank panics and other major events to evaluate the different predictions of stock return volatility.

4.1. The banking crisis of 1837

There was a major banking crisis in May 1837. This is one of the cases where many banks refused to redeem demand deposits for currency. Stock prices fell in early 1837 as investors seeking liquidity sold stocks [see Sobel (1988, ch. 2) for an interesting history of this episode]. Fig. 3a plots the unexpected stock return $\hat{e}_t(E)$[9] along with the one-lag Fourier (F), kernel (K), Hamilton (H), EGARCH(1, 2) (EG), and GARCH(1, 2) (G) estimates of the conditional standard deviation for 1837. Stock prices fell during early 1837, with monthly returns of -2, -5, -8, and -8 percent in February through May. On the other hand, the rise in stock prices in July 1837 of over

---

[8]Some of the forecasts of conditional standard deviation are over 200 percent per month from the Fourier models in this period.

[9]The unexpected stock returns $\hat{e}_t(E)$ in figs. 3a–3d are multiplied by 0.1 so they do not dominate the plots of the standard deviations. Thus, when E is -0.01 in one of these plots, the unexpected stock return was -10 percent that month.

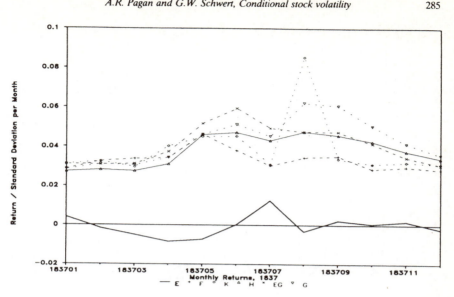

Fig. 3a. Unexpected stock returns, e_t, and estimates of conditional standard deviations from Fourier (F), kernel (K), Hamilton (H), EGARCH (EG), and GARCH (G) models, 1837.

12 percent is the third largest monthly return in the sample. This is characteristic of conditional heteroskedasticity – large returns follow large returns, with random signs. Among the volatility estimates, the Fourier estimate moves the least. The kernel estimate and the GARCH estimate increase in August 1837, following the erratic pattern of returns earlier in the year. The kernel estimate drops back to its previous level in September 1837, while the GARCH estimates gradually decay.

4.2. The banking panic of 1857

There was a major banking crisis in the Fall of 1857 [see Sobel (1988, ch. 3)]. Several major firms went bankrupt and there was a similar financial crisis in Europe. Fig. 3b plots the unexpected stock return $\hat{e}_t$ (E) along with the various conditional standard deviation estimates for the last half of 1857 and the first half of 1858. Stock prices fell 6, 14, and 13 percent in August, September, and October 1857. Then, in November 1857, prices rose by more than 16 percent. The returns for September–November 1857 are three of the four largest in absolute value for the 1835–1925 period. This episode is the best experiment to differentiate among the alternative variance estimators. Both the kernel and the Fourier estimates rise dramatically in October 1857,

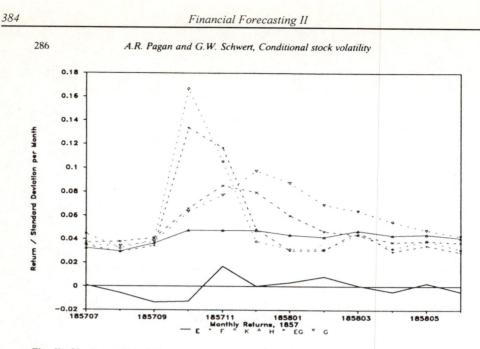

Fig. 3b. Unexpected stock returns, e_t, and estimates of conditional standard deviations from Fourier (F), kernel (K), Hamilton (H), EGARCH (EG), and GARCH (G) models, 1857–58.

and they decline sharply in December 1857. In contrast, the GARCH and EGARCH estimates rise gradually, peaking in December 1857 and gradually decaying after that. Hamilton's estimate rises and falls much less. Thus, the nonparametric estimates adapt more quickly to the fast increase in volatility and to its decrease when the panic subsided.

4.3. The start of the Civil War, 1860

It is not surprising that the beginning of the Civil War increased the volatility of stock returns. Fig. 3c plots the unexpected stock return $\hat{e}_t$ (E) along with the various conditional standard deviation estimates for the last half of 1860 and the first half of 1861. Stock prices fell 4, 10, and 5 percent in the last three months of 1860, rising about 10 percent in January 1861, only to fall 9 and 6 percent in April and May 1861. Again, the Fourier estimate of the conditional standard deviation rises the most in December 1860 and May 1861, returning to more normal levels in the next month. The other methods show a smaller increase in volatility in December 1860 and slight decay from that point.

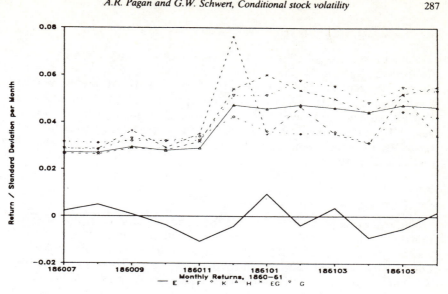

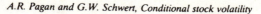

Fig. 3c. Unexpected stock returns, e_t, and estimates of conditional standard deviations from Fourier (F), kernel (K), Hamilton (H), EGARCH (EG), and GARCH (G) models, 1860–61.

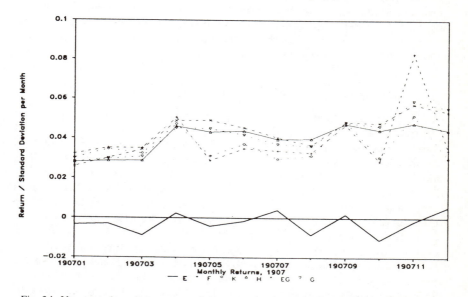

Fig. 3d. Unexpected stock returns, e_t, and estimates of conditional standard deviations from Fourier (F), kernel (K), Hamilton (H), EGARCH (EG), and GARCH (G) models, 1907.

4.4. The banking crisis of 1907

The banking crisis of 1907 is often credited with leading to the creation of the Federal Reserve System in 1914. Fig. 3d shows that stock prices fell by almost 9 percent in March, August, and October 1907. All the estimates of conditional standard deviations rose in April 1907, with the kernel and Fourier estimates dropping in May. The Fourier estimate jumps from October to November, then falls back to its previous level in December. The GARCH, EGARCH, and Hamilton estimates remain high throughout the second half of 1907.

4.5. Summary

The plots in figs. 3a–3d show that the nonparametric estimates of conditional volatility (kernel and Fourier) are different from the parametric estimates (GARCH, EGARCH, and Hamilton) in periods when stock prices fall. In particular, volatility rises fast after large negative unexpected returns. The parametric estimates all show slow adjustment to large volatility shocks, but the effects of these shocks persist after the crises subside. These plots reinforce the impression given by the goodness-of-fit regressions in tables 1, 2, and 3. The parametric and nonparametric methods of modeling conditional volatility capture different aspects of the data. The parametric methods use the persistent, smoother aspects of conditional volatility, while the nonparametric methods use the highly nonlinear response to large return shocks. Neither method subsumes the other.

5. Nesting parametric and nonparametric models

The previous evidence shows that parametric and nonparametric models for stock volatility capture different aspects of the data. One way to nest these models is to add Fourier terms to the parametric models. For example, we added the sine and cosine of lagged stock returns y_{t-1} to the GARCH$(1, 2)$ model in (6) for 1835–1925 and the log-likelihood increased by 4.8. The likelihood ratio test statistic of 9.6 has a p-value of 0.008. When Fourier terms were added to the EGARCH$(1, 2)$ model in (7), however, the log-likelihood increased by only 0.77, yielding a small test statistic with a p-value of 0.46. Thus, it seems that for the 1835–1925 period the EGARCH model captures the asymmetry in the relation between stock return and volatility.

We also added Fourier terms to GARCH and EGARCH models estimated over the entire 1835–1987 period. The χ^2 statistic for the Fourier terms is 16.8 in the GARCH model (with a p-value of 0.0002), which again shows the importance of asymmetries missed by the GARCH model. The χ^2 statistic is

11.8 for the EGARCH model, which has a *p*-value of 0.003. Thus, it seems there are important asymmetries missed by the EGARCH model over the longer sample period. It remains an open question whether the nonstationarity of the variance over this period affects the tests for the Fourier terms.

6. Conclusions and suggestions for future work

Our aim was to compare various measures of stock volatility. Taking the 1835–1925 period as the sample, it emerged that the nonparametric procedures tended to give a better explanation of the squared returns than any of the parametric models. Both Hamilton's and the GARCH model produced weak explanations of the data. Nelson's EGARCH model came closest to the explanatory power of the nonparametric models, because it reflects the asymmetric relation between volatility and past returns.

In out-of-sample prediction experiments, the nonparametric models fared worse than the parametric models. Nonparametric estimators of conditional moments are inefficient relative to parametric ones, and this is likely to show up in too much variability in the estimates of σ_t^2. An improved ability to capture the movements in σ_t^2 when returns decline therefore has to be set against this tendency, and it appears that even with a sample of the size used here nonparametric methods find it hard to overcome their inherent inefficiency. Previous uses of nonparametrics in this area, for example Pagan and Hong (1988), used the estimate of σ_t^2 in a regression to semiparametrically estimate risk coefficients, and hence the 'averaging' of $\hat{\sigma}_t^2$ makes the semiparametric and parametric estimators equivalent.

Our results imply that standard parametric models are not sufficiently extensive. Augmenting the GARCH and EGARCH models with terms suggested by nonparametric methods yields significant increases in explanatory power. This fact points to the need to merge the two traditions to capture a richer set of specifications than are currently employed. Nevertheless, our results emphasize that any extensions are best done in a parametric framework.

A secondary concern of the paper, which grew out of the data analysis, is that data taken over long periods cannot be assumed to be covariance stationary. Much work in this area ignores this question entirely, although the models proposed to fit the data imply covariance stationarity. A simple recursive variance test showed that the data could not be thought of as homogeneous before and after the Great Depression. This was illustrated by the fact that all the models performed poorly in predicting conditional variances in the 1926–1937 sample. If covariance nonstationarity is found to be a feature of many financial series, it forces us to examine what are likely to be good models of such data.

References

Black, Fischer, 1976, Studies of stock price volatility changes, Proceedings of the 1976 Meetings of the Business and Economics Statistics Section, American Statistical Association, 177–181.

Bollerslev, Tim, 1986, Generalized autoregressive conditional heteroskedasticity, Journal of Econometrics 31, 307–328.

Bollerslev, Tim, 1988, Integrated ARCH and cointegration in variance, Unpublished manuscript (Northwestern University, Evanston, IL).

Christie, Andrew A., 1982, The stochastic behavior of common stock variances: Value, leverage and interest rate effects, Journal of Financial Economics 10, 407–432.

Cowles, Alfred III and Associates, 1939, Common stock indexes, 2nd ed., Cowles Commission monograph no. 3 (Principia Press, Bloomington, IN).

Davidian, Marie and Raymond J. Carroll, 1987, Variance function estimation, Journal of the American Statistical Association 82, 1079–1091.

Engle, Robert F., 1982, Autoregressive conditional heteroskedasticity with estimates of the variance of United Kingdom inflation, Econometrica 50, 987–1007.

Engle, Robert F. and Tim Bollerslev, 1986, Modeling the persistence of conditional variances, Econometric Reviews 5, 1–50.

French, Kenneth R., G. William Schwert, and Robert F. Stambaugh, 1987, Expected stock returns and volatility, Journal of Financial Economics 19, 3–29.

Gallant, A. Ronald, 1981, On the bias in flexible functional forms and an essentially unbiased form: The Fourier flexible form, Journal of Econometrics 15, 211–244.

Hamilton, James D., 1988, Rational-expectations econometric analysis of changes in regime: An investigation of the term structure of interest rates, Journal of Economic Dynamics and Control 12, 385–423.

Hamilton, James D., 1989, A new approach to the economic analysis of nonstationary time series and the business cycle, Econometrica 57, 357–384.

Macaulay, Frederick R., 1938, The movements of interest rates, bond yields and stock prices in the United States since 1856 (National Bureau of Economic Research, New York, NY).

Mandelbrot, Benoit, 1963, The variation of certain speculative prices, Journal of Business 36, 394–419.

Nadaraya, E.A., 1964, On estimating regression, Theory of Probability and Its Applications 9, 141–142.

Nelson, Daniel B., 1988, Conditional heteroskedasticity in asset returns: A new approach, Unpublished manuscript (University of Chicago, Chicago, IL).

Pagan, Adrian R. and Aman Ullah, 1988, The econometric analysis of models with risk terms, Journal of Applied Econometrics 3, 87–105.

Pagan, Adrian R. and Yi-Soek Hong, 1989, Nonparametric estimation and the risk premium, in: W. Barnett, J. Powell, and G. Tauchen, eds., Semiparametric and nonparametric methods in econometrics and statistics (Cambridge University Press, Cambridge).

Pagan, Adrian R. and H. Sabau, 1987, Consistency tests for heteroskedastic and risk models, Unpublished manuscript (University of Rochester, Rochester, NY).

Sabau, H., 1988, Some theoretical aspects of econometric inference with heteroskedastic models, Unpublished doctoral dissertation (Australian National University, Canberra).

Schwert, G. William, 1989a, Why does stock market volatility change over time?, Journal of Finance 44, 1115–1153.

Schwert, G. William, 1989b, Business cycles, financial crises, and stock volatility, Carnegie–Rochester Conference Series on Public Policy 31, 83–126.

Schwert, G. William, 1990, Stock volatility and the crash of '87, Review of Financial Studies 3, forthcoming.

Silverman, B.W., 1986, Density estimation for statistics and data analysis (Chapman and Hall, London).

Smith, Walter B. and Arthur H. Cole, 1935, Fluctuations in American business, 1790–1860 (Harvard University Press, Cambridge, MA).

Sobel, Robert, 1988, Panic on Wall Street, Rev. ed. (E.P. Dutton, New York, NY).

Watson, G.S., 1964, Smooth regression analysis, Sankhya A 26, 359–372.

White, Halbert, 1980, A heteroskedasticity-consistent covariance matrix estimator and a direct test for heteroskedasticity, Econometrica 48, 817–838.

[22]

International Journal of Forecasting 3 (1987) 159–170
North-Holland

FORECASTING THE VOLATILITY OF CURRENCY EXCHANGE RATES *

Stephen J. TAYLOR

University of Lancaster, Lancaster, LA1 4YX, UK

Abstract: Currency volatility is defined to be the standard deviation of day-to-day changes in the logarithm of the exchange rate. After a discussion of statistical models for exchange rates, the paper describes methods for choosing and assessing volatility forecasts using open, high, low and close prices. Results for DM/$ futures prices at the IMM in Chicago from 1977 to 1983 show high and low prices are valuable when seeking accurate volatility forecasts. The best forecasts are a weighted average of present and past high, low and close prices, with adjustments for weekend and holiday effects. The forecasts can be used to value currency options.

Keywords: Forecasting, Exchange rates, Volatility, Futures prices, Statistical models, Options.

1. Introduction

Finding a better forecast of a future exchange rate than the relevant forward rate or futures price is extremely difficult. This paper makes no attempt to forecast exchange rates. Instead we consider forecasts of volatility, i.e., forecasts of the rate of price changes but not of their direction. Volatility is the name given by option traders to the standard deviation of certain price changes. If we suppose exchange rates are recorded once per day, with Z_t the price on day t, and if we also suppose that logarithmic price changes, $X_t = \log(Z_t/Z_{t-1})$, called returns, are independently and identically distributed (i.i.d.) then the volatility σ is defined to be the standard deviation of X_t. More complicated models are needed for financial prices since returns are not i.i.d. Suitable models are presented in section 2 with volatility defined as a conditional standard deviation.

This paper compares various volatility forecasts calculated from Chicago futures prices for the DM/$ rate. We consider daily open, high, low and close prices from 1977 to 1983 inclusive. In a recent book [Taylor (1986)] the author has investigated forecasts based upon closing prices alone. This paper seeks improved forecasts, primarily by using high and low prices since these prices are theoretically very helpful when estimating volatilities [Parkinson (1980), Garman and Klass (1980)]. Section 2 summarises some realistic price and volatility models, then section 3 presents theoretical forecasting results. The data is described in section 4. It is subdivided into two sets: prices from 1977 to 1981 are used to estimate parameters in section 5, then prices for 1982 and 1983 are used to assess various forecasts in section 6.

* This is an abbreviated and revised version of a paper presented at the Sixth International Symposium on Forecasting, Paris, June 1986. The longer paper is available upon request. Helpful comments by the editors and referees are gratefully acknowledged.

Volatility forecasts have important practical applications for option traders. The purchaser of a currency option owns the right, but not an obligation, to make a currency transaction at a later date at a previously agreed rate. Most traders suppose an option's price depends on the spot price, the exercise price, the time until the expiration date, domestic and foreign interest rates and the volatility σ; they implicitly assume returns are i.i.d. Once σ is specified, a fair option price can be calculated [Garman and Kohlhagen (1983), Gemmill (1986)]. Any trader possessing a superior forecast of σ would expect to make a riskless profit trading mispriced options using some arbitrage strategy. This possibility provides an incentive to seek better volatility forecasts.

2. Modelling prices, returns and volatilities

2.1. Two assumptions

Recall the notation Z_t for the price on trading day t, which will be supposed to be the closing price at a particular exchange, and the notation $X_t = \log(Z_t/Z_{t-1})$ for the return from day $t-1$ to day t. Theoretically, expected returns $E[X_t]$ are zero for futures [Black (1976)] but depend on domestic and foreign interest rates for spot currency. We will only consider currency futures and will assume expected returns are zero.

International markets process information quickly and the well-known efficient market hypothesis states that past prices Z_{t-i}, $i > 0$, are of no economic value when forecasting future prices Z_{t+j}, $j > 0$; only Z_t is important. It will be assumed that prices follow a random walk so returns are uncorrelated, i.e., the correlation between X_t and $X_{t+\tau}$ is zero for all integers t and all positive lags τ, as any small autocorrelation can be ignored when forecasting volatilities.

2.2. Discrete time models

Many researchers have observed that the standard deviation of returns appears to change with time. A suitable general model for futures returns is given by

$$X_t = V_t U_t, \tag{1}$$

with V_t a positive variable representing volatility and U_t a normal variable having zero mean and unit variance. A random walk is obtained by assuming that the U_t are independently and identically distributed. Also, I assume the processes $\{V_t\}$ and $\{U_t\}$ are stochastically independent.

In eq. (1), X_t, V_t and U_t are random variables. By the end of day t, numerous traders will be responsible for particular outcomes x_t, v_t and u_t. The actual volatility v_t is a conditional standard deviation for X_t. Given v_t, the observed return x_t is an observation from the normal distribution $N(0, v_t^2)$.

A special case of eq. (1) is the model implicitly assumed by many option traders, defined by supposing $V_t = \sigma$, for all t. There is ample evidence that this special model is inadequate even within the lifetime of a futures contract [e.g., Taylor (1986, pp. 52, 106)]. More detailed models, consistent with the general model, eq. (1), have often been investigated [e.g., Clark (1973), Hsu (1977), Ali and Giaccotto (1982)]. In particular, Tauchen and Pitts (1983) have described an economic model for the reaction of individual traders to separate items of information and then V_t is a function of the number of relevant information items during day t. Another approach has been developed in Engle (1982) and Engle and Bollerslev (1986). They have suggested ARCH models for which V_t is a deterministic function of past returns X_{t-i}, $i > 0$. It would then be possible to perfectly forecast V_{t+1}

using present and past returns although this is empirically disputable [Taylor (1986, ch. 4)]. Forecasts derived from ARCH models are similar to those presented here.

2.3. Overnight and open-market models

Prices will change overnight from the previous day's close Z_{t-1} to the price at which the market opens on day t, denoted Z_t^0. Define X_{1t}, the overnight return, as $\log(Z_t^0/Z_{t-1})$ and X_{2t}, the open-market return, as $\log(Z_t/Z_t^0)$. Then we assume

$$X_{it} = V_t U_{it}, \qquad i = 1, 2, \tag{2}$$

with $U_{1t} \sim N(0, \epsilon)$, $U_{2t} \sim N(0, 1 - \epsilon)$ and U_{1t} independent of U_{2t}. Clearly $U_t = \Sigma U_{it}$, summing over $i = 1, 2$. The term ϵ represents the proportion of daily variance attributable to the hours when the market is closed.

2.4. Continuous time models

Following common practise it will be assumed that prices change continually when the market is open and then follow a Brownian process. Let T be a real number representing trading time on a continuous scale. To model prices $Z(T)$ throughout the day let

$$\log[Z(T)] - \log[Z_t^0] = V_t[B(T) - B(t-1)], \qquad t-1 < T < t, \tag{3}$$

with $\{B(T), T \text{ real}\}$ a non-standardised Brownian process for which $B(T_2) - B(T_1)$ is normal with mean zero and variance $(1 - \epsilon)(T_2 - T_1)$ for any $T_2 > T_1$. Then $U_{2t} = B(t) - B(t-1)$. The notation $Z(T)$ is used for non-integer values of T. Daily high and low prices H_t and L_t are respectively defined by the maximum and minimum of $\{Z_t^0, Z_t, Z(T), t-1 < T < t\}$.

2.5. Seasonal effects

Some returns are calculated from prices separated by more than 24 hours as markets close for weekends and holidays. Consequently the volatility V_t may be seasonal. It will be supposed that a non-seasonal volatility V_t^* can be defined by

$$V_t^* = V_t \qquad \text{when } X_t \text{ is a 24 hour return,} \tag{4}$$

$$= V_t/s_v \quad \text{otherwise,}$$

for some constant $s_v > 1$. The proportion of a return's variance attributable to the hours when the market is closed is also seasonal. This proportion is now denoted ϵ_t to emphasise its time-dependence.

3. Forecasting volatility: theoretical results

3.1. Introducing related variables

It is impossible to calculate the exact volatility of prices on a particular day, then or later, because the volatility of prices changes frequently. Thus we cannot use current and past volatilities to forecast future volatilities v_{t+h}, $h > 0$, because the series $\{v_t\}$ is not observable. This section argues that forecasts of v_{t+h} should be constructed from forecasts of related, observable variables. Two examples of related variables are absolute returns

$$M_t = |X_t| = V_t |U_t| = V_t |U_{1t} + B(t) - B(t-1)|, \tag{5}$$

and the daily range of log(price), i.e., log(high/low), defined as

$$D_t = \log(H_t) - \log(L_t)$$

$$= V_t \{ \max[B(T), t-1 \leqslant T \leqslant t] - \min[B(T), t-1 \leqslant T \leqslant t] \}. \tag{6}$$

3.2. Relationships between the accuracy of forecasts

Suppose we try to forecast a random variable A_{t+h}, which is related to the volatility V_{t+h} by

$$A_{t+h} = V_{t+h} f(J_{t+h}), \qquad J_{t+h} = \{U_{1,t+h}, B(T), t+h-1 \leqslant T \leqslant t+h\}. \tag{7}$$

Eqs. (5) and (6) illustrate two possible functions f. The accuracy of forecasts $\hat{A}_{t+h}$ and $\hat{V}_{t+h}$ are assessed by their mean square errors

$$\text{MSE}(\hat{A}_{t+h}) = E\left[(A_{t+h} - \hat{A}_{t+h})^2\right] \quad \text{and} \quad \text{MSE}(\hat{V}_{t+h}) = E\left[(V_{t+h} - \hat{V}_{t+h})^2\right]. \tag{8}$$

Let $\hat{A}_{t+h}$ be defined using information I_t, one possible example being the current and past values $\{A_{t-i}, i \geqslant 0\}$. It will be assumed that any random variable constructed from I_t and V_{t+h} is independent of any random variable constructed from J_{t+h}. This is consistent with a perfectly efficient futures market. Then the best forecast of $f(J_{t+h})$ using I_t is simply its mean value, say $\mu_{f,t+h}$ abbreviated to μ_f.

Now suppose $\hat{A}_{t+h}$ and $\hat{V}_{t+h}$ are forecasts linked by

$$\hat{A}_{t+h} = \mu_f \hat{V}_{t+h}. \tag{9}$$

Then it can be shown, quickly, [cf. Taylor (1986, p. 99)] that

$$\text{var}(A_{t+h}) - \text{MSE}(\hat{A}_{t+h}) = \mu_f^2 \{\text{var}(V_{t+h}) - \text{MSE}(\hat{V}_{t+h})\}. \tag{10}$$

Consequently, if $\hat{A}_{t+h}$ is the optimal forecast of A_{t+h} using I_t, then the optimal forecast of V_{t+h} using the *same* information is defined by eq. (9).

This result suggests the following strategy for forecasting volatility: for suitable information sets $\{I_t\}$ and an appropriate related series $\{A_t\}$ seek optimal forecasts $\{\hat{A}_{t+h}\}$ and hence optimal forecasts $\{\hat{V}_{t+h}\}$ using eq. (9). It is necessary to calculate μ_f, which, in practise, requires assumptions that variables like U_{1t} and $B(T_2) - B(T_1)$ have normal distributions.

3.3. Results for some stationary models

Now consider some results for special stationary models which will be helpful when assessing empirical estimates of autocorrelations and mean square errors. This is only possible for non-sea-

S.J. Taylor / Forecasting the volatility of currency exchange rates 163

sonal processes and involves technical complications which some readers may prefer to skip. Let V_t^* be the non-seasonal volatility, eq. (4), let f_t^* be a non-seasonal adaptation of $f_t = f(J_t)$ and let $A_t^* = V_t^* f_t^*$ be the non-seasonal related variable. For example, f_t^* is simply f_t when the related variable is the absolute return M_t, whilst $f_t^* = f_t / \sqrt{(1 - \epsilon_t)}$ will be used when considering the daily range D_t. Now suppose the processes $\{V_t^*\}$ and $\{f_t^*\}$ are stationary. In an effort to keep the notation under control the stars are now suppressed for this subsection. Thus throughout the remainder of section 3.3 V_t refers to the non-seasonal volatility and likewise for A_t and f_t.

It can be shown that the autocorrelations $\rho_{\tau,A} = \text{cor}(A_t, A_{t+\tau})$ are a constant times the autocorrelations $\rho_{\tau,V} = \text{cor}(V_t, V_{t+\tau})$:

$$\rho_{\tau,A} = \rho_{\tau,V} \, \text{var}(V_t) / \left\{ \psi_f E[V_t^2] - E[V_t]^2 \right\}, \tag{11}$$

with $\psi_f = E[f_t^2] / E[f_t]^2 \geqslant 1$. When A_t is the absolute return M_t, $E[f_t^2] = 1$, $E[f_t] = \sqrt{(2/\pi)}$ and $\psi_f \approx 1.57$, whilst if A_t is the range D_t then $E[f_t^2] = 4 \log_e 2$, $E[f_t] = 2\sqrt{\{2/\pi\}}$ and $\psi_f \approx 1.09$ [Parkinson (1980, p. 62)]. Thus ranges would then be more highly autocorrelated than absolute returns.

The simplest appropriate stationary model for $\{V_t\}$ is given by supposing $\{\log(V_t)\}$ is Gaussian with autocorrelations ϕ^τ and variance denoted by β^2 [Taylor (1986, chs. 3 and 4)]. Then $\{V_t\}$ has autocorrelations similar to ϕ^τ for low β and

$$\rho_{\tau,A} \approx \phi^\tau \{\exp(\beta^2) - 1\} / \{\psi_f \exp(\beta^2) - 1\}. \tag{12}$$

Replacing $\approx$ by $=$ in eq. (12), the autocorrelation can be described by

$$\rho_{\tau,A} = K\phi^\tau, \tag{13}$$

for a constant K depending on β and ψ_f with $0 < K < 1$. An ARMA (1, 1) process has the same autocorrelations as in eq. (13) for certain parameter values. Thus it can be shown [cf. Taylor (1986, pp. 21–22, 101–102)] that the best forecast $\hat{A}_{t+1}$ linear in the variables $A_t, A_{t-1}, A_{t-2}, \ldots$, is given by

$$\hat{A}_{t+1} = \mu_A + (\phi - \theta) \sum_{i=0}^{\infty} \theta^i (A_{t-i} - \mu_A), \tag{14}$$

with $\mu_A = E[A_t]$ and θ the solution of the quadratic equation

$$\theta^2 - d\theta + 1 = 0, \qquad d = \{1 + \phi^2(1 - 2K)\} / \{\phi(1 - K)\}, \tag{15}$$

having $\theta < 1$. Further algebra gives the following relative *MSE* values for $\hat{A}_{t+1}$ and the linked forecast $\hat{V}_{t+1} = \hat{A}_{t+1} / \mu_f$:

$$RMSE(\hat{A}_{t+1}) = MSE(\hat{A}_{t+1}) / \text{var}(A_{t+1}) = \frac{1 - \phi^2}{1 - 2\phi\theta + \theta^2}, \tag{16}$$

$$RMSE(\hat{V}_{t+1}) = MSE(\hat{V}_{t+1}) / \text{var}(V_{t+1}) = \frac{1 - \phi^2}{1 - \phi\theta}. \tag{17}$$

4. Data considered

We consider the prices of deutschemark futures at the International Monetary Market in Chicago from 3 January 1977 to 30 December 1983. With two exceptions, each March, June, September and December futures contract provides prices for the three months preceding its delivery month.

Thus, for example, the June 1977 contract provides prices for March, April and May 1977. The exceptions to this general pattern occur at the ends of the period: the March 1977 contract only gives prices for January and February 1977 whilst the March 1984 contract is used for December 1983 alone.

Futures prices are studied because reliable prices are published by the IMM, including the important high and low prices. Furthermore, changes in futures prices, unlike spot changes, theoretically have zero mean. Care is needed when the contract studied changes once a quarter but it is only necessary to ensure that all calculations of daily returns and overnight returns use two prices for the same futures contract. So, for example, the return for 1 March 1977 is calculated from the closing prices of the June 1977 contract on 28 February and 1 March 1977. Futures prices are related to spot prices by a well-known arbitrage equation involving domestic and foreign interest rates. It follows that the volatility of the spot price will be very similar to the futures volatility for every contract.

Closed-market and open-market returns, x_{1t} and x_{2t}, have been calculated from appropriate closing prices, z_{t-1} and z_t, and an intermediate opening price z_t^0 by the formulae

$$x_{1t} = \log(z_t^0/z_{t-1}) \quad \text{and} \quad x_{2t} = \log(z_t/z_t^0), \tag{18}$$

for $t = 1, 2 \ldots, 1762$. Sample variances are presented on the next page for

(i)   all returns and for
(ii) ordinary Tuesdays to Fridays (z_t recorded 24 hours after z_{t-1}),
(iii) ordinary Mondays (z_t recorded 72 hours after z_{t-1}),
(iv) the rest (a holiday between the recording of z_t and z_{t-1}).

Adding the closed- and open-market variances gives the total variance. The estimate of ϵ, the proportion of variance attributable to the closed-market hours, is the closed-market variance divided by the total variance. All the estimates exceed 0.5. It is obvious that the average volatility is greater on Mondays and holidays than on other days and the same conclusion applies to the proportion ϵ.

5. Constructing forecasts from prices 1977–1981

The seven year period (1977–1983) has been split into five years for constructing forecasts (1977–1981) and two years for assessing these forecasts 'post-sample' (1982–1983). We consider deseasonalised absolute returns m_t^* and ranges d_t^*. These are defined using close, high and low prices (z_t, h_t, l_t) by

$$m_t = |\log(z_t/z_{t-1})|, \qquad d_t = \log(h_t/l_t), \tag{19}$$

$$m_t^* = m_t, \qquad d_t^* = d_t \quad \text{for 24 hour returns}, \tag{20a}$$

$$m_t^* = m_t/s_m, \qquad d_t^* = d_t/s_d \quad \text{for Mondays and holidays}, \tag{20b}$$

and I have used $s_m = 1.24$ and $s_d = 1.11$.

Category	Sample size	Variance $\times 10^4$		Estimate of ϵ
		Closed mkt	Open mkt	
(i) all	1762	0.220	0.169	0.565
(ii) Tues–Fri	1386	0.184	0.157	0.540
(iii) Mondays	318	0.345	0.209	0.622
(iv) Holidays	58	0.393	0.248	0.613

5.1. Autocorrelations and parameter estimates

The autocorrelations of the observations m_t^* and d_t^* can be used to help construct forecasts. These forecasts should be reasonable if the processes generating the observations are stationary. The forecasts may, however, be seriously suboptimal if the processes are nonstationary. There are 1258 observations for each series up to the end of 1981 from which autocorrelations $r_{\tau,m}$ and $r_{\tau,d}$ have been calculated for lags τ ranging from 1 to 50 days. All the autocorrelations are positive and they generally decrease as τ increases. The coefficients up to lag 5 and at various later lags are as shown in the table below. Clearly ranges are far more autocorrelated than absolute returns, as was predicted theoretically in the paragraph following eq. (11).

The sample autocorrelations $r_{\tau,m}$ and $r_{\tau,d}$ are compatible with generating processes having theoretical autocorrelations $K_M \phi^\tau$ and $K_D \phi^\tau$ [cf. eqs. (12), (13)]. An appropriate common estimate of the autoregressive parameter is $\hat{\phi} = 0.986$ and then $\hat{K} = 0.175$ for series m^* and $\hat{K} = 0.473$ for series d^*. Then using eq. (15) the estimates of the moving average parameter for an ARMA (1,1) model are $\hat{\theta} = 0.9245$ for series m^* and $\hat{\theta} = 0.8525$ for series d^*. More information about the estimation method is given in Taylor (1986, Section 3.9). It involves minimising the goodness-of-fit statistic 1258 $\Sigma(r_\tau - \hat{K}\hat{\phi}^\tau)^2$, summing over τ from 1 to 50. For the estimates presented here this statistic equals 52.7 for series m^* and 42.4 for series d^*.

5.2. Choosing a related variable

The methodology for forecasting volatility requires the selection of an observable related variable. Eq. (17) and the parameter estimates $\hat{\phi}$, $\hat{\theta}$ predict *RMSE* values for optimal volatility forecasts. These *RMSE* are respectively 0.314 and 0.174 for forecasts based on the deseasonalised quantities m_t^* and d_t^* defined by eqs. (19) and (20). Consequently, the related variable used for subsequent forecast comparisons in this paper will be the deseasonalised daily range d_t^*.

Lag	Series m^*	Series d^*
1	0.250	0.510
2	0.215	0.476
3	0.230	0.452
4	0.176	0.429
5	0.231	0.451
10	0.165	0.420
20	0.090	0.373
30	0.124	0.330
40	0.062	0.306
50	0.060	0.257

5.3. Empirical RMSE

Suppose a forecast $\hat{d}_{t+h}$ is made at time t for the quantity d^*_{t+h}, for times $t = t_1, \ldots, t_2$, and let $\bar{d}$ be the average value of d^* up to the end of 1981. Then the empirical $RMSE$ of the forecasts is defined to be

$$RMSE = \sum_{t=t_1}^{t_2} (d^*_{t+h} - \hat{d}_{t+h})^2 / \sum_{t=t_1}^{t_2} (d^*_{t+h} - \bar{d})^2. \tag{21}$$

The notation $RMSE(j)$ is used for forecast method j. In this section $h = 1$, $t_1 = 20$ and $t_2 = 1257$.

5.4. Stationary forecasts

First, suppose d^*_{t+1} is forecast using the present and past values d^*_{t-i}, $i \geq 0$, and a stationary ARMA(1,1) model. Then from eq. (14)

$$\hat{d}_{t+1} = \bar{d} + (\phi - \theta) \sum_{i=0}^{\infty} \theta^i (d^*_{t-i} - \bar{d}).$$

Inserting the estimates $\hat{\phi} = 0.986$ and $\hat{\theta} = 0.8525$ from section 5.1 and simplifying gives forecast 1($F1$)

$$F1 \qquad \hat{d}_{t+1} = 0.014\bar{d} + 0.1335d^*_t + 0.8525\hat{d}_t. \tag{22}$$

Here $\hat{d}_t$ is the forecast of d^*_t made at time $t - 1$. To begin the calculations I have let $\hat{d}_0 = \bar{d}$. The first forecast gives $RMSE(1) = 0.611$. This empirical figure is very close to the theoretical prediction, 0.609, provided by eq. (16).

Second, suppose the information used is present and past values m^*_{t-i}, $i \geq 0$, and again an ARMA(1,1) model is assumed. Then an appropriate forecast is

$$\hat{d}_{t+1} = b\hat{m}_{t+1},$$

$$\hat{m}_{t+1} = (1 - \phi)\bar{m} + (\phi - \theta)m^*_t + \theta\hat{m}_t,$$

for some constant b. Inserting a regression estimate $\hat{b} = 1.329$ and the estimates appropriate to series m^* ($\hat{\phi} = 0.986$, $\hat{\theta} = 0.9245$) and then simplifying gives forecast 2

$$F2 \qquad \hat{d}_{t+1} = 0.0186\bar{m} + 0.0817m^*_t + 0.9245\hat{d}_t. \tag{23}$$

The second forecast gives $RMSE(2) = 0.676$. This is 6 per cent worse than the first forecast and confirms that daily ranges are more informative than absolute returns.

5.5. Non-stationary forecasts

Many researchers dislike an assumption that financial data has been generated by a stationary model. It is indeed possible that volatility and related variables have non-stationary mean values. As the estimate $\hat{\phi}$ is almost 1 appropriate forecasts avoiding the stationarity assumption are given by letting $\phi = 1$ in the ARMA(1,1) forecasting equations. A value for θ can be obtained by minimising the empirical *RMSE* [cf. Taylor (1986, pp. 103–4)]. On this occasion $\theta = 0.88$ is appropriate. Then forecast 3 is an exponentially-weighted moving average of the d_t^*

$$F3 \qquad \hat{d}_{t+1} = 0.12d_t^* + 0.88\hat{d}_t, \tag{24}$$

with $RMSE(3) = 0.618$ marginally worse than $RMSE(1) = 0.611$. Likewise, forecast 4 is a weighted average of the m_t^* with a regression estimate $\hat{b} = 1.269$ giving

$$F4 \qquad \hat{d}_{t+1} = 0.1523\hat{m}_t + 0.88\hat{d}_t, \tag{25}$$

with $RMSE(4) = 0.686$, again slightly worse than the comparable stationary forecast.

5.6. Combined forecasts

Garman and Klass (1980) presented theoretical results for volatility estimates computed from various functions of daily ranges, closed-market returns and open-market returns. They argued that all three types of price-changes should be used in volatility estimates. I have evaluated several combinations of forecasts but only minor improvements upon forecast 1 have been obtained.

Regression methods give the following best combinations of the stationary and non-stationary forecasts

$$F5 = 0.831 \ F1 + 0.236 \ F2, \tag{26}$$

$$F6 = 0.730 \ F3 + 0.348 \ F4, \tag{27}$$

with $RMSE(5) = 0.608$ and $RMSE(6) = 0.607$ compared with $RMSE(1) = 0.611$.

5.7. Simple forecasts

The *RMSE* values describe the accuracy of a set of forecasts relative to the constant forecast defined by the historic mean $\bar{d}$ for a five-year period. Option traders do not use five years data to estimate volatility. A simple estimate of volatility suggested in textbooks is provided by the standard deviation of the twenty or so latest daily or weekly returns [e.g., Cox and Rubinstein (1985, pp. 255–7, 276–7)]. Consequently, we consider forecasts

$$\hat{d}_{t+1} = b\hat{v}_{t+1}, \qquad \hat{v}_{t+1} = \sqrt{\left[\sum_{i=0}^{N-1} m_{t-i}^{*2}/N\right]},$$

for constants b and N. For $N = 20$ regression gives $b = 0.987$ as best for minimising *RMSE* and hence forecast 7 (the 'state of the art' forecast) is

$$F7 \qquad \hat{d}_{t+1} = 0.987\sqrt{\left[\sum_{i=0}^{19} m_{t-i}^{*2}/20\right]}, \tag{28}$$

for which $RMSE(7) = 0.760$. Optimising over both b and N defines forecast 8 with $N = 15$ and $RMSE(8) = 0.757$

$$F8 \qquad \hat{d}_{t+1} = 0.987\sqrt{\left[\sum_{i=0}^{14} m_{t-i}^{*2}/15\right]}. \tag{29}$$

It may be argued that many option traders use high and low prices so we also consider a simple average of N ranges; firstly, $N = 20$ gives forecast 9 (the 'advanced state of the art' forecast [cf. Parkinson (1980), Cox and Rubinstein (1985, p. 277)])

$$F9 \qquad \hat{d}_{t+1} = \sum_{i=0}^{19} d^*_{t-i}/20, \tag{30}$$

with $RMSE(9) = 0.657$ and, secondly, the best N defines forecast 10 with $N = 10$

$$F10 \qquad \hat{d}_{t+1} = \sum_{i=0}^{9} d^*_{t-i}/10, \tag{31}$$

and this final forecast has $RMSE(10) = 0.639$.

6. Forecasting results out-of-sample 1982–1983

The ten forecasts have been assessed 'post-sample' for two years and for forecast horizons $h = 1$, 5, 10 and 20 trading days. Post-sample $RMSE$ figures are calculated using the same definition as before, i.e., eq. (21), but now with summation limits $t_1 = 1259\text{-}h$ and $t_2 = 1762\text{-}h$.

6.1. Forecasting for the next day

The table presents $RMSE(j)$ when $h = 1$ for the first five years and the final two years. *F5* and *F6* were the best forecasts both 'within-sample' (1977–81) and 'post sample' (1982–83). Thus it is best to use both daily ranges d_t and absolute returns m_t when forecasting volatility, rather than only one of these variables. Of the two variables the ranges are clearly the more informative ($RMSE(1) < RMSE(2)$, etc.).

Forecasts derived from stationary models gave slightly better predictions than their non-stationary alternatives. Sophisticated forecasts (*F1* to *F6*) would have been better than simple forecasts (*F7* to *F10*) and all the forecasts are better than the pre-1982 average $\bar{d}$. Within-sample the best sophisticated and simple forecasts were *F6* and *F10* respectively, with $RMSE(6)/RMSE(10) = 0.95$ both within- and post-sample. It is apparent that all the $RMSE$ figures are higher post-sample than within-sample. This suggests the actual volatilities were less variable in the later period.

Forecast	Information used	Model type	RMSE	
			1977–81	1982–83
1	Series d	Stationary	0.611	0.744
2	Series m	Stationary	0.676	0.793
3	Series d	Non-stationary	0.618	0.756
4	Series m	Non-stationary	0.686	0.880
5	Both d and m	Stationary	0.608	0.735
6	Both d and m	Non-stationary	0.607	0.738
7	Series m	Simple, $N = 20$	0.760	0.900
8	Series d	Simple, $N = 20$	0.657	0.802
9	Series m	Simple, best N	0.757	0.919
10	Series d	Simple, best N	0.639	0.781

Forecast	RMSE, h			
	1	5	10	20
1	0.744	0.815	0.886	0.959
2	0.793	0.833	0.889	0.957
3	0.756	0.836	0.927	1.054
4	0.880	0.928	1.013	1.150
5	0.735	0.802	0.872	0.947
6	0.738	0.808	0.895	1.023
7	0.900	0.961	1.050	1.072
8	0.802	0.871	0.963	1.043
9	0.919	0.875	1.072	1.161
10	0.781	0.874	0.955	1.112

6.2. Forecasting for later days

Stationary forecasts $\hat{d}_{t+h}$ and $\hat{d}_{t+1}$, both made at time t, should satisfy

$$\hat{d}_{t+h} - \bar{d} = \phi^{h-1}(\hat{d}_{t+1} - \bar{d}), \tag{32}$$

for the model considered. Eq. (32) applies to *F1*, *F2* and *F5* with $\phi = 0.986$. As *F3*, *F4* and *F6* arise by letting $\phi = 1$ it is natural to then let $\hat{d}_{t+h} = \hat{d}_{t+1}$ and this has also been done for the simple forecasts *F7* to *F10*. The table presents $RMSE(j)$ post-sample for $h = 1, 5, 10$ and 20.

F5 has the least *RMSE* for all the horizons h. This is a stationary forecast: it is based upon the assumption that the stochastic processes generating the d_t^* and the m_t^* are stationary. As h increases, the difference $RMSE(6) - RMSE(5)$ between the accuracies of the best stationary and non-stationary forecasts increases. Thus it appears best to use $\phi < 1$ in eq. (32) and so to assume predicted volatilities regress towards a mean level as the horizon h increases [cf. Cox and Rubinstein (1985, p. 280), Taylor (1986, pp. 108–110)]. For $h = 10$ and 20 the three stationary forecasts are the three best forecasts. Also, for $h = 20$ only these forecasts have $RMSE < 1$. Sophisticated forecasts are better than simple forecasts for all h, with $RMSE(6)/RMSE(10)$ between 0.92 and 0.94 for $h > 1$.

7. Concluding remarks

This paper has shown that volatility forecasts calculated from daily high and low prices are empirically better than forecasts calculated from daily closing prices. Beckers (1983) has also made this claim in support of the theoretical results of Parkinson (1980) and Garman and Klass (1980). The best forecasts use high, low *and* close prices. As the forecasting horizon increases it appears best to let the forecasts regress towards a mean value. It is possible that better forecasts can be constructed by considering further relevant information, in particular volatility figures implied by option prices in conjunction with certain option pricing models. I hope to discuss such forecasts in a later paper.

References

Ali, M.M. and C. Giaccotto, 1982, The identical distribution hypothesis for stock market prices – location and scale-shift alternatives, Journal of the American Statistical Association 77, 19–28.

Beckers, S., 1983, Variances of security price returns based on high, low and closing prices, Journal of Business 56, 97–112.

Black, F., 1976, The pricing of commodity contracts, Journal of Financial Economics 3, 167–179.

Clark, P.K., 1973, A subordinated stochastic process model with finite variance for speculative prices, Econometrica 41, 135–155.

Cox, J.C. and M. Rubinstein, 1985, Options markets (Prentice-Hall, Englewood Cliffs, NJ).

Engle, R.F., 1982, Autoregressive conditional heteroscedasticity with estimates of the variance of UK inflation, Econometrica 50, 987–1007.

Engle, R.F. and T. Bollerslev, 1986, Modelling the persistence of conditional variances, Econometric Reviews, forthcoming.

Garman, M.B. and M.J. Klass, 1980, On the estimation of security price volatilities from historical data, Journal of Business 53, 67–78.

Garman, M.B. and S.W. Kohlhagen, 1983, Foreign currency option values, Journal of International Money and Finance 2, 231–238.

Gemmill, G., 1986, A primer on the pricing of options on currencies and short-term interest rates, The Investment Analyst 81, 16–22.

Hsu, D.A. 1977, Tests for variance shift at an unknown time point, Applied Statistics 26, 279–284.

Parkinson, M., 1980, The extreme value method for estimating the variance of the rate of return, Journal of Business 53, 61–65.

Tauchen, G.E. and M. Pitts, 1983, The price variability-volume relationship on speculative markets, Econometrica 51, 485–505.

Taylor, S.J., 1986, Modelling financial time series (Wiley, Chichester).

Biography: Stephen J. TAYLOR, M.A., Ph. D. is a lecturer in Operational Research at the University of Lancaster. The author of *Modelling Financial Time Series* (Wiley, 1986) he is particularly interested in stock, currency and commodity prices, especially for futures and options contracts. Previous publications include articles in the *Journals of the Royal Statistical Society, Journal of Financial and Quantitative Analysis, Journal of the Operational Research Society, Applied Economics* and *The Investment Analyst*.

[23]

ANNALES D'ÉCONOMIE ET DE STATISTIQUE. – N° 60 – 2000

Value-at-Risk
and Extreme Returns

Jon DANIELSSON, Casper G. DE VRIES *

ABSTRACT. – We propose a semi-parametric method for unconditional Value-at-Risk (VaR) evaluation. The largest risks are modelled parametrically, while smaller risks are captured by the non-parametric empirical distribution function. A comparison of methods on a portfolio of stock and option returns reveals that at the 5 % level the RiskMetrics analysis is best, but for predictions of low probability worst outcomes, it strongly underpredicts the VaR while the semi-parametric method is the most accurate.

Valeurs-à-Risque et les rendements extrêmes

RÉSUMÉ. – Nous présentons une méthode semi-paramétrique pour évaluer la valeur-à-risque (VaR). Les risques les plus grands sont modélisés paramétriquement, alors que les petits risques sont approchés par la distribution empirique. Une comparaison des méthodes sur les rendements d'un portefeuille d'actions et options montre qu'au niveau de confiance de 5 %, la méthode proposée par J. P. MORGAN (*RiskMetrics*) est la meilleure, mais que pour les prédictions pour les plus grandes pertes à des bas niveaux de probabilité, la méthode semi-paramétrique est supérieure, la méthode *RiskMetrics* sous-évalue la VaR.

---

* J. DANIELSSON: London School of Economics; C.G. DE VRIES: Tinbergen Institute and Erasmus University Rotterdam.
Our e-mail is J.danielsson@lse.ac.uk and cdevries@few.eur.nl.
Our papers can be downladed from www.RiskResearch.org.
We wish to thank F. X. DIEBOLD, P. HARTMANN, D. PYLE, T. VORST, E. ZIVOT, and workshop participants at the London School of Economics, University of Edinburgh, Cambridge University, Pompeu Fabra University, Erasmus University Rotterdam and two referees for excellent comments. The University of Iceland research fund, the Fullbright program, and the Research Contribution of the Icelandic Banks supported this research. The first draft of this paper was written while the first author was visiting at the University of Pennsylvania, and we thank the university for its hospitality.

1 Introduction

A major concern for regulators and owners of financial institutions is catastrophic market risk and the adequacy of capital to meet such risk. Well publicized losses incurred by several institutions such as Orange County, Procter and Gamble, and NatWest, through inappropriate derivatives pricing and management, as well as fraudulent cases such as Barings Bank, and Sumitomo, have brought risk management and regulation of financial institutions to the forefront of policy making and public discussion.

A primary tool for financial risk assessment is the Value-at-Risk (VaR) methodology where VaR is defined as an amount lost on a portfolio with a given small probability over a fixed number of days. The major challenge in implementing VaR analysis is the specification of the probability distribution of extreme returns used in the calculation of the VaR estimate.

By its very nature, VaR estimation is highly dependent on good predictions of uncommon events, or catastrophic risk, since the VaR is calculated from the lowest portfolio returns. As a result, any statistical method used for VaR estimation has to have the prediction of tail events as its primary goal. Statistical techniques and rules of thumb that have been proven useful in analysis and prediction of intra-day and day-to-day risk, are not necessarily appropriate for VaR analysis. This is discussed in a VaR context by *e.g.* DUFFIE and PAN [1997] and JORION [2000].

The development of techniques to evaluate and forecast the risk of uncommon events has moved at a rapid rate, and specialized methods for VaR prediction are now available. These methods fall into two main classes: parametric prediction of conditional volatilities, of which the J. P. MORGAN RiskMetrics method is the best known, and non-parametric prediction of unconditional volatilities such as techniques based on historical simulation or stress testing methods.

In this paper, we propose a semi-parametric method for VaR estimation which is a mixture of these two approaches, where we combine non-parametric historical simulation with parametric estimation of the tails of the return distribution. These methods build upon recent research in extreme value-theory, which enable us to accurately estimate the tails of a distribution. DANIELSSON and DE VRIES [1997a] and DANIELSSON and DE VRIES [1997b] propose an efficient, semi-parametric method for estimating tails of financial returns, and this method is expanded here to the efficient estimation of *"portfolio tails"*.

We evaluate various methods for VaR analysis, and compare the traditional methods with our tail distribution estimator using a portfolio of stocks. First, we construct a number of random portfolios over several time periods, and compare the results of one step ahead VaR predictions. Second, we investigate multi-day VaR analysis. Third, we study the implications of adding an index option to the portfolio. Fourth, the issues relating to the determination of capital are discussed. Finally, we discuss the practical implementations of these methods for real portfolio management, with special emphasis on the ease of implementation and computational issues.

2 The Methodology of Risk Forecasting

2.1 Dependence

Financial return data are characterized by (at least) two stylized facts. First, returns are non-normal, with heavy tails. Second, returns exhibit dependence in the second moment. In risk forecasting, there is a choice between two general approaches. The risk forecast may either be conditioned on current market conditions, or can be based on the unconditional market risk. Both approaches have advantages and disadvantages, where the choice of methodology is situation dependent.

2.1.1 Unconditional Models

A pension fund manager has an average horizon which is quite the opposite from an options trader. It is well known that conditional volatility is basically absent from monthly return series, but the fat tail property does not fade. For longer horizon problems, an unconditional model is appropriate for the calculation of large loss forecasts. Furthermore, even if the time horizon is shorter, financial institutions often prefer unconditional risk forecast methods to avoid undesirable frequent changes in risk limits for traders and portfolio managers. For more in this issue, see DANIELSSON [2000]. For a typical large portfolio (in terms of number of assets), the conditional approach may also just not be feasible since this requires constructing and updating huge conditional variance-covariance matrices.

2.1.2 Conditional Models

Building on the realization that returns exhibit volatility clusters, conditional volatility forecasts are important for several applications. In many situations where the investment horizon is short, conditional volatility models may be preferred for risk forecasting. This is especially the case in intra-day risk forecasting where predictable patterns in intra-day volatility seasonality are an essential component of risk forecasting. In such situations both GARCH and Stochastic Volatility models have been applied successfully. In general, where there are predictable regime changes, *e.g.* intra-day patterns, structural breaks, or macroeconomic announcements, a conditional model is essential. In the case of intra-day volatility, DANIELSSON and PAYNE [2000] demonstrate that traders in foreign exchange markets build expectations of intra-day volatility patterns, where primarily unexpected volatility changes are important.

2.1.3 Conditionality *versus* Unconditionality in Risk Forecasting

Neither the conditional nor the unconditional approach is able to tell when disaster strikes, but GARCH type models typically perform worse when disaster strikes since the unconditional approach structures the portfolio against disasters, whereas GARCH does this only once it recognizes one has hit a high volatility regime. Per contrast, GARCH performs better in signalling the continuation of a high risk regime since it adapts to the new situation. The conditional GARCH methodology thus necessarily implies more volatile risk forecasts than the unconditional approach; see *e.g.* DANIELSSON [2000] who find that risk volatility from a GARCH model can be 4 times higher than for an unconditional model. Because the GARCH methodology quickly adapts to recent market developments, it meets the VaR constraint more frequently than the unconditional approach. But this frequency is just one aspect, the size of the misses also counts. Lastly, conditional hedging can be self defeating at times it is most needed due to macro effects stalling the market once many market participants receive sell signals from their conditional models, *cf.* the 1987 crash and the impact of portfolio insurance.

In the initial version of this paper, DANIELSSON and DE Vries [1997c], unconditional risk forecasts were recommended over the conditional type. At the time, empirical discussion of risk forecasting was in its infancy, and our purpose was primarily to introduce and demonstrate the uses of semi-parametric unconditional Extreme Value Theory (EVT) based methods. This approach was subsequently criticized, in particular by MCNEIL and FREY [1999], who propose a hybrid method, where a GARCH model is first estimated and EVT is applied to the estimated residuals. It is our present position that the choice of methodology should depend on the situation and question at hand, and that both the conditional and unconditional approach belong in the toolbox of the risk manager. In this paper, without prejudice, we focus only on the unconditional methods.

2.2 Data Features

In finance, it is natural to assume normality of returns in daily and multiday conditional and unconditional volatility predictions, in applications such as derivatives pricing. As the volatility smile effect demonstrates, however, for infrequent events the normal model is less useful. Since returns are known to be fat tailed, the conditional normality assumption leads to a sizable underprediction of tail events. Moreover, the return variances are well known to come in clusters. The popular RiskMetrics technique, in essence an IGARCH model, is based on conditional normal analysis that recognizes the clustering phenomenon and comes with frequent parameter updates to adapt to changing market regimes. The price one has to pay for the normality assumption and frequent parameter updating is that such model is not well suited for analyzing large risks. The normality assumption implies that one under estimates the chances of heavy losses. The frequent updating implies a high variability in the estimates and thus recurrent costly capital adjustments. For this reason, RiskMetrics focuses on the 5 % quantile, or the probability of losses that occur once every 20 days. These losses are so small that they can be handled by any financial institution. We argue below that RiskMetrics is ill suited for lower probability loses.

Furthermore, conditional parametric methods typically depend on conditional normality for the derivation of multi-period VaR estimates. Relaxation of the normality assumption leads to difficulties due to the *"square-root-of-time"* method, *i.e.* the practice of obtaining multi-period volatility predictions by multiplying the one day prediction by the square root of the length of the time horizon. As CHRISTOFFERSEN and DIEBOLD [2000] argue, conditional volatility predictions are not very useful for multi-day predictions. We argue that the appropriate method for scaling up a single day VaR to a multi-day VaR is the alpha-root rule, where alpha is the number of finite bounded moments, also known as the tail index. We implement the alpha-root method and compare it with the square-root rule.

As an alternative to the fully parametric approach to (unconditional) VaR forecasts, one can either use the historical returns as a sampling distribution for future returns as in Historical Simulation (HS) and stress testing, or use a form of kernel estimation to smooth the sampling distribution as in BUTLER and SCHACHTER [1996]. The advantages of historical simulation have been well documented by *e.g.* JACKSON, MAUDE, and PERRAUDIN [1997], MAHONEY [1996], and HENDRICKS [1996]. A disadvantage is that the low frequency and inaccuracy of tail returns leads to predictions which exhibit a very high variance, *i.e.* the variance of the highest order statistics is very high, and is in some cases even infinite. As a result, the highest realizations lead to poor estimates of the tails, which may invalidate HS as a method for stress testing. In addition, it is not possible to do out-of-sample prediction with HS, *i.e.* predict losses that occur less frequently than are covered by the HS sample period.

2.3 **Properties of Extreme Returns**

Value-at-Risk analysis is highly dependent on extreme returns or spikes. The empirical properties of the spikes, are not the same as the properties of the entire return process. A major result from empirical research of returns, is the almost zero autocorrelation and significant positive serial correlation in the volatility of returns. As a result volatilities can be relatively well predicted with a parametric model such as ARCH. If, however, one focuses only on spikes, the dependency is much reduced. This is due to the fact that the ARCH process is strong mixing (in combination with another technical condition). In DE HAAN, RESNICK, ROOTZEN, and DE VRIES [1989] it was demonstrated that the ARCH process satisfies these conditions so that if the threshold level, indicating the beginning of the tails, rises as the sample size increases, the spikes eventually behave like a Poisson process. In particular, for the ARCH(1) process DE HAAN, RESNICK, ROOTZEN, and DE VRIES [1989] obtain the tail index and the extremal index by which the mean cluster size has to be rescaled to obtain the associated independent process, see below.

Some evidence for the reduced dependency over larger thresholds is given in Table 1, which lists the number of trading days between the daily extremes for the SP-500 index along with the rank of the corresponding observation. Figure 1 shows the 1 % highest and lowest returns on the daily SP-500 index in the 1990's along with the 7 stocks used below in testing the VaR estimation techniques. No clear pattern emerges for these return series. In some cases we see clustering, but typically the extreme events are almost randomly scattered. Furthermore, there does not appear to be strong correlation in the tail events.

There were 2 days when 5 assets had tail events, no days with 4 tail events, 5 days with 3 events, 21 days with 2 events, 185 days with 1 event, and 1,558 days with no tail events. For the SP-500, two of the upper tail observations are on adjacent days but none of the lower tailed observations, and in most cases there are a number of days between the extreme observations. One does not observe market crashes many days in a row. There are indications of some clustering of the tail events over time. However, the measurement of a spike on a given day, is not indicative of a high probability of a spike the following few days. The modelling of the dependency structure of spikes would therefore be different than in *e.g.* GARCH models.

Another important issue is pointed out by DIMSON and MARSH [1996] who analyze spikes in 20 years of the British FTSE All Share Index, where they define spikes as fluctuations of 5 % or more. They find 6 daily spikes, however they also search for non-overlapping multi day spikes, and find 4 2-day spikes, 3 3-day, 3 4-day, 8 weekly, and up to 7 biweekly. Apparently, the number of spikes is insensitive to the time span over which the returns are defined. This is an example of the fractal property of the distribution of returns and the extremes in particular, and is highly relevant for spike forecasting when the time horizon is longer than one day.

On the basis of the above evidence, we conclude that for computing the VaR, which is necessarily concerned with the most extreme returns, the ARCH dependency effect is of no great importance. One can show, moreover, that the estimators are still asymptotically normal, albeit with higher variance due to the ARCH effect. Hence, it suffices to assume that the highest and lowest realizations are i.i.d.. This is corroborated by the evidence from CHRISTOFFERSEN and DIEBOLD [2000] that when the forecast horizon is several days, conditional prediction performs no better than using the unconditional distribution as predictive distribution. The reason is that most current history contains little information on the likelihood that a spike will occur, especially in the exponential weighting of recent history by RiskMetrics.

3 Modelling Extremes

3.1 Tail Estimation

Extreme value theory is the study of the tails of distributions. Several researchers have proposed empirical methods for estimation of tail thickness. The primary difficulty in estimating the tails is the determination of the start of the tails. Typically, these estimators use the highest/lowest realizations to estimate the parameter of tail thickness which is called the tail index. HILL [1975] proposed a moments based estimator for the tail index. The estimator is conditional on knowing how many extreme order statistics for a given sample size have to be taken into account. HALL [1990] suggested a bootstrap procedure for estimation of the start of the tail. His method is too restrictive to be of use for financial data, *e.g.*, it is not applicable to the Student-*t* distribution, which has been used repeatedly to model asset returns. Recently, DANIELSSON and DE VRIES [1997a] and DANIELSSON, DE HAAN, PENG, DE VRIES [2000] have proposed general estimation methods for the number of extreme order statistics that are in the tails, but presuppose i.i.d. data.[1] This method is used here to choose the optimal number of extreme order statistics. A brief formal summary of these results is presented in Appendix A.

It is known that only one limit law governs the tail behavior of data drawn from almost any fat tailed distribution.[2] The condition on the distribution $F(x)$ for it to be in the domain of attraction of the limit law is given by (7) in Appendix A. Since financial returns are heavy tailed, this implies that for obtaining the tail behavior we only have to deal with this limit distribution. By taking an expansion of $F(x)$ at infinity and imposing mild regularity conditions one can show that for most heavy tailed distributions the second order expansion of the tails is:

$$(1) \qquad F(x) \simeq 1 - ax^{-\alpha}\left[1 + bx^{-\beta}\right], \; \alpha, \beta > 0$$

for x large, while a, b, α, and β are parameters. In this expansion, the key coefficient is α, which is denoted as the tail index, and indicates the thickness of the tails. The parameter a determines the scale, and embodies the dependency effect through the extremal index; the other two parameters b and β are the second order equivalents to a and α. For example, for the Student-t or the non-normal stable densities, α equals the degrees of freedom or the characteristic exponent. For the ARCH process α equals the number of bounded moments of the unconditional distribution of the ARCH innovations.

HILL [1975] proposed a moments based estimator of the tail index which is estimated conditional on a threshold index M where all values $x_i > X_{M+1}$ are used in the estimation. The X_i indicate the decreasing order statistics, $X_1 \geqslant X_2 \geqslant \ldots \geqslant X_M \geqslant \ldots \geqslant X_n$, in a sample of returns x. DANIELSSON and DE VRIES [1997] discuss the following estimator for the tail probabilities, given estimates of α and the threshold:

$$(2) \qquad \hat{F}(x) = p = \frac{M}{n}\left(\frac{X_{M+1}}{x}\right)^{\hat{\alpha}}, \; x > X_{M+1}$$

where n is the number of observations, and p is the probability. This applies equally to the lower tails. By taking the inverse of $\hat{F}(x)$ we obtain an extreme quantile estimator:

$$(3) \qquad \hat{x}_p = \hat{F}^{-1}(x) = X_{M+1}\left(\frac{M}{np}\right)^{\frac{1}{\hat{\alpha}}}.$$

Note that $\hat{F}(x)$ is always conditional on a given sample. In order to use the distribution $\hat{F}(x)$ we need to specify the parameters α and the random variables M and X_{M+1}, before we can obtain a quantile estimate for a probability. The empirical and estimated distribution functions of the SP-500 index

---

1. For dependent data it is not known yet how to choose the number of highest order statistics optimally.

2. DANIELSSON and DE VRIES [1997a] discuss this issue in details some.

are presented in Figure 3. Some practical issues of the tail estimation are discussed below.

3.2 Multi-Period Extreme Analysis

The method for obtaining multi-period predictions follows from the work of FELLER [1971, VIII.8]. FELLER shows that the tail risk for fat tailed distributions is, to a first approximation, linearly additive. Assume that the tails of the distribution are symmetric in the sense that for a single period return $\Pr[|X| > x] \approx ax^{-\alpha}$ when x is large.[3] For the T-period return we then have

$$(4) \qquad \Pr[X_1 + X_2 + \ldots + X_n > x] \approx Tax^{-\alpha}.$$

The implication for portfolio analysis of this result has been discussed in the specific case of non-normal stable distributions by FAMA and MILLER [1972, p. 270]. In that case $\alpha < 2$ and the variance is infinite. DACOROGNA, MULLER, PICTET, and DE VRIES [1995] are the first to discuss the finite variance case when $\alpha > 2$. It is well known that the self-additivity of normal distributions implies that the $T^{1/2}$ scaling factor for multi-period VaR, *i.e.* the "*square-root-of-time rule*" implemented in RiskMetrics. But for heavy tailed distributions this factor is different for the largest risks. Heavy tailed distributions are self-additive in the tails, see *e.g.* (4). This implies a scaling factor $T^{1/\alpha}$ for VaR in a T-period analysis. With finite variance where $\alpha > 2$ and hence $T^{1/2} > T^{1/\alpha}$, *i.e.* the scaling factor for heavy tailed distributed returns is smaller than for normal distributed returns. In comparison with the normal model, there are two counter balancing forces. If daily returns are fat tailed distributed, then there is a higher probability of extreme losses and this increases the one day possible loss *vis-à-vis* the normal model. This is a level effect. But there is also a slope effect. Due to the above result, the multiplication factor (slope) used to obtain the multi-day extreme is smaller for fat tailed distributed returns than for normal returns. For this reason, extreme predictions from the two models cross at different probability levels if we consider different time horizons. This is demonstrated in Table 5.

3.3 Monte Carlo Evidence

In order to evaluate the performance of the estimated tail distribution in (2) DANIELSSON and DE VRIES [1997a] do extensive Monte Carlo experiments to evaluate the properties of the estimator. In Table 2, a small subset of the results is presented. We generate repeated samples of size 2000 from a Student-t distribution with 4 degrees of freedom and compare the average maxima, denoted here as the sample maxima by historical simulation (HS), from the samples with the average predicted value by $\hat{F}(x)$, denoted as extreme value (EV). The specific distribution was chosen since its tail behavior is similar to a typical return series. The Monte Carlo results are reported in Table 2.

---

3. For more general results and conditions on the tails, see GELUK, PENG, DE VRIES [2000].

Out-of-sample predictions were obtained by using the estimated tail of the distribution to predict the value of the maxima of a sample of size 4,000 and 6,000, the true values are reported as well. We can see that the tail estimator performs quite well in predicting the maxima while the sample averages yield much lower quality results. Note that the variance of HS approach is much higher than the variance by EV method. Moreover, HS is necessarily silent on the out of sample sizes 4,000 to 6,000, where EV provides an accurate estimate. Obviously, if one used the normal to predict the maximums, the result would be grossly inaccurate, and would in fact predict values about one third of the theoretical values. See also Figures 3 and 4 in Section 5 below for a graphical illustration of this claim.

4 Value-at-Risk and Common Methods

Value-at-Risk form the basis of the determination of market risk capital (see Section 6.1.3). The formal definition of Value-at-Risk (VaR) is easily given implicitly:

(5)
$$\Pr[\Delta P_{\Delta t} \leqslant VaR] = \pi,$$

where $\Delta P_{\Delta t}$ is a change in the market value of portfolio P over time horizon Δt with probability π. Equation (5) states that a loss equal to, or larger than the specific VaR occurs with probability π. Or conversely, (5) for a given probability π losses, equal to or larger than the VaR, happen. In this latter interpretation the VaR is written as a function of the probability π. Let $F(\Delta P_{\Delta t})$ be the probability distribution of $\Delta P_{\Delta t}$, then

(6)
$$F^{-1}(\pi) = VaR;$$

where $F^{-1}(\cdot)$ denotes the inverse of $F(\cdot)$. The major problem in implementing VaR analysis is the specification of the probability distribution $F(\cdot)$ which is used in the calculation in (5).

Two methods are commonly used to evaluate VaR:

1. Historical Simulation (Non Parametric, Unconditional Volatility)
2. Parametric Methods (Fully Parametric, Conditional Volatility)

Both these methods are discussed in this section. The semi-parametric extreme value (EV) method falls in between these two methodologies.

4.1 Historical Simulation

A popular method for VaR assessment is historical simulation (HS). Instead of making distributional assumptions about returns, past returns are used to predict future returns.

The advantage of historical simulation is that few assumptions are required, and the method is easy to implement. The primary assumption is that the distribution of the returns in the portfolio is constant over the sample period. Historical simulation has been shown to compare well with other methods, see *e.g.* MAHONEY [1996], however past extreme returns can be a poor predictor of extreme events, and as a result historical simulation should be used with care. The reason for this is easy to see. By its very nature HS has nothing to say about the probability outcomes which are worse than the sample minimum return. But HS also does not give very accurate probability estimates for the borderline in sample extremes, as is demonstrated below. Furthermore, the choice of sample size can have a large impact on the value predicted by historical simulation. In addition, the very simplicity of HS makes it difficult to conduct sensitivity experiments, where a VaR is evaluated under a number of scenarios.

A major problem with HS is the discreteness of extreme returns. In the interior, the empirical sampling distribution is very dense, with adjacent observations very close to each other. As a result the sampling distribution is very smooth in the interior and is the mean squared error consistent estimate of the true distribution. The closer one gets to the extremes, the longer the interval between adjacent returns becomes. This can be seen in Table 3 where the 7 largest and smallest returns on the stocks in the sample portfolio and SP-500 Index for 10 years are listed.

These extreme observations are typically the most important for VaR analysis, however since these values are clearly discrete, the VaR will also be discrete, and hence be either underpredicted or overpredicted. We see that this effect is somewhat more pronounced for the individual assets, than for the market portfolio SP-500, due to diversification. Furthermore, the variance of the extreme order statistics is very high; and can be infinite. As a result, VaR estimates that are dependent on the tails, will be measured discretely, with a high variance, making HS in many cases a poor predictor of the VaR. Results from a small Monte Carlo (MC) experiment demonstrating this are presented in Section 3.3. In Figure (2) we plot the 99th percentile of the S&P for the past 500 and 1,000 days, *i.e.* the 5th and 10th largest and smallest observations for the past 500 and 1,000 days respectively. It is clear from the figure that the window length in assessing the probability of spikes is very important, and this creates a serious problem. Note how rapidly the percentile changes when new data enter and exit the window. In VaR prediction with HS, the inclusion or exclusion of one or two days at the beginning of the sample can cause large swings in the VaR estimate, while no guidelines exist for assessing which estimate is the better.

BUTLER and SCHACHTER [1996] propose a variation of HS by use of a kernel smoother to estimate the distribution of returns, which is in essence an estimation of the distribution of returns. This type of methodology has both advantages and draw backs. The advantage is that a properly constructed kernel distribution provides a smooth sampling distribution. Hence sensitivity experiments can be readily constructed, and valuable insight can be gained about the return process. Furthermore, such distribution may not be as sensitive to the sample length as HS is. Note that these advantages are dependent on a properly constructed kernel distribution. In kernel estimation, the specific choice of a kernel and window length is extremely important. Almost all kernels are estimated with the entire data set, with interior observations dominating the kernel estimation. While even the most careful kernel estimation will provide good estimates for the interior, there is no reason to believe that the kernel will describe the tails adequately. Tail bumpiness is a common problem in kernel estimation. Note especially that financial data are thick tailed with high excess kurtosis. Therefore, a Gaussian kernel, which assumes that the estimated distribution has the same shape as the normal, is unsuitable for financial data.

A referee suggested that an optimal window length might be obtained from economic rather than statistical considerations. This is an appropriate recommendation for those who plan to apply kernel estimation to risk problems. In addition, we feel that a similar suggestion could also apply to the choice of number of extreme order statistics in EVT estimation, specifically that a money metric may be an appropriate side constraint; *cf.* PENG [1998].

4.2 Parametric Forecasting

In parametric forecasting, the predicted future volatility of an asset is an explicit function of past returns, and the estimated model parameters. The most common models are the unconditional normal with frequently updated variance estimate, or explicit models for conditional heteroscedasticity like the GARCH model, with normal innovations. The popular RiskMetrics approach which uses the frequently updated normal model is asymptotically equivalent to an IGARCH model. This implies a counterfactual hypothesis of an unconditional infinite variance. However, since in most cases, only short horizon conditional forecasts are made, this does not affect the results significantly. GARCH models with normal innovations have proved valuable in forecasting common volatilities, however they perform poorly in predicting extreme observations, or spikes, in returns. Furthermore, while the GARCH normal model unconditionally has heavy tails, conditionally, they are thin. The normality assumption is primarily a matter of convenience, and a GARCH model with non-normal innovations can easily be estimated, with the most common specification being the Student-t. The advantage of Student-t innovations is that they are thick tailed and hence will in general provide better predictive densities; note that the Student-t contains Gaussian errors as a special case. The disadvantages of non-normal innovations for the VaR exercise are several, *e.g.* multivariate versions of such models are typically hard to estimate and recursive forecasts of multi-step ahead VaR levels are difficult to compute, since the GARCH process is not self additive.

There are several reasons for the failure of RiskMetrics to adequately capture the tail probabilities. For example, the normal likelihood function weight values close to zero higher than large values, so the contribution of the large values to the likelihood function is relatively small. Since most observations are in the interior, they dominate the estimation, especially since tail events are may be 1-2 % of the observations. While a GARCH model with normal innovations preforms poorly, it does not imply that parametric forecasting will in general provide biased VaR estimates, however such a model would have to be constructed with the tails as the primary focus. See JACKSON, MAUDE, and PERRAUDIN [1997] for discussion on this issue.

There is yet another problem with the way RiskMetrics implements the GARCH methodology. Instead of going by the GARCH scheme for predicting future volatilities, RiskMetrics ignores GARCH and simply uses the square-root-of-time method which is only appropriate under an i.i.d. normal assumption. If the predicted next day volatility is $\hat{\sigma}_{t+1}^2$, then the predicted T day ahead volatility is $T\hat{\sigma}_{t+1}^2$ in the RiskMetrics analysis. This implies that for the next T days, returns are essentially assumed to be normally distributed with variance $T\hat{\sigma}_{t+1}^2$. The underlying assumption is that returns are i.i.d., in which case there would be no reason to estimate a conditional volatility model. Note that this problem can be by passed by using T day data to obtain T day ahead predictions as suggested in the RiskMetrics manual. But the methodology of entertaining different GARCH processes at different frequencies lacks internal consistency.

In Table 4, we show the six highest and lowest returns on the daily SP-500 index from 1990 to 1996, or 1,771 observations. We used the normal GARCH and Student-t GARCH models to predict the conditional volatility, and show, in the table, the probability of an outcome equal to or more extreme than the observed return, conditional on the predicted volatility for each observation. In addition, we show the probability as predicted by the extreme value estimator, and values of the empirical distribution function. We see from the table that the normal GARCH model performs very poorly in predicting tail events, while the Student-t GARCH model gives some what better results. Both methods are plagued by high variability and inaccurate probability estimates, while the extreme value estimator provides much better estimates.

5 Extreme Value Theory and VaR

Accurate prediction of extreme realizations is of central importance to VaR analysis. VaR estimates are calculated from the lower extreme of a portfolio forecast distribution; therefore, accurate estimation of the lower tail of portfolio returns is of primary importance in any VaR application. Most available tools, such as GARCH, are however designed to predict common volatilities, and therefore have poor tail properties. Even historical simulation (HS) has less than desirable sampling properties out in the tails. Therefore, a hybrid technique that combines sampling from the empirical distribution for common observations with sampling from a fitted tail distribution has the potential to perform better than either HS or fully parametric methods by themselves.

In Figure 3, the empirical distribution of the SP-500 index is plotted along with the fitted power tail distribution $F(x)$ and the estimated normal distribution. We see the problems with HS in the tails from Figure 3, *e.g.* discreteness of observations and the inability to provide out-of-sample low probability predictions. The normal distribution clearly under estimates the probability of the highest returns. On the other hand, the fitted distribution is a smooth function through the empirical distribution, both in and out of sample. For comparison, in figure 4 we plot the fitted distribution along with the normal distribution estimated from the sample mean and variance, and the distribution obtained from the normal GARCH(1,1) process if one conditions on the maximum observed past volatility. This means that the normal distribution, with the variance of the largest of the one day GARCH volatility predictions, is plotted. This gives the normal GARCH the maximum benefit of the doubt. Since this conditional distribution is still normal, it underestimates the extreme tails. There are several advantages in using the estimated power tail in VaR estimation. For example:

- In HS, the presence of an event like the '87 crash in the sample,will cause a large VaR estimate. However, since a '87 magnitude crash only occurs rarely, say once every 60 years, the presence of such an event in the sample will produce upward biased VaR estimates. And, hence, imposes too conservative capital provisions. By sampling from the tail distribution, the probability of a '87 type event will be much smaller, leading to better VaR estimates.
- The empirical distribution is sampled discretely out in the tails, with the variance of the extreme order statistics being very high. This implies that a VaR that relies on tail realizations will exhibit the same properties, with the resulting estimates being highly variable. A Monte Carlo example of this is given in Table 2.
- By sampling from the tail of the distribution, one can easily obtain the lowest return that occurs at a given desired probability level, say 0.1 %, greatly facilitating sensitivity experiments. This is typically not possible with HS by itself.
- The probability theory of tail observations, or extreme value theory, is well known, and the tail estimator therefore rests on firm statistical foundations. In contrast, most traditional kernel estimators have bad properties in the tails.

5.1 Estimated Tails and Historical Simulation

We propose combining the HS for the interior with the fitted distribution from (1) along the lines of DANIELSSON and DE VRIES [1997a]. Recall from above that the fitted distribution, $\hat{F}(x)$, is conditional on one of the highest order statistics X_{M+1}. Therefore, we can view X_{M+1} as the start of the tail, and use $\hat{F}(x)$ as the sampling distribution for extreme returns. Below this threshold X_{M+1} we can see the empirical distribution for interior returns. This can be implemented in the following algorithm, where $X_{M^{upper}+1}$ and $X_{M^{lower}-1}$ are the thresholds for the upper and lower tail respectively, and T is the window size.

Draw x^s from $\{x_t\}_{t=1}^{T}$ with replacement
if $x^s < X_{M^{lower}-1}$ then
   draw x^s from $\hat{F}(x)$ for the lower tail
else
   if $x^s > X_{M^{upper}+1}$ then
      draw x^s from $\hat{F}(x)$ for the uper tail
   else
      keep x^s
   end if
end if

Note that this guarantees that the combined density integrates out to one. We can then view x as one draw from the combined empirical and extreme value distributions, and we denote the method as the combined extreme value estimator and historical simulation method.

5.2 Tails of Portfolios

In general, multiple assets are used to construct a portfolio. We can implement simulations of portfolio returns with one of two methods, post fitting or pre-sampling. Results from implementing both methods are presented in Table 11 and discussed below. Note that while we would not necessarily expect strong interdependency between the tails of stock returns, strong tail *"correlation"* is often expected in exchange rates, *e.g.* in the EMS, large movements often occur at the same time for several countries.

5.2.1 Post-Fitting

In post-fitting, one proceeds along the lines of the combined extreme value and historical simulation procedures and applies the current portfolio weights to the historical prices to obtain a vector of simulated portfolio returns. This is exactly as in historical simulation. Subsequently, the tails of the simulated returns are fitted, and any probability-VaR combination can be read from the fitted tails. This procedure has several advantages. No restrictive assumptions are needed, the method can be applied to the largest of portfolios, and does not require significant additional computation time over HS. The primary disadvantage is that it carries with it the assumption of constant correlation across returns, while systematic changes in correlation may occur over time. However, in the results below this does not seem to cause any significant problems.

5.2.2 Presampling

In the presampling method, each asset is sampled independently from the hybrid extreme value estimator and empirical distribution, and subsequently scaled to obtain properly correlated returns. Then the value of the portfolio is calculated. The scaling is achieved as follows. Let Σ_t be the covariance matrix of the sample, and $L_t L_t' = \Sigma_t$ be the Cholesky transformation. The number of assets in the portfolio is K and the number of simulations is N. We then draw a KN matrix of simulated returns, denoted as $\tilde{X}_n$. Let the covariance matrix of $\tilde{X}_n$ be denoted by Ω_n, with the Cholesky transformation $M_n M_n' = \Omega_n$. Scale $\tilde{X}_n$ to an identity covariance matrix by $M_n^{-1} \tilde{X}_n$, which can then be scaled to the sample covariance by L_t. The matrix of simulated returns X is:

$$X_n = L_t M_n^{-1} \tilde{X}_n.$$

If $w = \{w_i\}_{i=1}^K$ is the vector of portfolio weights, the simulated return vector R is:

$$R_n = \sum_{i=1}^K w_i X_{t,n,i} \quad n = 1, N.$$

By sorting the simulated portfolio returns R, one can read off the tail probabilities for the VaR, in the same manner as in HS. By using this method, it is possible to use a different covariance matrix for sub samples than for the whole sample. This may be desirable when the covariance matrix of returns changes over time where it may yield better results to replace the covariance matrix Ω with the covariance matrix of the last part of the sample. If the effects of a regime change can be anticipated by imputing the appropriate changes in the covariance structure, such as in the case of monetary unification, the presampling approach has an advantage over the post-fitting method.

6 Estimation

To test the performance of our VaR procedure, we selected 6 US stocks randomly as the basis for portfolio analysis in addition to the JP Morgan bank stock price. The stocks in the tables are referred by their ticker tape symbols. The window length for HS and the combined extreme value-empirical distribution procedure was set at 6 years or 1,500 trading days. Note this is much larger than the regulatory window length of one year. The reason for this long period is that for accurate estimation of events that happen once every 100 days, as in the 1 % VaR, one year is not enough for accurate estimation. In general, one should try to use as large a sample as is possible. Using a smaller sample than 1,500 trading days in the performance testing was not shown to improve the results. Performance testing starts at Jan. 15. 1993, and the beginning of the sample is 1,500 days before that on Feb. 12, 1987. It is a stylized fact in empirical studies of financial returns, that returns exhibit several common properties, regardless of the underlying asset. This extends to the tails of returns. In Table 12, we present summary statistics on a wide range of financial returns for the period 1987-1996, and it is clear that the tails all have similar properties. Summary statistics for each stock return are listed in Table 7 for the entire sample period, and in Table 8 for the 1990-1996 testing period. The corresponding correlation matrixes are presented in Tables 9 and 10. The sample correlations drop in the 1990's. Given this change in correlation, we tested changing correlations in the pre-fitting method, but it did not have much impact for our data, and therefore we do not report those results here.

6.1 VaR Prediction

6.1.1 Interpretation of Results

Results are reported in Table 11. The VaR return estimates for each method are compared with the realized returns each day. The number of violations of the VaR estimates were counted, and the ratio of violations to the length of the testing period was compared with the critical value. This is done for several critical values. This is perhaps the simplest possible testing procedure. Several authors, most recently DAVÉ and STAHL [1997], propose much more elaborate testing procedures, *e.g.* the likelihood based method of DAVÉ and STAHL which is used to test a single portfolio. However by using a large number of random portfolios one obtains accurate measurements of the performance of the various methods, without resorting to specific distributional assumptions, such as the normality assumption of DAVÉ and STAHL. In addition, while the green, yellow, and red zone classification method proposed by BIS may seem attractive for the comparison, it is less informative than the ratio method used here.

The test sample length was 1,000 trading days, and the window size in HS and EV was 1,500. For the 1 % risk level, we expect a single violation of the VaR every 100 days, or 10 times over the entire testing period. This risk level is given in the eight column from the left in Table 11. At this risk level RiskMetrics yields too many violations, *i.e.* 16.3, on average, while the other methods give too few violations, or from 7.6 for HS to 9.3 for the presampling EV method, on average. If the number of violations is higher than the expected value, it indicates that the tails are underpredicted, thinner or lower than expected, and conversely too few violations indicate that the estimated tail is thicker than expected. In addition to the tail percentages, we show the implied number of days, *i.e.* how frequently one would expect a tail event to occur. If the number of days is large, we transform the days into years, assuming 260 trading days per year.

6.1.2 Comparison of Methods

For the 5th percentile, RiskMetrics performs best. The reason for this is that at the 5 % level we are sufficiently inside the sample so that the conditional prediction performs better than unconditional prediction. However, as we move to the tails, RiskMetrics consistently underpredicts the tail, with ever larger biases as we move farther into the tails. For example, at the 0.1 % level RiskMetrics predicts 5 violations, while the expected number is one. Therefore RiskMetrics will underpredict the true number of losses at a given risk level. Historical simulation has in a way the opposite problem, in that it consistently overpredicts the tails. Note that for HS we can not obtain estimates for lower probabilities than one over the sample size, or in our case probabilities lower than once every 1,500 days. Hence the lowest prediction, 0.75, is repeated in the last four columns in the table. Obviously for smaller sample sizes HS is not able to predict the VaR for even relatively high probabilities. Both EV estimators have good performance, especially out in the tails. The presampling version of the EV estimator can not provide estimates for the lowest probability. The simulation size was 10,000 and this limits the lowest probability at 1/10,000. The post fitting version has no such problems. It is interesting to note that the EV estimators do a very good job at tracking the expected value of exceedances. Even at the lowest probability, the expected value is 0.05 while the post fitting EV method predicts 0.06.

6.1.3 Implication for Capital Requirements

A major reason for the implementation of VaR methods is the determination of capital requirements (CR). Financial regulators determine the CR according to the formula

$$CR = 3 \times VaR + \text{constant}$$

Individual financial institutions estimate the VaR, from which the CR are calculated. If the banks underestimate the VaR they get penalized by an increase in the multiplicative factor or the additive constant. The multiplicative constant may be increased to 4. If, however, the financial institution over estimates the VaR, it presumably gets penalized by shareholders. Hence accurate estimation of the VaR is important. The scaling factor 3 appears to be somewhat arbitrary, and has come under criticism from financial institutions for being too high. STAHL [1997] argues that the factor is justified by applying Chebyshev's inequality to the ratio of the true and model VaR distributions. In this worst case scenario, STAHL calculates 2.7 as an appropriate scaling factor at the 5 % level, 4.3 at the 1 % level, and increasing with lower probabilities. But according to Table 11, this factor is much too high or conservative. By comparing the RiskMetrics and the EV results at the 5 % level, we see that they are very close to the expected number of violations, and in that case a multiplicative constant close to one would be appropriate. At the 0.1 % level, RiskMetrics has five times the expected number of violations and in that case a large multiplicative constant may be appropriate, but the EV method gives results close to the expected value, suggesting that the constant should be close to one if EV is used for VaR. While a high scaling factor may be justified in the normal case, by using the estimate of the tails, as we do with the EV method, the multiplicative factor can be taken much lower. Note that HS, implies too high capital requirements in our case, while RiskMetrics implies too low CR. The extreme value estimator method appears to provide accurate tail estimates, and hence the most accurate way to set capital requirements.[4]

DANIELSSON, HARTMANN, and DE VRIES [1998] raise an issue regarding implications for incentive compatibility. The banks want to keep capital requirements as low as possible, and are faced with a sliding multiplicative factor in the range from three to four. Given that using a simple normal model implies considerably smaller capital requirements than the more accurate historical simulation or extreme tail methods, or even RiskMetrics, and that the penalty for under predicting the VaR is relatively small, *i.e.* the possible increase from 3 to 4, it is in the banks best interest to use the VaR method which provides the lowest VaR predictions. This will, in general be close to the worst VaR method available. This may explain the current prevalence among banks of using a moving average normal model for VaR prediction. It is like using a protective sunblock, because one has to, but choosing the one with lowest protection factor because its cheapest, with the result that one still gets burned.

6.2 Multi-Day Prediction

While most financial firms use one day VaR analysis for internal risk assessment, regulators require VaR estimates for 10 day returns. There are two ways to implement a multi-day VaR. If the time horizon is denoted by T, one can either look at past non-overlapping T day returns, and use these in the same fashion as the one day VaR analysis, or extrapolate the one day VaR

---

4. For more general results and conditions on the tails, see GELUK, PENG, DE VRIES [2000].

returns to the T day VaR. The latter method has the advantage that the sample size remains as it is. Possibly for this reason, RiskMetrics implements the latter method by the so called "*square-root-of-time*" rule which implies that returns are normal with no serial correlation. However, for fat tailed data, a $T^{1/\alpha}$ is appropriate. See section 3.1 for discussion on this issue.

It is not possible to backtest the $T = 10$ day VaR estimates because we have to compare the VaR predictions with non-overlapping T day returns. This implies that the sample available for testing is T times smaller than the one day sample. Since we are looking at uncommon events, we need to back-test over a large number of observations. In our experience, 1,000 days is a minimum test length. Therefore, for 10 day VaR we would need 10,000 days in the test sample.

In order to demonstrate the multi-day VaR methods, we use the one day VaR at the last day of our sample, December 30, 1996 to obtain 10 day VaRs. This is the VaR prediction on the last day of the results in Table 1, the number of random portfolios was 500. In Table 5, we present the one day and 10 day VaR predictions from RiskMetrics type and extreme value post-fitting methods. The numbers in the table reflect losses in millions of dollars on a portfolio of 100 million dollars. We see in Table 5 the same result as in Table 11, *i.e.* RiskMetrics underpredicts the amount of losses *vis-à-vis* EV at the 0.05 % and 0.005 % probabilities, while for the 10 day predictions RiskMetrics over predicts the loss, relative to EV, even for very low risk levels. Recall that EV uses the multiplicative factor $T^{1/\alpha}$ while RiskMetrics uses $T^{1/2}$. Due to this, the loss levels of the two methods cross at different probability levels depending on the time horizon. The average α was 4.6, with the average scaling factor of 1.7 which is much smaller than $T^{1/2} = 3.7$. As a result, at the 0.05 % level RiskMetrics predicts a 10 day VaR of \$6.3m while EV only predicts \$5.1m, on average.

6.3 Options

The inclusion of liquid nonlinear derivatives like options in the portfolio does not cause much extra difficulty. In general one has to price the option by means of risk neutral probabilities. However, the risk neutral measure is not observed, at least not directly. This is a generic problem for any VaR method, and for this reason RiskMetrics proceeds under the assumption of risk neutrality, and the assumption is followed here as well. The extreme value method can be used to generate the data for the underlying asset, and these simulated data can be used to price the option under risk neutrality. A structured Monte Carlo method is easily implemented by the post fitting method.

For simulation of returns on an European option, the path of returns on the underlying is simulated from the current day until expiration, sampling each day return from the combined empirical and estimated distributions, as described above, with the mean subtracted, and summing up the one day returns to obtain a simulated return for the entire period, y_i. If P^F is the future spot price of the asset, then a simulated future price of the underlying is $P^F \exp[y_i]$, and the simulated payoff follows directly. By repeating this N times, we get a vector of simulated options payoffs, which is discounted back with the rescaled three month t-bill rate, the vector is averaged, and the price of the option is subtracted. We then update the current futures price by one day through an element from the historical return distribution of the underlying, and repeat the simulation. This is done for each realization in the historical sample. Together this gives us the value of the option, and a vector of option prices quoted tomorrow. Finally, we calculate the one day option returns and can treat these returns as any other asset in the portfolio.

We used the same data as in the VaR exercise above, and added a European put option on the SP-500 index to the portfolio. The VaR was evaluated with values on September 4, 1997, the future price of the index was 943 and the strike price was 950. We used random portfolio weights, where the option received a weight of 4.9 %, and evaluated the VaR on the portfolio with and without the option. The results are in Table 6, where we can see that the option results in lower VaR estimates than if it is left out. Interestingly, the differences in monetary value are the greatest at the two confidence levels in the middle.

7 Practical Issues

There are several practical issues in implementing the extreme value method, *e.g.* the length of the data set, the estimation of the tail shape, and the calculation of the VaR for individual portfolios.

For any application where we are concerned with extreme outcomes, or events that happen perhaps once every 100 days or less, as is typical in VaR analysis, the data set has to include a sufficient number of extreme events in order to obtain an accurate prediction of VaR. For example, if we are concerned with a 1 % VaR, or the worst outcome every 100 days, a window length of one year, or 250 days is not very sensible. In effect the degrees of freedom are around two, and the VaR estimates will be highly inaccurate. This is recognized by the Basle Committee which emphasizes stress testing over multiple tumultuous periods such as the 1987 Crash and the 1993 ERM crisis. In this paper, we use a window length of 1,500 days, or about 7 years, and feel that a much shorter sample is not practical. This is reflected when we apply our extreme value procedure to a short sample in Monte Carlo experiments. When the sample is small, say 500 days or two years, the estimate of the tail index is rather inaccurate. There is no way around this issue, historical simulation and parametric methods will have the same small sample problems. In general the sample should be as large as possible. The primary reason to prefer a relatively small sample size is if the correlation structure in the sample is changing over time. However, in that case one can use the presampling version of the tail estimator, and use a covariance matrix that is only estimated with the most recent realizations in the sample. In general, one would expect lower correlation in extremes among stocks than *e.g.* exchange rates; and we were not able to demonstrate any benefit for our sample by using a frequently updated covariance matrix. However, we would expect that to happen for a sample that includes exchange rates that belong to managed exchange rate systems like the EMS.

It is not difficult to implement the tail estimation procedure. Using the historical sample to construct the simulated portfolio is in general not computer intensive for even very large portfolios, and in most cases can be done in a spread sheet like Excel. The subsequent estimation of the tails may take a few seconds at most using an add-in module with a dynamic linklibrary (dll) to fit the tails. So the additional computational complexity compared with historical simulation is a few seconds.

8 Conclusion

Many financial applications are dependent on accurate estimation of downside risk, such as optimal hedging, insurance, pricing of far out of the money options, and the application in this paper, Value-at-Risk (VaR). Several methods have been proposed for VaR estimation. Some are based on using conditional volatilities, such as the GARCH based RiskMetrics method. Others rely on the unconditional historical distribution of returns, such as historical simulation. We propose the use of the extreme value method as a semi-parametric method for estimation of tail probabilities. We show that conditional parametric methods, such as GARCH with normal innovations, as implemented in RiskMetrics, underpredict the VaR for a sample of US stock returns at the 1 % risk level, or below. Historical simulation performs better in predicting the VaR, but suffers from a high variance and discrete sampling far out in the tails. Moreover, HS is unable to address losses which are outside the sample. The performance of the extreme value estimator method performs better than both RiskMetrics and historical simulation far out in the tails.

The reason for the improved performance of the EV method is that it combines some of the advantages of both the non-parametric HS approach and the fully parametric RiskMetrics method. By only modelling the tails parametrically, we can also evaluate the risk on observed losses. In addition, because we know that financial return data are heavy tailed distributed, one can rely on a limit expansion for the tail behavior that is shared by all heavy tailed distributions. The importance of the central limit law for extremes is similar to the importance of the central limit law, *i.e.* one does not have to choose a particular parametric distribution. Furthermore, this limit law shares with the normal distribution the additivity property, albeit only for the tails. This enables us to develop a straightforward rule for obtaining multi-period VaR from the single period VaR, much like the normal based square root of time rule. At a future date, we plan to investigate the cross section implication of this rule, which may enable us to deal in a single manner with very widely diversified trading portfolios. We demonstrated that adding non-linear derivatives to the portfolio can be implemented quite easily by using a structured Monte Carlo procedure. We also observed that the present incentives are detrimental to implementing these improved VaR techniques. The current Basle directives rather encourage the opposite, and we would hope that, prudence nonwithstanding, positive incentives will be forthcoming to enhance future improvements in the VaR methodology and implementation thereof in practice. ∎

• References

BUTLER J. S., SCHACHTER B. (1996). – « Improving Value-at-Risk Estimates by Combining Kernel Estimation with Historical Simulation », *Mimeo*, Vanderbilt University and Comptroller of the Currency.

CHRISTOFFERSEN P. F., DIEBOLD F. X. (2000). – « How Relevant is Volatility Forecasting for Financial Risk Management? », *Review of Economics and Statistics*, 82, pp. 1-11.

DACOROGNA M. M., MULLER U. A., PICTET O. V., DE VRIES C. G. (1995). – « The Distribution of External Foreign Exchange Rate Returns in Extremely Large Data Sets », Tinbergen Institute *Working Paper*, TI 95-70.

DANIELSSON J. (2000). – « (Un)Conditionality of Risk Forecasting », *Mimeo*, London School of Economics.

DANIELSSON J., DE HAAN L., PENG L., DE VRIES C. G. (2000). – « Using a Bootstrap Method to Choose the Sample Fraction in Tail Index Estimation », *Journal of Multivariate Analysis*, forthcoming.

DANIELSSON J., DE VRIES C. G. (1997a). – « Beyond the Sample: Extreme Quantile and Probability Estimation », *Mimeo*, Tinbergen Institute Rotterdam.

DANIELSSON J., DE VRIES C. G. (1997b). – « Tail Index and Quantile Estimation with Very High Frequency Data », *Journal of Empirical Finance*, 4, pp. 241-257.

DANIELSSON J., DE VRIES C. G. (1997c). – « Value at Risk and Extreme Returns », London School of Economics, Financial Markets Group *Discussion Paper*, no. 273.

DANIELSSON J., HARTMANN P., DE VRIES C. G. (1998). – « The Cost of Conservatism: Extreme Returns, Value-at-Risk, and the Basle "Multiplication Factor" », *Risk*, January 1998.

DANIELSSON J., PAYNE R. (2000). – « Dynamic Liquidity in Electronic Limit Order Markets », *Mimeo*, London School of Economics.

DAVÉ R. D., STAHL G. (1997). – « On the Accuracy of VaR Estimates Based on the Variance-Covariance Approach », *Mimeo*, Olsen & Associates.

DE HAAN L., RESNICK S. I., ROOTZEN H., DE VRIES C. G. (1989). – « Extremal Behavior of Solutions to a Stochastic Difference Equation with Applications to ARCH Processes », *Stochastic Process and their Applications*, 32, pp. 213-224.

DIMSON E., MARSH P. (1996). – « Stress Tests of Capital Requirements », *Mimeo*, London Business School.

DUFFIE D., PAN J. (1997). – « An Overview of Value-at-Risk », *The Journal of Derivatives*, Spring 1997, pp. 7-49.

FAMA E. T., MILLER M. H. (1972). – *The Theory of Finance*, Dryden Press.

FELLER W. (1971). – *An Introduction to Probability Theory and its Applications*, Wiley, New York, vol. ii, 2nd, ed. edn.

GELUK J., PENG L., DE VRIES C. (2000). – « Convolutions of Heavy Tailed Random Variables and Applications to Portfolio Diversification and MA(1) Time Series », *Journal of Applied Probability*, forthcoming.

HALL P. (1990). – « Using the Bootstrap to Estimate Mean Squared Error and Select Smoothing Parameter in Nonparametric Problems », *Journal of Multivariate Analysis*, 32, pp. 177-203.

HENDRICKS D. (1996). – « Evaluation of Value-at-Risk Models Using Historical Data », *Federal Reserve bank of New York Economic Policy Review*, April, pp. 39-69.

HILL B. M. (1975). – « A Simple General Approach to Inference about the Tail of a Distribution », *Annals of Statistics*, 35, pp. 1163-1173.

JACKSON P., MAUDE D. J., PERRAUDIN W. (1997). – « Bank Capital and Value-at-Risk », *Journal of Derivatives*, Spring 1997, pp. 73-111.

JORION P. (2000). – *Value-at-Risk*, McGraw Hill.

MORGAN J. P. (1995). – *RiskMetrics-Technical Manual*, Third edn.

MAHONEY J. M. (1996). – « Forecast Biases in Value-at-Risk Estimations: Evidence from Foreign Exchange and Global Equity Portfolios », *Mimeo*, Federal Reserve Bank of New York.

McNeil A. J., Frey R. (1999). – « Estimation of Tail-Related Risk Measures for Heteroskedastic Financial Time Series: An Extreme Value Approach », *Mimeo*, ETH Zurich.

Peng L. (1998). – « Second Order Condition and Extreme Value Theory », Ph.D. *Thesis*, Erasmus University Rotterdam, Tinbergen Institute, # 178.

Stahl G. (1997). – « Three Cheers », *Risk*, 10, pp. 67-69

APPENDIX A

Extreme Value Theory and Tail Estimators

This appendix gives an overview of the statistical methods used in obtaining estimates of the tail of a distribution. The following is a brief summary of results in DANIELSSON and DE VRIES [1997a] which also provide all the proofs. Let x be the return on a risky financial asset where the distribution of x is heavy tailed. Suppose the distribution function $F(x)$ varies regularly at infinity with tail index α:

(7) $$\lim_{t \to \infty} \frac{1 - F(tx)}{1 - F(t)} = x^{-\alpha}, \quad \alpha > 0, \quad x > 0.$$

This implies that the unconditional distribution of the returns is heavy tailed and that unconditional moments which are larger than α are unbounded. The assumption of regular variation at infinity as specified in (7) is essentially the only assumption that is needed for analysis of tail behavior of the returns x. Regular variation at infinity is a necessary and sufficient condition for the distribution of the maximum or minimum to be in the domain of attraction of the limit law (extreme value distribution) for heavy tailed distributed random variables.

A parametric form for the tail shape of $F(x)$ can be obtained by taking a second order expansion of $F(x)$ as $x \to \infty$. The only non-trivial possibility under mild assumptions is:

(8) $$F(x) = 1 - ax^{-\alpha} \left[1 + bx^{-\beta} + o\left(x^{-\beta}\right)\right], \beta > 0 \quad \text{as } x \to \infty$$

The tail index can be estimated by the HILL estimator (HILL [1975]), where M is the random number of exceedances over a high threshold observation X_{M+1}

(9) $$\frac{1}{\alpha} = \frac{1}{M} \sum_{i=M}^{n} \log \frac{X_i}{X_{M+1}},$$

The asymptotic normality, variance, and bias, are known for this estimator both for i.i.d. data and for certain stochastic processes like MA(1) and ARCH(1). It can be shown that a unique AMSE minimizing threshold level exists which is a function of the parameters and number of observations.[5] This value is estimated by the bootstrap estimator of DANIELSSON and DE VRIES [1997a] and DANIELSSON, DE HAAN, PENG and DE VRIES [2000], but presumes independent observations.

It is possible to use (8) and (9) to obtain estimators for out of sample quantile and probability (P, Q) combinations given that the data exhibit fat tailed distributed innovations. The properties of the quantile and tail probability esti-

---

5. Instead of minimizing the MSE of the tail index estimator, one can choose a different criterion and minimize the MSE of the quantile estimator (10), see PENG [1998].

mators below follow directly from the properties of $\widehat{1/\alpha}$. In addition, the out of sample (P,Q) estimates are related in the same fashion as the in sample (P,Q) estimates.

To derive the out of sample (P,Q) estimator consider two excess probabilities p and t with $p < 1/n < t$, where n is the sample size. Corresponding to p and t are the large quantiles, x_p and x_t, where for x_i we have $1 - F(x_i) = i$, $i = t, p$. Using the expansion of $F(x)$ in (8) with $\beta > 0$, ignoring the higher order terms in the expansion, and replacing t by M/n and x_t by the $(M + 1)$-th descending order statistic one obtains the estimator

$$(10) \qquad \hat{x}_p = X_{(M+1)} \left(\frac{m}{np} \right)^{\frac{1}{\hat{\alpha}}} .$$

It can be shown that the quantile estimator $\hat{x}_p$ is asymptotically normally distributed. A reverse estimator can be developed as well by a similar manipulation of (8)

$$(11) \qquad \hat{p} = \frac{M}{n} \left(\frac{x_t}{x_p} \right)^{\hat{\alpha}} .$$

The excess probability estimator $\hat{p}$ is also asymptotically normally distributed.

APPENDIX B

Figures and Tables

TABLE 1
Daily SP-500, 1990-96. Time Between Extreme Returns

Upper Tail			Lower Tail		
date	days	rank	date	days	rank
90-08-27	74	2	90-01-23	6	6
90-10-01	24	4	90-08-07	136	3
90-10-18	13	8	90-08-17	8	12
90-10-19	1	10	90-08-22	3	15
90-11-09	15	14	90-08-24	2	4
91-01-17	46	1	90-09-25	21	14
91-02-06	14	16	90-10-10	11	5
91-02-11	3	5	91-05-13	148	17
91-03-05	15	13	91-08-20	69	10
91-04-02	19	9	91-11-18	63	1
91-08-21	99	3	93-02-17	315	9
91-12-23	86	6	93-04-05	33	16
91-12-30	4	11	94-02-07	214	11
93-03-08	300	17	96-03-11	527	2
94-04-05	273	12	96-07-08	82	13
96-12-19	686	15	96-07-16	6	7

TABLE 2
Predicted and Expected Maxima of Student-t (4)

In Sample Prediction, 2000 observations	Theoretical	Average Values
Sample Maxima by HS	8.610	10.67 (4.45) [4.90]
Forecast Maximas by EV	8.610	8.90 (1.64) [1.66]
Out of Sample Prediction		
Forecast Maximas by EV for Sample of Size 4000	10.306	10.92 (2.43) [2.50]
Forecast Maximas by EV for Sample of Size 6000	11.438	12.32 (3.02) [3.14]

Sample size = 2,000, simulations 1,000, bootstrap iterations = 2,000. Standard errors in parenthesis, RMSE in brackets. HS denotes estimation by historical simulation and EV estimation with the method proposed by DANIELSSON and DE VRIES [1997b].

VALUE-AT-RISK AND EXTREME RETURNS   263

TABLE 3
Extreme Daily returns 1987-1996

JPM	25 %	12 %	8.8 %	6.7 %	6.5 %	6.4 %	6.3 %
	−41 %	−6.7 %	−6.3 %	−6.1 %	−6.0 %	−5.8 %	−5.7 %
MMM	11 %	7.1 %	5.9 %	5.7 %	5.7 %	5.0 %	4.8 %
	−30 %	−10 %	−10 %	−9.0 %	−6.2 %	−6.1 %	−5.6 %
MCD	10 %	7.9 %	6.3 %	6.2 %	5.4 %	5.0 %	5.0 %
	−18 %	−10 %	−8.7 %	−8.5 %	−8.3 %	−7.3 %	−6.9 %
INTC	24 %	11 %	9.9 %	9.0 %	8.9 %	8.6 %	8.6 %
	−21 %	−21 %	−16 %	−15 %	−14 %	−12 %	−12 %
IBM	12 %	11 %	11 %	10 %	9.4 %	7.4 %	6.5 %
	−26 %	−11 %	−11 %	−9.3 %	−7.9 %	−7.5 %	−7.1 %
XRX	12 %	8.0 %	7.8 %	7.5 %	7.1 %	6.8 %	6.3 %
	−22 %	−16 %	−11 %	−8.4 %	−7.5 %	−6.9 %	−6.2 %
XON	17 %	10 %	6.0 %	5.8 %	5.8 %	5.6 %	5.4 %
	−27 %	−8.7 %	−7.9 %	−6.6 %	−6.3 %	−5.7 %	−5.4 %
SP-500	8.7 %	5.1 %	4.8 %	3.7 %	3.5 %	3.4 %	3.3 %
	−23 %	−8.6 %	−7.0 %	−6.3 %	−5.3 %	−4.5 %	−4.3 %

TABLE 4
Observed Extreme Returns of the daily SP-500, 1990-1996, and the Probability of that Return as Predicted by the Normal GARCH, Student-t GARCH Model, the Extreme Value Estimation Method, and the Empirical Distribution. Due to Moving Estimation Windows Results Represent Different Samples

Observed	Probabilities			
Return	Normal	Student-*t*	EV Estimator	Empirical
−3.72 %	0.0000	0.0002	0.0007	0.0006
−3.13 %	0.0000	0.0010	0.0015	0.0011
−3.07 %	0.0002	0.0021	0.0016	0.0017
−3.04 %	0.0032	0.0071	0.0016	0.0023
−2.71 %	0.0098	0.0146	0.0026	0.0028
−2.62 %	0.0015	0.0073	0.0029	0.0034
3.66 %	0.0000	0.0011	0.0004	0.0006
3.13 %	0.0060	0.0096	0.0009	0.0011
2.89 %	0.0002	0.0022	0.0013	0.0017
2.86 %	0.0069	0.0117	0.0014	0.0023
2.53 %	0.0059	0.0109	0.0025	0.0028
2.50 %	0.0007	0.0038	0.0026	0.0034

TABLE 5
10 Day VaR Prediction on December 30, 1996 in Millions of US Dollars for a $100 Million Trading Portfolio

Risk Level	5 %	1.0 %	0.5 %	0.10 %	0.05 %	0.005 %
EV						
One day	$0.9	$1.5	$1.7	$2.5	$3.0	$5.1
10 day	$1.6	$2.5	$3.0	$4.3	$5.1	$8.9
RM						
One day	$1.0	$1.4	$1.6	$1.9	$2.0	$2.3
10 day	$3.2	$4.5	$4.9	$5.9	$6.3	$7.5

TABLE 6
Effect of Inclusion of Option in Portfolio

Confidence Level	VaR with Option	VaR without Option	Difference
95 %	$895,501	$1,381,519	$486,019
99 %	$1,474,056	$2,453,564	$979,508
99.5 %	$1,823,735	$2,754,562	$930,827
99.9 %	$3,195,847	$3,856,747	$669,900
99.99 %	$7,130,721	$6,277,714	− $853,007

TABLE 7
Summary Statistics. Jan. 27, 1984 to Dec. 31, 1996

	JPM	MMM	MCD	INTC	IBM	XRX	XON
Mean	0.05	0.04	0.07	0.09	0.01	0.04	0.05
S.D.	1.75	1.41	1.55	2.67	1.62	1.62	1.39
Kurtosis	100.28	68.07	8.36	5.88	25.71	16.44	49.23
Skewness	− 2.70	− 3.17	− 0.58	− 0.36	− 1.08	− 1.06	− 1.74
Minimum	− 40.56	− 30.10	− 18.25	− 21.40	− 26.09	− 22.03	− 26.69
Maximum	24.63	10.92	10.05	23.48	12.18	11.67	16.48

Note: JPM = J. P. Morgan; MMM = 3m; MCD = McDonalds; INTC = Intel; IBM = IBM; XRX = Xerox; XON = Exxon.
Source: DATASTREAM

VALUE-AT-RISK AND EXTREME RETURNS   265

TABLE 8
Summary Statistics. Jan. 2, 1990 to Dec. 31, 1996

	JPM	MMM	MCD	INTC	IBM	XRX	XON
Mean	0.05	0.04	0.05	0.15	0.03	0.06	0.04
S.D.	1.45	1.19	1.48	2.34	1.72	1.60	1.12
Kurtosis	1.83	3.78	1.51	2.86	6.67	9.46	1.10
Skewness	0.28	−0.32	0.05	−0.36	0.25	−0.35	0.11
Minimum	−6.03	−9.03	−8.70	−14.60	−11.36	−15.63	−4.32
Maximum	6.70	4.98	6.27	9.01	12.18	11.67	5.62

TABLE 9
Correlation Matrix. Jan. 27, 1984 to Dec. 31, 1996

	JPM	MMM	MCD	INTC	IBM	XRX	XON
JPM	1.00						
MMM	0.49	1.00					
MCD	0.42	0.44	1.00				
INTC	0.30	0.36	0.29	1.00			
IBM	0.38	0.42	0.34	0.40	1.00		
XRX	0.35	0.39	0.34	0.32	0.35	1.00	
XON	0.44	0.48	0.37	0.24	0.35	0.30	1.00

TABLE 10
Correlation Matrix. Jan. 2, 1990 to Dec. 31, 1996

	JPM	MMM	MCD	INTC	IBM	XRX	XON
JPM	1.00						
MMM	0.28	1.00					
MCD	0.28	0.28	1.00				
INTC	0.24	0.21	0.21	1.00			
IBM	0.18	0.19	0.19	0.32	1.00		
XRX	0.23	0.23	0.22	0.21	0.19	1.00	
XON	0.20	0.25	0.21	0.12	0.10	0.12	1.00

TABLE 11

Estimation Results. Average number of realized portfolios that were larger than VaR Predictions

Tail Percentage	0.005 %	0.01 %	0.025 %	0.05 %	0.1 %	0.25 %	0.5 %	1 %	2.5 %	5 %
Expected	0.05	0.1	0.25	0.5	1	2.5	5	10	25	50
Frequency Days / Frequency Years	77	38	15	7.7	3.8	1.5	200	100	40	20
RiskMetrics	1.58 (1.29)	2.00 (1.45)	2.72 (1.66)	3.55 (1.81)	4.85 (2.06)	7.29 (2.27)	10.65 (2.73)	16.28 (3.13)	30.26 (4.41)	52.45 (7.39)
Historical Simulation	0.75 (0.89)	0.75 (0.89)	0.75 (0.89)	0.75 (0.89)	0.95 (1.03)	1.90 (1.57)	3.69 (2.39)	7.66 (3.90)	20.50 (7.22)	43.24 (10.75)
Tail Kernel Presampling	0.09 (0.31)	0.09 (0.31)	0.37 (0.71)	0.68 (0.98)	1.21 (1.27)	2.54 (1.71)	4.82 (2.56)	9.32 (4.26)	22.35 (7.66)	44.02 (11.62)
Tail Kernel Post-Fitting	0.06 (0.23)	0.12 (0.35)	0.33 (0.62)	0.59 (0.82)	1.06 (1.13)	2.35 (1.72)	4.23 (2.55)	8.19 (3.86)	20.84 (7.35)(	43.14 11.10)

Observations in testing = 1,000 over period 930115 to 961230. Window size in HS and EK-HS = 1,500, initial starting date for window 870210, random portfolios = 500, simulation size in HS-extreme kernel = 10,000. Standard errors in parenthesis.

TABLE 12
10 Years, 2,600 Daily Returns, 1987-1996. With Predicted Maximum Daily Drop in one Year (250 days)

	mean	var	kurtosis	max	min	skew	upper tail				lower tail			
							α	m	$X_{(m+1)}$	max	α	m	$X_{(m+1)}$	max
Stock Index														
Hang Seng	0.06	2.7	144.5	8.9	-40.5	-6.5	3.5	32	3.5	3.6 %	2.2	49	-3.2	-3.3 %
Straights Times	0.03	1.5	64.4	11.5	-23.4	-3.7	3.1	36	2.5	2.6 %	2.2	59	-2.3	-2.3 %
Word	0.03	0.6	25.7	7.9	-10.0	-1.4	3.5	37	1.6	1.7 %	3.1	44	-1.6	-1.7 %
DAX	0.03	1.4	12.2	7.3	-13.7	-1.1	2.9	52	2.3	2.3 %	2.6	43	-2.7	-2.8 %
FT All Share	0.03	0.7	25.9	5.7	-12.1	-2.0	2.9	58	1.5	1.5 %	3.1	86	-1.3	-1.3 %
SP-500	0.04	1.0	115.8	8.7	-22.8	-5.1	3.8	26	2.3	2.4 %	2.5	51	-1.9	-1.9 %
Miscellaneous Assets														
Gold Bullion	0.00	0.5	7.6	3.6	-7.2	-1.0	4.8	16	2.2	2.2 %	3.0	33	-1.9	-1.9 %
US Bonds	0.00	0.9	73.5	17.8	-10.7	1.7	2.4	86	1.3	1.4 %	2.5	79	-1.4	-1.5 %
US Stocks														
JPM	0.03	3.3	106.9	24.6	-40.6	-3.1	3.5	31	4.2	4.3 %	3.1	48	-3.2	-3.3 %
MMM	0.04	2.1	72.5	10.9	-30.1	-3.6	4.5	29	3.4	3.5 %	2.4	52	-2.8	-2.9 %
MCD	0.06	2.5	6.6	10.0	-18.3	-0.7	5.2	22	4.1	4.2 %	3.0	45	-3.3	-3.4 %
INTC	0.13	6.8	5.1	23.5	-21.4	-0.5	4.7	29	6.3	6.6 %	2.8	37	-6.2	-6.4 %
IBM	0.01	2.9	23.5	12.2	-26.1	-1.2	3.2	28	4.3	4.5 %	2.9	38	-3.8	-3.9 %
XRX	0.03	2.6	16.9	11.7	-22.0	-1.2	3.6	29	4.0	4.1 %	2.7	50	-3.3	-3.4 %
XON	0.04	2.0	56.7	16.5	-26.7	-2.0	3.5	34	3.1	3.2 %	2.7	70	-2.3	-2.4 %
Forex														
FRF/USD	-0.01	0.4	-0.8	2.7	-3.2	0.0	6.2	16	2.0	2.0 %	8.2	17	-2.1	-2.1 %
DM/USD	-0.01	0.5	-0.9	3.2	-3.0	0.0	7.0	16	2.2	2.2 %	6.7	16	-2.1	-2.2 %
YEN/USD	-0.01	0.4	0.2	3.4	-3.6	-0.2	4.9	16	1.9	2.0 %	4.7	18	-2.1	-2.1 %
GBP/USD	-0.01	0.4	-0.5	3.3	-2.8	0.3	9.5	16	2.3	2.3 %	6.3	17	-1.9	-2.0 %

FIGURE 1

1 % Largest and Smallest Daily Returns on Stocks in Portfolio

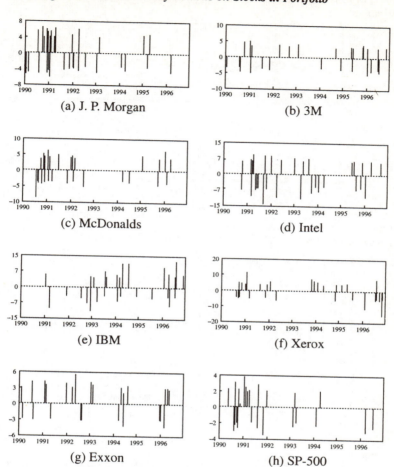

(a) J. P. Morgan

(b) 3M

(c) McDonalds

(d) Intel

(e) IBM

(f) Xerox

(g) Exxon

(h) SP-500

FIGURE 2
1 % Largest and Smallest Returns on SP-500 over 500 and 1,000 Day Windows

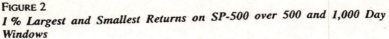
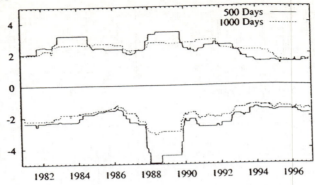

FIGURE 3
Distribution of SP-500 Returns 1990-1996 with Fitted Upper Tail

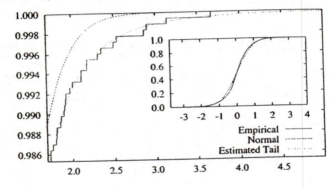

FIGURE 4
Distribution of SP-500 Returns 1990-1996 and Highest GARCH Prediction

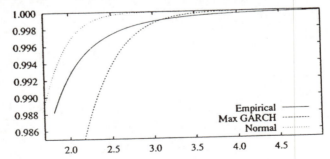

[24]

ELSEVIER   Journal of Empirical Finance 4 (1997) 187–212

Journal of
EMPIRICAL
FINANCE

Forecasting the frequency of changes in quoted foreign exchange prices with the autoregressive conditional duration model [1]

Robert F. Engle [a], Jeffrey R. Russell [b,*]

[a] *Department of Economics 0508, University of California, San Diego, La Jolla, CA 92093-0508, USA*
[b] *University of Chicago, Graduate School of Business, 1101 East 58th St., Chicago, IL 60537, USA*

Abstract

This paper applies the Autorecressive Conditional Duration model to Foreign Exchange quotes arriving on Reuters screens. The Autoregressive Conditional Duration model, developed in Engle and Russell (1995) [Engle, R., Russell, J., 1995. Autoregressive conditional duration; a new model for irregularly spaced time series data, University of California, San Diego, unpublished manuscript.], is a new statistical model for the analysis of data that does not arrive in equal time intervals. When Dollar/Deutschmark data are examined, it is clear that many of the price quotes are simply noisy repeats of the previous quote. By systematically thinning the sample, a measure of the time between price changes is developed. These price durations are modeled with the ACD to obtain estimates of the instantaneous intensity of price changes. This measure is related to standard measures of volatility but is formulated in a way that incorporates the information in the irregular sampling intervals. A simple market microstructure model implies that the bid–ask spread should have predictive power for the volatility which is supported by the data. A model of price leadership however, is not supported. © 1997 Elsevier Science B.V.

---

[*] Corresponding author.

[1] The authors would like to thank David Brillinger, Sir David Cox, Clive Granger, Andrew Karolyi, and Gennady Samorodnitsky for their comments and suggestions. Useful comments were also received from participants at the 1995 Olsen and Associates meetings on high frequency data analysis. The research was supported in part by National Science Foundation Grant SES-9122056. Jeffrey Russell is grateful for financial support from the Sloan Foundation and the UCSD Project in Econometric Analysis Fellowship.

188   *R.F. Engle, J.R. Russell / Journal of Empirical Finance 4 (1997) 187–212*

1. Introduction

The foreign exchange market is a massive market with international participants trading billions of dollars 24 h a day. Transactions are carried out in split seconds between parties across the globe. As the market is a dealer market there are no systematic accounts of the movements in the market except for the advertised quotes which appear continuously on trading desks over the Reuters screens. These update traders on a second by second basis giving bid and ask prices for the major players in the market. Transactions then occur bilaterally and are not systematically recorded.

Often investigators are interested in studying the behavior of the exchange rate process. See, for example, Bollerslev and Domowitz (1993) or Goodhart et al. (1993). Price quote data inherently arrive in irregular time intervals. Since the majority of time series techniques are based on equally spaced intervals between arrivals of data, there is a natural inclination of the econometrician to choose some fixed interval and aggregate the information within each interval. The choice of an interval is potentially a very important part of the analysis. If too short of an interval is chosen then most of the data points will be zeros and heteroskedasticity of a particular form will be introduced. On the other hand if too lone, an interval is chosen, then features of the data will be smoothed and potentially hidden.

Engle and Russell (1995) developed a model for data that do not arrive in equal time intervals. Their paper proposed a new point process model for intertemporally correlated event arrival times. Rather than aggregate to some fixed interval, it is proposed to treat the arrival times of the data as a point process with an intensity defined conditional on past activity. Because the model formulation focuses on the intertemporal correlations of the durations (time interval between events), the model is called the autoregressive conditional duration (ACD) model.

Point processes frequently incorporate other information which modifies or 'marks' the arrival times. Engle and Russell (1995) describe an algorithm for modeling marks by focusing only on some types of events. For the FX data analyzed in this paper, it is apparent that many of the quotes are simply repeats of previous quotes. At some point, however, a quote will arrive that is different. This paper uses the thinning algorithm discussed in Engle and Russell to model the intensity of quote arrivals which signify price chances. The model is called the ACD model for price based durations.

This model predicts how long it will be until prices change. A trader might be interested in knowing this time interval as it could influence the speed with which he places an order. Each time the price changes, there is an interval of time during which he can trade at that price. If the market is slow, this interval may be quite long, while in an active market, the price may last much less than a minute. If the trader is using an automated trading, system, then the system itself must recognize that sometimes a delay will have no impact on the available prices while at others it may eliminate the opportunity.

By modeling the time it takes for prices to move a certain amount, the model is essentially a volatility model or more precisely the inverse of a volatility model. Because the model allows weakly exogenous and lagged dependent variables to influence the intensity of the price process, simple LM tests can be performed to investigate the determinants of price volatility. The hypothesis of price leadership can be examined since the sources of the quotes are recorded.

Each price duration can potentially be interpreted as the delayed response of the market makers quotes to an information event as in the Glosten and Milgrom (1985) model. Market makers infer the direction and size of a new piece of privately available information by examining the requests to buy or sell assets. As some of the agents may be privately informed, the market makers will set and adjust bid and ask quotes in response to excess demand or supply which serves as a signal of the news. Both the speed of adjustment and the bid–ask spread depend upon the fraction of the traders assumed to be informed and whether they are successful in disguising themselves as liquidity traders. Easley and O'Hara (1992), Easley et al. (1994, 1995) point out that market makers do not in general even know whether there has been an information event. Thus, slow trading can be interpreted as evidence that there has been no new information, and the price adjustment will be consequently slowed. Thus the time until prices change can be given a structural interpretation in terms of the rate at which information is released and the rate at which the market incorporates this information into prices.

Section 2 of the paper will present the ACD model with both the statistical underpinnings and the motivation. Section 3 describes the data and Section 4 gives the results. Section 5 gives further analysis of the model and tests some interesting hypotheses, Section 6 develops a relation between the price duration measure of volatility and standard measures of volatility and Section 7 concludes.

2. The ACD model

The statistical problem is to estimate the probability of an event such as a quote arrival at each point in time. This requires specifying the stochastic process of the arrival times, estimating the parameters and computing the probabilities of events. The instantaneous probability of an event is called the intensity of the process and in dependent processes such as the ones considered here is conditional on past information. Once the intensity is parameterized, the likelihood can be computed and parameters estimated and checked.

Engle and Russell (1995) proposed the ACD class of statistical models for arrival times which are dependent. The data are simply a list of times and possibly characteristics, or marks, associated with the arrival times. They considered the arrival rates of IBM transactions on the NYSE, while this paper will develop similar models for the arrival rates on Reuters screens of foreign exchange quotes on the Dollar Deutschmark.

190   *R.F. Engle, J.R. Russell / Journal of Empirical Finance 4 (1997) 187–212*

Consider the stochastic process which is simply a sequence of times $\{t_1, t_2, \ldots, t_n, \ldots\}$. As these are points distributed in time, this is called a 'point process' and the times are called 'arrival times' of the point process. Corresponding to these arrival times is a counting process, $N(t)$ which is the number of events which have occurred by the time t. Obviously, $N(t)$ is a non-decreasing function of time with $N(t_0) = 0$.

Defining the 'conditional intensity' of a process as

$$\lambda\left(t; N(t), t_1, \ldots, t_{N(t)}\right)$$
$$= \lim_{\Delta t \to 0} \frac{P\left(N(t + \Delta t) > N(t) | N(t), t_1, \ldots, t_{N(t)}\right)}{\Delta t}, \tag{1}$$

the intensity over the next instant is potentially a function of the entire past history of the process. This expression generalizes the familiar Poisson process where λ is a constant, and the inhomogeneous Poisson process where it depends only upon t but not past arrivals. The Eq. (1) is used to characterize 'self exciting point processes' as described in Snyder and Miller (1991) and attributed variously to Rubin (1972), or Hawkes (1971). Self exciting processes allow the past events to influence the future evolution of the process. Such processes have been used to model dependent point processes such as earthquakes, electron emissions and nerve cell firings. The model nests a variety of point processes described in the literature. If the intensity depends only on $N(t)$ but not the timing of events, then the process is a 'birth process', and if it depends only on the m most recent arrival times, it is called a m-memory self exciting process.

Once the local properties of the process are specified by a parameterization of Eq. (1), the probabilities of counts and waiting times are all fully specified. In particular the likelihood function of the observed times can be derived from the intensity process. It is convenient to write this likelihood function in terms of the durations which are the intervals between successive arrival times. Let $x_i = t_i - t_{i-1}$ for $i = 1, \ldots, N(T)$ be the data set. Then the log likelihood can be expressed in terms of the conditional density function of x_i as:

$$L\left(x_1, \ldots, x_{N(T)}; \theta\right) = \sum_{i=1}^{N(T)} \log f\left(x_i | x_1, \ldots, x_{i-1}; \theta\right) \tag{2}$$

The ACD model is a new and convenient class of specifications for the self exciting process. The model does not necessarily have limited memory and is easy to estimate by maximum likelihood. The simplest specifications allow analytic forecasts of waiting times. The crucial assumption for the ACD model is that the time dependence can be summarized by a function ψ which is the conditional expected duration given past information and has the property that x_i/ψ_i are independent and identically distributed. That is, the density of these 'standardized durations' satisfy:

$$\psi_i = E\left[x_i | x_{i-1}, \ldots, x_1; \theta\right] \tag{3}$$

and

$$x_i/\psi_i \text{ are i.i.d.}$$ (4)

This can also be written as

$$x_i = \psi_i \varepsilon_i$$ (5)

where ε is an i.i.d. series of disturbances with a distribution which must be specified. Associated with this distribution is a hazard function given by the probability density of ε divided by the survival function of ε which is simply one minus the cumulative distribution function. The hazard function of ε is often called the baseline hazard since it does not depend upon any conditioning information. If f is the density of ε, the baseline hazard is given by:

$$h_0(t) = \frac{f(t)}{\int_t^\infty f(u)\,du}$$ (6)

It is natural to call the model autoregressive conditional duration or ACD because it parameterizes the conditional duration in terms of the lagged durations.

From Eqs. (3) and (5) it is apparent that there is a vast set of ACD model specifications defined by different distributions of ε and specifications of ψ. For example, a natural starting point is to assume that durations are conditionally exponential. In this case, the conditional intensity is given by

$$\lambda\big(t|x_{N(t)}, \ldots, x_1\big) = \psi_{N(t)+1}^{-1}$$ (7)

which is therefore constant from one arrival to the next, although it has a step function at each arrival time. A simple m-memory specification of the intensity is given by:

$$\psi_i = \omega + \sum_{j-1}^{m} \alpha_j x_{i-j} \quad \text{for } \alpha_j \geq 0,\ \omega > 0,\ \forall i,\ i = 1, \ldots, N,\ j = 1, \ldots, m$$

(8)

A natural generalization of this model introduces infinite memory by including q lagged durations:

$$\psi_i = \omega + \sum_{j-1}^{m} \alpha_j x_{i-j} + \sum_{j=1}^{q} \beta_j \psi_{i-j} \quad \text{for } \alpha_j,\ \beta_j \geq 0,\ \omega > 0,\ \forall i,\ i = 1, \ldots, N,$$

$$j = 1, \ldots, m, q$$ (9)

This model called the ACD(m, q) is convenient because it allows various moments to be calculated by expectation. For example, the conditional mean of x_i is ψ_i, the conditional duration, but the unconditional mean is

$$E(x_i) = \frac{\omega}{1 - \sum_{j=1}^{m} \alpha_j - \sum_{j=1}^{q} \beta_j}.$$ (10)

192   *R.F. Engle, J.R. Russell / Journal of Empirical Finance 4 (1997) 187–212*

This is most easily seen by taking expectations of both sides of Eq. (9) although the proof also requires that all roots of an associated difference equation lie outside the unit circle. In the ACD(1, 1) case this requires that $\alpha + \beta < 1$. Similarly, in the ACD(1, 1) case, the conditional variance of x is ψ_i^2 but the unconditional variance is given by σ^2 where

$$\sigma^2 = \mu^2 (1 - \beta^2 - 2\alpha\beta)/(1 - \beta^2 - 2\alpha\beta - 2\alpha^2). \tag{11}$$

Since $\alpha > 0$, the unconditional standard deviation will exceed the mean exhibiting 'excess dispersion' as often noticed in duration data sets. From taking repeated expectations, multistep forecasts of durations can be computed directly. That is, the expected duration of the nth transaction can be computed directly from Eq. (9).

Readers who are familiar with the ARCH class of models will immediately recognize the relationship to models of conditional variance. The ACD(1, 1) is analogous to the GARCH(1, 1) and will have many of the same properties. Just as the GARCH(1, 1) is often a good starting point, the ACD(1, 1) seems like a natural starting point. However, as there are many alternative volatility models, there are many interesting possibilities here. For recent surveys on ARCH models and lists of different classes, see Bollerslev et al. (1994), Bollerslev et al. (1992) and Bera and Higgins (1992). The ARCH model was originally introduced by Engle (1982) and GARCH by Bollerslev (1986).

The specifications in Eqs. (7) and (9) can be generalized in many ways. The durations in Eq. (7) are assumed to be conditionally exponential but there are countless ways to relax this restriction. One popular suggestion is the Weibull. Engle and Russell (1995) found that a conditional Weibull density appeared to fit the data better than the conditional exponential density for most models estimated on the stock market data examined in that paper. For the Weibull distribution, the hazard is a slightly more complicated form

$$\lambda\left(t | x_{N(t)}, \ldots, x_1\right) = \left(\Gamma\left(1 + (1/\gamma)\right)\psi_{N(t)+1}^{-1}\right)^{\gamma}\left(t - t_{N(t)}\right)^{\gamma - 1}\gamma \tag{12}$$

where $\Gamma(\cdot)$ is the gamma function and γ is the Weibull parameter. The conditional intensity is now a two parameter family which can exhibit either increasing or decreasing hazard functions. This makes especially long durations more or less likely than for the exponential depending on whether γ is greater or less that unity respectively. When $\gamma = 1$, this simplifies to Eq. (7).

In practice, additional variables may well enter the ACD model. Of particular importance is time itself. There are systematic variations in the arrival rate of price quotes over the day and over the week. Thus the conditional expected duration typically depends upon t directly. Thus the specification in Eq. (3) may naturally be generalized to give

$$\psi_i(x_{i-1}, \ldots, x_1; \theta)\Phi(t_{i-1}) = E[x_i | x_{i-1}, \ldots, x_1; \theta] \tag{13}$$

where it is assumed that the seasonal function of time is separable multiplicatively from the stochastic component.

More interestingly, economic variables can enter the equation which determines the frequency of transactions. From this version of the model one can test hypothesis on economic determinants of the rates of transactions. It is here that the information loss due to thinning can be assessed and hypothesis about market microstructure such as price setting behavior with potentially asymmetric information and price leadership are examined.

3. Data

The foreign exchange data were provided by Olsen and Associates (O & A). The data set contains several variables extracted from the Reuters screens including bid–ask quotes and associated arrival times. The foreign exchange market operates around the clock 7 days a week and the complete data set is one year covering October 1, 1992 through September 30, 1993. The typical rate of quote arrivals differs dramatically on weekends and weekdays and between business hours in different countries and in different time zones. In order to utilize days with a common typical pattern, only Tuesdays, Wednesdays and Thursdays are analyzed. This subsample consists of 51 days and 303,408 observations on the Deutschmark–Dollar exchange rate for the months of May through August.

Although the primary focus of the paper is on price based durations (price durations), it is useful initially to describe the quote arrival rate and quote based durations (quote durations). For the O & A data set a typical weekday has almost 6000 quote arrivals. On average a quote arrives every 15 s. Seasonal patterns in the rate of arrival of quotes have been examined in several papers [2]. The first task is to model this rate. Assuming the separability of time function and stochastic function as in Eq. (13), the elimination of the time of day effect is comparable to seasonal adjustment. The strategy followed here is to regress the duration on a function purely of the time of day to obtain a consistent (but inefficient) estimator of the typical shape. Dividing, the durations by their estimated typical shape gives a 'seasonally adjusted' set of durations.

Fig. 1 presents the expected duration conditioned on time-of-day alone. This expectation was formed by regressing the observed duration on 96 time-of-day binary variables, each 15 min long. The day of week was neglected so Tuesdays, Wednesdays, and Thursdays are assumed to have the same seasonal component. Notice that this plot reveals the same patterns as previous studies of quote frequency, although it looks roughly like the inverse. In particular, instead of observing a trough for a lack of quote arrivals during the Japanese lunch hour as observed in Bollerslev and Domowitz (1993), we observe a corresponding spike for particularly long durations between quote updates. Analogous to the previous

---

[2] See Bollerslev and Domowitz (1993) and Muller et al. (1990) for example.

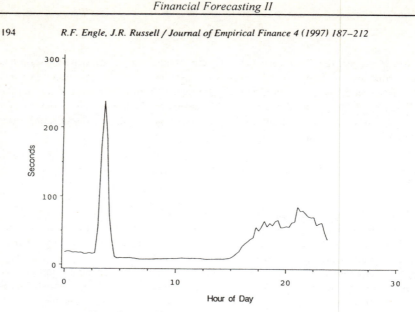

Fig. 1. Expected quote duration conditioned on time of day.

studies, we find the most quote activity in the middle of the day between hours 5 and 14. During this time quotes are arriving at a rate of just under 1 every 9 s on average. At the other extreme, during the Japanese lunch hour (hours 3–4 GMT), quotes arrive at a rate of around 1 every 4 min.

Fig. 2 presents a plot of the histogram of raw durations up to 300 s. Most of the quotes are recorded in intervals of multiples of 6 s because the recording device checks for new quotes every six seconds. In the few exceptions where quotes arrived off multiples of 6 s, the durations were rounded up to the nearest 6 s interval. The majority of the quotes (nearly 60% arrive within 6 s of the previous quote. Furthermore, approximately 97% of the quotes arrive within 24 s of the previous quote.

An interesting feature of the quote durations is the presence of autocorrelation even after partialling out the time-of-day effects. In particular, consider the 'seasonally adjusted' series

$$\tilde{x}_i = \frac{x_i}{\Phi(t_{i-1})} \quad \text{where } \Phi(t_{i-1}) \equiv E(x_i|t_{i-1}). \tag{14}$$

This adjusted series now has a mean of approximately 1. The autocorrelations and partial autocorrelations for the month of May are presented in Table 1 with the Ljung-Box statistic. The Ljung Box is calculated for the seasonally adjusted series using 15 lags. This will have the usual Chi-squared distribution with 15 degrees of freedom. There are 71,557 observations in this sample with a corresponding

R.F. Engle. J.R. Russell / Journal of Empirical Finance 4 (1997) 187–212 195

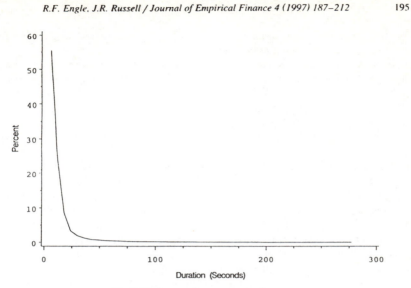

Fig. 2. Histogram of raw quote durations.

Ljung-Box statistic of 3019. The null hypothesis of white noise is easily rejected with the test statistic well above the critical value of 24.99 at the 5% level. The long sets of positive autocorrelations are indicative of duration clustering, suggest-

Table 1
Autocorrelations and partial autocorrelations for price durations

	Quote durations (May)		Price durations (Tues. Wed. Thurs. full sample)	
	acf	pacf	acf	pacf
lag 1	0.083	0.083	0.120	0.120
lag 2	0.076	0.070	0.109	0.096
lag 3	0.064	0.053	0.080	0.058
lag 4	0.053	0.039	0.066	0.042
lag 5	0.059	0.045	0.080	0.057
lag 6	0.048	0.031	0.075	0.049
lag 7	0.050	0.033	0.051	0.021
lag 8	0.038	0.020	0.063	0.036
lag 9	0.048	0.031	0.059	0.032
lag 10	0.040	0.022	0.060	0.031
lag 11	0.049	0.031	0.062	0.032
lag 12	0.043	0.023	0.056	0.025
lag 13	0.039	0.019	0.047	0.016
lag 14	0.040	0.020	0.059	0.030
lag 15	0.042	0.022	0.043	0.011
	Ljung-Box 3019.25		Ljung-Box 1307.58	
	Sample size 71557		Sample size 16277	

196 *R.F. Engle. J.R. Russell / Journal of Empirical Finance 4 (1997) 187–212*

ing periods of relatively high quote activity and others of relatively low quote activity beyond a seasonal component [3].

In order to define price durations a further transformation of the data is necessary. A new series for the midpoint of the bid and ask quotes is constructed. Define

$$p_i = \frac{(\text{ask}_i + \text{bid}_i)}{2} \tag{15}$$

This will be referred to as the price series. Now, consider the time series data consisting of N arrival times and N associated prices indexed by i $\{(t_1, p_1), \ldots, (t_N, P_N)\}$. From these pairs the price based arrival times are defined by selectively deleting some of the pairs. It is the history and the current value of the price that determine if the point is deleted. For $i = 2, \ldots, N$, delete the current point if the price is 'close' to the last retained point [4]. In essence only the points at which the price has changed significantly since the occurrence of the last price change are kept. In order to minimize the effects of errant quotes two consecutive points were required to have changed significantly since the last price change. Hence one errant quote will not trigger a price change. A more formal definition of the retained series is as follows:

(i) Retain point 1.

(ii) Retain point $i > 1$ if abs($p_i - p_j$) > c and abs($p_{i+1} - p_j$) > c where j is the index of the most recent retained point, and c is a constant.

Reindexing the retained series by i' for $i' = 1, \ldots, N'$ for $N' < N$ the price durations are then defined as $x_{i'}^p(c) = t_{i'} - t_{i'-1}$ for $i'(c) > 1$. For simplicity the dependence on c will be dropped. As discussed in Engle and Russell (1995) retaining some points of the point process and deleting others is known as thinning a point process. In this case, the thinning is a function of the price marks.

Clearly the value of c is what characterizes a significant price change. If $c = 0$ then we would count every single movement in the midpoint as a price change. We might expect, however, that there will be some movements in the midpoint as a function of individual bank decisions that reflect idiosyncratic portfolio adjustment that should not be considered as a movement in the fundamental price at which individuals are exchanging. In order to better capture movements in the price at which transactions are occurring, we will choose a threshold value of c greater than 0. A histogram for the spread is presented in Fig. 3. Most spreads are 0.0005 accounting for 46% and 0.001 which accounts for 47%. Another 4% are just under 0.00075. To minimize the impact of asymmetric quote setting due to portfolio adjustment by individual banks we will set $c = 0.0005$ (five pips). This

---

[3] Although not reported, the autocorrelations were present in various subsamples of the day.

[4] Note that the first point is retained.

R.F. Engle, J.R. Russell / Journal of Empirical Finance 4 (1997) 187–212   197

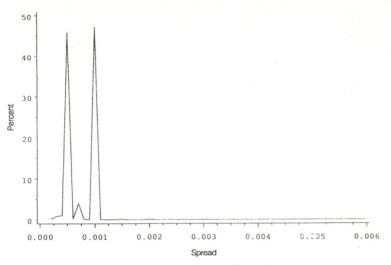

Fig. 3. Histogram of observed spreads.

means that a price change will be triggered only when the midpoint of the quote moves by half the largest observed spread (0.001). This choice of c yields a sample size of 16,277 or 5.36% of the original sample. The minimum price duration is 6 s, the maximum is 11,556 s (or just over 3 h), and the average for the sample is 258 s (or just over 4 min). Fig. 4 presents the histogram for the price durations. Not surprising is the lack of price durations at 6 s. The most common price duration is 18 s accounting for 5% of the of all price durations.

Fig. 5 presents the seasonal component for the price durations. This component was calculated in the same manner as for the quote durations. It is apparent that price changes occur most frequently when the American market overlaps with the European markets between the hours of 12:30 and 15:30 GMT. At this time the price changes on average once every 100 seconds or once every minute and 40 s. When the European market closes, price changes occur much less frequently. They become as infrequent as once every half hour around 22:00 GMT.

The seasonally adjusted series is again formed by partialling out the seasonal component using the same technique as was used for the quote durations. The mean of the new series is approximately unity. The standard deviation is 1.28. The standard deviation for the exponential distribution should be equal to the mean. Relative to the exponential, there is clear excess dispersion in the data. Table 1 presents the autocorrelations and partial autocorrelations for the new series. The long sets of positive autocorrelations are present again indicating price duration clustering. Prices tend to experience periods of rapid movement and periods of

198   *R.F. Engle, J.R. Russell / Journal of Empirical Finance 4 (1997) 187–212*

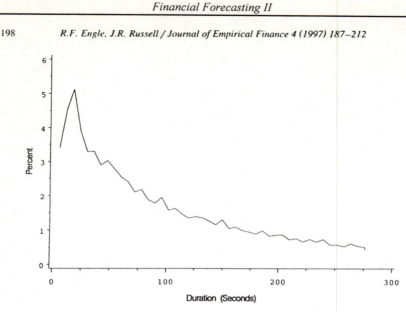

Fig. 4. Histogram of price durations.

slow movement. The autocorrelations are much larger than those for the quote durations (about 1.5 times as large). The Ljung-Box associated with 15 lags is 1044 indicating significant autocorrelations again.

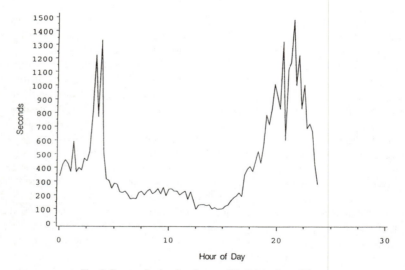

Fig. 5. Expected price duration conditioned on time of day.

The plot of the estimated seasonal component suggests that the price movements change characteristics as markets around the world open and close. A natural question is whether price duration clustering occurs only during certain parts of the day. That is, could a particular portion of the day be responsible for the large autocorrelations. Indeed we find evidence suggesting that the autocorrelations are driven by a particular time of day. The boundaries of when particular markets around the world are 'open' are rather vague. Unlike the NYSE, there is no official opening and closing of the market. Furthermore, active periods in markets around the world overlap. One possible way of dividing the day is to define two periods of the day; a high activity period when Europe and Asia are active from hours 5 through 14, and a low period from hours 17 through 24. This resulted in price duration sample sizes of 8638 and 1938 respectively. The autocorrelations and partial autocorrelations for these two periods, after partialing out the seasonal component, are presented in Table 2. It is apparent that the structure of the autocorrelations is different for these two subperiods of the day. In particular, the low activity period contains several negative autocorrelations corresponding to the 4th, 8th, 9th, 10th, 12th, and 15th lag. The null hypothesis of white noise is clearly not rejected with a test statistic of 15.0. It is apparent that the autocorrelations observed for the day as a whole were generated in the high activity period. The low activity period essentially says that there is nothing to model. Consequently, the model will be estimated on the high activity period only.

Table 2
Autocorrelations and partial autocorrelations for price durations

	Hours 5–14		Hours 17–24	
	acf	pacf	acf	pacf
lag 1	0.123	0.123	0.038	0.038
lag 2	0.098	0.084	0.026	0.025
lag 3	0.098	0.078	0.012	0.010
lag 4	0.068	0.042	−0.017	−0.018
lag 5	0.088	0.063	0.020	0.021
lag 6	0.086	0.056	0.017	0.016
lag 7	0.053	0.020	0.011	0.009
lag 8	0.064	0.033	−0.009	−0.011
lag 9	0.072	0.042	−0.016	−0.016
lag 10	0.075	0.043	−0.020	−0.018
lag 11	0.057	0.021	0.029	0.031
lag 12	0.052	0.018	−0.019	−0.021
lag 13	0.078	0.047	0.045	0.045
lag 14	0.067	0.031	0.004	0.001
lag 15	0.033	−0.007	−0.021	−0.020
	Ljung-Box 772.94		Ljung-Box 15.07	
	Sample size 8638		Sample size 1938	

200   *R.F. Engle, J.R. Russell / Journal of Empirical Finance 4 (1997) 187–212*

4. Results

This section will present results for ACD model estimates for the 4 month subsample of price based durations over the active period of the day containing hours 5 through 14. Due to the non linearity of the model, the BHHH algorithm was used with numerical derivatives. The algorithm has no trouble converging for the sample and the results appear robust to initial values imposed.

Parameter estimates for the Weibull ACD (1, 1) (WACD(1, 1)) are presented in Table 3. The top of the figure presents the model estimated for hours 5–14 price durations data with the seasonal portion partialed out. For hours 5–14 the seasonal component appears to be relatively less important than for the day as a whole so estimates for the raw price durations are presented at the bottom of Table 3. With the expected exception of the constant term the models appear very similar. Furthermore, all coefficients for both sets of data are significant according to the t-ratios. The t-ratio for the parameter γ is presented for the null hypothesis of $\gamma = 1$ which would be the case if the true model were exponential ACD. The null hypothesis of an exponential is easily rejected with a t-ratio against this null of 1 of 12.92 and 15.61 for the normalized and raw price durations respectively. $\gamma < 1$ implies that the hazard is decreasing in t. Equivalently, the longer the observed duration of no price change, the less likely a trade will occur at that time.

For a constant unconditional mean to exist lemma 1 of Engle and Russell (1995) requires $(\alpha + \beta) < 1$. For these estimates the sum is approximately 0.9762 for the first sample and 0.9696 for the second suggesting that the process is not integrated. The implied unconditional mean obtained from lemma 1 is 1.01 and 198.42 for the first and second data sets respectively. The actual unconditional

Table 3

Parameter estimates for price durations hours 5–14 GMT.

$\psi_{i'} = \omega + \alpha X_{i'-1} + \beta \psi_{i'-1}$ and γ is the Weibull parameter

	Estimate	Std. error	t-ratio
De-seasonalized price durations			
ω	0.02420	0.00351	6.8789
α	0.07315	0.00487	15.002
β	0.90313	0.00692	130.42
γ	0.90782	0.00713	12.923 *
Raw price durations			
ω	6.0140	0.74590	8.0627
α	0.09807	0.00557	17.584
β	0.87161	0.00766	113.68
γ	0.89137	0.00695	15.618 *

* $H_0: \gamma = 1$.

mean for the second data set is 191.45 with standard deviation of 264. It is useful to examine the standardized series:

$$\hat{\varepsilon} = \left(\frac{\tilde{x}_{i'}^{p}}{\psi_{i'}} \right)^{\gamma} \tag{16}$$

Correct specification implies that this series should be i.i.d. exponential with $\lambda = 1$ for both data sets. First order conditions imply a mean of one for this series. However, the standard deviation of the series should be unity as well. Although the standard deviation has been reduced from 1.31 to 1.12 there is still evidence of excess dispersion in the first data set. Similarly, for the second data set the standard deviation of the standardized series suggests excess dispersion with a value of 1.15. Correct specification also implies that these standardized series are i.i.d. The Ljung-Box statistics associated with 15 lags are 20.3 and 16.84. This has been reduced from 772.9 and 935 for the first and second data set respectively. In both cases, the null hypothesis of white noise is not rejected at the 5% level. The WACD(1, 1) captures the autocorrelations observed in both data sets. The implied unconditional means are very close to those observed so the models have desirable forecasting properties.

The one-step forecast of the expected price duration is given by

$$E\left(x_{i'+1}^{p} | I_{i'} \right) = E\left(\tilde{x}_{i'+1}^{p} | I_{i'} \right) \Phi\left(t_{i'} \right) = \psi_{i'+1} \Phi\left(t_{i'} \right). \tag{17}$$

Fig. 6 presents the one-step forecast of the WACD(1, 1) model estimated with a seasonal component. The day was chosen arbitrarily. The dashed line is the

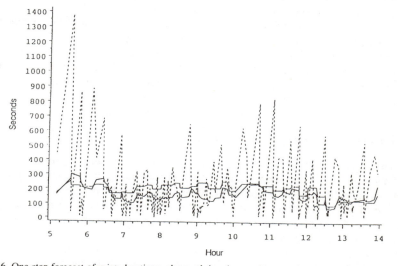

Fig. 6. One-step forecast of price durations, observed durations and seasonal component for WACD(1, 1) for an arbitrary day.

202   *R.F. Engle, J.R. Russell / Journal of Empirical Finance 4 (1997) 187–212*

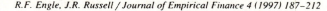

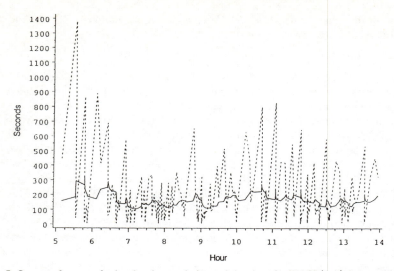

Fig. 7. One-step forecast of price durations and observed durations for WACD(1, 1) for an arbitrary day.

observed durations. The two solid lines are the seasonal spline and the one-step forecast. It is apparent from the graph that the one-step forecast of $\tilde{x}^p_{i'}$ is substantially more variable than the seasonal component. At times the forecast is nearly half the expected value conditioned on time of day alone. In particular, hours 7 through 9:30 exhibit a conditional expectation around 125 s while the seasonal component alone suggests around 225 s.

Fig. 7 presents the one-step forecast plots for the same day but for the data set with no seasonal component. We still observe significant variability in the one-step forecast and the forecasting characteristics are very similar for this period of the day.

5. Testing market microstructure hypotheses

There are several interesting questions that can now be addressed by introducing additional predetermined variables which theoretically could contain information useful in forecasting the price durations. Such hypotheses can easily be tested using LM tests on various variables suggested by theory. The three hypotheses to be examined all relate to the method by which the market participants set prices. One hypothesis is that there is a price leader who commonly signals changes in prices which other bidders follow. A second is that large numbers of quotes between price events signal rapid market adjustment and shorter durations. Third is that market makers concerned about informed traders set the bid ask spread

R.F. Engle, J.R. Russell / Journal of Empirical Finance 4 (1997) 187–212 203

widest when the probability of informed trading is greatest and this is also when they adjust quotes most rapidly leading to short price durations.

It is well known that the LM statistic can be obtained from $N * R^2$ where R^2 is the R-squared from regressing a vector of ones on the scores evaluated under the null hypothesis. The R-squared can be obtained from the first iteration of the BHHH algorithm taken from the maximum likelihood estimates under the null. The test statistic will have the usual chi-squared distribution.

One way of examining the price leadership question is to test if the quote activity of a large player in the market helps to forecast price durations. The quote activity of the largest quote contributor, Deutsche Bank-Asia, is highly autocorrelated for hours 5–14. For this firm we find periods of high quote activity (frequent quote postings) and periods of low activity. Do prices tend to change more rapidly following frequent quote updates from this bank? Deutsche Bank-Asia posted 17,149 quotes between the hours of 5 and 14 in the 4 month sample. The autocorrelations, partial autocorrelations, and the Ljung-Box statistic for the duration between quote updates for Deutsche Bank-Asia are presented in Table 4. The set of large positive autocorrelations yields a Ljung-Box statistic of 3420. The estimated parameters of the quote duration model for Deutsche Bank-Asia are presented in Table 5. For this model the sum of $(\alpha + \beta$ is 0.9233. Excess dispersion is still present in the standardized series having been reduced from 1.51 to 1.30. Although the null hypothesis for the standardized series of white noise is rejected, the Ljung-Box has been greatly reduced from 3420 for the demeaned

Table 4

Autocorrelations and partial autocorrelations for Deutsche Bank-Asia quote durations

Deutsche Bank-Asia quote durations		
	acf	pacf
lag 1	0.275	0.275
lag 2	0.234	0.171
lag 3	0.178	0.087
lag 4	0.068	−0.032
lag 5	0.062	0.007
lag 6	0.039	0.006
lag 7	0.044	0.026
lag 8	0.064	0.043
lag 9	0.073	0.041
lag 10	0.042	−0.007
lag 11	0.063	0.028
lag 12	0.034	−0.005
lag 13	0.048	0.025
lag 14	0.067	0.041
lag 15	0.047	0.010
	Ljung-Box 3420.36	
	Sample size 17149	

Table 5
Parameter estimates for quote durations – Deutsche Bank-Asia
$\psi_i = \omega + \alpha X_{i-1} + \beta \psi_{i-1}$ and γ is Weibull parameter

	Coefficient	Std. error	*t*-ratio
ω	0.0769424	0.0045514	16.905
α	0.1021910	0.0004780	25.498
β	0.8213549	0.0074811	109.79
γ	1.100348	0.0041622	24.107 [*]

[*] $H_0: \gamma = 1$.

series to 47.76 for the standardized series. Plots of the one-step forecast for these durations are presented with the seasonal component in Fig. 8.

Two tests are performed to examine the predictive power of the quote rate of Deutsche Bank-Asia. The first examines the predictive power for the most recent quote duration for Deutsche Bank-Asia prior to the current price duration for the market as a whole. The second test examines if the most recent one-step forecast of Deutsche Bank-Asia's quote activity has predictive ability for the future price durations against the null of a WACD(1, 1).

$x_{i'-1}^{DBA}$ is the most recent quote duration prior to time $t_{i'}$, for Deutsche Bank-Asia and

$\psi_{i'-1}^{DBA}$ is the most recent one-step quote duration forecast prior to time $t_{i'}$, for Deutsche Bank-Asia.

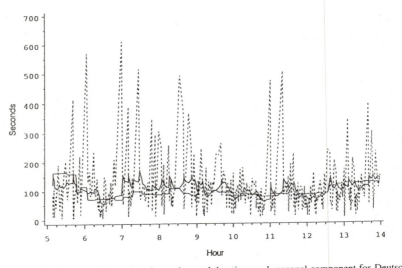

Fig. 8. One-step forecast of quote durations, observed durations and seasonal component for Deutsche Bank-Asia.

Table 6
LM test statistics for predictability of price durations

	$\psi_{i'-1}^{DBA}$	$x_{i'-1}^{DBA}$	$\bar{x}_{i'-1}$	$\bar{s}_{i'-1}$
Test statistic	1.29	0.34	0.881	10.59
Direction	$(-)$	$(-)$	$(+)$	$(-)$

$\psi_{i'-1}^{DBA}$ is the one-step forecast for the Deutsche Bank-Asia quote duration immediately preceding the price duration.
$x_{i'-1}^{DBA}$ is the Deutsche Bank-Asia quote duration immediately preceding the price duration.
$\bar{x}_{i'-1}$ is the average rate of arrival of quotes over the previous price duration $i'-1$.
$\bar{s}_{i'-1}$ is the average spread observed over price duration $i'-1$.
$\chi_{5\%}^2(1) = 3.84$.

The LM statistics for this section are presented in Table 6. The LM test fails to reject the null hypothesis of no linear relationship for both variables. The test statistics are 1.29 and 0.34 for the duration and forecast respectively. Both statistics are far below the 5% critical value of 3.84. Hence, these tests provide no evidence in favor of price leadership.

The second hypothesis is that quote arrivals carry information about the intensity of the market which has been ignored in the thinned price duration process. These quote arrivals are observed by all agents including the market makers and therefore may reveal the intensity of activity in the market or the rate of information flow [5]. To test this hypothesis, a random variable was constructed as the average arrival rate of quotes over the previous price duration. That is,

$$\bar{x}_{i'} = \frac{1}{n_{i'}} \sum_{k=i_{min}}^{i_{max}} x_k \qquad (18)$$

where $i_{min} \equiv i \in \{1, 2, \ldots, N(T)\}|t_i > t_{i'-1}$, $i_{max} \equiv i \in \{2, 3, \ldots, N(T)\}|t_i = t_{i'}$ and $n = (i_{max} - i_{min})$.

The LM statistic is 0.881 suggesting that lagged durations have no predictive power for price durations. Thus suggests that thinning the quotes to focus only on the price changes loses little information. The deleted quotes appear not to influence economic price setting behavior.

The third hypothesis tests whether bid–ask spreads help predict price durations. There is a vast literature associated with the determination of bid–ask spreads. See for example the excellent discussion in O'Hara (1995). The two general classes of models of price setting are inventory and information models. The former visualize the market makers as risk averse agents who set prices to control their inventories and set spreads to cover transaction costs plus whatever market power they can obtain. Since all the quotes are from potential market makers, the market

---

[5] This hypothesis has recessed recent attention in stock market literature. See, for example, Jones et al. (1994).

206   *R.F. Engle, J.R. Russell / Journal of Empirical Finance 4 (1997) 187–212*

power of each should be minimal. Possibly when fewer quotes are being issued, the market power could be greater and thus spreads could increase. Unless transaction costs vary systematically with volatility, there need be no relation between spread and volatility so at best, the inventory model would predict a weak positive relation between spread and price durations.

The information models such as Glosten and Milgrom (1985) or Easley and O'Hara (1992) on the other hand suppose that there are agents with superior information to that of the risk neutral market makers. Thus the market makers set bid and ask quotes to reflect the possibility of trading with an informed agent. The greater this possibility, the greater the spread. Similarly, if there are many informed traders, the market maker will rapidly adjust both bid and ask prices in response to observed buy or sell orders. Thus the prices will move rapidly and the price durations will be short whenever the market maker has knowledge that he faces high proportions of informed traders. The market makers may well have access to this information through mechanisms such as eloquently discussed by Lyons (1993). Thinking of a price duration as an information event, which is only gradually incorporated into prices, the length of time for price adjustment and the initial bid ask spread should be negatively related.

Yet another strand of literature is the relation between volume and volatility. It is widely found that volume and volatility are closely contemporaneously related. See for example Tauchen and Pitts (1993) Lamoureux and Lastrapes (1990) and Jain and Joh (1988). The larger the volume, the greater the liquidity in the market and consequently, the smaller the required bid ask spread. It is easily seen that high volume stocks have relatively small spreads: presumably this is due either to increasing returns in the transaction technology or increasing numbers of liquidity traders. In either case, this association would predict that bigger spreads would lead to longer price durations.

To test these theories, data on the spread must be constructed. Associated with each price duration is a set of deleted quotes; the measure of bid and ask spread used is the average percent bid–ask spread over all the quote arrivals associated with each particular price duration. More formally,

$$\bar{S}_{i'} = \frac{100}{n_{i'}} \sum_{k=i_{\min}}^{i_{\max}} \log(\text{ask}_k) - \log(\text{bid}_k) \tag{19}$$

where $i_{\max}$, $i_{\min}$ and $n_{i'}$ are defined as above.

The minimum average percent spread is 0.00000118, the maximum average percent spread is 0.24783, with an average of 0.04684 and a standard deviation of 0.01905. The LM test statistic for $\bar{S}_{i'-1}$, is 10.59 which easily rejects the null hypothesis suggesting that prices change more rapidly following larger bid–ask spreads [6]. To follow up on this, a WACD(1, 1) model with the lagged spread was

---

[6] For the purposes of the test the spread series was multiplied by 10^5 for numerical accuracy.

Table 7
Parameter estimates for price durations with lagged spread
$\psi_{i'} + \alpha X_{i'-1} + \beta \psi_{i'-1} + \eta \bar{S}_{i'-1}$ and γ is Weibull parameter

	Coefficient	Std. error	t-ratio
ω	0.1294009	0.0045514	8.21571
α	0.0852118	0.0004780	18.0392
β	0.8782600	0.0074811	131.027
η	-174.7711	31.09269	-5.62097
γ	0.8920969	0.00692483	15.5820 *

* $H_0 : \gamma = 1$.

estimated. These results are shown in Table 7. The model predicts that a tenth of a percent increase in the average spread will reduce the expectation of the following duration by 17.4 s [7]. This effect is consistent with the asymmetric information model but not with the other two models.

6. A relationship between price durations and volatility

The price duration is a measure of the time per unit price change. Intuitively, this is related to measures of volatility. Rather than measure the expected price change per unit time, the ACD price duration model measures the expected time per unit price change. Clearly the motivation for applying the ACD price duration model to transaction type data is in the irregular spacing of the data. However, it might be interesting to relate the price durations to standard measures of volatility. This section will develop a relationship between the price duration based volatility and standard measures of volatility.

One way of identifying a relationship between price durations and standard measures of volatility is to assume that p_i follows a diffusion process. We can then think of the quote arrivals as a snapshot of the current location of p_i. From this viewpoint the ACD price duration model is a model for the expected time for the diffusion process, given an initial point p_j to escape some symmetric boundary $2c$ units wide. This type of problem has been examined in the context of continuous-time stochastic processes and is called a crossing time problem. If we make the more restrictive assumption that the diffusion parameter is constant within each price duration, but possibly time varying across price durations, then

---

[7] Some caution has to be used in interpreting this result. There might be a mechanical reason to observe this relationship. If a large spread is observed because the specialist moved either just the bid down or just the ask up then a price change (as measured by the midpoint) will be more likely to occur at this time.

Appendix A shows that the expected crossing time is c^2/σ^2. Matching this to ψ gives an implied diffusion variance of:

$$\tilde{\sigma}_i^2 = \frac{c^2}{\psi_i} \tag{21}$$

Hence can be interpreted as the instantaneous volatility measured in seconds.

An alternative interpretation of Eq. (21) is useful. Instead of assuming that the underlying price process is a diffusion process which is constant until a trade occurs and then shifts to a new rate, it is more natural to think of the prices as being only defined when there is a price setting transaction. Thus the underlying process is a binomial process with increments of $\pm c$ which takes expected time Ψ. Thus the expected variance per unit time is also simply

$$\hat{\sigma}_i^2 = \frac{c^2}{\psi_i} \tag{22}$$

These implied instantaneous volatility measures were calculated for the raw price durations using the estimated conditional durations. It is convenient to adjust the unintuitive units of squared price change per second to the more common percent annual standard deviation by multiplying the $\hat{\sigma}_i$ by the square root of the number of weekday trading seconds in a year. This is approximately the square root of (252 weekdays/year)(24 h/day)(60 min/h)(60 s/min). Essentially, this aggregates each diffusion parameter up to what the annual percent standard

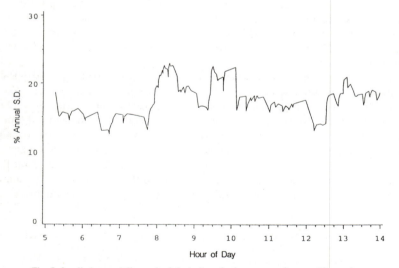

Fig. 9. Implied annual % standard deviation of price process for an arbitrary day.

R.F. Engle, J.R. Russell / Journal of Empirical Finance 4 (1997) 187–212   209

deviation would be for the entire year if the diffusion parameter were constant for trading on weekdays for the whole year. The volatility over the weekend is ignored in this calculation. Fig. 9 presents the one-step forecast of the implied annualized volatility for an arbitrary day.

7. Conclusions

A measure and forecasts for the intensity of price changes as measured by the midpoint of the bid–ask spread for the Dollar/Deutschmark rate was proposed. Significant autocorrelations of the price durations were observed in this data set which the ACD model of Engle and Russell (1995) was able to successfully model. Both seasonal time of day effects and stochastic effects were observed and modeled. Using a Weibull density for the hazard proved superior to the exponential. This model provides a framework in which the instantaneous probability of events can be forecast.

When the durations are measured in terms of price change events, the ACD model becomes a volatility model. A simple analogy with brownian crossing times, and with a binomial process which has random time intervals, gives a formula for the volatility per unit time. The annualized instantaneous volatility of the FX rates can then be observed and measured over the day and during particularly interesting events.

The model is easily generalized to allow for other exogenous and lagged dependent variables to enter the model formulation. LM tests and model estimates with the significant variables shed new light on the performance of the FX market as revealed by the Reuters quotes. Various theoretical models of price setting behavior in this market suggest particular variables to introduce into the model.

The first model tests the hypothesis that one bank takes the role of price leadership so that their quotes are more influential in determining price movements than others. Lagged quote durations and expected quote durations of Deutsche Bank-Asia, were not significant for the ACD model for the price quotes of the entire market judging from LM tests.

The second hypothesis is that the quote arrival rate carries information useful in addition to the price duration in measuring volatility. The average quote duration during the previous price duration was tested for significance in the ACD. The *t*-statistic was under 1 indicating no evidence that thinning the process to remove price uninformative quotes sacrificed any efficiency either statistically or economically.

The third hypothesis examines the impact of the past bid ask spread on future volatility. Evidence was uncovered, using LM tests and then by re-estimating the model, suggesting that the lagged average spread, defined by averaging over all quotes received in the previous price duration, helps predict price durations. In

210   *R.F. Engle, J.R. Russell / Journal of Empirical Finance 4 (1997) 187–212*

particular, a tenth of a percent increase in the average spread reduces the expectation of the following price duration by 17.4 s. This is relative to a sample average near 100 s and a standard deviation of the average percent spread of around 0.02. This result is interpreted as supporting the asymmetric information model of price setting; market makers can assess the probability of facing informed traders and when doing so set big spreads and adjust prices rapidly.

Appendix A

This section develop the relationship between the price durations and volatility used in Section 6.

Following Karatzas and Shreve (1991) let W_t be Brownian motion defined for $0 < t < \infty$ with drift $\mu = 0$ and constant diffusion parameter assumed to be normalized to 1. Karatzas and Shreve propose the problem for Brownian motion defined on the state space $[0, a]$ where a is positive and finite. Let T_a is denote the first passage time defined as

$$T_a = \inf\{t \geq 0; W_t = a\}.$$

Let T_0 denote the first passage time for 0. Let t_{min} denote $\min(T_0, T_a)$. Then for some initial value $W_t = x$ $0 \leq x \leq a$ and $t > 0$, the distribution of t_{min} is shown to be (Karatzas and Shreve (1991), p. 99)

$$P^x[t_{min} \in dt; a, x]$$

$$= \frac{1}{\sqrt{2\pi t^3}} \sum_{n=-\infty}^{\infty} \left[(2na + x)\exp\left\{ \frac{(-2na + x)^2}{2t} \right\} \right.$$

$$\left. + (2na + a - x)\exp\left\{ \frac{(-2na + a - x)^2}{2t} \right\} \right] dt \quad (A.1)$$

The Laplace transform of Eq. (A.1) is shown (p. 100) to be

$$E^x[\exp(-\alpha(t_{min}))] = \frac{\cosh((x - (a/2))\sqrt{2\alpha})}{\cosh((a/2)\sqrt{2\alpha})} \quad (A.2)$$

Differentiating with respect to α and evaluating at $\alpha = 0$ yields

$$E(t_{min}) = x(a - x). \quad (A.3)$$

Setting $a = 2c$ and $x = c$ yields and dividing a and x by the standard deviation yields

$$E(t_{min}) = \frac{c^2}{\sigma^2}$$

(A.4)

Then, at time t_i, $E(t_{min}) = E(x_i) = \psi_i$. Hence, we get the desired result

$$\sigma_i^2 = \frac{c^2}{\psi_i}.$$

(A.5)

References

Bera, A., Higgins, M., 1992. Survey of ARCH Models: Properties, Estimation and Testing. Department of Economics, University of Illinois, unpublished manuscript.

Bollerslev, T., 1986. Generalized autoregressive conditional heteroskedasticity. Journal of Econometrics 31, 307–327.

Bollerslev, T., Domowitz, I., 1993. Trading patterns and prices in the interbank foreign exchange market. The Journal of Finance 48, 1421–1443.

Bollerslev, T., Engle, R., Nelson, D., 1994. ARCH models, in: Engle, R., McFadden. D. (Eds.), Handbook of Econometrics IV, North Holland.

Bollerslev, T., Chou, R.Y., Kroner, K.F., 1992. ARCH Modeling in Finance. Journal of Econometrics 52, 5–49.

Easley, D., O'Hara, M., 1992. Time and the process of security price adjustment. The Journal of Finance 19, 69–90.

Easley, D., Kiefer, N., O'Hara, M., 1994.

Easley, D., Kiefer, N., O'Hara, M., 1995.

Engle, R., 1982. Autoregressive conditional heteroskedasticity with estimates of the variance of U.K. inflation. Econometrica 50, 987–1008.

Engle, R., Russel, J., 1995. Autoregressive Conditional Duration; A New Model for Irregularly Spaced Time Series Data, University of California, San Diego unpublished manuscript.

Glosten, L.R., Milgrom, P., 1985. Bid ask and transaction prices in a specialist market with heterogenously informed agents. Journal of Financial Economics 14, 71–100.

Goodhart, C.A.E., Hall, S., Henry, S., Pesaran, B., 1993. News effects in a high-frequency model of the Sterling–Dollar exchange rate. Journal of Applied Econometrics 8 (1), 1–13.

Hawkes, A.G., 1971. Spectra of some self-exciting and mutually exciting point processes. Biometrika 58, 83–90.

Jain, P.J., Joh, G., 1988. The dependence between hourly prices and trading volume. Journal of Financial and Quantitative Analysis 23, 269–284.

Jones, J.J., Kaul, G., Lipson, M.L., 1994. Transactions, volume, and volatility. The Review of Financial Studies 7, 631–651.

Karatzas, Shreve, 1991. Brownian Motion and Stochastic Calculus, 2nd Ed., Springer-Verlag. New York.

Lamoureux, C.G., Lastrapes, W.D., 1990. Heteroskedasticity in stock return data: Volume versus GARCH effects. Journal of Finance 45, 221–229.

Lyons, R., 1993. Tests of Microstructure Hypotheses Using Foreign Exchange Markets, Working Paper, University of California at Berkeley.

Muller, U.A., Dacorogna, M.M., Olsen, R.B., Pictet, O.V., Schwarz, M., Morgenegg, C., 1990.

Statistical study of foreign exchange rates, empirical evidence of a price change scaling law, and intraday analysis. Journal of Banking and Finance 14, 1189–1208.

O'Hara, M., 1995. Market Microstructure Theory, Basil Blackwell.

Rubin, I., 1972. Regular point processes and their detection. IEEE Trans. on Information Theory 18, 547–557.

Snyder, D.L., Miller, M.I., 1991. Random Point Processes in Time and Space, 2nd Ed., Springer-Verlag.

Tauchen, G., Pitts, M., 1993. The price variability-volume relationship on speculative markets. Econometrica 51, 485–505.

B
Options-implied Volatility

[25]

Forecasting Stock-Return Variance: Toward an Understanding of Stochastic Implied Volatilities

Christopher G. Lamoureux
Washington University in St. Louis

William D. Lastrapes
University of Georgia

We examine the behavior of measured variances from the options market and the underlying stock market. Under the joint hypotheses that markets are informationally efficient and that option prices are explained by a particular asset pricing model, forecasts from time-series models of the stock-return process should not have predictive content given the market forecast as embodied in option prices. Both in-sample and out-of-sample tests suggest that this hypothesis can be rejected. Using simulations, we show that biases inherent in the procedure we use to imply variances cannot explain this result. Thus, we provide evidence inconsistent with the orthogonality restrictions of option pricing models that assume that variance risk is unpriced. These results also have implications for optimal variance forecast rules.

According to the Black and Scholes (1973) model of option valuation, equilibrium option prices are determined by the absence of arbitrage profits. This con-

We are grateful to Don Andrews, Kerry Back, Phil Dybvig, Ravi Jagannathan, Andrew Lo (the editor), Chester Spatt (the executive editor), and an anonymous referee for numerous suggestions. But we wish to absorb all culpability. Address correspondence to Christopher G. Lamoureux, John M. Olin School of Business, Washington University in St. Louis, Campus Box 1133, One Brookings Drive, St. Louis, MO 63130-4899.

The Review of Financial Studies 1993 Volume 6, number 2, pp. 293–326
© 1993 The Review of Financial Studies 0893-9454/93/$1.50

The Review of Financial Studies / v 6 n 2 1993

dition depends on the assumption that the variance of the underlying stock returns is constant over time or deterministically changing through time. The model is a powerful economic tool because market behavior can be understood without explicitly specifying and estimating preferences of agents.

A problem with the empirical implementation of the Black–Scholes model is that the variance assumption is inconsistent with the data. Since stochastic volatility is manifest in time-series models of stock returns as well as in the empirical variances implied from the Black–Scholes model itself, models of option pricing have been developed in which the variance of the underlying asset returns varies randomly through time. Hull and White (1987) derive a closed-form solution for European call option prices under the assumption that volatility risk is unpriced. They show that, given certain conditions on the stochastic process governing underlying returns, the option price equals the expected value of the Black–Scholes price over the distribution of average variance.

While the stochastic volatility generalization has been shown by Hull and White (1987) and others to improve the explanatory power of the Black–Scholes model, the full implications of the stochastic volatility option pricing models have not been adequately tested. In particular, a clear test of whether the strong assumption of market indifference to volatility risk is consistent with the data is missing in the empirical finance literature. Although this assumption may be unattractive from a theoretical perspective, it does afford simplification of both valuation and variance extraction, and the model lends itself to unambiguous empirical testing. We examine this issue by testing an important implication of the *class* of models represented by Hull and White (1987) in which volatility risk is unpriced. If option markets are informationally efficient, then information available at the time market prices are set cannot be used to predict actual return variance better than the variance forecast embedded in the option price, which represents the subjective expectation of the market. That is, the forecast error of the subjective expectation should be orthogonal to all available information.

To test this orthogonality restriction, we interpret the variance implied from equating the observed market option price to the Hull and White model price as the market's assessment of return variance. However, implying a variance from the closed-form expression of Hull and White may distort, or bias, the market forecast, even assuming that the joint null hypothesis is true since the Black–Scholes formula is nonlinear (Jensen's inequality) and the variance and stock processes may be instantaneously correlated. We carefully calibrate simulations of the stock-price and variance processes for each of the stocks in the sample to examine the extent to which such bias exists. The simulations demonstrate that this distortion is trivial for our sample of at-the-money options. Furthermore, we couch our statistical inference in the context of the simulations to account for the possible sources of distortion. This procedure enables us to refer to our empirical exercise as a formal test of an asset pricing model. If we did not control for the distortion or couch our inference in terms of this distortion, our exercise would simply be an examination of the extent to which filtering the options and stock-price data with the Black–Scholes model has information.

We test the orthogonality restriction for at-the-money call options on individual stocks by comparing the forecast performance of the implied variance from the model with time-series representations of stock-return volatility. We use a simple time-series model of serial dependence in volatility, the generalized autoregressive conditional heteroskedasticity (GARCH) process of Engle (1982) and Bollerslev (1986), to capture available information that can explain the evolution of return variance. Two types of tests of the orthogonality restriction are performed: in-sample and out-of-sample. The in-sample, regression-based tests incorporate the implied variance into the GARCH equation of the return process to measure the marginal predictive power of past information on variance. We then compare the out-of-sample forecast performance of the implied variance with time-series models using standard measures of average forecast error and encompassing regressions. The out-of-sample encompassing analysis helps us to explore an important issue: regardless of the outcome of tests of the orthogonality restrictions, does filtering market data through the model provide information about the future evolution of return variance that is not evident in the past time series of stock returns? This issue is relevant to constructing optimal variance forecast rules.

Our research design differs from most previous tests of stochastic volatility option pricing models. Melino and Turnbull (1990), for example, test such a model for foreign exchange options. They estimate a stochastic volatility process for the underlying asset, then price options on this asset using the parameters from the process and the option pricing model. This price is found to predict the actual option price better than a constant variance price. However, they also find that current information can explain some of the model's forecast error. By testing the implications of the option pricing model in measures of variance rather than option price, we exploit different information than Melino and Turnbull to test the orthogonality restrictions. More importantly, our forecast comparisons are performed ultimately out-of-sample. Out-of-sample analysis is more natural than in-sample analysis for scrutinizing models that depend on the infor-

The Review of Financial Studies / v 6 n 2 1993

mation set of agents at any point in time, since the econometrician's conditioning set is a proper subset of the information available to the agents in the economy.

Our work in this article complements concurrent, independent research by Day and Lewis (1992), which also compares implied volatilities from option pricing models with GARCH models. Essentially four major differences occur in the articles. (1) We broaden the data sample by using daily data on individual stocks, whereas Day and Lewis use weekly data on stock indices. (2) As noted, we provide simulation evidence to quantify the extent to which implying variances under Black–Scholes distorts the actual variance forecast *under the null hypothesis* for each stock in our sample. Thus, unlike Day and Lewis we interpret our analysis as a formal test of a specific asset pricing model. (3) Given the daily frequency of data, we are better able than Day and Lewis to adjust for the inconsistencies between the forecast horizons of the time-series models and the maturity of the options in the sample. (4) Perhaps most importantly, we take considerable care to purge problems related to measurement error by effectively using intraday data to construct the daily series. Day and Lewis, for example, use closing prices in both option and stock markets, which do not even close at the same time. To attenuate this problem, they imply the price of the underlying asset from the option price, under the assumption that the model which they are testing is true. Because our data are carefully mapped into our research design, we substantially reduce these errors-in-variables problems.

Although our empirical strategy is discussed in the context of the model developed by Hull and White (1987), we wish to emphasize that we do not attempt to test all of the implications of their model. These authors were interested in explaining the biases of the Black–Scholes restrictions when volatility is stochastic as a function of moneyness and maturity of the option. This aim requires exploiting a broader range of options than we use to infer moments beyond the mean of the subjective distribution of variance. Our strategy is to focus solely on the orthogonality restrictions implied by this *class* of models, hence our reliance on the market's expectation of return variance. In other words, we are not testing the null hypothesis that Black–Scholes is true against the stochastic variance alternative. We are treating the stochastic volatility option pricing model as a special case of more general models of asset pricing that include the possibility of pricing volatility risk.

Both the in-sample tests and the out-of-sample encompassing tests suggest that, while the implied variance helps predict future volatility, the orthogonality restriction of the joint null hypothesis is rejected. One possible reason for the rejection of the null is that volatility risk is priced. Therefore, further attempts to learn from the data should explicitly model a risk premium on the variance process, as in Heston (1993), for example. Assuming constant relative-risk aversion and using a Fourier inversion formula [Stein and Stein (1991)], Heston has obtained a closed-form expression for an option on an asset with stochastic volatility that allows for the volatility process to be priced.

In the following section, we lay out the analytical framework of the study. We describe the Hull and White (1987) model, state explicitly the orthogonality restrictions that it implies jointly with the assumption of market efficiency, and outline the general test strategy. We also characterize stochastic volatility in the data by using the GARCH model, and we report simulation results to quantify certain biases in our implied variances. In Section 2, we describe the options data used in this study, the specific in-sample and out-of-sample tests of the orthogonality restriction undertaken, and the results from these tests. We offer conclusions in Section 3.

1. Analytical Framework

1.1 Theoretical model and test strategy

The framework for the empirical analysis in this article is the model developed by Hull and White (1987), which is an application of Garman (1976). The model represents the class of stochastic volatility options pricing models, including those of Scott (1987), Wiggins (1987), and Johnson and Shanno (1987), that assumes volatility risk does not affect the option price. The Hull–White (HW) model is based upon the following continuous-time process for the underlying stock:

$$dS = \phi S \; dt + \sqrt{V} S \; dw, \tag{1}$$

$$dV = \mu V \; dt + \xi V \; dz, \tag{2}$$

where S is the stock price, and the Brownian motions dw and dz have an instantaneous correlation of ρ. Under the assumption that volatility risk is not priced and $\rho = 0$, a call option on this stock at time t will be priced as

$$p_t = \int \mathrm{BS}(\overline{V}_t) h(\overline{V}_t \mid I_t) \; d\overline{V}_t = \mathrm{E}[\mathrm{BS}(\overline{V}_t) \mid I_t], \tag{3}$$

where

$$\overline{V}_t = \frac{1}{T-t} \int_t^T V_i \; di,$$

$h(\overline{V}_t \mid V_t)$ is the density of $\overline{V}_t$ conditional on the current V_t, T is the expiration date of the option, I_t is the information set at time t, and

The Review of Financial Studies / v 6 n 2 1993

BS($\cdot$) is the Black–Scholes pricing formula. Thus, the HW price is the mean Black–Scholes price, evaluated over the conditional distribution of average variance $\overline{V}_t$.

To price options according to (3), market participants must form a subjective conditional density on $\overline{V}_t$. If these participants are rational, then the subjective density of the market equals the actual density, $h(\overline{V}_t \mid I_t)$. The focus of our study is on the mean of this distribution:

$$\mathrm{E}(\overline{V}_t \mid I_t) = \int \overline{V}_t h(\overline{V}_t \mid I_t) \, d\overline{V}_t.$$

The average variance can be decomposed as

$$\overline{V}_t = \mathrm{E}(\overline{V}_t \mid I_t) + \mu_t,$$

where u_t is orthogonal to the conditional expectation and, therefore, to any information available to agents up to time t. Thus, if option market participants are rational (in the mean sense), then the subjective mean, $\mathrm{E}^s(\overline{V}_t \mid I_t)$, equals the actual mean, $\mathrm{E}(\overline{V}_t \mid I_t)$, and the subjective forecast error, $u_t^s = \overline{V}_t - \mathrm{E}^s(\overline{V}_t \mid I_t)$, is orthogonal to all available information. This orthogonality condition is tested in this article.

The market's conditional expectation of variance is not directly observable. But given market prices on options, the HW model implies a variance that can be used to estimate the expectation. Because the variance of the underlying asset is the only unknown argument in the Black–Scholes formula, the implied variance (discussed in more detail later) is the value of that argument that equates the market price to the theoretical Black–Scholes price. It is evident from (3) that the implied variance is not in general a good predictor of the market's evaluation of variance, since the conditional density h is unaccounted for. However, Cox and Rubinstein (1985, p. 218, figure 5, 6) show that the Black–Scholes formula is essentially a linear function of the standard deviation for at-the-money options, so that $\mathrm{E}[BS(\overline{V}_t) \mid I_t]$ approximately equals $BS[\mathrm{E}(\overline{V}_t) \mid I_t]$.[1] For this reason, we use a sample of at-the-money options and therefore interpret the implied variance as the market's assessment of average stock-return variance over the remaining life of the option, $\mathrm{E}^s(\overline{V}_t \mid I_t)$, under the assumption that the HW model is valid.

We test whether the forecast error constructed from $\overline{V}_t$ and the implied variance is orthogonal to past information, using in-sample and out-of-sample tests. This orthogonality condition is based on a joint hypothesis: (a) option markets are informationally efficient, so

---

[1] While this linearity has formally been expressed in terms of the standard deviation, our analysis is conducted in terms of the variance. Simulations reported in Section 1.3 show that the linearity applies to the variance as well, for our data. Feinstein (1989) analyzes implied volatilities and confirms the linearity documented by Cox and Rubinstein.

observed option prices contain all relevant, available information; and (b) the HW pricing model is correct, so the implied variances are valid estimates of the subjective variance of the market.

The test design is analogous to tests in the international finance literature that examine the hypothesis that forward exchange rates are optimal predictors of future spot exchange rates [e.g., Hansen and Hodrick (1980)]. If the foreign exchange market is informationally efficient, then the difference between the realized future spot rate and the market's subjective expectation of that rate is orthogonal to obtainable information. As with our approach, an economic model must be used to link the market's expectation to observable variables (i.e., market prices). Given this link, the forecast error can be measured and regressed on past information available to traders. The primary difference between the exchange rate tests and our own is that we exploit option price data to focus on the variance, not the mean, of the underlying asset.

1.2 Characterization of stochastic volatility

Tests of the orthogonality restrictions will lack power unless information available to the market can be used to predict return volatility. We show in this subsection that the returns in our sample are accurately characterized by the GARCH process, a parametric model of persistence in conditional variance. As such, the model links return volatility to the past behavior of the return process itself, which is included in I_t. Under the null hypothesis, GARCH momentum will be fully used by options traders in forming expectations of variance; thus, the GARCH model will have no marginal predictive power over the implied variance.

Consider the following GARCH (1, 1) model for stock returns:

$$r_t = \bar{r} + \epsilon_t, \tag{4}$$

$$\epsilon_t \mid \epsilon_{t-1}, \epsilon_{t-2}, \ldots \sim N(0, b_t), \tag{5}$$

$$b_t = C + \alpha \epsilon_{t-1}^2 + \beta b_{t-1} + \gamma \zeta_{t-1}, \tag{6}$$

where r_t is the return over day t; $\bar{r}$, C, α, β, and γ are parameters, and ζ_{t-1} is a vector of exogenous variables. In this section, we constrain γ to be zero, so (6) is the conventional GARCH specification. It is easily verified that if $\alpha + \beta = 1$ there is no mean reversion in the variance. In this case, the conditional variance is integrated, and unconditional variance is undefined. Persistence of shocks to variance increases rapidly as this sum approaches unity from below. The return process is stationary if $\alpha + \beta < 1$.

The GARCH model is a discrete-time approximation to the diffusion process in Equations (1) and (2) and is therefore consistent with the

The Review of Financial Studies / v 6 n 2 1993

HW model. We can think of the actual stock price and its variance as being generated in continuous time by (1) and (2), but with the data observed discretely (daily). It is evident that (4) is the discrete-time analog to (1), where $\bar{r}$ approximates the drift ϕ. To see how (6) maps into (2) (assuming $\gamma = 0$), subtract h_{t-1} from both sides of (6) to obtain

$$h_t - h_{t-1} = [C/h_{t-1} - (1 - \alpha - \beta)]h_{t-1} + \alpha h_{t-1}(\theta_{t-1}^2 - 1), \quad (6)$$

where we have used the identity $\epsilon_t^2 = h_t\theta_t^2$, and θ is an i.i.d. standardized normal random variable. Nelson (1990) has shown that as the time interval goes to zero this expression approaches the diffusion in (2), where $C/h_{t-1} - (1 - \alpha - \beta)$ approaches $\mu \, dt$ and α approaches $\xi\sqrt{dt/2}$. This approximation is not unique, but it is consistent with our use of the GARCH model in the subsequent analysis.

It is not intuitive that the continuous-time limit of the GARCH process has two sources of randomness [dw and dz in (2)], whereas the discrete-time process appears to have a single source of randomness [ϵ is the only stochastic term in (4) to (6)]. The intuition for this is as follows. By definition, the conditional variance of *next period's* residual is not stochastic in the GARCH framework. However, the (conditional) forecast of the variance over the next two periods depends on the realization of ϵ_{t+1} and hence is random. Now, as the interval between time periods shrinks to its limit, the ability to distinguish between time $t + 1$ and time t is lost, which yields the second source of randomness in the limiting case.

The GARCH model is estimated for a sample of daily returns for 10 individual stocks over the period April 19, 1982, to March 30, 1984 (496 trading days), except for company 10, the sample for which begins June 30, 1982. The sample is chosen to conform to our tests of the orthogonality restrictions, as discussed in the following section. The return data come from the CRSP tapes; daily returns are thus calculated as the rate of change of the last transaction price of the day.

Estimates from the GARCH model are reported in Table 1, for each of the 10 companies, as model 2. Ticker symbols are provided in Table 1, and we use these in reference to particular companies. Maximum likelihood estimation of the GARCH model is carried out by using a variant of the Berndt, Hall, Hall, and Hausman optimization algorithm that constrains parameter estimates in the variance equations to be nonnegative [Biegler and Cuthrell (1985)]. First derivatives are calculated numerically.[2]

---

[2] We tested all 10 companies for the presence of an AR(1) process in returns, allowing for GARCH residuals. All 10 had positive first-order serial correlation, but this was significant at the 10 percent level for only one company (number 10). The magnitude of this serial correlation is trivial: the largest first-order serial correlation coefficient (company 10) is .13; the median is .06.

The evidence in Table 1 shows that the GARCH model provides a good fit for the 10 stocks in the sample. In all cases but one, the GARCH parameters are statistically different from zero at small significance levels, according to the asymptotic t-statistics. For DEC (panel B), α is significant at a 10 percent level. For most of the stocks, the sum $\alpha + \beta$ exceeds .9.

1.3 Characterization of bias

The interpretation of our tests relies on equating the variance implied from the data and the Black–Scholes model with the market's subjective variance of returns over the remaining life of the option. However, there are potentially important ways in which the implied variance can be expected to differ from the subjective variance, even assuming the HW model is valid and markets are efficient. In this subsection, we attempt to quantify this bias in order to determine if it affects our inferences.

The implied variance may deviate from the subjective variance as a result of measurement error in the option price and nonsynchronous stock and option prices. However, because of our careful choice and handling of the data, as discussed in Section 2.1, the bias from this source is likely to be trivial and will not influence our results.

Two other sources of bias, however, are potentially more serious. First, as noted, the virtual linearity of the Black–Scholes formula for at-the-money options means that the implied variance will only be an approximation of the true subjective variance. Without further analysis, however, it is not clear how good the approximation will be. Hull and White (1987), for example, indicate that large values for the standard deviation of the variance process can lead to large biases in implied variances even for at-the-money options. Second, the stock return distribution may be skewed, implying a nonzero ρ and additional bias. In order to understand the importance, *in our data,* of the linearity approximation and the assumption that $\rho = 0$, we perform a Monte Carlo simulation of the continuous-time process for returns in (1) and (2). The simulation allows ρ to be nonzero. The magnitude of the bias from these two sources is measured by comparing the implied variance from the simulated data with the actual variance inherent in this data.

We calibrate the simulation to be consistent with the market data used in this study. Because the GARCH model approximates the diffusion process, the parameters in (1) and (2) are constructed from the GARCH estimates in Table 1. For example, $\xi = \sqrt{2}\alpha$, dt is taken to be 1, and α is estimated directly from the GARCH model. Sample values for ρ are obtained by estimating the sample correlation between r_t and h_t, the fitted value from the GARCH equation (6).

The Review of Financial Studies / v 6 n 2 1993

Table 1
Specifications of conditional variance

Model	$\mathscr{L}$	$\bar{r}$ (*t*-stat.)	C (*t*-stat.)	α (*t*-stat.)	β (*t*-stat.)	γ (*t*-stat.)
A						
1	−2281.8	0.648 (0.56)	590.52 (18.98)			
2	−2270.3	0.385 (0.33)	238.15 (1.99)	0.110 (2.04)	0.484 (2.10)	
3	−2275.0	0.000 (0.00)	262.62 (3.53)			0.576 (3.79)
4	−2264.9	−0.034 (−0.03)	58.85 (1.02)	0.058 (1.76)	0.612 (2.82)	0.237 (1.60)

A: Computer Sciences Corp. (CSC) (20536310)

Model	$\mathscr{L}$	$\bar{r}$ (*t*-stat.)	C (*t*-stat.)	α (*t*-stat.)	β (*t*-stat.)	γ (*t*-stat.)
1	−2292.0	0.484 (0.42)	614.71 (38.71)			
2	−2280.2	0.011 (0.01)	413.79 (2.44)	0.094 (1.77)	0.228 (0.74)	
3	−2292.1	0.489 (0.42)	613.55 (9.80)			0.000 (0.00)
4	−2280.2	0.008 (0.01)	404.80 (2.45)	0.095 (1.76)	0.230 (0.70)	0.157 (0.85)

B: Digital Equipment Corp. (DEC) (25384910)

Model	$\mathscr{L}$	$\bar{r}$ (*t*-stat.)	C (*t*-stat.)	α (*t*-stat.)	β (*t*-stat.)	γ (*t*-stat.)
1	−2511.9	0.910 (0.52)	492.31 (9.68)			
2	−2482.0	1.338 (0.88)	11.56 (2.06)	0.020 (5.00)	0.969 (138.43)	
3	−2485.6	0.583 (0.59)	0.00 (0.00)			1.629 (9.70)
4	−2475.2	0.562 (0.34)	31.37 (0.39)	0.081 (2.89)	0.373 (1.34)	0.843 (1.86)

C: Datapoint (DPT) (23810020)

Model	$\mathscr{L}$	$\bar{r}$ (*t*-stat.)	C (*t*-stat.)	α (*t*-stat.)	β (*t*-stat.)	γ (*t*-stat.)
1	−2259.2	0.678 (0.65)	538.12 (20.00)			
2	−2245.3	0.474 (0.46)	40.18 (1.84)	0.056 (2.67)	0.869 (15.52)	
3	−2251.9	0.301 (0.29)	0.0 (0.00)			1.348 (3.62)
4	−2243.7	0.298 (0.28)	0.00 (0.00)	0.057 (2.36)	0.791 (8.15)	0.204 (1.46)

D: Federal Express (FDX) (31330910)

Model	$\mathscr{L}$	$\bar{r}$ (*t*-stat.)	C (*t*-stat.)	α (*t*-stat.)	β (*t*-stat.)	γ (*t*-stat.)
1	−2464.3	1.855 (1.14)	1230.98 (18.40)			
2	−2450.7	1.972 (1.26)	55.20 (1.73)	0.052 (2.60)	0.904 (24.43)	
3	−2451.8	1.489 (0.95)	0.00 (0.00)			1.768 (3.94)
4	−2445.8	1.274 (0.83)	0.00 (0.00)	0.050 (1.32)	0.678 (2.63)	0.480 (1.01)

E: National Semiconductor (NSM) (63764010)

Model	$\mathscr{L}$	$\bar{r}$ (*t*-stat.)	C (*t*-stat.)	α (*t*-stat.)	β (*t*-stat.)	γ (*t*-stat.)
1	−2492.8	−0.359 (−0.21)	1443.24 (29.08)			
2	−2476.5	1.599 (0.97)	188.51 (3.08)	0.089 (3.56)	0.783 (12.63)	
3	−2482.3	0.616 (0.35)	321.59 (2.60)			1.402 (7.01)
4	−2477.4	0.625 (0.34)	230.78 (1.96)	0.000 (0.00)	0.194 (0.85)	1.166 (3.28)

F: Paradyne (PDN) (69911310)

Forecasting Stock-Return Variance

Table 1
Continued

Model	$\mathscr{L}$	$\bar{r}$ (*t*-stat.)	C (*t*-stat.)	α (*t*-stat.)	β (*t*-stat.)	γ (*t*-stat.)
		G: Rockwell (ROK) (77434710)				
1	−2181.0	1.558 (1.73)	392.10 (20.84)			
2	−2171.7	1.590 (1.73)	31.86 (1.33)	0.048 (2.00)	0.871 (11.02)	
3	−2175.5	1.558 (1.77)	161.21 (2.71)			1.011 (3.74)
4	−2167.9	1.427 (1.59)	25.98 (0.94)	0.043 (0.12)	0.742 (3.80)	0.253 (1.28)
		H: Storage Technologies (STK) (86211110)				
1	−2443.6	−1.328 (−0.85)	1134.58 (23.09)			
2	−2423.7	−1.548 (−1.09)	96.26 (3.06)	0.079 (3.76)	0.836 (19.90)	
3	−2428.2	−2.015 (−1.34)	0.000 (0.00)			1.505 (5.57)
4	−2421.1	−1.762 (−1.19)	0.00 (0.00)	0.093 (2.16)	0.573 (3.54)	0.513 (2.01)
		I: Tandy Corp. (TAN) (87538210)				
1	−2337.2	0.362 (0.30)	738.35 (19.11)			
2	−2311.3	−0.548 (−0.49)	49.97 (2.38)	0.112 (3.50)	0.819 (16.06)	
3	−2325.4	−0.248 (−0.21)	0.00 (0.00)			1.350 (4.35)
4	−2307.9	−0.66 (−0.59)	0.00 (0.00)	0.128 (2.72)	0.656 (4.72)	0.287 (1.39)
		J: Toys R US (TOY) (89233510)				
1	−1980.2	2.082 (1.63)	680.39 (20.64)			
2	−1962.2	2.086 (1.80)	8.14 (1.48)	0.040 (3.64)	0.946 (59.12)	
3	−1968.6	1.674 (1.35)	0.00 (0.00)			1.311 (5.06)
4	−1961.9	−1.615 (1.28)	0.00 (0.00)	0.102 (1.57)	0.381 (1.22)	0.682 (1.80)

Model: $r_t = \bar{r} + \epsilon_t$

1. $\epsilon_t \sim N(0, C)$

2. $\epsilon_t \sim N(0, b_t)$

$b_t = C + \alpha\epsilon_{t-1}^2 + \beta b_{t-1}$

3. $\epsilon_t \sim N(0, b_t)$

$b_t = C + \gamma\zeta_{t-1}$

4. $\epsilon_t \sim N(0, b_t)$

$b_t = C + \alpha\epsilon_{t-1}^2 + \beta b_{t-1} + \gamma\zeta_{t-1}$

ζ_t represents the daily implied variance from minimizing the sum-of-squared errors from all option midpoint quotes on day t, for the nearest to-the-money option, intermediate term to expiration. All returns are daily percentages times 1000. *t*-stat. represents the asymptotic Student's *t* statistic. This may be biased as a result of the departure from normality of $\epsilon_t b_t^{-.5}$. $\mathscr{L}$ represents the value of the log-likelihood function at its optimum for each model. All models are estimated using daily data from April 19, 1982 through March 30, 1984; except TOY, which starts June 30, 1982 (423 days).

The Review of Financial Studies / v 6 n 2 1993

Given these parameter values, which are grounded in the data, the simulation proceeds as follows for each company in the sample. Risk-neutral pricing and (1) and (2) are assumed to be true. Also, the sample value of ρ is assumed to be true, as are the (time-dependent) values of μ and (time-independent) values of ξ obtained from the GARCH estimates. Finally, ϕ is assumed to be the average daily return on the riskless asset and takes the value 0.000245. Given these parameter values, the stock-return process is simulated 1000 times over the life of the option according to (1) and (2), where we approximate the continuous-time process by dividing the 135-day remaining life of the option into discrete, daily increments.[3] This experiment yields an estimate of the actual price for the (European) call option. Under risk-neutral valuation, this estimate is computed as the mean of the discounted terminal value of the option over the 1000 trials. The method described in Section 2 is then used to impute a variance from the simulated price and the initial value of the stock price, where stock and strike prices are chosen to be at-the-money. The simulations also define the actual mean cumulative variance over the option's remaining life, $E(\overline{V}_t \mid I_t)$. Under the null hypothesis, this conditional mean equals the subjective variance. Bias is then defined as the difference between the simulated actual mean cumulative variance and the implied variance from the model.

If there were no computational limits to the simulation, there would be no reason to generate only 1000 replications of the process. In the limit as the number of realizations approaches infinity, the empirical distribution of $\overline{V}$ approaches its true distribution. However, given practical constraints, it is impossible to determine how many finite simulations are required to obtain a good estimate of the true distribution. Our strategy is to use 1000 simulations to compute the option price and $E(\overline{V}_t \mid I_t)$, and to repeat this procedure 100 times. With 100 realizations of the option price (and thus the implied variance) we are able to construct a confidence interval around mean bias, which quantifies the numerical bias in the experiment.[4]

As a check on the possible numerical bias from using only 1000 draws, the foregoing procedure is modified so that 10,000 draws of the stock and variance evolution are made (the 10,000-draw simulation is conducted independently from the 1000-draw simulation).

---

[3] The antithetic variate technique of using each pair of draws four times, discussed in Hull and White (1987), is used in this regard. Equations (11) of that article (see notes to our Table 2), with normally distributed random variates, form the basis for the simulation.

[4] In effect, the simulation experiment utilizes 100,000 simulations (1000 realizations, 100 times) to construct estimates of bias. The comparable alternative strategy—100,000 realizations with no repetitions—yields only one estimate of option price, so no confidence interval can be constructed. Though 100,000 simulations may be sufficient to ensure a precise estimate of the true option price and the distribution of $\overline{V}$, there is no way to determine this from the alternative strategy.

Here 1,000,000 draws are taken for each stock. The effect of the size of the simulation is seen by comparing the results as we go from 1000 to 10,000 draws.

The results from the Monte Carlo experiments are contained in Table 2. Sample means and standard errors are reported over the 100 repetitions of the simulated mean cumulative variance $E(\overline{V}_t \mid I_t)$, the implied variance, and inherent bias. These values are computed and reported for three values of initial variance $[V(0)]$. The middle value of $V(0)$ is the unconditional variance, C, taken from Table 1, specification 1. Simulations using 10,000 draws are only conducted for the middle value of $V(0)$ and are reported last for each company in the table.

The results show that mean bias inherent in the analytic approximation using the option pricing model is never more than 1.3 percent of the actual variance. The variance nested in the Monte Carlo analysis appears to be trivial because standard errors of the bias are also small: two-standard-error confidence intervals around the mean bias never include 3 percent in absolute value. When 10,000 trials are repeated, the two-standard-error bounds are always less than 1.5 percent in absolute value. Note also that the mean implied volatility from the 10,000-draw simulations is always within two numerical standard errors of the 1000-draw simulation.

From the simulation results obtained by Hull and White (1987), we might expect large bias for cases in which α is large. For example, they show that for $\xi = 3$ on an annual basis, which approximately corresponds to $\alpha = .11$ (as for CSC and TAN in our data), the bias of the implied variance is 20 percent. However, their result holds for $\mu = 0$; that is, the variance process follows a random walk. Our findings of low bias are likely due to mean reversion in the estimated discrete-time variance process. Also, for companies like DPT and TOY that have strong persistence in variance, estimated α values are relatively small.

As a sensitivity check, the experiments for several companies were repeated with much higher values of ρ in absolute value. For instance, FDX with $V(0)$ of 538.12 and ρ of $-.8$ generates a mean bias of 0.59 percent (two-standard-error confidence interval: $[-.69, 1.86]$); when ρ is set to .8, the mean bias becomes -1.28 percent (two-standard-error confidence interval: $[-2.78, 0.22]$). This result is representative of those for all 10 stocks. We conclude that under the HW model with risk-neutral probabilities, our variance extraction procedure appears to be insensitive to the nonlinearity assumption and skewness in the context of our data. We will refer to these results to ascertain the potential effects of the inherent bias on inferences from the forecast-based tests of the orthogonality restrictions.

The Review of Financial Studies / v 6 n 2 1993

Table 2
Bias inherent in analytic approximation

Draws	$V(0)$	Simulated variance (std. err.)	Implied variance (std. err.)	Bias (%) (2 std. err. range)
	A: CSC, $\rho = 0.2962$
1000	438.56	589.49 (0.01)	593.86 (4.12)	−0.74 (−2.14, 0.66)
1000	590.52	591.02 (0.01)	596.54 (4.14)	−0.93 (−2.33, 0.47)
1000	750.52	592.84 (0.01)	599.52 (4.17)	−1.13 (−2.53, 0.28)
10,000	590.52	591.04 (0.004)	592.50 (1.26)	−0.25 (−0.67, 0.18)
	B: DEC, $\rho = -0.1872$
1000	354.71	614.06 (0.01)	617.19 (4.29)	−0.51 (0.89, −1.91)
1000	614.71	614.42 (0.01)	619.43 (4.14)	−0.81 (−2.15, 0.53)
1000	834.71	615.36 (0.01)	621.98 (4.17)	−1.07 (−2.43, 0.27)
10,000	614.71	614.39 (0.003)	614.98 (1.30)	−0.10 (−0.52, 0.33)
	C: DPT, $\rho = -0.1059$
1000	332.31	681.07 (0.03)	679.87 (4.81)	0.18 (−1.24, 1.59)
1000	492.31	763.05 (0.03)	762.97 (5.49)	0.01 (−1.43, 1.45)
1000	642.31	840.19 (0.04)	841.14 (6.13)	−0.11 (−1.57, 1.35)
10,000	492.31	763.09 (0.01)	757.56 (1.66)	0.72 (0.29, 1.16)
	D: FDX, $\rho = 0.0493$
1000	378.12	522.16 (0.02)	524.68 (3.59)	−0.48 (−1.86, 0.89)
1000	538.12	536.66 (0.03)	540.46 (3.72)	−0.71 (−2.10, 0.68)
1000	798.12	560.59 (0.03)	566.48 (3.91)	−1.05 (−2.44, 0.34)
10,000	538.12	536.67 (0.01)	536.79 (1.12)	−0.02 (−0.44, 0.39)
	E: NSM, $\rho = 0.2085$
1000	880.98	1196.00 (0.10)	1205.98 (9.58)	−0.83 (−2.44, 0.76)
1000	1230.98	1251.91 (0.11)	1265.30 (10.12)	−1.07 (−2.69, 0.55)
1000	1580.98	1308.22 (0.11)	1325.03 (10.67)	−1.28 (−2.92, 0.35)
10,000	1230.98	1252.03 (0.03)	1254.77 (3.10)	−0.20 (−0.70, 0.28)
	F: PDN, $\rho = -0.0408$
1000	1043.24	1457.01 (0.09)	1465.23 (11.58)	−0.56 (−2.15, 1.02)
1000	1443.24	1476.86 (0.09)	1488.33 (10.20)	−0.78 (−2.16, 0.60)
1000	1843.24	1497.19 (0.09)	1511.89 (12.05)	−0.98 (−2.59, 0.63)

Forecasting Stock-Return Variance

Table 2
Continued

Draws	$V(0)$	Simulated variance (std. err.)	Implied variance (std. err.)	Bias (%) (2 std. err. range)
10,000	1443.24	1476.97 (0.03)	1475.35 (3.64)	0.11 (−0.40, 0.60)
		G: ROK, $\rho = 0.0360$		
1000	262.10	382.81 (0.01)	384.55 (2.54)	−0.45 (−1.78, 0.87)
1000	392.10	393.62 (0.01)	396.39 (2.63)	−0.70 (−2.04, 0.63)
1000	522.10	404.61 (0.01)	408.40 (2.72)	−0.94 (−2.28, 0.41)
10,000	392.10	393.60 (0.005)	393.83 (0.79)	−0.06 (−0.46, 0.34)
		H: STK, $\rho = -0.2735$		
1000	884.58	1115.95 (0.09)	1114.47 (8.19)	0.13 (−1.34, 1.60)
1000	1134.58	1135.74 (0.09)	1136.07 (8.38)	−0.03 (−1.50, 1.45)
1000	1484.58	1163.81 (0.09)	1166.63 (8.64)	−0.24 (−1.73, 1.24)
10,000	1134.58	1135.84 (0.03)	1127.21 (2.56)	0.76 (0.31, 1.21)
		I: TAN, $\rho = -0.0563$		
1000	518.35	707.59 (0.16)	704.63 (4.82)	0.42 (−0.94, 1.78)
1000	738.35	729.40 (0.17)	727.98 (5.01)	0.19 (−1.18, 1.57)
1000	1008.35	756.52 (0.18)	756.91 (5.23)	−0.05 (−1.43, 1.33)
10,000	738.35	729.59 (0.06)	722.75 (1.53)	0.94 (0.005, 1.36)
		J: TOY, $\rho = 0.1518$		
1000	530.39	558.84 (0.09)	559.12 (3.99)	−0.05 (−1.48, 1.38)
1000	680.39	625.41 (0.10)	626.52 (4.53)	−0.18 (−1.63, 1.27)
1000	880.39	714.29 (0.13)	716.49 (5.26)	−0.31 (−1.78, 1.16)
10,000	680.39	625.34 (0.03)	622.22 (1.38)	0.50 (0.06, 0.94)

Model: $dS = \phi S\,dt + \sqrt{V}S\,dw,$ (1)

$$dV = \mu V\,dt + \xi V\,dz.$$ (2)

S is the stock price. The Brownian motions dw and dz have an instantaneous correlation of ρ. Following Hull and White (1987), risk-neutral option valuation is performed by simulating the following two equations:

$$S_t = S_{t-1}\,\exp[(r_f - V_{t-1}/2)\Delta t + u_t\sqrt{V_{t-1}\Delta t}],$$ (1′)

$$V_t = V_{t-1}\,\exp[(\mu - \xi^2/2)\Delta t + \rho u_t \xi \sqrt{\Delta t} + \sqrt{1 - \rho^2}\nu_t \xi \sqrt{\Delta t}].$$ (2′)

The relevent time increment (Δt) is taken to be one day. In all cases the option expires in 135 days. (1′) and (2′) are simulated 1000 times (draws), using the four-way control variate technique described in Hull and White (1987). [The simulation is repeated using 10,000 simulations, 100 times for the middle value of $V(0)$. The results from this experiment are reported for each company—using the middle value of $V(0)$—below the first horizontal line.] This provides a single

The Review of Financial Studies / v 6 n 2 1993

2. Tests of the Orthogonality Restriction

2.1 Tests and data

We test the orthogonality restrictions in two basic ways. The first set of tests, in Section 2.2, analyzes the marginal predictive power of the past behavior of the return process, given the implied variance, using in-sample regressions and classical statistical tests. Section 2.3 contains results from out-of-sample tests of forecastability. We investigate the ability of implied variance to predict actual volatility out-of-sample to models using past information by comparing root mean square errors and by estimating encompassing regressions.

The implied variances used in this study are constructed from option and contemporaneous stock-price data for 10 individual stocks with publicly traded options on the Chicago Board Options Exchange (CBOE) for the period April 19, 1982, through March 31, 1984. On the floor of the CBOE there are multiple competing market makers for each of these options. A clerk records every time one of the market makers quotes a bid price that is higher than the bids of the other market makers. Similarly, the clerk records all ask quotes that are lower than extant asks. Both the bid and ask quotes at such points are posted—time-stamped to the nearest second—along with the most recent stock price to have crossed the ticker. We refer to the highest bid and lowest ask quotes as the inside spread. The best bid and best ask quotes are not necessarily from the same market maker. Our data, taken from the Berkeley options database, consist of every inside spread during each day in our sample. Each option inside spread is paired with the most recent stock price from the ticker, recorded by the clerk.

The sample of data and extraction techniques used in this study are chosen to avoid as much as possible errors in the measurement of the implied variance. The stocks in our sample paid no cash dividends from 1981 through 1985; therefore, the options are essentially European. The sample period has no special significance. It starts nine years following the inception of public trading in listed options, so market makers should be adroit at their job. It also allows isolation of non-dividend-paying stocks and is a relatively calm period (com-

---

(market) option price (and market cumulative variance forecast) from which an implied volatility is computed analytically, following Black–Scholes. This will be exactly correct in those cases where Black–Scholes is exactly linear in V and where $\rho = 0$. This simulation to obtain an implied volatility is repeated 100 times to provide the mean and standard errors of the inherent bias (the source of variation is numeric, not sampling error). u and v are independent normal $(0, 1)$ random deviates. $S(0) = Xe^{-r\tau}$, $r_f = 0.000245$. The values of μ and ξ are derived from the GARCH $(1, 1)$ estimates of the variance equation for each company (see Table 1), following Nelson (1990). The value of ρ is computed as the sample correlation between the GARCH $(1, 1)$ conditional variance on day t (given information up to day t-1) and the return on day t. All variances are daily times 1 million.

pared to, say, late 1987), so the ticker should report up-to-the-minute stock transaction prices.

Note that we are not using transaction prices from the options market. At any point in time when the market is open, the option price is assumed to be the midpoint of the inside bid–ask spread. Although actual transaction prices may include price pressure effects, and (latest) transaction prices from both markets at a fixed point in time (such as closing) will always be asynchronous, our data suffer from neither of these problems.

However, the daily return series may embody noise due to the bid–ask spread "bounce." The subset of stocks with listed options in 1982 consisted of actively traded and generally large stocks in terms of market value of equity. For these stocks, relative spreads tend to be small, and the observed price process should be an excellent instrumental variable for the latent "true" price. By the same token, the most recent stock price matched to the option from the Berkeley tapes may contain some noise. Again, to the extent that this noise is well-behaved, the procedure used to imply a single variance from the entire day's data should serve to trivialize the errors-in-variables problem.

Only those options that were closest to being at-the-money are used. Furthermore, of the three expiration dates available for most companies and most days, the intermediate-term option is used throughout the analysis. The number of quotes in a day varies significantly across the sample, but the average number of quotes per day per company is about 50 for the at-the-money, intermediate-term call option.

We construct time series of implied variances for each stock in the sample as follows. On each day, at-the-money options are isolated by choosing those options with the closest discounted (at the risk-free rate) strike price to stock price at option market close. Of these, for those options that expire at the intermediate term, a single daily implied variance is computed by minimizing over variance the sum of squared errors from actual midpoint quotes to the Black–Scholes model value at that variance.[5] The model value is taken to be a function of the yield on the U.S. Treasury bill maturing as closely as possible to the intermediate-term expiration date and the most recent transaction price of the stock from the NYSE, which is the simultaneous stock price reported on the Berkeley tape.[6] As noted, there are

---

[5] A quadratic hill-climbing algorithm is used that has good convergence properties. This technique was suggested by Whaley (1982) and is more efficient than that used by Brenner and Galai (1987), namely, implying a variance from each option and using the daily average.

[6] We collected daily Treasury-bill yields from the *Wall Street Journal*. For options that mature in six months or less, there is always a one-day difference in the maturity date of the Treasury bill and

The Review of Financial Studies / v 6 n 2 1993

on average 50 quote pairs used to define a single implied variance per day. Options quote midpoints and the corresponding stock prices that violate the Black–Scholes lower boundary condition are discarded. Otherwise, all qualifying options within the day are treated equally. This procedure assumes that the variance is constant within a day.

2.2 Regression-based tests

In this subsection we test the orthogonality restrictions by examining the significance of the GARCH coefficients (α and β) in the conditional variance specification after accounting for option market forecasts of volatility. Hence, we define ζ_{t-1} in (6) to be the implied variance given information at time $t - 1$, and we allow γ to be a free parameter. From the discussion in Section 1.2, the conditional variance h_t corresponds to the instantaneous variance of the diffusion, V_t. If the life of the option T is one day, then $\overline{V}_t$ and V_t are identical for the discrete-time approximation. The general conditional variance equation in (6) then can be interpreted as a regression of $\overline{V}_t$ on the subjective variance, as measured by the implied variance, and past information. The orthogonality restriction of the joint hypothesis implies that the GARCH coefficients in (6) are zero (i.e., that the GARCH variables have no marginal predictive power).

This test is subject to an obvious and important criticism. Whereas h_t is the conditional variance of daily returns, in this study ζ_{t-1} is the implied variance from an option that matures at a horizon greater than a day (between 64 and 129 trading days). Under the HW model, the implied variance represents the market's prediction of average daily volatility over the remaining life of the option. Thus, given this specification, ζ_t is not an exact predictor of the dependent variable h_t. Day and Lewis (1992) use weekly return horizons with index options that mature in a month and are therefore subject to the same criticism. We conduct these tests as a preliminary characterization of the orthogonality restrictions and account for this maturity mismatch problem with out-of-sample tests in Section 2.2 below.

The results of the in-sample, regression-based tests are shown in Table 1. The table contains the estimation results for the unrestricted model in (4) to (6) (specification 4) and three restricted specifications. Specification 1 is a homoskedastic model where the restriction

---

the option expiration date. Since 12-month bills are only auctioned every four weeks, there is sometimes an eight-day difference between the maturity of the applicable Treasury bill and the expiration of the option. There are three days in the sample period where the Treasury-bill market was closed, but the NYSE and CBOE were open. In these cases, the previous day's rate data were substituted. The Berkeley database is missing data for the dates July 1, 1983, and December 23, 1983. For these dates, we use the options data from the previous day to replace the missing values.

$\alpha = \beta = \gamma = 0$ is imposed. Specification 2 is standard GARCH(1, 1) where γ is restricted to equal 0 (and is discussed in Section 1.2). Specification 3 restricts the conditional heteroskedasticity to be entirely manifest in the option market's variance forecast. A likelihood ratio test (LRT) on the restrictions imposed on specification 2 by specification 1 suggests that the null hypothesis of no GARCH ($\alpha = \beta = 0$) can be rejected at the 1 percent level for all 10 companies, assuming conditional normality, which confirms the inferences in Section 1.2. As discussed there, nontrivial variance clustering is an important characteristic of most of the companies.

From specification 3, we can reject the null that ζ has no explanatory power for actual daily variance for all companies except DEC, even given the maturity mismatch problem. In all other cases, this coefficient is significant and positive. The coefficient on ζ exceeds unity in eight cases.

The joint null hypothesis of informational efficiency and the HW model can be tested against the alternative that allows GARCH terms to have incremental predictive ability by comparing specifications 3 and 4. Using the LRT, we reject the null hypothesis at standard significance levels for 7 of the 10 companies: CSC, FDX, NSM, ROK, STK, TAN, and TOY.[7] Statistical inference for the remaining three companies is hindered by the fact that the nonnegativity constraints imposed in estimation are binding in the variance equation.[8]

Despite different sample periods, assets, horizons, and so forth, these results are consistent with those of Day and Lewis (1992)—past information improves the market forecast of volatility. However, this result must be interpreted with caution since the maturity mismatch problem may bias the test against the implied variance. In the next subsection we make adjustments for this problem in the context of out-of-sample forecast comparisons.

2.3 Out-of-sample tests
The incompatibility of forecast horizons that arises in the regression-based tests is eliminated in this subsection by transforming GARCH forecasts of daily variance to forecasts of average daily variance over the remaining life of the corresponding option. On any day t in the sample ($t = 1,...,495$), we can construct a forecast of h_t by using the fitted value of Equation (6) with γ equal to zero. By recursive substitution of this GARCH equation, the forecast for h_{t+k} can be con-

---

[7] The LRT is more appropriate that Wald tests given the potential collinearity between ϵ_{t-1}^2, h_{t-1}, and ζ_{t-1}.

[8] These constraints bind in some other cases (e.g., FDX), but here the constraint is binding in both specifications 3 and 4.

The Review of Financial Studies / v 6 n 2 1993

structed for any $k > 0$, given information at t. To obtain a GARCH forecast that is directly comparable to our interpretation of the implied variances, we construct the GARCH forecasts for $h_{t+1}, h_{t+2}, \ldots, h_{t+N}$, where N is the number of days left in the life of the intermediate-term option on day t. Denote the mean over these N forecasts by G_t. The forecast horizons for G_t and the implied variance are identical by construction. The joint null hypotheses imply that G_t is not a better predictor of N-step ahead realized return volatility than the implied variance; that is, the orthogonality restriction means that G_t cannot be used to improve the forecast in the implied variance. In this subsection, we compare the forecast performance of implied variance with the GARCH forecast G and a naive forecasting model.

To ensure that forecast comparisons are not biased in favor of the time-series model, we are careful to construct the GARCH forecasts by using information available to traders at the time the forecasts are made. Thus, forecast comparisons are made out-of-sample. We estimate both rolling and updating GARCH models. The rolling structure uses a constant sample size of 300 observations, adding the return on day $t - 1$ and deleting the return on day $t - 301$ from the sample used to estimate GARCH on each day t. The updating procedure simply adds information as time progresses to construct an updated forecast. Because the GARCH model is estimated only from stock-return data (and is therefore not tied down to the options sample), the first sample begins 301 trading days before April 19, 1982, the first day of our implied variance sample. The GARCH model is reestimated 495 times, for each procedure, to construct out-of-sample forecasts that are up-to-date. In addition to GARCH, we also consider the updated sample variance of past returns as a naive forecast of variance:

$$H_t = \frac{1}{t} \sum_{i=1}^{t} \hat{\epsilon}_i^2,$$

where $\hat{\epsilon}_i^2$ is the estimated residual from Equation (4), with $\alpha = \beta = \gamma = 0$.

Forecasting performance is judged by comparing the ability of the forecasts to predict the out-of-sample mean of the squared return residuals from Equation (4) over the remaining life of the intermediate-term option. To be precise, assume that this option on day t has N days to maturity. Then the realized volatility over this period is given by

$$z_t = \frac{1}{N} \sum_{i=1}^{N} \hat{\epsilon}_{t+i}^2.$$

Note that z_t is constructed to be compatible with the interpretation of the implied variance and G_t. Comparisons are based upon the out-of-sample mean error

$$ME = \frac{1}{495} \sum_{t=1}^{495} (z_t - x_t),$$

where x_t is alternatively the implied variance at time t, the two GARCH forecasts, and H_t, mean absolute error

$$MAE = \frac{1}{495} \sum_{t=1}^{495} |z_t - x_t|,$$

and root mean square error

$$RMSE = \left[\frac{1}{495} \sum_{t=1}^{495} (z_t - x_t)^2 \right]^{.5}.$$

The results of this exercise are contained in Table 3. The implied variance has the smallest RMSE for only two companies (DPT and TOY). For the remaining companies, the GARCH and the naive forecasts have lower RMSE than the implied variance. Thus, for these companies, using past information on the stock-return process can improve the market's forecast. The following points are also evident from the table:

1. The updating GARCH outperforms rolling GARCH for all 10 companies under RMSE criterion.[9]

2. The updated sample variance has the lowest RMSE in 5 of 10 cases. This relative forecasting performance is at odds with the results of Akgiray (1989). Akgiray finds that GARCH variance forecasts are convincingly superior to historical variance as a forecast using the RMSE criterion for stock index data. However, Akgiray uses a forecast horizon of only 20 days. We replicated his analysis with a 100-day horizon (representative of the average number of calendar days in the horizon in this study) and found that the relative rankings of historical variance and GARCH were overturned, which is consistent with our results.

3. The ME for implied variance is positive for all companies, which indicates that the implied variance is systematically lower than the actual volatility in this period. This characteristic of the forecasting performance of implied volatilities is readily visible in Figures 1 and 2. Here we plot the realized mean squared returns over the option's life, the updated sample variance, and the implied variance for two

---

[9] In a study that examines the forecast efficiency of GARCH (in terms of expected utility), West et al. (1990) find that rolling GARCH is superior to updating. The data in that paper are weekly foreign exchange rates.

The Review of Financial Studies / v 6 n 2 1993

Table 3
Comparisons of out-of-sample variance forecasts

	Implied variance	Updated G_t	Rolling G_t	H_t
		A: CSC		
ME	33.48	−11.04	−12.14	−20.32
MAE	187.26	132.05	147.85	133.67
RMSE	232.15	150.61	169.84	150.32
		B: DEC		
ME	257.00	188.80	107.23	239.22
MAE	308.37	306.09	331.32	300.41
RMSE	392.84	375.86	389.23	300.72
		C: DPT		
ME	281.63	−829.87	−899.04	−327.47
MAE	402.04	905.79	1051.97	593.85
RMSE	541.84	1537.71	1719.35	670.95
		D: FDX		
ME	143.41	−22.91	−4.89	−25.89
MAE	179.12	185.86	211.14	184.84
RMSE	241.21	213.12	233.74	212.61
		E: NSM		
ME	547.96	115.72	−5.66	141.25
MAE	557.17	367.14	447.95	381.81
RMSE	693.59	535.82	592.99	536.92
		F: PDN		
ME	644.95	372.79	136.16	386.43
MAE	689.63	571.96	674.26	584.19
RMSE	917.84	751.40	812.22	760.52
		G: ROK		
ME	177.74	−4.38	0.25	−12.99
MAE	203.28	94.51	115.09	99.67
RMSE	243.78	114.91	135.86	114.93
		H: STK		
ME	434.22	115.36	59.76	−125.06
MAE	496.36	431.79	520.75	414.72
RMSE	635.48	538.00	616.10	513.18
		I: TAN		
ME	203.32	−50.24	−51.02	−53.56
MAE	275.50	279.86	307.21	283.17
RMSE	389.52	350.04	393.33	343.31
		J: TOY		
ME	71.15	−79.78	−136.79	−60.62
MAE	241.51	266.82	275.33	256.89
RMSE	296.57	330.84	363.50	319.96

GARCH (G), historical (H), and implied variance are each being used to forecast the mean of the daily variance over the remaining life of the option. For each day in the sample, each forecast is compared to the actual mean of the daily variance. In this table, only those options with days to maturity of between 90 and 180 days are used. Only call options that are closest-to-the-money are used. The realized variable is measured as the sample average of $\epsilon^2 = (r_t − \bar{r})^2$ over the remaining life of the option, where $\bar{r}$ is the unconditional mean of the return process.

As defined in the text, ME refers to mean forecast error, MAE refers to mean absolute error, and RMSE refers to root mean square error. Rolling GARCH forecasts use 300 days prior to the day from which the forecast is being made. Updated GARCH adds an additional observation for each forecast. All returns are daily percentages times 1000.

Forecasting Stock-Return Variance

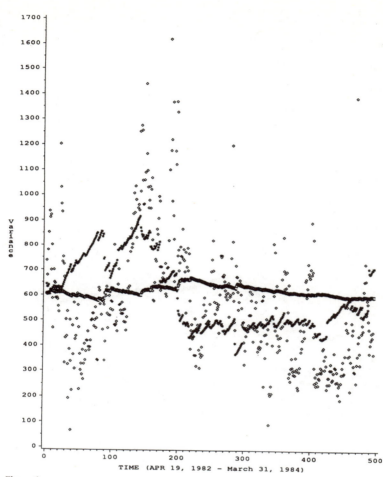

Figure 1
Daily variance measures for CSC (April 19, 1982 through March 31, 1984)
Two forecasts of the average stock-return variance over horizon $t + N$ are compared with the actual average variance over that horizon for each day in the sample period. We plot the updated sample variance (using at least the past 300 daily returns) and the variance implied from simultaneous stock price and option quotes over the day on the closest-to-the money call option that matures in N (trading) days ($64 \leq N \leq 129$). Both measures can be thought of as predictors of the average variance over the remaining life of the option. The actual variance of the stock return (which was, in fact, realized) over the forecast horizon is also plotted. The three variance measures plotted are (CCC) the updated sample variance; ($\Diamond\Diamond\Diamond$) the implied variance; and (***) the actual variance over the forecast horizon. If the joint null hypothesis of the paper were true, then the implied variance would be an unbiased predictor of the actual realized variance, and the historical sample variance would be orthogonal to the prediction error.

315

The Review of Financial Studies / v 6 n 2 1993

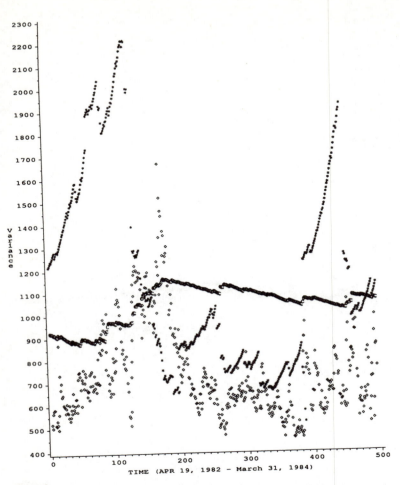

Figure 2
Daily variance measures for STK (April 19, 1982 through March 31, 1984)
Two forecasts of the average stock-return variance over the period $t + 1$ through $t + N$ are compared
with the actual average variance over that period. On day t in the sample, we plot the updated
sample variance (using at least the past 300 daily returns) and the variance implied from simultaneous stock price and option quotes over the day on the closest-to-the money call option that
matures in N (trading) days ($64 \le N \le 129$). Both measures can be thought of as predictors of
the average variance over the remaining life of the option. The actual variance of the stock return
(which was, in fact, realized) over the forecast horizon is also plotted. The three variance measures
plotted are (CCC) the updated sample variance; ($\Diamond\Diamond\Diamond$) the implied variance; and (***) the
actual variance over the forecast horizon. If the joint null hypothesis of the paper were true, then
the implied variance would be an unbiased predictor of the actual realized variance, and the
historical sample variance would be orthogonal to the prediction error.

representative companies, CSC (with relatively low persistence in variance) and STK (with relatively high persistence).

As noted by Fair and Shiller (1990, pp. 375–376), simply comparing out-of-sample forecasts using RMSE has limitations. Further insights into the nature of the different forecast models can be obtained by regressing the realized mean squared residuals on the three alternative out-of-sample forecasts:

$$z_t = \beta_0 + \beta_1 \zeta_t + \beta_2 G_t + \beta_3 H_t + u_t. \qquad (7)$$

All variables are as defined before, except note that G_t is the updated GARCH forecast, conditional on information available at time t, of the mean variance; rolling GARCH is not used here because updating GARCH dominates it under RMSE, and these two are highly correlated.

This regression is in the spirit of the encompassing literature [Hendry and Richard (1982)]. If a forecast contains no useful information regarding the evolution of the dependent variable, we would expect the coefficient on that forecast to be insignificantly different from zero. The orthogonality restriction implies that the alternative time-series models contain no information not incorporated in the implied variance that can be used to predict realized volatility. Thus, the encompassing regressions are closely related to the in-sample regression tests. However, this design avoids the maturity mismatch problem, and the forecasts are conditioned on information available at period t. As pointed out by Fair and Shiller (1990), this test also avoids the inherent ambiguity of RMSE comparisons.[10]

Ordinary least squares (OLS) is a consistent estimator of these regression coefficients. However, because the forecast horizon exceeds the frequency of the available data, the error term will be a moving average process. Since generalized least squares is inconsistent (as the forecast errors are not strictly exogenous), we take the approach of obtaining a consistent estimator of the variance covariance matrix of the OLS estimators by generalized method of moments (GMM). An early example of this procedure is Hansen and Hodrick (1980).

To construct this consistent estimator, we use the Bartlett kernel approximation to the spectral density at frequency 0 of the residuals to weight lagged values as suggested by Newey and West (1987). As noted by Andrews (1991), the asymptotic theory for this estimator

---

[10] Fair and Shiller (1990) use this empirical strategy to infer the information content of alternative models of real GNP growth. In particular, they examine the forecasting performance of a structural model and various time-series models of aggregate output. Although the economic issue in our article differs from Fair and Shiller, it is clear that the questions we ask are analogous to theirs. Thus, their methods of inference are appropriate for our analysis.

317

The Review of Financial Studies / v 6 n 2 1993

Table 4
Encompassing tests of variance forecasts

β_0 (GMM t)	β_1 (GMM t)	β_2 (GMM t)	β_3 (GMM t)	r^2 M^*
		A: CSC		
2014.269	0.276	−2.580		0.357
(5.39)	(3.81)	(−4.32)		50
2950.717	0.272	0.522	−4.566	0.451
(4.72)	(3.81)	(0.98)	(−3.47)	54
		B: DEC		
981.366	0.382	−1.012		0.222
(7.52)	(1.60)	(−3.96)		42
1069.920	0.361	−0.890	−0.327	0.227
(3.26)	(1.16)	(−2.49)	(−0.30)	66
		C: DPT		
445.920	0.531	0.129		0.418
(3.18)	(1.82)	(2.92)		60
3692.963	0.970	0.093	−2.360	0.575
(2.64)	(3.97)	(2.12)	(−2.49)	51
		D: FDX		
1585.291	1.116	−2.641		0.304
(3.38)	(2.35)	(−2.71)		75
3161.79	0.831	1.736	−6.938	0.508
(3.87)	(2.99)	(1.29)	(−2.70)	85
		E: NSM		
2084.680	1.462	−1.659		0.387
(3.65)	(4.28)	(−2.80)		59
4955.058	0.490	0.366	−4.093	0.839
(9.73)	(2.21)	(1.57)	(−7.17)	73
		F: PDN		
1997.741	0.118	−0.632		0.030
(2.96)	(0.52)	(−0.93)		184
2388.188	0.212	1.074	−2.175	0.086
(2.63)	(0.79)	(1.94)	(−2.34)	196
		G: ROK		
1988.798	−0.452	−3.775		0.356
(6.69)	(−0.48)	(−5.02)		98
2141.949	−0.100	−1.556	−2.504	0.375
(4.81)	(−1.24)	(−0.80)	(−1.02)	119
		H: STK		
2491.690	1.300	−2.166		0.402
(4.24)	(3.01)	(−3.27)		47
5073.759	0.619	−0.389	−3.792	0.637
(3.41)	(2.28)	(0.96)	(−2.54)	86
		I: TAN		
1858.705	0.748	−1.907		0.215
(4.24)	(3.01)	(−3.27)		47
5030.08	0.390	0.730	−6.351	0.488
(3.41)	(2.28)	(0.96)	(−2.54)	86
		J: TOY		
824.120	1.171	−1.273		0.227
(4.23)	(2.56)	(−2.85)		59
4053.326	0.660	0.028	−5.999	0.555
(4.91)	(2.57)	(−0.02)	(−4.32)	87

Model: $z_t = \beta_0 + \beta_1 \zeta_t + \beta_2 G_t + \beta_3 H_t + u_t$.

Forecasting Stock-Return Variance

requires that the lag length used to accumulate the variance go to infinity with the sample size. Therefore, selection of lag length is not obvious. We use the method of Andrews (1991) to estimate optimally this lag length.[11]

Table 4 contains the results of the optimal forecast weighting tests. Two regressions are reported. In the first, β_3 is constrained to be 0, and the second is the unrestricted model. In the table, we report the automatic bandwidth obtained from the Andrews procedure, M^*; the t-statistics are computed by using M^* in the Newey–West weighting scheme. All tests were conducted with a bandwidth of 32, 66, and 132, as well. None of the following inferences are sensitive to the choice of bandwidth.

In general, the optimal out-of-sample forecast of mean realized volatility places a statistically significant positive weight on the implied variance from the options market, no significant weight on the GARCH forecast, and a large significant negative weight on the updated sample variance. DEC, PDN, and ROK are exceptions to this pattern. Only DEC has a significantly negative coefficient on the GARCH forecast. In all 10 cases the intercept is positive and statistically significant. This result is consistent with earlier evidence that during this period variance forecasts are biased downward.

These regression results suggest the importance of the point made by Fair and Shiller (1990). RMSE comparisons suppress a large amount of information about the problem of constructing an optimal forecast. Despite having the lowest RMSE in only two cases, implied variance has significant forecast weight in seven cases. Symmetrically, note that in the two cases where implied variance had the lowest RMSE

---

[11] Andrews (1991) has developed the asymptotic theory to estimate the optimal lag length or bandwidth for a given sample of size T as a function of the autocovariance structure of the matrix V, where $V = \epsilon'X$, ϵ is a $T \times 1$ vector of the OLS residuals, and X is the $T \times K$ matrix of regressors. In our case, the first column is a vector of 1. We estimate a univariate AR(1) process for each column of V. The K AR(1) coefficients and residual variances are then used to compute $\hat{\alpha}(1)$ by using Equation (6.4) in Andrews (1991, p. 835). We use weights of 1 for $p = 2,...,K$ and 0 for $p = 1$ (which Andrews notes yields a scale-invariant covariance matrix, page 834). Since we are using the triangular (Bartlett) kernel estimator as in Newey and West (1987), we obtain the optimal bandwidth by plugging $\hat{\alpha}(1)$ into Andrews' Equation (6.2) (page 834). The result of this equation is equal to M^* + 1, where M^* is the optimal bandwidth used to compute the variance–covariance matrix, as in Newey and West. M^* increases with the cubed root of T.

←

β_3 is restricted to be 0 in the first model and a free parameter in the second. z_t is the realized mean $(r_t - \bar{r})^2$ during the period $t + 1$ through $t + N$, where $t + N$ is the maturity date of the option. ζ_t is the implied variance from all quotes on the at-the-money, intermediate-term options (that expire at time $t + N$) on day t. G_t is N-step ahead (updated) GARCH (1, 1) variance forecast (conditional on information available at time t). H_t is the updated sample variance measured through day t. M^* is the optimal bandwidth used to estimate the Bartlett kernel in the Newey–West variance–covariance matrix [following Andrews (1991)]. GMM t refers to the Student's t-statistic computed using this matrix. All returns are daily percentages times 1000. All variances are on a daily basis.

The Review of Financial Studies / v 6 n 2 1993

Table 5
Implied volatility forecast "errors" and the level of variance

Company	β_0 (GMM t)	β_1 (GMM t)	r^2 M^*
CSC	3601.40 (4.36)	−5.77 (−4.32)	0.26 24
DEC	905.16 (6.63)	−1.54 (−4.39)	0.12 38
DPT	3557.52 (2.35)	−2.16 (−2.18)	0.28 54
FDX	2869.53 (4.41)	−4.81 (−4.43)	0.48 75
NSM	4622.75 (10.62)	−3.73 (−9.61)	0.82 46
PDN	2381.30 (2.57)	−1.67 (−2.11)	0.18 101
ROK	1721.33 (1.75)	−3.64 (−1.54)	0.11 47
STK	5092.60 (5.68)	−4.47 (−5.28)	0.62 77
TAN	4790.36 (5.45)	−5.74 (−5.37)	0.48 29
TOY	3987.13 (5.56)	−6.13 (−5.64)	0.51 69

Model: $z_t - \zeta_t = \beta_0 + \beta_1 H_t + u_t$.

z_t is the realized mean $(r_\tau - \bar{r})^2$ during the period $t + 1$ through $t + N$, where $t + N$ is the maturity date of the option. ζ_t is the implied variance from all quotes on the at-the-money, intermediate-term options that expire at time $t + N$ on day t. H_t is the updated sample variance measured through day t. M^* is the optimal bandwidth used to estimate the Barlett kernel in the Newey–West variance–covariance matrix [following Andrews (1991)]. GMM t refers to the Student's t-statistic computed using this matrix. All returns are daily percentages times 1000. All variances are on a daily basis.

(DPT and TOY), the historical variance has significant forecasting power.

The results reported in this table suggest that the joint null hypothesis of market efficiency and the HW model is rejected at standard significance levels. However, it is not the case that filtering the data with the HW model is uninformative. To an agent confronted with deriving an optimal variance forecast, the norm here is to exploit information in both the historical path of stock prices and contemporaneous option and stock prices.

An alternative regression is run, and the results are provided in Table 5. Here the dependent variable is defined as the variance-measured model error: $z_t - \zeta_t$. The regressor is the updated sample variance estimate at time t. Test statistics are derived from the GMM covariance matrix as in Table 4. Except for ROK (also an outlier in the optimal forecast analysis, with an insignificant negative weight on ζ_t), the intercept in this regression is positive and significant. The coefficient on the current variance estimate is negative and significant. Note that the order of magnitude of the intercept is the same as the dependent variable itself. The r^2 values reported in Table 5 are high.

In half of the cases, more than 45 percent of the variance-measured pricing error is explained by the evolution of the current variance.

2.4 Interpretation of results

The results of the different experiments conducted are in general inconsistent with the joint hypothesis of the stochastic variance option pricing model and informational efficiency. This inference is robust across the in- and out-of-sample experimental designs. The tests uncover two facts for the 10 companies in the sample:

1. Implied variance tends to underpredict realized variance (see mean error in Table 3 and the significantly positive intercept in Table 5).

2. Forecasts of variance from past returns contain relevant information not contained in the market forecast constructed under the HW assumptions. The optimal weight placed on these forecasts of realized variance is negative (see Tables 4 and 5).

We refer to the results in Table 2 and ask whether these characteristics can be due solely to the bias inherent in our procedure for implying volatilites under the assumptions of zero correlation between the instantaneous rate of change in the stock price and the instantaneous variance and linearity of the pricing model. The smallest percentage bias in the data is for CSC. Here the mean error of implied variance from Table 3 is 33.48, and the level of variance is 590.52 (see Table 1, specification 1), a percentage error of 5.67. From Table 2, under the joint null, we would expect a percentage error of -0.25 percent; if the estimated percentage error fell between -0.67 and 0.18 percent, we would be unable to reject the null at an approximate 5 percent level of significance.[12] For Tandy, as a more representative company, the expected bias under the null is 0.94 percent, with a two-standard-error range of 0 to 1.36 percent. The bias in the data is 27.54 percent. In all 10 cases, the out-of-sample forecasting error lies well outside the calibrated two-standard-error confidence interval. Thus, the documented underprediction of implied variances cannot be attributed to the two potential sources of bias.

Also, from Table 2, we ask whether the empirical relationship between the forecast error of the implied variance and the current variance is solely a result of the approximation procedure used to imply variances. It is possible that the negative coefficient on H_t (or G_t) in the encompassing regressions picks up a tendency for the bias

---

[12] Recognizing that the unconditional variance is estimated with sampling error, add two standard errors to this estimate, and the percentage error is 5.1. The inference is unchanged.

The Review of Financial Studies / v 6 n 2 1993

in implied variance, though small, to change with the level of variance. Note from Table 2 that in all 10 cases the inherent percentage bias is inversely related to the level of variance, $V(0)$. However, the magnitude of this phenomenon is very different from that manifest in the data. Federal Express is a typical case. From the three sets of values in Table 2 (generated with 1000 draws, 100 times), the change in absolute bias divided by the change in level of variance is -0.008. From Table 5, the change in the forecast error relative to a change in historical variance is -4.81.[13] Therefore, whereas we expect a negative coefficient on historical variance, the size of this coefficient computed from actual data is too large to be the result of the inherent biases in the experimental design.

Since the biases inherent in our extraction procedure are unlikely to be the reason for the rejection of the null hypothesis, we can speculate as to the potential causes. One interpretation of the statistically significant negative effect of the updated sample variance is that market participants totally ignore the information contained in past realizations of returns. An alternative interpretation is that the market overreacts to recent volatility shocks: too much weight is placed on the recent past of the variance process. A current increase to volatility raises the sample variance, but the negative β_3 suggests that this shock is temporary. However, options traders impute a permanence to the shock, leading to an underprediction of variance [Stein (1989)].

Given informational efficiency, our results can be explained by the existence of a risk premium applied to the nontraded variance process. Recall that an assumption underlying the use of the implied variance from the model as an instrument for the market's forecast of variance is that volatility risk is unpriced. The option price is independent of risk preferences if agents are risk-neutral, or if the instantaneous variance is uncorrelated with aggregate consumption and, therefore, is uncorrelated with marginal utility of wealth. If this assumption is false, then observed option prices will include a risk premium. For example, if variance uncertainty gives negative utility to traders, the observed option price will be lower than the risk-neutral price, *ceteris paribus*. When the observed price is applied to the Black–Scholes formula, the implied variance will be correspondingly lower than actual variance. As noted, we document this underprediction by the implied variance for all stocks in the sample. The negative coefficient on the current level of variance means that

---

[13] The regression coefficient reported in Table 5 is a first derivative analogous in its interpretation to the ratio of changes reported. Although the magnitude of change in the variance level is large in Table 2, the size and sign of the pseudoderivative are virtually identical across companies and independent of the size of change in $V(0)$.

the risk premium is time dependent. Specifically, the implied variance rises relative to the future (realized) volatility as the stock's variance rises. Thus the variance risk premium embedded in option prices diminishes as the stock's variance increases.[14]

Melino and Turnbull (1990) use numerical methods to evaluate a partial differential equation in the spirit of Garman (1976), and they find evidence to support the notion that a nonzero risk premium on the variance process exists in the Canadian dollar–U.S. dollar exchange rate option market. They restricted the price of variance risk to be a constant. Our results suggest that such a risk premium is time-varying in the stock market.

Our empirical analysis is confined to constructing an optimal variance forecast. Since we reject the joint null hypothesis of market efficiency and stochastic variance option pricing model-based pricing of these options, these results do not indicate that one could take the optimal variance forecasts and use them to "beat" the option market. It is plausible that the market's forecast as embodied in option prices is optimal, but that filtering the prices through the simple option pricing model distorts the forecast. Thus, if one used the "optimal forecast" from the regressions, the profits generated by that strategy would be offset by volatility risk if this trader's utility function is the same as the market's.

Although we have motivated this experiment as a test of the restrictions of an asset pricing model, the tests also provide insights into the nature of the variance process for these individual stocks. The poor out-of-sample performance of GARCH at the 90- to 180-calendar-day horizons appears inconsistent with its good in-sample fit and good forecast performance at short horizons [see Akgiray (1989)]. This set of results is consistent with a variance process that is subject to highly persistent shocks at low frequencies and quickly dampening shocks at high frequencies. This property of stock-return variances and its relationship to GARCH has been suggested by Lamoureux and Lastrapes (1990). Theoretical analysis of this phenomenon is provided by Nelson (1992). GARCH treats all innovations equally; therefore, it overstates the persistence of high-frequency shocks, which leads to excellent short-term forecasts but poor long-term forecasts.

As a final note, Back (1993) has developed an equilibrium model of informed trader behavior in the spirit of Kyle (1985), where the monopolistically informed trader may trade with an uninformed market maker in either the stock or option market. Back shows that the only equilibrium that does not generate arbitrage opportunities for

---

[14] There is no reason to suspect a priori that this risk premium would be the same across stocks. It is a function of the correlation between the variance process and marginal utility. To the extent that stock variances include common factors, the risk premiums will be related.

The Review of Financial Studies / v 6 n 2 1993

the informed trader is one in which the stock's variance is stochastic and in which the option price contains information about the future variance that is not publicly available elsewhere. Thus, the option allows a finer partition of information than is available from an information set that excludes the current option price. Empirically, this theoretical result could be rejected if, for example in our analysis, we found that the optimal forecast weight on implied variance could not be statistically distinguished from zero. For 7 of the 10 companies, the implied variance has a statistically positive weight. This result is consistent with Back's model.

3. Conclusions

We examine the joint hypothesis of a class of stochastic volatility option pricing models and informational efficiency in the options markets using a criterion function based on the variance of the underlying stock returns. To examine this hypothesis, we represent the subjective variance of the market as the implied variance from the data and the option pricing model. By utilizing discrete-time simulations of the continuous-time return process, calibrated to our data, we show that potential biases between these two variance concepts are small and do not affect the inferences of our tests of the joint hypothesis.

Using both in-sample and out-of-sample tests, we reject the implication of the hypothesis that available information cannot be used to improve the market's variance forecast embedded in observable prices *as measured by this class of models*. This result is robust across the different test designs and to inherent measurement bias and is consistent with the results of Melino and Turnbull (1990) and Day and Lewis (1992). If the market is efficient, our results suggest that the fundamental assumptions of the model are not sufficient to account for the properties of the data. In particular, equilibrium models of option pricing that do not assume investor indifference to volatility risk appear necessary to reconcile the theory and data. The data suggest that the market premium on variance risk is time varying; it is a decreasing function of the level of the stock's variance. Results concerning the nature of this risk premium are uniform (and strikingly similar) across the 10 stocks used in our analysis.

Although the option pricing model is rejected as the price-determining market mechanism, filtering the data with the simple model does contain useful information that is not contained in the historical price process of the underlying stock for forecasting the stock's variance over a 180- to 90-calendar-day horizon. This result has normative implications for optimal variance forecast rules, even in the absence of the "correct" equilibrium option pricing model capable of explaining the data.

References

Akgiray, V., 1989, "Conditional Heteroskedasticity in Time Series of Stock Returns: Evidence and Forecasts," *Journal of Business,* 62, 55–80.

Andrews, D. W. K., 1991, "Heteroskedasticity and Autocorrelation Consistent Covariance Matrix Estimation," *Econometrica,* 59, 817–858.

Back, K., 1993, "Asymmetric Information and Options," *Review of Financial Studies,* 6, forthcoming.

Biegler, L. J., and J. E. Cuthrell, 1985, "Improved Feasible Path Optimization for Sequential Modular Simulators. II: The Optimization Algorithm," *Computers and Chemical Engineering,* 9, 257–267.

Black, F., and M. S. Scholes, 1973, "The Pricing of Options and Corporate Liabilities," *Journal of Political Economy,* 81, 637–654.

Bollerslev, T., 1986, "Generalized Autoregressive Conditional Heteroskedasticity," *Journal of Econometrics,* 31, 307–327.

Brenner, M., and D. Galai, 1987, "On the Prediction of the Implied Standard Deviation," in *Advances in Futures and Options Research,* JAI Press, Greenwich, Conn.

Cox, J. C., and M. Rubinstein, 1985, *Options Markets,* Prentice-Hall, Englewood Cliffs, N.J.

Day, T. E., and C. M. Lewis, 1992, "Stock Market Volatility and the Information Content of Stock Index Options," *Journal of Econometrics,* 52, 267–287.

Engle, R. F., 1982, "Autoregressive Conditional Heteroskedasticity with Estimates of the Variance of U.K. Inflation," *Econometrica,* 50, 987–1007.

Fair, R. C., and R. J. Shiller, 1990, "Comparing Information in Forecasts from Econometric Models," *American Economic Review,* 80, 375–389.

Feinstein, S. P., 1989, "A Theoretical and Empirical Investigation of the Black–Scholes Implied Volatility," unpublished thesis, Yale University.

Garman, M., 1976, "A General Theory of Asset Valuation under Diffusion State Processes," working paper, University of California, Berkeley.

Hansen, L. P., and R. J. Hodrick, 1980, "Forward Exchange Rates as Optimal Predictors of Future Spot Rates: An Econometric Analysis," *Journal of Political Economy,* 88, 829–853.

Hendry, D. F., and J-F. Richard, 1982, "On the Formulation of Empirical Models in Dynamic Economics," *Journal of Econometrics,* 20, 3–33.

Heston, S., 1993, "A Closed-Form Solution for Options with Stochastic Volatility with Applications to Bond and Currency Options," *Review of Financial Studies,* 6, 327–343.

Hull, J., and A. White, 1987, "The Pricing of Options on Assets with Stochastic Volatilities," *Journal of Finance,* 42, 281–300.

Johnson, H., and D. Shanno, 1987, "Option Pricing When the Variance is Changing," *Journal of Financial and Quantitative Analysis,* 22, 143–151.

Kyle, A. S., 1985, "Continuous Auctions and Insider Trading," *Econometrica,* 53, 1315–1335.

Lamoureux, C. G., and W. D. Lastrapes, 1990, "Persistence in Variance, Structural Change, and the GARCH Model," *Journal of Business and Economic Statistics,* 8, 225–234.

Melino, A., and S. Turnbull, 1990, "Pricing Foreign Currency Options with Stochastic Volatility," *Journal of Econometrics,* 45, 239–265.

The Review of Financial Studies / v 6 n 2 1993

Nelson, D. B., 1990, "ARCH Models as Diffusion Approximations," *Journal of Econometrics,* 45, 7–38.

Nelson, D. B., 1992, "Filtering and Forecasting with Misspecified ARCH Models. I: Getting the Right Variance with the Wrong Model," *Journal of Econometrics,* 52, 61–90.

Newey, W. K., and K. D. West, 1987, "A Simple, Positive Semi-Definite Heteroskedasticity and Autocorrelation Consistent Covariance Matrix," *Econometrica,* 55, 703–708.

Scott, L. O., 1987, "Option Pricing When the Variance Changes Randomly," *Journal of Financial and Quantitative Analysis,* 22, 419–438.

Stein, E. M., and J. C. Stein, 1991, "Stock Price Distributions with Stochastic Volatility: An Analytic Approach," *Review of Financial Studies,* 4, 727–752.

Stein, J. C., 1989, "Overreactions in the Options Market," *Journal of Finance,* 44, 1011–1023.

West, K. D., H. J. Edison, and D. Cho, 1990, "A Utility Based Comparison of Some Models of Exchange Rate Volatility," working paper, University of Wisconsin.

Whaley, R. E., 1982, "Valuation of American Call Options on Dividend Paying Stocks: Empirical Tests," *Journal of Financial Economics,* 10, 29–58.

Wiggins, J. B., 1987, "Option Values under Stochastic Volatility: Theory and Empirical Estimates," *Journal of Financial Economics,* 19, 351–372.

[26]

The Informational Content of Implied Volatility

Linda Canina
Brown University

Stephen Figlewski
New York University

Implied volatility is widely believed to be informationally superior to historical volatility, because it is the "market's" forecast of future volatility. But for S&P 100 index options, the most actively traded contract in the United States, we find implied volatility to be a poor forecast of subsequent realized volatility. In aggregate and across subsamples separated by maturity and strike price, implied volatility has virtually no correlation with future volatility, and it does not incorporate the information contained in recent observed volatility.

One of the most attractive features of the Black–Scholes option pricing model is that its parameters are almost all observable. The one input that must be forecast is the volatility of the underlying asset. Unfortunately, price volatility of most optionable securities varies considerably over time, and accurate prediction is far from easy. The two basic approaches are either to compute the realized volatility over the recent past from historical price data or to calculate the "implied volatility" (IV) from current option prices in the market by solving the pricing model for the volatility that sets the model and market prices equal.

We would like to thank the Interactive Data Corporation and Yogi Thambiah for supplying the data used in this study. Helpful comments from Clifford Ball, Stephen Brown, Stephen Cecchetti, William Greene, Barry Schachter, William Silber, Bruce Tuckman, Robert Whaley, Robert Stambaugh (the editor), and an anonymous referee, as well as seminar participants at Boston College, Cornell, Duke, New York University, Ohio State, and Virginia Polytechnic Institute and State University, are gratefully acknowledged. Address correspondence to Stephen Figlewski, New York University Stern School of Business, 44 West 4th Street, New York, NY 10012.

The Review of Financial Studies 1993 Volume 6, number 3, pp. 659–681
© 1993 The Review of Financial Studies 0893-9454/93/$1.50

The Review of Financial Studies / v 6 n 3 1993

It has become almost an article of faith in the academic finance profession that the implied volatility is the "market's" volatility forecast, and that it is a better estimate than historical volatility. Indeed, researchers often use implied volatility in other models as an ex ante measure of perceived asset price risk.[1] Here, we examine that proposition as it pertains to the most active options market in the United States, options on the Standard and Poors 100 Index (frequently called by their ticker symbol, OEX options). The results we obtain from analyzing over 17,000 OEX call option prices conflict sharply with the conventional wisdom.

We begin the analysis in Section 1 with a discussion of the logic behind the conventional wisdom and a critical examination of how it should be tested. Section 2 describes our data and methodology. If implied volatility is the market's prediction of actual volatility over the time remaining to an option's expiration date, daily observations on IV involve sequential forecasts for overlapping time periods. This leads to serial dependence in the time series of forecast errors and to a statistical problem in testing the model. In addition, simultaneous trading in multiple contracts with different strike prices and overlapping expirations creates further cross-correlations if the data sample contains observations on more than one option per day. Previous studies dealt with the problem by aggregating and excluding data to create nonoverlapping observations. Unfortunately, such procedures can severely reduce the power of statistical tests. Instead, we maximize the amount of information obtained from the data by adopting an estimation procedure that makes use of the entire data sample and corrects for the time dependence directly.

Section 3 presents our estimation results. In brief, they show that for OEX index options, implied volatility is an inefficient and biased forecast of realized future volatility that does not impound the information contained in recent historical volatility. In fact, the statistical evidence shows little or no correlation at all between implied volatility and subsequent realized volatility.

1. Volatility Forecasts and Implied Volatility

1.1 Realized volatility, implied volatility, and the market's volatility forecast

It is widely accepted that the implied Black–Scholes volatility computed from the market price of an option is a good estimate of the

---

[1] See Patell and Wolfson (1979, 1981) or Poterba and Summers (1986) for examples of the use of implied volatility as a proxy for the market's risk assessment. Implied volatility has also been used as a proxy for the true instantaneous price volatility of the underlying asset, as in Stein's (1989) study of the "term structure" behavior of implied volatility.

"market's" expectation of the volatility of the underlying asset, and that the market's expectation is informationally efficient.

Black and Scholes assume that the price for the underlying stock follows a logarithmic diffusion process with constant instantaneous mean and volatility. However, there is an obvious conflict in applying an approach that assumes the asset price process has a known constant volatility to a situation in which volatility must be forecast because it changes randomly over time. Investors who were fully rational in valuing options should use a pricing model that deals rigorously with the stochastic nature of volatility, as in Hull and White (1987) or Wiggins (1987). Stochastic volatility models require the investor to forecast not just a single volatility parameter but the entire joint probability distribution for asset returns and changes in volatility and also the market price of volatility risk. These requirements make these models significantly more difficult to implement than Black–Scholes and other constant-volatility models. During the period covered by our data sample, ending in 1987, option traders had easy access to theoretical values, implied volatilities, deltas, and so on, for traded options from the standard fixed-volatility models, but formal stochastic volatility models were not in general use. Even today, it is common practice for option traders to make trading and hedging decisions by picking a point forecast for volatility—perhaps the implied volatility, an estimate computed from historical prices, or some subjectively determined combination of the two—and then inserting this point estimate into the Black–Scholes or binomial model. Similarly, academic investigators almost invariably use implied volatilities from standard fixed-volatility models to measure the market's volatility expectations.

Thus, we consider the analysis in this subsection to be more valid as a description of the approach taken by many actual investors and researchers than as optimal behavior in a world of stochastic volatility. One way to interpret our empirical work is as a test of whether the "rule of thumb" strategy of computing implied volatility from a standard fixed-volatility model is an efficient way to obtain a volatility forecast.

For a series of prices $\{S_0, S_1, ..., S_T\}$, the realized volatility σ is defined as the annualized standard deviation of the continuously compounded returns, $\{R_1, R_2, ..., R_T\}$, where $R_t \equiv \ln(S_t/S_{t-1})$, $\bar{R}$ is the sample mean of the R_n, and K is the number of observation intervals in a year:[2]

$$\sigma = \left(\frac{K}{T-1} \sum_{t-1}^{T} (R_t - \bar{R})^2 \right)^{1/2}. \tag{1}$$

---

[2] Equation (1) is widely used as a *consistent* estimator of volatility, but while the expression in the large parentheses yields an unbiased estimate of the variance, taking the square root to obtain the

The Review of Financial Studies / v 6 n 3 1993

In the later discussion of our empirical work, the annualized volatility that will be realized over the remaining lifetime of a τ-period option as of date t will be denoted $\sigma_t(\tau)$. In this section, we simplify the notation by suppressing the explicit dependence on t and τ.

One estimate of future volatility can be obtained from historical prices by assuming that the recent realized level of volatility will continue in the future. Another estimate comes from current option prices. Given the observable parameters and an option valuation formula, there is a one-to-one correspondence between the option price and the volatility input. Computing the implied volatility, IV, from the observed market price then gives an estimate of the "market's" volatility forecast,

$$IV = E_{MKT}[\sigma], \tag{2}$$

where $E_{MKT}[\sigma]$ denotes the market's (subjective) expectation for σ.[3]

By definition, realized volatility can be written as its expected value conditional on an information set Φ plus a zero-mean random error that is orthogonal to Φ:

$$\sigma = E[\sigma|\Phi] + \epsilon, \qquad E[\epsilon|\Phi] = 0.$$

This formulation leads to the well-established regression test for the rationality of a forecast,

$$\sigma = \alpha + \beta F(\Phi) + u, \tag{3}$$

where $F(\Phi)$ is the forecast of σ based on the information set Φ and u is the regression residual.[4] If the forecast is the true expected value of σ conditional on Φ, regressing realized values of σ on their expectations should produce regression estimates of 0.0 and 1.0 for α and β, respectively. Deviation from those values is evidence of bias and inefficiency in the forecasts.

Since the forecast error must be orthogonal to any rationally formed forecast, Equation (3) should hold with $\alpha = 0$ and $\beta = 1$ for any Φ. Running (3) on forecasts derived from a more inclusive information set does not change the expected coefficient estimates, but a better forecast should produce a higher R^2. Further, if one regresses σ on two forecasts, $F_1(\Phi_1)$ and $F_2(\Phi_2)$, where the second is derived from a subset of the information used in forming the first ($\Phi_1 \supset \Phi_2$),

---

volatility is a nonlinear transformation that introduces a small bias in a finite sample by Jensen's inequality. It is common practice to treat this bias as negligible.

[3] Again, we ignore the bias in a forecast of σ obtained as the square root of an unbiased forecast of σ^2.

[4] Theil (1966) is credited with introducing this test of forecast rationality and analyzing it in detail. It has been widely applied to test the rationality of expectations, as in Pesando (1975) (for inflation expectations) or Brown and Maital (1981) (for a broad selection of economic variables).

$$\sigma = \alpha + \beta_1 F_1(\Phi_1) + \beta_2 F_2(\Phi_2) + u, \tag{4}$$

the slope coefficient of the first, β_1, should still be 1.0 and the less-informed forecast should have $\beta_2 = 0$. Analyzing the relative information content of two different forecasts by means of a regression like (4) is known as an "encompassing regression" test. Fair and Shiller (1990) discuss this approach in detail and use it to evaluate the forecasting performance of different macroeconomic models.

The tests we report are based on Equations (3) and (4), with implied volatility and historical volatility as the conditional forecasts.

1.2 Empirical evidence on implied volatility

Early studies by Latané and Rendleman (1976) (LR), Chiras and Manaster (1978) (CM), and Beckers (1981) all use the basic Black–Scholes European option model or a variant of it in computing IVs for American calls on dividend-paying stocks.[5] In the tests presented here, we derive the IVs from a binomial model that adjusts for dividends and captures the value of early exercise. This resolves the problem of analyzing American options but does not address the many other issues raised by the possibility that the "market" may not be using exactly the same model we are. For example, the market's option model may allow nonlognormal price changes or price jumps. Using the wrong model violates (2): the computed IV will differ from the market's real volatility forecast.

In the early studies, stock-price volatility was typically treated as if it were a constant parameter, so the exact timing and periodicity of the data sample used in estimating it did not matter much. This tacit assumption gave rise to problems in the way data were handled, including use of sparse monthly data spanning long time periods to estimate historical volatility, estimating "realized" volatility over periods that did not match option maturity, and, in at least one case, analyzing "forecasts" of volatility over periods prior to the date the forecast was made.[6] Only Beckers (1981) recognizes the importance of timing, in that he uses daily data to estimate historical volatility

---

[5] LR, in fact, made no adjustment for dividend payout. CM corrected this mistake by using Merton's continuous-payout European call formula. Beckers, recognizing the problem posed by the possibility of early exercise, adopted an ad hoc adjustment to the European formula.

[6] For example, in LR's study of option prices from October 1973 through June 1974, historical volatility was computed from four years of monthly data ending at the beginning of the sample period. This long time period with sparsely distributed monthly data contrasts with the one to six months of daily data that options traders typically use to compute historical volatility and makes it likely that the estimates were contaminated by stale data. CM also used monthly data, but only from the 24 months immediately preceding the date of the option price. However, in trying to establish the relative forecasting accuracy of historical volatility versus implied volatility, both LR and CM computed "realized" volatility figures for time periods that did not match option maturities. In fact, one of LR's realized volatility series included stock prices observed six months prior to the first option price in their sample.

The Review of Financial Studies / v 6 n 3 1993

from the previous three months of stock prices and realized volatility over the period from the observation date to option expiration.

Recent papers by Day and Lewis (1990) (DL) and Lamoureux and Lastrapes (1993) (LL) also examine implied volatility as a source of information. Both studies find that IV contributes a statistically significant amount of information about volatility over the (short-term) forecasting horizon covered by the models, but they also find that IV does not fully impound the information that the model is able to extract from historical prices. LL also examine forecasting volatility through option expiration and find that IV alone is less accurate than the models that incorporate historical prices in 8 out of 10 cases.

2. Data and Methodology

The data sample is drawn from the set of closing prices for all call options on the OEX index from March 15, 1983, shortly after index option trading opened, through March 28, 1987. We eliminated options with fewer than 7 or more than 127 days to expiration and those that were more than 20 points in- or out-of-the-money.[7] Also, some of the recorded option prices violated the lower arbitrage boundary—that the call price should be greater than the current stock price minus the present value of the strike price plus future dividends. An option's price equals the boundary value if volatility is zero. In the case of a boundary violation, implied variance would have to be negative, so those options were also excluded from the sample. This left a total of 17,606 observations. At the outset, there were contracts traded for two expiration dates, September and December 1983. Starting in December 1983, the expiration cycle was changed so that there were always one-, two-, three-, and four-month maturities.

These are American options, and the OEX index portfolio contains mostly dividend-paying stocks. To take into account the value of early exercise, we used a binomial model with 500 time steps,[8] a very fine grid size (e.g., 10 steps per day for an option with 50 days to expiration). In selecting a measure of the riskless interest rate, we have tried to take into account both the relevant lending and borrowing rates faced by options traders. Instead of Treasury-bill rates, we used the average of the Eurodollar deposit rate and the broker call rate on each date. We treated dividends as if future payouts were known, and

---

[7] Note that the level of the OEX index was over 200 for most of the sample period, so an option with a strike price 20 points away from the current level of the index is not actually very far in- or out-of-the-money in percentage terms.

[8] In fact, because the dividend stream on the OEX index portfolio is much less lumpy than that of an individual stock, rational early exercise is unlikely, and American option values are quite close to those derived from the dividend-adjusted Black–Scholes European option formula.

Table 1
Summary statistics of implied volatility by maturity group

Maturity group (i)	Days to expiration	Number of obs	IV mean	Sample standard deviation
All		17,606	0.168	0.055
1	7–35	4,088	0.195	0.080
2	29–63	5,196	0.166	0.046
3	57–98	4,709	0.158	0.039
4	85–127	3,613	0.152	0.035

The table shows the breakdown of implied volatilities for OEX call options between March 15, 1983, and March 28, 1987, into four maturity groups corresponding to the number of contract months to expiration. For example, the first group ($i = 1$) contains the near-month options. The rightmost columns give the mean and the standard deviation of implied volatilities within each group.

we used the actual stream of dividends paid over the option's life. Annualized implied volatilities were then calculated to the nearest 0.001 by an iterative search procedure.

On each date, there are prices, and therefore implied volatilities, for many different options. We find that the IVs for OEX options observed at a given point in time vary systematically across the different strikes and maturity months, where maturity month refers to the near-, second-, third-, and fourth-month expiration dates. This regular cross-sectional structure is illustrated in Tables 1 and 2 and Figures 1 and 2 for subsamples of the data, broken up according to maturity month and the extent to which the options are in- or out-of-the-money.

The extent to which the options are in- or out-of-the-money is simply $S - X$, the current level of the index minus the option's strike price. To save space we will hereafter refer to this quantity as the

Table 2
Summary statistics of implied volatility by intrinsic-value group

Group (j)	Intrinsic value	Number of obs	Mean	Standard deviation
All		17,606	0.168	0.055
1	−20--15.01	1,800	0.167	0.038
2	−15--10.01	2,761	0.158	0.034
3	−10--5.01	3,069	0.154	0.034
4	−5--0.01	3,093	0.155	0.036
5	0–5	2,907	0.158	0.043
6	5.01–10	2,127	0.179	0.058
7	10.01–15	1,230	0.209	0.082
8	15.01–20	619	0.263	0.121

The table shows the breakdown of implied volatilities for OEX call options between March 15, 1983, and March 28, 1987, into eight intrinsic-value groups corresponding to the amount the option is in- or out-of-the-money. For example, the first group ($j = 1$) contains the options that are between 15 and 20 points out-of-the-money. The rightmost columns give the mean and the standard deviation of implied volatilities within each group.

The Review of Financial Studies / v 6 n 3 1993

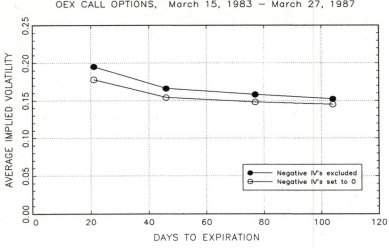

Figure 1
Implied volatility vs. time to expiration OEX call options, March 15, 1983–March 27, 1987

option's "intrinsic value," although this usage is somewhat unconventional (because it takes negative values for out-of-the-money options).

Table 1 shows that the average implied volatility in the sample is a decreasing function of time-to-option expiration. The mean for the entire set of 17,606 observations is 0.168, while the averages for our four maturity groups decline monotonically from 0.195, for near-month options, to 0.152, for those expiring in the fourth month.

Latané and Rendleman (1976) pioneered the practice of forming a weighted-average implied standard deviation (WISD) using multiple options on the same stock. This makes sense if the only reason IVs for two options on the same asset will differ is random noise in the sampling process. But with time-varying volatility, options expiring on different dates may reasonably be priced using different volatilities. Other differences are often observed, such as a regular structure of IVs across strike prices for options with a given maturity, and these constitute evidence against the hypothesis that IV is the market's fully rational volatility forecast.[9] Regularity in IV differences suggests

---

[9] That there seems to be a systematic structure to implied volatilities is quite well known. For example, the observed "overpricing" of deep-out-of-the-money options has given rise to numerous theories and articles over the years. Rubinstein (1985) provides an extensive analysis of implied volatilities from individual stocks that reveals several regular patterns. A pattern observed in a number of markets, that of IVs that are lowest at-the-money and become progressively higher the further the option is in- or out-of-the-money, is known to traders as the "smile."

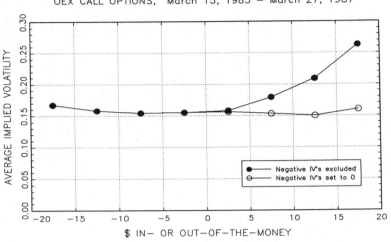

IMPLIED VOLATILITY VS INTRINSIC VALUE
OEX CALL OPTIONS, March 15, 1983 — March 27, 1987

Figure 2
Implied volatility vs. intrinsic value OEX call options, March 15, 1983–March 27, 1987

the existence of *systematic* factors that lead investors to price particular options high or low relative to others.[10] It is therefore inappropriate simply to average together IVs from options with different
expirations or IVs measured on different dates as if they were just
multiple noisy observations on the same parameter.[11]

The most striking result in Table 2 is that deep in-the-money calls
appear to have much higher IVs than at-the-money options. Beckers
also finds this pattern in his study of individual stock options. In his
sample, IVs for deep-in-the-money near-to-expiration calls are as much
as 10 times the IVs for the corresponding at-the-money options. One
explanation for this phenomenon is that in constructing the sample
we were obliged to exclude the calls that would have negative IVs
because their prices violated the lower boundary. Deep-in-the-money
options are quite insensitive to volatility, meaning a large change in
the implied volatility is produced by a small change in the option's

---

[10] Using a careful analysis of transactions data, Harvey and Whaley (1992) also find several interesting
regularities in the time pattern of implied volatilities drawn from OEX options, including a day-
of-the-week effect. Call IVs are low on Fridays and high on Mondays, but puts do not show the
same pattern.

[11] LR, for example, computed their WISDs, one per week, and then averaged them over the whole
39-week sample period into a single IV for each stock. By contrast, Beckers found the IV drawn
from a single at-the-money option to be at least as accurate a predictor of future volatility as the
weighted-average IV.

The Review of Financial Studies / v 6 n 3 1993

price. At the same time, these options are rather illiquid, and they trade less frequently than those nearer to the money, so they have wider bid–ask spreads and nonsynchronous data is a larger problem. Thus, there is relatively more "noise" in the prices of these calls, and apparent boundary violations are most frequent for them. In forming our sample, we are potentially introducing a bias by keeping calls whose prices were artificially high due to trading noise but eliminating them when noise drove their prices below the boundary.

To see how this bias might affect the results, we constructed a broader sample including the calls that violated the boundary and arbitrarily assigned them an IV of 0. The second curves in Figures 1 and 2 plot the results from this procedure. Figure 2 shows how this alters the estimates of mean IVs for the deep-in-the-money calls and brings them much closer to the values observed for the other option groups. We suspect that Beckers' results may also be partly due to eliminating option prices that violated the lower arbitrage boundary.

When the market prices embody a regular volatility structure that seems to reflect systematic factors other than predicted future volatility, we do not know which option's IV, if any, represents the market's true expectation. It is also clear that simply averaging different IVs together would contaminate our estimate of the market's volatility forecast with price effects relating to those other factors. Accordingly, we subdivide the sample into groups, which we analyze separately, according to maturity and intrinsic value. This allows us to test whether any group of options, such as those that are at-the-money and near to expiration, provides a more useful IV.

The sample is broken into four maturity groups, and each of those is divided into eight intrinsic-value groups. This produces 32 subsamples, which we denote as subsample (i, j), where i represents the maturity group and j the intrinsic value group. For example, subsample $(1, 2)$—maturity group 1 and intrinsic-value group 2—contains implied volatilities for the near-month options that are between 15 and 10 points out-of-the-money. The subsample break points are displayed in Tables 1 and 2. Break points for the intrinsic value groups are set 5 points apart, corresponding to the contract strike prices. Since options expire on the third Friday of the delivery month, the near-month calls may have up to 35 days to expiration, while in other months the second-month options might mature in as few as 29 days.[12] Our subsamples are constructed such that each contains a maximum of one option price per day.

Equation (3) is estimated separately for each subgroup. We rewrite

[12] Technically, expiration is on the Saturday following the third Friday, but since Friday is the last date the options can be traded and their payoffs are based on Friday's closing stock prices, expiration is effectively at the close on the third Friday.

(3) to bring out its dependence on maturity, intrinsic value, and the time period:

$$\sigma_t(\tau) = \alpha + \beta \cdot IV_t(i, j) + u_{t,i,j}, \tag{5}$$

where $IV_t(i, j)$ is the implied volatility computed at time t from the option in maturity group i and intrinsic-value group j, and $u_{t,i,j}$ represents the regression disturbance. The symbol $\sigma_t(\tau)$ is the realized volatility of returns over the period between t and $t + \tau$, the option's expiration date, annualized by multiplying the calculated volatility per trading day by $\sqrt{260}$. In the tests reported here, the realized volatility $\sigma_t(\tau)$ is computed over the remaining life of the option as the annualized sample standard deviation of log returns including cash dividends; that is, $\ln[(S_s + D_s)/S_{s-1}]$ for $t < s \le t + \tau$.

As long as the regressors and disturbances are uncorrelated with one another, the least-squares estimates of α and β will be unbiased and consistent. However, when daily data are used, the disturbances $u_{t,i,j}$ will be serially correlated. Since the realized volatility involves each day's return, from $t + 1$ to expiration at $t + \tau$, $\sigma_t(\tau)$ is only fully known on the day after the expiration date. The forecast errors are therefore correlated for IVs computed from any pair of options whose remaining lifetimes overlap.

Define X_n as the row vector of the independent variables for observation n in the sample; that is, $X_n = (1 \quad IV)_n$. X is the $N \times 2$ matrix of the X_n. [X is $N \times 3$ for regressions based on Equation (4).] Let u_n be the regression error for observation n, and let u denote the N vector of the u_n. Following Hansen (1982), we compute

$$\hat{\Psi} = N^{-1} \sum_{n=1}^{N} (\hat{u}_n)^2 X_n' X_n$$

$$+ N^{-1} \sum_{k=1}^{N} \sum_{n=k+1}^{N} Q(k, n) \hat{u}_k \hat{u}_n (X_n' X_k + X_k' X_n), \tag{6}$$

where u_k and u_n are the fitted residuals for observations k and n from the OLS regression. $Q(k, n)$ is an indicator function taking the value 1 if there is an overlap between the periods to expiration for the two options, and 0 otherwise.

The estimated covariance matrix for the coefficients is

$$\hat{\Omega} = (X'X)^{-1} \hat{\Psi} (X'X)^{-1}. \tag{7}$$

The procedure we have just described is consistent, but a question remains as to its performance in small samples (and how large a sample has to be before it is no longer "small"). Another important question is how much statistical power is gained by making use of

The Review of Financial Studies / v 6 n 3 1993

all available data rather than restricting the analysis to nonoverlapping observations. The Appendix describes the results of a simulation study with a data sample constructed to be like the one we examine here. We find the corrected standard errors to be reasonably close to the true values. Moreover, incorporating the overlapping data points leads to a standard error on the β coefficient between one-quarter and one-eighth of what would be obtained with only nonoverlapping data, depending on the option maturity.

3. The Forecasting Performance of Implied Volatility

To test the predictive power of implied volatility, the regression equation (5) was fitted separately for each of the 32 subsamples. The equations were estimated by OLS, and for hypothesis testing the consistent estimate of the coefficient covariance matrix, shown in Equations (6) and (7), was computed.

The results are presented in Table 3 by subsample. For example, for the subsample of options that expire in the second month ($i = 2$) that are between \$0 and \$5 out-of-the-money ($j = 4$), the intercept is 0.113 and the estimated slope coefficient is 0.163, with standard errors of 0.017 and 0.101, respectively. The adjusted R^2 is .053. Thus, the hypothesis that $\alpha = 0$ and $\beta = 1.0$, and implied volatility is an unbiased forecast of future realized volatility, is strongly rejected for this subsample.

The results obtained for subsample (2, 4) are representative of what we find generally in Table 3: in every subsample, implied volatility fails the unbiasedness test. Indeed, the slope coefficient is estimated to be significantly different from *zero* at the 5 percent significance level in only 6 out of the 32 subsamples, and 3 of these were negative. In the group of three significant positives, the coefficient on implied volatility ranged from 0.138 to 0.229, and the adjusted R^2 was between .035 and .067. Far from demonstrating that implied volatility in OEX options is an unbiased and efficient forecast of subsequent realized volatility, these results show that, in most cases, implied volatility has no statistically significant correlation with realized volatility at all.

We do see that the options that are expected to be the most efficiently priced—those that are at- or slightly out-of-the-money (intrinsic-value groups 3, 4, and 5) and near to expiration (maturity group 1)—do produce significant positive β's and some of the highest R^2's. Nevertheless, the results in Table 3 appear to constitute a strong rejection of the null hypothesis.

However, it could be that OEX volatility is just very hard to predict accurately. In that case, the market's information set simply contains very little useful information for predicting $\sigma_t(\tau)$, and the estimation

Informational Content of Implied Volatility

Table 3
Realized volatility over the remaining life of the option regressed on implied volatility:
Equation (5) $\sigma_t(\tau) = \alpha + \beta \cdot IV_t(i, j) + u_{t,i,j}$

Maturity group	Intrinsic value							
	−20 to −15.01, $j = 1$	−15 to −10.01, $j = 2$	−10 to −5.01, $j = 3$	−5 to −0.01, $j = 4$	0 to 5.00, $j = 5$	5.01 to 10, $j = 6$	10.01 to 15, $j = 7$	15.01 to 20, $j = 8$
Maturity $i = 1$; $\tau = 7$ to 35								
α	0.152	0.125	0.101	0.098	0.113	0.143	0.158	0.161
SE	0.026	0.019	0.015	0.013	0.011	0.012	0.014	0.012
β	−0.063	0.065	0.205	0.229	0.138	−0.025	−0.070	−0.047
SE	0.104	0.087	0.080	0.069	0.058	0.045	0.042	0.028
R^2	.004	.003	.044	.067	.035	.000	.032	.037
N	336	611	691	697	675	513	343	222
Maturity $i = 2$; $\tau = 29$ to 63								
α	0.125	0.111	0.109	0.113	0.123	0.143	0.161	0.182
SE	0.027	0.020	0.018	0.017	0.016	0.016	0.014	0.015
β	0.110	0.178	0.188	0.163	0.102	−0.020	−0.100	−0.171
SE	0.143	0.109	0.099	0.101	0.084	0.070	0.054	0.060
R^2	.010	.049	.062	.053	.025	.000	.055	.197
N	564	792	851	852	836	685	407	209
Maturity $i = 3$; $\tau = 57$ to 98								
α	0.116	0.112	0.112	0.118	0.127	0.143	0.162	0.176
SE	0.024	0.024	0.021	0.018	0.017	0.017	0.013	0.009
β	0.171	0.191	0.188	0.144	0.081	−0.015	−0.108	−0.157
SE	0.138	0.143	0.125	0.110	0.093	0.080	0.053	0.070
R^2	.038	.062	.070	.046	.019	−.001	.061	.147
N	507	731	803	810	789	593	324	152
Maturity $i = 4$; $\tau = 85$ to 127								
α	0.135	0.120	0.121	0.131	0.139	0.154	0.155	0.159
SE	0.026	0.022	0.019	0.017	0.016	0.016	0.015	0.010
β	0.060	0.138	0.129	0.062	0.002	−0.093	−0.075	−0.084
SE	0.155	0.136	0.121	0.109	0.102	0.072	0.046	0.044
R^2	.002	.033	.035	.009	−.002	.031	.022	.019
N	393	627	724	734	607	336	156	36

The table reports regression results from Equation (5) for OEX call options between March 15, 1983, and March 28, 1987, for each of the 32 subsamples defined by maturity and intrinsic value. The coefficients are fitted by OLS, but the standard errors (labeled SE) are corrected for intercorrelation as described in Section 2. N is the number of observations in the subsample. $IV_t(i, j)$ is the implied volatility computed from the date t price of the call option from maturity group i (expiring at $t + \tau$), and intrinsic-value group j. $\sigma_t(\tau)$ is the realized volatility of the OEX index from date t to $t + \tau$. $u_{t,i,j}$ is the regression residual. The hypothesis that $IV_t(i, j)$ is an informationally efficient forecast of $\sigma_t(\tau)$ requires $\alpha = 0.0$ and $\beta = 1.0$. The hypothesis is overwhelmingly rejected in every subsample.

results are dominated by the forecast errors. In order to check whether volatility is predictable at all from data available to the market, we estimated each of the regressions by using a historical measure of volatility as the independent variable, in place of implied volatility:

$$\sigma_t(\tau) = \alpha + \beta \cdot VOL60_t(i, j) + u_{t,i,j}, \tag{8}$$

where $VOL60_t(i, j)$ is the annualized standard deviation of the log returns of the S&P 100 stock index portfolio over the 60-day period

The Review of Financial Studies / v 6 n 3 1993

preceding the date of the implied volatility, for all of the dates t corresponding to implied volatility observations contained in subsample (i, j). A 60-day sample period was used for historical volatility because it was approximately equal to the average forecast horizon in our sample, but tests using historical volatilities computed from 30 and 120 days of data yielded similar results. As before, the equation was fitted with OLS, and the covariance matrix was adjusted for heteroskedasticity and time dependence by using Equation (7).

The results are reported in Table 4. The contrast with the previous table is striking. The largest slope coefficient is 0.589, all of the estimated values are positive, and most are significantly different from zero at the 5 percent level.[13]

Table 4 shows that the future volatility of the OEX index was partly forecastable from publicly available information on historical volatility. Note, though, that the historical volatility estimate also fails the rationality test. Even so, the fact that (measured) implied volatility is a less accurate forecast than historical volatility confirms that it is not informationally efficient.

Table 5 reports the results for the "encompassing regression" test. Equation (4) in this case becomes

$$\sigma_t(\tau) = \alpha + \beta_1 \cdot \mathrm{IV}_t(i, j) + \beta_2 \cdot \mathrm{VOL60}_t(i, j) + u_{t,i,j}. \qquad (9)$$

The estimated coefficient on historical volatility in Table 5 is significantly greater than zero in most of the regressions, and its value is comparable to that in the corresponding Table 4 regression. The coefficient on IV is nowhere significantly greater than zero and is negative for 28 out of 32 subsamples. The table clearly shows the overall message of our tests—that implied volatility is a poor forecast of subsequent realized volatility, and it does not accurately impound the information contained in a readily available historical volatility estimate.

The subsamples we have analyzed so far contain a maximum of one observation per day, but the same procedure can be applied equally well to the case in which there is any number of observations per day. This allows estimation on more aggregated samples without the loss of information that occurs when the data points themselves are aggregated, as they are in forming WISDs.

---

[13] Note that since neither realized nor historical volatility is a function of option intrinsic value, the differences among the eight regressions reported for each maturity group in Table 4 are due only to the differences in the dates whose observations are included in the subsamples. Nearly identical sample composition leads to nearly identical regressions, as in subsamples (2, 3) and (2, 4). There is a small amount of regularity in the differences among subsamples, because the options exchange tends not to introduce options at strikes far below the current index. This means there will only be deep-in-the-money options when the market price has risen substantially after listing. This results in a lower average τ for intrinsic-value groups 7 and 8 (52.9 and 45.8 days, respectively, compared with an average τ of between 59.8 and 61.8 days for intrinsic-value groups 1 to 6).

Table 4

Realized volatility over the remaining life of the option regressed on historical volatility:
Equation (8) $\sigma_t(\tau) = \alpha + \beta \cdot \text{VOL60}_t(i, j) + u_{t,i,j}$

Maturity group	Intrinsic value							
	−20 to −15.01, $j = 1$	−15 to −10.01, $j = 2$	−10 to −5.01, $j = 3$	−5 to −0.01, $j = 4$	0 to 5.00, $j = 5$	5.01 to 10, $j = 6$	10.01 to 15, $j = 7$	15.01 to 20, $j = 8$
Maturity $i = 1$; $\tau = 7$ to 35								
α	0.070	0.058	0.054	0.055	0.057	0.063	0.056	0.104
SE	0.037	0.025	0.023	0.023	0.025	0.028	0.031	0.040
β	0.483	0.556	0.576	0.573	0.562	0.521	0.573	0.270
SE	0.272	0.180	0.172	0.172	0.181	0.196	0.212	0.255
R^2	.059	.106	.119	.118	.108	.087	.094	.016
N	336	611	691	697	675	513	343	222
Maturity $i = 2$; $\tau = 29$ to 63								
α	0.088	0.078	0.074	0.074	0.074	0.068	0.075	0.085
SE	0.027	0.024	0.024	0.024	0.025	0.027	0.033	0.042
β	0.381	0.441	0.464	0.464	0.467	0.499	0.453	0.394
SE	0.181	0.166	0.165	0.165	0.170	0.185	0.218	0.268
R^2	.085	.132	.151	.151	.150	.158	.117	.064
N	564	792	851	852	836	685	407	209
Maturity $i = 3$; $\tau = 57$ to 98								
α	0.091	0.079	0.078	0.078	0.077	0.073	0.069	0.091
SE	0.029	0.029	0.028	0.028	0.029	0.032	0.033	0.041
β	0.367	0.439	0.445	0.444	0.454	0.478	0.504	0.368
SE	0.188	0.193	0.191	0.192	0.193	0.211	0.218	0.266
R^2	.112	.183	.188	.186	.190	.203	.197	.063
N	507	731	803	810	789	593	324	152
Maturity $i = 4$; $\tau = 85$ to 127								
α	0.091	0.077	0.077	0.078	0.071	0.067	0.059	0.108
SE	0.033	0.027	0.026	0.026	0.026	0.029	0.031	0.033
β	0.367	0.459	0.455	0.446	0.497	0.522	0.589	0.242
SE	0.207	0.174	0.171	0.176	0.178	0.202	0.221	0.223
R^2	.105	.208	.220	.212	.240	.240	.286	.000
N	393	627	724	734	607	336	156	36

The table reports regression results from Equation (8) for OEX call options between March 15, 1983, and March 28, 1987, for each of the 32 subsamples defined by maturity and intrinsic value. The coefficients are fitted by OLS, but the standard errors (labeled SE) are corrected for intercorrelation as described in Section 2. N is the number of observations in the subsample. $\text{VOL60}_t(i, j)$ is the historical volatility computed from the OEX index values on dates $t - 60$ to $t - 1$. Each $\text{VOL60}_t(i, j)$ subsample is set up to match the corresponding $\text{IV}_t(i, j)$ subsample in Table 3. That is, for each IV in subsample (i, j) of Table 3, subsample (i, j) of Table 4 contains the historical volatility estimated from the previous 60 days' prices. $\sigma_t(\tau)$ is the realized volatility of the OEX index from date t to $t + \tau$. $u_{t,i,j}$ is the regression residual. The hypothesis that $\text{VOL60}_t(i, j)$ is an informationally efficient forecast of $\sigma_t(\tau)$ requires $\alpha = 0.0$ and $\beta = 1.0$. The hypothesis is rejected in every subsample.

We have applied this procedure to fit Equation (5) on more aggregated samples of our data. Using the entire data sample in one grand regression ($i = 1,...,4$ and $j = 1,...,8$) yields

$$\hat{\sigma}_t(\tau) = \underset{(0.012)}{0.136} + \underset{(0.050)}{0.022} \cdot \text{IV}_t(i, j), \qquad \begin{array}{l} N = 17{,}606 \\ R^2 = .002 \end{array}$$

and Table 6 shows the results of aggregating across maturity and

Financial Forecasting II

The Review of Financial Studies / v 6 n 3 1993

Table 5
Realized volatility over the remaining life of the option regressed on implied volatility and historical volatility: Equation (9) $\sigma_t(\tau) = \alpha + \beta_1 \cdot IV_t(i, j) + \beta_2 \cdot VOL60_t(i, j) + u_{t,i,j}$

	Intrinsic value							
Maturity group	−20 to −15.01, $j = 1$	−15 to −10.01, $j = 2$	−10 to −5.01, $j = 3$	−5 to −0.01, $j = 4$	0 to 5.00, $j = 5$	5.01 to 10, $j = 6$	10.01 to 15, $j = 7$	15.01 to 20, $j = 8$
Maturity $i = 1$; $\tau = 7$ to 35								
α	0.082	0.061	0.053	0.055	0.056	0.069	0.076	0.120
SE	0.039	0.023	0.022	0.023	0.024	0.025	0.031	0.039
β_1	−0.056	−0.022	0.043	0.077	0.038	−0.024	−0.063	−0.048
SE	0.097	0.087	0.106	0.100	0.070	0.041	0.038	0.027
β_2	0.478	0.567	0.488	0.488	0.522	0.521	0.554	0.275
SE	0.272	0.204	0.241	0.241	0.223	0.198	0.210	0.253
R^2	.062	.105	.119	.122	.109	.087	.120	.054
N	336	611	691	697	675	513	343	222
Maturity $i = 2$; $\tau = 29$ to 63								
α	0.092	0.078	0.074	0.074	0.074	0.075	0.095	0.122
SE	0.030	0.024	0.024	0.024	0.024	0.029	0.035	0.026
β_1	−0.062	−0.010	0.001	−0.008	−0.026	−0.061	−0.100	−0.174
SE	0.142	0.122	0.106	0.097	0.080	0.050	0.045	0.052
β_2	0.423	0.451	0.473	0.473	0.492	0.529	0.451	0.416
SE	0.197	0.206	0.203	0.203	0.196	0.192	0.236	0.198
R^2	.086	.131	.150	.150	.150	.171	.172	.270
N	564	792	851	852	836	685	407	209
Maturity $i = 3$; $\tau = 57$ to 98								
α	0.091	0.080	0.079	0.079	0.078	0.079	0.088	0.128
SE	0.030	0.029	0.028	0.028	0.028	0.033	0.036	0.037
β_1	−0.006	−0.040	−0.020	−0.037	−0.042	−0.066	−0.108	−0.147
SE	0.128	0.134	0.123	0.107	0.081	0.060	0.043	0.069
β_2	0.372	0.474	0.478	0.478	0.489	0.507	0.504	0.313
SE	0.208	0.224	0.230	0.230	0.217	0.216	0.228	0.259
R^2	.110	.184	.188	.187	.193	.218	.260	.191
N	507	731	803	810	789	593	324	152
Maturity $i = 4$; $\tau = 85$ to 127								
α	0.099	0.080	0.079	0.082	0.076	0.081	0.072	0.118
SE	0.033	0.025	0.024	0.024	0.023	0.025	0.029	0.034
β_1	−0.146	−0.147	−0.143	−0.152	−0.163	−0.148	−0.096	−0.096
SE	0.138	0.146	0.135	0.117	0.088	0.043	0.024	0.035
β_2	0.468	0.589	0.587	0.587	0.639	0.584	0.608	0.294
SE	0.231	0.236	0.234	0.234	0.204	0.193	0.204	0.222
R^2	.122	.229	.244	.253	.307	.320	.327	.033
N	393	627	724	734	607	336	156	36

The table reports regression results from Equation (9) for OEX call options between March 15, 1983, and March 28, 1987, for each of the 32 subsamples defined by maturity and intrinsic value. The coefficients are fitted by OLS but the standard errors (labeled SE) are corrected for intercorrelation as described in Section 2. N is the number of observations in the subsample. $IV_t(i, j)$ is the implied volatility computed from the date t price of the call option from maturity group i (expiring at $t + \tau$), and intrinsic value group j. $VOL60_t(i,j)$ is the historical volatility computed from the OEX index values on dates $t - 60$ to $t - 1$ for each observation in subsample (i, j). $\sigma_t(\tau)$ is the realized volatility of the OEX index from date t to $t + \tau$. $u_{t,i,j}$ is the regression residual. The hypothesis that $IV_t(i, j)$ is an informationally efficient forecast of $\sigma_t(\tau)$ and that it fully impounds the information contained in $VOL60_t(i, j)$ requires $\alpha = 0.0$, $\beta_1 = 1.0$, and $\beta_2 = 0.0$. In fact, the estimate for β_1 is negative in 28 out of 32 subsamples. β_2 is significantly less than 1.0 nearly everywhere, but significantly positive in most subsamples.

Table 6
Realized volatility regressed on implied volatility for samples aggregated across maturities and intrinsic values: Equation (5) $\sigma_i(\tau) = \alpha + \beta \cdot IV_j(i, f) + u_{i,j}$

Results by intrinsic-value group for all maturities (for $i = 1,...,4$)

	Intrinsic value							
	−20 to −15.01, $j = 1$	−15 to −10.01, $j = 2$	−10 to −5.01, $j = 3$	−5 to −0.01, $j = 4$	0 to 5.00, $j = 5$	5.01 to 10, $j = 6$	10.01 to 15, $j = 7$	15.01 to 20, $j = 8$
α	0.142	0.123	0.113	0.116	0.125	0.145	0.156	0.157
SE	0.017	0.019	0.017	0.015	0.014	0.014	0.013	0.011
β	0.020	0.106	0.165	0.148	0.085	−0.030	−0.072	−0.051
SE	0.075	0.094	0.093	0.083	0.073	0.056	0.038	0.026
R^2	.012	.042	.038	.025	.006	.001	.086	.065
N	1800	2761	3069	3093	2907	2127	1230	619

Results by maturity group for all intrinsic values (for $j = 1,...,8$)

	Maturity group			
	Near month 7–35 days $i = 1$	2nd month 29–63 days $i = 2$	3rd month 57–98 days $i = 3$	4th month 85–127 days $i = 4$
α	0.132	0.134	0.132	0.136
SE	0.009	0.015	0.017	0.017
β	0.025	0.037	0.056	0.032
SE	0.030	0.071	0.096	0.101
R^2	.003	.004	.009	.003
N	4088	5196	4709	3613

The table reports regression results from Equation (5) for OEX call options between March 15, 1983, and March 28, 1987. In the top panel each of the eight subsamples aggregates across all maturities within the specified intrinsic-value group, while the bottom panel aggregates across all intrinsic values within a specified maturity group. The coefficients are fitted by OLS, but the standard errors (labeled SE) are corrected for intercorrelation as described in Section 2. See the notes to Table 3 for further discussion of the variables.

intrinsic value separately. In all cases, the results only confirm what was shown in the disaggregated subsamples: implied volatility is not a rational forecast of future volatility.

One final issue that we can evaluate is whether the errors-in-variables problem caused by nonsynchronous prices can account for the results we have seen. We obtained transactions data for the time period spanned by our sample, for options with maturities in the second month ($i = 2$), and have replicated the regressions reported in Table 3. Because of small differences in the dates represented in the two data sets, we formed matching samples in the following way. On each date for which there were both transactions prices and a closing-price observation that was included in the Table 3 regression, we took the last recorded option transaction of the day prior to the NYSE close and matched it with the simultaneously observed level of the OEX index. Table 7 compares the results from estimating Equation (5) on these transactions data with those obtained from closing prices, as in Table 3. We find only small differences in the

Financial Forecasting II

The Review of Financial Studies / v 6 n 3 1993

Table 7
Realized volatility regressed on implied volatility: comparison between closing prices and transactions prices: Equation (5) $\sigma_i(\tau) = \alpha + \beta \cdot IV_i(i, j) + u_{i,j}$

	Intrinsic value							
Maturity group	-20 to -15.01, $j = 1$	-15 to -10.01, $j = 2$	-10 to -5.01, $j = 3$	-5 to -0.01, $j = 4$	0 to 5.00, $j = 5$	5.01 to 10, $j = 6$	10.01 to 15, $j = 7$	15.01 to 20, $j = 8$
	Maturity $i = 2$: Closing prices							
α	0.125	0.109	0.107	0.111	0.121	0.141	0.161	0.175
SE	0.028	0.019	0.016	0.016	0.016	0.017	0.014	0.014
β	0.108	0.193	0.190	0.170	0.114	-0.007	-0.092	-0.133
SE	0.150	0.107	0.098	0.090	0.085	0.078	0.055	0.052
R^2	.009	.056	.070	.061	.030	.001	.048	.122
N	520	733	780	778	756	607	329	161
	Maturity $i = 2$: Transactions prices							
α	0.129	0.119	0.121	0.126	0.133	0.142	0.163	0.172
SE	0.016	0.014	0.013	0.012	0.011	0.011	0.012	0.012
β	0.079	0.127	0.111	0.078	0.036	-0.008	-0.110	-0.116
SE	0.085	0.079	0.076	0.068	0.058	0.052	0.038	0.035
R^2	.009	.038	.038	.026	.008	.001	.093	.149
N	520	733	780	778	756	607	329	161

See the notes to Table 3. This table compares the results from estimating Equation (5) on recorded closing prices for the option and the index, as in Table 3, with synchronous prices drawn from transactions data. For dates during the sample period for which both transactions data and closing prices are available, we take the last trade price for the option prior to the close of the NYSE and match it with the simultaneously observed level of the OEX index.

estimated coefficients: the α's are almost identical, and the β's tend to be lower in the regressions with transactions prices. Although the standard errors are somewhat smaller with transactions data, none of the estimated β's is significantly positive and three of the eight point estimates are negative. It is evident from this table that the use of slightly nonsynchronous closing-price data does not explain the negative results we obtained before.

4. Conclusion

It is widely accepted that an option's implied volatility is a good estimate of the "market's" expectation of the asset's future volatility, but our results from a large sample of prices for the most actively traded option contract strongly refute that view. How should one interpret what we have found?

One possibility is to point to problems in the testing procedure. However, our strong belief is that despite the potential technical criticisms our procedures were reasonable and the results were so clear that further perfecting of the methodology would not change the basic conclusions. At the very least, we observe that if there is actually a strong correlation between IV and realized volatility, but it cannot be detected with this methodology, one cannot expect the normal procedure of simply computing IVs from recorded closing option prices to give useful volatility estimates.

We also tend to reject the conclusion that options traders are irrational. Although we cannot rule out irrationality entirely without independent data on market expectations, given the enormous amount of evidence that financial markets are largely efficient it would be surprising if options traders were clearly inferior to other investors in this regard.

The interpretation we favor is based on the fact that along with investors' volatility forecasts an option's market price also impounds the net effect of the many factors that influence option supply and demand but are not in the option model. These include liquidity considerations, interaction between the OEX option and the (occasionally mispriced) S&P 500 index futures contract, investor tastes for particular payoff patterns, and so on. Option pricing theories ignore such factors because, in a frictionless market, unlimited arbitrage drives the price to the model value regardless of what trading strategies other market participants follow. In the real world, however, the arbitrage between an OEX option and the underlying index is a difficult and very costly strategy that requires continuously buying and selling 100 stocks to maintain a delta neutral hedge.[14] In practice, there is little arbitrage trading of OEX options against the underlying stocks; most hedging by professionals is said to be done with S&P 500 futures. Thus, many factors can affect the price of an OEX option without inducing arbitrage to offset them, and the implied volatility will impound the net price effect of all of them.[15]

Several conclusions and conjectures result from this interpretation. One is that how accurate implied volatility is as a forecast of future volatility should be related to how easy the arbitrage trade is. Options on futures contracts are at one extreme, since they are traded on the same trading floors as the underlying futures, and transactions costs are very low.[16] At the other extreme would probably lie options on broad stock indexes like OEX and the S&P 500. In between are

---

[14] Figlewski (1989) shows in a simulation analysis that both the transactions costs and the risk borne by an arbitrageur who attempts to follow a model-based arbitrage strategy are very large, leading to wide bands around the model price within which arbitrage will not be done.

[15] Evidence that arbitrage involving stock index options is difficult to do and that "mispricings" do not seem to be easily arbitraged away is provided by Evnine and Rudd (1985). Using intraday data, they document numerous violations of arbitrage relations, including put-call parity, for both OEX and major market index options.

[16] Both Feinstein (1989) and Park and Sears (1985) present evidence that implied volatilities from stock index futures options contain a significant amount of information about futures volatility. (However, Feinstein also finds that implied volatility from S&P 500 futures options does not pass the rationality regression test.)

The Review of Financial Studies / v 6 n 3 1993

options on individual stocks, for which the arbitrage is possible but somewhat costly.

Another conclusion from our results is that since both IV and historical volatility fail the rationality test neither is an appropriate volatility forecast for OEX options. To compute the true expected value of future volatility from the information contained in stock and options prices, one must treat implied volatility as an element of the information set from which the conditional expectation will be derived and not as the conditional expectation itself. As inputs to the calculation, it is perfectly reasonable to combine both implied and historical volatilities without regard for whether either individually passes the rationality test. Moreover, since this is the way a rational economist should use OEX index options prices in forecasting future volatility, we should expect a rational investor to do the same thing. To measure the "market's" volatility estimate, therefore, we must not just take the implied volatility. We should attempt to compute the true conditional expectation of the future volatility from the market's information set.

Appendix

This Appendix reports Monte Carlo simulation results that allow us to evaluate the performance of the estimation procedure from two perspectives. We would like to know, first, how close the corrected standard errors are likely to be to the true values and, second, how much additional statistical power is gained by using all of the available daily data in the estimation rather than restricting the analysis to nonoverlapping observations.

We generated random series of returns, designed to look as much as possible like the actual data in our sample of OEX returns. First, the sample mean and volatility of the OEX index, μ_k and σ_k, were computed for each calendar month k in our data. Then a random series of returns R_t was created for that month by using Equation (A1):

$$R_t = \mu_k + \sigma_k z_t, \tag{A1}$$

where z_t represents a random draw from a standard normal distribution, and μ_k and σ_k are the mean and volatility of returns, here expressed in terms of their values per trading day. This process was repeated month by month until a return for each day in the sample had been generated. Then for each day the "realized" volatility of the simulated series was computed from that point to the expiration date for the option maturity being considered, exactly as we did with the actual OEX returns.

The results we obtained in the analysis of actual prices suggested virtually no connection between IV and subsequent realized volatility.

Table A1
Monte Carlo simulations of estimated coefficient standard errors for different procedures

Maturity	$i = 1$		$i = 2$		$i = 3$		$i = 4$	
	α	β	α	β	α	β	α	β
Overlapping Sample								
True standard deviation	0.0208	0.1285	0.0186	0.1174	0.0176	0.1122	0.0153	0.1023
OLS std errors								
Mean	0.0062	0.0377	0.0045	0.0284	0.0041	0.0262	0.0039	0.0263
Standard dev	0.0008	0.0047	0.0006	0.0040	0.0007	0.0040	0.0006	0.0042
Corrected std errors								
Mean	0.0202	0.1214	0.0173	0.1031	0.0159	0.0927	0.0142	0.0811
Standard dev	0.0040	0.0237	0.0047	0.0279	0.0053	0.0310	0.0053	0.0308
Nonoverlapping Sample								
True standard deviation	0.0139	0.4770	0.0178	0.6989	0.0205	0.7934	0.0190	0.7840
OLS std errors								
Mean	0.0145	0.4729	0.0181	0.6827	0.0207	0.7609	0.0193	0.7446
Standard dev	0.0020	0.0763	0.0038	0.1463	0.0046	0.1974	0.0055	0.2496

The table presents summary results on the estimated coefficient standard errors from regressions like Equation (5): $\sigma_r(\tau) = \alpha + \beta \cdot IV_r(i, j) + u_{i,j}$, for intrinsic-value group 4 (at- to 5 points out-of-the-money), run on 10,000 simulated returns series. See the Appendix for details of the sample construction. The "overlapping sample" makes use of all simulated data points, while the "nonoverlapping sample" restricts the sample to only observations for which the periods to option expiration do not overlap. "True standard deviation" is the sample standard deviation of the estimated parameter across the 10,000 regressions. "OLS std errors" are uncorrected for correlation in the residuals, while "corrected std errors" are corrected by using the methodology described in Section 2. "Mean" and "standard dev" refer to the sample average and standard deviation of the standard error estimates across the 10,000 regressions.

To create a simulated IV series with the same distributional characteristics as the actual IVs but having no correlation with the simulated volatilities, we simply chose randomly from the set of observed IVs for intrinsic-value group 4 (at- to slightly-out-of-the-money). To maintain the same pattern of serial correlation among the IVs as is present in the actual data, we carried out the selection in batches, as follows. For the first observation pertaining to a given expiration date, we randomly chose an IV for an option with the same number of days to maturity from the data sample. The IVs were then taken in order from the sample of actual IVs until a new expiration date was called for, at which point another random selection was made. In essence, this procedure randomly selects about one month of observations at a time from the series of actual IVs.

The series of realized volatilities computed from the simulated returns was then regressed on the series of randomly selected implied volatilities in two ways, first with the full sample of overlapping observations as we did in the paper and, again, using only nonoverlapping observations. OLS standard errors were calculated for both cases, and the corrected standard errors were computed for the overlapping

The Review of Financial Studies / v 6 n 3 1993

sample. The coefficient estimates were also recorded so that their true standard deviations across simulations could be computed. This process was repeated 10,000 times for each maturity group, $i = 1, 2, 3, 4$.

Table A1 shows the results. For each maturity group, we show the standard errors on the two regression coefficients. The first line gives the true standard deviations of the coefficient estimates across the 10,000 regressions. For example, for the second maturity group the true standard error of the estimate of β was 0.1174. Next we show the uncorrected OLS results, both the average values for the estimated standard errors and the sample standard deviations of those estimates in the 10,000 regressions. With no adjustment, the OLS estimates are severely biased downward and show very little variability across regressions. The next lines show that the corrected standard errors are much closer to the true values on average (e.g., 0.1031 versus the true value of 0.1174 for β in the second maturity group), although they are still slightly downward biased and also somewhat variable across regressions. These results give us confidence that the standard error correction procedure we used is effective in removing the effect of cross-correlation in the residuals.

The lower portion of Table A1 reveals how much more accurate the coefficients estimated from the overlapping data are compared with those computed by using only nonoverlapping observations from the same data sample. To run these regressions, we took only nonoverlapping data points for 18, 40, 75, and 100 days to expiration for maturity groups 1, 2, 3, and 4, respectively. Although there is little difference in the accuracy with which the regression constant is estimated, there is a large increase in the true standard errors for the slope coefficients, up to a factor of about 8 for maturity group 4. Because there is no cross-correlation in the residuals, the OLS standard error estimates are consistent for this case, as is apparent in the table. Notice, however, that even in this case where the true slope coefficient is zero by construction and we have four years of data, the standard errors that come out of the nonoverlapping regressions are so large that if the estimate of the slope coefficient turned out to be 0.0 it would still be impossible to reject the hypothesis that $\beta = 1.0$ for any but the first maturity group, and only a marginal rejection would be possible there!

References

Beckers, S., 1981, "Standard Deviations Implied in Option Prices as Predictors of Future Stock Price Variability," *Journal of Banking and Finance*, 5, 363–381.

Brown, B. W., and S. Maital, 1981, "What Do Economists Know? An Empirical Study of Experts' Expectations," *Econometrica*, 49, 491–504.

Chiras, D. P., and S. Manaster, 1978, "The Information Content of Option Prices and a Test of Market Efficiency," *Journal of Financial Economics,* 6, 213–234.

Day, T. E., and C. M. Lewis, 1990, "Stock Market Volatility and the Information Content of Stock Index Options," *Journal of Econometrics,* 52, 267–287.

Evnine, J., and A. Rudd, 1985, "Index Options: The Early Evidence," *Journal of Finance,* 40, 743–756.

Fair, R. C., and R. J. Shiller, 1990, "Comparing Information in Forecasts from Econometric Models," *American Economic Review,* 80, 375–389.

Feinstein, S., 1989, "Bias, Forecast Efficiency, and Information in the Black–Scholes Implied Volatility," Working Paper, Yale School of Management.

Figlewski, S., 1989, "Options Arbitrage in Imperfect Markets," *Journal of Finance,* 44, 1289–1311.

Hansen, L. P., 1982, "Large Sample Properties of Generalized Method of Moments Estimators," *Econometrica,* 50, 1029–1054.

Harvey, C. R., and R. E. Whaley, 1992, "Market Volatility Estimation and the Pricing of S&P 100 Options," *Journal of Financial Economics,* 31, 43–73.

Hull, J., and A. White, 1987, "The Pricing of Options on Assets with Stochastic Volatilities," *Journal of Finance,* 42, 281–300.

Lamoureux, C. G., and W. D. Lastrapes, 1993, "Forecasting Stock Return Variance: Toward an Understanding of Stochastic Implied Volatilities," *Review of Financial Studies,* 6, 293–326.

Latané, H. A., and R. J. Rendleman, 1976, "Standard Deviations of Stock Price Ratios Implied in Option Prices," *Journal of Finance,* 31, 369–381.

Park, H. Y., and R. S. Sears, 1985, "Estimating Stock Index Futures Volatility through the Prices of their Options," *Journal of Futures Markets,* 5, 223–237.

Patell, J. M., and M. A. Wolfson, 1979, "Anticipated Information Releases Reflected in Call Option Prices," *Journal of Accounting and Economics,* 1, 117–140.

Patell, J. M., and M. A. Wolfson, 1981, "The Ex Ante and Ex Post Price Effects of Quarterly Earnings Announcements Reflected in Option and Stock Prices," *Journal of Accounting Research,* 2, 434–458.

Pesando, J. E., 1975, "A Note on the Rationality of the Livingston Price Expectations," *Journal of Political Economy,* 83, 849–858.

Poterba, J. M., and L. Summers, 1986, "The Persistence of Volatility and Stock Market Fluctuations," *American Economic Review,* 76, 1142–1151.

Rubinstein, M., 1985, "Nonparametric Tests of Alternative Option Pricing Models Using All Reported Trades and Quotes on the 30 Most Active CBOE Option Classes from August 23, 1976 through August 3, 1978," *Journal of Finance,* 40, 455–480.

Stein, J., 1989, "Overreactions in the Options Market," *Journal of Finance,* 44, 1011–1023.

Theil, H., 1966, *Applied Economic Forecasting,* North-Holland, Amsterdam, chap. 2.

Wiggins, J., 1987, "Option Values under Stochastic Volatility: Theory and Empirical Estimates," *Journal of Financial Economics,* 19, 351–372.

[27]

ELSEVIER   Journal of Banking & Finance 19 (1995) 803–821

Journal of
BANKING &
FINANCE

Conditional volatility and the informational efficiency of the PHLX currency options market

Xinzhong Xu [a,*], Stephen J. Taylor [b]

[a] *Department of Accounting and Finance, University of Manchester, Manchester M13 9PL, UK*
[b] *Department of Accounting and Finance, Lancaster University, Lancaster LA1 4YX, UK*

Received January 1993; final version received November 1993

Abstract

The relative performance of implied and historical volatility predictors is compared for four exchange rates from 1985 to 1991. For three currencies, ARCH models estimated up to 1989 show that PHLX implied volatilities provide specifications for daily conditional variances which can not be significantly improved by using past returns. This result is consistent with the informational efficiency of the Philadelphia currency options market. Out-of-sample forecasts of the average volatility over four-week periods are evaluated for 1990 and 1991. Once more the implied predictors are superior to historical predictors.

Keywords: ARCH models; Forecasting; Informational efficiency; Options; Volatility

JEL classification: G13; G14

1. Introduction

Options markets are often viewed as markets for volatility trading. Options prices provide forecasts of the future average variance of returns from the underlying asset over the life of the option. The ability of the volatility forecast implied by options prices to predict future volatility is considered a measure of the

---

* Corresponding author. Tel. 44 161 275 4030, Fax 44 161 275 4023.

information content of option prices (Day and Lewis, 1992a). Until recently most research into information content has focused on relationships between implied volatility and measures of the subsequent realised volatility (Latane and Rendleman, 1976; Chiras and Manaster, 1978; Gemmill 1986; Shastri and Tandon, 1986; Scott and Tucker, 1989). This prior research concludes that volatility predictors calculated from option prices are better predictors of future volatility than standard deviations calculated from historical asset price data. However, Canina and Figlewski (1993) claim that neither implied volatilities nor historical volatilities have much predictive power for the S&P 100 index.

Day and Lewis (1992a) develop a new methodology based upon ARCH models. They examine the information content of implied volatilities, obtained from call options on the S&P 100 index, relative to ARCH estimates of conditional volatility by adding the implied volatility to ARCH models as an exogenous variable. They find that both implied volatility and historical series of asset returns contain incremental information. The null hypothesis that returns contain no volatility information additional to that found in options prices is rejected. Likewise, the hypothesis that options prices have no additional information is rejected. These results imply that the US stock options market either does not use all publicly available information in setting options prices or that the dividend-adjusted version of the Black–Scholes formula used for computing implied volatility is misspecified. Similar results have been found by Day and Lewis (1992b) for the conditional volatility of oil futures and by Lamoureux and Lastrapes (1993) for the conditional volatility of individual stocks. However, it should be noted that these ARCH tests might be unreliable because the implied volatility variable used in the tests is not necessarily appropriate. The ARCH conditional volatility is always for the next period, typically the next day or week. As an implied volatility for the next period rarely exists, Day and Lewis (1992a) use implied volatilities obtained from options having short times to maturity, which range from 7 to 36 days. The implied volatilities used by Lamoureux and Lastrapes (1993) correspond to maturities of between 64 and 129 trading days. It is known that implied volatilities at any moment in time vary for different times to option expiry. This term structure of volatility expectations has been ignored in previous applications of ARCH methodology. This paper includes an empirical evaluation of whether or not this methodological issue is important.

The relative importance of implied and historical volatility predictors is examined once more in this paper using ARCH models, but we go one step further. The first implied predictor used here is an estimate of the volatility expectation for the next period calculated from the volatility term structure model developed in Xu and Taylor (1994). Results for this predictor are compared with results for a second predictor defined by short-maturity implied volatilities. We study four exchange rate series and find that for three series the implied volatility information alone gives optimal predictions of one-period-ahead conditional volatility. Consequently the volatility information provided by currency returns has no incremental

X. Xu, S.J. Taylor / Journal of Banking & Finance 19 (1995) 803–821   805

predictive power. This is consistent with the informational efficiency of the Philadelphia currency options market. Out-of-sample forecast comparisons confirm this conclusion. The choice of implied volatility predictor (term structure or short maturity) does not affect the conclusions for our data.

The rest of the paper is organised as follows. Section 2 describes the data and a method for estimating volatility expectations for any set of future periods. Exchange rates and options prices from January 1985 to February 1992 are analyzed. Within-sample calculations are confined to the period until November 1989. The subsequent data are reserved for out-of-sample forecasting evaluations. Section 3 discusses briefly the definitions of ARCH models and the specifications of empirical tests of the informational efficiency of the options market. The empirical within-sample results are presented in Section 4 followed by out-of-sample forecasting results in Section 5. The paper concludes with a summary in Section 6.

2. Data and implied volatility methodology

2.1. Datasets

The primary source database for the options prices is the transaction report compiled daily by the Philadelphia Stock Exchange (PHLX). Daily closing option prices and the simultaneous spot exchange rate quotes have been used for the (British) Pound, (Deutsche) Mark, (Japanese) Yen and (Swiss) Franc quoted against the US Dollar from January 2, 1985 to January 8, 1992. However, the transaction report is not available for some trading days. For some other days the report is not complete or in a few cases it is clearly erroneous. Prices have been collected manually from the Wall Street Journal (WSJ) whenever necessary. Approximately 10% of our implied volatilities are calculated from WSJ prices [1].

Uninformative options records are removed from the database. Options which violate boundary conditions, or are either deep in- or out-of-the-money, or have time to expiry less than ten calendar days are not considered. In addition, all implied volatilities more than five standard deviations distant from their sample mean are excluded.

The interest rates used are London euro-currency rates, collected from Datas-

---

[1] For the period from December 18, 1990 to March 15, 1991 there is no data for the Swiss franc in the PHLX database and the WSJ did not list the closing SF/$ spot exchange rate, so spot rates were collected from Datastream while option prices were collected from the WSJ. This affects the accuracy of implied volatilities calculated from option prices and in turn affects the performance of implied volatility forecasts, and thus the results for the Swiss franc in Section 5 should be interpreted with some caution.

tream. Daily closing prices for futures [2] contracts traded at the International Monetary Market (IMM) in Chicago are also collected from Datastream. Each futures contract is used for the three months prior to its expiration month. At the rollover date, the closing price of the new contract on the previous day before the rollover is used in the calculation of the relative price change. Results from estimating ARCH models show that the choice of method and timing for rolling over futures contracts has insignificant effects.

The IMM closes at 1.20 p.m. while the PHLX closes at 2.00 p.m., and this could lead to bias in favour of the informational efficiency of the options market. However, it has been checked that the conclusions presented in Section 4 do not change even if we use the options estimate of volatility expectations from the previous day.

2.2. Computation of implied volatility

Implied volatilities have been calculated from American model prices, approximated by the very accurate functions derived in Barone-Adesi and Whaley (1987). The calculations use an interval subdivision method, which always converges to an unique solution.

All the implied volatilities are calculated for nearest-the-money options; the selected exercise price on a specific day for a specific maturity minimises $|S-X|$. [3] Nearest-the-money options are chosen for two reasons. First, given the widely reported 'strike bias' or 'smile effect' (Shastri and Wethyavivorn, 1987; Sheikh, 1991; Taylor and Xu, 1994), including out-of-the-money and in-the-money options would introduce further noise into volatility expectation estimates. Second, the approximation that the implied volatility of a rationally priced option will equal the mean expected volatility over the time to expiry is generally considered more satisfactory for an at-the-money option than for all other options (Stein, 1989; Day and Lewis, 1992a; Heynen et al., 1994).

2.3. Estimating the term structure of volatility expectations

Implied volatilities have a term structure. One set of volatility expectations is obtained by estimating a time-varying term structure model for volatility expectations. Complete details are given in Xu and Taylor (1994).

---

[2] The volatility of currency futures prices is identical to the volatility of spot exchange rates if domestic and foreign interest rates are non-stochastic. Differences between spot and futures volatilities will be minimal as the futures maturities are always less than four months. Futures prices, rather than spot prices, were available to us from Datastream for the whole period under study.

[3] Equal forward and exercise prices define the at-the-money option in theoretical arguments but these arguments are usually developed for European options.

Market agents will have expectations at time t about price volatility during future time periods. Suppose they form expectations of the quantities

$$\text{var}(R_{t+\tau}), \text{ with } R_{t+\tau} = \ln P_{t+\tau} - \ln P_{t+\tau-1}, \tau = 1, 2, 3, \ldots \tag{1}$$

where P refers to the price of the asset upon which options are traded.

The volatility term structure model involves two factors representing short-term ($\tau = 1$) and long-term ($\tau \to \infty$) annualised volatility expectations, denoted α_t and μ_t, respectively. As the horizon τ increases, the volatility expectations are assumed to revert towards the long-term expectation and the rate of reversion, ϕ, is assumed to be the same for all t. Then the expected volatility at time t for an interval of general length T, from time t to time $t + T$, is the quantity v_T given by

$$v_T^2 = \mu_t^2 + \frac{1 - \phi^T}{T(1 - \phi)}(\alpha_t^2 - \mu_t^2) \tag{2}$$

providing it is assumed that subsequent asset prices, $\{P_{t+\tau}, \tau > 0\}$, follow a random walk.

Kalman filtering methodology applied to implied volatilities provides estimates for the term structure parameters, particularly ϕ, and also time series of short-term and long-term volatility expectation estimates, $\{\hat{\alpha}_t\}$ and $\{\hat{\mu}_t\}$.

3. ARCH methodology

3.1. Specifications of ARCH models using returns information

The expected variance for the next time interval, $t + 1$, can be obtained from returns up to time t by using the conditional variance h_{t+1} from an ARCH model. In general:

$$h_{t+1} = \text{var}(R_{t+1} | I_t) \tag{3}$$

where I_t denotes the information set of all observed returns up to time t. The most successful and parsimonious models are the GARCH(1,1) model of Bollerslev (1986) and the Exponential ARCH(1,0) model of Nelson (1991). These models have provided satisfactory descriptions of numerous financial time series (Bollerslev et al., 1992).

The GARCH(1,1) model defines the conditional variance recursively using residual terms, which are returns minus their conditional means, thus:

$$\varepsilon_t = R_t - E[R_t | I_{t-1}] \tag{4}$$

and

$$h_{t+1} = c + a\varepsilon_t^2 + bh_t. \tag{5}$$

A few examples of applications are Akgiray (1989), Baillie and Bollerslev (1989), Baillie and DeGennaro (1990) and Hsieh (1989).

Nelson (1991) introduces models whose conditional variances are an asymmetric function of the residuals ε_t. The Exponential ARCH(1,0) model involves standardised residuals, z_t,

$$z_t = \varepsilon_t / h_t^{\frac{1}{2}}, \tag{6}$$

and an AR(1) specification for $\ln(h_t)$:

$$\ln(h_{t+1}) - \lambda = \rho[\ln(h_t) - \lambda] + \theta z_t + \gamma(|z_t| - E[|z_t|]). \tag{7}$$

Examples of equity studies are Nelson (1991) and Poon and Taylor (1992).

3.2. Tests of the informational efficiency of the options market

As noted in Section 2.3, an estimate $\hat{\alpha}_t^2$ of expected short-term squared volatility can also be obtained from a term structure model for option prices. The estimate can be rescaled to give a variance estimate for one period rather than an annualised quantity. The estimate is then for the following unobservable conditional variance

$$\alpha_t^2 = \text{var}(R_{t+1} | M_t). \tag{8}$$

Here α_t is not an annualised figure and M_t is the information used by options market agents when they set prices at time t. The set M_t is presumed to include observed returns I_t. Day and Lewis (1992a) use implied volatility from short maturity options to approximate α_t. To evaluate their methodology we use the implied volatility from an option with the least time to maturity but greater than nine calendar days.

Options prices will provide optimal predictions of volatility when options markets use information efficiently and the pricing model correctly specifies the relationship between prices and volatility expectations. Information other than options prices should not have incremental predictive power when this joint hypothesis is true.

To test the hypothesis that options prices give optimal one-period-ahead volatility predictions two ARCH models are estimated. The first model only uses options information, the second model also uses returns information. For a GARCH(1,1) specification the two models are

$$h_{t+1} = c + d\hat{\alpha}_t^2 \tag{9}$$

and

$$h_{t+1} = c + a\varepsilon_t^2 + bh_t + d\hat{\alpha}_t^2. \tag{10}$$

For the symmetric version of Exponential ARCH(1,0) the models are

$$\ln(h_{t+1}) = \lambda + \delta \ln(\hat{\alpha}_t^2) \tag{11}$$

and

$$\ln(h_{t+1}) = \lambda(1 - \rho) + \rho \ln(h_t) + \gamma(|z_t| - E[|z_t|]) + \delta \ln(\hat{\alpha}_t^2). \tag{12}$$

X. Xu, S.J. Taylor / Journal of Banking & Finance 19 (1995) 803–821   809

Likelihood ratio tests of the null hypothesis $a = b = 0$ or $\rho = \gamma = 0$ can be evaluated by comparing $LR = 2(L_1 - L_0)$ with χ_2^2, with L_0 and L_1 the maximum log-likelihoods either for (9) and (10) or (11) and (12). These tests make strong and possibly optimistic assumptions about the asymptotic distribution of the likelihood ratio [4]. The relative information content of the two sets of estimates for α_t^2 can be assessed by comparing their maximum values of the log-likelihood.

Estimates $\hat{\mu}_t^2$ of the squared long-term expectation should have no incremental power to predict short-term volatility if market expectations are rational. This hypothesis is tested by including an additional term $e\hat{\mu}_t^2$ in (9) and (10) and a term $\eta \ln(\hat{\mu}_t^2)$ in (11) and (12).

3.3. Seasonal volatility effects

It is known that returns measured over more than 24 hours often have higher variances than 24-hour returns. The equations for h_t require revisions to allow for this seasonality. It is assumed that equations (5), (7) and (9)–(12) all apply to a non-seasonal conditional variance h_{t+1}^* defined to be the conditional variance h_{t+1} divided by a seasonal term. We replace h_t, h_{t+1}, and ε_t by h_t^*, h_{t+1}^* and ε_t^* (where $\varepsilon_t^* = h_t^{*\,1/2} z_t$) and assume

$$h_t / h_t^* = \begin{cases} 1 \text{ if close } t \text{ is 24 hours after close } t - 1, \\ M \text{ if } t \text{ falls on a Monday and } t - 1 \text{ on a Friday} \\ H \text{ if a holiday occurs between close } t \text{ and close } t - 1. \end{cases} \tag{13}$$

ARCH models for h_t^* combined with (13) define appropriate models for h_t.

The options estimates $\hat{\alpha}_t^2$ and $\hat{\mu}_t^2$ need to reflect the seasonal effects measured by M and H. Annualised estimates $\hat{\alpha}_{A,t}^2$ have been converted into non-seasonal, daily estimates using appropriate calendar constants for currency markets, as follows:

$$\hat{\alpha}_t^2 = \hat{\alpha}_{A,t}^2 / (196 + 48M + 8H). \tag{14}$$

3.4. The conditional distribution

Empirical evidence decisively rejects the hypothesis that the distribution of a return R_t conditional upon the information set I_{t-1} of past returns is Normal for high frequency data (Engle and Bollerslev, 1986; Baillie and Bollerslev, 1989; Taylor, 1994). Two empirically better conditional distributions are the scaled t and the generalised error distribution (GED) (Taylor, 1994). The shape of the condi-

---

[4] We recognise that asymptotic theory for ARCH models is difficult (Bollerslev et al. 1992, Section 2.6, and sometimes unreliable (Lumsdaine, 1995), consequently we use very small nominal significance levels.

810 *X. Xu, S.J. Taylor / Journal of Banking & Finance 19 (1995) 803–821*

tional distribution z_t then depends on the degrees-of-freedom ω for the scaled t and the tail-thickness parameter ν for the GED. Normal distributions are given by $\omega \to \infty$ and $\nu = 2$.

3.5. Estimation

Model parameters occur in the definitions of the non-seasonal conditional variance, the seasonal multipliers and the conditional distribution. All of these parameters can be simultaneously estimated by maximising the likelihood function for a set of observed returns and volatility expectations implied by options prices. The likelihood function for a given parameter vector is calculated from the conditional variances and the standardised return residuals (Bollerslev et al., 1992; Taylor, 1994).

4. Empirical results within-sample

All the results presented from estimating ARCH models are for the period from January 1985 to November 1989. Prices for 1990 and 1991 are used in Section 5 for ex ante forecast evaluations.

4.1. ARCH models that only use returns information

Initial comparisons are made between the GARCH(1,1) model and the symmetric Exponential ARCH(1,0) model (i.e. $\theta = 0$ in (7)) and between the three most popular conditional distributions, the Normal, the scaled-t and the GED. Comparisons are also made between two ways to define the conditional mean return: either always zero, which is reasonable for futures data, or the appropriate figure defined by five dummy variables, one for each day of the week. To maximise the log-likelihood an initial value for the conditional variance is required. Empirical evidence suggests that the choice of initial value does not matter much, and we report the results as if the initial value is an additional parameter.

The following conclusions are obtained for all models estimated. There is no significant increase in the maximum log-likelihood when dummy variables define the conditional mean, consequently it is assumed to be zero. There is no uniform statistical result across the currencies about the significance of the variance dummy variables, but all the point estimates are well above one. Consequently these dummy variables are included in all the models discussed here.

The results presented in Table 1 reflect the above conclusions. The results for the scaled-*t* distribution are not reported to save space because the GED distribution is always slightly superior to the scaled-*t* distribution. The differences in maximum log-likelihoods between the GED and the Normal conditional distribution all exceed 20 for the GARCH(1,1) and symmetric Exponential ARCH(1,0)

X. Xu, S.J. Taylor / Journal of Banking & Finance 19 (1995) 803–821

Table 1

Parameter estimates for GARCH(1,1) and Exponential ARCH(1,0) models. Maximum likelihood estimates and the maxima of the log-likelihood function for ARCH models fitted to daily BP/$, DM/$, JY/$ and SF/$ exchange rates between January 1985 and November 1989. The ARCH models contain seasonal dummy variables M and H for Mondays and holidays, and the estimates of these parameters are not given here. The conditional distribution is GED with tail-thickness parameter ν. The special case $\nu = 2$ defines a Normal distribution. The conditional mean is equal to zero.

GARCH(1,1): $h_t = h_t^*$, Mh_t^*, Hh_t^*, and $h_{t+1}^* = c + a\varepsilon_t^2(h_t^*/ht) + bh_t^*$

	$10^5 c/(1-a-b)$	a	$a+b$	ν	$\ln(L)$
BP	6.0576	0.0466	0.9839	2	4254.01
	5.9589	0.0391	0.9877	1.1854	4297.04
DM	6.1391	0.0837	0.9569	2	4292.89
	6.0004	0.0738	0.9583	1.2528	4327.31
JY	4.9830	0.1012	0.8712	2	4391.42
	5.1111	0.0960	0.9189	1.0336	4478.84
SF	7.4797	0.0642	0.9617	2	4152.34
	7.3561	0.0599	0.9611	1.3778	4173.67

Exponential ARCH(1,0): $h_t = h_t^*$, Mh_t^*, Hh^*, and $\ln(h_{t+1}^*) = (1-\rho)\lambda + \rho \ln(h_t^*)$ $+ \gamma(|z_t| - E[|z_t|])$

	λ	γ	ρ	ν	$\ln(L)$
BP	−9.4316	0.1206	0.9795	2	4251.67
	−9.8054	0.1095	0.9835	1.1802	4296.03
DM	−9.5816	0.1708	0.9594	2	4295.11
	−9.8108	0.1574	0.9617	1.2571	4329.18
JY	−9.8369	0.2155	0.8604	2	4388.97
	−9.9819	0.2089	0.9117	1.0299	4477.72
SF	−9.3939	0.1347	0.9689	2	4155.43
	−9.5704	0.1260	0.9687	1.3855	4176.14

models. As the Normal distribution is the GED with $\nu = 2$, doubling log-likelihood differences and comparing test values with χ_1^2 shows they are all statistically significant at the 0.1% significance level. A fat-tailed, non-Normal conditional distribution enhances the descriptive accuracy of the model. Comparing the log-likelihoods for GARCH(1,1) and symmetric Exponential ARCH(1,0) reveals very small differences. The differences between GARCH and Exponential ARCH are 1.01 for the Pound, −1.87 for the Mark, 1.12 for the Yen and −2.47 for the Franc when the conditional distribution is GED. There is thus no clear-cut difference between the two models.

Now we consider more general ARCH models with the GED conditional distribution. First, consider the asymmetric specification for the volatility response in the Exponential ARCH(1,0) model. The increases in maximum log-likelihoods are less than 0.7 for all four currencies; the hypothesis $\theta = 0$ can not be rejected at the 10% significance level. As noted by Taylor (1994), there are plausible theories for a negative θ in stock models but none for a non-zero θ in a currency model. Price and volatility innovations can therefore be assumed independent when pricing currency options.

Table 2

Parameter estimates for GARCH(1,1) models including the term structure volatility expectations, with GED conditional distributions. The terms $\hat{\alpha}_t$ and $\hat{\mu}_t$ are respectively short- and long-term volatility expectations obtained from a term structure model. $h_t = h_t^*$, Mh_t^*, Hh_t^*, and $h_{t+1}^* = c + a\varepsilon_t^2(h_t^*/h_t)$ $+ bh_t^* + d\hat{\alpha}_t^2 + e\hat{\mu}_t^2$

$10^5 \times c$	a	b	d	e	ν	$\ln(L)$
Panel A: British Pound						
0.0735 (3.81)	0.0391 (2.56)	0.9485 (108.35)			1.1854 (17.73)	4297.04
			1.0000		1.2297 (20.57)	4300.23
1.2065 (3.53)			0.8459 (9.19)		1.2307 (17.74)	4312.17
1.1858 (3.22)	0.0297 (0.64)	0.0000	0.8276 (8.07)		1.2313 (17.75)	4312.41
0.5960 (0.81)			0.7538 (6.21)	0.1771 (1.22)	1.2344 (17.73)	4313.02
0.6152 (1.01)	0.0138 (0.43)	0.0000	0.7456 (6.11)	0.1682 (1.15)	1.2347 (17.73)	4313.11
Panel B: Deutsche Mark						
0.2500 (6.02)	0.0738 (3.81)	0.8846 (52.78)			1.2528 (17.62)	4327.31
			1.0000		1.2494 (20.77)	4328.74
1.1266 (3.84)			0.7941 (10.23)		1.3289 (17.51)	4349.69
1.1260 (3.84)	0.0000	0.0000	0.7943 (10.24)		1.3282 (17.51)	4349.69
1.1262 (3.84)			0.7945 (10.24)	0.0000	1.3285 (17.51)	4349.69
1.1265 (3.84)	0.0000	0.0000	0.7944 (10.23)	0.0000	1.3285 (17.51)	4349.69
Panel C: Japanese Yen						
0.4147 (6.39)	0.0960 (3.13)	0.8229 (26.41)			1.0366 (18.87)	4478.84
			1.000		0.9982 (24.57)	4442.75
1.6907 (4.83)			0.7139 (6.82)		1.0278 (19.15)	4480.48
1.5515 (4.40)	0.1252 (2.28)	0.0000	0.6185 (5.77)		1.0419 (19.03)	4485.21
1.6854 (4.51)			0.7151 (6.37)	0.0000	1.0278 (19.18)	4480.48

Table 2 (continued)

$10^5 \times c$	a	b	d	e	ν	$\ln(L)$
1.5476	0.1255	0.0000	0.6185	0.0000	1.0462	4485.21
(4.40)	(2.29)		(5.78)		(19.03)	

Panel D: Swiss Franc

$10^5 \times c$	a	b	d	e	ν	$\ln(L)$
0.2860	0.0570	0.9041			1.3777	4173.67
(7.42)	(3.52)	(56.60)			(17.42)	
			1.0000		1.4512	4181.43
					(19.40)	
1.3539			0.8864		1.4519	4192.13
(2.83)			(8.98)		(17.12)	
1.3537	0.0000	0.0000	0.8864		1.4519	4192.13
(2.83)			(8.98)		(17.12)	
1.3533			0.8864	0.0000	1.4519	4192.13
(2.83)			(8.98)		(17.12)	
1.3536	0.0000	0.0000	0.8864	0.0000	1.4519	4192.13
(2.83)			(8.98)		(17.12)	

Notes: The numbers in parentheses are t-statistics estimated using the hessian and numerical second derivatives. All parameters are constrained to be non-negative. When a parameter estimate is zero or smaller than 10^{-6} then no estimated standard error is reported.

Second, consider higher order ARCH models. Results not reported here show such models have nothing extra to offer. Results for the tests of the informational efficiency of the currency options market are reported later for GARCH(1,1) and symmetric Exponential ARCH(1,0) models with the GED conditional distribution. However, not unexpectedly, all the conclusions also stand for other distributions and higher order ARCH models.

4.2. Informational efficiency of the currency options market

Tables 2 and 3 present the model estimates used for tests of informational efficiency. Table 2 uses market volatility expectations for the next period given by the term structure model outlined in Section 2.3. Table 3 uses the short-maturity implied volatility.

Eq. (10) includes options market volatility information as an exogenous variable in the GARCH(1,1) model for the conditional volatility. The increases in maximum log-likelihoods compared with those from the standard GARCH(1,1) model, i.e. Eq. (5), are as follows:

	Pound	Mark	Yen	Franc
Table 2	15.37	22.38	6.37	18.37
Table 3	18.47	22.34	4.94	17.36

Table 3

Parameter estimates for GARCH(1,1) models including short-maturity implied volatilities, with GED conditional distributions. The term $\hat{\alpha}_t$ is the implied volatility for the shortest maturity option with more than nine calendar days to expiry. $h_t = h_t^*$, Mh_t^*, Hh_t^*, and $h_{t+1}^* = c + a\varepsilon_t^2(h_t^*/h_t) + bh_t^* + d\hat{\alpha}_t^2$

$10^5 \times c$	a	b	d	ν	$\ln(L)$
Panel A: British Pound					
0.0735	0.0391	0.9485		1.1854	4297.04
(3.81)	(2.56)	(108.3)		(17.73)	
			1.0000	1.2632	4315.33
				(18.75)	
0.0000			1.0313	1.2524	4315.49
			(18.75)	(17.76)	
0.0000	0.0061	0.0000	1.0250	1.2524	4315.51
	(0.19)		(15.74)	(17.75)	
Panel B: Deutsche Mark					
0.2500	0.0738	0.8846		1.2528	4327.31
(6.02)	(3.81)	(52.78)		(17.62)	
			1.0000	1.3196	4349.49
				(17.85)	
0.0000			0.9719	1.3320	4349.64
			(19.42)	(17.42)	
0.0000	0.0000	0.0429	0.9295	1.3321	4349.65
		(1.43)	(3.11)	(17.40)	
Panel C: Japanese Yen					
0.4147	0.0960	0.8299		1.0336	4478.84
(6.39)	(3.13)	(26.41)		(18.87)	
			1.0000	1.0470	4473.03
				(22.11)	
0.9941			0.8698	1.0245	4478.53
(2.08)			(6.02)	(19.13)	
0.6033	0.1202	0.4017	0.3922	1.0420	4483.78
(1.72)	(2.58)	(1.56)	(1.64)	(18.98)	
Panel D: Swiss Franc					
0.2860	0.0570	0.9041		1.3777	4173.67
(7.42)	(3.52)	(56.00)		(17.42)	
			1.0000	1.4669	4187.16
				(18.56)	
0.5761			0.9993	1.4480	4190.66
(1.22)			(10.23)	(17.09)	
0.2339	0.0000	0.2144	0.8211	1.4515	4191.03
(0.47)		(0.80)	(3.08)	(17.05)	

Notes: The numbers in parentheses are *t*-statistics estimated using the hessian and numerical second derivatives. All parameters are constrained to be non-negative. When a parameter estimate is zero or smaller than 10^{-6} then no estimated standard error is reported.

Doubling these increases and comparing these test values with χ_1^2 shows clearly that the hypothesis that the options prices have no incremental information content can be rejected at the 0.5% significance level for each currency.

The more important question is whether options market volatility information is sufficient for predicting the next day's conditional volatility. As Eq. (9) only includes options market volatility information in the conditional variance equation, it is nested within Eq. (10). Thus a likelihood ratio test can again be used. The decreases in maximum log-likelihoods are as follows:

	Pound	Mark	Yen	Franc
Table 2	0.24	0.00	4.73	0.00
Table 3	0.02	0.01	5.25	0.37

Doubling these numbers and comparing these test values with χ_2^2 shows that the null hypothesis that returns contain no volatility information in addition to that already conveyed by options prices can not be rejected for any currency at the 0.5% significance level. The null can be rejected at the 1% level for the Yen. To conclude, the options market was informationally efficient for the three European currencies, the Pound, the Mark and the Franc, from 1985 to 1989; however, no such firm conclusion can apply to the Yen.

When the options market forms rational volatility expectations, long-term expectations have no incremental power to predict short-term conditional volatility. This null hypothesis is tested by evaluating the increases in maximum log-likelihood when the term structure estimate of long-term volatility is an additional variable in Eqs. (9) and (10). The results in Table 2 show the null hypothesis must be accepted.

The hypothesis that market expectations from option prices are unbiased estimates for one-period-ahead future volatility implies $c = 0$ and $d = 1$ in Eq. (9). Likelihood ratio tests are once more appropriate. The results in Table 2 reject the hypothesis at the 0.5% level for all four currencies. The results in Table 3 show much less evidence for bias. The term structure expectations for the next day are extrapolations and this can explain the bias identified by Table 2.

The maximum log-likelihoods in Tables 2 and 3 are very similar for our preferred model (Eq. 9, so $a = b = 0$). The higher values are in Table 2 for three currencies and in Table 3 for the Pound.

Tests of the informational efficiency of the options market using the symmetric Exponential ARCH(1,0) specification lead to the same conclusions as those reported above for the GARCH(1,1) specification.

5. Out-of-sample volatility forecasting

The tests in Section 4 characterise within-sample properties of volatility information because the likelihoods of both the ARCH and term structure models are maximised over the complete sample period. The direction of any within-sample biases is unknown (Day and Lewis, 1992a). In this section we compare the *ex ante* forecasting ability of historical volatility predictors, forecasts from standard ARCH models and options market forecasts over a longer time horizon than considered in Section 4.

The data cover seven years and we require a large sample to estimate the parameters in both the ARCH models and the volatility term structure model. Less than two and a half years of data remain after using five years to select and estimate the ARCH and term structure models. A four-week forecast horizon allows us to evaluate 30 non-overlapping, four-week ahead forecasts for the period from October 18, 1989 to February 4, 1992.

The non-seasonal, realised volatility is calculated ex post as follows:

$$V_{R,t} = \sqrt{\frac{1}{N} \sum_{i=1}^{N} \varepsilon_{t+1}^{*2}} \tag{15}$$

where N is the number of trading periods in some four-week interval. Note that the non-seasonal quantity ε_t^{*2} is one of R_t^2, R_t^2/M or R_t^2/H, with the choice determined by Eq. (13). The benchmark forecast is the simple historical volatility over the last four weeks, i.e.

$$V_{H,t} = \sqrt{\frac{1}{N} \sum_{i=0}^{N-1} \varepsilon_{t-i}^{*2}} = V_{R,t-N}. \tag{16}$$

The ARCH forecast for the realised volatility of the returns over N future periods can be obtained from N single-period forecasts all made at the same time. In the case of the GARCH(1,1) model, the volatility forecast can be calculated by:

$$V_{G,t} = \sqrt{\frac{1}{N} \sum_{i=1}^{N} \hat{h}_{t+i}} \tag{17}$$

where

$$h_{t+1}^* = c + a\varepsilon_t^{*2} + bh_t^*$$

and

$$\hat{h}_{t+i} = \frac{c}{1-a-b} + (a+b)^{i-1}\left(h_{t+1}^* - \frac{c}{1-a-b}\right), \quad i = 1, 2, 3, \ldots$$

All of the preceding volatility measures are annualised by multiplying by $(196 + 48M + 8H)^{1/2}$.

Forecasts can be derived from option prices, both from the term structure model and from a matched maturity option. The forecasts from the term structure model, $V_{TS,t}$, can be calculated from Eq. (2) with T equal to 28 calendar days. The matched forecast at time t is the implied volatility for an option whose time to maturity is nearest to 28 calendar days, denoted $V_{M,t}$.

The parameters in both the GARCH model and the term structure model of implied volatility are re-estimated as new observations come in on a rolling basis. We use a constant sample size of 250 weeks of daily data by adding the latest four weeks of observations and deleting the first four weeks of observations in the previous sample [5].

Forecasting performance is initially evaluated using the mean forecast error (ME), the mean absolute error (MAE) and the root mean square error ($RMSE$), calculated from forecasts $V_{F,t}$ given by one of the five methods above and realised figures $V_{R,t}$ as follows:

$$ME = \frac{1}{n} \sum_{t \in S} (V_{F,t} - V_{R,t})$$

$$MAE = \frac{1}{n} \sum_{t \in S} |V_{F,t} - V_{R,t}|$$

$$RMSE = \left[\frac{1}{n} \sum_{t \in S} (V_{F,t} - V_{R,t})^2 \right]^{1/2}$$

Here S indicates the set of times at which ex ante forecasts are produced and n denotes the number of forecasts made using each method [6]. For this study, $n = 30$.

The results, listed in Table 4, clearly demonstrate the superiority of the two volatility forecasts computed from options prices [7]. The smallest $RMSE$ is obtained by the options forecasts for each currency. The differences in Table 4 between the two options forecasts are minimal. The options forecasts also have the smallest MAE for the Pound, the Mark and the Yen while the ARCH forecast with the GED conditional distribution achieves the smallest MAE for the Franc [8]. The ME values for both options forecasts are very small (less than 1% of the average volatility) for the Mark, the Yen and the Franc and are not statistically different from zero at the 5% level, although the ME nearest zero is obtained by the historical volatility forecast for the Pound and the Yen and by the ARCH forecast for the Mark and the Franc.

---

[5] We also estimated parameters and forecast the volatility on a continual updating basis, which only adds new observations. The results, not reported here in detail, are not very different from the results based on the rolling method; the only significant result, which is rather data related, is reported in footnote 8. Our results differ from the findings of Lamoureux and Lastrapes (1993), however the underlying assets, the number of observations in the rolling samples, and the forecasting horizon are all different.

[6] Note that an optimal forecast will not have $MAE = RMSE = 0$ because $V_{R,t}$ is only a point estimate of the asset's price volatility which is unobservable.

[7] Replacing $V_{R,t}$ and $V_{R,t}$ by $V_{R,t}$ in the definition of ME, MAE and $RMSE$ provides identical conclusions to those presented in the text.

[8] Using the updating method to re-estimate parameters reduces the effect of the inferior data for the Swiss franc (footnote 1) and then the implied volatility forecast also has the smallest MAE.

818 *X. Xu, S.J. Taylor / Journal of Banking & Finance 19 (1995) 803–821*

Table 4
Comparisons of alternative out-of-sample volatility forecasts. The implied forecasts are estimates of the market's volatility expectation for the next 28 days obtained either from a term structure model or the option with maturity closest to 28 days. The numbers tabulated are mean forecast error (*ME*), mean absolute errors (*MAE*) and root mean square errors (*RMSE*)

	Historical voltatility	GARCH(1,1)		Implied volatility	
		Normal	GED	Term structure	Matched
Panel A: British Pound (Average Realised Volatility = 0.11433)					
ME	−0.001038	0.001737	0.002015	0.005234	0.004447
MAE	0.033370	0.029240	0.029384	0.028412	0.029083
RMSE	0.041493	0.036214	0.036531	0.032527	0.033399
Panel B: Deutsche Mark (Average Realised Volatility = 0.12121)					
ME	−0.001736	0.001095	−0.000083	0.000788	0.000279
MAE	0.032874	0.032247	0.031692	0.025364	0.025945
RMSE	0.040840	0.040525	0.039836	0.032931	0.034312
Panel C: Japanese Yen (Average Realised Volatility = 0.10585)					
ME	−0.000217	0.007983	0.008441	0.000469	−0.000369
MAE	0.037799	0.030106	0.030415	0.025612	0.025727
RMSE	0.045695	0.034854	0.035267	0.030865	0.030763
Panel D: Swiss Franc (Average Realised Volatility = 0.12789)					
ME	−0.001915	0.000674	0.000355	−0.001246	−0.002130
MAE	0.028903	0.023740	0.023654	0.024342	0.023883
RMSE	0.034371	0.029103	0.029066	0.028720	0.028315

The forecasts from the ARCH model offer a marked improvement over naive historical volatility forecasts for all four currencies. The ARCH forecasts have up to 20% smaller *MAE*s and *RMSE*s than naive historical volatility forecasts. Comparing the ARCH forecasts with different conditional distributions reveals that forecasts from non-Normal models do not convincingly outperform forecasts from Normal models. Some caution should be exercised in interpreting these results as we only predict 30 four-week realised volatilities.

Lamoureux and Lastrapes (1993) perform encompassing regressions of the realised volatility on their three alternative out-of-sample forecasts and argue that the regressions provide further insight into the nature of the different forecast models. Like them we are interested in the incremental predictive power of the forecasts. Care is required because all forecasts are highly correlated. We apply the stepwise regression technique to select statistically significant regressors from the forecasts. The only forecast selected for the Pound, the Mark and the Yen is the term structure implied predictor (5% significance level, *F*-test). This implies no bivariate predictor is significantly more accurate than the term structure predictor. A similar conclusion has been obtained by Day and Lewis (1992b) for oil futures. However, no forecast is significant for the Swiss franc. The poor performance in the case of the Swiss franc could well be due to the block of inferior data mentioned in footnote 1. The within-sample and out-of-sample methodologies give the same conclusion that the volatility forecast obtained from option prices is optimal: returns from the underlying asset do not contain significant incremental information for predicting future volatility.

Finally we perform the test of the null hypothesis that the volatility forecast from option prices is an unbiased estimate for the four-week ahead realised volatility. We run regressions of the realised volatility on the term structure forecast with and without a constant term. The results show that the unbiased hypothesis cannot be rejected. The slope coefficients are all very close to 1 when the constant term is suppressed.

6. Summary

This paper examines the informational efficiency of the currency options market at the Philadelphia Stock Exchange using an ARCH methodology. By using likelihood ratio tests, we find that volatility forecasts estimated from call and put options prices contain incremental information relative to standard ARCH specifications for conditional volatility which only use the information in past returns. This is found for all four currencies. Furthermore, when predicting one-period-ahead volatility, the hypothesis that past returns have no incremental information content in addition to the information conveyed by the options market can not be rejected for the Pound, the Mark and the Franc, and is only marginally rejected for the Yen. We also find that market agents are rational in forming their expectations about future volatility, as the long-term expected volatility has no extra power when predicting short-term volatility.

The out-of-sample volatility forecasts confirm the above results. The two implied volatility forecasts markedly outperform the forecasts from past returns (the historical volatility forecast and forecasts from ARCH models) when predicting four-week ahead realised volatility. Further tests support the hypothesis that the options market's volatility expectations are unbiased predictions of future volatility.

These results suggest that the Philadelphia currency options market is informationally efficient in setting prices and the volatility expectations in option prices provide superior predictors of both one-period-ahead and longer horizon (i.e. four weeks) conditional volatilities. This conclusion contrasts with the lack of informational efficiency identified for US stock options markets by Day and Lewis (1992a), Lamoureux and Lastrapes (1993) and Canina and Figlewski (1993). The superior informational efficiency of the currency options market is consistent with the arguments developed in the final section of Canina and Figlewski (1993): they expect efficiency to be enhanced in an environment which permits low cost arbitrage trading.

The ultimate efficiency test is whether excessive profits can be made by some trading strategy. As Harvey and Whaley (1992) find, even if superior forecasts of future volatility are made then abnormal returns are not necessarily possible when transaction costs are taken into account. This issue will be explored in future research.

Acknowledgements

Xu was at the Financial Options Research Centre, University of Warwick when the paper was written and revised. We thank two anonymous referees, Stewart Hodges, Michael Selby, Martin Walker and participants at the 1993 meeting of the European Finance Association for their helpful comments and advice. We thank the Philadelphia Stock Exchange for providing their currency options data.

References

Akgiray, V., 1989, Conditional heteroscedasticity in time series of stock returns: evidence and forecasts, Journal of Business 62, 55–80.

Baillie, R.T. and T. Bollerslev, 1989, The message in daily exchange rates: a conditional-variance tale, Journal of Business and Economic Statistics 7, 297–305.

Baillie, R.T. and R.P. DeGennaro, 1990, Stock returns and volatility, Journal of Financial and Quantitative Analysis 25, 203–214.

Barone-Adesi, G. and R.E. Whaley, 1987, Efficient analytic approximation of American option values, Journal of Finance 42, 301–320.

Bollerslev, T., 1986, Generalised autoregressive conditional heteroscedasticity, Journal of Econometrics 31, 307–327.

Bollerslev, T., R.Y. Chou and K.F. Kroner, 1992, ARCH modeling in finance: a review of the theory and empirical evidence, Journal of Econometrics 52, 5–59.

Canina, L., and S. Figlewski, 1993, The informational content of implied volatility, Review of Financial Studies 6, 659–681.

Chiras, D.P., and S. Manaster, 1978, The information content of option prices and a test of market efficiency, Journal of Financial Economics 6, 213–234.

Day, T.E., and C.M. Lewis, 1992a, Stock market volatility and the information content of stock index options, Journal of Econometrics 52, 289–311.

Day, T.E., and C.M. Lewis, 1992b, Initial margin policy and volatility in the crude oil future market, Proceedings of the Options Conference, FORC, Warwick University.

Engle, R. and T. Bollerslev, 1986, Modelling the persistence of conditional variances. Econometric Reviews 5, 1–50.

Gemmill, G.T., 1986, The forecasting performance of stock options on the London Traded Options Market, Journal of Business Finance and Accounting 13, 535–546.

Harvey, C.R., and R.E. Whaley, 1992, Market volatility prediction and the efficiency of the S&P 100 index option market, Journal of Financial Economics 31, 43–73.

Heynen, R., A.G.Z. Kemna and T. Vorst, 1994, Analysis of the term structure of implied volatilities, Journal of Financial and Quantitative Analysis 29, 31–56.

Hsieh, D.A., 1989, Modelling heteroscedasticity in daily foreign-exchange rates, Journal of Business and Economic Statistics 7, 307–317.

Lamoureux, C.B. and W.D. Lastrapes, 1993, Forecasting stock return variance: toward an understanding of stochastic implied volatilities, Review of Financial Studies 6, 293–326.

Latane, H. and R.J. Rendleman, 1976, Standard deviation of stock price ratios implied by option premia, Journal of Finance 31, 369–382.

Lumsdaine, R.L., 1995, Finite sample properties of the maximum likelihood estimator in GARCH(1,1) and IGARCH(1,1) models: a Monte Carlo investigation, Journal of Business & Economic Statistics 13, 1–10.

Nelson, D.B., 1991, Conditional heteroscedasticity in asset returns: a new approach, Econometrica 59, 347–370.

Poon, S. and S.J. Taylor, 1992, Stock returns and volatility: an empirical study of the UK stock market, Journal of Banking and Finance 16, 37–59.

Scott, E. and A.L. Tucker, 1989, Predicting currency return volatility, Journal of Banking and Finance 13, 839–851.

Shastri, K. and K. Tandon, 1986, An empirical test of a valuation model for American options on futures contracts, Journal of Financial and Quantitative Analysis 10, 377–392.

Shastri, K. and K. Wethyavivorn, 1987, The valuation of currency options for alternate stochastic processes, Journal of Financial Research 10 (No. 2), 283–293.

Sheikh, A.M., 1991, Transaction data tests of S&P 100 call option pricing, Journal of Financial and Quantitative Analysis 26, 459–475.

Stein, J.C., 1989, Overreactions in the options market, Journal of Finance 44, 1011–1023.

Taylor, S.J., 1994, Modelling stochastic volatility, Mathematical Finance 4, 183–204.

Taylor, S.J. and X. Xu, 1994, The magnitude of implied volatility smiles: theory and empirical evidence for exchange rates, The Review of Futures Markets 13, 355–380.

Xu, X. and S.J. Taylor, 1994, The term structure of volatility implied by foreign exchange options, Journal of Financial and Quantitative Analysis 29, 57–74.

Name Index

Abdel, A.B. 140
Abraham, B. 176
Adams, K.J. 27, 30
Agiakloglou, C. 45
Akaike, H. 71
Akgiray, V. 322, 326, 329, 481, 491, 522
Aldous, D. 297
Alexander, D. 123, 124, 125
Alexander, S.S. 276
Ali, M.M. 390
Allen, H. 219, 279
Allen, H.L. 103
Andersen, T. 285
Anderson, B.D.O. 176
Andrews, D.W.K. 485, 487, 488
Ansley, C.F. 177
Arbor, P. 28
Argy, V. 252
Armstrong, J.S. 312
Arnold, C.M. 281
Artis, M.J. 128

Bachelor, R.A. 110
Back, K. 491
Balassa, B. 181
Baldwin, R. 140
Ball, R. 225, 323
Ballie, R.T. 125, 156, 163, 329, 522, 524
Banz, R.W. 298
Barkoulas, J.T. 41
Barone-Adesi, G. 521
Barron, A.R. 156, 159
Batchelor, R.A. 4
Bates, J.M. 101
Baum, C.F. 41
Beckers, S. 399, 499
Belkaoui, A. 59
Belongia, M.T. 3, 18
Bennington, G.A. 298
Benveniste, A. 161
Bera, A. 438
Berg, A. 188
Berndt, E.K. 329
Biegler, L.J. 468
Bilson, J. 79, 90, 277
Bilson, J.F.O. 102, 175, 178
Black, F. 330, 366, 371, 390, 461

Blake, D. 103
Blanco, H. 205
Bliss, R.R. 27
Blume, M. 238, 240, 241, 276
Bodie, Z. 340
Bollerslev, T. 163, 285, 299, 321, 329, 345, 366, 390, 434, 438, 439, 463, 522, 524, 525
Bonomo, V. 15
Boothe, P. 102, 139
Brailsford, T.J. 321, 322, 330, 331
Branson, W. 252
Branson, W.H. 69, 276
Brealey, R.A. 300
Breeden, D.T. 236, 251
Breen, W.J. 298
Brenner, M. 477
Brock, W.A. 140, 277, 280
Brown, B.W. 498
Brown, P. 323, 324
Brown, R.G. 302
Buse, A. 28
Butler, J.S. 405, 410

Cagan, P. 178
Calvo, G.A. 202
Campbell, J.Y. 229, 330
Canina, L. 534
Carleton, W.T. 25
Chang, P.H.K. 226, 232, 280
Cheung, Y.W. 41, 45, 56, 279
Chin, M.D. 157
Chinn, M. 279
Chiras, D.P. 499, 519
Chou, R. 345
Christ, C.F. 74
Christie, A.A. 330, 366, 371
Christoffersen, P.F. 405, 406
Cicarelli, J. 19, 20
Clark, P.K. 139, 390
Clemen, R.T. 102
Clements, K.W. 181
Cleveland, W.A. 142
Cleveland, W.S. 142
Cole, C.S. 26, 27
Condoyanni, L. 324
Cooper, I.A. 25
Cootner, P. 138

Cornell, B. 67, 235, 244, 249
Cornerll, W. 276
Corsetti, G. 186, 188, 198
Cowles, A. 368
Cox, J.C. 26, 397, 398, 465
Crane, D.B. 101
Crotty, J.R. 101
Cumby, R. 79, 90
Curcio, R. 280
Cuthbertson, K. 124
Cuthrell, J.E. 468
Cybenko, 156, 158
Cyriax, G. 101

Dacorogna, M.M. 408
Danielsson, J. 285, 288, 402, 403, 404, 407, 408, 417, 423
Dave, R.D. 416
Davenport, J.M. 112
Day, T.E. 464, 478, 479, 492, 499, 519, 521, 523, 531, 533, 534
De Haan, L. 405, 407, 423
De Jong, F. 321
De Vries, C.G. 402, 404, 405, 407, 408, 417, 423
Dechert, W.D. 140
DeGennaro, R.P. 329, 522
Devlin, S.J. 142
Dickens, R. 300
Diebold, F.X. 102, 113, 124, 139, 140, 145, 157, 165, 170, 406
Dietrich, J.K. 235, 238, 244, 249, 276
Dimson, E. 298, 300, 322, 326, 327, 332, 333, 334, 337, 406
Dittmar, R. 225, 228
Dominguez, K.M. 277
Domowitz, I. 140, 434, 439
Dooley, M. 235, 236, 237, 239, 240, 244, 258
Dooley, M. 280
Dornbusch, R. 90, 175, 181, 252
Driskell, R.A. 83
Dua, P. 3, 4
Duffie, D. 402
Durbin, J. 178
Dutta, S. 58, 59

Easley, D. 435, 452
Ederington, L. 58, 59
Edwards, R. 281
Efron, B. 277, 280, 286, 290
Eichenbaum, M. 231
Elman, J.L. 159, 160
Engel, C. 157, 229, 259, 260
Engle, E. 157

Engle, R. 345, 433, 434, 435, 438, 442, 446, 455, 524
Engle, R.F. 124, 125, 126, 133, 138, 140, 321, 329, 330, 366, 390, 463
Engle, T. 299
Epstein, R.A. 15
Evans, C.L. 231
Evnine, J. 513

Fabozzi, F.J. 28
Faff, R.W. 321, 322, 330, 331
Fair, R.C. 68, 70, 75, 485, 487, 499
Fama, E.F. 26, 27, 138, 183, 228, 238, 239, 240, 241, 252, 276, 408
Fang, H. 41
Feige, E. 79
Feinstein, S.P. 465
Feller, W. 408
Fernstein, S. 513
Fielitz, B.D. 41
Figlewski, S. 101, 513, 519, 534
Figliuoli, L. 283, 292
Finn, M.G. 102
Fisher, P.G. 125
Flood, R. 140, 186
Fortune, P. 225
Frankel, J. 103, 229, 231
Frankel, J.A. 69, 70, 81, 82, 90, 174, 175, 177, 188
French, K. 345, 367, 370, 371
French, K.R. 26, 300
Frenkel, J. 241
Frenkel, J.A. 67, 83, 175, 181
Frey, R. 404
Friedman, M. 3, 4, 10, 110, 232
Froot, K. 103, 140
Froot, K.A. 231, 276
Fukunaga, K. 58
Furman, J. 187, 204

Galai, D. 477
Gallant, A.R. 139, 140, 142, 376
Garbade, K. 177
Garber, P. 140
Garber, P. 205
Garman, M. 465, 491
Garman, M.B. 389, 390, 397, 399
Geluk, J. 408, 417
Gemmill, G. 390, 519
Genberg, H. 252
Gerencser, L. 162
Geweke, J. 42, 43, 46, 79
Giaccotto, C. 390
Glaessner, T. 70, 83

Glassman, D. 102, 139
Glosten, L.R. 321, 330, 435, 452
Goldfield, S.M. 174
Goldstein, M. 188
Goodhart, C. 283, 285, 292
Goodhart, C.A.E. 107, 434
Goodman, S.H. 103
Granger, C. 75, 76
Granger, C.W.J. 46, 101, 124, 125, 126
Greene, M.T. 41
Grossman, S.F. 26, 27
Grossman, S.J. 229
Guerard, J.B. 102

Haache, G. 68
Hafer, R.W. 3
Hakkio, C.S. 79, 140
Hall, P. 406
Halttunen, H. 69
Hamilton, J. 157
Hamilton, J.D. 140, 259, 260, 366, 372, 384
Hansen, L.P. 79, 104, 467, 485, 505
Hardy, C.C. 281
Hartmann, P. 417
Harvey, A.C. 177, 180
Harvey, C.R. 535
Hassler, U. 43
Hathaway, N. 323
Hawkes, A.G. 436
Hayes, R. 58
Haynes, S. 70
Hein, S.E. 3, 18
Henderson, D. 276
Hendricks, D. 405
Hendry, D.F. 177, 485
Henriksson, R.D. 157, 165, 167
Hentschel, L. 330
Heston, S. 465
Heynen, R. 521
Higgins, M. 438
Hill, B.M. 406, 423
Hill, J. 28
Hinckley, D.V. 277
Hinich, M. 140
Hodrick, R. 256
Hodrick, R.J. 79, 104, 140, 239, 252, 467, 485
Holden, K. 116
Hong, T. 345, 352, 367, 375, 387
Hooper, P. 70, 73, 81, 82, 181
Hornik, K. 156, 158, 163
Horrigan, J. 58
Howrey, E.P. 19
Hsieh, D.A. 102, 139, 140, 156, 259, 267, 522
Hsu, D.A. 390

Hull, J. 26, 342, 462, 464, 465, 469, 472, 473, 475, 497

Iman, R.L. 112
Ingersoll, J. 26
Isard, P. 83, 174
Ito, T. 230, 285

Jackson, P. 405, 411
Jaffe, J. 324
Jagannathan, R. 321
Jain, P.J. 452
Jensen, M.C. 224, 298
Jevons, W.S. 298
Joh, G. 452
Johansen, S. 124, 125, 126
Johnson, H. 465
Jorion, P. 27, 402
Joyeux, R. 46

Kalman, R.E. 175
Kamara, A. 26, 28, 29, 33
Kaminsky, G. 187, 188, 189, 191, 209
Kane, A. 345
Kaplan, R. 58, 59
Kato, K. 324
Kaufman, P. 281
Kearns, P. 321
Kendall, M.G. 60
Kim, J.W. 58, 60
Kirman, A. 103, 177
Klass, M.J. 389, 397, 399
Kocherlakota, N.R. 228
Kohlhagen, S.W. 390
Kolb, R.A. 4
Kroner, K. 345
Krugman, P. 186
Kuan, C.M. 157, 160, 161, 163, 169, 170
Kyle, A.S. 491

Labys, W.C. 41
Lai, K.S. 41
Lai, M. 41
Lakonishok, J. 277
Lamoureux, C.G. 329, 452, 491, 499, 519, 532, 533, 534
Lastrapes, W.D. 329, 452, 491, 499, 519, 532, 533, 534
Latane, H.A. 499, 502, 519
Leahy, M.P. 231
Leamer, E. 297
LeBaron, B. 140, 231, 277, 290
Ledolter, J. 176
Lee, E.J.Q. 241

Levi, M. 298
Levich, R. 157, 165, 241, 249, 280
Levich, R.M. 225, 226, 256, 276
Lewis, C.M. 464, 478, 479, 492, 499, 519, 521, 523, 531, 533, 534
Lillien, D.M. 140
Lim, L. 28
Lippmann, R. 58
Litterman, R.B. 72, 75, 79, 128
Lizondo, S. 188
Ljung, L. 170
Lo, A.W. 229, 280, 297, 298
Logue, D.E. 235, 238, 244
Loopesko, B. 90, 91
Lucas, R.E. 174, 178
Lui, Y.-H. 279
Lyons, R. 140, 452
Lyons, R.K. 230

Macaulay, F.R. 368
MacDonald, R. 102, 104, 105, 124
Mack, G.A. 4
Mackinlay, A.C. 229, 297, 298
Maddala, G.S. 33
Magee, J. 281
Mahoney, J.M. 410
Maital, S. 498
Malkiel, B.G. 224, 225
Manaster, S. 499, 519
Mandelbrot, B. 138, 367
Mariano, R.S. 165
Marion, N. 186
Mark, N.C. 229
Marks, S.G. 345
Marsh, P.R. 298, 300, 322, 326, 327, 332, 333, 334, 337, 405, 406
Martin, L. 59
Masson, P. 69
Mathur, I. 290
Maude, D.J. 405, 411
McCormick, F. 241
McCulloch, J.H. 75
McMahon, P.C. 156
McNeil, A.J. 404
Meese, R.A. 70, 71, 78, 79, 81, 85, 89, 91, 97, 102, 107, 123, 124, 125, 128, 129, 139, 145, 153, 174, 175, 176, 177, 178, 179, 180, 181, 183, 229
Melino, A. 463, 491, 492
Melitz, J. 90
Melvin, M.T. 230
Mendoza, E.G. 202
Menkhoff, L. 280
Merton, R. 346

Merton, R.C. 5, 157, 165, 167, 236, 251, 297, 300
Milesi-Ferretti, G.M. 202, 204, 211
Milgrom, P. 435, 452
Miller, M.H. 408
Miller, M.I. 436
Mingo, K. 59
Mishkin, F. 27
Mizon, G.E. 177
Mizrach, B. 157, 165
Mole, D. 279
Moore, J.R. 176
Moorthy, V. 224
More, J. 163
Morgan, J.P. 402
Morton, J. 181
Morton, J.E. 70, 73, 81, 82
Muller, U.A. 408
Murphy, J. J. 220, 224, 281
Mussa, M. 67, 175
Muth, J.F. 27

Nadaraya, E.A. 374
Nason, J.A. 124, 157, 170
Nason, J.M. 140
Neely, C. 225, 228, 231
Nelson, C. 74
Nelson, D.B. 330, 366, 367, 476, 491, 522
Nerlove, M. 139, 145
Newbold, P. 45, 75, 76, 101
Newey, W.K. 485
Ng, V.K. 321, 330
Nychka, D.W. 142

O'Hara, M. 435, 451, 452
Obstfeld, M. 79, 90, 140
Officer, R. 300
Onochie, J. 41
Osler, C.L. 226, 232, 280, 290, 292

Pagan, A.R. 124, 126, 321, 334, 352, 367, 371, 375, 387
Pan, J. 402
Park, H.Y. 513
Park, T.H. 32
Parkinson, M. 389, 398, 399
Parzen, E. 72
Pattell, J.M. 496
Patterson, D. 140
Pattillo, C. 188
Paulos, J.A. 225
Pauly, P. 102, 113, 140
Payne, R. 285, 288, 403
Peel, D.A. 116

Peng, L. 407, 408, 411, 417, 423
Perraudin, W. 405, 411
Perron, P. 31
Pesando, J. 18, 498
Pesaran, M.H. 157, 165, 170
Pesenti, P. 186, 188, 198
Pfeifer, P.E. 5
Phillips, P.C.B. 31
Pictet, O.V. 408
Pinches, G. 59
Pitts, M. 390, 452
Poon, S.-H. 321
Porter, R.D. 174
Porterba, J.M. 300, 496
Porter-Hudak, S. 42, 43, 46
Poterba, J. 344
Praetz, P. 236
Prell, M.J. 3
Prescott, D.M. 153
Pring, M. 281

Radlet, S. 186, 187, 188, 198
Ramanathan, R. 101
Ray, B. 46
Razin, A. 202, 204, 211
Reichenstein, W. 26, 27
Reinhart, C. 188
Rendleman, R.J. 499, 502, 519
Resnick, S.I. 405
Richard, J.F. 485
Rissanen, J. 157, 161, 162
Robins, R.P. 140
Robinson, P. 43
Robinson, P.M. 141, 142
Rogoff, K. 70, 71, 78, 81, 85, 89, 91, 97, 102,
    107, 123, 124, 125, 128, 129, 139, 145, 174,
    175, 176, 177, 178, 179, 180, 181, 183, 229
Roll, R. 225
Rootzen, H. 405
Rose, A.K. 124, 125, 153, 188
Rosenberg, B. 300
Ross, S.A. 26
Roubini, N. 186, 188, 198
Rubenstein, M. 397, 398, 465, 502
Rubin, I. 436
Rudd, A. 513
Rumelhart, D.E. 160
Runkle, D.E. 321
Russell, J. 433, 434, 435, 438, 442, 446, 455

Sabau, H. 371
Sachs, J. 186, 187, 188, 198
Saidi, N. 174
Samuelson, P.A. 35, 261

Sarantis, N. 125, 126, 131, 134, 135
Sargent, T.J. 71, 82
Schachter, B. 405, 410
Scheinkman, J.A. 140
Schinasi, G.J. 123, 124, 125
Schlumberger, M. 280
Schmalensee, R. 342
Schnader, M.H. 4, 5
Schneeweis, T. 28
Scholes, M.S. 461
Schulmeister, S. 259
Schwartz, G. 71
Schwarz, G. 161
Schwert, G.W. 300, 321, 329, 334, 345, 352, 367,
    370, 371, 373, 382
Schwert, W. 33
Scott, E. 519
Scott, L.O. 465
Sears, R.S. 513
Seguin, P.J. 390, 329
Selover, P.D. 125
Shabacker, R.W. 281
Shafer, J. 90, 91, 235, 236, 237, 239, 240, 244,
    258, 280
Shanno, D. 465
Shastri, K. 519, 521
Sheffrin, S.M. 83
Shekhar, S. 58, 59
Shiller, R.J. 485, 487, 499
Shleifer, A. 232
Shoesmith, G.L. 132
Siegel, J.J. 75, 228
Silverman, B.W. 374, 376
Simpson, T.D. 174
Sims, C. 128, 140
Sims, C.A. 73, 79
Singleton, C. 58, 59, 79
Skillings, J.H. 4
Sklarew, A. 281
Smith, C. 346
Snyder, D.L. 436
Sobel, R. 382, 383
Soderstrom, T. 170
Somanath, V.S. 124
Sowell, F. 56
Spudeck, R. 18
Srivastava, S. 239, 252
Stahl, G. 416
Stambaugh, R. 345, 367, 371
Stein, E.M. 465, 490
Stein, J.C. 465, 496, 521
Stekler, H.O. 4, 5, 110
Stengos, T. 153
Stewart, C. 125, 126, 131, 134, 135

Stiglitz, J. 187, 204
Stiglitz, J.E. 229
Stone, J.A. 70
Stuart, A. 60
Summers, L. 232, 300, 344, 496
Surkan, A. 58, 59
Swamy, P.A.V.B. 123, 124, 125
Sweeney, R. 258, 259, 261, 272, 276, 280
Sweeney, R.J. 225, 235, 236, 238, 239, 241, 244,
    249, 252
Switzer, L.N. 32
Szakmary, A. 290

Tauchen, G. 139, 140, 452
Tauchen, G.E. 390
Taylor, M.P. 124, 219, 279
Taylor, S.J. 157, 321, 389, 390, 391, 393, 397,
    519, 521, 524, 525, 526
Taylor, T.S. 102, 103
Tendon, K. 519
Thaler, R.H. 228, 276
Theil, H. 498
Thomas, L. 280
Thomas, L.R. 26, 123, 124, 125, 225, 226
Timmerman, A. 157, 165, 170
Tornell, A. 187, 188, 198, 201
Townend, J. 68
Trippi, R. 342
Tryon, R. 79
Tse, Y.K. 321, 322, 326, 328, 334
Tucker, A.L. 519
Tung, S.H. 321, 322, 326, 328, 334
Turnbull, S. 463, 491, 492

Ullah, A. 141, 352, 367
Urwitz, T. 101
Urwitz, U. 58, 59

Van Deventer, D.R. 27, 30

Velasco, A. 188
Vishny, R.W. 232

Watson, G.S. 374
Weiss, A.A. 139, 140
Weller, P. 225, 228, 231
West, K.D. 485
Westerfield, J.M. 71, 139
Westerfield, R. 324
Wethyavivorn, K. 521
Whaley, R.E. 477, 521, 535
White, A. 26, 342, 462, 464, 465, 469, 472, 473,
    475, 497
White, H. 153, 157, 160, 161, 163, 170, 366, 380,
    381
Wiggins, J. 342, 497
Willett, T.D. 235, 238, 244
Williamson, J. 134
Winkler, R.L. 101
Wohar, M. 45
Wolf, C.C.P. 123
Wolff, C.C.P. 176, 181
Wolff, C.P. 102
Wolfson, M.A. 496
Wong, K.A. 324
Wong, Y.-P. 279,
Woo, W.T. 251
Wooldridge, J. 345
Working, H. 73
Wright, J.H. 46

Xu, X. 519, 521

Yakowitz, S.J. 142
Yau, J. 28
Yoo, B.S. 125, 126, 133

Zhang, W. 128

The International Library of Critical Writings in Financial Economics

1. The Theory of Corporate Finance
   (Volumes I and II)
   Michael J. Brennan

2. Futures Markets
   (Volumes I, II and III)
   A.G. Malliaris

3. Market Efficiency: Stock Market
   Behaviour in Theory and Practice
   (Volumes I and II)
   Andrew W. Lo

4. Microstructure: The Organization of
   Trading and Short Term Price Behavior
   (Volumes I and II)
   Hans R. Stoll

5. The Debt Market
   (Volumes I, II and III)
   Stephen A. Ross

6. Options Markets
   (Volumes I, II and III)
   *George M. Constantinides and
   A.G. Malliaris*

7. Empirical Corporate Finance
   (Volumes I, II, III and IV)
   Michael J. Brennan

8. The Foundations of Continuous Time
   Finance
   Stephen M. Schaefer

9. International Securities
   (Volumes I and II)
   *George C. Philippatos and Gregory
   Koutmos*

10. Behavioral Finance
    (Volumes I, II and III)
    Hersh Shefrin

11. Asset Pricing Theory and Tests
    (Volumes I and II)
    Robert R. Grauer

12. International Capital Markets
    (Volumes I, II and III)
    G. Andrew Karolyi and René M. Stulz

13. Financial Forecasting
    (Volumes I and II)
    Roy Batchelor and Pami Dua

Future titles will include:

Emerging Markets
Geert Bekaert and Campbell R. Harvey

Foreign Exchange Markets
Richard J. Sweeney

Financial Econometrics
Andrew W. Lo

Financial Markets and the Real Economy
John H. Cochrane